SEARCH ALGORITHMS AND APPLICATIONS

Edited by **Nashat Mansour**

Search Algorithms and Applications
Edited by Nashat Mansour

Published by InTech
Janeza Trdine 9, 51000 Rijeka, Croatia

Publishing Process Manager Ivana Lorkovic

Technical Editor Teodora Smiljanic

Cover Designer InTech Design Team

Additional hard copies can be obtained from orders@intechopen.com

Search Algorithms and Applications, Edited by Nashat Mansour
p. cm.
ISBN 978-953-307-156-5

For EU product safety concerns:
IN TECH d.o.o., Prolaz Marije Krucifikse Kozulić 3, 51000 Rijeka, Croatia,
info@intechopen.com or visit our website at intechopen.com.

Meet the editor

Nashat Mansour is a Professor of Computer Science at the Lebanese American University. He received B.E. and M.Eng.Sc. degrees in Electrical Engineering from the University of New South Wales, Australia, and M.S. in Computer Engineering and Ph.D. in Computer Science from Syracuse University, USA. His research interests include: application of metaheuristics and data mining to real-world problems, software testing, parallel computing, protein structure prediction, and gene-disease association. Dr. Mansour has published many papers in international journals and conference proceedings.

Contents

Preface

Search algorithms aim to find solutions or objects with specified properties and constraints in a large solution search space or among a collection of objects. A solution can be a set of value assignments to variables that will satisfy the constraints or a substructure of a given discrete structure. In addition, there are search algorithms, mostly probabilistic, that are designed for the prospective quantum computer.

This book demonstrates the wide applicability of search algorithms for the purpose of developing useful and practical solutions to problems that arise in a variety of problem domains. Although it is targeted to a wide group of readers: researchers, graduate students, and practitioners, it does not offer an exhaustive coverage of search algorithms and applications.

The chapters are organized into three sections: Population-based and quantum search algorithms, Search algorithms for image and video processing, and Search algorithms for engineering applications. The first part includes: two proposed swarm intelligence algorithms and an analysis of parallel implementation of particle swarm optimization algorithms on graphic processing units; an enhanced genetic algorithm applied to the bioinformatics problem of predicting protein structures; an analysis of quantum searching properties and a search algorithm based on quantum walk. The second part includes: a search method based on simulated annealing for equalizing spatial and spectral quality in satellite images; search algorithms for object recognition in computer vision and remote sensing images; an enhanced diamond search algorithm for efficient block motion estimation; an efficient search pattern based algorithm for video compression. The third part includes: heuristic search algorithms applied to aspects of the physical layer performance optimization in wireless networks; music inspired harmony search algorithm for maintenance planning and economic dispatch; search algorithms based on neural network approximation for multi-objective design optimization in electromagnetic devices; search algorithms for adaptive filtering and for finding frequent inter-transaction itemsets; formal concept search technique for finding document clusters; search algorithms for navigation, robotics, geophysics, and fluid dynamics.

I would like to acknowledge the efforts of all the authors who contributed to this book. Also, I thank Ms. Ivana Lorkovic, from InTech Publisher, for her support.

March 2011

Nashat Mansour

Part 1

Population Based and Quantum Search Algorithms

1

Two Population-Based Heuristic Search Algorithms and Their Applications

Weirong Chen, Chaohua Dai and Yongkang Zheng
Southwest JiaotongUniversity
China

1. Introduction

Search is one of the most frequently used problem solving methods in artificial intelligence (AI) [1], and search methods are gaining interest with the increase in activities related to modeling complex systems [2, 3]. Since most practical applications involve objective functions which cannot be expressed in explicit mathematical forms and their derivatives cannot be easily computed, a better choice for these applications may be the direct search methods as defined below: *A direct search method for numerical optimization is any algorithm that depends on the objective function only through ranking a countable set of function values.* Direct search methods do not compute or approximate values of derivatives and remain popular because of their simplicity, flexibility, and reliability [4]. Among the direct search methods, hill climbing methods often suffer from local minima, ridges and plateaus. Hence, random restarts in search process can be used and are often helpful. However, high-dimensional continuous spaces are big places in which it is easy to get lost for random search. Resultantly, augmenting hill climbing with memory is applied and turns out to be effective [5]. In addition, for many real-world problems, an exhaustive search for solutions is not a practical proposition. It is common then to resort to some kind of heuristic approach as defined below: *heuristic search algorithm for tackling optimization problems is any algorithm that applies a heuristic to search through promising solutions in order to find a good solution.* This heuristic search allows the bypass of the "combinatorial explosion" problem [6]. Those techniques discussed above are all classified into heuristics involved with random move, population, memory and probability model [7]. Some of the best-known heuristic search methods are genetic algorithm (GA), tabu search and simulated annealing, etc.. A standard GA has two drawbacks: premature convergence and lack of good local search ability [8]. In order to overcome these disadvantages of GA in numerical optimization problems, differential evolution (DE) algorithm has been introduced by Storn and Price [9].

In the past 20 years, swarm intelligence computation [10] has been attracting more and more attention of researchers, and has a special connection with the evolution strategy and the genetic algorithm [11]. Swarm intelligence is an algorithm or a device and illumined by the social behavior of gregarious insects and other animals, which is designed for solving distributed problems. There is no central controller directing the behavior of the swarm; rather, these systems are self-organizing. This means that the complex and constructive collective behavior emerges from the individuals (agents) who follow some simple rules and communicate with each other and their environments. Swarms offer several advantages over traditional systems based on deliberative agents and central control: specifically robustness, flexibility, scalability, adaptability, and suitability for analysis. Since 1990's, two typical swarm intelligence algorithms have emerged. One is the particle swarm optimization (PSO) [12], and the other is the ant colony optimization (ACO) [13].

In this chapter, two recently proposed swarm intelligence algorithms are introduced. They are seeker optimization algorithm (SOA) [3, 14-19] and stochastic focusing search (SFS) [20, 21], respectively.

2. Seeker Optimization Algorithm (SOA) and its applications

2.1 Seeker Optimization Algorithm (SOA) [3, 14-19]

Human beings are the highest-ranking animals in nature. Optimization tasks are often encountered in many areas of human life [6], and the search for a solution to a problem is one of the basic behaviors to all mankind [22]. The algorithm herein just focuses on human behaviors, especially human searching behaviors, to be simulated for real-parameter optimization. Hence, the seeker optimization algorithm can also be named as human team optimization (HTO) algorithm or human team search (HTS) algorithm. In the SOA, optimization process is treated as a search of optimal solution by a seeker population.

2.1.1 Human searching behaviors

Seeker optimization algorithm (SOA) models the human searching behaviors based on their memory, experience, uncertainty reasoning and communication with each other. The algorithm operates on a set of solutions called seeker population (i.e., swarm), and the individual of this population are called seeker (i.e., agent). The SOA herein involves the following four human behaviours.

A. Uncertainty Reasoning behaviours

In the continuous objective function space, there often exists a neighborhood region close to the extremum point. In this region, the function values of the variables are proportional to their distances from the extremum point. It may be assumed that better points are likely to be found in the neighborhood of families of good points. In this case, search should be intensified in regions containing good solutions through focusing search [2]. Hence, it is believed that one may find the near optimal solutions in a narrower neighborhood of the point with lower objective function value and find them in a wider neighborhood of the point with higher function value.

"Uncertainty" is considered as a situational property of phenomena [23], and precise quantitative analyses of the behavior of humanistic systems are not likely to have much relevance to the real-world societal, political, economic, and other type of problems. Fuzzy systems arose from the desire to describe complex systems with linguistic descriptions, and a set of fuzzy control rules is a linguistic model of human control actions directly based on a human thinking about the operation. Indeed, the pervasiveness of fuzziness in human thought processes suggests that it is this fuzzy logic that plays a basic role in what may well be one of the most important facets of human thinking [24]. According to the discussions on the above human focusing search, the uncertainty reasoning of human search could be described by natural linguistic variables and a simple fuzzy rule as "If {*objective function value* is *small*} (i.e., *condition* part), Then {*step length* is *short*} (i.e., *action* part)". The understanding and linguistic description of the human search make a fuzzy system a good candidate for simulating human searching behaviors.

B. Egotistic Behavior

Swarms (i.e., seeker population here) are a class of entities found in nature which specialize in mutual cooperation among them in executing their routine needs and roles [25]. There are two extreme types of co-operative behavior. One, *egotistic,* is entirely pro-self and another, *altruistic,* is entirely pro-group [26]. Every person, as a single sophisticated agent, is uniformly egotistic, believing that he should go toward his personal best position $\vec{p}_{i,best}$ through cognitive learning [27].

C. Altruistic Behavior

The altruistic behavior means that the swarms co-operate explicitly, communicate with each other and adjust their behaviors in response to others to achieve the desired goal. Hence, the individuals exhibit entirely pro-group behavior through social learning and simultaneously move to the neighborhood's historical best position or the neighborhood's current best position. As a result, the move expresses a self-organized aggregation behavior of swarms [28]. The aggregation is one of the fundamental self-organization behaviors of swarms in nature and is observed in organisms ranging from unicellular organisms to social insects and mammals [29]. The positive feedback of self-organized aggregation behaviors usually takes the form of attraction toward a given signal source [28]. For a "black-box" problem in which the ideal global minimum value is unknown, the neighborhood's historical best position or the neighborhood's current best position is used as the only attraction signal source for the self-organized aggregation behavior.

C. Pro-Activeness Behavior

Agents (i.e., seekers here) enjoy the properties of pro-activeness: agents do not simply act in response to their environment; they are able to exhibit goal-directed behavior by taking the initiative [30]. Furthermore, future behavior can be predicted and guided by past behavior [31]. As a result, the seekers may be pro-active to change their search directions and exhibit goal-directed behaviors according to the response to his past behaviors.

2.1.2 Implementation of Seeker Optimization Algorithm

Seeker optimization algorithm (SOA) operates on a search population of s D-dimensional position vectors, which encode the potential solutions to the optimization problem at hand. The position vectors are represented as $\vec{x}_i = [x_{i1}, \cdots, x_{ij}, \cdots, x_{iD}]$, i=1, 2, ⋯, s, where x_{ij} is the jth element of $\vec{x}_i$ and s is the population size. Assume that the optimization problems to be solved are minimization problems.

The main steps of SOA are shown as Fig. 1. In order to add a social component for social sharing of information, a neighborhood is defined for each seeker. In the present studies, the population is randomly divided into three subpopulations (all the subpopulations have the same size), and all the seekers in the same subpopulation constitute a neighborhood. A search direction $\vec{d}_i(t) = [d_{i1}, \cdots, d_{iD}]$ and a step length vector $\vec{\alpha}_i(t) = [\alpha_{i1}, \cdots, \alpha_{iD}]$ are computed (see Section 1.1.3 and 1.1.4) for the ith seeker at time step t, where $\alpha_{ij}(t) \geq 0$, $d_{ij}(t) \in \{-1,0,1\}$, i=1,2,⋯,s; j=1,2,⋯,D. When $d_{ij}(t) = 1$, it means that the i-th seeker goes towards the positive direction of the coordinate axis on the dimension j; when $d_{ij}(t) = -1$, the seeker goes towards the negative direction; when $d_{ij}(t)=0$, the seeker stays at the current position on the corresponding dimension. Then, the *j*th element of the *i*th seeker's position is updated by:

$$x_{ij}(t+1)=x_{ij}(t)+\alpha_{ij}(t)d_{ij}(t) \tag{1}$$

Since the subpopulations are searching using their own information, they are easy to converge to a local optimum. To avoid this situation, an inter-subpopulation learning strategy is used, i.e., the worst two positions of each subpopulation are combined with the best position of each of the other two subpopulations by the following binomial crossover operator:

$$x_{k_n j,\text{worst}}=\begin{cases}x_{lj,\text{best}} & \text{if } R_j\le 0.5\\ x_{k_n j,\text{worst}} & \text{else}\end{cases} \tag{2}$$

where R_j is a uniformly random real number within [0,1], $x_{k_n j,\text{worst}}$ is denoted as the *j*th element of the *n*th worst position in the *k*th subpopulation, $x_{lj,\text{best}}$ is the *j*th element of the best position in the *l*th subpopulation, the indices *k*, *n*, *l* are constrained by the combination $(k,n,l)\in\{(1,1,2), (1,2,3), (2,1,1), (2,2,3), (3,1,1), (3,2,2)\}$, and $j=1,\cdots,D$. In this way, the good information obtained by each subpopulation is exchanged among the subpopulations and then the diversity of the population is increased.

2.1.3 Search direction

The gradient has played an important role in the history of search methods [32]. The search space may be viewed as a gradient field [33], and a so-called empirical gradient (EG) can be determined by evaluating the response to the position change especially when the objective function is not be available in a differentiable form at all [5]. Then, the seekers can follow an EG to guide their search. Since the search directions in the SOA does not involve the magnitudes of the EGs, a search direction can be determined only by the signum function of a better position minus a worse position. For example, an empirical search direction $\vec{d}=sign(\vec{x}'-\vec{x}'')$ when $\vec{x}'$ is better than $\vec{x}''$, where the function $sign(\cdot)$ is a signum function on each element of the input vector. In the SOA, every seeker *i* (i=1,2,$\cdots$,s) selects his search direction based on several EGs by evaluating the current or historical positions of himself or his neighbors. They are detailed as follows.

According to the egotistic behavior mentioned above, an EG from $\vec{x}_i(t)$ to $\vec{p}_{i,best}(t)$ can be involved for the *i*th seeker at time step *t*. Hence, each seeker *i* is associated with an empirical direction called as egotistic direction $\vec{d}_{i,ego}(t)=[d_{i1,ego},d_{i2,ego},\cdots,d_{iD,ego}]$:

$$\vec{d}_{i,ego}(t)=sign(\vec{p}_{i,best}(t)-\vec{x}_i(t)) \tag{3}$$

On the other hand, based on the altruistic behavior, each seeker *i* is associated with two optional altruistic direction, i.e., $\vec{d}_{i,alt_1}(t)$ and $\vec{d}_{i,alt_2}(t)$:

$$\vec{d}_{i,alt_1}(t)=sign(\vec{g}_{i,best}(t)-\vec{x}_i(t)) \tag{4}$$

$$\vec{d}_{i,alt_2}(t)=sign(\vec{l}_{i,best}(t)-\vec{x}_i(t)) \tag{5}$$

where $\vec{g}_{i,best}(t)$ represents the neighborhood's historical best position up to the time step t, $\vec{l}_{i,best}(t)$ represents the neighborhood's current best position. Here, the neighborhood is the one to which the ith seeker belongs.

Moreover, according to the pro-activeness behavior, each seeker i is associated with an empirical direction called as pro-activeness direction $\vec{d}_{i,pro}(t)$:

$$\vec{d}_{i,pro}(t) = sign(\vec{x}_i(t_1) - \vec{x}_i(t_2)) \tag{6}$$

where $t_1, t_2 \in \{t, t-1, t-2\}$, $\vec{x}_i(t_1)$ and $\vec{x}_i(t_2)$ are the best one and the worst one in the set $\{\vec{x}_i(t), \vec{x}_i(t-1), \vec{x}_i(t-2)\}$ respectively.

According to human rational judgment, the actual search direction of the ith seeker, $\vec{d}_i(t) = [d_{i1}, d_{i2}, \cdots, d_{iD}]$, is based on a compromise among the aforementioned four empirical directions, i.e., $\vec{d}_{i,ego}(t)$, $\vec{d}_{i,alt_1}(t)$, $\vec{d}_{i,alt_2}(t)$ and $\vec{d}_{i,pro}(t)$. In this study, the jth element of $\vec{d}_i(t)$ is selected applying the following proportional selection rule (shown as Fig. 2):

$$d_{ij} = \begin{cases} 0 & \text{if } r_j \le p_j^{(0)} \\ 1 & \text{if } p_j^{(0)} < r_j \le p_j^{(0)} + p_j^{(1)} \\ -1 & \text{if } p_j^{(0)} + p_j^{(1)} < r_j \le 1 \end{cases} \tag{7}$$

where i=1,2,⋯,s, j=1,2,⋯,D, r_j is a uniform random number in [0,1], $p_j^{(m)}$ $(m \in \{0,1,-1\})$ is defined as follows: In the set $\{d_{ij,ego}, d_{ij,alt_1}, d_{ij,alt_2}, d_{ij,pro}\}$ which is composed of the jth elements of $\vec{d}_{i,ego}(t)$, $\vec{d}_{i,alt_1}(t)$, $\vec{d}_{i,alt_2}(t)$ and $\vec{d}_{i,pro}(t)$, let $num^{(1)}$ be the number of "1", $num^{(-1)}$ be the number of "-1", and $num^{(0)}$ be the number of "0", then $p_j^{(1)} = \frac{num^{(1)}}{4}$, $p_j^{(-1)} = \frac{num^{(-1)}}{4}$, $p_j^{(0)} = \frac{num^{(0)}}{4}$. For example, if $d_{ij,ego} = 1, d_{ij,alt_1} = -1$, $d_{ij,alt_2} = -1, d_{ij,pro} = 0$, then $num^{(1)}$ =1, $num^{(-1)}$=2, and $num^{(0)}$=1. So, $p_j^{(1)} = \frac{1}{4}, p_j^{(-1)} = \frac{2}{4}, p_j^{(0)} = \frac{1}{4}$.

2.1.4 Step length

In the SOA, only one fuzzy rule is used to determine the step length, namely, "If {*objective function value* is *small*} (i.e., *condition* part), Then {*step length* is *short*} (i.e., *action* part)". Different optimization problems often have different ranges of fitness values. To design a fuzzy system to be applicable to a wide range of optimization problems, the fitness values of all the seekers are descendingly sorted and turned into the sequence numbers from 1 to s as the inputs of fuzzy reasoning. The linear membership function is used in the conditional part (fuzzification) since the universe of discourse is a given set of numbers, i.e., {1,2,⋯,s}. The expression is presented as (8).

$$\mu_i = \mu_{\max} - \frac{s - I_i}{s-1}(\mu_{\max} - \mu_{\min}) \tag{8}$$

where I_i is the sequence number of $\vec{x}_i(t)$ after sorting the fitness values, $\mu_{\max}$ is the maximum membership degree value which is assigned by the user and equal to or a little less than 1.0. Generally, $\mu_{\max}$ is set at 0.95.

In the action part (defuzzification), the Gaussian membership function $\mu(\alpha_{ij}) = e^{-\alpha_{ij}^2/(2\delta_j^2)}$ $(i=1,\cdots,s; j=1,\cdots,D)$ is used for the jth element of the ith seeker's step length. For the Bell function, the membership degree values of the input variables beyond [-$3\delta_j$, $3\delta_j$] are less than 0.0111 ($\mu(\pm 3\delta_j)$=0.0111), which can be neglected for a linguistic atom [34]. Thus, the minimum value $\mu_{\min}$=0.0111 is fixed. Moreover, the parameter δ_j of the Gaussian membership function is the jth element of the vector $\vec{\delta} = [\delta_1,\cdots,\delta_D]$ which is given by:

$$\vec{\delta} = \omega \cdot abs(\vec{x}_{best} - \vec{x}_{rand}) \tag{9}$$

where $abs(\cdot)$ returns an output vector such that each element of the vector is the absolute value of the corresponding element of the input vector, the parameter ω is used to decrease the *step length* with time step increasing so as to gradually improve the search precision. In general, the ω is linearly decreased from 0.9 to 0.1 during a run. The $\vec{x}_{best}$ and $\vec{x}_{rand}$ are the best seeker and a randomly selected seeker in the *same* subpopulation to which the ith seeker belongs, respectively. Notice that $\vec{x}_{rand}$ is different from $\vec{x}_{best}$, and $\vec{\delta}$ is shared by all the seekers in the same subpopulation. Then, the *action* part of the fuzzy reasoning (shown in Fig. 3) gives the jth element of the ith seeker's step length $\vec{\alpha}_i = [\alpha_{i1},\cdots,\alpha_{iD}]$ (i=1,2,···,s; j=1,2,···,D):

$$\alpha_{ij} = \delta_j \sqrt{-\log(RAND(\mu_i,1))} \tag{10}$$

where δ_j is the jth element of the vector $\vec{\delta}$ in (9), the function $\log(\cdot)$ returns the natural logarithm of its input, the function $RAND(\mu_i,1)$ returns a uniform random number within the range of $[\mu_i,1]$ which is used to introduce the randomicity for each element of $\vec{\alpha}_i$ and improve local search capability.

2.1.5 Further analysis on the SOA

Unlike GA, SOA conducts focusing search by following the promising empirical directions until to converge to the optimum for as few generations as possible. In this way, it does not easily get lost and then locates the region in which the global optimum exists.

Although the SOA uses the same terms of the personal/population best position as PSO and DE, they are essentially different. As far as we know, PSO is not good at choosing step length [35], while DE sometimes has a limited ability to move its population large distances across the search space and would have to face with stagnation puzzledom [36]. Unlike PSO and DE, SOA deals with search direction and step length, independently. Due to the use of fuzzy rule: "If {*fitness value* is *small*}, Then {*step length* is *short*}", the better the position of the seeker is, the shorter his step length is. As a result, from the worst seeker to the best seeker, the search is changed from a coarse one to a fine one, so as to ensure that the population can not only keep a good search precision but also find new regions of the search space. Consequently, at every time step, some seekers are better for "exploration", some others better for "exploitation". In addition, due to self-organized aggregation behavior and the decreasing parameter ω in (9), the feasible search range of the seekers is decreasing with time step increasing. Hence, the population favors "exploration" at the early stage and "exploitation" at the late stage. In a word, not only at every time step but also within the whole search process, the SOA can effectively balance exploration and exploitation, which could ensure the effectiveness and efficiency of the SOA [37].

According to [38], a "nearer is better (NisB)" property is almost always assumed: most of iterative stochastic optimization algorithms, if not all, at least from time to time look around a good point in order to find an even better one. Furthermore, the reference [38] also pointed out that an effective algorithm may perfectly switch from a NisB assumption to a "nearer is worse (NisW)" one, and vice-versa. In our opinion, SOA is potentially provided with the NisB property because of the use of fuzzy reasoning and can switch between a NisB assumption and a NisW one. The main reason lies in the following two aspects. On the one hand, the search direction of each seeker is based on a compromise among several empirical directions, and different seekers often learn from different empirical points on different dimensions instead of a single *good point* as mentioned by NisB assumption. On the other hand, uncertainty reasoning (fuzzy reasoning) used by SOA would let a seeker's step length "uncertain", which uncertainly lets a seeker nearer to a certain *good point*, or farer away from another certain *good point*. Both the two aspects can boost the diversity of the population. Hence, from Clerc's point of view [38], it is further proved that SOA is effective.

```
begin
t←0;
generating s positions uniformly and randomly in search
space;
repeat
      evaluating each seeker;
      computing d_i(t) and α_i(t) for each seeker i;
      updating each seeker's position using (1);
      t←t+1;
until the termination criterion is satisfied
end.
```

Fig. 1. The main step of the SOA.

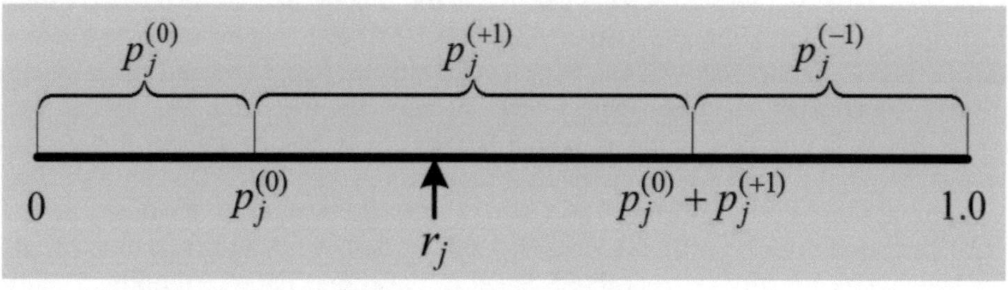

Fig. 2. The proportional selection rule of search directions

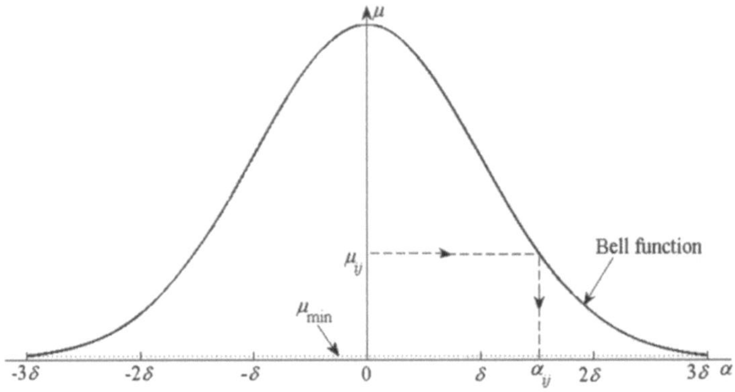

Fig. 3. The *action* part of the Fuzzy reasoning.

2.2 SOA for benchmark function optimization (Refs.[3,16, 18)

Twelve benchmark functions (listed in Table 1) are chosen from [39] to test the SOA with comparison of PSO-w (PSO with adaptive inertia weight) [40], PSO-cf (PSO with constriction factor) [41], CLPSO (comprehensive learning particle swarm optimizer) [42], the original DE [9], SACP-DE (DE with self-adapting control parameters) [39] and L-SaDE (the self-adaptive DE) [43]. The *Best, Mean* and *Std* (standard deviation) values of all the algorithms for each function over 30 runs are summarized in Table 2. In order to determine whether the results obtained by SOA are statistically different from the results generated by other algorithms, the *T*-tests are conducted and listed in Table 2, too. An *h* value of one indicates that the performances of the two algorithms are statistically different with 95% certainty, whereas *h* value of zero implies that the performances are not statistically different. The *CI* is confidence interval. The Table 2 indicates that SOA is suitable for solving the employed multimodal function optimizations with the smaller *Best, Mean* and *std* values than most of other algorithms for most of the functions. In addition, most of the *h* values are equal to one, and most of the *CI* values are less than zero, which shows that SOA is statistically superior to most of the other algorithms with the more robust performance. The details of the comparison results are as follows. Compared with PSO-w, SOA has the smaller *Best, Mean* and *std* values for all the twelve benchmark functions. Compared with PSO-cf, SOA has the smaller *Best, Mean* and *std* values for all the twelve benchmark functions expect that PSO-cf also has the same *Best* values for the functions 2-4, 6, 11 and 12. Compared with CLPSO, SOA has the smaller *Best, Mean* and *std* values for all the twelve benchmark functions expect that CLPSO also has the same *Best* values for the functions 6, 7, 9, 11 and 12. Compared with SPSO-2007, SOA has the smaller *Best, Mean* and *std* values for all the twelve benchmark functions expect that SPSO-2007 also has the same *Best* values for the functions 7-12. Compared with DE, SOA has the smaller *Best, Mean* and *std* values for all the twelve benchmark functions expect that DE also has the same *Best* values for the functions 3, 6, 9, 11 and 12. Compared with SACP-DE, SOA has the smaller *Best, Mean* and *std* values for all the twelve benchmark functions expect that SACP-DE can also find the global optimal solutions for function 3 and has the same *Best* values for the functions 6, 7, 11 and 12. Compared with L-SaDE, SOA has the smaller *Best, Mean* and *std* values for all the twelve benchmark functions expect that L-SaDE can also find the global optimal solutions for function 3 and has the same *Best* values for the functions 6, 9 and 12.

Functions	n	S	$f_{\min}$
$f_1(\vec{x}) = \sum_{i=1}^{n} i x_i^4 + rand[0,1)$	30	$[-1.28,1.2$	$f_1(\vec{0}) = 0$
$f_2(\vec{x}) = -20\exp(-0.2\sqrt{\frac{1}{n}\sum_{i=1}^{n} x_i^2}) - \exp(\frac{1}{n}\sum_{i=1}^{n}\cos(2\pi x_i)) + 20 + e$	30	$[-32,32]^n$	$f_2(\vec{0}) = 0$
$f_3(\vec{x}) = \frac{1}{4000}\sum_{i=1}^{n} x_i^2 - \prod_{i=1}^{n}\cos(\frac{x_i}{\sqrt{i}}) + 1$	30	$[-600,600$	$f_3(\vec{0}) = 0$
$f_4(\vec{x}) = \frac{\pi}{n}\{10\sin^2(\pi y_1) + \sum_{i=1}^{n-1}(y_i - 1)^2[1 + 10\sin^2(\pi y_{i+1})]$ $+(y_n - 1)^2\} + \sum_{i=1}^{n} u(x_i, 10, 100, 4)$	30	$[-50,50]^n$	$f_4(-\vec{1}) = 0$
$f_5(\vec{x}) = 0.1\{\sin^2(3\pi x_1) + \sum_{i=1}^{n-1}(x_i - 1)^2[1 + \sin^2(3\pi x_{i+1})]$ $+(x_n - 1)^2[1 + \sin^2(2\pi x_n)]\} + \sum_{i=1}^{n} u(x_i, 5, 100, 4)$	30	$[-50,50]^n$	$f_5(1,\ldots,1)=0$
$f_6(\vec{x}) = \sum_{i=1}^{11}[a_i - \frac{x_1(b_i^2 + b_i x_2)}{b_i^2 + b_i x_3 + x_4}]^2$	4	$[-5,5]^n$	$f_6(0.1928,0.1908,0.1231,0.1358)=3.0749\times10^{-4}$
$f_7(\vec{x}) = 4x_1^2 - 2.1x_1^4 + \frac{1}{3}x_1^6 + x_1 x_2 - 4x_2^2 + 4x_2^4$	2	$[-5,5]^n$	$f_7(-0.09,0.71)=-1.031628$
$f_8(\vec{x}) = (x_2 - \frac{5.1}{4\pi^2}x_1^2 + \frac{5}{\pi}x_1 - 6)^2 + 10(1 - \frac{1}{8\pi})\cos(x_1) + 10$	2	$[-5,15]^n$	$f_8(9.42,2.47) = 0.$
$f_9(\vec{x}) = [1 + (x_1 + x_2 + 1)^2(19 - 14x_1 + 3x_1^2 - 14x_2 + 6x_1x_2 + 3x_2^2)] \times$ $[30 + (2x_1 - 3x_2)^2 \times (18 - 32x_1 + 12x_1^2 + 48x_2 - 36x_1x_2 + 27x_2^2)]$	2	$[-2,2]^n$	$f_9(0,-1) = 3$
$f_{10}(\vec{x}) = -\sum_{i=1}^{4} c_i \exp[-\sum_{j=1}^{3} a_{ij}(x_j - p_{ij})^2]$	3	$[0,1]^n$	$f_{10}(0.114,0.556,0$
$f_{11}(\vec{x}) = -\sum_{i=1}^{7}[(\vec{x} - a_i)(\vec{x} - a_i)^T + c_i]^{-1}$	4	$[0,10]^n$	$f_{11}(\approx\vec{4}) = -10.40$
$f_{12}(\vec{x}) = -\sum_{i=1}^{10}[(\vec{x} - a_i)(\vec{x} - a_i)^T + c_i]^{-1}$	4	$[0,10]^n$	$f_{12}(\approx\vec{4}) = -10.53$

Table 1. The employed benchmark functions.

function	Index	PSO-ω	PSO-cf	CLPSO	SPSO-2007	DE	SACP-DE	L-SaDE	SOA
1	*Best*	2.7136e-3	1.0861e-3	3.3596e-3	7.6038e-3	1.8195e-3	3.7152e-3	1.0460e-3	4.0153e-5
	Mean	7.1299e-3	2.5423e-3	5.1258e-3	5.0229e-2	4.3505e-3	5.5890e-3	4.2653e-3	9.7068e-5
	Std	2.3404e-3	9.7343e-4	1.1883e-3	3.5785e-2	1.2317e-3	1.1868e-3	1.7366e-3	4.8022e-5
	h	1	1	1	1	1	1	1	-
	CI	[-0.0081 - 0.0060]	[-0.0029 - 0.0020]	[-0.0056 - 0.0045]	[-0.0663 - 0.0339]	[-0.0048 - 0.0037]	[-0.0060 - 0.0050]	[-0.0050 - 0.0034]	-
2	*Best*	7.3196e-7	2.6645e-15	6.3072e-4	1.7780e+0	8.5059e-8	5.2355e-9	1.2309e-11	2.6645e-15
	Mean	1.7171e-6	8.0458e-1	8.2430e-4	3.1720e+0	1.6860e-7	1.12625e-8	7.0892e-11	2.6645e-15
	Std	8.8492e-7	7.7255e-1	1.2733e-4	9.1299e-1	7.3342e-8	4.1298e-9	4.1709e-11	0
	h	1	1	1	1	1	1	1	-
	CI	[-2.12e-6 - 1.32e-6]	[-1.1543 - 0.4549]	[-8.82e-4 - 7.67e-4]	[-3.5853 - 2.7587]	[-2.02e-7 - 1.35e-7]	[-1.31e-8 - 9.39e-9]	[-8.98e-11 -5.20e-11]	-
3	*Best*	2.2204e-15	0	1.7472e-7	6.6613e-16	0	0	0	0
	Mean	8.3744e-3	1.9984e-2	2.4043e-6	1.0591e-2	4.9323e-4	0	0	0
	Std	7.7104e-3	2.1321e-2	3.6467e-6	1.1158e-2	2.2058e-3	0	0	0
	h	1	1	1	1	0	-	-	-
	CI	[-0.0118 - 0.0049]	[-0.0296 - 0.0103]	[-4.06e-6 - 7.54e-7]	[-0.0156 - 0.0055]	[-0.0015 5.0527e-4]	-	-	-
4	*Best*	1.2781e-13	1.5705e-32	1.8074e-7	5.2094e-22	2.9339e-15	2.2953e-17	2.5611e-21	1.5705e-32
	Mean	2.6878e-10	1.1402e-1	5.7391e-7	1.3483e+0	2.5516e-14	1.3700e-16	8.0092e-20	1.5808e-30
	Std	6.7984e-10	1.8694e-1	2.4755e-7	1.3321e+0	1.8082e-14	8.7215e-17	7.9594e-20	3.8194e-30
	h	0	1	1	1	1	1	1	-
	CI	[-5.75e-10 3.70e-11]	[-0.1986 - 0.0294]	[-6.86e-7 - 4.62e-7]	[-1.9513 - 0.7453]	[-3.4e-14 - 1.7e-14]	[-1.8e-16 - 9.8e-17]	[-1.12e-19 -4.41e-20]	-
5	*Best*	1.6744e-12	1.3498e-30	4.2229e-6	1.0379e-19	2.5008e-14	3.8881e-16	1.0668e-21	6.1569e-32
	Mean	1.0990e-3	1.0987e-3	6.8756e-6	1.3031e+1	1.0165e-13	9.7736e-16	3.4614e-19	3.3345e-29
	Std	3.4744e-3	3.3818e-3	2.7299e-6	1.1416e+1	7.1107e-14	8.4897e-16	4.7602e-19	8.3346e-29
	h	0	0	1	1	1	1	1	-
	CI	[-0.0027 4.6368e-4]	[-0.0026 4.3212e-4]	[-8.11e-6 - 5.64e-6]	[-18.1990 - 7.8633]	[-1.3e-13 - 6.9e-14]	[-1.4e-15 - 5.9e-16]	[-5.62e-1 1.31e-19]	-
6	*Best*	3.0750e-4	3.0749e-4	3.0749e-4	3.0749e-4	3.0749e-4	3.0749e-4	3.0749e-4	3.0749e-4
	Mean	4.9063e-4	4.4485e-4	3.5329e-4	4.9463e-4	4.4485e-4	3.0750e-4	3.0750e-4	3.0749e-4
	Std	3.8608e-4	3.3546e-4	2.0478e-4	1.7284e-4	3.3546e-4	3.0191e-9	2.8726e-9	9.6334e-20
	h	1	0	0	1	0	1	1	-

	CI	[-3.57e-4 - 9.49e-5]	[-2.89e-4 1.45e-5]	[-1.39e-4 4.69e-5]	[-2.65e-4 - 1.09e-4]	[-2.89e-4 1.45e-5]	[-1.15e-8 - 8.74e-9]	[-1.14e-8 - 8.7e-9]	-
7	*Best*	-1.031626	-1.031627	-1.031628	-1.031628	-1.031627	-1.031628	-1.031627	-1.031628
	Mean	-1.031615	-1.031612	-1.031617	-1.031627	-1.031619	-1.031617	-1.031613	-1.031628
	Std	8.6069e-6	7.8874e-6	7.4529e-6	3.5817e-6	8.4157e-6	8.0149e-6	9.0097e-6	7.6401e-13
	h	1	1	1	0	1	1	1	-
	CI	[-1.72e-5 - 9.49e-6]	[-2.00e-5 - 1.28e-5]	[-1.53e-5 - 8.54e-6]	[-2.47e-6 7.76e-6]	[-1.28e-5 - 5.21e-6]	[-1.52e-5 - 7.99e-6]	[-1.92e-5 - 1.11e-5]	-
8	*Best*	3.97890e-1	3.97898e-1	3.97897e-1	3.97887e-1	3.97902e-1	3.97888e-1	3.97889e-1	3.97887e-1
	Mean	3.97942e-1	3.97939e-1	3.97947e-1	3.97892e-1	3.97947e-1	3.97932e-1	3.97941e-1	3.97887e-1
	Std	3.3568e-5	3.0633e-5	3.1612e-5	1.8336e-5	3.0499e-5	3.3786e-5	3.76524e-5	1.2874e-7
	h	1	1	1	0	1	1	1	-
	CI	[-6.95e-5 - 3.93e-5]	[-6.52e-5 - 3.74e-5]	[-7.37e-5 4.51e-5]	[-1.277e-5 3.92e-6]	[-7.38e-5 - 4.62e-5]	[-6.00e-5 - 2.94e-5]	[-7.09e-5 - 3.69e-5]	-
9	*Best*	3.0000	3.0000	3	3	3	3.0000	3	3
	Mean	3.0000	3.0000	3.0000	3.0000	3	3.0000	3.0000	3
	Std	4.0898e-12	3.1875e-12	1.7278e-13	2.6936e-12	9.9103e-15	2.6145e-8	5.4283e-13	2.7901e-15
	h	1	1	1	1	1	1	1	-
	CI	[-5.1e-12 - 1.5e-12]	[-4.5e-12 - 1.61e-12]	[-3.1e-13 - 1.6e-13]	[-2.7e-12 - 2.6e-13]	[-8.5e-14 - 7.6e-14]	[-2.6e-8 - 2.6e-9]	[-6.4e-13 - 1.5e-13]	-
10	*Best*	-3.86174	-3.86260	-3.86254	-3.86278	-3.86256	-3.86251	-3.86228	-3.86278
	Mean	-3.86120	-3.86142	-3.86131	-3.86196	-3.86115	-3.86137	-3.86104	-3.86278
	Std	4.1892e-4	7.0546e-4	6.6908e-4	3.6573e-3	7.9362e-4	6.1290e-4	6.8633e-4	2.0402e-15
	h	1	1	1	0	1	1	1	-
	CI	[-0.0018 - 0.0014]	[-0.0017 - 0.0010]	[-0.0018 - 0.0012]	[-0.0025 8.3672e-4]	[-0.0020 - 0.0013]	[-0.0017 - 0.0011]	[-0.0021 - 0.0014]	-
11	*Best*	-1.0403e+1	-1.0403e+1	-1.0403e+1	-1.0403e+1	-1.0403e+1	-1.0403e+1	-1.0402e+1	-1.0403e+1
	Mean	-8.8741e+0	-9.3713e+0	-7.5794e+0	-8.5881e+0	-1.0403e+1	-1.0307e+1	-1.0307e+1	-1.0403e+1
	Std	3.2230e+0	2.5485e+0	3.6087e+0	3.2342e+0	6.6816e-7	1.9198e-1	1.6188e-1	5.8647e-11
	h	1	0	1	1	1	1	1	-
	CI	[-2.9785 - 0.0791]	[-2.1852 0.1220]	[-4.4570 - 1.1900]	[-3.2788 - 0.3508]	[-7.32e-7 -1.27e-7]	[-0.1828 - 0.0090]	[-0.1692 - 0.0226]	-
12	*Best*	-1.0536e+1	-1.0536e+1	-1.0536e+1	-1.0536e+1	-1.0536e+1	-1.0536e+1	-1.0534e+1	-1.0536e

								+1
Mean	-8.4159e+0	-8.6726e+0	-9.2338e+0	-9.7313e+0	-1.0536e+1	-1.0432e+1	-1.0437e+1	-1.0536e+1
Std	3.4860e+0	3.3515e+0	2.7247e+0	2.0607e+0	4.3239e-7	3.1761e-1	1.3003e-1	3.0218e-11
h	1	1	1	0	1	0	1	-
CI	[-3.6885 - 0.5526]	[-3.3809 - 0.3467]	[-2.5360 - 0.0692]	[-1.7379 0.1277]	[-4.86e-7 - 9.43e-8]	[-0.2481 0.0394]	[-0.1586 - 0.0409]	-

Table 2. The Comparisons of SOA with Other Evolutionary Methods on Benchmark Functions

2.3 SOA for optimal reactive power dispatch (Ref.[16])

2.3.1 Problem formulation

The objective of the reactive power optimization is to minimize the active power loss in the transmission network, which can be defined as follows:

$$P_{\text{loss}} = f(\vec{x}_1, \vec{x}_2) = \sum_{k \in N_E} g_k (V_i^2 + V_j^2 - 2V_i V_j \cos\theta_{ij}) \quad (11)$$

Subject to

$$\begin{cases} P_{Gi} - P_{Di} = V_i \sum_{j \in N_i} V_j (G_{ij} \cos\theta_{ij} + B_{ij} \sin\theta_{ij}) & i \in N_0 \\ Q_{Gi} - Q_{Di} = V_i \sum_{j \in N_i} V_j (G_{ij} \sin\theta_{ij} - B_{ij} \cos\theta_{ij}) & i \in N_{PQ} \\ V_i^{\min} \le V_i \le V_i^{\max} & i \in N_B \\ T_k^{\min} \le T_k \le T_k^{\max} & k \in N_T \\ Q_{Gi}^{\min} \le Q_{Gi} \le Q_{Gi}^{\max} & i \in N_G \\ Q_{Ci}^{\min} \le Q_{Ci} \le Q_{Ci}^{\max} & i \in N_C \\ S_l \le S_l^{\max} & l \in N_l \end{cases} \quad (12)$$

where $f(\vec{x}_1, \vec{x}_2)$ denotes the active power loss function of the transmission network, $\vec{x}_1$ is the control variable vector $[V_G \; K_T \; Q_C]^T$, $\vec{x}_2$ is the dependent variable vector $[V_L \; Q_G]^T$, V_G is the generator voltage (continuous), T_k is the transformer tap (integer), Q_C is the shunt capacitor/inductor (integer), V_L is the load-bus voltage, Q_G is the generator reactive power, $k=(i,j)$, $i \in N_B$, $j \in N_i$, g_k is the conductance of branch k, θ_{ij} is the voltage angle difference between bus i and j, P_{Gi} is the injected active power at bus i, P_{Di} is the demanded active power at bus i, V_i is the voltage at bus i, G_{ij} is the transfer conductance between bus i and j, B_{ij} is the transfer susceptance between bus i and j, Q_{Gi} is the injected reactive power at bus i, Q_{Di} is the demanded reactive power at bus , N_E is the set of numbers of network branches, N_{PQ} is the set of numbers of PQ buses, N_B is the set of numbers of total buses, N_i is the set of numbers of buses adjacent to bus i (including bus i), N_0 is the set of numbers of total buses excluding slack bus, N_C is the set of numbers of possible reactive power source installation buses, N_G is the set of numbers of generator buses, N_T is the set of numbers of transformer branches, S_l is the power flow in branch l, the superscripts "min" and "max" in equation (12) denote the corresponding lower and upper limits, respectively.

The first two equality constraints in (12) are the power flow equations. The rest inequality constraints are used for the restrictions of reactive power source installation, reactive generation, transformer tap-setting, bus voltage and power flow of each branch.

Control variables are self-constrained, and dependent variables are constrained using penalty terms to the objective function. So the objective function is generalized as follows:

$$f = P_{loss} + \lambda_V \sum_{N_V^{\lim}} \Delta V_L^2 + \lambda_Q \sum_{N_Q^{\lim}} \Delta Q_G^2 \tag{13}$$

where λ_V, λ_Q are the penalty factors, $N_V^{\lim}$ is the set of numbers of load-buses on which voltage outside limits, □ $N_Q^{\lim}$ is the set of numbers of generator buses on which injected reactive power outside limits, ΔV_L and ΔQ_G are defined as:

$$\Delta V_L = \begin{cases} V_L^{\min} - V_L & \text{if } V_L < V_L^{\min} \\ V_L - V_L^{\max} & \text{if } V_L > V_L^{\max} \end{cases} \tag{14}$$

$$\Delta Q_G = \begin{cases} Q_G^{\min} - Q_G & \text{if } Q_G < Q_G^{\min} \\ Q_G - Q_G^{\max} & \text{if } Q_G > Q_G^{\max} \end{cases} \tag{15}$$

2.3.2 Implementation of SOA for reactive power optimization

The basic form of the proposed SOA algorithm can only handle continuous variables. However, both tap position of transformations and reactive power source installation are discrete or integer variables in optimal reactive power dispatch problem. To handle integer variables without any effect on the implementation of SOA, the seekers will still search in a continuous space regardless of the variable type, and then truncating the corresponding dimensions of the seekers' real-value positions into the integers [44] is only performed in evaluating the objective function.

The fitness value of each seeker is calculated by using the objective function in (13). The real-value position of the seeker consists of three parts: generator voltages, transformer taps and shunt capacitors/inductors. After the update of the position, the main program is turned to the sub-program for evaluating the objective function where the latter two parts of the position are truncated into the corresponding integers as [44]. Then, the real-value position is changed into a mixed-variable vector which is used to calculate the objective function value by equation (13) based on Newton-Raphson power flow analysis [45]. The reactive power optimization based on SOA can be described as follows [16].

Step 1. Read the parameters of power system and the proposed algorithm, and specify the lower and upper limits of each variable.

Step 2. Initialize the positions of the seekers in the search space randomly and uniformly. Set the time step t=0.

Step 3. Calculate the fitness values of the initial positions using the objective function in (13) based on the results of Newton-Raphson power flow analysis [45]. The initial historical best position among the population is achieved. Set the personal historical best position of each seeker to his current position.

Step 4. Let $t = t + 1$.
Step 5. Select the neighbors of each seeker.
Step 6. Determine the search direction and step length for each seeker, and update his position.
Step 7. Calculate the fitness values of the new positions using the objective function based on the Newton-Raphson power flow analysis results. Update the historical best position among the population and the historical best position of each seeker.
Step 8. Go to Step 4 until a stopping criterion is satisfied.

2.3.3 Simulation results

To evaluate the effectiveness and efficiency of the proposed SOA-based reactive power optimization approach, standard IEEE 57-bus power system is used.

Since proposed in 1995, PSO [46] and DE [9, 47] have received increasing interest from the evolutionary computation community as two of the relatively new and powerful population-based heuristic algorithms, and they both have been successfully applied to reactive power optimization problems [12, 48-53]. So, the proposed method is compared mainly with the two algorithms and their recently modified versions.

Since the original PSO proposed in [46] is prone to suffer from the so-called "explosion" phenomena [41], two improved versions of PSO: PSO with adaptive inertia weight (PSO-w) and PSO with a constriction factor (PSO-cf), were proposed by Shi, et al. [40] and Clerc, et al. [41], respectively. Considering that the PSO algorithm may easily get trapped in a local optimum when solving complex multimodal problems, Liang, et al. [42] proposed a variant of PSO called comprehensive learning particle swarm optimizer (CLPSO), which is adept at complex multimodal problems. Furthermore, in the year of 2007, Clerc, et al. [54] developed a "real standard" version of PSO, SPSO-07, which was specially prepared for the researchers to compare their algorithms. So, the compared PSOs includes PSO-w(learning rate $c_1 = c_2=2$, inertia weight linearly decreased from 0.9 to 0.4 with run time increasing, the maximum velocity $v_{\max}$ is set at 20% of the dynamic range of the variable on each dimension) [40], PSO-cf ($c_1= c_2=2.01$ and constriction factor $\chi=0.729844$) [41], CLPSO(its parameters follow the suggestions from [42] except that the refreshing gap $m=2$) and SPSO-07 [54].

Since the control parameters and learning strategies in DE are highly dependent on the problems under consideration, and it is not easy to select the correct parameters in practice, Brest, et al. [39] presented a version of DE with self-adapting control parameters (SACP-DE) based on the self-adaptation of the two control parameters: the crossover rate *CR* and the scaling factor *F*, while Qin, et al. [43] proposed a self-adaptive differential evolution (SaDE) where the choice of learning strategy and the two control parameters *F* and *CR* are not required to be pre-specified. So, the compared set of DEs consists of the original DE (DE: DE/rand/1/bin, F=0.5, CR=0.9) [9]), SACP-DE [39] and SaDE [43]. For the afore-mentioned DEs, since the local search schedule used in [43] can clearly improve their performances, the improved versions of the three DEs with local search, instead of their corresponding original versions, are used in this study and denoted as L-DE, L-SACP-DE and L-SaDE, respectively. Moreover, a canonical genetic algorithm (CGA) and an adaptive genetic algorithm (AGA) introduced in [55] are implemented for comparison with SOA. The *fmincon*-based nonlinear programming method (NLP) [45, 56] is also considered.

All the algorithms are implemented in Matlab 7.0 and run on a PC with Pentium 4 CPU 2.4G 512MB RAM. For all the evolutionary methods in the experiments, the same population size *popsize*=60 except SPSO-2007 whose popsize is automatically computed by the algorithm, total 30 runs and the maximum generations of 300 are made. The NLP method uses a different uniformly random number in the search space as its start point in each run. The transformer taps and the reactive power compensation are discrete variables with the update step of 0.01p.u. and 0.048 p.u., respectively. The penalty factors λ_V and λ_Q in (13) are both set to 500.

The IEEE 57-bus system shown in Fig. 4 consists of 80 branches, 7 generator-buses and 15 branches under load tap setting transformer branches. The possible reactive power compensation buses are 18, 25 and 53. Seven buses are selected as PV-buses and $V\theta$-bus as follows: PV-buses: bus 2, 3, 6, 8, 9, 12; $V\theta$-bus: bus 1. The others are PQ-buses. The system data, variable limits and the initial values of control variables were given in [57]. In this case, the search space has 25 dimensions, i.e., the 7 generator voltages, 15 transformer taps, and 3 capacitor banks. The variable limits are given in Table 3.

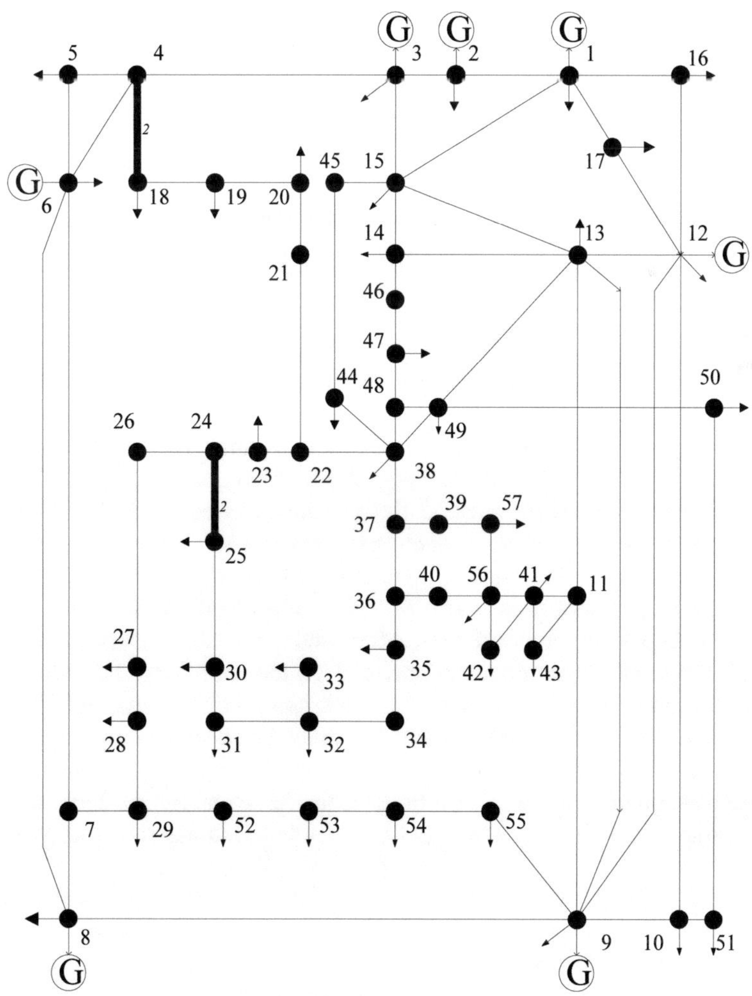

Fig. 4. Network configuration of IEEE 57-bus power system

Limits of Generation Reactive Power							
Bus	1	2	3	6	8	9	12
Q_G^{max}	1.5	0.5	0.6	0.25	2.0	0.09	1.55
Q_G^{min}	-0.2	-0.17	-0.1	-0.08	-1.4	-0.03	-1.5
Limits of Voltage and Tap Setting							
V_G^{max}	V_G^{min}	V_{PQ}^{max}	V_{PQ}^{min}	T_k^{max}	T_k^{min}		
1.06	0.94	1.06	0.94	1.1	0.9		
Limits of Reactive Power Sources							
Bus	18	25	53				
Q_C^{max}	0.1	0.059	0.063				
Q_C^{min}	0.0	0.0	0.0				

Table 3. The Variable Limits (p.u.)

The system loads are given as follows:

$$P_{load}=12.508 \text{ p.u.}, Q_{load}=3.364 \text{ p.u.}$$

The initial total generations and power losses are as follows:

$$\sum P_G=12.7926 \text{ p.u.}, \sum Q_G=3.4545 \text{ p.u.},$$

$$P_{loss}=0.28462 \text{ p.u.}, Q_{loss}=-1.2427 \text{ p.u.}$$

There are five bus voltages outside the limits in the network: V_{25}=0.938, V_{30}=0.920, V_{31}=0.900, V_{32}=0.926, V_{33}= 0.924.

To compare the proposed method with other algorithms, the concerned performance indexes including the best active power losses (*Best*), the worst active power losses (*Worst*), the mean active power losses (*Mean*) and the standard deviation (*Std*) are summarized in Table 4 over total 30 runs. In order to determine whether the results obtained by SOA are statistically different from the results generated by other algorithms, the *T*-tests are conducted, and the corresponding *h* and *CI* values are presented in Table 4, too. Table 4 indicates that SOA has the smallest *Best, Mean* and *Std.* values than all the listed other algorithms, all the *h* values are equal to one, and all the confidence intervals are less than zero and don't contain zero. Hence, the conclusion can be drawn that SOA is significantly better and statistically more robust than all the other listed algorithms in terms of global search capacity and local search precision.

The best reactive power dispatch solutions from 30 runs for various algorithms are tabulated in Table 5 and Table 6. The P_{SAVE}% in Table 6 denotes the saving percent of the reactive power losses. Table 6 demonstrates that a power loss reduction of 14.7443% (from 0.28462 p.u. to 0.2426548 p.u.) is accomplished using the SOA approach, which is the biggest reduction of power loss than that obtained by the other approaches. The corresponding bus voltages are illustrated in Fig. 5 - Fig.8 for various methods. From Fig. 8, it can be seen that all the bus voltages optimized by SOA are kept within the limits, which implies that the proposed approach has better performance in simultaneously achieving the two goals of voltage quality improvement and power loss reduction than the other approaches on the employed test system.

The convergence graphs of the optimized control variables by the SOA are depicted in Fig. 9 - Fig. 11 with respect to the number of generations. From these figures, it can be seen that, due to the good global search ability of the proposed method, the control variables have a serious vibration at the early search phase, and then converge to a steady state at the late search phase, namely, a near optimum solution found by the method.

In this experiment, the computing time at every function evaluation is recorded for various algorithms. The total time of each algorithm is summarized in Table 7. Furthermore, the average convergence curves with active power loss vs. computing time are depicted for all the algorithms in Fig. 12. From Table 7, it can be seen that the computing time of SOA is less than that of the other evolutionary algorithms except SPSO-07 because of its smaller population size. However, Fig. 12 shows that, compared with SPSO-07, SOA has faster convergence speed and, on the contrary, needs less time to achieve the power loss level of SPSO-07. At the same time, SOA has better convergence rate than CLPSO and three versions of DE. Although PSO-w and PSO-cf have faster convergence speed at the earlier search phase, the two versions of PSO rapidly get trapped in premature convergence or search stagnation with the bigger final power losses than that of SOA. Hence, from the simulation results, SOA is synthetically superior to the other algorithms in computation complexity and convergence rate.

Algorithms	*Best*	*Worst*	*Mean*	*Std.*	*h*	*CI*
NLP	0.2590231	0.3085436	0.2785842	1.1677×10^{-2}	1	[-4.4368×10^{-2}, -3.4656×10^{-2}]
CGA	0.2524411	0.2750772	0.2629356	6.2951×10^{-3}	1	[-2.2203×10^{-2}, -1.8253×10^{-2}]
AGA	0.2456484	0.2676169	0.2512784	6.0068×10^{-3}	1	[-1.0455×10^{-2}, -6.6859×10^{-3}]
PSO-w	0.2427052	0.2615279	0.2472596	7.0143×10^{-3}	1	[-6.7111×10^{-3}, -2.3926×10^{-3}]
PSO-cf	0.2428022	0.2603275	0.2469805	6.6294×10^{-3}	1	[-6.3135×10^{-3}, -2.2319×10^{-3}]
CLPSO	0.2451520	0.2478083	0.2467307	9.3415×10^{-4}	1	[-4.3117×10^{-3}, -3.7341×10^{-3}]
SPSO-07	0.2443043	0.2545745	0.2475227	2.8330×10^{-3}	1	[-5.6874×10^{-3}, -3.9425×10^{-3}]
L-DE	0.2781264	0.4190941	0.3317783	4.7072×10^{-2}	1	[-1.0356×10^{-1}, -7.4581×10^{-2}]
L-SACP-DE	0.2791553	0.3697873	0.3103260	3.2232×10^{-2}	1	[-7.7540×10^{-2}, -5.7697×10^{-2}]
L-SaDE	0.2426739	0.2439142	0.2431129	4.8156×10^{-4}	1	[-5.5584×10^{-4}, -2.5452×10^{-4}]
SOA	**0.2426548**	**0.2428046**	**0.2427078**	$\mathbf{4.2081\times10^{-5}}$	-	-

Table 4. Comparisons of the Results of Various Methods on IEEE 57-Bus System over 30 Runs (p.u.)

Variable	Base Case	NLP	CGA	AGA	PSO-w	PSO-cf	CLPSO	SPSO-07	L-DE	L-SACP-DE	L-SaDE	SOA
Generator Voltage V_G												
V_{G1}	1.04	1.06	0.9686	1.0276	1.06	1.06	1.0541	1.0596	1.0397	0.9884	1.0600	1.06
V_{G2}	1.01	1.06	1.0493	1.0117	1.0578	1.0586	1.0529	1.0580	1.0463	1.0543	1.0574	1.0580
V_{G3}	0.985	1.0538	1.0567	1.0335	1.04378	1.0464	1.0337	1.0488	1.0511	1.0278	1.0438	1.0437
V_{G6}	0.98	1.06	0.9877	1.0010	1.0356	1.0415	1.0313	1.0362	1.0236	0.9672	1.0364	1.0352
V_{G8}	1.005	1.06	1.0223	1.0517	1.0546	1.06	1.0496	1.06	1.0538	1.0552	1.0537	1.0548
V_{G9}	0.98	1.06	0.9918	1.0518	1.0369	1.0423	1.0302	1.0433	0.94518	1.0245	1.0366	1.0369
V_{G12}	1.015	1.060	1.0044	1.0570	1.0334	1.0371	1.0342	1.0356	0.99078	1.0098	1.0323	1.0336
Transformer Tap Ratio												
$T_{4\text{-}18}$	0.97	0.91	0.92	1.03	0.9	0.98	0.99	0.95	1.02	1.05	0.94	1
$T_{4\text{-}18}$	0.978	1.06	0.92	1.02	1.02	0.98	0.98	0.99	0.91	1.05	1	0.96
$T_{21\text{-}20}$	1.043	0.93	0.97	1.06	1.01	1.01	0.99	0.99	0.97	0.95	1.01	1.01
$T_{24\text{-}26}$	1.043	1.08	0.9	0.99	1.01	1.01	1.01	1.02	0.91	0.98	1.01	1.01
$T_{7\text{-}29}$	0.967	1	0.91	1.1	0.97	0.98	0.99	0.97	0.96	0.97	0.97	0.97
$T_{34\text{-}32}$	0.975	1.09	1.1	0.98	0.97	0.97	0.93	0.96	0.99	1.09	0.97	0.97
$T_{11\text{-}41}$	0.955	0.92	0.94	1.01	0.9	0.9	0.91	0.92	0.98	0.92	0.9	0.9
$T_{15\text{-}45}$	0.955	0.91	0.95	1.08	0.97	0.97	0.97	0.96	0.96	0.91	0.97	0.97
$T_{14\text{-}46}$	0.9	0.98	1.03	0.94	0.95	0.96	0.95	0.95	1.05	1.08	0.96	0.95
$T_{10\text{-}51}$	0.93	0.98	1.09	0.95	0.96	0.97	0.98	0.97	1.07	0.99	0.96	0.96
$T_{13\text{-}49}$	0.895	0.98	0.9	1.05	0.92	0.93	0.95	0.92	0.99	0.91	0.92	0.92
$T_{11\text{-}43}$	0.958	0.98	0.9	0.95	0.96	0.97	0.95	1	1.06	0.94	0.96	0.96
$T_{40\text{-}56}$	0.958	0.98	1	1.01	1	0.99	1	1	0.99	0.99	1	1
$T_{39\text{-}57}$	0.98	1.08	0.96	0.94	0.96	0.96	0.96	0.95	0.97	0.96	0.96	0.96
$T_{9\text{-}55}$	0.94	1.03	1	1	0.97	0.98	0.97	0.98	1.07	1.1	0.97	0.97
Capacitor Banks												
Q_{C18}	0	0.08352	0.084	0.0168	0.05136	0.09984	0.09888	0.03936	0	0	0.08112	0.09984
Q_{C25}	0	0.00864	0.00816	0.01536	0.05904	0.05904	0.05424	0.05664	0	0	0.05808	0.05904
Q_{C53}	0	0.01104	0.05376	0.03888	0.06288	0.06288	0.06288	0.03552	0	0	0.06192	0.06288
P_{loss}	0.28462	).2590231	).2524411	).2456484	0.2427052	0.2428022	0.2451520	0.2443043	0.2781264	0.2791553	0.2426739	0.2426548

Table 5. Values of Control Variable & P_{loss} After Optimization by Various Methods for IEEE 57-Bus Sytem (p.u.)

Algorithms	$\sum P_G$	$\sum Q_G$	P_{loss}	Q_{loss}	$P_{SAVE}\%$
NLP	12.7687	3.1578	0.2590231	-1.1532	8. 9934
CGA	12.7604	3.0912	0.2524411	-1.1176	11.3059
AGA	12.7536	3.0440	0.2456484	-1.1076	13.6925
PSO-w	12.7507	3.0300	0.2427052	-1.0950	14.7266
PSO-cf	12.7508	2.9501	0.2428022	-1.0753	14.6925
CLPSO	12.7531	3.0425	0.2451520	-1.0853	13.8669
SPSO-07	12.7523	3.0611	0.2443043	-1.0845	14.1647
L-DE	12.7861	3.3871	0.2781264	-1.2158	2.28150
L-SACP-DE	12.7871	3.2712	0.2791553	-1.2042	1.92000
L-SaDE	12.7507	2.9855	0.2426739	-1.0758	14.7376
SOA	12.7507	2.9684	**0.2426548**	-1.0756	**14.7443**

Table 6. The Best Solutions for All the Methods on IEEE 57-Bus System (p.u.)

Algorithms	Shortest time (s)	Longest time (s)	Average time (s)
CGA	353.08	487.14	411.38
AGA	367.31	471.86	449.28
PSO-w	406.42	411.66	408.48
PSO-cf	404.63	410.36	408.19
CLPSO	423.30	441.98	426.85
SPSO-07	121.98	166.23	137.35
L-DE	426.97	443.22	431.41
L-SACP-DE	427.23	431.16	428.98
L-SaDE	408.97	413.03	410.14
SOA	382.23	411.02	391.32

Table 7. The Average Computing Time for Various Algorithms

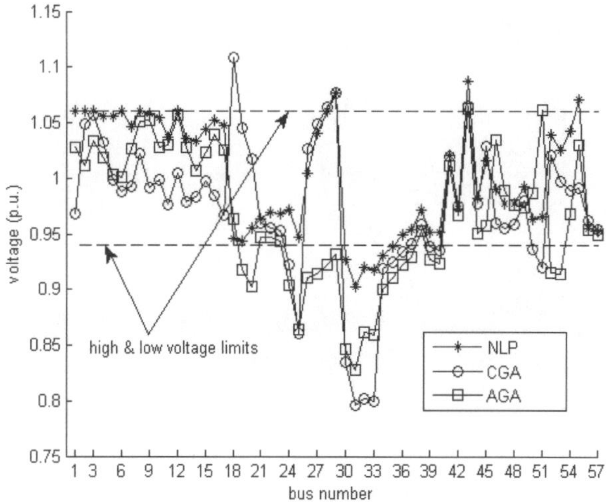

Fig. 5. Bus voltage profiles for NLP and GAs on IEEE 57-bus system

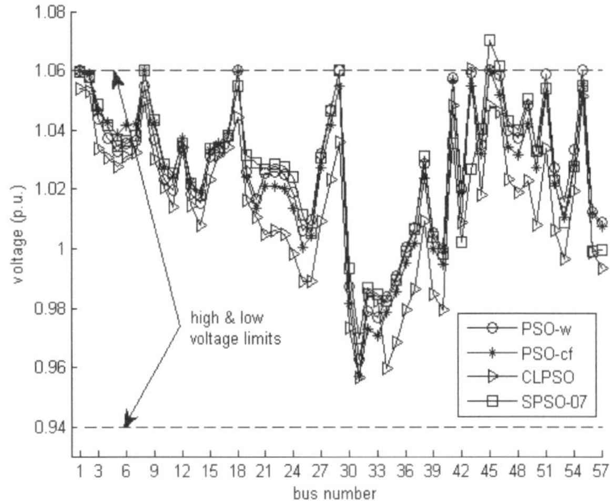

Fig. 6. Bus voltage profiles for PSOs on IEEE 57-bus system

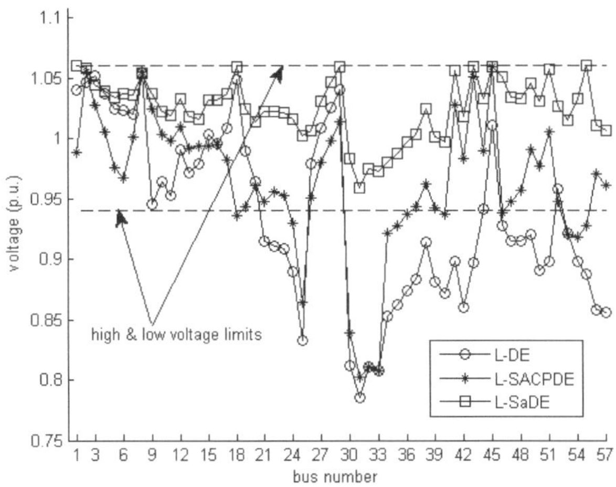

Fig. 7. Bus voltage profiles for DEs on IEEE 57-bus system

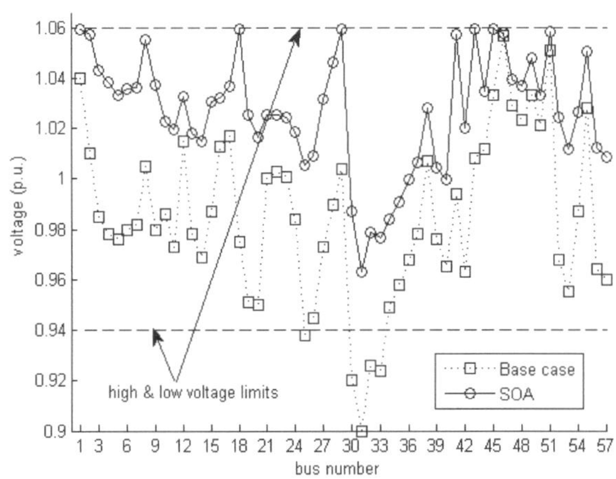

Fig. 8. Bus voltage profiles before and after optimization for SOA on IEEE 57-bus system

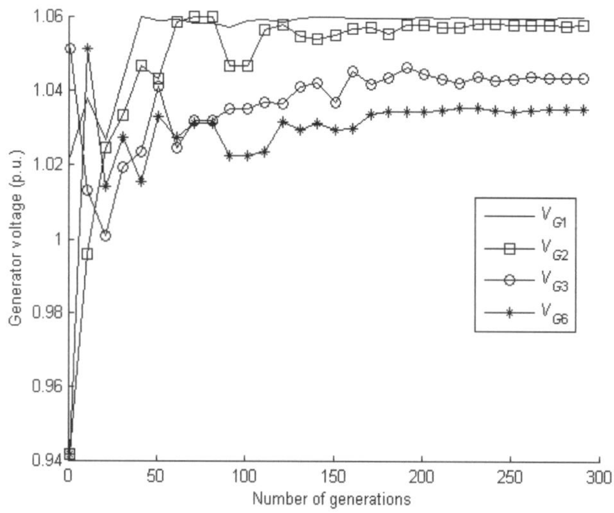

(a)

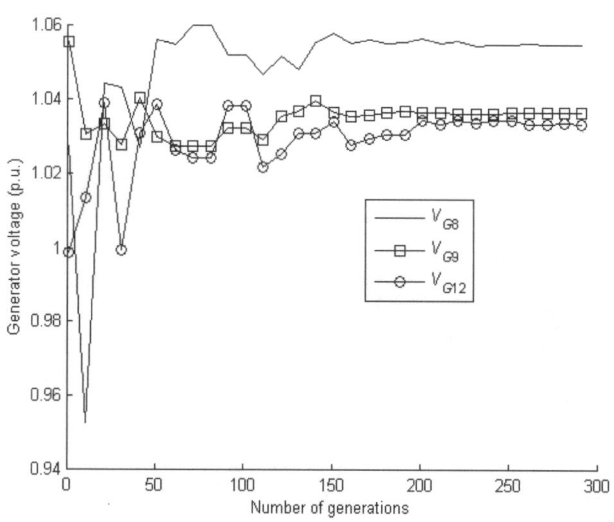

(b)

Fig. 9. Convergence of generator voltages V_G for IEEE 57-bus system

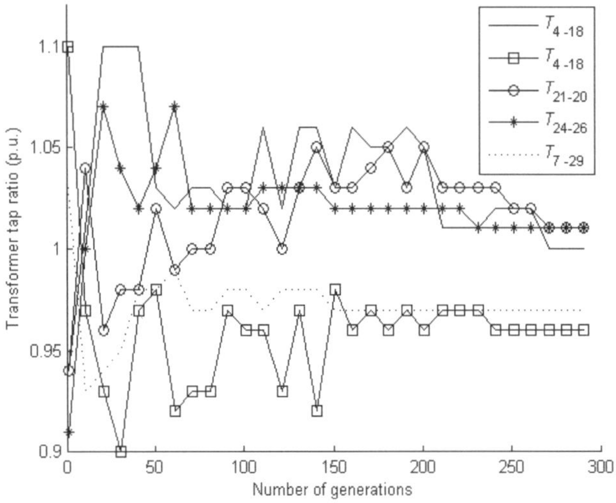

Transformer tap ratio (p.u.)
Number of generations
1.1
1.05
1
0.95
0.9
0
50
100
150
200
250
300
T4 -18
T4 -18
T21-20
T24-26
T7 -29

(a)

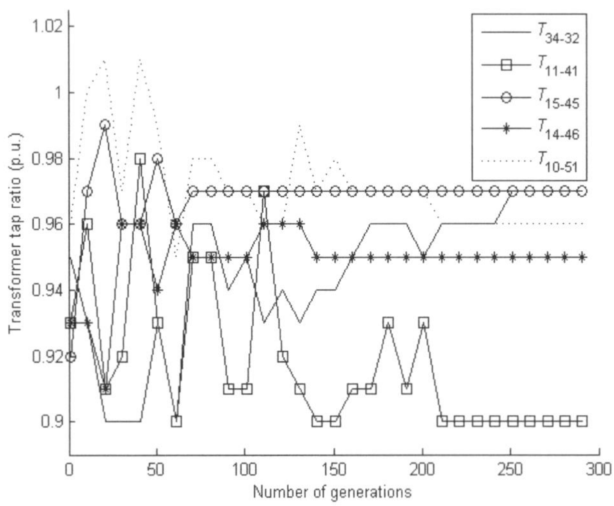

Transformer tap ratio (p.u.)
Number of generations
1.02
1
0.98
0.96
0.94
0.92
0.9
0
50
100
150
200
250
300
T34-32
T11-41
T15-45
T14-46
T10-51

(b)

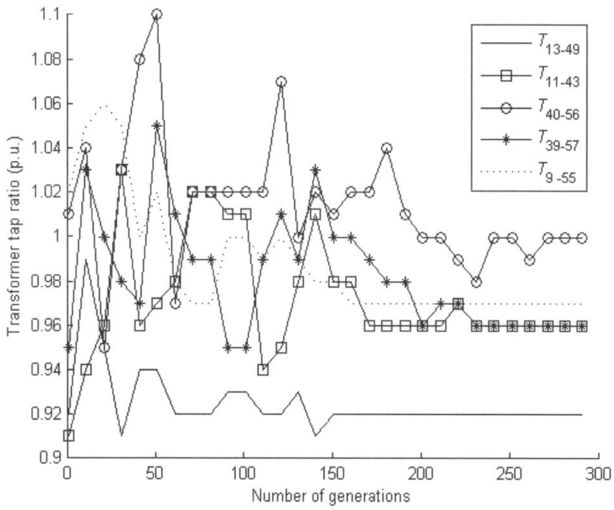

(c)

Fig. 10. Convergence of transformer taps T for IEEE 57-bus system

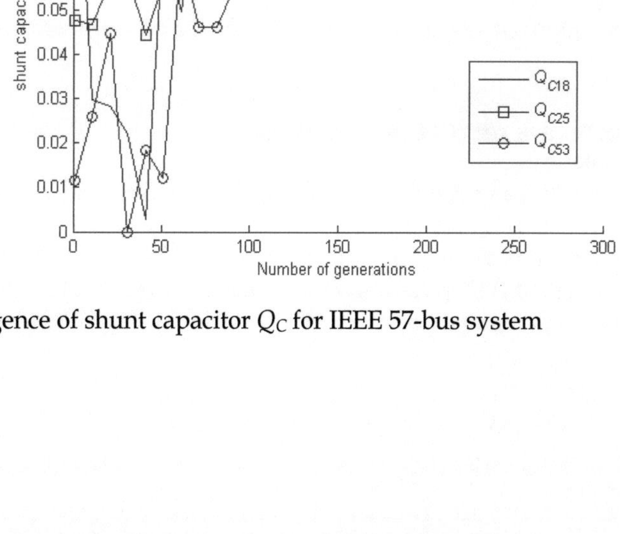

Fig. 11. Convergence of shunt capacitor Q_C for IEEE 57-bus system

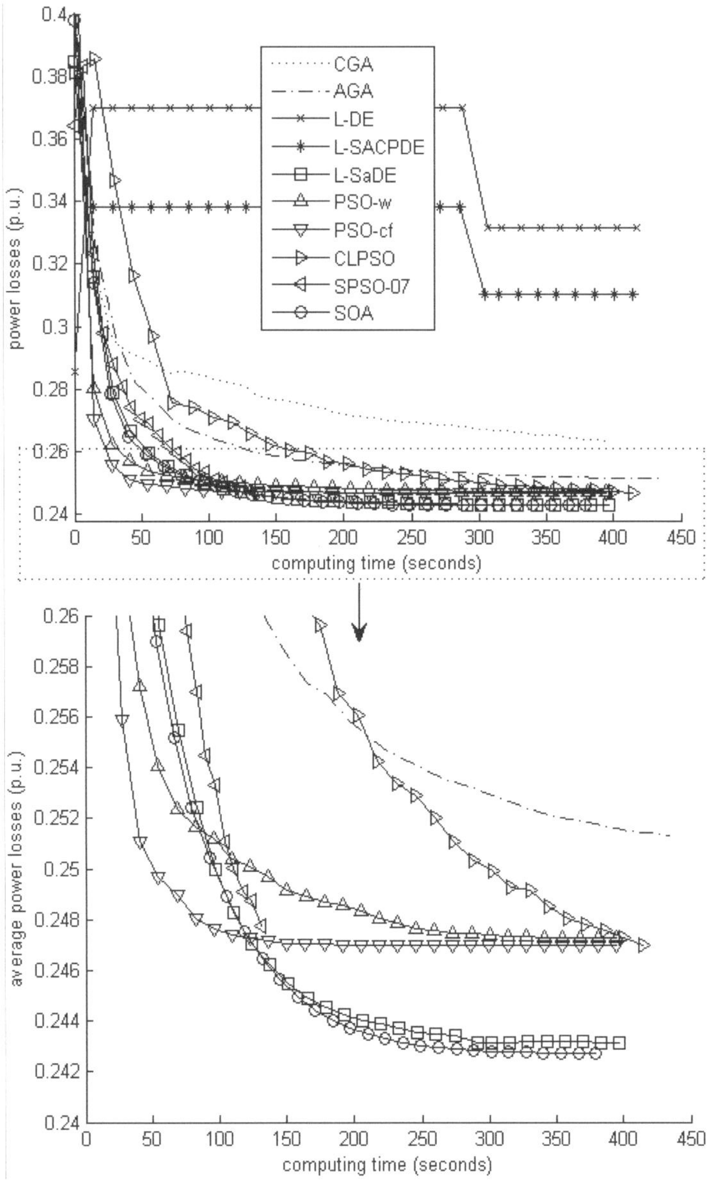

Fig. 12. Convergence graphs of various algorithms on IEEE 57-bus system (power loss vs. time)

2.4 SOA for multi-objective reactive power dispatch

2.4.1 Problem formulation

The multi-objective functions of the ORPD include the technical and economic goals. The economic goal is mainly to minimize the active power transmission loss. The technical goals are to minimize the load bus voltage deviation from the ideal voltage and to improve the voltage stability margin (VSM) [58]. Hence, the objectives of the ORPD model in this chapter are active power loss (P_{loss}), voltage deviation (ΔV_L) and voltage stability margin (VSM).

A. The Active Power Loss

The active power loss minimization in the transmission network can be defined as follows [16, 17, 44]:

$$\min P_{\text{loss}} = f(\vec{x}_1, \vec{x}_2) = \sum_{k \in N_E} g_k (V_i^2 + V_j^2 - 2V_i V_j \cos\theta_{ij}) \tag{16}$$

Subject to

$$\begin{cases} P_{Gi} - P_{Di} = V_i \sum_{j \in N_i} V_j (G_{ij}\cos\theta_{ij} + B_{ij}\sin\theta_{ij}) & i \in N_0 \\ Q_{Gi} - Q_{Di} = V_i \sum_{j \in N_i} V_j (G_{ij}\sin\theta_{ij} - B_{ij}\cos\theta_{ij}) & i \in N_{PQ} \\ V_i^{\min} \le V_i \le V_i^{\max} & i \in N_B \\ T_k^{\min} \le T_k \le T_k^{\max} & k \in N_T \\ Q_{Gi}^{\min} \le Q_{Gi} \le Q_{Gi}^{\max} & i \in N_G \\ Q_{Ci}^{\min} \le Q_{Ci} \le Q_{Ci}^{\max} & i \in N_C \\ S_l \le S_l^{\max} & l \in N_l \end{cases} \tag{17}$$

where $f(\vec{x}_1, \vec{x}_2)$ denotes the active power loss function of the transmission network, $\vec{x}_1$ is the control variable vector $[V_G \; K_T \; Q_C]^T$, $\vec{x}_2$ is the dependent variable vector $[V_L \; Q_G]^T$, V_G is the generator voltage (continuous), T_k is the transformer tap (integer), Q_C is the shunt capacitor/inductor (integer), V_L is the load-bus voltage, Q_G is the generator reactive power, $k=(i,j)$, $i \in N_B$, $j \in N_i$, g_k is the conductance of branch k, θ_{ij} is the voltage angle difference between bus i and j, P_{Gi} is the injected active power at bus i, P_{Di} is the demanded active power at bus i, V_i is the voltage at bus i, G_{ij} is the transfer conductance between bus i and j, B_{ij} is the transfer susceptance between bus i and j, Q_{Gi} is the injected reactive power at bus i, Q_{Di} is the demanded reactive power at bus , N_E is the set of numbers of network branches, N_{PQ} is the set of numbers of PQ buses, N_B is the set of numbers of total buses, N_i is the set of numbers of buses adjacent to bus i (including bus i), N_0 is the set of numbers of total buses excluding slack bus, N_C is the set of numbers of possible reactive power source installation buses, N_G is the set of numbers of generator buses, N_T is the set of numbers of transformer branches, S_l is the power flow in branch l, the superscripts "min" and "max" in equation (17) denote the corresponding lower and upper limits, respectively.

B. Voltage Deviation

Treating the bus voltage limits as constraints in ORPD often results in all the voltages toward their maximum limits after optimization, which means the power system lacks the required reserves to provide reactive power during contingencies. One of the effective ways to avoid this situation is to choose the deviation of voltage from the desired value as an objective function [59], i.e.:

$$\min \Delta V_L = \sum_{i=1}^{N_L} \left| V_i - V_i^* \right| / N_L \tag{18}$$

where ΔV_L is the per unit average voltage deviation, N_L is the total number of the system load buses, V_i and V_i^* are the actual voltage magnitude and the desired voltage magnitude at bus *i*.

C. Voltage Stability Margin

Voltage stability problem has a closely relationship with the reactive power of the system, and the voltage stability margin is inevitably affected in optimal reactive power flow (ORPF) [58]. Hence, the maximal voltage stability margin should be one of the objectives in ORPF [49, 58, 59]. In the literature, the minimal eigenvalue of the non-singular power flow Jacobian matrix has been used by many researchers to improve the voltage stability margin [58]. Here, it is also employed [58]:

$$\max\ VSM = \max(\min\ |\mathrm{eig}(Jacobi)|) \tag{19}$$

where *Jacobi* is the power flow Jacobian matrix, eig(*Jacobi*) returns all the eigenvalues of the Jacobian matrix, min(eig(*Jacobi*)) is the minimum value of eig(*Jacobi*), max(min(eig(*Jacobi*))) is to maximize the minimal eigenvalue in the Jacobian matrix.

D. Multi-objective Conversion

Considering different sub-objective functions have different ranges of function values, every sub-objective uses a transform to keep itself within [0,1]. The first two sub-objective functions, i.e., active power loss and voltage deviation, are normalized:

$$f_1 = \begin{cases} 0 & \text{if } P_{\text{loss}} < P_{\text{loss}_{\min}} \\ \dfrac{P_{\text{loss}} - P_{\text{loss}_{\min}}}{P_{\text{loss}_{\max}} - P_{\text{loss}_{\min}}} & \text{if } P_{\text{loss}_{\min}} \le P_{\text{loss}} \le P_{\text{loss}_{\max}} \\ 1 & \text{if } P_{\text{loss}} > P_{\text{loss}_{\max}} \end{cases} \tag{20}$$

$$f_2 = \begin{cases} 0 & \text{if } \Delta V_L < \Delta V_{L_{\min}} \\ \dfrac{\Delta V_L - \Delta V_{L_{\min}}}{\Delta V_{L_{\max}} - \Delta V_{L_{\min}}} & \text{if } \Delta V_{L_{\min}} \le \Delta V_L \le \Delta V_{L_{\max}} \\ 1 & \text{if } \Delta V_L > \Delta V_{L_{\max}} \end{cases} \tag{21}$$

where the subscripts "min" and "max" in equations (20) and (21) denote the corresponding expectant minimum and possible maximum value, respectively.

Since voltage stability margin sub-objective function is a maximization optimization problem, it is normalized and transformed into a minimization problem using the following equation:

$$f_3 = \begin{cases} 0 & \text{if } VSM > VSM_{\max} \\ \dfrac{VSM_{\max} - VSM}{VSM_{\max} - VSM_{\min}} & \text{else} \end{cases} \tag{22}$$

where the subscripts "min" and "max" in equation (22) denote the possible minimum and expectant maximum value, respectively.

Control variables are self-constrained, and dependent variables are constrained using penalty terms. Then, the overall objective function is generalized as follows:

$$\min\ f = \omega_1 f_1 + \omega_2 f_2 + \omega_3 f_3 + \lambda_V \sum_{N_V^{\lim}} \Delta V_L^2 + \lambda_Q \sum_{N_Q^{\lim}} \Delta Q_G^2 \tag{23}$$

where ω_i (i=1,2,3) is the user-defined constants which are used to weigh the contributions from different sub-objectives; λ_V, λ_Q are the penalty factors; $N_V^{\lim}$ is the set of numbers of load-buses on which voltage outside limits, □ $N_Q^{\lim}$ is the set of numbers of generator buses on which injected reactive power outside limits; ΔV_L and ΔQ_G are defined as:

$$\Delta V_L = \begin{cases} V_L^{\min} - V_L & \text{if } V_L < V_L^{\min} \\ V_L - V_L^{\max} & \text{if } V_L > V_L^{\max} \end{cases} \tag{24}$$

$$\Delta Q_G = \begin{cases} Q_G^{\min} - Q_G & \text{if } Q_G < Q_G^{\min} \\ Q_G - Q_G^{\max} & \text{if } Q_G > Q_G^{\max} \end{cases} \tag{25}$$

2.4.2 Implementation of SOA for reactive power optimization

The fitness value of each seeker is calculated by using the objective function in (23). The real-value position of the seeker consists of three parts: generator voltages, transformer taps and shunt capacitors/inductors. According to the section 3.4 of this paper, after the update of the position, the main program is turned to the sub-program for evaluating the objective function where the latter two parts of the position are truncated into the corresponding integers as [44, 55]. Then, the real-value position is changed into a mixed-variable vector which is used to calculate the objective function value by equation (23) based on Newton-Raphson power flow analysis [45]. The reactive power optimization based on SOA can be described as follows [17].

Step 1. Read the parameters of power system and the proposed algorithm, and specify the lower and upper limits of each variable.

Step 2. Initialize the positions of the seekers in the search space randomly and uniformly. Set the time step t=0.

Step 3. Calculate the fitness values of the initial positions using the objective function in (23) based on the results of Newton-Raphson power flow analysis [45]. The initial historical best position among the population is achieved. Set the historical best position of each seeker to his current position.

Step 4. Let t=t+1.

Step 5. Determine the neighbors, search direction and step length for each seeker.

Step 6. Update the position of each seeker.

Step 7. Calculate the fitness values of the new positions using the objective function based on the Newton-Raphson power flow analysis results. Update the historical best position among the population and the historical best position of each seeker.

Step 8. Go to Step 4 until a stopping criterion is satisfied.

2.4.3 Simulation results

To evaluate the effectiveness and efficiency of the proposed SOA-based reactive power optimization approach, the standard IEEE 57-bus power system is used as the test system.

For the comparisons, the following algorithms are also considered: PSO-w (learning rate $c_1 = c_2=2$, inertia weight linearly decreased from 0.9 to 0.4 with run time increasing, the maximum velocity v_{max} is set at 20% of the dynamic range of the variable on each dimension) [40], PSO-cf ($c_1= c_2=2.01$ and constriction factor χ=0.729844) [41], CLPSO (its parameters follow the suggestions from [42] except that the refreshing gap m=2) and SPSO-07 [54], the original DE (DE: DE/rand/1/bin, F=0.5, CR=0.9) [39]), SACP-DE and SaDE. For the afore-mentioned DEs, since the local search schedule used in [43] can clearly improve their performances, the improved versions of the three DEs with local search, instead of their corresponding original versions, are used in this study and denoted as L-DE, L-SACP-DE and L-SaDE, respectively.

Moreover, a canonical genetic algorithm (CGA) and an adaptive genetic algorithm (AGA) introduced in [55] are considered for comparison with SOA.

All the algorithms are implemented in Matlab 7.0 and run on a PC with Pentium 4 CPU 2.4G 512MB RAM. In the experiments, the same population size *popsize*=60 for the IEEE 57-bus system except SPSO-2007 whose popsize is automatically computed by the algorithm, total 30 runs and the maximum generations of 300 are made. The transformer taps and the reactive power compensation are discrete variables with the update step of 0.01p.u. and 0.048 p.u., respectively.

The main parameters involved in SOA include: the population size s, the number of subpopulations, and the parameters of membership function of Fuzzy reasoning (including the limits of membership degree value, i.e., μ_{max} and μ_{min} in (8) and the limits of ω, i.e., ω_{max} and ω_{min} in (9)). In this paper, s=60 for IEEE 57-bus system and s=80 for IEEE 118-bus system, K=3, μ_{max}=0.95, μ_{max}=0.0111, ω_{max}=0.8, ω_{min}=0.2 for both the test systems.

The IEEE 57-bus system [45] shown in Fig. 4 consists of 80 branches, 7 generator-buses and 15 branches under load tap setting transformer branches. The possible reactive power compensation buses are 18, 25 and 53. Seven buses are selected as PV-buses and $V\theta$-bus as follows: PV-buses: bus 2, 3, 6, 8, 9, 12; $V\theta$-bus: bus 1. The others are PQ-buses. The system data, operating conditions, variable limits and the initial generator bus voltages and transformer taps were given in [57], or can be obtained from the authors of this paper on request. The model parameters in the equations (20)-(23) are set as: $P_{loss_{max}} = 0.5, P_{loss_{min}} = 0.2$, $\Delta V_{L_{max}} = 1$, $\Delta V_{L_{min}} = 0$, VSM_{max}=0.4, VSM_{min}=0.05, ω_1=0.6, ω_2=0.2, ω_3=0.2, λ_V=500 and λ_Q=500.

The system loads are : P_{load}=12.508 p.u., Q_{load} =3.364 p.u. The initial total generations and power losses are: $\sum P_G$=12.7926 p.u., $\sum Q_G$=3.4545 p.u., P_{loss}=0.28462 p.u., Q_{loss}= -1.2427 p.u. There are five bus voltages outside the limits: V_{25}=0.938, V_{30}=0.920, V_{31}=0.900, V_{32}=0.926, V_{33}= 0.924.

To compare the proposed method with other algorithms, the concerned performance indexes including the *best*, *worst*, *mean* and standard deviation (*Std.*) of the overall and sub-objective function values are summarized in Tables 8 - 11. In order to determine whether the results obtained by SOA are statistically different from the results generated by other algorithms, the T-tests [56] are conducted. An h value of one indicates that the performances of the two algorithms are statistically different with 95% certainty, whereas h value of zero implies that the performances are not statistically different. The CI is confidence interval.

The corresponding h and CI values for overall function values and active power losses are presented in Tables 8 and 9, respectively. The best reactive power dispatch solutions from 30 runs for various algorithms are tabulated in Table 12 where $P_{SAVE}\%$ denotes the saving percent of the reactive power losses. The corresponding bus voltages are illustrated in Fig. 13. The total time of each algorithm is summarized in Table 13. The average convergence curves for overall function value vs. computing time and active power loss vs. computing time are depicted for all the algorithms in Figs. 14 and 15, respectively.

Table 8 indicates that SOA has the smallest *Best, Mean, Worst* and *Std.* values of overall function than all the listed other algorithms except that SOA has the a little larger *Worst* value than that of PSO-w, only the h values for SOA vs. CLPSO and SOA vs. L-SaDE are equal to zeroes (Accordingly, their confidence intervals contain zero). Table 9 indicates that SOA has the smallest *Best, Mean, Worst* and *Std.* values of power loss than all the listed other algorithms except that SOA has the a little larger *Worst* value than that of L-SaDE with h=0 and CI containing zero. Tables 10 and 11 show that SOA has the better or comparable other two sub-objective values, i.e., voltage stability margin (VSM) and voltage deviation (ΔV_L). Table 12 demonstrates that a power loss reduction of 13.4820% (from 0.28462 p.u. to 0.246248 p.u.) is accomplished using the SOA approach, which is the biggest reduction of power loss than that obtained by the other approaches. Hence, the conclusion can be drawn that SOA is better than, or comparable to, all the other listed algorithms in terms of global search capacity and local search precision. Furthermore, from Fig. 13, it can be seen that all the bus voltages optimized by SOA are acceptably kept within the limits.

From Table 13, it can be seen that the average computing time of SOA is less than that of other algorithms except SPSO-07 because of its smaller population size. However, Figs. 14 and 15 show that, compared with SPSO-07, SOA has faster convergence speed and, on the contrary, needs less time to achieve the overall function value and power loss level achieved by SPSO-07. At the same time, SOA also has better convergence rate than GAs, DEs and PSOs.

Algorithms	*Best*	*Worst*	*Mean*	*Std.*	*h*	*CI*
CGA	0.192750	0.195206	0.194024	4.8798×10^{-4}	1	[-0.0684, -0.0378]
AGA	0.192284	0.193994	0.193030	4.4517×10^{-4}	1	[-0.0674, -0.0368]
PSO-w	0.191851	**0.191977**	0.191901	$\mathbf{4.2691\times10^{-5}}$	1	[-0.0727, -0.0292,]
PSO-cf	0.116954	0.192593	0.188312	16797×10^{-2}	1	[-0.0634, -0.0314]
CLPSO	0.120773	0.192739	0.148663	3.3476×10^{-2}	0	[-0.0257, 0.0102]
SPSO-2007	0.191918	0.193559	0.192551	3.9668×10^{-4}	1	[-0.0669, -0.0363,]
L-DE	0.232519	0.388413	0.314205	4.0455×10^{-2}	1	[-0.1923, -0.1543]
L-SACP-DE	0.237277	0.395611	0.317571	4.1949×10^{-2}	1	[-0.1959, -0.1574]
L-SaDE	0.116819	0.192131	0.154692	3.8257×10^{-2}	0	[-0.0324, 0.0049]
SOA	**0.116495**	0.192083	**0.140927**	3.4163×10^{-2}	-	-

Table 8. The Results of Overall Objective Function Values for Various Algorithms on IEEE 57-bus System over 30 Runs (p.u.)

Algorithms	*Best*	*Worst*	*Mean*	*Std.*	*h*	*CI*
CGA	0.267170	0.419747	0.323181	4.2147×10^{-2}	1	[-0.0787, -0.0529]
AGA	0.258072	0.369785	0.296744	3.5776×10^{-2}	1	[-0.0507, -0.0280,]
PSO-w	0.259729	0.324923	0.283945	2.2313×10^{-2}	1	[-0.0363 -0.0168]
PSO-cf	0.247866	0.393221	0.297066	3.2551×10^{-2}	1	[-0.0502, -0.0291,]
CLPSO	0.257968	0.340029	0.273334	1.9252×10^{-2}	1	[-0.0235, -0.0083,]
SPSO-2007	0.274210	0.386235	0.307093	2.7961×10^{-2}	1	[-0.0591, -0.0402]
L-DE	0.291864	0.5069975	0.373198	5.4894×10^{-2}	1	[-0.1320, -0.0996]
L-SACP-DE	0.273183	0.4438575	0.343407	4.5156×10^{-2}	1	[-0.0997, -0.0723]
L-SaDE	0.246712	**0.282335**	0.260983	1.3426×10^{-2}	0	[-0.0101, 0.0030]
SOA	**0.246248**	0.287541	**0.257410**	$\mathbf{1.1918\times10^{-2}}$	-	-

Table 9. The Results of Active Power Loss for Various Algorithms on IEEE 57-bus System over 30 Runs (p.u.)

Algorithms	*Best*	*Worst*	*Mean*	*Std.*
CGA	0.186249	0.173969	0.1798794	2.4399×10^{-3}
AGA	0.188582	0.180030	0.1848524	2.2259×10^{-3}
PSO-w	0.190745	0.190117	**0.1904974**	2.1346×10^{-4}
PSO-cf	**0.190754**	0.1870317	0.1895324	122285×10^{-3}
CLPSO	0.187857	0.1783987	0.183922	3.0781×10^{-3}
SPSO-2007	0.190411	0.182206	0.187245	1.9834×10^{-3}
L-DE	0.1778431	0.165211	0.171368	3.4560×10^{-3}
L-SACP-DE	0.183051	0.159702	0.170998	5.7523×10^{-3}
L-SaDE	0.190638	0.1853272	0.1882648	1.9748×10^{-3}
SOA	0.190709	0.176374	0.187451	2.6388×10^{-3}

Table 10. The Results of Voltage Stability Margin for Various Algorithms on IEEE 57-bus System over 30 Runs (p.u.)

Algorithms	CGA	AGA	PSO-w	PSO-cf	CLPSO	SPSO-2007	LDE	L-SACP-DE	L-SaDE	SOA
Best	0	0	0	0	0	0	2.886554	2.317914	0	0
Worst	0	0	0	0	0.291757	0	0.561878	0.634840	0	0
Mean	0	0	0	0	0.014588	0	1.777176	1.890710	0	0
Std.	0	0	0	0	6.5239×10^{-2}	0	6.0402×10^{-1}	7.9319×10^{-1}	0	0

Table 11. The Results of Voltage Deviation for Various Algorithms on IEEE 57-bus System over 30 Runs (p.u.)

Algorithms	$\sum P_G$	$\sum Q_G$	P_{loss}	Q_{loss}	P_{SAVE}%	VSM	ΔV_L
CGA	12.7752	3.1744	0.267170	-1.1565	6.1308	0.179828	0
AGA	12.7661	3.0679	0.258072	-1.1326	9.3276	0.185845	0
PSO-w	12.7677	3.1026	0.259729	-1.1598	8.7453	**0.190117**	0
PSO-cf	12.7559	3.0157	0.247866	-1.1137	12.9132	0.1870317	0
CLPSO	12.7660	3.1501	0.257968	-1.1295	9.3642	0.1849117	0.291757
SPSO-2007	12.7822	3.1818	0.274210	-1.2532	3.6576	0.1877947	0
L-DE	12.7999	3.3656	0.291864	-1.2158	-1.2380	0.1701207	2.886554
L-SACP-DE	12.7812	3.2085	0.273183	-1.1868	4.0185	0.183051	4.282957
L-SaDE	12.7549	3.0191	0.246712	-1.1209	13.2696	0.186182	0
SOA	12.7543	2.9837	**0.246248**	-1.0914	**13.4820**	0.186895	0

Table 12. The Best Dispatch Solutions for Various Algorithms on IEEE 57-bus System (p.u.)

Algorithms	CGA	AGA	PSO-w	PSO-cf	CLPSO	SPSO-2007	LDE	L-SACP-DE	L-SaDE	SOA
Shortest time (s)	1265.34	1273.44	1216.91	1188.45	1399.48	433.36	1210.73	1212.95	1273.42	1192.83
Longest time (s)	1295.02	1323.91	1244.64	1268.00	1448.84	495.97	1239.86	1235.03	1368.03	1288.66
Average time (s)	1284.11	1293.78	1229.98	1225.14	1426.19	480.94	1224.27	1221.51	1306.86	1221.10

Table 13. The Computing Time for Various Algorithms on IEEE 57-bus System over 30 Runs

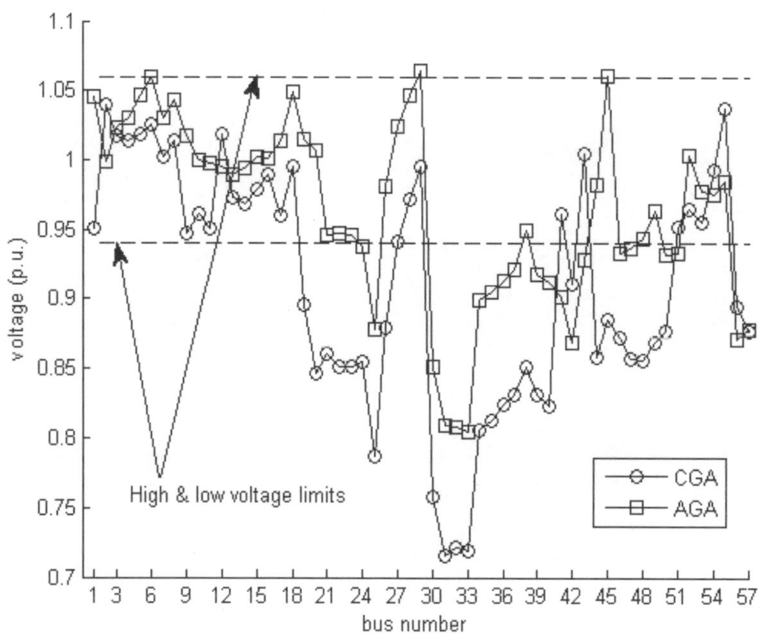

(a)

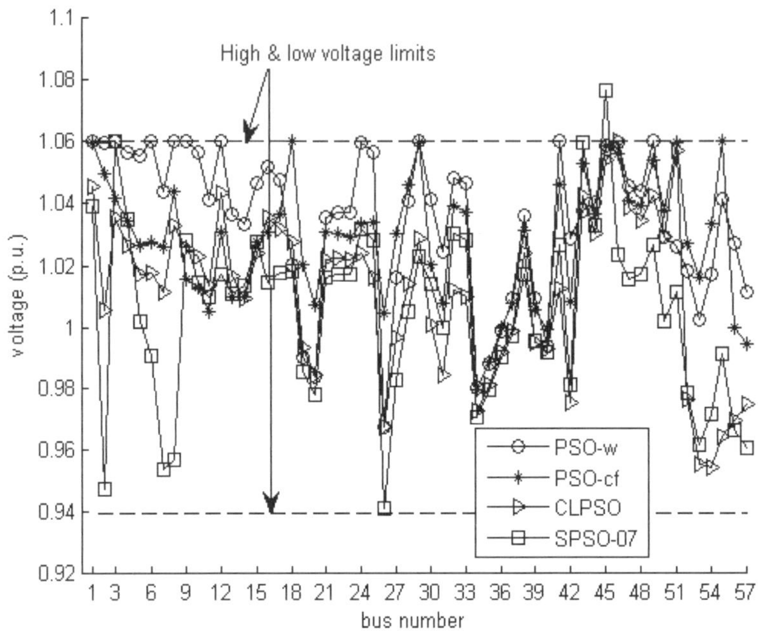
High & low voltage limits
voltage (p.u.)
1.1
1.08
1.06
1.04
1.02
1
0.98
0.96
0.94
0.92
PSO-w
PSO-cf
CLPSO
SPSO-07
1 3 6 9 12 15 18 21 24 27 30 33 36 39 42 45 48 51 54 57
bus number

(b)

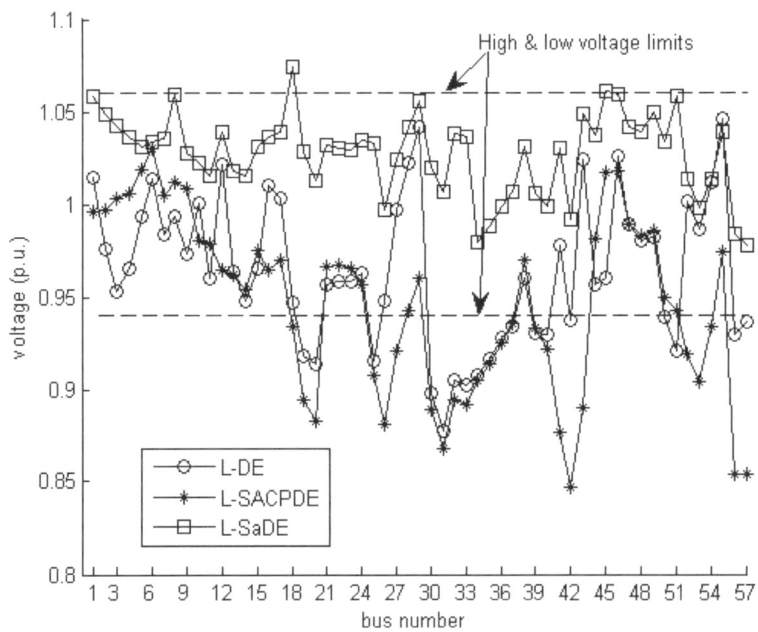
High & low voltage limits
voltage (p.u.)
1.1
1.05
1
0.95
0.9
0.85
0.8
L-DE
L-SACPDE
L-SaDE
1 3 6 9 12 15 18 21 24 27 30 33 36 39 42 45 48 51 54 57
bus number

(c)

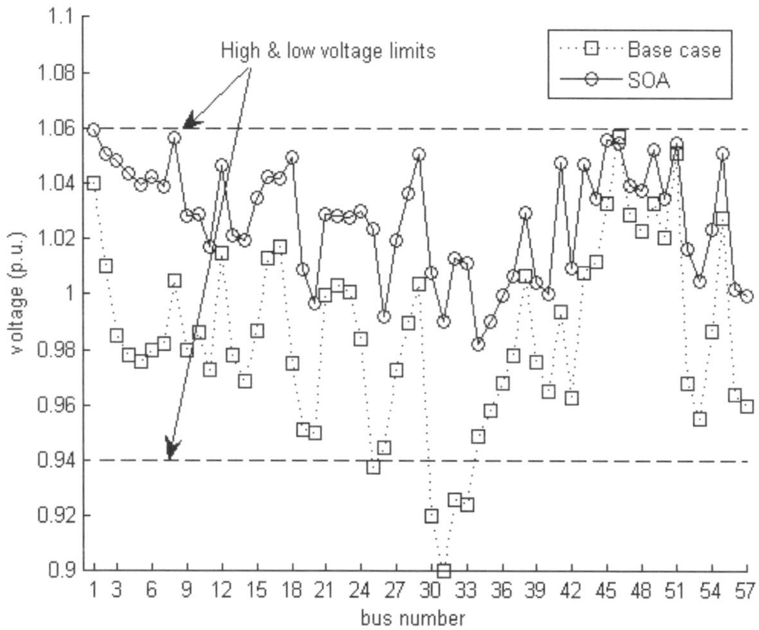

(d)

Fig. 13. Bus voltage profiles for various algorithms on IEEE 57-bus

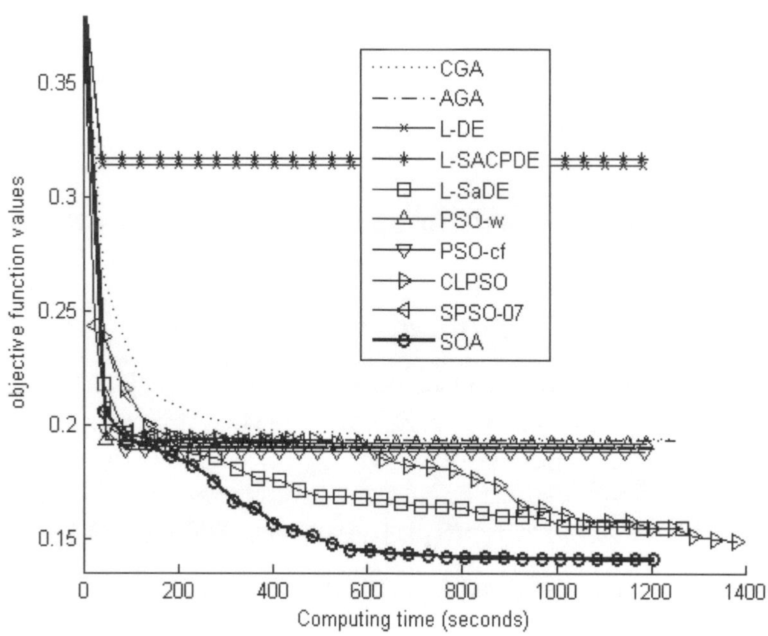

Fig. 14. Convergence Graphs of various algorithms on IEEE 57-bus (overall objective function values vs. time)

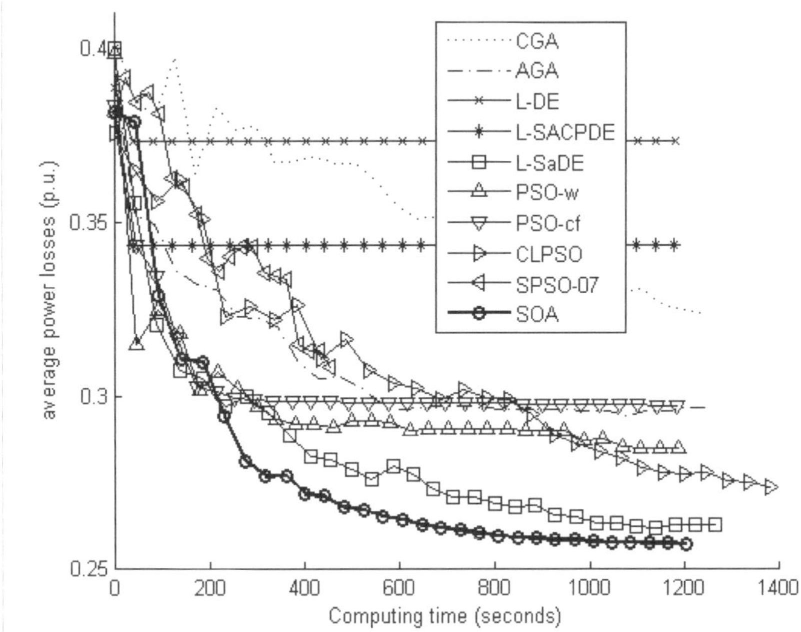

Fig. 15. Convergence Graphs of various algorithms on IEEE 57-bus (power loss vs. time)

3. Stochastic Focusing Search (SFS) and its application

3.1 Stochastic Focusing Search (SFS) (Ref.[20, 21])

Stochastic focusing search (SFS) is a simplified and improved version of PSO. In the SFS, particles make a focusing search around the best position so far and stochastically update their positions within a neighborhood of the best position with a decreasing search radius. Unlike PSO, the velocity and position iteration of the SFS is implemented according to the following equations:

$$\vec{v}_i(t) = \begin{cases} Rand() \times (R_{ti} - \vec{x}_i(t-1)) & \text{if } fun(\vec{x}_i(t-1)) \geq fun(\vec{x}_i(t-2)) \\ \vec{v}_i(t-1) & \text{if } fun(\vec{x}_i(t-1)) < fun(\vec{x}_i(t-2)) \end{cases} \tag{26}$$

$$\vec{x}_i(t) = \vec{v}_i(t) + \vec{x}_i(t-1) \tag{27}$$

where $Rand()$ returns a uniformly random number in the range [0, 1], $fun(\vec{x}_i(t))$ is the objective function value of $\vec{x}_i(t)$, R_{ti} is a random selected point (position) in the neighborhood space R_t of $\vec{g}_{best}$. R_t is defined as: $\left[\vec{g}_{best} - \frac{w(\vec{g}_{best} - \vec{x}_{\min})}{(\vec{x}_{\max} - \vec{x}_{\min})^{1-w}}, \vec{g}_{best} + \frac{w(\vec{x}_{\max} - \vec{g}_{best})}{(\vec{x}_{\max} - \vec{x}_{\min})^{1-w}}\right]$, where $\vec{x}_{\max}$ and $\vec{x}_{\min}$ are the search space borders. When w is linearly decreased from 1 to 0, R_t is deflated from the entire search space to the best point $\vec{g}_{best}$.

According to Eq. (26), if a particle holds a good velocity at the time step *t*-1 (i.e., $fun(\vec{x}_i(t-1)) < fun(\vec{x}_i(t-2))$), its velocity keeps the same one as the past; else, the particle randomly selects a position within a neighborhood of the best position so far. Moreover, the SFS also uses a greedy selection, namely: if the new position obtained by Eq. (27) is worse the early position (i.e., $fun(\vec{x}_i(t-1)) < fun(\vec{x}_i(t))$), the particle will come back to the early position (i.e., $\vec{x}_i(t) = \vec{x}_i(t-1)$).

According to Eqs. (26) and (27), it can be seen that each individual particle makes a search in a decreasing R_t with time step increasing. It is of significance to select an appropriate w to not only assure the global convergence ability but also avoid a local extremum. In this study, w is defined as:

$$w = (\frac{G-t}{G})^{\delta} \tag{28}$$

where G is the maximum generation, δ is a positive number. It is indicated that w is decreased from 1 to 0 with the increasing of time step *t*.

To improve the global searching ability and avoid a local extremum, the particles are categorized into multiple subpopulations. The number of subpopulations μ is decreasing from particles size s to 1 according to the indexes of the particles with the inertia weight w'.

$$w' = (\frac{G-t}{G})^{\delta'} \tag{29}$$

$$\mu = \lfloor w's + 1 \rfloor \tag{30}$$

It can be seen that w' has the same form of w from equation (29). w' decreases with the run time increasing so as to decrease the subpopulations μ. In every subpopulation, there will be a different $\vec{g}_{best}$, which is the best position of the subpopulation. The pseudocode of the SFS is presented in Fig. 16.

```
begin
    t←0;
    generating s positions uniformly and randomly in the whole search space;
    evaluating each particle;
    repeat
        t←t+1;
        finding the respective g_best in every subpopulation;
        updating and evaluating each particle's position using (3) and (4) with the
        greedy selection;
    until the stop condition is satisfied
end.
```

Fig. 16. The pseudo code of the main algorithm

3.2 SFS for benchmark function optimization (Ref.[20])

3.2.1 The benchmark functions

In order to evaluate the novel algorithm, a test suite of benchmark functions previously introduced by Yao, Liu and Lin [60] was used (listed in Table 14), the ranges of their search spaces, their dimensionalities, and their global minimum function values (ideal values) are

Functions	n	S	f_{min}
$f_1(\vec{x})=\sum_{i=1}^{n}x_i^2$	30	$[-5.12,5.12]^n$	$f_1(\vec{0})=0$
$f_2(\vec{x})=\sum_{i=1}^{n}\lvert x_i\rvert+\prod_{i=1}^{n}\lvert x_i\rvert$	30	$[-10,10]^n$	$f_2(\vec{0})=0$
$f_3(\vec{x})=\sum_{i=1}^{n}(\sum_{j=1}^{i}x_j)^2$	30	$[-100,100]^n$	$f_3(\vec{0})=0$
$f_4(\vec{x})=\max_i\{\lvert x_i\rvert,1\le i\le n\}$	30	$[-100,100]^n$	$f_4(\vec{0})=0$
$f_5(\vec{x})=\sum_{i=1}^{n-1}(100(x_{i+1}-x_i^2)^2+(x_i-1)^2)$	30	$[-30,30]^n$	$f_5(\vec{1})=0$
$f_6(\vec{x})=\sum_{i=1}^{n}(\lfloor x_i+0.5\rfloor)^2$	30	$[-100,100]^n$	$f_6(\vec{p})=0,\ -0.5\le p_i\le 0.5$
$f_7(\vec{x})=\sum_{i=1}^{n}ix_i^4+rand[0,1)$	30	$[-1.28,1.28]^n$	$f_7(\vec{0})=0$
$f_8(\vec{x})=-\sum_{i=1}^{n}(x_i\sin(\sqrt{\lvert x_i\rvert}))$	30	$[-500,500]^n$	$f_8(42\vec{0}.97)=-12569.5$
$f_9(\vec{x})=\sum_{i=1}^{n}(x_i^2-10\cos(2\pi x_i)+10)$	30	$[-5.12,5.12]^n$	$f_9(\vec{0})=0$
$f_{10}(\vec{x})=-20\exp(-0.2\sqrt{\frac{1}{n}\sum_{i=1}^{n}x_i^2})$ $-\exp(\frac{1}{n}\sum_{i=1}^{n}\cos(2\pi x_i))+20+e$	30	$[-32,32]^n$	$f_{10}(\vec{0})=0$
$f_{11}(\vec{x})=\frac{1}{4000}\sum_{i=1}^{n}x_i^2-\prod_{i=1}^{n}\cos(\frac{x_i}{\sqrt{i}})+1$	30	$[-600,600]^n$	$f_{11}(\vec{0})=0$
$f_{12}(\vec{x})=\frac{\pi}{n}\{10\sin^2(\pi y_1)$ $+\sum_{i=1}^{n-1}(y_i-1)^2[1+10\sin^2(\pi y_{i+1})]$ $+(y_n-1)^2\}+\sum_{i=1}^{n}u(x_i,10,100,4)$	30	$[-50,50]^n$	$f_{12}(-\vec{1})=0$
$f_{13}(\vec{x})=0.1\{\sin^2(3\pi x_1)$ $+\sum_{i=1}^{n-1}(x_i-1)^2[1+\sin^2(3\pi x_{i+1})]$ $+(x_n-1)^2[1+\sin^2(2\pi x_n)]\}$ $+\sum_{i=1}^{n}u(x_i,5,100,4)$	30	$[-50,50]^n$	$f_{13}(1,\ldots,1)=0$
$f_{14}(\vec{x})=(0.002$ $+\sum_{j=1}^{25}(j+\sum_{i=1}^{2}(x_i-a_{ij})^6)^{-1})^{-1}$	2	$[-65.54, 65.54]^n$	$f_{14}(-3\vec{1}.95)=0.998$
$f_{15}(\vec{x})=\sum_{i=1}^{11}[a_i-\frac{x_1(b_i^2+b_ix_2)}{b_i^2+b_ix_3+x_4}]^2$	4	$[-5,5]^n$	$f_{15}(0.1928,0.1908,0.1231,0.1358)$ $=3.075\times10^{-4}$
$f_{16}(\vec{x})=4x_1^2-2.1x_1^4+\frac{1}{3}x_1^6+x_1x_2-4x_2^2+4x_2^4$	2	$[-5,5]^n$	$f_{16}(-0.09,0.71)=-1.0316$
$f_{17}(\vec{x})=(x_2-\frac{5.1}{4\pi^2}x_1^2+\frac{5}{\pi}x_1-6)^2$ $+10(1-\frac{1}{8\pi})\cos(x_1)+10$	2	$[-5,15]^n$	$f_{17}(9.42,2.47)=0.398$

$f_{18}(\vec{x})=[1+(x_1+x_2+1)^2(19-14x_1+3x_1^2-14x_2+6x_1x_2+3x_2^2)]\times[30+(2x_1-3x_2)^2\times(18-32x_1+12x_1^2+48x_2-36x_1x_2+27x_2^2)]$	2	$[-2,2]^n$	$f_{18}(0,-1)=3$
$f_{19}(\vec{x})=-\sum_{i=1}^{4}c_i\exp[-\sum_{j=1}^{3}a_{ij}(x_j-p_{ij})^2]$	3	$[0,1]^n$	$f_{19}(0.114,0.556,0.852)=-3.86$
$f_{20}(\vec{x})=-\sum_{i=1}^{4}c_i\exp[-\sum_{j=1}^{6}a_{ij}(x_j-p_{ij})^2]$	6	$[0,1]^n$	$f_{20}(0.201,0.15,0.477,0.275,0.311,0.657)=-3.32$
$f_{21}(\vec{x})=-\sum_{i=1}^{5}[(\vec{x}-a_i)(\vec{x}-a_i)^T+c_i]^{-1}$	4	$[0,10]^n$	$f_{21}(\approx\vec{4})=-10.3$
$f_{22}(\vec{x})=-\sum_{i=1}^{7}[(\vec{x}-a_i)(\vec{x}-a_i)^T+c_i]^{-1}$	4	$[0,10]^n$	$f_{21}(\approx\vec{4})=-10.6$
$f_{23}(\vec{x})=-\sum_{i=1}^{10}[(\vec{x}-a_i)(\vec{x}-a_i)^T+c_i]^{-1}$	4	$[0,10]^n$	$f_{21}(\approx\vec{4})=-10.7$

Table 14. The 23 Benchmark Functions

also included in Table 14. The problem set contains a diverse set of problems, including unimodal as well as multimodal functions, and functions with correlated and uncorrelated variables. Functions f_1 - f_5 are unimodal. Function f_6 is the step function, which has one minimum and is discontinuous. Function f_7 is a noisy quartic function. Functions f_8 - f_{13} are multimodal functions where the number of local minima increases exponentially with the problem dimension. Functions f_{14} - f_{23} are low-dimensional functions which have only a few local minima. As still a preliminary study on the new algorithm, the optimization problems listed above are considered in this paper, and the more experiments are needed for future studies.

Where n is the dimension size of the functions, $f_{\min}$ is the ideal function value, and $S\in R^n$ (search space).

Where G is the maximum generation, Func. = Functions, Algo. = Algorithms, Accuracy stands for the fixed accuracy level, *Best* stands for the best function value over 30 runs, *Mean* indicates the mean best function values, *Std. Dev.* stands for the standard deviation, Time stands for the average CPU time (seconds) consumed within the fixed number of generations. Succ.Gens. and Succ. Time stand for the average generation and average CPU time (seconds) achieving the fixed accuracy, Succ. Runs stands for the success number over 30 runs.

3.2.2 Experimental setup

The algorithms used for comparison are differential evolution (DE) algorithm [47], particle swarm optimization with inertia weight (PSO-w) [40], PSO with constriction factor (PSO-cf) [41], and comprehensive learning particle swarm optimizer (CLPSO) [42]. In all the experiments, the same population size *popsize*=100, total 30 runs are made, and the experiments results are listed in Table 15 -Table 17. The initial population is generated uniformly and randomly in the range as specified in Table 14. The parameters of the PSO-w are that: learning rate c_1=c_2=2, inertia weight linearly decreased from 0.9 to 0.4 with run time increasing, the maximum velocity $v_{\max}$ is set at 20% of the dynamic range of the variable on each dimension; the parameters of the PSO-cf are that: c_1= c_2=2.01 and constriction factor χ=0.729844. The parameters of the CLPSO follow the suggestions from [42] except that the refreshing gap m=2 for functions f_{14}-f_{23}. The parameters of the SFS are that: $\delta=\delta'=14$. All the algorithms are run on a PC with Pentium 4 CPU 2.4GHz.

Func.	Accuracy	Algo.	*Best*	*Mean*	*Std. Dev.*	Time	Succ.Gens.	Succ. Time	Succ. Runs
f_1 (G =1500)	1e-6	DE	5.20e-14	3.74e-13	3.94e-13	5.4	933.4	3.7	30
		PSO-w	1.79e-15	1.66e-13	4.59e-13	18.2	1056.3	12.1	30
		PSO-cf	4.50e-45	2.28e-41	4.54e-41	19.8	349.8	4.3	30
		CLPSO	3.22e-13	2.73e-12	1.68e-12	24.4	924.6	16.3	30
		SFS	5.40e-34	8.78e-32	3.06e-31	18.5	573.8	7.55	30
f_2 (G =2000)	1e-6	DE	6.17e-10	3.74e-09	2.20e-09	9.0	1553.9	7.6	30
		PSO-w	5.36e-12	6.67e-11	7.98e-11	26.2	1545.7	19.3	30
		PSO-cf	3.29e-29	1.60e-00	4.22e-00	30.1	1612.7	22.5	23
		CLPSO	1.63e-09	3.82e-09	1.73e-09	33.6	1453.8	21.3	30
		SFS	3.36e-18	1.34e-14	7.28e-14	27.18	1323.7	18.7	30
f_3 (G=5000)	1e-6	DE	1.10e-11	1.85e-10	1.49e-10	32.8	3762.0	25.9	30
		PSO-w	2.00e-02	2.40e-01	2.23e-01	75.0	5000	75.0	0
		PSO-cf	3.01e-19	3.33e+02	1.78e+03	86.3	2736.1	42.5	26
		CLPSO	3.37e-02	4.20 e-01	3.62e-01	93.9	5000	93.9	0
		SFS	4.02e-23	3.03e-21	3.11e-21	81.1	2093.7	35.6	30
f_4 (G =5000)	1e-6	DE	6.83e-13	3.10e-02	8.70e-02	23.9	4423.3	20.2	9
		PSO-w	1.18e-02	7.02e-02	4.66e-02	63.4	5000	63.4	0
		PSO-cf	1.48e-16	7.13e-13	2.19e-12	73.2	2893.4	42.4	30
		CLPSO	6.88e-04	2.05e-03	1.25e-03	83.9	5000	83.9	0
		SFS	6.97e-19	3.77e-17	5.31e-17	68.5	2970.6	40.7	30
f_5 (G =20000)	1e-6	DE	0	3.47e-31	2.45e-30	84.1	3966	16.2	30
		PSO-w	1.05e-02	1.82e+03	1.27e+03	251.5	20000	251.5	0
		PSO-cf	1.87e-12	7.32e+03	2.46e+03	271.8	17837	242.4	9
		CLPSO	1.68e-01	3.63e+01	3.12e+01	349.1	20000	349.1	0
		SFS	7.00e-21	6.56e-16	1.81e-15	241.1	13827	172.4	30
f_6 (G =1500)	1e-6	DE	0	0	0	7.3	357.0	1.6	30
		PSO-w	0	0	0	19.3	921.7	12.7	30
		PSO-cf	0	0	0	20.7	189.0	2.6	30
		CLPSO	0	0	0	25.7	723.5	12.5	30
		SFS	0	0	0	21.8	109.9	1.52	30
f_7 (G =5000)	1e-4	DE	1.97e-03	4.66e-03	1.30e-03	29.5	5000	29.5	0
		PSO-w	2.99e-03	6.28e-03	2.17e-03	72.5	5000	72.5	0
		PSO-cf	9.86e-04	2.45e-03	1.38e-03	75.0	5000	75.0	0
		CLPSO	1.03e-03	2.98e-03	9.72e-04	93.5	5000	93.5	0
		SFS	4.74e-05	9.53e-05	3.26e-05	73.9	3860.8	64.1	18

Table 15. The simulation results for f_1-f_7

Func.	Accuracy	Algo.	*Best*	*Mean*	*Std. Dev.*	Time	Succ.Gens	Succ. Time	Succ. Runs
f_8 (G =5000)	-12000	DE	-11719	-11234	455.5	41.5	5000	41.5	0
		PSO-w	-10495	-9363.3	445.3	72.8	5000	72.8	0
		PSO-cf	-10398	-9026.1	656.9	83.3	5000	83.3	0
		CLPSO	-12569	-12271	177.8	92.1	1774.2	28.4	30
		SFS	-8952	-7216	721.9	74.3	5000	74.3	0
f_9 (G =5000)	1e-3	DE	9.95e-00	8.10e+01	3.23e+01	36.1	5000	36.1	0
		PSO-w	7.96e-00	2.10e+01	8.01e-00	67.0	5000	67.0	0
		PSO-cf	2.69e+01	6.17e+01	1.84e+01	78.9	5000	78.9	0
		CLPSO	9.91e-01	4.13e+00	1.79e+00	84.3	5000	84.3	0
		SFS	2.98e-00	6.93e-00	1.68e-00	75.6	5000	75.6	0
f_{10} (G =1500)	1e-3	DE	5.79e-08	1.71e-07	7.66e-08	7.7	844.5	4.4	30
		PSO-w	1.39e-07	1.66e-06	2.66e-06	21.0	1344.3	18.6	30
		PSO-cf	2.67e-15	5.59e-01	7.30e-01	22.5	845.4	12.6	19
		CLPSO	3.31e-06	6.81e-06	1.94e-06	27.1	1334.6	23.9	30
		SFS	2.66e-15	8.82e-15	3.95e-15	21.5	552.8	8.2	30
f_{11} (G =2000)	1e-3	DE	0	4.44e-04	1.77e-03	10.8	714.4	4.0	30
		PSO-w	0	1.59e-01	2.19e-02	28.5	1833.7	25.3	7
		PSO-cf	0	1.11e-02	1.25e-02	30.9	1351.5	21.1	7
		CLPSO	1.64e-14	2.96e-04	1.46e-03	36.7	1423.7	25.3	29
		SFS	0	0	0	30.4	337.2	5.1	30
f_{12} (G =1500)	1e-3	DE	3.40e-15	3.67e-14	4.07e-14	9.5	594.7	3.8	30
		PSO-w	8.85e-15	2.21 e-00	5.52e-00	29.0	1154.6	21.4	30
		PSO-cf	1.57e-32	1.66e+01	1.81 e+01	31.9	698.1	15.7	21
		CLPSO	8.80e-12	4.80e-11	3.96e-11	35.2	1023.9	23.5	30
		SFS	2.60e-32	7.51e-31	2.08e-30	22.5	201.9	3.2	30
f_{13} (G=1500)	1e-3	DE	4.13e-14	2.91e-13	2.88e-13	9.8	748.8	5.0	30
		PSO-w	8.23e-07	5.72e+02	3.57e+02	37.0	778.7	18.8	29
		PSO-cf	1.35e-32	2.40e+02	2.40e+02	33.6	606.8	13.6	22
		CLPSO	1.18e-10	6.42e-10	4.46e-10	38.6	637.3	16.7	30
		SFS	2.21e-32	4.90e-31	1.37e-30	22.4	266.5	4.2	30

Table 16. The simulation results for f_8-f_{13}

Func.	Accuracy	Algo.	Best	Mean	Std. Dev.	Time	Succ.Gens	Succ. Time	Succ. Runs
f_{14} (G=100)	0.998+1e-3	DE	0.998	0.998	2.88e-16	1.2	32.5	0.3	30
		PSO-w	0.998	1.026	1.52e-01	1.4	43.4	0.7	30
		PSO-cf	0.998	0.998	8.69e-13	1.52	19.9	0.3	30
		CLPSO	0.998	0.998	5.63e-10	2.1	37.5	0.8	30
		SFS	0.998	0.998	1.43e-16	1.8	25.6	0.4	30
f_{15} (G =4000)	3.175×1e-4	DE	3.0749c-04	4.7231e-02	3.55e-04	31.5	3859.7	29.9	2
		PSO-w	3.0749e-04	2.0218e-03	5.47e-03	40.3	2837.0	29.0	22
		PSO-cf	3.0749e-04	2.0225e-03	5.47e-03	43.1	824.5	8.9	27
		CLPSO	3.2847e-04	5.3715e-04	6.99e-05	67.7	1413.7	24.1	29
		SFS	3.0749e-04	3.0749e-04	2.01e-19	54.5	612.9	8.7	30

f_{16} (G =100)	-1.0317	DE	-1.0316	-1.0316	6.77e-13	0.6	24.7	0.1	30
		PSO-w	-1.0316	-1.0316	8.80e-12	0.9	20.7	0.2	30
		PSO-cf	-1.0316	-1.0316	5.92e-12	0.9	20.6	0.2	30
		CLPSO	-1.0316	-1.0316	8.50e-14	1.5	79.4	1.3	30
		SFS	-1.0316	-1.0316	5.90e-16	1.1	15.2	0.2	30
f_{17} (G =100)	0.3981	DE	0.3979	0.3979	1.14e-08	0.6	37.6	0.2	30
		PSO-w	0.3979	0.3979	2.33e-12	0.9	32.4	0.3	30
		PSO-cf	0.3979	0.3979	5.25e-12	0.9	21.4	0.2	30
		CLPSO	0.3979	0.3979	1.08e-13	1.5	83.8	1.4	30
		SFS	0.3979	0.3979	0	1.1	16.2	0.2	30
f_{18} (G =100)	3+1e-4	DE	3	3	3.31e-15	0.7	25.8	0.1	30
		PSO-w	3	3	2.50e-11	1.0	48.1	0.5	30
		PSO-cf	3	3	2.05e-11	1.0	31.1	0.3	30
		CLPSO	3	3	5.54e-13	1.6	49.1	0.8	30
		SFS	3	3	3.33e-15	1.1	24.8	0.2	30
f_{19} (G =100)	-3.86+1e-4	DE	-3.8628	-3.8628	1.97e-15	0.7	14.6	0.1	30
		PSO-w	-3.8628	-3.8628	2.66e-11	1.1	14.9	0.2	30
		PSO-cf	-3.8628	-3.8628	2.92e-12	1.1	9.1	0.1	30
		CLPSO	-3.8628	-3.8628	6.07e-12	1.7	28.2	0.4	30
		SFS	-3.8628	-3.8621	2.60e-15	1.1	17.1	0.2	30
f_{20} (G =200)	-3.32+0.01	DE	-3.322	-3.215	0.036	1.4	188.1	1.3	19
		PSO-w	-3.322	-3.256	0.066	2.8	141.7	2.1	17
		PSO-cf	-3.322	-3.277	0.058	2.8	91.2	1.3	15
		CLPSO	-3.322	-3.274	0.059	3.5	122.2	2.1	13
		SFS	-3.322	-3.322	1.36e-15	2.4	44.9	0.55	30
f_{21} (G =100)	-10	DE	-10.15	-10.15	4.67e-06	1.0	48.2	0.5	30
		PSO-w	- 6.57	- 2.01	1.10e-00	1.2	100	1.2	0
		PSO-cf	-10.15	- 6.23	3.25e-00	1.3	86.4	1.1	13
		CLPSO	-10.14	- 9.57	4.28e-01	1.8	80.2	1.5	17
		SFS	-10.15	-10.15	5.70e-15	1.6	21.1	0.3	30
f_{22} (G =100)	-10	DE	-10.40	-10.40	2.07e-07	1.2	39.5	0.5	30
		PSO-w	- 4.61	- 2.14	8.34e-01	1.2	100	1.2	0
		PSO-cf	-10.40	- 6.47	3.56e-00	1.4	49.5	0.7	21
		CLPSO	-10.34	- 9.40	1.12e-00	1.9	43.2	0.8	23
		SFS	-10.40	-10.40	4.66e-16	1.6	19.2	0.3	30
f_{23} (G =100)	-10	DE	-10.54	-10.54	3.21e-06	1.3	38.1	0.5	30
		PSO-w	- 6.63	- 2.20	1.01e-00	1.4	100	1.4	0
		PSO-cf	-10.54	- 8.11	3.47e-01	1.8	51.5	0.9	19
		CLPSO	-10.46	- 9.47	1.25e-00	2.0	47.4	1.0	25
		SFS	-10.54	-10.54	1.65e-15	1.7	18.0	0.3	30

Table 17. The simulation results for f_{14}-f_{23}

3.2.3 Unimodal functions

The results of 30 independent runs for functions f_1 - f_7 are summarized in Table 15. From Table 15, SFS is successful over all the 30 runs for f_1 - f_6. For f_7, it is successful in 18 runs but all the PSOs failed over all the runs. Moreover, PSOs has more time consumption of achieving the fixed accuracy than that of SFS except that PSO-cf has smaller time consumption for f_1. Although DE has less time consumption within the fixed number of generations than SFS and PSOs, it failed in 21 runs for f_4 and all the 30 runs for f_7.

3.2.4 Multimodal functions

1. Multimodal functions with many local minima: Multimodal functions with many local minima are often regarded as being difficult to optimize. f_8 - f_{13} are such functions where the number of local minima increases exponentially as the dimension of the function increases. The dimensions of f_8-f_{13} were all set to 30 in our experiments as [60]. Table 16 gives the results of 30 independent runs. From Table 16, SFS is successful over all the 30 runs for functions f_{10}-f_{13} but f_8 and f_9. For functions f_{10}-f_{13}, SFS has faster convergence speed with the fewer generations and computation time to achieve the fixed accuracy level than DE and PSOs except DE for f_{10} and f_{11}.
2. Multimodal functions with only a few local minima: For functions f_{14}-f_{23}, the number of local minima and the dimension are small. Table 17 summarizes the results over 30 runs. From Table 17, it is apparent that SFS performs better than DE and PSOs for functions f_{14}-f_{23}.

Table 15 - Table 17 indicates that SFS is suitable for solving the most employed unimodal and multimodal function optimizations with better convergence ability. Compared with the three modified PSOs, SFS has better global search ability with more successful runs for the benchmark functions. The Tables also show that SFS has often higher computational complexity with more time consumption within the given generations than DE but PSO-cf and CLPSO.

4. References

[1] Andrew Sohn. Parallel bidirectional heuristic search on the EM-4 multiprocessor. In: Proceedings of the Sixth IEEE Symposium on Parallel and Distributed Processing, Dallas, TX, USA, 1994, pp. 100-107.

[2] Raphael B., Smith I.F.C.. A direct stochastic algorithm for global search. Applied Mathematics and Computation, 2003, vol.146, issues 2-3, pp. 729–758.

[3] Chaohua Dai, Weirong Chen, Yonghua Song and Yunfang Zhu. Seeker optimization algorithm: A novel stochastic search algorithm for global numerical optimization, Journal of Systems Engineering and Electronics, 2010, vol. 21, no. 2, pp. 300-311.

[4] Robert Michael Lewisa, Virginia Torczon, Michael W. Trosset. Direct search methods: then and now. Journal of Computational and Applied Mathematics, 2000, vol.124, issues 1-2, pp.191-207.

[5] Stuart J. Russell, Peter Norvig. Artificial Intelligence: A Modern Approach. Second Edition. Hongkong: Pearson Education Asia Limited and Beijing: Tsinghua University Press, 2006, pp.120-122.

[6] Mathias Kern. Parameter adaptation in heuristic search: a population-based approach. Ph.D. thesis, Department of Computer Science, University of Essex, 2006.

[7] Mills Patrick, Tsang Edward, Zhang Qingfu, et al. A survey of AI-based meta-heuristics for dealing with local optima in local search. Technical Report Series, Report Number CSM-416, September 2004. Department of Computer Science, University of Essex, Colchester CO4 3SQ. (Available: http://cswww.essex.ac.uk/CSP/)

[8] Nurhan Karaboga. Digital IIR filter design using differential evolution algorithm. EURASIP Journal on Applied Signal Processing, 2005, no.8, pp. 1269-1276.
[9] Storn R. and Price K.. Differential evolution - A simple and efficient heuristic for global optimization over continuous spaces. Journal of Global Optimization, 1997, vol.11, no. 4, pp.341-359.
[10] Kennedy, J., Eberhart, R., and Shi, Yu. Swarm Intelligence. Morgan Kaufmann, San Francisco, CA, 2001.
[11] Bonabeau E., Dorigo M., Theraulaz G.. Inspiration for optimization from social insect behavior. Nature, 2002, vol.406, no.6, pp.39-42.
[12] Valle Y. del, Venayagamoorthy G., Mohagheghi S., et al. Particle swarm optimization: basic concepts, variants and applications in power systems. IEEE Transactions on Evolutionary Computation, 2008, vol.12, no.2, pp.171-195.
[13] Marco Dorigo, Mauro Birattari, and Thomas Stützle. Ant colony optimization: artificial ants as a computational intelligence technique. IEEE Computing Intelligence Magazine, 2006, vol.1, no.4, pp.28-39.
[14] Chaohua Dai, Yunfang Zhu and Weirong Chen. Seeker optimization algorithm, Lecture Notes in Artificial Intelligence, Y. Wang, Y. Cheung, and H. Liu (Eds.), Springer-Verlag Berlin Heidelberg: Revised selected paper from CIS 2006, pp. 167–176, 2007.
[15] Chaohua Dai, Weirong Chen, and Yunfang Zhu. Seeker optimization algorithm for digital IIR filter design, IEEE Transactions on Industrial Electronics, 2010, vol. 57, no. 5, pp. 1710-1718.
[16] Chaohua Dai, Weirong Chen, Yunfang Zhu and Xuexia Zhang. Seeker optimization algorithm for optimal reactive power dispatch, IEEE Transactions on Power Systems, 2009, vol. 24, no. 3, pp. 1218-1231.
[17] Chaohua Dai, Weirong Chen, Yunfang Zhu and Xuexia Zhang. Reactive power dispatch considering voltage stability with seeker optimization algorithm, Electric Power System Research, 2009, vol. 79, no. 10, pp. 1462-1471.
[18] Chaohua Dai, Weirong Chen, Zhanli Cheng, et al. Seeker Optimization Algorithm for Global Optimization: a Case Study on Optimal Modeling of Proton Exchange Membrane Fuel Cell (PEMFC). International Journal of Electrical Power and Energy Systems, accepted.
[19] Chaohua Dai, Weirong Chen, Yunfang Zhu, et al. Seeker optimization algorithm for tuning the structure and parameters of neural networks. Neurocomputing, accepted.
[20] Yongkang Zheng, Weirong Chen, Chaohua Dai, Weibo Wang. Stochastic focusing search: A novel optimization algorithm for real-parameter optimization. Journal of Systems Engineering and Electronics, 2009, vol. 20, no. 4, pp. 869-876.
[21] Yongkang Zheng, Weirong Chen, Chaohua Dai, et al. Optimization algorithm with stochastic focusing search (in Chinese). Control Theory & Applications, 2009, vol. 26, no. 8, pp. 915-917.
[22] Donald A. Pierre. Optimization Theory with Applications. New York: Dover Publications, Inc., 1986.
[23] Zimmermann Hans-Jürgen. "A fresh perspective on uncertainty modeling: uncertainty vs. uncertainty modeling," in Fuzzy sets and operations research for decision support. Edited by Da Ruan, Chonghu Huang, Beijing: Beijing Normal University Press, 2000, pp.40-57.
[24] Zadeh L. A.. The concept of linguistic variable and its application to approximate reasoning. Information Science, 1975, vol.8, no. 3, pp.199-246.

[25] Vignesh Kumar, Ferat Sahin. Cognitive maps in swarm robots for the mine detection application. in Proc. of IEEE International Conference on Systems, Man and Cybernetics, 2003, vol.4, pp.3364-3369.

[26] Eustace D, Barnes DP, Gray JO. Co-operant mobile robots for industrial applications. in Proc. of the Inter. Conf. on Industrial Electronics, Control, and Instrumentation, 1993, vol.1, Maui, HI, USA , pp.39-44.

[27] James Kennedy. The particle swarm: Social adaptation of knowledge. In: Proceedings of IEEE International Conference on Evolutionary Computation, 1997, Indianapolis, IN, USA, pp. 303-308.

[28] Vito Trianni, Roderich Groß, Thomas H. Labella, et al. Evolving aggregation behaviors in a swarm of robots. W. Banzhaf et al. (Eds.): ECAL 2003, LNAI 2801, pp.865–874.

[29] Camazine S., Deneubourg J.-L., Franks N., Sneyd J., Theraulaz G., and Bonabeau E. Self-Organization in Biological Systems. Princeton University Press, Princeton, NJ, 2001.

[30] Wooldridge M., Jennings N. R.. Intelligent agents: theory and practice. The Knowledge Engineering Review, 1995, vol.10, no.2, pp.115-152.

[31] Icek Ajzen. Residual effects of past on later behavior: Habituation and reasoned action perspectives. Personality and Social Psychology Review, 2002, vol.6, no.2, pp.107–122.

[32] Joel D. Hewlett, Bogdan M. Wilamowski, and Günhan Dündar. Optimization using a modified second-order approach with evolutionary enhancement. IEEE Trans. Ind. Electron., vol.55, no.9, pp.3374-3380, 2008.

[33] Steels L. Cooperation between distributed agents through self organization. in Dernazean Y, Müller J-P, eds. Decentralized AI: Proc. of the First European Workshop on Modeling Autonomous Agents in a Multi-Agent World (MAAMAW-89), pp.175-196, 1990.

[34] Deyi Li. Uncertainty reasoning based on cloud models in controllers. Computers and Mathematics with Applications, vol.35, no.3, pp.99-123, 1998.

[35] Yu Liu, Zheng gin, and Zhewen Shi. Hybrid particle swarm optimizer with line search. in Proc. of the 2004 IEEE Inter. Conf. on Systems, Man and Cybernetics, pp.3751-3755, 2004.

[36] W. B. Langdon and Riccardo Poli. Evolving problems to learn about particle swarm and other optimizers. CEC-2005, vol.1, pp.81-88, 2005.

[37] D.E. Goldberg. Genetic algorithms in search, optimization and machine learning. Reading, MA: Addison Wesley, 1989.

[38] Clerc, M. "When nearer is better," Online at https://hal.archives-ouvertes.fr/hal-00137320, 2007.

[39] J. Brest, S. Greiner, B. Bošković, et al. Self-adapting control parameters in differential evolution: a comparative study on numerical benchmark problems. IEEE Trans. Evol. Comput., vol.10, no.6, pp. 646-657, 2006.

[40] Y. Shi and R. Eberhart, A modified particle swarm optimizer. in Proc. IEEE World Congr. Comput. Intell., pp.69-73, May 1998.

[41] M. Clerc and J. Kennedy, The particle swarm - explosion, stability, and convergence in a multidimensional complex space. IEEE Trans. Evol. Comput., vol.6, no.1, pp.58-73, Feb. 2002.

[42] J. J. Liang, A.K. Qin, Ponnuthurai Nagaratnam Suganthan, et al. Comprehensive learning particle swarm optimizer for global optimization of multimodal functions. IEEE Trans. Evol. Comput., vol.10, no.3, pp.67-82, 2006.

[43] A. K. Qin and P. N. Suganthan. Self-adaptive differential evolution algorithm for numerical optimization. in Proc. of IEEE Congress on Evolutionary Computation, Edinburgh, Scotland, pp.1785-1791, 2005.

[44] B. Zhao, C.X. Guo, Y.J. Cao, A multi-agent based particle swarm optimization approach for reactive power dispatch. IEEE Trans. Power Syst., vol.20, no.2, pp.1070-1078, 2005.
[45] Ray D. Zimmerman, Carlos E. Murillo-Sánchez and Deqiang Gan. Matlab Power System Simulation Package (Version 3.1b2), Available at http://www.pserc.cornell.edu/matpower/, 2006.
[46] J. Kennedy and R. Eberhart, Particle swarm optimization. in Proc. IEEE Int. Conf. Neural Netw., vol.4, pp.1942-1948, Nov. 1995.
[47] R. Storn and K. Price. Differential evolution - a simple and efficient adaptive scheme for global optimization over continuous spaces. Tech. Rep. TR-95-012, International Computer Science Institute, Berkeley, Calif, USA, March 1995.
[48] Manoj Fozdar, C. M. Arora and V. R. Gottipati. Recent trends in intelligent techniques to power systems. in Proc. of the 42nd International Universities Power Engineering Conference, pp.580-591, 2007.
[49] H. Yoshida, Y. Fukuyama, K. Kawata, et al. A particle swarm optimization for reactive power and voltage control considering voltage security assessment. IEEE Trans. Power Syst., 2001, vol.15, no.4, pp.1232-1239.
[50] Ahmed A. A. Esmin, Germano Lambert-Torres, Antônio C. Zambroni de Souza. "A hybrid particle swarm optimization applied to loss power minimization," IEEE Trans. Power Syst., 2005, vol.20, no.2, pp.859-866.
[51] John G. Vlachogiannis and Kwang Y. Lee. "A comparative study on particle swarm optimization for optimal steady-state performance of power systems," IEEE Trans. Power Syst., 2006, vol.21, no.4, pp.1718-1728.
[52] M. Varadarajan, K.S. Swarup, Network loss minimization with voltage security using differential evolution. Electric Power Systems Research, 2008, vol.78, pp.815-823.
[53] M. Varadarajan, K.S. Swarup, Differential evolutionary algorithm for optimal reactive power dispatch. Int. J. Electr. Power Energ. Syst, 2008, vol. 30, no. 8, pp. 435-441.
[54] Standard PSO 2007 (SPSO-07) on the Particle Swarm Central, Programs section: http://www.particleswarm.info, 2007.
[55] Q. H. Wu, Y. J. Cao, and J. Y. Wen, Optimal reactive power dispatch using an adaptive genetic algorithm. Int. J. Elect. Power Energy Syst., 1998, vol.20, no. 8, pp.563-569.
[56] Statistics Toolbox 5.0, The MathWorks, Inc.
[57] Juan Yu, "New models and algorithms of optimal reactive power flow and applications in voltage stability risk assessment," A Ph.D. thesis submitted to Chongqing University, pp:107-112, Chongqing, China, 2008. (in Chinese).
[58] Xiong Hugang, Cheng Haozhong, Li Haiyu. Optimal reactive power flow incorporating static voltage stability based on multi-objective adaptive immune algorithm. Energy Conversion and Management, 2008, vol. 49, no. 5, pp. 1175-1181.
[59] Wen Zhang and Yutian Liu. Multi-objective reactive power and voltage control based on fuzzy optimization strategy and fuzzy adaptive particle swarm. Int. J. Electr. Power Energy Syst., 2008, vol. 30, no. 9, pp. 525-532.
[60] Xin Yao, Yong Liu, and Guangming Lin. Evolutionary programming made faster. IEEE Transactions on Evolutionary Computation, 1999, vol. 3, no. 2, pp. 82-102.

2

Running Particle Swarm Optimization on Graphic Processing Units

Carmelo Bastos-Filho, Marcos Oliveira Junior and Débora Nascimento
University of Pernambuco
Brazil

1. Introduction

Particle swarm optimization (PSO) is a computational intelligence technique widely used to solve optimization problems. It was inspired on the social behavior of flocks of birds. In the PSO algorithm, the search space is bounded and each possible position within the search space represents a solution for the optimization problem.

During the algorithm execution, the particles adjust their velocities and positions based on the best position reached by itself and on the best position reached by its neighborhood during the search process. Some issues are quite important for the convergence velocity and the quality of the solutions, among them we can cite: the communication scheme to exchange information among the particles (topology) (Bratton & Kennedy (2007); Kennedy & Mendes (2002)), the equation used to update the velocity of the particles (Eberhart & Shi (2000)), the mechanisms to avoid explosion states (Clerc & Kennedy (2002)) and the quality of the Random Number Generator (RNGs) (Bastos-Filho et al. (2009)).

PSO is inherently parallel since the fitness can be evaluated for each particle individually. Hence, PSO is naturally suitable for parallel implementations.

In the recent years, the use of Graphic Processing Units (GPUs) have been proposed for some general purpose computing applications. GPUs have shown great advantages on applications requiring intensive parallel computing. Despite GPU based architectures require an additional CPU time to assign the tasks for the GPUs, the speed up obtained by GPU based architectures in relation to simple CPU architectures is higher for application where the processing is much more focused on floating point and matrix operations.

The major benefit to implement the PSO in GPU based architectures is the possibility to reduce the execution time. It is quite possible since the fitness evaluation and the update processes of the particles can be parallelized through different threads. Nevertheless, some issues regarding GPU-based PSOs should be analyzed.

In this chapter, we analyze and discuss some advantages and drawbacks of PSO algorithms implemented on GPU-based architectures. We describe the steps needed to implement different PSO variations in these architectures. These variations include different topologies such as Global, Local, Focal, Four Cluster and von Neumann. Two different approaches used to update the particles are analyzed as well.

We also consider some other relevant aspects such as: (1) how to determine the number of particle for a specific GPU architecture; (2) in which memory the variables should be allocated; (3) which RNG should be used to accelerate the execution; and (4) when and where is necessary to state synchronization barriers. The analysis of these aspects is crucial to provide high performance for GPU-based PSOs. In order to show this, we performed simulation using a parallel processing platform developed by NVIDIA, called CUDA (NVIDIA, 2010).

2. Particle Swarm optimization

Particle Swarm Optimization (PSO) is a stochastic, bio-inspired, population-based global optimization technique. James Kennedy and Russel C. Eberhart first described the algorithm in 1995 (Kennedy & Eberhart (1995)). It is based on the social behaviour of biological organisms, specifically the ability of groups of animals to work as a whole in searching desirable positions in a given area.

Each particle in the swarm represents a point in the fitness function domain. Each particle i has four attributes: its current position in the D-dimensional space $\vec{x}_i = (x_{i1}, x_{i2}, ..., x_{id})$, its best position found so far during the search $\vec{p}_i = (p_{i1}, p_{i2}, ..., p_{id})$, the best position found by its neighborhood so far $\vec{n}_i = (n_{i1}, n_{i2}, ..., n_{id})$ and its current velocity $\vec{v}_i = (v_{i1}, v_{i2}, ..., v_{id})$ (Bratton & Kennedy (2007)). The position and the velocity of every particle are updated iteratively according to its current best position $\vec{p}_i$ and the best position of its neighborhood $\vec{n}_i$ by applying the following update equations for each particle in each dimension d:

$$v_{id} = v_{id} + c_1 \cdot r_1 \cdot (p_{id} - x_{id}) + c_2 \cdot r_2 \cdot (n_{id} - x_{id}), \tag{1}$$

$$x_{id} = x_{id} + v_{id}, \tag{2}$$

where c_1 and c_2 in the Equation (1) are non negative constants. They are the cognitive and the social acceleration constants, respectively, and they weight the contribution of the cognitive and social components. The values r_1 and r_2 are two different random variables generated at each iteration for each dimension from a uniform distribution in the interval [0,1].

Particles velocities can be clamped to a maximum value in order to prevent an explosion state. Their positions are also bounded by search space limits in order to avoid inutile exploration of space (Bratton & Kennedy (2007)).

The original PSO updates the velocities fully considering the previous velocity of the particles. The first and most famous variation of this updating process uses an inertia factor (ω) (Eberhart & Shi (2000)). It was designed to adjust the influence of the previous velocity of the particles. It helps to switch the search mode of the swarm from exploration to exploitation along the search process. The resulting velocity update equation is stated as follows:

$$v_{id} = \omega \cdot v_{id} + c_1 \cdot r_1 \cdot (p_{id} - x_{id}) + c_2 \cdot r_2 \cdot (n_{id} - x_{id}). \tag{3}$$

Similar to the parameter ω, a parameter χ, known as the constriction factor, was proposed by Clerc (Clerc & Kennedy (2002)). The factor χ is defined according to the following equation:

$$\chi = \frac{2}{|2 - \varphi - \sqrt{\varphi^2 - 4\varphi}|}, \ \varphi = c_1 + c_2. \tag{4}$$

This constriction factor is applied to the entire velocity update equation as shown in the following equation:

$$v_{id} = \chi \cdot [v_{id} + c_1 \cdot r_1 \cdot (p_{id} - x_{id}) + c_2 \cdot r_2 \cdot (n_{id} - x_{id})]. \tag{5}$$

The effects are similar to those obtained by inertia weight approach. The χ parameter controls the exploration-exploitation abilities of the swarm.

2.1 Population topologies

The uniqueness of the PSO algorithm lies in the dynamic interaction of the particles (Kennedy & Mendes (2002)). Even when it is using different types of update equations, the performance depends on the information exchange mechanism inside the swarm.

The information flow scheme through the particles is determined by the communication method used by the swarm (Ferreira de Carvalho & Bastos-Filho (2009)). The topology of the swarm defines the neighborhood of each particle, that is the subset of particles which it is able to communicate with (Bratton & Kennedy (2007)).

Previous investigation performed by Watts (Watts (1999); Watts & Strogatz (1998)) showed that some aspects can affect the flow of information through social networks. These aspects included the degree of connectivity among the nodes; the average number of neighbors in common per node; and the average shortest distance between nodes.

Kennedy and Mendes analyzed these factors on the particle swarm optimization algorithm (Kennedy & Mendes (2002)) and showed that the presence of intermediaries slows down the information. On the other hand, it moves faster between connected pairs of individuals. Thus, when a distance between nodes are too short, the population tends to rapidly toward the best solution found in earlier iterations. On simple unimodal problems, it usually result in a faster convergence on the global optimum.

However, the fast convergence might lead to a premature suboptimal point on multi-modal problems (Bratton & Kennedy (2007)). In this case, a structure with intermediaries could help to reach better results.

The first PSO model used a dynamic topology with a Euclidean distance based neighborhood, where the distance between particles determines which particles were close enough to communicate with (Heppner & Grenander (1990)). It was abandoned due to the high computational cost, albeit the similarity to the natural behavior of bird flocks (Bratton & Kennedy (2007)).

The global topology is the structure proposed in the first PSO approach and is still used by researchers. It uses a global neighborhood mechanism known as *gbest*. Particles can share information globally through a fully-connected structure, as shown in Figure 1. This arrangement leads to a fast convergence, since the information spreads quickly.

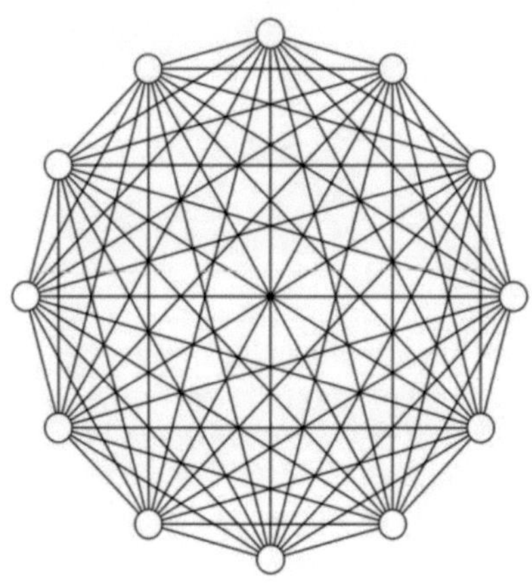

Fig. 1. The Global Topology.

The usual alternative to the global topology is the ring topology, depicted in Figure 2. In this structure, each particle has one neighbor on each side. The information spreads slowly along the graph, thus different regions of the search space is explored, but it slows down the convergence.

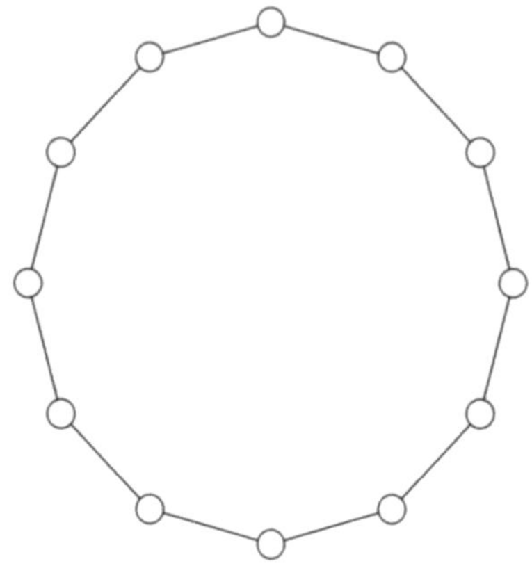

Fig. 2. The Ring Topology.

The dichotomic behaviour of the global and ring topologies suggests to consider structures to balance the previous approaches. Some other topologies were recently proposed.
The four clusters topology consists in clusters of particles connected among themselves by several gateways (Mendes et al. (2003)), as shown in Figure 3. Each gateway particle act as an informant that disseminates the information acquired by its own cluster.

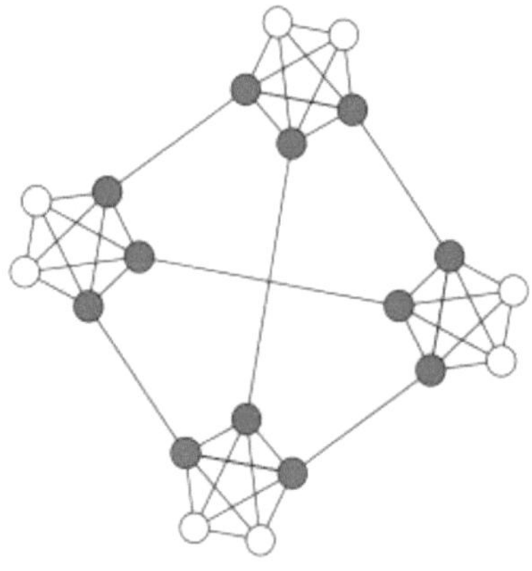

Fig. 3. The Four Clusters Topology.

The topology depicted in Figure 4 is known as focal topology. One single particle is the focus of the swarm, it updates its position based on the performance of the other particles (Ferreira de Carvalho & Bastos-Filho (2009)). If the focus improves its position, this information will be transmitted to the entire neighborhood.
In the von Neumann topology, the particles are connected as a grid. Each particle has neighbors above, below, and on each side (Kennedy & Mendes (2002)), as shown in Figure 5. This structure is commonly used to represent neighborhoods in the Evolutionary Computation and Cellular Automata communities (Mendes et al. (2004)). Kennedy and Mendes pointed this topology as the most consistent in their experiments in (Kennedy & Mendes (2002)).

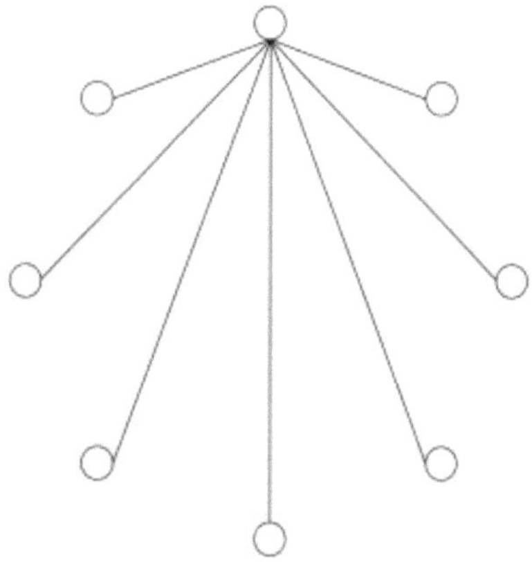

Fig. 4. The Focal Topology.

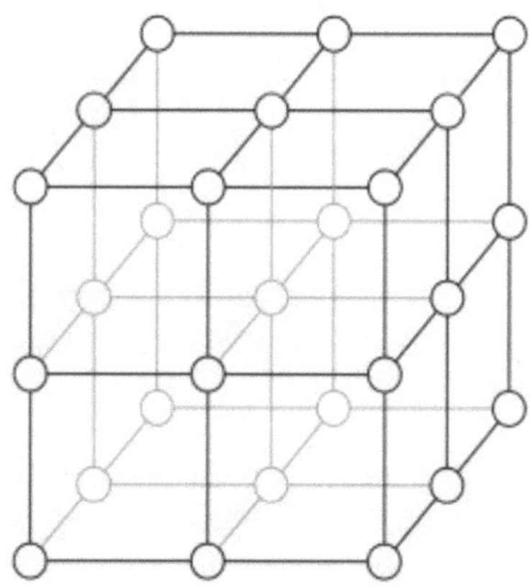

Fig. 5. The von Neumann Topology.

3. GPU computing

GPU parallel computing follows an architecture called SIMT (Single Instruction – Multiple Threads) (NVIDIA (2010)). In the SIMT paradigm, the same instruction set is executed on different data processors at the same time. In our case, the data processors are on the GPUs. The GPU SIMT architecture presents a lower overhead for parallel computing, which is suitable for intensive and repetitive computations.

The GPUs are specially well-suited to tackle problems that can be expressed as data-parallel computations, where the same set of commands can be executed in parallel on many data processing elements. Data-parallel processing maps these data elements to parallel processing threads.

Traditionally, GPUs were designed for image and graphic processing. However, The GPUs have became popular in recent years through the CUDA (Compute Unified Device Architecture), which is a technology that enables programmers and developers to write software to solve complex computational problems by automatically distributing these threads to many-core graphic processors.

The CUDA parallel programming model allows the programmer to divide the main problem in many sub-problems that can be executed independently in parallel. Each sub-problem can be decomposed in many modules where each module can be executed cooperatively and in parallel. In CUDA terminology, each sub-problem corresponds to a block of threads, where each thread is a module. The function that is performed to solve the sub-problem is called kernel. When a kernel function is invoked by the CPU, it runs on each thread within the corresponding block.

Each thread that executes a kernel function is identified by its thread identifier that is accessible within the kernel with two built-in variables *threadIdx* and *blockIdx*.

Blocks of threads are organized into a one-dimensional or two-dimensional grid of thread blocks. The number of thread blocks in a grid is defined by the size of the data being processed or the number of processors in the system. The maximum number of threads inside a block is defined by the number of processor inside the GPU and its architecture. On the current GPUs, a thread block may contain up to 1024 threads. However, the simulations in this chapter were made with GPUs that supports up to 512 threads.

Threads within a block can cooperate among themselves by sharing data through some shared memory and synchronizing their execution to coordinate memory accesses. Each thread has a private local memory. Each block of threads has a shared memory visible to all threads of the block and with the same lifetime of the block. All threads can access the same global memory. There is a memory hierarchy in the architecture, the memory with fastest access is the local memory and the one with the slowest is the global memory. On the other hand, the largest memory is the global memory and the smallest is the local memory.

3.1 Previous GPU-based particle Swarm optimization approaches

Few parallel PSO implementations on GPU have been developed. They have all shown great speed-up performances when compared to CPU versions. Nevertheless, there is a absence of analysis of the performance impact on the parallel model when using different topologies.

Zhou & Tan (2009) have presented a model of the Standard Particle Swarm Optimization (SPSO) (Bratton & Kennedy (2007)) on CUDA. In their analysis, there is no other topology, but the local ring structure. Furthermore, the implementation is not CPU-free since it needs to generate random numbers on the *host*. Zhu & Curry (2009) presented a SPSO model that combines CPU and GPU codes on the particles best solution updates. Likewise, they carried out the analysis only on the ring topology. On the other hand, Mussi et al. (2009) did not only focus their studies on the local ring topology, they implemented the global topology and also used their PSO model to detect signs on the road.

Moreover, none of these studies presented any analysis of the impact of the location of the synchronization barriers on PSO performance. For instance, the different location of the synchronization barriers is what allows to generate a synchronous PSO, where the best position is obtained after all particles have been totally updated, or a asynchronous PSO, which updates the best position based on the current status of the particles during the optimization process.

4. Our GPU-based Particle Swarm optimization proposals

4.1 First Considerations

There are some first considerations to be analyzed when modeling the particle swarm optimization technique on the CUDA platform. The algorithm correctness must be guaranteed, once race conditions on a parallel implementation may lead to wrong results. Furthermore, since we want to run the algorithm as fast as possible, it is worth to discuss the main issues that may slow it down.

4.1.1 Memory bottleneck

There is a huge bottleneck on data transferring between the host and the device. Any transfer of this kind can harm the performance. Thus, this operation should be avoided when it is possible. One way to get rid of it is to move more code from the host to the device.
On the same way, as shown in Section 3, there is a memory hierarchy present on CUDA platform. The access to the shared memory is faster than the access to the global memory, despite both memory are placed in the GPU. Then, if there is data that must be accessed by all threads in a block, the shared memory is the best choice. However, there are two issues on using it: it is only shared by threads inside one block, if there are more blocks, it will not work right; and as it follows a memory hierarchy, the memory space is not very large, then there will be problems that are not suitable for the shared memory.

4.1.2 Synchronization barriers

Another issue to be pointed out relies on the synchronization barriers. A barrier placed on the code allows a thread to wait until all the other threads have reached the same barrier. They guarantee the correctness of the algorithm running on the GPU, but can mitigate the performance.
On the original PSO algorithm, each particle updates its neighborhood $\vec{n}_i$ after all particles have been totally updated. This first approach is known as synchronous PSO. On the other hand, the asynchronous PSO updates the $\vec{n}_i$ based on the current status of the other particles. It means that a particle can adjust its $\vec{n}_i$ before some other particle j updates its $\vec{n}_j$.
Hence, the synchronous PSO must be implemented carefully with barriers to prevent any race condition that could generate mistaken results. These barriers guarantee the correctness but it comes with a caveat. Since the particles need to wait for all others, all these barriers harm the performance. As a result, the execution of the asynchronous approach is faster than the synchronous one due its absence of synchronization barriers. However, the results will be probably worse, since the information acquired is not necessarily updated.

4.1.3 Random number generation

Bastos-Filho et al. (2009) showed that the random number generator (RNG) used in the PSO technique needs a minimum quality for the algorithm to perform well. However, the classic RNGs can not be executed parallel, since they need a current state and a seed to run.
Most of GPU-based PSO proposed get rid of it pre-generating all random numbers needed to run the algorithm on the CPU. Some other PSO implementations use a GPU version of the Mersenne Twister generator (Matsumoto & Nishimura (1998); Podlozhnyuk (2007)). Both approaches are not CPU-free and the numbers are not generated on demand.
GPU-based random numbers generators are discussed by Nguyen (2007) and Thomas et al. (2009). Bastos-Filho et al. (2010) presented a CPU-free approach for generating random numbers on demand based on the Xorshift generator (Marsaglia (2003)). They also analyzed the quality of the random numbers generated with the PSO algorithm and showed that the quality of the RNG is similar to the frequently RNGs used by researchers.

4.1.4 Hardware limitation

The GPUs present in the current video cards have a huge parallel computation capacity. However, they have also some limitation that may reduce their performance.
Although the GPUs are famous by their parallel high precision operations, there are GPUs with only single precision capacity. Since many computational problems need double

precision computation, this limitation may lead to wrong results and then turn these GPUs inappropriate to solve these kind of problems.
Another issue on the GPU is the maximum number of threads running in parallel in a block. It is defined by the number of processors and the architecture. Therefore, each GPU has its own limitation. This way, application that needs to overpass this limitation have to be executed sequentially with more blocks what might result in wrong computations.
The global memory space is not a big deal for the majority of the applications. However, the other levels of memory – such as the shared memory and the local memory – are not as huge as the global memory. This limitation may harm the performance, since many applications need to store data on a low speed memory – the global memory.
The NVIDIA CUDA platform classify the NVIDIA GPUs with what they call Compute Capability NVIDIA (2010). The cards with double-precision floating-point numbers has Compute Capability 1.3 or 2.x. The cards with 2.x Capability can run 1024 threads in a block and has 48 KB of shared memory space, the other ones only can execute 512 threads and have 16 KB of shared memory space.

4.2 Data structures, kernel functions and GPU-operations

The swarm is modeled with four unidimensional NxD-elements arrays, where N is the number of particles and D is the number of dimensions. The four arrays represent the velocity $\vec{v}_i$, the position $\vec{x}_i$, the best position reached $\vec{p}_i$ and the best position in the neighborhood $\vec{n}_i$ – respectively vx, xx, px and nb – for all the particles of the swarm. For example, the first element of the xx array corresponds to the first dimension of the first particle position vector; the Nth element is the first dimension of the second particle, and so far.
The GPU used to run the algorithm only executes 512 thread simultaneously. Due to this, more than one block is needed to run the algorithm. Once the threads need to communicate through blocks, the vectors used by the algorithm must be stored in the global memory. It will harm the performance but it can be overcomed by using more advanced GPUs cards.
The modulus operation and the integer division are widely used through the pseudocodes. The first one is expressed by the % character and it returns the division rest of the operators. The integer division is actually a simple division operation attributed to a integer variable, it means that only the integer value is stored.
In order to know which particle belongs the Kth element of an array, one can use the modulus operation and the integer division operation. By instance, the particle has index $p = K/D$ and it represents the dimension $d = K\%D$.
The synchronization barrier shown on Section 4.1.2 is expressed on the pseudocodes by the command *synchronization-barrier()*. In the CUDA platform, it is expressed as *__syncthreads()*.
The kernel function calls are written in the code with the $<<a, b>>$ parameters. It means that the function will be executed by a threads in b blocks. It is very similar to the CUDA platform, but, in this case, it is used built-in variable types.
The *particle* variable presented on the codes is actually what defines a thread on the GPU. In the CUDA platform, it is obtained using built-in variables shown on Section 3.
The *first-thread-of-the-particle* is also seen on the codes, it is a boolean that indicates if the current thread is the thread with the duty to manipulate the first dimension of the vectors. It is used to avoid many threads executing the same operation on the same data.

4.3 The synchronous PSO

The synchronous version of the PSO needs a parallel model with barriers to assure that the particles will use the best information available from their neighborhood. For this, we split the code in kernel functions. After each call of a kernel function, there is an implicit synchronization barrier, which means that every thread has terminated its execution before the next kernel function be executed. The main code of the synchronous PSO with the kernel function calls is shown on Pseudocode 1.

Pseudocode 1 The Main Part of the Synchronous PSO on GPU.

```
for 1 to number-of-runs
  initialize-particles << 512, 2 >>;
  fitness-evaluation << 30, 1 >>;
  initialize-pbest << 30, 1 >>;
  do
      fitness << 30, 1 >>;
      update-pbestx << 512, 2 >>;
      update-pbest << 30, 1 >>;
      find-nbest << 30, 1 >>;
      update-particles << 512, 2 >>;
  while (iteration < number-of-iterations)
```

The implicit barrier avoids the particles to be updated before the best information has been found. However, searching for the best particle in the neighborhood may be computationally expensive, once it is a sequential search. The worst case is in the global topology where the order is $O(n)$.

Since the particles are actually arrays, one way to get rid of it is to use a method called Reduction Method. It reduces the searching order to $O(\log n)$. First, it compares in parallel the odd index elements of an array with the even index ones. Then, each thread copies the best one to the odd index element. Subsequently, the threads compare the elements with index being multiple of 2 and copy in parallel the best one to the element with the smallest index. And so forth with the elements multiples of $4, 8, 2^n < N/2$, where N is the number of elements in the array. In the end, the best value is in the first element of the array.

This method is described on Pseudocode 2 and it is used by the Global topology, the Four Clusters topology and the Focal topology.

Pseudocode 2 The Reduction Method with a 32-elements Array.

```
for s = 1 to 16 with increment s = s*2
  if (thread-idx % 2*s == 0)
      if (array[thread-idx] > array[thread-idx])
          array[thread-idx] = array[thread-idx];
  synchronization-barrier().
```

The *find-nbest* kernel has the duty to search the best neighbour of each particle. Each thread acts as a particle and search on its own neighborhood. Thus, the difference between the topologies lies in this kernel. They are shown in the following subsections.

4.3.1 Synchronous GPU-based PSO using the Global Topology

In the global topology, all particles are able to communicate with the other particles. Then, the best particle in a neighborhood is actually the best particle in the swarm. Thus, basically the global topology is the reduction method being used.
The kernel function is shown on the Pseudocode 3. Differently to the Pseudocode 2, there is an auxiliary variable *index* in the code. It is used to not override the *pbest* values.

Pseudocode 3 The *find-nbest* Kernel for the Global Topology.

```
for (int s = 1; s <=16; s = s*2)
  if (particle % 2*s == 0)
      if (pbest[index[particle]] > pbest[index[particle+s]])
          index[particle] = index[particle+s];
  synchronization-barrier();
best-neighbour[particle] = index[0];
```

4.3.2 Synchronous GPU-based PSO using the Ring topology

A particle in a swarm with the ring topology has only two neighbours. They are modeled here with the contiguous elements of an array. Thus, a thread knows its neighbours using the modulus operator, as shown on Pseudocode 4.

Pseudocode 4 The *find-nbest* Kernel for the Ring Topology.

```
best-neighbour[particle] = particle;
neighbour = (particle - 1) % number-of-agents;
if (pbest[best-neighbour[particle]] > pbest[neighbour])
  best-neighbour[particle] = neighbour;
neighbour = (particle + 1) % number-of-agents;
if (pbest[best-neighbour[particle]] > pbest[neighbour])
  best-neighbour[particle] = neighbour;
```

4.3.3 Synchronous GPU-based PSO using the von Neumann topology

The von Neumann topology is similar to the Ring topology. A particle has neighbors above, below, and on each side. This structure is a grid that can be defined by the number of columns and the number of rows.
The modulus operator and the integer division are used in the code. They are used with the variables *columns* and *rows* – respectively, the number of columns and the number of rows of the grid – to determine the neighbours. The code is described on Pseudocode 5.

4.3.4 Synchronous GPU-based PSO using the Four clusters topology

The Four Clusters topology is a composition of the Ring topology and the Global topology. First, each cluster find its best particle in the sub-swarm, then each gateway particle in the cluster communicates with others gateway to disseminate information.
The Reduction Method is used in the code but with a lower number of iterations. Thus, it finds the best particle in the current cluster. Then, using the modulus operator and the

Pseudocode 5 The *find-nbest* Kernel for the von Neumann Topology.

```
best-neighbour[particle] = particle;
x = particle % columns;
y = particle / columns;
neighbour = y * columns + (x - 1) % columns;
if (pbest[best-neighbour[particle]] > pbest[neighbour])
    best-neighbour[particle] = neighbour;
neighbour = y * columns + (x + 1) % columns;
if (pbest[best-neighbour[particle]] > pbest[neighbour])
    best-neighbour[particle] = neighbour;
neighbour = ((y - 1) % rows) * columns + x;
if (pbest[best-neighbour[particle]] > pbest[neighbour])
    best-neighbour[particle] = neighbour;
neighbour = ((y + 1) % rows) * columns + x;
if (pbest[best-neighbour[particle]] > pbest[neighbour])
    best-neighbour[particle] = neighbour;
```

integer division, the gateways communicate with the other clusters. The code is presented on Pseudocode 6.

Pseudocode 6 The *find-nbest* Kernel for the Four Clusters Topology.

```
for (int s = 1; s <=4; s = s*2)
    if (particle % 2*s == 0)
        if (pbest[index[particle]] > pbest[index[particle+s]])
            index[particle] = index[particle+s];
    synchronization-barrier();
gbest-cluster = particle / clusters;
gbest-cluster = gbest-cluster * clusters;
best-neighbour[particle] = gbest-cluster;
y = particle / agents-per-cluster;
x = particle % agents-per-cluster;
neighbour = particle + agents-per-cluster * (y - x + 1);
if (neighbour > number-of-agents)
    neighbour = particle;
if (pbest[best-neighbour[particle]] > pbest[neighbour])
    best-neighbour[particle] = neighbour;
```

4.3.5 Synchronous GPU-based PSO using the Focal topology

The Focal topology is very similar to the Global topology. The focus find the best particle in the swarm but this information flows slowly through the swarm.

The kernel function is described on Pseudocode 7. The focus is the particle with the index "0" in the array. First all particles are compared with the focus, then the Reduction Method is used to find the best particle in the swarm.

Pseudocode 7 The *find-nbest* Kernel for the Focal Topology.

```
best-neighbour[particle] = particle
if (pbest[particle] > pbest[0])
    best-neighbour[particle] = 0;
for (int s = 1; s <=16; s = s*2)
    if (particle % 2*s == 0)
        if (pbest[index[particle]] > pbest[index[particle+s]])
            index[particle] = index[particle+s];
    synchronization-barrier();
best-neighbour[0] = index[0];
```

4.4 The Asynchronous PSO

In the asynchronous PSO, all barriers used to assure no race condition on the synchronous PSO are removed. Thus, it allows the best particle variable value to be changed at any time if other particle finds a better position. Once it runs in parallel and it presents race conditions, there is no guarantee that the best information will be considered. The main code is presented on Pseudocode 8.

Pseudocode 8 The Main Part of the Asynchronous PSO on GPU.

```
for 1 to number-of-runs
    initialize-particles << 512, 2 >>;
    do
        iteration << 512, 2 >>;
    while (iteration < number-of-iterations)
```

The whole PSO algorithm lies in the kernel function *iteration*. The function is shown on Pseudocode 9. The difference between the topologies is presented in the line 4. In the following subsections, these differences are presented.

4.4.1 Asynchronous GPU-based PSO using the Global topology

In the global topology, the best particle in the neighborhood is actually the best one in the swarm. In fact, each particle claims to be the best after have compared with the current best one. In the asynchronous PSO, many particles claim to be the best at the same time and try to change the best value found so far by the swarm. Then, there is a race condition here what means that it is not guaranteed that the best value will actually have the best particle value. The asynchronous PSO with global topology is shown in the Pseudocode 10.

4.4.2 Asynchronous GPU-based PSO using the Ring topology

Each particle in a ring topology has two neighbours. The neighborhood of a particle is composed by the elements located after and before its index in the array. The code of this topology is presented in Pseudocode 11 and it is similar to the one in Pseudocode 4. The differences between them are only noticed at runtime, since the functions may be executed asynchronously by threads in different multi-processors in the asynchronous version.

Pseudocode 9 The *iteration* Kernel Function of the Asynchronous PSO on GPU.

```
if (the-first-thread-of-particle)
    minval[particle] = fitness-evaluation();
synchronization-barrier();
...
synchronization-barrier();
dimension = index % number-of-dimensions;
pbest-index = dimension + best-neighbour[particle]*number
            -of-dimensions;
vx[index] = factor*(vx[index] + c*random*(pbestx[index]-xx[index])
            + c*random*(pbestx[pbest-index] - xx[index]));
if (vx[index] > maxv)
    vx[index] = maxv;
else if (vx[index] < -maxv)
    vx[index] = -maxv;
xx[index] = xx[index] + vx[index];
if (xx[index] > maxx)
    xx[index] = maxx;
    vx[index] = -vx[index];
if (xx[index] < minx)
    xx[index] = minx;
    vx[index] = -vx[index];
```

Pseudocode 10 The Global Topology for the GPU-based Asynchronous PSO.

```
if (minval[particle] <= pbest[particle])
    if (the-first-thread-of-particle)
        pbest[particle] = minval[particle];
    pbestx[thread] = xx[index];
    if (the-first-thread-of-particle)
        if (pbest[particle] < pbest[gbest])
            gbest = particle;
```

Pseudocode 11 The Focal Topology for the GPU-based Asynchronous PSO.

```
if (minval[particle] <= pbest[particle])
    if (the-first-thread-of-particle)
        pbest[particle] = minval[particle];
    pbestx[thread] = xx[index];
best-neighbour[particle] = particle;
if (the-first-thread-of-particle)
    neighbour = (particle - 1)%number-of-agents;
    if (pbest[best-neighbour[particle]] > pbest[neighbour])
        best-neighbour[particle] = neighbour;
    neighbour = (particle + 1)%number-of-agents;
    if (pbest[best-neighbour[particle]] > pbest[neighbour])
        best-neighbour[particle] = neighbour;
```

4.4.3 Asynchronous GPU-based PSO using the von Neumann Topology

The von Neumann topology has similar behaviour when compared to the Ring topology. A particle has neighbours above, below, and on each side. This structure is a grid that can be defined by the number of columns and the number of rows.

The modulus operator and the integer division are used for this purpose. They are used with the variables *columns* and *rows* – respectively, the number of columns and the number of rows of the grid – to determine the neighbours. The code is described in Pseudocode 12 and it is very similar to the one presented in Pseudocode 5. Once the functions may be executed asynchronously by threads in different multi-processors, the differences between the synchronous and asynchronous versions are only noticed at runtime.

Pseudocode 12 The von Neumann Topology for the GPU-based Asynchronous PSO.

```
if (minval[particle] <= pbest[particle])
    if (the-first-thread-of-particle)
        pbest[particle] = minval[particle];
    pbestx[thread] = xx[index];
best-neighbour = particle;
x = particle % columns;
y = particle / columns;
neighbour = y * columns + (x-1)%columns;
if (pbest[best-neighbour[particle]] > pbest[neighbour])
    best-neighbour[particle] = neighbour;
neighbour = y * columns + (x+1)%columns;
if (pbest[best-neighbour[particle]] > pbest[neighbour])
    best-neighbour[particle] = neighbour;
neighbour = ((y - 1)%rows)*columns + x;
if (pbest[best-neighbour[particle]] > pbest[neighbour])
    best-neighbour[particle] = neighbour;
neighbour = ((y + 1)%rows)*columns + x;
if (pbest[best-neighbour[particle]] > pbest[neighbour])
    best-neighbour[particle] = neighbour;
```

4.4.4 Asynchronous GPU-based PSO using the Four clusters topology

In the Four Clusters topology, the particles first find the best particle in each cluster, likewise the Global topology. Then, the gateways present in each sub-swarm communicate with other clusters.

In the asynchronous PSO, the Global topology presented inside each cluster is affected in the same way as seen in Section 4.4.1. The race condition in the code means that it is not guaranteed that the best particle is the last one to set the best value found so far by the swarm. The code is described in Pseudocode 13. It uses the modulus operator and the integer division with the variable *agents-per-clusters* that is the number of particles inside each cluster.

Pseudocode 13 The Four Clusters Topology for the GPU-based Asynchronous PSO.

```
if (minval[particle] <= pbest[particle])
    if (the-first-thread-of-particle)
        pbest[particle] = minval[particle];
    pbestx[thread] = xx[index];
if (the-first-thread-of-particle)
    first-of-cluster = particle/clusters;
    first-of-cluster = first-of-cluster * clusters;
    best-neighbour[particle] = particle;
    if (pbest[best-neighbour[first-of-cluster]] < pbest[particle])
        best-neighbour[first-of-cluster] = particle ;
    best-neighbour[particle] = best-neighbour[first-of-cluster]
    y = particle / agents-per-cluster;
    x = particle % agents-per-cluster;
    neighbour-cluster = particle + agents-per-cluster*(x + y - 1);
    if (neighbour-cluster > number-of-agents)
        neighbour-cluster = particle;
    if (pbest[particle] > pbest[neighbour-cluster])
        best-neighbour[particle] = neighbour-cluster;
```

4.4.5 Asynchronous GPU-based PSO using the Focal topology

Since the Focal topology is very similar to the Global topology, once the focus first find the best particle in the swarm, the asynchronous PSO using the Focal topology is affected similarly as shown in Section 4.4.1. There is no guarantee that the best value found so far by the swarm will be set in the end by the best particle.

The code is described in Pseudocode 14 and the focus is the particle with index "0".

5. Experiments

In this section we present the performed experiments to compare the performance of synchronous and asynchronous PSO running on CUDA for each of the topologies analysed previously. Well known benchmark functions were chosen to perform the experiments.

5.1 Benchmark functions

Four benchmark functions were used to employ the simulations and are described in equations (6) to (9). All the functions are used for minimization problems. Two of these

Pseudocode 14 The Focal Topology for the GPU-based Asynchronous PSO.

```
if (minval[particle] <= pbest[particle])
    if (the-first-thread-of-particle)
        pbest[particle] = minval[particle];
    pbestx[thread] = xx[index];
if (the-first-thread-of-particle)
    best-neighbour[particle] = particle;
    if ((pbest[particle] < pbest[0]) && particle != 0)
        best-neighbour[0] = particle;
    else
        best-neighbour[particle] = 0;
```

functions (Rosenbrock and Schwefel) are uni-modal problems, and the others two (Rastrigin and Griewank) are multimodal functions that contains many local optima.
The first one is Rosenbrock function. It has a global minimum located in a banana-shaped valley. The region where the minimum point is located is very easy to reach, but the convergence to the global minimum point is hard to achieve. The function is defined as follows:

$$F_{Rosenbrock}(\vec{x}) = \sum_{i=1}^{n} x^2 \left[100(x_{i+1} - x_i^2)^2 + (1 - x_i)^2 \right]. \tag{6}$$

The second is the generalized Rastrigin, a multi-modal function that induces the search to a deep local minima arranged as sinusoidal bumps:

$$F_{Rastrigin}(\vec{x}) = 10n + \sum_{i=1}^{n} \left[x_i^2 - 10cos(2\pi x_i) \right]. \tag{7}$$

The third and the fourth ones are Griewank and Schwefel functions:

$$F_{Griewank}(\vec{x}) = 1 + \sum_{i=1}^{n} \frac{x_i^2}{4000} - \prod_{i=1}^{n} cos\left(\frac{x_i}{\sqrt{i}}\right), \tag{8}$$

$$F_{Schwefel}(\vec{x}) = \sum_{i=1}^{n} \left(\sum_{j=1}^{i} x_j \right). \tag{9}$$

5.2 Simulations setup

The PSO using the constriction factor, as shown on Section 2, was used to perform all the simulations in this chapter. To compose the constriction factor (χ) we used $\kappa = 1$, $c_1 = 2.05$ and $c_2 = 2.05$ ($\phi \geq 4$) values. All the simulations were performed using 32 particles for all five PSO topologies (Four Clusters, Focal, Global, Local and von Neumann). We run 50 trial to evaluate the average fitness.
Each simulation of the Four Clusters topology uses 4 clusters, each one with 8 particles. The focus of the Focal topology is the first particle of the swarm. All swarms were randomly initialized in an area far from the optimal solution in every dimension. This allows a fair convergence analysis between the topologies. All the random numbers needed by the PSO algorithm were generated as proposed by Bastos-Filho et al. (2010).

6. Results

The results of the experiments involving all the four benchmark functions are described in this section. In the Section 6.1 the results of the comparison between the synchronous and asynchronous algorithm for each one of the considered topologies are presented. Section 6.2 presents a performance analysis in terms of elapsed time to run the algorithm.

6.1 Fitness Analysis

The average value of the best fitness achieved for the Rosenbrock function for five different topologies using the synchronous and the asynchronous algorithm is shown in Figure 6.
Figures 6 (a) and 6 (b) show the convergence curve for Rosenbrock in the Four Clusters and the Focal topologies, respectively. When we compare the results for synchronous and asynchronous algorithm in each oh these topologies, we observe a worse performance for the last one. It is what we expected, since some data were not considered during the velocity update processes due to lack of synchronization barriers. On the other hand, for the topologies Global, Local and von Neumann, presented in Figures 6 (c), 6 (d) and 6 (e), respectively, the results are quite similar, although the loss of information by the asynchronous versions.
Figure 7 show the average value of the best fitness achieved in the Griewank function. The analysis for this function is quite different. In this case, despite it needs more iterations to reach the convergence, the lack of synchronicity helps to avoid the swarm to be trapped on local minima.
The comparison of the average and the (standard deviation of the fitness) for Rastrigin and Schwefel functions for each topology are presented in Table 1 and Table 2. Table 1 shows the results for the synchronous algorithm performance, while Table 2 shows the results for the asynchronous version.
A similar behaviour observed for Griewank can be observed for the Rastrigin function. It is quite expected since both are highly multimodal functions.

Function	Topology	Mean	SD
Rastrigin	Focal	52.31488	13.55017
	Four Clusters	73.07843	39.9018
	Global	53.09091	14.55321
	Local	67.16104	32.97102
	von Neumann	55.72031	32.49462
Schwefel	Focal	$2 \cdot 10^{-12}$	$1.41 \cdot 10^{-11}$
	Four Clusters	$2 \cdot 10^{-12}$	$1.41 \cdot 10^{-11}$
	Global	$4 \cdot 10^{-11}$	$2.82 \cdot 10^{-11}$
	Local	$2.4 \cdot 10^{-11}$	$1.69 \cdot 10^{-10}$
	von Neumann	$4 \cdot 10^{-12}$	$2.82 \cdot 10^{-11}$

Table 1. The Average Value and Standard Deviation of the Fitness After 50 Trials of 10,000 Evaluations for the Synchronous Version.

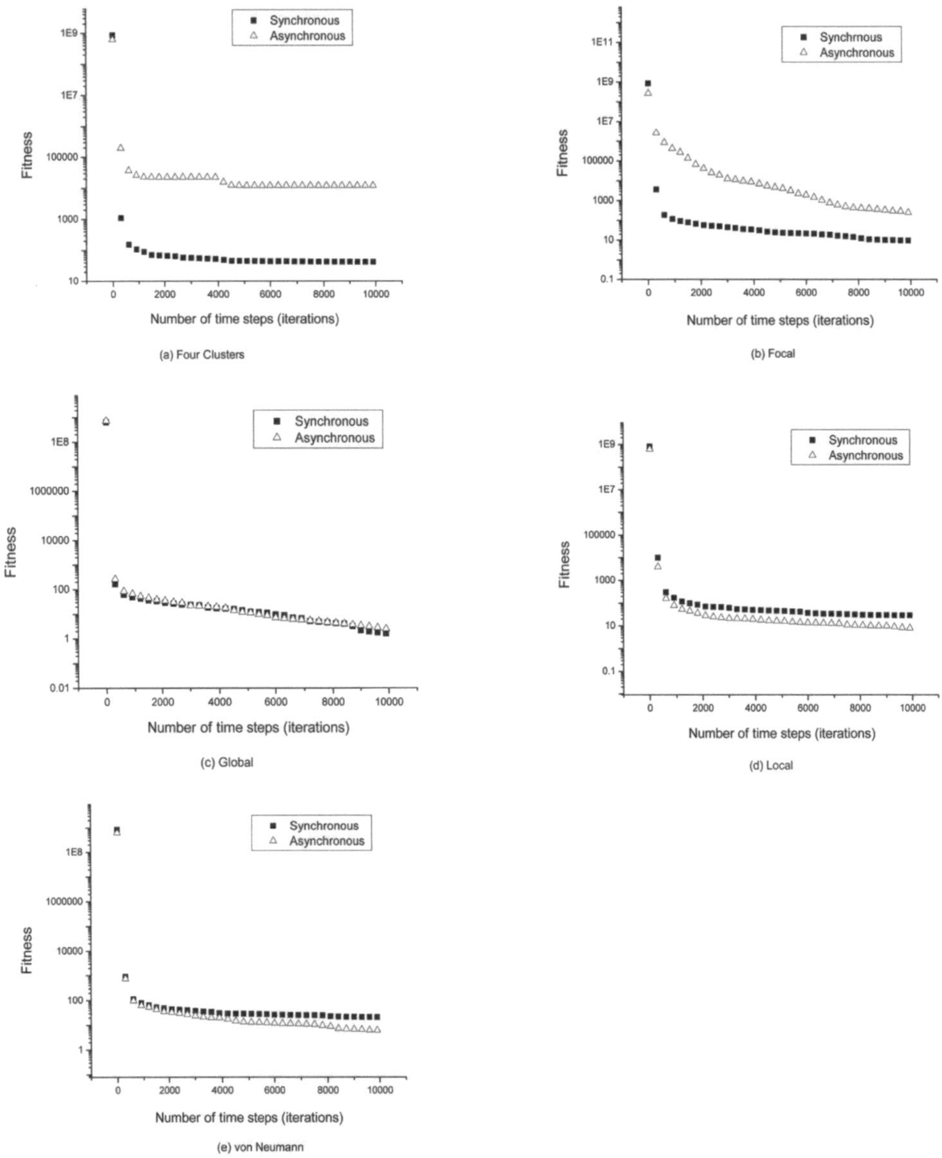

Fig. 6. The Best Fitness Comparison of the Five PSO Topologies for Rosenbrock Function.

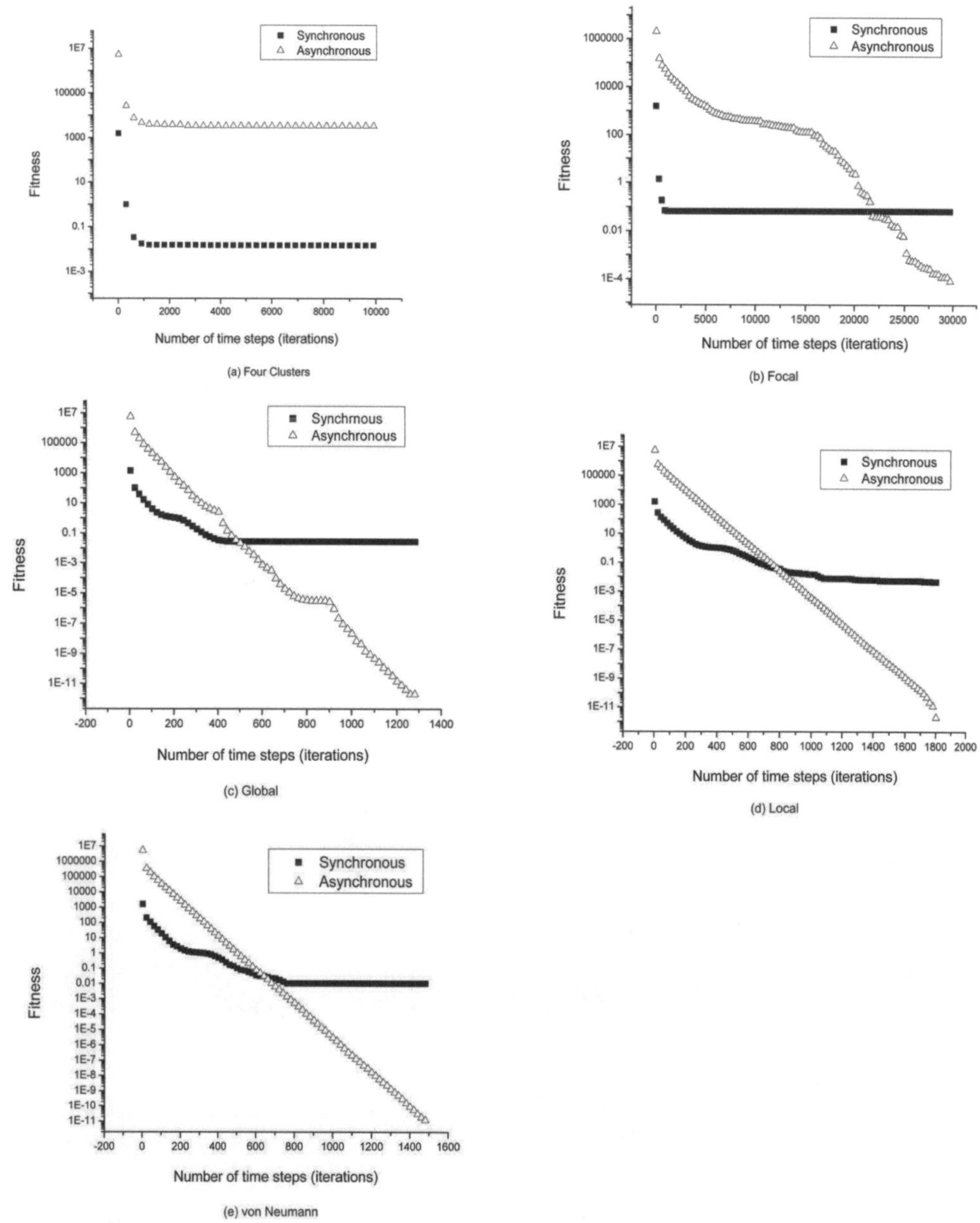

Fig. 7. The Best Fitness Comparison of the Five PSO Topologies of the Griewank Function.

Function	Topology	Mean	SD
Rastrigin	Focal	155.23031	26.16508
	Four Clusters	55.79153	15.49237
	Global	50.96177	13.36732
	Local	41.8803	10.2887
	von Neumann	33.26468	7.79463
Schwefel	Focal	$2 \cdot 10^{-12}$	$1.41 \cdot 10^{-11}$
	Four Clusters	19.6835	61.97515
	Global	$2 \cdot 10^{-11}$	$1.41 \cdot 10^{-11}$
	Local	$4 \cdot 10^{-12}$	$1.9794 \cdot 10^{-10}$
	von Neumann	$1.6 \cdot 10^{-11}$	$3.70328 \cdot 10^{-11}$

Table 2. The Average Value and Standard Deviation of the Fitness After 50 Trials of 10,000 Evaluations for the Asynchronous Version.

6.2 Performance analysis

The Figure 8(a) and Figure 8(b) show the elapsed time for the synchronous and asynchronous PSO for Rosenbrock and Griewank functions in Four Clusters, Focal, Global, Local and von Neumann topologies. One can note that the elapsed time for the asynchronous algorithm is lower than the synchronous algorithm for both Rosenbrock and Griewank functions. It is also expected due to lack of synchronization barriers. However, when we compare the performance between the five topologies, we can note that the synchronous algorithm results are quite similar for both Griewank and Rosenbrock functions. In other hand, when we compare the asynchronous algorithm results, a minor difference in terms of performance between the topologies can be observed.

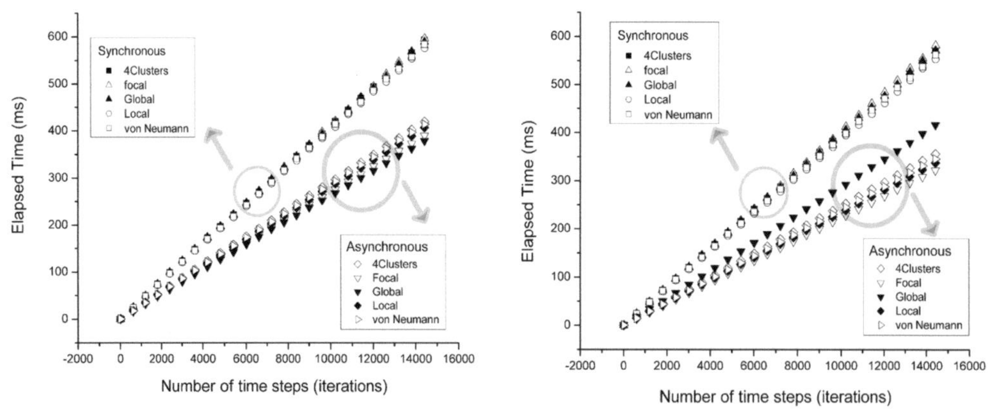

(a) Rosenbrock

(b) Griewank

Fig. 8. The Elapsed Time for the GPU-based PSO Execution for Rosenbrock and Griewank Functions Asynchronous and Synchronous.

7. Conclusion

In this chapter, we have presented some concerns that should be carried out to implement a GPU-based PSO algorithm. We also have analysed the performance of the PSO with different topologies in terms of best value achieved and the time needed to execute the algorithm.
We have shown in Section 4.1 that there is a memory bottleneck when transferring data between the GPU and the CPU. The random number generator should run in the GPU in order to avoid data transfer.
We also have presented results for two approaches to update the particles. The synchronization barriers placed in the code influence the algorithm runtime and performance. As shown in Section 6, the behaviour of the algorithm running on the GPU with different functions depends on the approach used to update the particles. For instance, when optimizing the Rosenbrock function with the GPU-based PSO using topology Local, Global or von Neumann, the asynchronous PSO presented similar results to the synchronous one. As the asynchronous is faster, thus it is better use it in this case. On the other hand, by using the Focal topology or the Four Clusters topology, the asynchronous version shows a bad performance and the speed-up reached by using the asynchronous PSO is not worth, then the best choice is the synchronous version.
We also showed that, in some cases, one can remove the synchronization barriers, specially for multimodal search spaces.

8. Acknowledgments

The authors would like to thank FACEPE, CNPq, UPE and POLI (Escola Politécnica de Pernambuco).

9. References

Bastos-Filho, C., Andrade, J., Pita, M. & Ramos, A. (2009). Impact of the quality of random numbers generators on the performance of particle swarm optimization, *Systems, Man and Cybernetics, 2009. SMC 2009. IEEE International Conference on* pp. 4988 –4993.

Bastos-Filho, C., Oliveira Junior, M., Nascimento, D. & Ramos, A. (2010). Impact of the random number generator quality on particle swarm optimization algorithm running on graphic processor units, *Hybrid Intelligent Systems, 2010. HIS '10. Tenth International Conference on* pp. 85–90.

Bratton, D. & Kennedy, J. (2007). Defining a standard for particle swarm optimization, *Swarm Intelligence Symposium, 2007. SIS 2007. IEEE* pp. 120 –127.

Clerc, M. & Kennedy, J. (2002). The particle swarm - explosion, stability, and convergence in a multidimensional complex space, *Evolutionary Computation, IEEE Transactions on* 6(1): 58 –73.

Eberhart, R. & Shi, Y. (2000). Comparing inertia weights and constriction factors in particle swarm optimization, *Evolutionary Computation, 2000. Proceedings of the 2000 Congress on* 1: 84 –88 vol.1.

Ferreira de Carvalho, D. & Bastos-Filho, C. J. A. (2009). Clan particle swarm optimization, *International Journal of Intelligent Computing and Cybernetics* 2(2): 197–227.
URL: *http://dx.doi.org/10.1108/17563780910959875*

Heppner, F. & Grenander, U. (1990). A stochastic nonlinear model for coordinated bird flocks, *in* E. Krasner (ed.), *The ubiquity of chaos*, AAAS Publications, pp. 233–238.

Kennedy, J. & Eberhart, R. (1995). Particle swarm optimization, Vol. 4, pp. 1942–1948 vol.4. URL: *http://dx.doi.org/10.1109/ICNN.1995.488968*

Kennedy, J. & Mendes, R. (2002). Population structure and particle swarm performance, Vol. 2, pp. 1671 –1676.

Marsaglia, G. (2003). Xorshift rngs, *Journal of Statistical Software* 8(14): 1–6. URL: *http://www.jstatsoft.org/v08/i14*

Matsumoto, M. & Nishimura, T. (1998). Mersenne twister: a 623-dimensionally equidistributed uniform pseudo-random number generator, *ACM Trans. Model. Comput. Simul.* 8: 3–30. URL: *http://doi.acm.org/10.1145/272991.272995*

Mendes, R., Kennedy, J. & Neves, J. (2003). Watch thy neighbor or how the swarm can learn from its environment, *Swarm Intelligence Symposium*, 2003. SIS 2003. IEEE, pp. 88 – 94.

Mendes, R., Kennedy, J. & Neves, J. (2004). The fully informed particle swarm: simpler, maybe better, *Evolutionary Computation, IEEE Transactions on* 8(3): 204 – 210.

Mussi, L., Cagnoni, S. & Daolio, F. (2009). Gpu-based road sign detection using particle swarm optimization, *Intelligent Systems Design and Applications, 2009. ISDA '09. Ninth International Conference on* pp. 152 –157.

Nguyen, H. (2007). *GPU Gems 3*, Addison-Wesley Professional.

NVIDIA (2010). *NVIDIA CUDA Programming Guide 3.1.*

Podlozhnyuk, V. (2007). Parallel Mersenne Twister, *Technical report*, nvidia Corp.

Thomas, D. B., Howes, L. & Luk, W. (2009). A comparison of cpus, gpus, fpgas, and massively parallel processor arrays for random number generation. URL: *http://doi.acm.org/10.1145/1508128.1508139*

Watts, D. J. (1999). *Small worlds: The dynamics of networks between order and randomness*, Princeton University Press, Princeton, NJ.

Watts, D. J. & Strogatz, S. H. (1998). Collective dynamics of 'small-world' networks., *Nature* 393(6684): 440–442. URL: *http://dx.doi.org/10.1038/30918*

Zhou, Y. & Tan, Y. (2009). Gpu-based parallel particle swarm optimization, *Evolutionary Computation, 2009. CEC '09. IEEE Congress on* pp. 1493 –1500.

Zhu, W. & Curry, J. (2009). Particle swarm with graphics hardware acceleration and local pattern search on bound constrained problems, *Swarm Intelligence Symposium, 2009. SIS '09. IEEE* pp. 1 –8.

3

Enhanced Genetic Algorithm for Protein Structure Prediction based on the HP Model

Nashat Mansour[1], Fatima Kanj[1] and Hassan Khachfe[2]
[1]*Department of Computer Science and Mathematics, Lebanese American University,*
[2]*Department of Biology and Biomedical Sciences, Lebanese International University,*
Lebanon

1. Introduction

Proteins are organic compounds that are made up of combinations of amino acids and are of different types and roles in living organisms. Initially a protein is a linear chain of amino acids, ranging from a few tens up to thousands of amino acids. Proteins fold, under the influence of several chemical and physical factors, into their 3-dimensional structures which determine their biological functions and properties. Misfolding occurs when the protein folds into a 3D structure that does not represent its correct native structure, which can lead to many diseases such as Alzheimer, several types of cancer, etc… (Prusiner, 1998). Hence, predicting the native structure of a protein from its primary sequence is an important and challenging task especially that this protein structure prediction (PSP) problem is computationally intractable.

The primary structure of a protein is a linear sequence of amino acids connected together via peptide bonds. Proteins fold due to hydrophobic effect, Vander Waals interactions, electrostatic forces, and Hydrogen bonding (Setubal & Meidanis, 1997). The secondary structures are three-dimensional structures characterized by repeating bonding patterns of α-helices and β-strands. Proteins further fold into a tertiary structure forming a bundle of secondary structures and loops. Furthermore, the aggregation of tertiary structure regions of separate protein sequences leads to quaternary structures. These structures are depicted in Fig. 1 (Rylance, 2004).

Computational approaches for PSP can be classified as: homology modeling, threading, and *ab initio* methods (Floudas, 2007). Approaches in the first two groups use known protein structures from protein data banks (PDB). Approaches in the third group solely rely on the given amino acid sequence. A survey of PSP approaches appeared in Sikder and Zomaya (2005). Homology modeling uses sequences of known structures in the PDB to align with the target protein's sequence for which the 3D structure is to be predicted (Kopp & Schwede, 2004; Notredame, 2002; Pandit et al., 2006).

Threading is similar to homology modeling. But, instead of finding similar sequences to deduce the native conformation of the target protein, threading assumes that the target structure is similar to another existing structure, which should be searched for (Lathrop et al., 1998; Jones 1998; Skolnick et al., 2004). The threading of a sequence to a fold is evaluated by either environment-based or knowledge-based mean-force-potentials derived from the PDB.

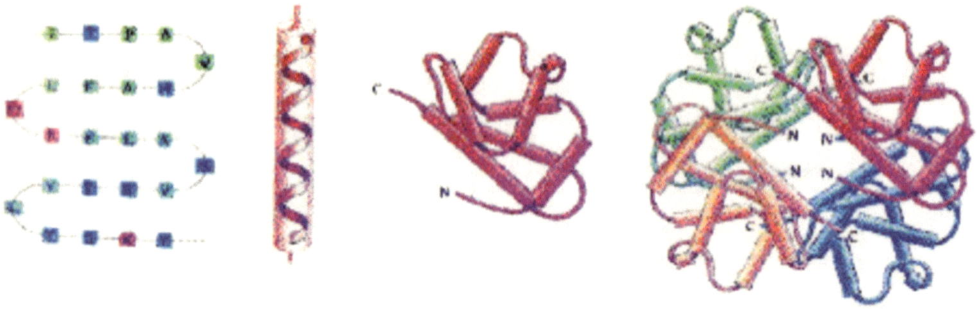

Fig. 1. Primary, secondary, tertiary and quaternary structures

Ab initio approaches do not rely on known structures in the PDB. Instead, they predict the 3D structure of proteins given their primary sequences. The underlying strategy is to find the best possible structure based on a chosen energy function. Based on the laws of physics, the most stable structure is the one with the lowest possible energy (Anfinsen, 1973). The main challenge of these approaches is to search for the most stable structure in a huge search space. Models such as the Hydrophobic-Polar (HP) models have been developed in order to reduce the size of the search space. Other models use the detailed representation of proteins with all the corresponding atoms, based on force fields.

Force field models use an energy objective function that evaluates the structure of a protein. This function attempts to represent the actual physical forces and chemical reactions occurring in a protein. Atoms are modeled as points in 3D with zero volume but with finite mass and charge, and bonds among atoms are modeled as Newtonian springs. The energy function is usually based on molecular mechanics and force fields components such as bond lengths, bond angles, dihedral angles, van der Waals interactions, electrostatic forces, etc.... Examples of force-field based methods are found in: Schulze-Kremer (2000), Klepeis and Floudas (2003), Datta et al. (2008), Li et al. (2006), Srinivasan and Rose (2000) and Mansour et al. (2009).

The HP model simplifies the protein by assigning each amino acid to be a point in a 2D or 3D lattice (Unger and Moult, 1993b) which is either hydrophobic (H) or polar (P) (Dill, 1985). According to this model, the most stable structure is the one with the hydrophobic amino acids lying in its core. The underlying concept is that hydrophobic amino acids tend to avoid contact with the solvent and hence tend to move inside the structure whereas the polar ones remain on the outside. The main energy function used in this model is the total number of the hydrophobic interactions between the amino acids and the goal is to have a lattice with minimum energy, i.e., with maximum number of H-H contacts. The objective is to fold a string of Hs and Ps on a three dimensional coordinates system in a self-avoiding walk. Candidate solutions are represented as a string of characters (b, f, u, d, l, r) representing the six directions: backward, forward, up, down, left and right.

Despite the reduction in search space, the problem of predicting protein structures in the HP model is still intractable (Unger and Moult, 1993a). Hence, heuristic and meta-heuristics algorithms have been reported for finding good sub-optimal solutions. In the early nineties, Unger and Moult (1993b) developed a genetic algorithm (GA) combined with the Monte Carlo method to fold proteins on a two dimensional lattice and they extended their work later to a 3D lattice. Later, a standard GA was developed (Patton et al., 1995) and it outperformed that of Unger and Moult (1993b) by reaching higher number of hydrophobic contacts with less number of energy evaluations. More recently, Johnson et al. (2006) proposed a genetic algorithm with a backtracking method to resolve the collision problem.

Heuristic methods based on assumptions about the folding mechanism were proposed, such as the hydrophobic zipper (Dill et al., 1993), the constrained hydrophobic core construction algorithm (Yue & Dill, 1995), and the contact interactions method (Toma & Toma, 1996). A branch and bound algorithm was developed by Chen and Huang (2005). The algorithm evaluates the importance of every possible position of the hydrophobic amino acids and only those promising locations are preserved for more branching at every level.

Methods based on the Monte Carlo (MC) algorithm have also been proposed: the MC based growth algorithm (Hsu et al., 2003), and the evolutionary MC algorithm (Liang & Wong, 2001). Further, a modified particle swarm optimization algorithm for the protein structure prediction problem in the 2D toy model was proposed by Zhang and Li (2007). An Ant Colony Optimization algorithm was proposed by Shmygelska and Hoos (2005) for both 2D and 3D lattice models.

In this paper, we present a genetic algorithm for the protein structure prediction problem based on the cubic 3D hydrophobic polar (HP) model. This algorithm is enhanced with heuristics that repair infeasible outcomes of the crossover operation and ensure that the mutation operation leads to fitter and feasible candidate solutions. The PSP solutions produced by this GA are experimentally evaluated by comparing them with previously published results.

The rest of the paper is organized as follows. Section 2 describes the GA algorithm for the PSP problem. Section 3 presents our experimental results. Section 4 concludes the paper.

2. Enhanced genetic algorithm

Genetic Algorithms simulate the concept of natural evolution (Holland, 1975). They are based on the operations of population reproduction and selection for the purpose of achieving optimal results. Through artificial evolution, successive generations search for fitter adaptations in order to solve a problem. Each generation consists of a population of chromosomes, and each chromosome represents a possible solution. The Darwinian principle of reproduction and survival of the fittest and the genetic operations of recombination and mutation are used to create a new offspring population from the current population. The process is repeated for many generations with the aim of maximizing the fitness of the chromosomes. In the following subsections, we describe an enhanced genetic algorithm (EGA) that is adapted for solving the protein structure prediction problem. A flowchart of this EGA is given in Fig. 2.

2.1 Chromosomal representation

A Chromosome in the population is encoded as an array of length N-1, where N is the number of amino acids in the respective protein. Each element in the array represents the position X_d of the corresponding amino acid d with respect to the preceding one and its value can be one of six characters {b, f, u, d, l, r}. These characters represent the following six directions, respectively {backward, forward, up, down, left, right}. In Fig. 3, a sample 3D

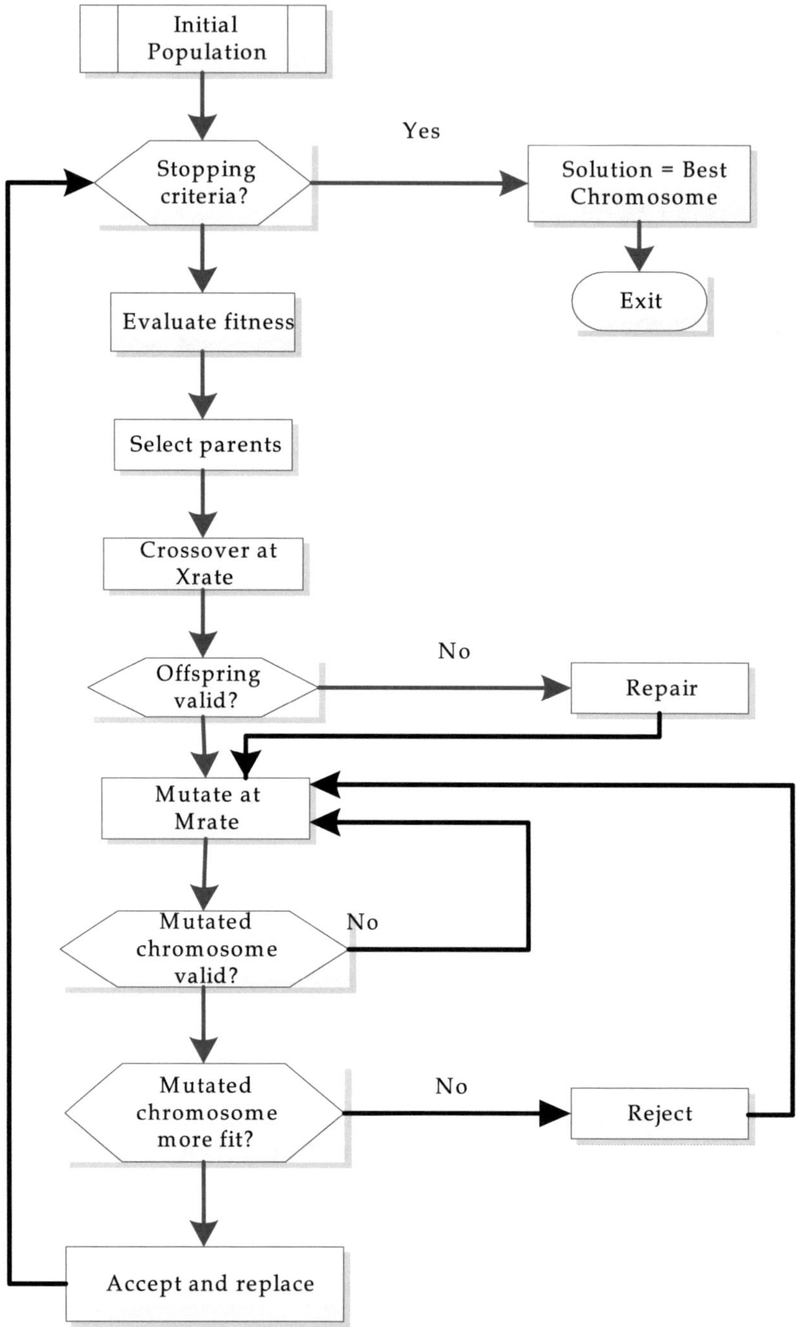

Fig. 2. Flowchart for the EGA.

structure is illustrated. This structure is represented as bbburdfulurrur, which is an array of directions (of length 14) is representing a protein sequence containing 15 amino acids where the first amino acid is omitted since it is the reference point. The gray balls represent the polar amino acids whereas the black balls represent the hydrophobic ones.

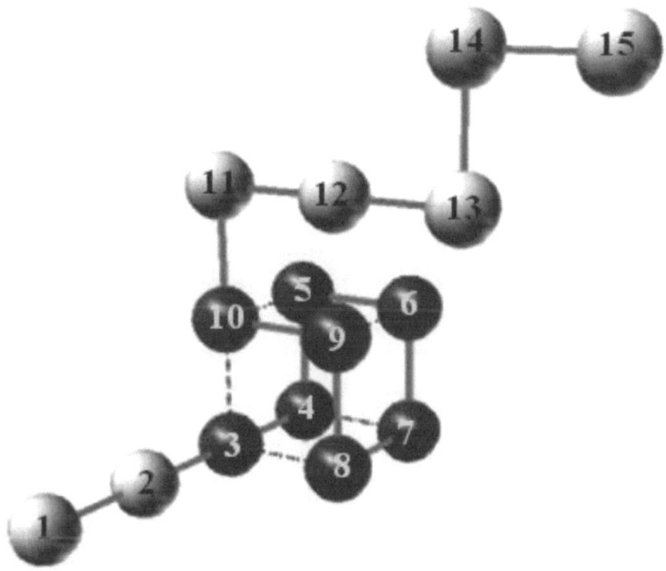

Fig. 3. A candidate PSP solution

GA's population is an array of POP Chromosomes. The initial population of PSP solutions is randomly generated. That is, each position X_d of amino acid d (d = 1, 2,..., N-1) is assigned a random value for the chromosome i (i = 0, 1, ..., POP-1). In our implementation, we use POP = 200.

2.2 Fitness function

The fitness function is given by the sum of the hydrophobic contacts (H-H) between non adjacent amino acids. Since we are using the cubic lattice, the maximum number of possible contacts per amino acid is four, except for the first and last amino acids, which might have up to five contacts. The goal is to maximize the fitness value of the chromosomes to obtain protein structures with the most compact hydrophobic core and, thus, with the lowest energy. For example, in Fig. 3, the fitness value of the displayed structure is 5. The hydrophobic contacts are displayed in dotted lines and there are five of them between the following pairs of hydrophobic amino acids: (3, 8), (3, 10), (4, 7), (5, 10) and (6, 9).
Evaluating the fitness value of a chromosome is simple. Every hydrophobic amino acid in the sequence is checked for any non-adjacent (not connected by a bond) hydrophobic amino acids in the six positions around it on the lattice, at a distance 1, and the number of these amino acids is counted.

2.3 Reproduction scheme and convergence

The whole population is considered a single reproduction unit within which tournament selection is performed. In this selection method, chromosomes are compared in a "tournament," with the higher-fitness chromosome being more likely to win. The tournament process is continued by sampling, with replacement, from the original population until a full complement of parents has been chosen. We use the binary tournament method, where we randomly select two pairs of chromosomes (i.e. 2 tournaments with 2 members each) and choose as the two parents the winner chromosomes

that have the higher fitness value from each pair. The tournament selection method is chosen since it is not very sensitive to the scaling of the fitness function.
To ensure that good candidate solutions are preserved, the best-so-far protein structure is saved. Convergence is detected when the best-so-far structure does not change its fitness value for 10 generations. After convergence, the best-so-far protein structure becomes the final PSP solution found.

2.4 Genetic operators and acceptance heuristics

The genetic operators employed in GA are 1-point crossover and mutation at the rates 0.5 and 0.1, respectively. Crossover is applied to pairs of chromosomes provided by tournament selection, where position k along the chromosome is selected at random between 1 and N, and all genes between k and N are swapped to create two new chromosomes. That is, the amino acids that lie between k and N will have their location in space (represented by the direction with respect to the preceding amino acid) exchanged. This may lead to collisions which occur if two or more amino acids lie at the same point on the cubic 3D lattice. If collisions occur, the protein structure becomes invalid. Invalid structures are repaired using a heuristic repair function, if possible; otherwise, the initial structure is restored. The repair function detects a collision and tries to repair it locally by finding an alternative empty location for the amino acid which caused the collision. If no such location is available, then it searches for previous amino acids whose locations can be modified. If modifications are performed for more than three amino acids or if none can be modified, then it is assumed that the structure cannot be repaired and the pre-crossover protein structure is returned.
Mutation is applied to randomly selected genes; that is the position of amino acid, d, in the 3D cubic lattice is changed to another position randomly selected from {b, f, u, d, l, r}. Eventually, the new offspring population replaces the parent population. But, if this mutation leads to an invalid protein structure, it is rejected and mutation will be repeated until a valid structure is found. Furthermore, the fitness value of this valid structure is computed. If the fitness of the mutated structure is higher than that of the initial pre-mutation structure, the mutated structure is accepted; otherwise, the initial structure is restored.

3. Experimental results

In this section, we report the empirical results of the proposed GA and compare them to those of published techniques: one by Patton et al. (1995), which proposed a standard genetic algorithm for this problem and reported better results than those achieved by Unger and Moult (1993b); the second is by Johnson et al. (2006), which reports better results than those achieved by Patton et al. (1995) for the smaller sequences.
We use two sets of benchmark sequences employed first by Unger and Moult (1993b). These are amino acid sequences of Hs and Ps generated randomly: 10 sequences are of length 27 and 10 sequences of length 64 (Tables 1 and 2). We evaluate the results using the following metrics:

- Fitness value: It is the total number of non consecutive H-H contacts.
- Number of fitness evaluations: This is the number of times the fitness function is computed to reach the final fitness score for a specific sequence. This metric is used as an indicator of the efficiency of our algorithm.

We executed our EGA program on a PC running MS-Windows XP operating system with a 2.33 GHz CPU and 2 GByte RAM memory.

Seq #	Sequence
273d.1	Phphphhhpphphpppppppppppphhp
273d.2	Phhppppppppppphhpphhpphpphph
273d.3	Hhhhpppphpppppphhhppppppppph
273d.4	Hhhpphhhhppphphpphhpphppphh
273d.5	Hhhhpppphphhppphhpppppppppp
273d.6	Hpppppphphhhpphhppphppppphph
273d.7	Hpphphhppphpppppphphhphphphh
273d.8	Hpppppppppppphphppppppppphphh
273d.9	Pppppphhhppphphhppphpphppp
273d.10	Ppppphhphphphphpphhphhphppp

Table 1. Benchmark sequences of length 27

Seq #	Sequence
643d.1	pphhhhhppphhppppphhppphpppppphphppphpphpphppppphppphhphhpphpphp
643d.2	pphphpphpphhhphhhhpphhhpppphphppphphppphphpppppphphpphphppphpphpp
643d.3	hphhpphhphpppppphhhphhhhpphpphphhppphphpphhhphhphppppphhhhhhhhppp
643d.4	hpphhpphpphphpphpppphppppphphphhhpphphppphphpphhpphpphpphphhhph
643d.5	hppphhpphphppphppphphhppphhphphhphpphppphpphphhhpphpphpphhhphhhh
643d.6	hpphhphhhhpppppphhpphppppphhppphpphphhphppppphhpppphpppppphpppphphh
643d.7	pppphppphppphhhhphhpppppphpphphhphphpppppphpppppppppphhhhppppphhpph
643d.8	ppphhhpphphpphpphhppphpphpphhphppphpppppppphphhhphhhhhpphhppphpph
643d.9	hpphpphhhppppphphppphphhphhhhhppppphphphppppphphppphhphpppphpphhphp
643d.10	pphpphpphhhppphphpphpphpppppphpphhhpphpphpphphppppppphhhppppphphp

Table 2. Benchmark sequences of length 64

Tables 3 and 4 show the results of our EGA in comparison with the previously published results of Johnson et al. (2006) for proteins with lengths 27 and the results of Patton et al. (1995) for 64 amino acids, respectively .

Table 3 results show that the proposed EGA produces fitness values that as the same as those of the technique of Johnson et al. (2006) in 9 out of 10 cases with a better value in the remaining case. However, the numbers of evaluations of fitness values is significantly less in the afore-mentioned 9 cases; it is greater in the 10th case where EGA clearly managed to search larger areas of the search space that enabled it to find a fitter protein structure.

Table 4 results show that the proposed EGA produces fitter protein structures than Patton et al. (1995) in 70% of the 10 cases, whereas the remaining 30% of the cases are identical.

4. Conclusion and future work

We have proposed a genetic algorithm that is enhanced with heuristic methods. These heuristics are incorporated into the crossover and mutation operations for the purposes of dealing with infeasible intermediate candidate solutions and of guiding the search into fitter regions of the search space. The empirical work shows that this enhanced genetic algorithm gives better results in terms of the protein structures, the algorithm efficiency, or both. Future work would consider larger proteins and visualization of the results. Furthermore, predicting the structures of large proteins is likely to require parallel processing in order to reduce execution time.

Seq #	Proposed EGA		Johnson et al. (2006)	
	Fitness	#Fitness Eval.	Fitness	#Fitness Eval.
273d.1	9	1,450	9	15,854
273d.2	10	5,473	10	19,965
273d.3	8	1,328	8	7,991
273d.4	15	5,196	15	23,525
273d.5	8	1,184	8	3,561
273d.6	12	18,012	11	14,733
273d.7	13	4,920	13	23,112
273d.8	4	654	4	889
273d.9	7	1,769	7	5,418
273d.10	11	3,882	11	5,592

Table 3. Results for sequences of length 27

Seq #	Proposed EGA	Patton et al. (1995)
	Fitness	Fitness
643d.1	28	27
643d.2	32	30
643d.3	40	38
643d.4	35	34
643d.5	36	36
643d.6	31	31
643d.7	25	25
643d.8	35	34
643d.9	34	33
643d.10	27	26

Table 4. Results for sequences of length 64

5. Acknowledgement

This work was partially supported by the Lebanese American University and the National Council for Scientific Research.

6. References

Anfinsen, C.B. (1973). Principles that govern the folding of proteins, *Science*, 181-187.

Chen, M. and Huang, W. (2005). A Branch and Bound Algorithm for the Protein Folding Problem in the HP Lattice Model. *Genomics, Proteomics & Bioinformatics*, Vol. 3, No. 4.

Datta, A., Talukdar, V. and Konar, A. (2008). Neuro-Swarm Hybridization for Protein Tertiary Structure Prediction. In proceedings of the 2nd National Conference on Recent Trends in Information Systems (ReTIS-08), Jadavpur University, Kolkata.

Dill, K. A. (1985). Theory for the folding and stability of globular proteins. *Biochemistry*, 24, 6, 1501-1509.

Dill, K.A., Fiebig, K.M. and Chan, H.S. (1993). Cooperativity in Protein-Folding Kinetics. *Proceedings of the National Academy of Sciences of the United States of America*, 90, 1942-1946.

Floudas, C.A. (2007). Computational methods in protein structure prediction. *Biotechnology and Bioengineering*, 97(2), 207-213.

Holland, J. (1975). *Adaptation in Natural and Artificial Systems*. University of Michigan Press. Michigan.

Hsu, H.P., Mehra, V., Nadler, W. and Grassberger, P. (2003). Growth Algorithm for Lattice Heteropolymers at Low Temperatures. *Journal of Chemical Physics*, 118, 444-51.

Johnson, C. and Katikireddy, A. (2006). A Genetic Algorithm with Backtracking for Protein Structure Prediction. *Proceedings of the 8th Annual Conference on Genetic and Evolutionary Computation, Washington, USA.*

Jones, D.T. (1998). THREADER: protein sequence threading by double dynamic programming. In *Computational Methods in Biology* (ed. Salzberg, S., Searl, D. and Kasif, S.). Amsterdam: Elsevier Science.

Klepeis, J.L. and Floudas, C.A. (2003). *Ab initio* tertiary structure prediction of proteins. *Journal of Global Optimization*, 25, 113–140.

Kopp, J. and Schwede, T. (2004). Automated protein structure homology modeling: a progress report. *Pharmacogenomics Journal*, 5, 4, 405-416.

Lathrop, R.H. et al. (1998). Computational Methods in Molecular Biology. *Elsevier Press*, 12, 227-283.

Li, W., Wang, T., Li, E., Baker, D., Jin, L., Ge, S., Chen, Y. and Zhang, Y. (2006). Parallelization and performance characterization of protein 3D structure prediction of Rosetta. *IEEE 20th Int. Parallel and Distributed Processing Symposium*, Rhodes Island, Greece.

Liang, F. and Wong, W.H. (2001). Evolutionary Monte Carlo for protein folding simulations. *Journal of Chemical Physics*, 115, 7, 3374-3380.

Notredame, C. (2002). Recent progress in multiple sequence alignment: a survey. *Pharmacogenomics Journal*, 3(1), 131-144.

Mansour, N., Kehyayan, C., and Khachfe, H. (2009). Scatter search algorithm for protein structure prediction. *International Journal of Bioinformatics Research and Applications*, Vol. 5, No. 5, 501-515.

Pandit, S.B., Zhang, Y., and Skolnick, J. (2006). Tasser-lite: an automated tool for protein comparative modeling. *Biophysics Journal*, 91, 11, 4180-4190.

Patton, A. L., Punch, W. F. and Goodman, E. D. (1995). A standard GA approach to native protein conformation prediction. *In Proceedings of the 6th International Conference on Genetic Algorithms.*

Prusiner, S.B. (1998). Prions. Proceedings of the National Academy of Sciences of the United States of America, 95, 13363-13383.

Rylance, G. (2004). Applications of Genetic Algorithms in Protein Folding Studies. First year report, School of Chemistry, University of Birmingham, England.

Schulze-Kremer, S. (2000). Genetic algorithms and protein folding. *Methods in Molecular Biology*, 143, 175-222.

Setubal, J. and Meidanis, J. (1997). *Introduction to computational molecular biology*. Boston: PWS Publishing Company.

Shmygelska, A. and Hoos, H. H. (2005). An Ant Colony Optimization Algorithm for the 2D and 3D Hydrophobic Polar Protein Folding Problem, *BMC Bioinformatics*, 6(30).

Sikder, A.R. and Zomaya, A.Y. (2005). An Overview of Protein-Folding Techniques: Issues and Perspectives. *International Journal of Bioinformatics Research and Applications*, 1, 1, 121-143.

Skolnick, J., Kihara, D. and Zhang, Y. (2004). Development and large scale benchmark testing of the PROSPECTOR 3 threading algorithm. *Proteins*, 56, 502-518.

Srinivasan, R. and Rose, G.D. (2002). Ab initio prediction of protein structure using LINUS. *PROTEINS: Structure, Function, and Genetics*, 47, 489-495.

Toma, L. and Toma, S. (1996). Contact interactions method: A new algorithm for protein folding simulations. *Protein Science*, 5, 147-153.

Unger, R. and Moult, J. (1993a). Finding the Lowest Free Energy Conformation of a Protein is an NP-Hard Problem: Proof and Implications. *Bulletin of Mathematical Biology*, 1183-1198.

Unger, R. and Moult, J. (1993b). Genetic algorithms for protein folding simulations. *Journal of Molecular Biology*, 231, 75-81.

Yue, K. and Dill, K.A. (1995). Forces of Tertiary Structural Organization in Globular Proteins. *Proceedings of the National Academy of Sciences of the United States of America*, 92, 146-150.

Zhang, X. and Li, T. (2007). Improved Particle Swarm Optimization Algorithm for 2D Protein Folding Prediction. *The 1st International Conference on Bioinformatics and Biomedical Engineering*, 53-56.

4

Quantum Search Algorithm

Che-Ming Li[1], Jin-Yuan Hsieh[2] and Der-San Chuu[3]
[1]*Department of Physics and National Center for Theoretical Sciences, National Cheng Kung University, Tainan 70101*
[2]*Department of Mechanical Engineering, Ming Hsin University of Science and Technology, Hsin-Fong 30401*
[3]*Department of Electrophysics, National Chiao Tung University, Hsinchu 30050 Taiwan*

1. Introduction

For a search problem associated with a unsorted database, the remarkable Grover's quantum algorithm (1) provides a quadratic speedup over its classical counterpart. The search problem can be described as follows: for a given function f, there exists one unknown element in the set $\{0, 1, ..., N-1\}$ that satisfies $f(x) = -1$, say $x = \tau$, whereas the other $N-1$ ones give $f(x) = 1$. How many times of evaluations of f are required to determine the element τ for $f(\tau) = -1$? Through a conventional algorithm, one needs $O(N)$ trials to achieve this aim. How about the utility of quantum algorithm for the search?

For the scenario in the quantum world, the search problem can be rephrased in the quantum mechanical language: for a given unitary operator I_τ, that is sometimes called the *oracle operator*, and a set of state vectors (orthonormal basis): $\mathbf{s} = \{|0\rangle, |1\rangle, ..., |N-1\rangle\}$, $I_\tau |x\rangle = |x\rangle$ for all states in the set except $I_\tau |x\rangle = -|x\rangle$ for $x = \tau$. How many queries of I_τ are required to determine $|\tau\rangle$? By Grover's algorithm, one needs only $O(\sqrt{N})$ quantum mechanical steps to find the marked state $|\tau\rangle$ out. It has been shown that Grover's algorithm is optimal since it needs minimal oracle calls to perform a quantum search (2).

The quantum searching process will be briefly reviewed as follows. The first step of Grover's algorithm is to prepare a superposition state of all elements with uniform probability amplitude:

$$|s\rangle = \frac{1}{\sqrt{N}} \sum_{x=0}^{N-1} |x\rangle . \tag{1}$$

Then apply the Grover kernel $G = -I_\eta I_\tau$ to $|s\rangle$, where I_η is a unitary operator and contains no bias against the marked state. For large N, after about $m = \pi\sqrt{N}/4$ repetitions of G operations, the probability to observe $|\tau\rangle$ is close to one, i.e.,

$$G^m |s\rangle \sim |\tau\rangle . \tag{2}$$

Since every single G involves one query of I_τ, only $O(\sqrt{N})$ searching steps are required for a quantum search task.

In what follows, we will first investigate on the general SU(2) formulation for the kernel of Grover's searching operator G. The discussions of quantum searching certainty, robustness, and the analog analogue version of the Grover's algorithm will be given afterwards.

2. Kernel of Grover's searching operator G

Suppose in a two-dimensional complex Hilbert space we have a marked state $|\tau\rangle$ to be searched by successively operating a Grover's kernel G on an arbitrary initial state $|s\rangle$. The Grover kernel is a product of two unitary operators I_τ and I_η, given by (3)

$$I_\tau = I + (e^{i\phi} - 1)\,|\tau\rangle\,\langle\tau|\,, \tag{3}$$

$$I_\eta = I + (e^{i\theta} - 1)U\,|\eta\rangle\,\langle\eta|\,U^{-1}, \tag{4}$$

where U is an arbitrary unitary operator, $|\eta\rangle \in \mathbf{s}$, and ϕ and θ are two phase angles. Note that in the original designation of Grover, the phase angles $\phi = \theta = \pi$ are chosen for phase flips of the state vectors. The Grover kernel can be expressed in a matrix form in the following set of basis vectors:

$$|I\rangle = |\tau\rangle\,, \quad |II\rangle = (U\,|\eta\rangle - U_{\tau\eta}\,|\tau\rangle)/l, \tag{5}$$

where $U_{\tau\eta} = \langle\tau|\,U\,|\eta\rangle$ and $l = (1 - |U_{\tau\eta}|^2)^{1/2}$. Let us suppose that $U_{\tau\eta} = \sin(\beta)e^{i\alpha}$, we then have

$$U\,|\eta\rangle = \sin(\beta)e^{i\alpha}\,|I\rangle + \cos(\beta)\,|II\rangle\,, \tag{6}$$

and the Grover kernel can now be written as

$$\begin{aligned} G =& -I_\eta I_\tau \\ =& -\begin{bmatrix} e^{i\phi}(1+(e^{i\theta}-1)\sin^2(\beta)) & (e^{i\theta}-1)\sin(\beta)\cos(\beta)e^{i\alpha} \\ e^{i\phi}(e^{i\theta}-1)\sin(\beta)\cos(\beta)e^{-i\alpha} & 1+(e^{i\theta}-1)\cos^2(\beta) \end{bmatrix}. \end{aligned} \tag{7}$$

3. Quantum searching with certainty

In the searching process, the Grover kernel is successively operated on the initial state $|s\rangle$. We suppose that after m iterations the final state $G^m\,|s\rangle$ will be orthogonal to the basis vector $|II\rangle$, which means that the probability for finding the marked state $|\tau\rangle$ will exactly be unity, i.e.,

$$\langle II|\,G^m\,|s\rangle = 0, \tag{8}$$

which implies that

$$|\langle\tau|\,G^m\,|s\rangle| = |\langle I|\,G^m\,|s\rangle| = 1. \tag{9}$$

For the matrix of Eq. (7), the eigenvalues of the Grover kernel G are

$$\lambda_{1,2} = -e^{i(\frac{\phi+\theta}{2} \pm w)}, \tag{10}$$

where the angle w is defined by

$$\cos(w) = \cos(\frac{\phi-\theta}{2}) - 2\sin(\frac{\phi}{2})\sin(\frac{\theta}{2})\sin^2(\beta). \tag{11}$$

Furthermore, the normalized eigenvectors associated with these eigenvalues can be derived:

$$|g_1\rangle = \begin{bmatrix} e^{-i\frac{\phi}{2}}e^{i\alpha}\cos(x) \\ \sin(x) \end{bmatrix}, \quad |g_2\rangle = \begin{bmatrix} -\sin(x) \\ e^{i\frac{\phi}{2}}e^{-i\alpha}\cos(x) \end{bmatrix}. \tag{12}$$

Here the angle x is defined by

$$\sin(x) = \sin(\frac{\theta}{2})\sin(2\beta)/\sqrt{l_m}, \tag{13}$$

where

$$l_m = 2\sin(w)(\sin(w) + \sin(\frac{\phi-\theta}{2}) + 2\cos(\frac{\phi}{2})\sin(\frac{\theta}{2})\sin^2(\beta)). \quad (14)$$

Then the matrix G^m can be expressed in the eigenbasis of G by $G^m = \lambda_1^m |g_1\rangle\langle g_1| + \lambda_2^m |g_2\rangle\langle g_2|$, and we have

$$G^m = (-1)^m e^{im(\frac{\phi+\theta}{2})} \begin{bmatrix} e^{imw}\cos^2(x) + e^{-imw}\sin^2(x) & e^{-i\frac{\phi}{2}}e^{i\alpha}i\sin(mw)\sin(2x) \\ e^{i\frac{\phi}{2}}e^{-i\alpha}i\sin(mw)\sin(2x) & e^{imw}\sin^2(x) + e^{-imw}\cos^2(x) \end{bmatrix}. \quad (15)$$

We proceed to consider the initial state $|s\rangle$. Here we assume that the initial state $|s\rangle$ is more general than the uniform superposition state (1):

$$|s\rangle = \sin(\beta_0)|I\rangle + \cos(\beta_0)e^{iu}|II\rangle. \quad (16)$$

Hence from the condition of searching with certainty, $\langle II|G^m|s\rangle = 0$, we have:

$$-\sin(mw)\sin(\frac{\phi}{2} - \alpha - u)\sin(2x)\sin(\beta_0) + \cos(mw)\cos(\beta_0) = 0, \quad (17)$$

$$\sin(mw)\cos(\frac{\phi}{2} - \alpha - u)\sin(2x)\sin(\beta_0) - \sin(mw)\cos(2x)\cos(\beta_0) = 0. \quad (18)$$

After substituting the angle x into Eq. (18), the equation can be reduced to the following condition:

$$(\sin(\frac{\phi-\theta}{2}) + 2\cos(\frac{\phi}{2})\sin(\frac{\theta}{2})\sin^2(\beta))\cos(\beta_0) = \sin(\frac{\theta}{2})\sin(2\beta)\cos(\frac{\phi}{2} - \alpha - u)\sin(\beta_0), \quad (19)$$

which is identical to the relation derived by Long et al. (4):

$$\tan(\frac{\phi}{2}) = \tan(\frac{\theta}{2})(\frac{\cos(2\beta) + \sin(2\beta)\tan(\beta_0)\cos(\alpha+u)}{1 - \tan(\beta_0)\tan(\frac{\theta}{2})\sin(2\beta)\sin(\alpha+u)}). \quad (20)$$

For Eq. (17), under the satisfaction of the matching condition (19), or (20), we can have a formula for evaluating the number of iterations m:

$$\cos(mw + \sin^{-1}(\sin(\beta_0)\sin(\frac{\phi}{2} - \alpha - u))) = 0. \quad (21)$$

Then one can compute the number m:

$$m = \lceil f \rceil, \quad (22)$$

where $\lceil\rceil$ denotes the smallest integer greater than the quantity in it, and the function f is given by

$$f = \frac{\frac{\pi}{2} - \sin^{-1}(\sin(\beta_0)\sin(\frac{\phi}{2} - \alpha - u))}{\cos^{-1}(\cos(\frac{\phi-\theta}{2}) - 2\sin(\frac{\phi}{2})\sin(\frac{\theta}{2})\sin^2(\beta))}. \quad (23)$$

It can be shown also that if the matching condition is fulfilled, then after m searching iterations the final state will be

$$G^m|s\rangle = e^{i\delta}|\tau\rangle = e^{i\left[m(\pi + \frac{\phi+\theta}{2}) + \Omega\right]}|\tau\rangle, \quad (24)$$

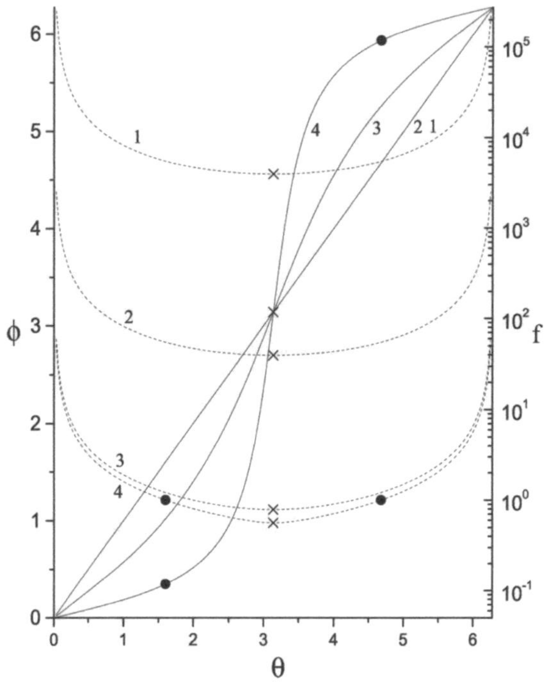

Fig. 1. Variations of $\phi(\theta)$ (solid) and $f(\theta)$ (broken), for $\alpha + u = 0$, $\beta_0 = 10^{-4}$, and $\beta = 10^{-4}$ (1), 10^{-2} (2), 0.5 (3) and 0.7 (4), respectively. The cross marks denote the special case of Høyer (6), while the black cirles correspond to the optimal choices of ϕ_{op} and θ_{op} for $\alpha + u = 0$, $\beta_0 = 10^{-4}$ and $\beta = 0.7$. The solid straight line 1 corresponds the case $\phi = \theta$, while the solid curve 2 is only approximately close to the former.

where the angle Ω is defined by

$$\Omega = \tan^{-1}(\cot(\frac{\phi}{2} - \alpha - u)). \tag{25}$$

The matching condition (19), or (20), relates the angles ϕ, θ, β, β_0 , and $\alpha + u$ for finding a marked state with certainty. If β, β_0 and $\alpha + u$ are designated, then $\phi = \phi(\theta)$ is deduced by the matching condition. As $\phi(\theta)$ is determined, we then can evaluate the value of $f = f(\phi(\theta), \theta)$ by (23) and consequently decide the number of iterations m by (22). It is worth to note that as $\alpha + u = 0$ and $\beta = \beta_0$, the matching condition recovers $\phi = \theta$ automatically since then Eq. (20) becomes an identity, and accordingly one has

$$f = \frac{\frac{\pi}{2} - \sin^{-1}(\sin(\frac{\phi}{2})\sin(\beta))}{2\sin^{-1}(\sin(\frac{\phi}{2})\sin(\beta))}, \text{ for } \phi = \theta, \tag{26}$$

which is the case discussed in Ref. (5). We also note that the matching condition (19) will recover the relation by Høyer (6):

$$\tan(\frac{\phi}{2}) = \tan(\frac{\theta}{2})\cos(2\beta), \text{ for } \cos(\phi/2 - \alpha - u) = 0. \tag{27}$$

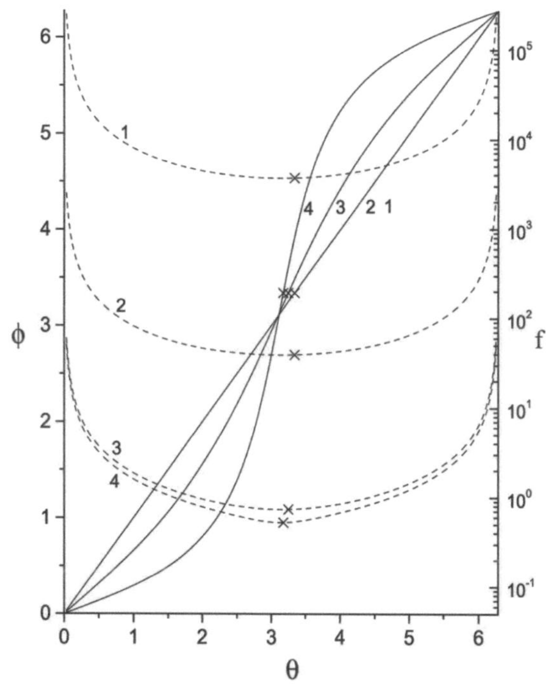

Fig. 2. Variations of $\phi(\theta)$ (solid) and $f(\theta)$ (broken), for $\alpha + u = 0.1$, $\beta_0 = 0.1$, and $\beta = 10^{-4}$ (1), 10^{-2} (2), 0.5 (3) and 0.7 (4), respectively. The cross marks denote the special case of Høye (6). The solid curves 1 and 2 are almost identical, and both of them are only approximately close to the line $\phi = \theta$.

In Figs. 1 and 2 we have shown by the cross marks some particular examples of this special case.

Observing Figs. 1 and 2, one realizes that for every designation of β, β_0 and $\alpha + u$, the optimal choices for ϕ and θ is $\phi = \theta = \pi$, since then the corresponding f is minimum under the fact $df/d\theta = (\partial f/\partial\phi)(d\phi/d\theta) + \partial f/\partial\theta = 0$, for $\phi = \theta = \pi$. We thus denote the optimal value of m by

$$m_{op} = \lceil \min(f) \rceil = \left\lceil \frac{\frac{\pi}{2} - \sin^{-1}(\sin(\beta_0)\cos(\alpha + u))}{2\beta} \right\rceil. \tag{28}$$

With the choice of m_{op}, however, one needs to modify the phases θ and $\phi(\theta)$ to depart from π so that the matching condition is satisfied again. For example, if $\alpha + u = 0$, $\beta_0 = 10^{-4}$ and $\beta = 0.7$ are designated, then the minimum value of f will be $\min(f) = 0.56$. So we choose $m_{op} = 1$ and the modified phases are $\theta_{op} = (1 \pm 0.490)\pi$ and $\phi_{op} = (1 \pm 0.889)\pi$, respectively. This example has been shown by the marked black circles in Fig. 1. It is worth to note again that under the choice of m_{op} the modified ϕ and θ for the special case considered by Long (5) will be

$$\phi_{op} = \theta_{op} = \lceil \min(f) \rceil = 2\sin^{-1}\left(\frac{\sin(\frac{\pi}{4m_{op}+2})}{\sin(\beta)}\right), \tag{29}$$

where

$$m_{op} = \left\lceil \frac{\frac{\pi}{2} - \beta}{2\beta} \right\rceil, \tag{30}$$

This is in fact a special case in which the phases ϕ_{op} and θ_{op} can be given by a closed-form formula.

4. Phase error tolerance in a quantum search algorithm

In Section 3 we have given a general review of quantum search algorithm with SU(2) formulation. To give a detailed discussion about phase error tolerance in a quantum search algorithm, in what follows we will focus on the original version of Grover's algorithm, which means that the unitary operator U shown in Eq. (4) corresponds to a specific transformation. Grover's quantum search algorithm (1) is achieved by applying Grover kernel G on an uniform superposition state (1), which is obtained by applying Walsh-Hadamard transformation on a initial state, in a specific operating step such that the probability amplitude of marked state is amplified to a desired one. Specifically, Grover's kernel is composed of phase rotations and Walsh-Hadamard transformations. The phase rotations include two kinds of operations: π-inversion of the marked state and π-inversion of the initial state. As shown in Section 3, the phases, π, can be replaced by two angles, ϕ and θ, under the phase matching criterion, which is the necessary condition for quantum searching with certainty. In other words, the relation between ϕ and θ will affect the degree of success of quantum search algorithm.

There have been several studies concern with the effect of imperfect phase rotations. Long *et al.* (7) have found that, a given expected degree of success $P_{\max}$, the tolerated angle difference between two phase rotations, δ, due to systematic errors in phase inversions is about $2/\sqrt{NP_{\max}}$, where N is the size of the database. Høyer (6) has shown that after some number of iterations of Grover kernel, depending on N and unperturbed θ, it will give a solution with error probability $O(1/N)$ under a tolerated phase difference $\delta \sim O(1/\sqrt{N})$. The same result is also redrived by Biham *et al.* (8). A roughly close conclusion, $\delta O(1/N^{2/3})$, is presented by Pablo-Norman and Ruiz-Altaba (9).

The result of Long *et al.* (7) is based on the approximate Grover kernel and the assumptions of large N and small δ. However, one can find that the main inaccurancy comes from the approximate Grover kernel. Since all parameters in Grover kernel connect with each other exquisitely, any reduction to the structure of Grover's kernel would destroy this penetrative relation, so accumulative errors emerge from the iterations to a quantum search. In what follows, we will use the tool derived from SU(2) formulation discussed in Section 3 to get an improved criterion for tolerated error in phase rotation and the required number of qubits for preparing a database (10). In addition, a concise formula for evaluating minimum number of iterations to achieve a maximum probability will also be acquired.

Let us follow the derivation detailed in Section 3 for the analysis of error tolerance. If the operator U is Walsh-Hadamard transformation W, the orthonormal set becomes

$$|I\rangle = |\tau\rangle \text{ and } |\tau_\perp\rangle = (W|\eta\rangle - W_{\tau\eta}|\tau\rangle)/l\,, \tag{31}$$

where $W_{\tau\eta} = \langle\tau| W |\eta\rangle$ and $l = (1 - |W_{\tau\eta}|^2)^{1/2}$. Since $W_{\tau\eta} = \sin(\beta)$ we have

$$|s\rangle = W|\eta\rangle = \sin(\beta)|\tau\rangle + \cos(\beta)|\tau_\perp\rangle\,, \tag{32}$$

and the Grover kernel can now be written as

$$\begin{aligned} G &= -I_\eta I_\tau \\ &= -\begin{bmatrix} e^{i\phi}(1+(e^{i\theta}-1)\sin^2(\beta)) & (e^{i\theta}-1)\sin(\beta)\cos(\beta) \\ e^{i\phi}(e^{i\theta}-1)\sin(\beta)\cos(\beta) & 1+(e^{i\theta}-1)\cos^2(\beta) \end{bmatrix}. \end{aligned} \tag{33}$$

After m number of iterations, the operator G^m can be expressed as

$$G^m = (-1)^m e^{im(\frac{\phi+\theta}{2})} \begin{bmatrix} e^{imw}\cos^2(x) + e^{-imw}\sin^2(x) & e^{-i\frac{\phi}{2}} i\sin(mw)\sin(2x) \\ e^{i\frac{\phi}{2}} i\sin(mw)\sin(2x) & e^{imw}\sin^2(x) + e^{-imw}\cos^2(x) \end{bmatrix}. \quad (34)$$

Then the probability of finding a marked state is

$$\begin{aligned} P &= 1 - |\langle\tau| G^m |s\rangle|^2 \\ &= 1 - (\cos(mw)\cos(\beta) - \sin(mw)\sin(\frac{\phi}{2})\sin(2x)\sin(\beta))^2 \\ &\quad - \sin^2(mw)(\cos(\frac{\phi}{2})\sin(2x)\sin(\beta) - \cos(2x)\cos(\beta))^2. \end{aligned} \quad (35)$$

By the equation $\partial P/\partial(\cos(mw)) = 0$, the minimum number of iterations for obtaining the maximum probability, $P_{\max}(\cos(m_{\min}w))$, is evaluated:

$$m_{\min}(\beta,\phi,\theta) = \frac{\cos^{-1}(\sqrt{\frac{b-2a}{2b}})}{w}, \quad (36)$$

where

$$\begin{aligned} a &= \sin(2x)\cos(2\beta) + \cos(2x)\cos(\frac{\phi}{2})\sin(2\beta), \\ b &= (2+\sin^2(2x) + (3\sin^2(2x)-2)\cos(4\beta) - 2\sin^2(2x)\cos(\phi)\sin^2(2\beta)) \\ &\quad +2\sin(4x)\cos(\frac{\phi}{2})\sin(4\beta). \end{aligned}$$

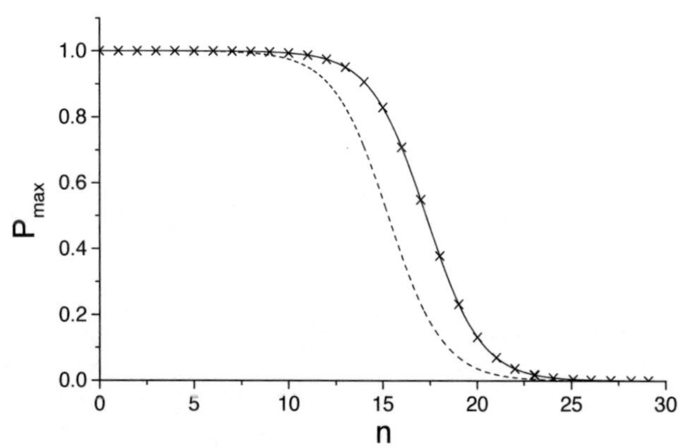

Fig. 3. Variations of exact vaule of $P_{\max}$ (n)(cross marks), $16\beta^2\sin^2(\frac{\theta}{2})/(\delta^2+16\beta^2\sin^2(\frac{\theta}{2}))$ (solid), and $4\beta^2/(\delta^2+4\beta^2)$ (dash) for $\theta=\pi$, $\delta=0.01$ where $\beta=\sin^{-1}(2^{-n/2})$.

For a sure-success search problem, the phase condition, $\phi = \theta$, with $m_{\min} = (\pi/2 - \sin^{-1}(\sin(\phi/2)\sin(\beta))/w$, is required. However, when effects of imperfect phase inversions are considered, the search is not certain, then the new condition to phase error, $\delta = \phi - \theta$, and the size of database should be derived in order to accomplish the search with a reduced maximum probability. Now, we suppose the database is large, i.e., if $\sin(\beta) \ll 1$, and a phase error δ is small, where $|\delta| \ll 1$, one has the following approximation:

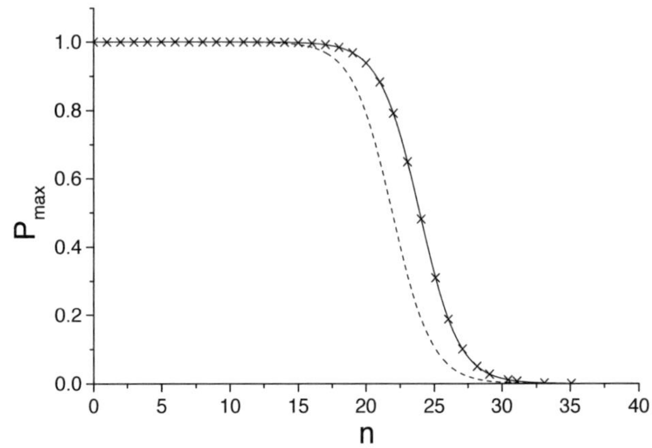

Fig. 4. Variations of exact value of $P_{\max}$ (n)(cross marks), $16\beta^2 \sin^2(\frac{\theta}{2})/(\delta^2 + 16\beta^2 \sin^2(\frac{\theta}{2}))$ (solid), and $4\beta^2/(\delta^2 + 4\beta^2)$ (dash) for $\theta = \pi$, $\delta = 0.001$ where $\beta = \sin^{-1}(2^{-n/2})$.

$$
\begin{aligned}
\cos(w) &= \cos(\frac{\delta}{2}) - 2\sin(\frac{\theta}{2} + \frac{\delta}{2})\sin(\frac{\theta}{2})\sin^2(\beta) \\
&\approx 1 - (\frac{\delta^2}{8} + 2\beta^2 \sin^2(\frac{\theta}{2})), \\
\sin(w) &= (1 - \cos^2(w))^{1/2} \\
&\approx \frac{(\delta^2 + 16\beta^2 \sin^2(\frac{\theta}{2}))^{1/2}}{2}, \\
\sin(2x) &= \frac{4\beta \sin(\frac{\theta}{2})}{(\delta^2 + 16\beta^2 \sin^2(\frac{\theta}{2}))^{1/2}}.
\end{aligned}
$$

The probability P (Eq.35) then can be expressed approximately as

$$
\begin{aligned}
P &\approx 1 - \cos^2(mw)\cos^2(\beta) - \sin^2(mw)\cos^2(2x) \\
&= \sin^2(mw)\sin^2(2x),
\end{aligned} \tag{37}
$$

with a maximum value, by setting $\sin^2(mw) = 1$,

$$
P_{\max} \approx \sin^2(2x) = \frac{16\beta^2 \sin^2(\frac{\theta}{2})}{\delta^2 + 16\beta^2 \sin^2(\frac{\theta}{2})}. \tag{38}
$$

From Fig. 3 and Fig. 4, one can realize the function (38) depicted by solid line coincides with the exact value which is obtained by Eq. (35) and Eq. (36) as shown by cross marks. On the contrary, the result of Long *et al.*,

$$
P_{\max} \approx \frac{4\beta^2 \sin^2(\frac{\theta}{2})}{\delta^2 + 4\beta^2 \sin^2(\frac{\theta}{2})}, \tag{39}
$$

is an underestimation depicted by dash lines.

5. Family of sure-success quantum search algorithms

Even in the case of large N, where high success rate in finding the marked state is expected by using the standard Grover's algorithm, inevitable noises including decoherence and gate inaccuracies can significantly affect the efficiency of the algorithm. To overcome such drawback , one might either apply the fault-tolerant computation (11) to reduce gate imperfections and decoherence, or limit the size of the quantum database to depress the effect of the uncertainty of the phase inversion operations. In another way, one can also, if possible, consider implementing a modified algorithm which is itself robust against phase imperfections and or decoherence. Recently, Hu (12) introduced an interesting family of algorithms for the quantum search. Although these algorithms are more complicated than the standard Grover's algorithm, they can be proved to be robust against imperfect phase inversions, so the limitation of the size of database can be greatly relieved. In what follows the algorithms introduced by Hu (12) will be analyzed intently in detail, and the robustness of the family in resisting the effect of imperfect phase inversions will be shown later on.

Let us denote the phase inversion of marked state $I_\tau = 1 + (e^{i\phi} - 1)\,|\tau\rangle\,\langle\tau|$ as usual and the phase inversion of the initial state $I_s = 1 + (e^{i\theta} - 1)\,|s\rangle\,\langle s|$. Instead of applying G^n on the initial state $|s\rangle$, Hu (12) presented and utilized the operators $A_{2n} = (I_s^\dagger I_\tau^\dagger I_s I_\tau)^n$ and $A_{2n+1} = GA_{2n}$ to accomplish a quantum search with certainty, and named the former the even member and the latter the odd member of the family $\{A_n, n = 1, 2, ...\}$ because they require even ($2n$) and odd ($2n+1$) oracle calls in computation, respectively. The arrangement $I_s^\dagger I_\tau^\dagger I_s I_\tau$ is shown to have cancellation effect on phase errors in each iteration of the algorithm A_{2n} and A_{2n+1} and as a whole can ensure the robustness against imperfect phase inversion.

Consider a two-dimensional Hilbert space spanned by the marked state $|\tau\rangle$ and the state $|\tau_\perp\rangle$, which is orthogonal to $|\tau\rangle$. The initial state, as a uniform superposition of all states, then can be expressed by $|s\rangle = W\,|0\rangle = \sin(\beta)\,|\tau\rangle + \cos(\beta)\,|\tau_\perp\rangle$, where $\sin(\beta) \equiv \sqrt{M/N}$ and M is the number of the target states. The eigenvalues of the operator $I_s^\dagger I_\tau^\dagger I_s I_\tau$ are $\lambda_{1,2} = \cos(\omega) \pm i\sin(\omega)$ and the corresponding eigenvectors are computed (13; 14) as

$$
\begin{aligned}
|\lambda_1\rangle &= \cos(x)\,|\tau\rangle + i\sin(x)e^{i(\frac{\phi}{2}-\gamma)}\,|\tau_\perp\rangle\,, \\
|\lambda_2\rangle &= i\sin(x)e^{-i(\frac{\phi}{2}-\gamma)}\,|\tau\rangle + \cos(x)\,|\tau_\perp\rangle\,,
\end{aligned} \tag{40}
$$

where the rotation x and the related parameters are defined by

$$
\tan(x) = \frac{2r\sin(\frac{\phi}{2})\sin(\frac{\theta}{2})\sin(2\beta)}{\sin(\omega) + \sin^2(\frac{\theta}{2})\sin(\phi)\sin^2(2\beta)}, \tag{41}
$$

$$
\cos(\omega) = 1 - 2\sin^2(\frac{\theta}{2})\sin^2(\frac{\phi}{2})\sin^2(2\beta), \tag{42}
$$

$$
re^{i\gamma} = \cos(\frac{\theta}{2}) + i\sin(\frac{\theta}{2})\cos(2\beta). \tag{43}
$$

Then in n iterations of the operator of $I_s^\dagger I_\tau^\dagger I_s I_\tau$ we will have $A_{2n} = (I_s^\dagger I_\tau^\dagger I_s I_\tau)^n = \lambda_1^n\,|\lambda_1\rangle\,\langle\lambda_1| + \lambda_2^n\,|\lambda_2\rangle\,\langle\lambda_2|$, which can be expressed in the following matrix form:

$$
A_{2n} = \begin{bmatrix} \cos(nw) + i\sin(nw)\cos(2x) & \sin(2x)\sin(nw)e^{-i(\frac{\phi}{2}-\gamma)} \\ -\sin(2x)\sin(nw)e^{i(\frac{\phi}{2}-\gamma)} & \cos(nw) - i\sin(nw)\cos(2x) \end{bmatrix}, \tag{44}
$$

where $\sin(2x)$ and $\cos(2x)$ are given by

$$\sin(2x) = (\frac{1-\sin^2(\frac{\theta}{2})\sin^2(2\beta)}{1-\sin^2(\frac{\theta}{2})\sin^2(\frac{\phi}{2})\sin^2(2\beta)})^{1/2}, \tag{45}$$

$$\cos(2x) = \frac{\sin(\frac{\theta}{2})\cos(\frac{\phi}{2})\sin(2\beta)}{(1-\sin^2(\frac{\theta}{2})\sin^2(\frac{\phi}{2})\sin^2(2\beta))^{1/2}}. \tag{46}$$

When the quantum search is carried out by using the even member A_{2n}, the component of the final state after n iterations of $(I_s^\dagger I_\tau^\dagger I_s I_\tau)$ in the basis state $|\tau_\perp\rangle$ is expressed by $\langle\tau_\perp| A_{2n} |s\rangle = RE_e + iIM_e$, and accordingly the exact success rate in finding the marked state $|\tau\rangle$ then is given by

$$p = 1 - |\langle\tau_\perp| A_{2n} |s\rangle|^2 = 1 - (RE_e^2 + IM_e^2), \tag{47}$$

where

$$RE_e = \cos(n\omega)\cos(\beta) - \sin(n\omega)\sin(2x)\cos(\frac{\phi}{2} - \gamma)\sin(\beta), \tag{48}$$

$$IM_e = -\frac{\sin(n\omega)\sin(\beta)}{(1-\sin^2(\frac{\theta}{2})\sin^2(\frac{\phi}{2}\sin^2(2\beta)))^{1/2}}\sin(\frac{\theta+\phi}{2}). \tag{49}$$

It is clear that when $IM_e = 0$, one obtains the n-independent phase matching condition, $\phi = -\theta$, for A_{2n}, and the success rate then becomes

$$p = 1 - RE_e^2 = 1 - \cos^2(n\omega - \alpha), \tag{50}$$

where $\alpha = \sin^{-1}(\sin(\beta)\cos(\phi/2+\gamma))$. The 100% success rate for the search problem can be achieved as by setting $\cos(n\omega - \alpha) = 0$. For a search with certainty, since n is a positive integer, one therefore has to expect the iteration number given by

$$n_e(\theta,\beta) = \lceil f_e(\theta,\beta) \rceil, \tag{51}$$

and the function $f_e(\theta,\beta)$ is given by

$$f_e(\theta,\beta) = \frac{\frac{\pi}{2} + \alpha(\theta,\beta)}{\omega(\theta,\beta)}. \tag{52}$$

Given β, the function f_e has its minimal value as $\theta = \pi$ (and $\phi = -\pi$ thereby), as if minimal oracle calls are demanded in the computation, we should have the optimal phase θ_{op} associated with

$$f_e(\theta_{op},\beta) = \lceil f_e(\pi,\beta) \rceil. \tag{53}$$

For example, if given $\beta = 1$, we have $\lceil f_e(\pi,1) \rceil = 1$, and the optimal phase angle $\theta_{op} = \pi \pm 1.304$ follows in the algorithm using the even member A_{2n}. In usual operation, however, the quantum database is large, i.e., $\sin(\beta) \ll 1$, and the phase $\theta = \pi$ and $\phi = -\pi$ are fixed, then the required iterations are estimated by $n \sim \pi/8\beta$ and the maximal success rate will be approximately evaluated

$$p_{\max} \sim 1 - \beta^2, \text{ for } \theta = \pi,$$

which is the same result obtained as if the standard Grover algorithm is implemented. That is, as the phase $\theta = \pi$ is fixed, the present algorithm (A_{2n}) is equivalent to the standard algorithm (G^m) with even oracle calls required in the computation. Nevertheless, since in a real operation, imperfections in the phase inversions are inevitable. In what follows,one can

show that the present algorithm is robust against small phase imperfections in a quantum computation and provides a maximal success rate that is similar to the one given above.
In the absence of decoherence and error correction, constant phase errors are considered to cause the phase ϕ and θ to be $\phi = \pi + \phi_e$ and $\theta = \pi + \theta_e$, where $|\phi_e| \ll 1$ and $|\theta_e| \ll 1$. By introducing the constant phase imperfections, one then has the following approximations, when $\beta \ll 1$,

$$\sin(2x) \sim 1 - \frac{1}{2}\beta^2\phi_e^2, \cos(2x) \sim \beta\phi_e,$$
$$\cos(\frac{\phi}{2} - \gamma) \sim -1 + \frac{1}{8}(\theta_e - \phi_e)^2, \sin(\frac{\phi}{2} - \gamma) \sim \frac{1}{2}(\theta_e - \phi_e),$$
$$\omega \sim 4\beta(1 - \frac{1}{8}(\theta_e^2 + \phi_e^2) + \frac{4}{3}\beta^2).$$

Then, since the errors are unknown in advance of the computation, the iteration number is also considered to be $n \sim \pi/8\beta$, and one thus has $\cos(n\omega) \sim \pi(\theta_e^2 + \phi_e^2)/16 - 2\pi\beta^2/3$ and $\sin(n\omega) \sim 1$. The approximation of RE_e and IM_e accordingly are evaluated by

$$RE_e \sim \beta + \frac{\pi}{16}(\theta_e^2 + \phi_e^2) - \frac{2}{3}\pi\beta^2, \qquad (54)$$
$$IM_e \sim -\frac{1}{2}\beta(\theta_e + \phi_e).$$

The maximal success rate now is approximately derived by

$$p_{\max} \sim 1 - \beta^2 - (\text{H.O.T.}), \qquad (55)$$

where H.O.T. represents high order terms higher than second-degree in the small parameters β, θ_e and ϕ_e. Expression (55) clearly shows that the reduction of the probability due to the introduction of the phase errors in fact can almost be neglected. Then, through it, we can see that the present algorithm is robust against systematic phase imperfections.
We proceed to analyze the algorithm using the odd member A_{2n+1} by the same procedure as in analyzing the even member. In this case, one obtains

$$p_{\max} = 1 - (RE_o^2 + IM_o^2), \qquad (56)$$

where

$$RE_o = \cos(nw)[\cos(\frac{\theta - \phi}{2}) - 4\sin(\frac{\theta}{2})\sin(\frac{\phi}{2})\sin^2(\beta)]\cos(\beta)$$
$$+ \sin(nw)\{\cos(2x)[\sin(\frac{\theta - \phi}{2}) - 4\sin(\frac{\theta}{2})\sin(\frac{\phi}{2})\sin^2(\beta)]\cos\beta$$
$$- \sin(2x)[\cos(\gamma + \frac{\theta}{2}) + 4\sin(\gamma)\sin(\frac{\theta}{2})\cos^2(\beta)]\sin\beta\},$$
$$IM_o = \cos(\beta)\sin(\frac{\theta - \phi}{2})(\cos(nw) - \sin(nw)\frac{\cos(2x)\sin(\frac{\phi}{2})}{\cos(\frac{\phi}{2})}). \qquad (57)$$

For $IM_o = 0$, one has the phase matching condition, $\phi = \theta$, for A_{2n+1}. The 100% success rate then can be ensured when the iteration steps at $n_o(\theta, \beta) = \lceil f_o(\theta, \beta) \rceil$, where

$$f_o(\theta, \beta) = \frac{\frac{\pi}{2} - \cos^{-1}(\frac{\cos(\beta)(1 - 4\sin^2(\frac{\theta}{2})\sin^2(\beta))\sqrt{1 - \sin^4(\frac{\theta}{2})\sin^2(2\beta)}}{\sqrt{1 - \sin^2(\frac{\theta}{2})\sin^2(2\beta)}})}{\omega(\theta, \beta)}. \qquad (58)$$

Note that in this case the inequality $1 - 4\sin(\theta/2)^2 \geq 0$ should be demanded since then the meaningful requirement $f_o \geq 0$ can then be fulfilled. Given β, the function $f_o(\theta, \beta)$ also has its minimal value at $\theta = \pi$ (then $\phi = \pi$), as the optimal choice of the phase θ_{op} should be estimated by

$$f_o(\theta_{op}, \beta) = \lceil f_o(\theta, \beta) \rceil, \tag{59}$$

when minimal oracle calls are demanded in a search with certainty. For $\beta = 1$, the choice of the phase should be $\theta_{op} = \phi_{op} = \pi \pm 1.870$, for example. The standard Grover algorithm with odd oracle calls can be recovered when $\theta = \phi = \pi$ is fixed. In usual operations, when phase imperfections are introduced, i.e., as $\theta = \pi + \theta_o$ and $\phi = \pi + \phi_o$, where both θ_o and ϕ_o are small errors in the phases, they also produce almost negligible reductions in the success rate as given by an expression like Eq. (55).

6. Analog quantum search

Several researchers have proposed other ways to solve the quantum search problem, such as the *analog analogue* version of the Grover's algorithm (15–17) and the adiabatic evolution to quantum search (18–20). The former is to be considered here. It is proposed that the quantum search computation can be accomplished by controlled Hamiltonian time evolution of a system, obeying the Schrödinger equation

$$i\frac{d\,|\Psi(t)\rangle}{dt} = H\,|\Psi(t)\rangle\,, \tag{60}$$

where the constant $\hbar = 1$ is imposed for convenience. Farhi and Gutmann (15) presented the time-independent Hamiltonian $H_{fg} = E_{fg}(|w\rangle\langle w| + |s\rangle\langle s|)$, where $|w\rangle$ is the marked state and $|s\rangle$ denotes the initial state. Later, Fenner (16) proposed another Hamiltonian $H_f = E_f i(|w\rangle\langle s| - |s\rangle\langle w|)$. Recently, Bae and Kwon (17) further derived a generalized quantum search Hamiltonian

$$H_g = E_{fg}(|w\rangle\langle w| + |s\rangle\langle s|) + E_f(e^{i\phi}\,|w\rangle\langle s| + e^{-i\phi}\,|s\rangle\langle w|), \tag{61}$$

where ϕ is an additional phase to the Fenner Hamiltonian. Unlike the Grover algorithm, which operates on a state in discrete time, a quantum search Hamiltonian leads to the evolution of a state in continuous time, so the 100% probability for finding the marked state can be guaranteed in the absence of all kinds of imperfection occurring in a quantum operation. Both the Hamiltonian H_{fg} and H_f can help to find the marked state with 100% success. However, Bae and Kwon (17) addressed that the generalized Hamiltonian H_g can accomplish the search with certainty only when $\phi = n\pi$ is imposed, where n is arbitrary integer. In what follows, one can show that the generalized Hamiltonian H_g can be derived by an analytical method, which is distinct to the one implemented by Bae and Kwon (17), and the same method will lead to arbitrary chosen phase ϕ, depending on when the measurement on the system is undertaken and how large the system energy gap is provided. Since Hamiltonian-controlled system is considered, the energy-time relation will play an essential role in the problem. Therefore, the evaluation of the measuring time for the quantum search becomes crucially important. Here, the general Hamiltonian for the time-controlled quantum search system will be reviewed first. The exact time for measuring the marked state will be deduced. Finally, the role played by the phase ϕ in the quantum search will be discussed, and both the measuring time and the system energy gap as variations with ϕ will be given.

Suppose that a two-dimensional, complex Hilbert space is spanned by the orthonormal set $|w\rangle$, which is the marked state, and $|w_\perp\rangle$, which denotes the unmarked one. An initial state $|s\rangle = |\Psi(0)\rangle$, which corresponds to the quantum database discussed in the previous sections, is designed to evolve under a time-independent quantum search Hamiltonian given by (21)

$$H = E_1 |E_1\rangle \langle E_1| + E_2 |E_2\rangle \langle E_2|, \tag{62}$$

where E_1 and E_2 are two eigenenergies of the quantum system, $E_1 > E_2$, and $|E_1\rangle$ and $|E_2\rangle$ are the corresponding eigenstates satisfying the completeness condition $|E_1\rangle \langle E_1| + |E_2\rangle \langle E_2| = \mathbf{1}$. The eigenstates can be assumed by

$$\begin{aligned} |E_1\rangle &= e^{i\alpha} \cos(x) |w\rangle + \sin(x) |w_\perp\rangle, \\ |E_2\rangle &= -\sin(x) |w\rangle + e^{-i\alpha} \cos(x) |w_\perp\rangle. \end{aligned} \tag{63}$$

where x and α are two parameters to be determined later based on the required maximal probability for measuring the marked state. Then the Hamiltonian can be written in the matrix form

$$H = \begin{bmatrix} E_p + E_o \cos(2x) & E_o \sin(2x) e^{i\alpha} \\ E_o \sin(2x) e^{-i\alpha} & E_p - E_o \cos(2x) \end{bmatrix}. \tag{64}$$

where $E_p = (E_1 + E_2)/2$ is the mean of eigenenergies and $E_o = (E_1 - E_2)/2$ represents half of the system energy gap. The major advantage of using the controlled Hamiltonian time evolution is that the marked state can always be searched with certainty in the absence of quantum imperfections. The crucial key of the present problem in turn is to decide when to measure the marked state by the probability of unity. So in what follows the relation between all the unknowns appearing in the system will be deduced in detail and the exact measuring time for finding the marked state with certainty will be evaluated later on.

The time evolution of the initial state is given by $|\Psi(t)\rangle = e^{-iHt} |s\rangle$. Therefore, the probability of finding the marked state will be $P = \left|\langle w| e^{-iHt} |s\rangle\right|^2 = 1 - \left|\langle w_\perp| e^{-iHt} |s\rangle\right|^2$. Without loss of generality, let us consider the problem of searching one target from N unsorted items. The general form of the initial state considered in this study is given by

$$|s\rangle = e^{iu} \sin(\beta) |w\rangle + \cos(\beta) |w_\perp\rangle, \tag{65}$$

where $\sin(\beta) \equiv 1/\sqrt{N}$ and u denotes the relative phase between the two components in the initial state. Note that the relative phase u may arise from a phase decoherence or an intended design during the preparation of the initial state. Now, because of $e^{-iHt} = e^{-iE_1 t} |E_1\rangle \langle E_1| + e^{-iE_2 t} |E_2\rangle \langle E_2|$, one can deduce

$$\begin{aligned} \langle w_\perp| e^{-iHt} |s\rangle = e^{-iE_p t}((&\cos(\beta)\cos(E_o t) - \sin(\alpha - u)\sin(2x)\sin(\beta)\sin(E_o t)) \\ &+ i(\cos(2x)\cos(\beta) - \cos(\alpha - u)\sin(2x)\sin(\beta))\sin(E_o t)). \end{aligned} \tag{66}$$

To accomplish the quantum search with maximal probability, the time-independent term $(\cos(2x)\cos(\beta) - \cos(\alpha - u)\sin(2x)\sin(\beta))$ must be vanished and thus the unknown x can be determined by

$$\cos(2x) = \frac{\sin(\beta)\cos(\alpha - u)}{\cos(\gamma)}, \text{ or } \sin(2x) = \frac{\cos(\beta)}{\cos(\gamma)}, \tag{67}$$

where γ is defined by $\sin(\gamma) = \sin(\beta)\sin(\alpha - u)$. The probability for finding the marked state then becomes

$$P = 1 - \left|\langle w_{\perp}| e^{-iHt} |s\rangle\right|^2$$
$$= 1 - \frac{\cos^2(\beta)}{\cos^2(\gamma)} \cos^2(E_0 t + \gamma). \tag{68}$$

If the size of database N is large, then $\gamma \ll 1$ and the marked state $|w\rangle$ will be measured at $t = \pi/(2E_o)$ by a probability $p = 1 - \tan^2\gamma \sim 1$, according to (68). Expression (68) also indicates that, by setting $\cos^2(E_0 t + \gamma) = 0$, one can measure the marked state with unit probability, no matter how large N is, at the time instants

$$t_j = \frac{(2j-1)\pi/2 - \sin^{-1}(\sin(\beta)\sin(\alpha - u))}{E_o}, j = 1, 2, ... \tag{69}$$

In what follows, let us only focus on the first instant $t_1 = (\pi/2 - \sin^{-1}(\sin(\beta)\sin(\alpha - u)))/E_o$. It is clear that a larger E_o, or equivalently a larger system energy gap, will lead to a shorter time for measuring the marked state with certainty. Meanwhile, as can be seen in (68), the probability for measuring the marked state varies with time as a periodic function whose frequency is the Bohr frequency E_o/π, so a larger E_o will also result in a more difficult control on the measuring time. In other words, the measuring time should be controlled more precisely for a higher Bohr frequency in the state evolution since then a small error in the measuring time will cost a serious drop of the probability. However, the energy gap E_o depends on the size of database N, as will be mentioned later.
With the relations $\sin(2x)$ and $\cos(2x)$, the present Hamiltonian now can be written by

$$H = \begin{bmatrix} E_p + E_o \frac{\sin(\beta)\cos(\alpha-u)}{\cos(\gamma)} & E_o \frac{\cos(\beta)}{\cos(\gamma)} e^{i\alpha} \\ E_o \frac{\cos(\beta)}{\cos(\gamma)} e^{-i\alpha} & E_p - E_o \frac{\sin(\beta)\cos(\alpha-u)}{\cos(\gamma)} \end{bmatrix}, \tag{70}$$

which is represented in terms of the energies E_p and E_o and the phase α. Alternatively, if we let

$$E_{fg} = \frac{(E_p - E_o \frac{\sin(\beta)\cos(\alpha-u)}{\cos(\gamma)})}{\cos^2(\beta)},$$
$$E_f e^{i(\phi-u)} = \frac{E_o}{\cos(\gamma)} e^{i(\alpha-u)} - E_{fg}\sin(\beta), \tag{71}$$

or inversely,

$$E_p = E_{fg} + E_f \cos(\phi - u)\sin(\beta),$$
$$E_o = ((E_f \cos(\phi - u) + E_{fg}\sin(\beta))^2 + E_f^2 \sin^2(\phi - u)\cos^2(\beta))^{\frac{1}{2}}, \tag{72}$$

then the Hamiltonian can also be expressed by

$$H = \begin{bmatrix} E_{fg}(1 + \sin^2(\beta)) + 2E_f\cos(\phi - u)\sin(\beta) & e^{iu}(E_f e^{i(\phi-u)} + E_{fg}\sin(\beta))\cos(\beta) \\ e^{-iu}(E_f e^{-i(\phi-u)} + E_{fg}\sin(\beta))\cos(\beta) & E_{fg}\cos^2(\beta) \end{bmatrix}, \tag{73}$$

which in turn is represented in terms of the energies E_{fg} and E_f and the phase ϕ. The Hamiltonian shown in (73) in fact can be expressed as $H_g = E_{fg}(|w\rangle\langle w| + |s\rangle\langle s|) + E_f(e^{i\phi}|w\rangle\langle s| + e^{-i\phi}|s\rangle\langle w|)$, which is exactly of the same form as the Bae and Kwon Hamiltonian H_g shown in (61). However, Bae and Kwon (17) only consider the case $u = 0$. In both the presentations (70) and (73) of the Hamiltonian H, the corresponding measuring time for finding the marked state $|w\rangle$ with certainty is at

$$t_1 = \frac{\frac{\pi}{2} - \sin^{-1}(\sin(\beta)\sin(\alpha - u))}{E_o} = \frac{\frac{\pi}{2} - \sin^{-1}\left(\frac{E_f \sin(\beta)\sin(\phi - u)}{((E_f\cos(\phi-u)+E_{fg}\sin(\beta))^2+E_f^2\sin^2(\phi-u))^{\frac{1}{2}}}\right)}{((E_f\cos(\phi - u) + E_{fg}\sin(\beta))^2 + E_f^2\sin^2(\phi - u)\cos^2(\beta))^{\frac{1}{2}}}. \tag{74}$$

Equation (74) indicates that when the phase difference $\alpha - u$, or $\phi - u$, is imposed and the energy gap E_o or the energies E_f and E_{fg} are provided, the measurement at the end of a search should be undertaken at the instant t_1. To discuss further, one first considers the case $u = 0$, i.e., the case where neither phase decoherence nor intended relative phase is introduced in the preparation of the initial state $|s\rangle$. If $\phi = n\pi$, or $\alpha = n\pi$, is imposed, then the present Hamiltonian reduces to that considered by Bae and Kwon (17) to serve for a search with certainty when the measurement is undertaken at $t_1 = \pi/(2E_o) = \pi/(2|(-1)^n E_f + E_{fg}\sin(\beta)|)$. If $E_f = 0$, or if $E_o = E_{fg}\sin(\beta)$ and $\alpha = 0$, is imposed, then the present Hamiltonian reduces to the Farhi and Gutmann Hamiltonian H_{fg}, which serves for a search with certainty at $t_1 = \pi/(2E_o) = \pi/(2E_{fg}\sin\beta)$. Further, when $E_{fg} = 0$ and $\phi = \pi/2$, or $E_p = 0$ and $\alpha = \pi/2$ is chosen, the present Hamiltonian will reduce to the Fenner Hamiltonian H_f associated with the measuring time $t_1 = (\pi - 2\beta)/(2E_o) = (\pi - 2\beta)/(2E_f\cos\beta)$. In general, the phase ϕ, or α, in fact can be imposed *arbitrary* for a search with certainty as the condition $u = 0$ is imposed.

However, if inevitable phase decoherence in the preparation of the initial state $|s\rangle$ is considered, then the phase u must be assumed to be arbitrary. Accordingly, the probability for finding the marked state will not be unity at all. For example, if following the treatment of Bae and Kwon (17) by setting $t_1 = \pi/(2E_o)$, then we only have a probability for finding the marked state given by

$$p = 1 - \frac{\cos^2(\beta)\sin^2(\beta)\sin^2(u)}{1 - \sin^2(\beta)\sin^2(u)}. \tag{75}$$

It is easy to show that the probability shown in (75) is always greater than or equal to the lower bound $p_{min} = 1 - \sin^2(\beta) = 1 - 1/N$. Of course, if the nonzero phase u is introduced by an intended design, not an inevitable phase decoherence, then a search with certainty can be accomplished for an arbitrary ϕ, or α, when associated with the measuring time shown in (74). For example, if $u = \pi/2$ is the phase designated, the ideal measuring time should be $t_1 = (\pi - 2\beta)/(2E_o)$, which is the same as the Fenner's t_1. Again if the phase decoherence is introduced into the system and changes the phase from $\pi/2$ to an undesired u, then one eventually obtains a poor probability $p = 1 - (1 + \sin^2(u) - 2\sin(u))\sin^2(\beta)$. Moreover if the phase error occurs randomly in a quantum database, then one is unable to be sure when to take a measurement, and the probability for finding the marked state even drops off seriously in some cases. For investigating the effect of the random uncontrollable parameter u on p at a fixed measuring time, one has to average over all possible values of $p(\beta, u)$ about all arbitrary values of phase parameter u. Fig. 5 shows the variation of the mean probability $\bar{p}$ with β for cases of Bae-Kwon, Farhi-Gutmann and Fenner at the specific measuring times, $t_{1,BK} = t_{1,FG} = \pi/(2E_o)$ and $t_{1,F} = (\pi - 2\beta)/(2E_o)$, those Hamiltonian suggest in such a case. The same character of their proposals is that $\bar{p}$ is sensitive to a phase decoherence as the database is small. The mean success probabilities of Bae-Kwon and Farhi-Gutmann are the same and always greater than the one of Fenner. Then the Hamiltonians presented by Bae and Kwon, and Farhi and Gutmann are more robust against the phase decoherence than the one proposed by Fenner especially for low values of N.

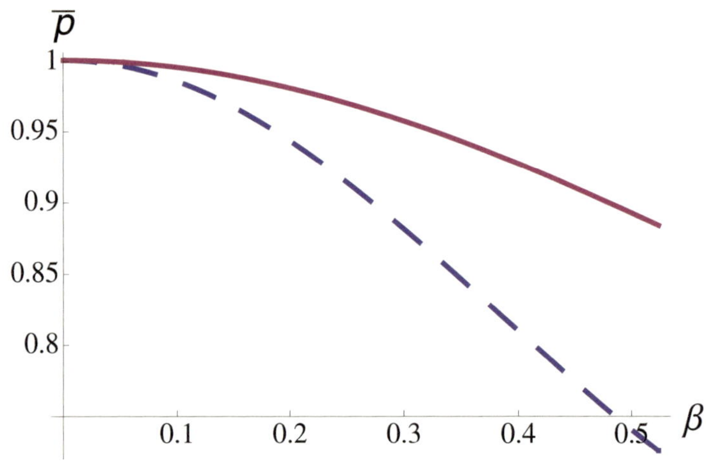

Fig. 5. The variation of $\bar{p}(\beta)$ for cases of Bae-Kwon(solid), Farhi-Gutmann(solid), and Fenner(broken) at the specific measuring times, $t_{1,BK} = t_{1,FG} = \pi/(2E_o)$ and $t_{1,F} = (\pi - 2\beta)/(2E_o)$.

A brief review on the comparison between E_{fg} and E_f, which has been discussed in Ref. (22), can be given now and the implication behind the analog quantum search first presented by Farhi and Gutmann (18) will be recalled. Suppose there is a $(N-1)$-fold degeneracy in a quantum system and its Hamiltonian is read as $H_0 = E\,|w\rangle\,\langle w|$, then our assignment is to find the unknown state $|w\rangle$. Since one does not yet know what $|w\rangle$ is, it is natural to add a well known Hamiltonian, $H_D = E\,|s\rangle\,\langle s|$, such that the initial state of the system $|s\rangle$ can be drove into $|w\rangle$. The total Hamiltonian therefore becomes $H = H_0 + H_D = E(|w\rangle\,\langle w| + |s\rangle\,\langle s|)$, which is just the Hamiltonian of Farhi and Gutmann (18) H_{fg}. It can be simplified under the large database limit,

$$H_{fg} \approx E(|w\rangle\,\langle w| + |s\rangle\,\langle s|) + E\sin(\beta)(|w\rangle\,\langle s| + |s\rangle\,\langle w|). \tag{76}$$

From it one can realize that the driving Hamiltonian induces transitions between $|w\rangle$ and $|s\rangle$ with a mixing amplitude $O(E\sin(\beta))$, which causes $|s\rangle$ to evolve to $|w\rangle$. By Eq. (72), thus it is rational to assume $E_f \sim E_{fg}\sin(\beta)$, and therefore the energy gap E_o should be proportional to $\sin\beta$, or $1/\sqrt{N}$. The measuring time then is easily found to be $t_1 \propto \sqrt{N}$ from Eq. (74). However, if consider the case $E_f \gg E_{fg}$, like the extreme situation considered by Fenner (16), then one encounters with $E_o \sim E_f\cos(\phi - u)$ and accordingly the measuring time t_1 is independent of the size of database N. Therefore, in an usual case the assumption $E_f \sim E_{fg}\sin(\beta)$ is reasonable.

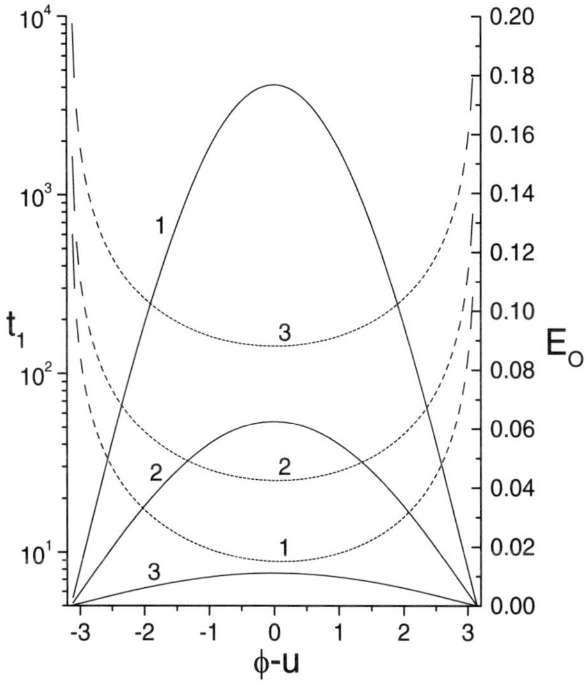

Fig. 6. Variations of $t_1(\phi - u)$ (broken) and $E_o(\phi - u)$ (solid), for $\beta = 0.085$ (1), $\beta = 0.031$ (2), and $\beta = 0.0055$ (3).

An interesting phenomenon occurs when the critical condition $E_f = E_{fg}\sin(\beta)$ is considered. Fig. 6 shows the variations of t_1 and E_o with the phase difference $\phi - u$ in such a case. It is observed that when $\phi - u = \pm\pi$ the energy gap E_o becomes zero and then the eigenstates of the quantum search system correspond to the common eigenvalue $E = E_1 = E_2$ and become degenerate. In such case, the Hamiltonian becomes proportional to the identity $\mathbf{1}(= |w\rangle\langle w| + |w_\perp\rangle\langle w_\perp|)$. Therefore, the initial state $|s\rangle$ does not evolve at all and the probability for finding the marked state $|w\rangle$ indeed is the initial one, viz., $p = \sin^2(\beta) = 1/N$, which can also be deduced using Eq. (68). In other words, the quantum search system is totally useless as long as $\phi - u = \pm\pi$ is imposed under the critical condition $E_f = E_{fg}\sin(\beta)$. When $\phi - u \neq \pm\pi$, both t_1 and E_o are finite, as can be seen from Fig. 6, and therefore the quantum search system becomes efficient again and is capable of finding the marked state with certainty, especially when the phase difference is imposed around $\phi - u = 0$. As a conclusion, for an efficient, useful quantum search system, the critical condition mentioned above should be avoided and in fact the reasonable condition $E_f \sim E_{fg}\sin(\beta)$ is recommended to be imposed.

7. Summary

A general SU(2) formulation is introduced to investigate the quantum search algorithm. In Sections 2 and 3, we show that the matching condition (19) for finding a marked state with certainty for arbitrary unitary transformations and an initial state can be derived from the general SU(2) formulation. Furthermore, one can also benefit from the same approach to evaluate the required number of iterations for the search such as Eqs. (22) and (23). With a given degree of maximum success, in Section 4 we derive a generalized and improved criterion for the tolerated error and the corresponding size of the quantum database under the inevitable gate imperfections. In Section 5, we consider a family of sure-success quantum algorithms and prove the matching conditions for both groups and give the corresponding formulae for evaluating the iterations or oracle calls required in the search. In addition, we show this kind of algorithms is robust against small phase imperfections in quantum gate operations. In the final section, we apply the same method as used for quantum search in the quantum circuit model to the analogue quantum search. A generalized Hamiltonian driving the evolution of quantum state in the analog search system is derived. Both the measuring time and the system energy gap suitable for a quantum search with or without certainty can be evaluated with the general results.

8. Acknowledgements

C.-M. Li is supported partially by the NSC, Taiwan, under the grant No. 99-2112-M-006-003.

9. References

[1] L. K. Grover, in Proceedings of 28th Annual ACM Symposium on the Theory of Computation, (ACM Press, New York, 1996).
[2] C. Zalka, Phys. Rev. A 60, 2746 (1999).
[3] C.-M. Li, J.-Y. Hsieh, and D.-S. Chuu, Phy. Rev. A 65, 052322 (2002).
[4] G. L. Long, L. Xiao, Y. Sun, e-print arXiv:quant-ph/0107013.
[5] G. L. Long, Phys. Rev. A 64, 022307 (2001).
[6] P. Høyer, Phys. Rev. A 62, 052304 (2000).
[7] G. L. Long, Y. S. Li, W. L. Zhang, and C. C. Tu, Phys. Rev. A 61, 042305 (2000).
[8] E. Biham *et al.*, Phys. Rev. A 63, 012310 (2000).
[9] B. Pablo-Norman and M. Ruiz-Altaba, Phys. Rev. A 61, 012301 (2000).
[10] C.-M. Li, J.-Y. Hsieh, and D.-S. Chuu, Chin. J. Phys. 42, 585 (2004).
[11] J. Preskill, Proc. R. Soc. London, Ser A 454, 385 (1998).
[12] C. R. Hu, Phys. Rev. A 66, 042301 (2002).
[13] C.-M. Li, J.-Y. Hsieh, and D.-S. Chuu, Int. J. Quantum Inf, 2, 285 (2004).
[14] C.-M. Li, J.-Y. Hsieh, and D.-S. Chuu, Chin. J. Phys. 45, 637 (2007).
[15] E. Farhi and S. Gutmann, Phys. Rev. A 57, 2403 (1998).
[16] S. A. Fenner. e-print arXive:quant-ph/0004091.
[17] J. Bae and Y. Kwon, Phys. Rev. A 66, 012314 (2002).
[18] E. Farhi, J. Goldstone, S. Gutmann, and M. Sipser, e-print arXiv:quant-ph/0001106.
[19] W. van Dam, M. Mosca, and U. Vazirani, in Proceedings of the 42nd Annual Symposium on the Foundations of Computer Science (IEEE Computer Society Press, New YTork, 2001), pp. 279-287.
[20] J. Roland and N. J. Cerf, Phys. Rev. A 65, 042308 (2002).
[21] C.-M. Li, J.-Y. Hsieh, and D.-S. Chuu, J. Phys. Soc. Jpn. 74, 2495 (2005).
[22] L. K. Grover and A. M. Sengupta, Phys. Rev. A 65, 032319 (2002).

5

Search via Quantum Walk

Jiangfeng Du, Chao Lei, Gan Qin, Dawei Lu and Xinhua Peng
University of Science and Technology of China
China

1. Introduction

For an unsorted database, it takes long time to find a special element. If the number of elements in the database increases, the searching time is proportional to the size of the database N. It is expected that there is no efficient search algorithm in the classical realm. The conceive of quantum computer may bring us the hope of improving the solution to the searching problems, just as to some other intractable problems such as factoring large numbers and discrete logarithm. The first quantum algorithm for searching an unsorted database is discovered by Grover, which is named as Grover algorithm (Grover (1997)). Grover algorithm can search the unsorted database with a quadratic speed up, soon after that it is proved to be the fastest speed up with the quantum computer. Although unlike some other quantum algorithms that make exponentially speed up upon the corresponding classical algorithms, it can not prevent us to treat Grover algorithm as an elegant harvest of the quantum computer since for very large unsorted database the quadratic speed up is not a trivial achievement. Suppose a classical search needs 10^6 steps, and 1 step costs 8.64 seconds, then the total calculation spends 100days. While the corresponding quantum search needs 10^3 steps, and thus the total calculation spends only 0.1 day!

Besides Grover algorithm, quantum walk is another approach to achieve quadratic speed up. Furthermore, quantum walk is soon generalized to other searching problems such as element distinctness, substructure finding etc. These problems can not be solved by Grover algorithm efficiently. This is far from ending. As we know, quantum computer is still a beautiful dream, which drives many people to double the effort to find the search algorithm based on conventional quantum computer or quantum walk. Some people may suspect that the decoherence can shatter the dream of building a quantum computer. But such pessimism would be taken away considering quantum walk may play an important role in many natural processes, such as photosynthesis. It is not surprising at all that someday the dream will come true.

In this chapter we will focus on the search algorithm based on quantum walk. The structure of this chapter is as follows, section 2 is the introduction of the quantum walk, including the coined and continuous quantum walk; section 3 is the search algorithm via quantum walk, for the general searching and the special searching problems; section 4 is focused on the physical implementation of quantum-walk-based search algorithm using an NMR quantum computer; in section 5 we will introduce the application of quantum walk in nature such as photosynthesis, in which the high efficiency of the energy transfer is still an enigma. And finally section 6 is the conclusion and proposals for the further study.

2. Quantum walk

Random walk is known as the Markovian chain which has been applied on the algorithms generally, it was quantized after the concept of quantum computer is formed. In this section we shall introduce the concept of quantum walk developed from the classical random walk and then the two forms of quantum walk - coined and continuous quantum walk.

2.1 Classical random walk

In principle, the random walk can be defined on arbitrary graph. Without loss of generality, we could focus on the random walk on one dimensional lattice. Suppose there are N lattice points arrayed on a line, each labeled by an integer, negative or positive, such as in Fig. 1, the lattices are labeled form -9 to 9 . At any time we can be at only one lattice point. Then we start at lattice 0 for example, we flip a coin to decide if we go to the left lattice or the right lattice, if the coin is up, we go to left, otherwise we go to right, then we flip the coin again to decide the next left or right. So at each step we flip a coin to decide which direction to go. After T steps, we can calculate the possibility on each lattice, for example we can see the Fig. 2. For this case we set the probability going to each direction to be 0.5. Of course, we can also set the probability different if necessary.

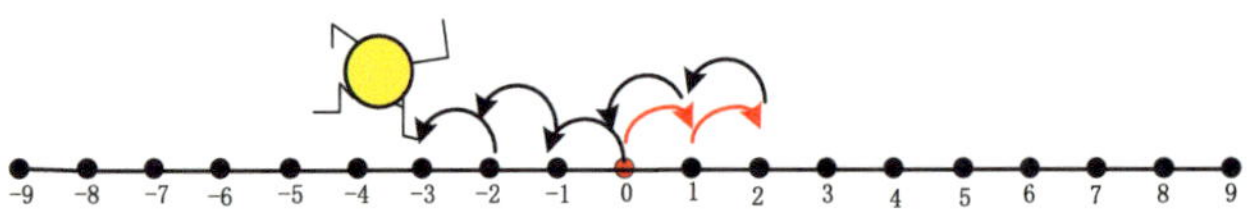

Fig. 1. In the case of the one dimensional lattice, a walker just has two direction to choose. In classical random walk, going to left or right may be decided by flipping a coin with two sides. This picture is from (Kendon et al. (2007)).

T \ i	-5	-4	-3	-2	-1	0	1	2	3	4	5
0						1					
1					$\frac{1}{2}$		$\frac{1}{2}$				
2				$\frac{1}{4}$		$\frac{1}{2}$		$\frac{1}{4}$			
3			$\frac{1}{8}$		$\frac{3}{8}$		$\frac{3}{8}$		$\frac{1}{8}$		
4		$\frac{1}{16}$		$\frac{1}{4}$		$\frac{3}{8}$		$\frac{1}{4}$		$\frac{1}{16}$	
5	$\frac{1}{32}$		$\frac{5}{32}$		$\frac{5}{16}$		$\frac{5}{16}$		$\frac{5}{32}$		$\frac{1}{32}$

Fig. 2. In this table $T$is the number of steps of the classical random walk in one dimensional lattice, i is the number that labels the position of the lattice. From this table we can know that after T steps, the walker will be at the center (or the start place) with the maximum probability (Kempe (2003)).

From a formal derivation we can get the probability distribution of the walker on each lattice. For details we can consult the book of 'A modern Course in Statistical Physics' (Reichl (1998)).

According to probability theory, the probability distribution of the random walker on the position after a time long enough is

$$\rho(x,T) = \frac{1}{\sqrt{2\pi T}} \exp(-\frac{x^2}{2T}) \tag{1}$$

where x is the position on one dimensional lattice, T is the step number.
Fig. 3 is the probability density of the distribution as the function of the position and the step number. Fig. 4 shows the results after some typical steps. It is not difficult to conclude that after many steps, the probability of the position of the random walker become flat on the lattice, tending to a Gauss distribution. The average position is 0 and the covariance of the position is

$$\sigma^2 = T \tag{2}$$

So statistically the walker's departure from the center is proportional to the square root of the step number.

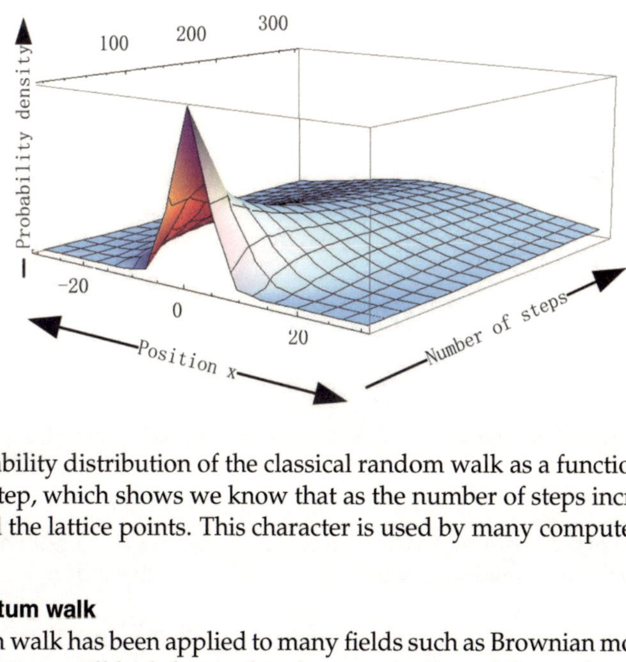

Fig. 3. The probability distribution of the classical random walk as a function of the position and number of step, which shows we know that as the number of steps increases, the walker will diffuse to all the lattice points. This character is used by many computer algorithms.

2.2 Coined quantum walk

Classical random walk has been applied to many fields such as Brownian motion, randomized algorithm etc.. But we still look forward to the quantization of the random walk to get more powerful applications, mainly attributed to the superposition principle of quantum realm. This was done by Y. Aharonov, L. Davidovich, and N. Zagury in 1993 (Aharonov et al. (1993)). For an intuitional view, the quantum walk can be regarded as the quantization of the classical random walk. However, in the classical random walk, the walker can go to only one lattice at a time. In contrast, the quantum walker can turn to both sides until it is measured, which is showed in Fig. 5.
Formally, we should define the quantum walk in Hilbert space. For simplicity we focus on the one dimensional lattice.

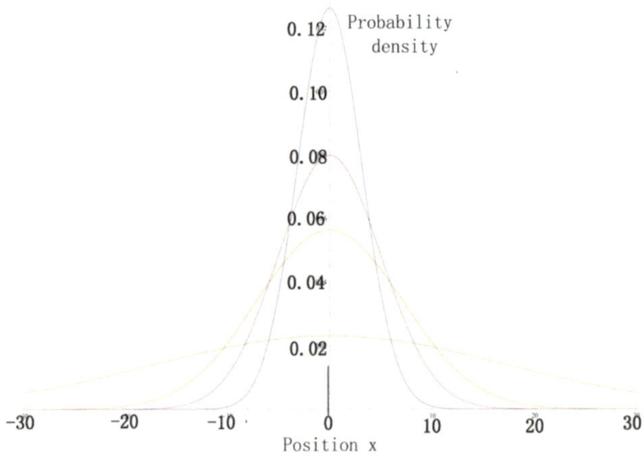

Fig. 4. Probability distribution of the classical random walk after some special steps.(green: T=300; yellow: T=50; red: T=25; blue: T=10).

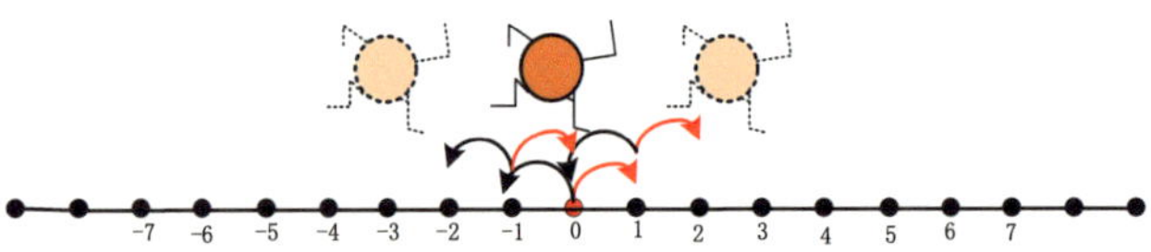

Fig. 5. The illustration of quantum walk in an intuitionistic way. Here the walker can go left and right simultaneously, which is one of the most amazing properties of quantum mechanics, first illustrated by Feynman with the tool of path integral. This picture comes from (Kendon et al. (2007)).

In the coined quantum walk, we should define two Hilbert space:

$$H = H_c \otimes H_p \tag{3}$$

where H_c is the coin Hilbert space and H_p is the position space, having the following forms:

$$H_p = \{|x\rangle ; x \in \mathbb{Z}\}, H_c = \{|+1\rangle, |-1\rangle\} \tag{4}$$

where the integer x is the position. In the coin space +1 means go to right and -1 means go to left. In quantum walk, the walking process can be realized by the shift operator:

$$S = |+1\rangle \langle +1| \otimes \sum_x |x+1\rangle \langle x| + |-1\rangle \langle -1| \otimes \sum_x |x-1\rangle \langle x| \tag{5}$$

And the coin operator is :

$$C = \begin{pmatrix} a & b \\ c & d \end{pmatrix} \tag{6}$$

The S and C operator are all unitary and hermitian, so for each step the evolution of the coin and space is also unitary as follows :

$$U = S(C \otimes I) \tag{7}$$

The state of the quantum coin can be a superposition of up and down, which is different from the classical case. As a result, the initial condition in quantum walk can be supposed as

$$|\Psi_{in}\rangle = (\alpha\,|+1\rangle + \beta\,|-1\rangle) \otimes |x\rangle \tag{8}$$

After T steps, the final state before measurement is:

$$U^T\,|\Psi_{in}\rangle \tag{9}$$

Then we can perform the measurement of the position of the walker and get the position distribution according to the quantum mechanical rule.
As an example, we can set two quantum register: the coin register and the position register. The coin register has two possible state |+1> or |-1>, and the position register can be the state |x>, where x is an integer.
The walking process is to flip the coin first and then shift, and we can set the coin operator as:

$$C = \frac{1}{\sqrt{2}}\begin{pmatrix} 1 & 1 \\ 1 & -1 \end{pmatrix} \tag{10}$$

Flipping leads to the following changes of the states:
$|+1> \rightarrow (|+1> + |-1>)/\sqrt{2}, |-1> \rightarrow (|+1> - |-1>)/\sqrt{2}$

Shift is :
$|+1>|x> \rightarrow |+1>|x+1>, |-1>|x> \rightarrow |-1>|x-1>$

We can also understand why the quantum walk is different from the classical random walk with the help of path integral method as illustrated in Fig. 6 (Pérez Delgado (2007)).
In Fig. 6, the dotted line is all the possible paths and the real line is one of them. The classical walker can only select one of the paths to walk, while the quantum walker can walk in all possible paths simultaneously, with the probability amplitude of every path interfering to each other.
If the initial state of the coin is |-1>, then we can get the possibility distribution as Fig. 7 shows.
Otherwise if we set the initial state of the coin to $\frac{1}{\sqrt{2}}(|+1\rangle + i\,|-1\rangle)$, then the possibility distribution is as Fig. 8 shows. This is very different from classical random walk whose possibility distribution is independent of the initial conditions.
Another difference of quantum walk from classical random walk is the diffusion rate of the walker from the center. As we know from section 2.1, the deviation of the walker is proportional to the root of the step number N, but in quantum walk, the deviation of the walker is proportional to N, which get a quadric speed up(for a detail see the Fig. 9).

2.3 Continuous time quantum walk

Continuous time quantum walk is introduced by Edward Farhi and Sam Gutmann in 1998 (Farhi & Gutmann (1998)). In contrast with the coined quantum walk, the continuous quantum walk does not need a coin, and is often defined with the tool of graphs.

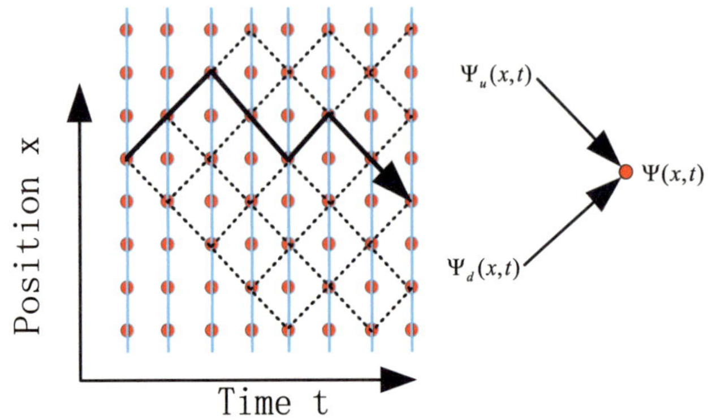

Fig. 6. Illustration of the quantum walk with the tool of path integral (Pérez Delgado (2007)). The red point stands for the lattice and the dotted line is all the possible path. In classical random walk, the walker can only choose one of the paths (the real line) with a probability, but in quantum walk one can walk in all possible paths simultaneously. The probability amplitude of every path can then interfere to each other if allowed.

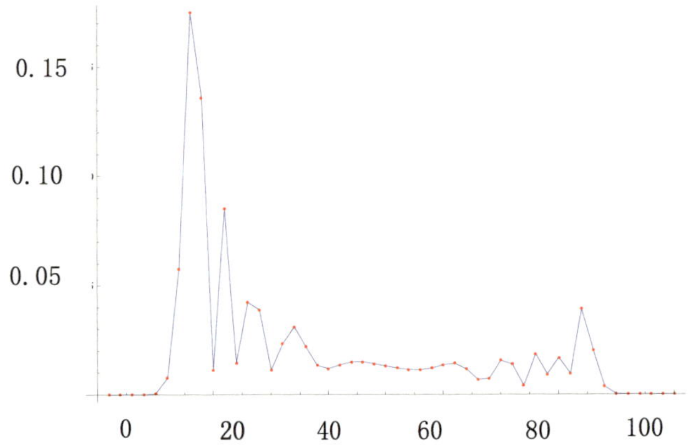

Fig. 7. Probability distribution of quantum walk with the initial state |-1> of the coin. The walker starts at the position x=50 and the number of steps is 50.

It is convenient to illustrate the continuous time quantum starting from the classical random walk on a graph. The process can be described by a matrix M, which transforms the probability distribution on the vertex of graph:

$$p_i^{t+1} = \sum_j M_{ij} p_j^t \tag{11}$$

where M_{ij} is the matrix element of M, the probability at the i th vertex at time t.
The next step is to make the transform process continuous, which requires to jump to only the neighbor vertex. Then we should use the infinitesimal generator matrix H to describe the walk process, i.e.

$$\frac{dp_i(t)}{dt} = -\sum_j H_{ij} p_j(t) \tag{12}$$

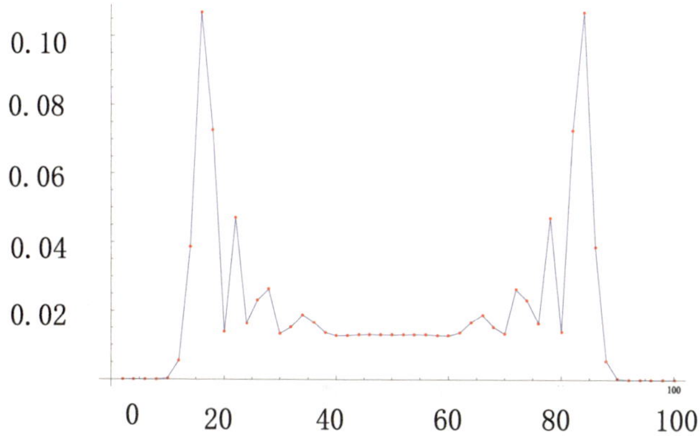

Fig. 8. Probability distribution of quantum walk with another initial state of the coin of $\frac{1}{\sqrt{2}}(|+1\rangle + i|-1\rangle$. The walker starts at x=50. By comparing Fig. 7 and Fig. 8 we can easily find that the probability distribution of quantum walk depends on the initial state of the coin, which is different from the classical random walk, whose probability distribution is independent of the initial state of the coin.

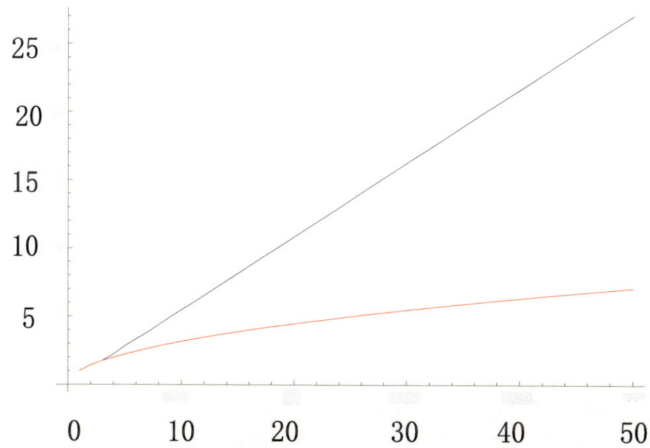

Fig. 9. The diffusion rate of the walker from the center, which is characterized by the deviation of the walker's position from the center (i.e. the start place of the walker). The horizontal axis represents the number of the steps T and the vertical axis represents the deviation of the position. In this picture the blue line is the case of quantum walk and the red line is the case of the classical random walk. It can be concluded that the diffusion rate of the quantum walk is quadratic speed up upon the classical random walk.

Solving the equation we get:

$$p(t) = \exp(-Ht)p(0) \tag{13}$$

where p is the vector of probability distribution.

Equation (12) has the similiar form with the Schrödinger equation, so the classical random walk is quantized in a continuous form.

3. Search algorithm via quantum walk

In section 2.2 we have know that in one dimensional lattice the walker departs from the center quadratically faster than classical random walk, however it is not a search. Search is the reverse process: starting in a uniform superposition of all the databases and returning to the marked item. So it is not difficult to understand why the quantum walk based search algorithm is quadratic speed up upon the classical search algorithm. Generally coined quantum walk can make quantum walk faster than the continuous time quantum walk(Ambainis (2005)).

Quantum walk can also be simulated by quantum circuit(Douglas & Wang (2009)), thus we can realized the quantum based search algorithm by the quantum computer in principle. This makes quantum walk not only a conceived tool for algorithm, but also useful for the computation theory to explore more efficient algorithms for intractable problems. For a review of the algorithm application of quantum walk we can see the article of Andris Ambainis and Vivien M Kendon (Ambainis (2003); Kendon (2006))

3.1 Searching on graphs

In this subsection we will focus on the search on graphs. Searching on graphs is to find a marked vertex of the graph. Sometimes one is also interested in finding a marked edge or even a marked subgraph, which is generalized from the search of vertex.

Searching on the graph can be done by coined quantum walk (Shenvi et al. (2003)) or continuous time quantum walk (Childs & Goldstone (2004)), we will focus on the coined quantum walk based search algorithm most of the time. Hitherto the quantum walk is all defined on highly symmetric graphs such as hypercube.

In section 2.2 we have introduced the coined quantum walk on one dimensional lattice just for illustration. In order to interpret the search algorithm via quantum walk it is necessary to get the definition of quantum walk on graph. This will be showed with the example of hypercube of dimension n. The first quantum walk based search algorithm is discovered by Neil Shenvi, Julia Kempe, and K. Birgitta Whaley (Shenvi et al. (2003)), which is called SKW algorithm. As an example we will illustrate the SKW algorithm without loss of generality.

The only difference between the quantum walk on higher dimensional graph and that on a line is the dimension of the Hilbert space of coin and position. In graph the position is replaced by the vertex and the dimension of the coin Hilbert space is the degree of the graph. For an n dimensional hypercube, the degree of every vertex is n and the number of the total nodes is $N = 2^n$, thus the Hilbert space of the vertex and coin is:

$$H = H_v \otimes H_c \tag{14}$$

where H_v is the vertex space and H_c is the coin space respectively which have the form:

$$H_v = \{|x\rangle : x \in \mathbb{Z}_N\} \tag{15}$$

$$H_c = \{|c\rangle : c \in \mathbb{Z}_d\} \tag{16}$$

where N is the number of the total nodes and d is the degree of every vertex.

Then we can define the coin operator and the shift operator on the Hilbert space of the coin and vertex in the following forms (Shenvi et al. (2003)):

$$S = \sum_{d=0}^{n-1} \sum_{\vec{x}} |d, \vec{x} \oplus \vec{e}_d\rangle \langle d, \vec{x}| \tag{17}$$

$$C = C_0 \otimes I \tag{18}$$

where $\vec{e}_d$is the d th basis vector on the hypercube. C_0 is an $n \times n$ unitary operator acting on the coin space and I is an identity operator. To implement the search algorithm it is natural to apply a marked coin operator. In the SKW algorithm for instance the marked coin operator is as follows:

$$C' = C_0 \otimes I + (C_1 - C_0) \otimes \left|\vec{0}\right\rangle \left\langle\vec{0}\right| \tag{19}$$

The marked coin can be any $n \times n$ unitary operator, for detail information we can see the literature (Shenvi et al. (2003)).
The more generalized searching target on the graph can be an edge or even a subgraph (Hilley et al. (2009)). Element distinctness is another algorithm that can be viewed as a quantum walk based search (Ambainis (2007))

3.2 Searching the exits

Another algorithm of search using quantum walk is found by Andrew M. Childs et al in 2003, which is the first quantum walk based algorithm. This algorithm uses the exponential speed up of hitting time of quantum walk upon classical random walk (Childs et al. (2003)). Contrast of the unsorted database, the algorithm found by Andrew M. Childs et al. is based on a particular sort of network (Fig. 10). Suppose that we are at the entrance of the network, our task is to find another exit as fast as possible. For classical case the best strategy may be to choose a direction randomly, i.e. the classical random walk. It still takes the time increasing exponentially with the wide of the network. One may be lost in the middle of the network. In quantum walk, however, one can choose all the possible paths simultaneously and reach the exit with the time increasing polynomially with the wide of the network, which makes an exponential speed up.

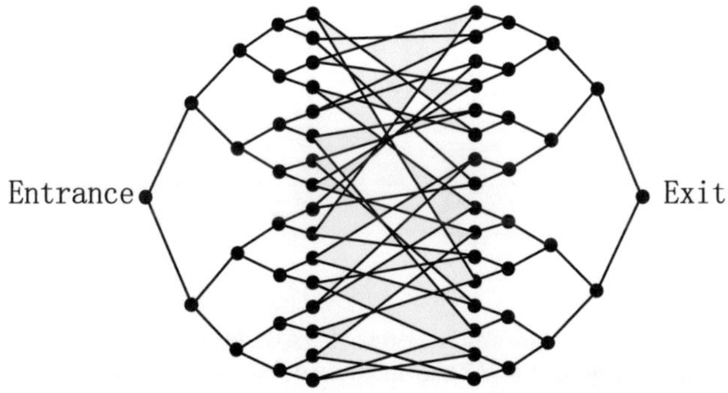

Fig. 10. The network of the first algorithm found by Andrew M. Childs et al. that is based on quantum walk (Childs et al. (2003)).

4. Physical implementation of quantum walk based search

4.1 Introduction to the SKW algorithm

The quantum random walk search algorithm proposed by Shenvi, Kempe and Whaley (SKW algorithm, Shenvi et al. (2003)) is one of the novel algorithms which exhibits the superiority of quantum computation. It belongs to the discrete-time quantum random walk model. Similar to Grover's quantum search algorithm, the SKW algorithm performs an oracle search on a

database of N items with $O(\sqrt{N})$ calls, where N is the size of the search space. Whereas, when the diffusion step of Grover algorithm cannot be implemented efficiently, this algorithm may be still available, which is a significant advantage comparing to the Grover algorithm. Afterwards various optimizations of the SKW algorithm have been brought up to reduce the complexity (Ambainis (2005); Chandrashekar (2008); Reitzner et al. (2009); Tulsi (2008)).
The original problem can be described as follows: given a function $f(x)$, $f(x) = 1$ if $x = a$, otherwise $f(x) = 0$. The goal is to find a, where $0 \leqslant a \leqslant 2^n - 1$. It is equivalent to search for a single marked node among the $N = 2^n$ nodes on the n-cube.
The coined quantum walk model requires a flipping coin and defines a two-step procedure consisting of a coin-flip step and coin-controlled walk step. The two steps can be expressed as $U = SC$, where C denotes a unitary operation corresponding to flipping the quantum coin (coin-flip step) and S is a permutation matrix which performs a controlled shift based on the state of the coin space (coin-controlled walk step). Specially, in the SKW algorithm, an oracle is needed to realize the searching procedure. The oracle acts by applying a marking coin C_1 to the marked node and the original coin C_0 to the unmarked nodes, which is defined as a new coin operator C'. After applying $U' = SC'$ for $t_f = \frac{\pi}{2}\sqrt{2^n}$ times, we gain the marked node with probability $\frac{1}{2} - O(1/n)$ by measurement.
A simple case for $n = 2$ is considered. We need three qubits to demonstrate the algorithm, with one coin qubit (labeled by qubit 0) and two database qubits (labeled by qubit 1 and 2). The target node is one of the four computational bases $|00\rangle_{12}, |01\rangle_{12}, |10\rangle_{12}, |11\rangle_{12}$, named by 1-out-of-4 algorithm. The network is shown in Fig.11. Now we describe the searching process in details. Suppose the initial state is a pure state $|000\rangle$.

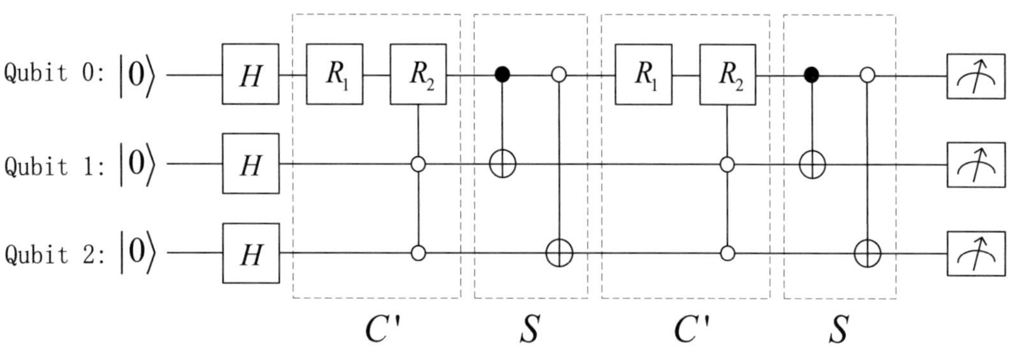

Fig. 11. Quantum network for the algorithm of 1-out-of-4 searching, with the target state being $|00\rangle_{12}$. Qubit 0 is the coin qubit, while qubit 1 and 2 are database qubits. The Hadamard gates are applied to produce an equal superposition over all the computational bases. The solid circle represents 1-control gate whereas the open circle represents the opposite. The purpose of oracle C' is to implement $C_1 = R_x^0(\pi/2)$ (rotating qubit 0 around the x axis by angle $\pi/2$) when the database is $|00\rangle_{12}$ and $C_0 = R_x^0(3\pi/2)$ otherwise. It is equivalent to be replaced by $R_1 = R_x^0(3\pi/2)$ and $R_2 = R_x^0(-\pi)$. The two controlled-not gates are inverting qubit 1 if qubit 0 is $|1\rangle_0$ and inverting qubit 2 if qubit 0 is $|0\rangle_0$, respectively. The measurement requires all the populations' reconstruction. Similar circuits can be obtained in a straightforward manner for other target states. For instance, if the goal is $|10\rangle_{12}$, we need only change the controlled condition of the three-body-interaction gate to state $|10\rangle_{12}$.

(I) Applying a Hadamard operation to every qubit to prepare the state

$$|\psi_i\rangle = \frac{|0\rangle_0 + |1\rangle_0}{\sqrt{2}} \otimes \frac{|0\rangle_1 + |1\rangle_1}{\sqrt{2}} \otimes \frac{|0\rangle_2 + |1\rangle_2}{\sqrt{2}}, \quad (20)$$

which is exactly an equal superposition over all the computational bases.
(II) Perform the oracle C' on the coin qubit depending on the state of database qubits, namely, $C_1 = R_x^0(\pi/2) = e^{-i\pi\sigma_x/4}$ if the database qubits are on the target state $|\tau\sigma\rangle_{12}$, and $C_0 = R_x^0(3\pi/2) = e^{-i3\pi\sigma_x/4}$ otherwise. Therefore, the whole coin operation is

$$C' = C_0 \otimes (E_{12} - |\tau\sigma\rangle_{12\,12}\langle\tau\sigma|) + C_1 \otimes |\tau\sigma\rangle_{12\,12}\langle\tau\sigma| \tag{21}$$

where E_{12} is the identity operator. Then the database qubits undergo the shift operation S conditioned on the state of coin qubit:

$$\begin{aligned} |0\rangle_0\,|00\rangle_{12} &\Longleftrightarrow |0\rangle_0\,|01\rangle_{12} \\ |0\rangle_0\,|10\rangle_{12} &\Longleftrightarrow |0\rangle_0\,|11\rangle_{12} \\ |1\rangle_0\,|00\rangle_{12} &\Longleftrightarrow |1\rangle_0\,|01\rangle_{12} \\ |1\rangle_0\,|01\rangle_{12} &\Longleftrightarrow |1\rangle_0\,|11\rangle_{12} \end{aligned} \tag{22}$$

(III) Repeat step (II) twice to implement the quantum walk, which will reach the final state

$$\left|\psi_f\right\rangle = (SC')^2\,|\psi_i\rangle \tag{23}$$

(IV) Measure all the populations of the database qubits. For example, in the case of finding $|00\rangle_{12}$, we can obtain that the probabilities of $|00\rangle_{12}, |01\rangle_{12}, |10\rangle_{12}, |11\rangle_{12}$ are 0.5, 0.25, 0.25, 0, respectively.
For other target states, with the controlled condition changed to the target node similar networks can be given easily. The results have an analogy with the aforementioned one.

4.2 NMR experimental implementation

Now we turn to our NMR quantum computer to implement the SKW algorithm. The three qubits are represented by the three ^{1}H spins in a sample of 1-Bromo-2,3-Dichlorobenzene oriented in liquid-crystal solvent (ZLI-1132). The molecular structure is shown in Fig.12(a). The system Hamiltonian can be described as

$$\begin{aligned} \mathcal{H} = &\sum_{j=1}^{3} 2\pi\nu_j I_z^j + \sum_{j,k,j<k\leqslant 3} 2\pi J_{jk}(I_x^j I_x^k + I_y^j I_y^k + I_z^j I_z^k) \\ &+ \sum_{j,k,j<k\leqslant 3} 2\pi D_{jk}\left(2I_z^j I_z^k - I_x^j I_x^k - I_y^j I_y^k\right) \end{aligned} \tag{24}$$

where ν_j is the resonance frequency of the jth spin, D_{jk} and J_{jk} are the dipolar coupling strengths and scalar coupling strengths between spins j and k, respectively. All the sums are restricted to the spins within one molecule. All experiments were carried out on a Bruker Avance 500 MHz spectrometer at room temperature. The spectrum of the thermal equilibrium state $\rho_{th} = \sum_{i=1}^{3} \sigma_z^i$ followed by a $\pi/2$ hard pulse is shown in Fig.12(b). With some initially guessed parameters assuming the molecular geometry, we iteratively fit the calculated and observed spectra through the parameters' perturbation (Suryaprakash (2000)). The values of parameters are listed in Table.1(a).
Since the system Hamiltonian has nondiagonal elements, the eigenstates are not Zeeman product states any more but linear combinations of them. To simplify the measurement of

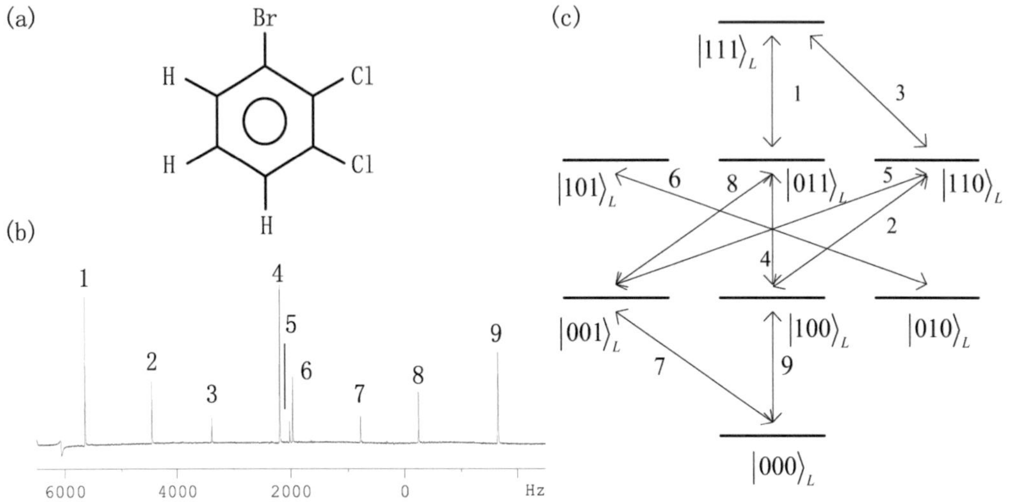

Fig. 12. (a) Molecular structure of 1-Bromo-2,3-Dichlorobenzene in which the three protons form a 3-qubit system. (b) Spectrum of the thermal equilibrium state followed by a $\pi/2$ hard pulse. All the observable transitions are labeled according to the descending orders of the frequencies. (c) Diagram of corresponding transitions in the eigenbasis.

(a)

	H_1	H_2	H_3
H_1	1945.5	-1633.3	-1341.7
H_2	8	2094.8	-339.35
H_3	8	1.4	2147.2

(b)

spin 1 No.9	$UR_y^1(\pi/2)$	$UR_y^1(\pi/2)R_y^2(\pi)$	$UR_y^1(\pi/2)R_y^3(\pi)$	$UR_y^1(\pi/2)R_y^{2,3}(\pi)$
	$P(1)-P(5)$	$P(3)-P(7)$	$P(2)-P(6)$	$P(4)-P(8)$
spin 2 No.8	$UR_y^2(\pi/2)$	$UR_y^2(\pi/2)R_y^1(\pi)$	$UR_y^2(\pi/2)R_y^3(\pi)$	$UR_y^2(\pi/2)R_y^{1,3}(\pi)$
	$P(2)-P(4)$	$P(6)-P(8)$	$P(1)-P(3)$	$P(5)-P(7)$
spin 3 No.7	$UR_y^3(\pi/2)$	$UR_y^3(\pi/2)R_y^1(\pi)$	$UR_y^3(\pi/2)R_y^2(\pi)$	$UR_y^3(\pi/2)R_y^{1,2}(\pi)$
	$P(1)-P(2)$	$P(5)-P(6)$	$P(3)-P(4)$	$P(7)-P(8)$

Table 1. (a) The parameters for fitting the spectrum of 1-Bromo-2,3-Dichlorobenzene (Hertz). The diagonal elements are chemical shifts of the three protons, the upper-right off-diagonal elements are dipolar coupling strengths, and the lower-left ones are scalar coupling strengths. (b) The read-out pulses and corresponding values of $P(i) - P(j)$. The results are shown on the transitions of No.9, 8 and 7.

populations (marked from $P(1)$ to $P(8)$), we found a feasible unitary matrix U to realize the transformation between the computational basis and eigenbasis, which satisfies

$$H_L = UH_S U^{\dagger}, \tag{25}$$

where H_S is the system Hamiltonian and H_L is a diagonal Hamiltonian (i.e., the Hamiltonian in the eigenbasis). With adding the pulse of implementing transformation matrix U after the original readout pulses in liquid NMR and combining with the normalization $\sum_{i=1}^{8} P(i) = 1$, we can obtain all eight population values straightforwardly. Table. 1 (b) shows all the available values of $P(i) - P(j)$ through different read-out pulses (for more explanations and details see Lu et al. (2010).

The experiment was divided into three steps: the psesudo-pure state preparation, quantum random walk searching process, and population measurement. Starting from the thermal equilibrium state, firstly we need to create the PPS $\rho_{000} = \frac{1-\epsilon}{8}\mathbf{1} + \epsilon\,|000\rangle\,\langle 000|$, where ϵ represents the polarization of the system and $\mathbf{1}$ is the identity matrix. We used shape pulses based on GRadient Ascent Pulse Engineering (GRAPE) algorithm (Baugh et al. (2007); Khaneja et al. (2005); Ryan et al. (2008)) and gradient pulses to realize the PPS preparation, with the numerical simulated fidelity 0.977.

The quantum random walk searching process contains two parts actually: The preparation of initial state $|+\rangle^{\otimes 3}$ ($|+\rangle = (|0\rangle + |1\rangle)/\sqrt{2}$) and two iterations of unitary evolution. We packed them together and calculated one GRAPE pulse of 20ms and 250 segments whose fidelity is higher than 0.990. The reading-out operators listed in Table.1(b) are also performed when generating the GRAPE pulses of 20ms with the fidelity 0.990. The probabilities of gaining $|00\rangle$, $|01\rangle$, $|10\rangle$, $|11\rangle$ are 0.513, 0.232, 0.197, and 0.058, respectively, which demonstrates that we have completed searching $|00\rangle$ based on the SKW algorithm.

Besides $|00\rangle$, we altered the target states to $|01\rangle$, $|10\rangle$ and $|11\rangle$. The experimental results are plotted in Fig. 13. It can be seen the experimental and theoretical results are mostly consistent with little error. The slight difference between theory and experiment may be attributed to decoherence, the RF field inhomogeneity and imperfect implementation of GRAPE pulses.

In summary, we experimentally implemented a search algorithm based on the quantum random walk (the SKW algorithm) in the case of 1-out-of-4. This algorithm performs an oracle search on a database of N items with $O(\sqrt{N})$ calls, with a speedup similar to the Grover search algorithm. The experiment was carried out on an NMR quantum information processor with strongly dipolar coupled spins. We used GRAPE pulses to realize high-fidelity unitary operations and provided an effective way to measure the populations of the density matrix. The experimental results agree well with the theoretical expectations, which exhibits the superiority of the algorithm.

5. Quantum walk based search in nature

One of the astonishing phenomena of nature is the photosynthesis, which supplies all the chemical energy of our earth and acts as an important form of energy storage. However the high efficiency of the energy transfer in photosynthesis is still an enigma, the method of quantum walk has been introduced to try to explain the process of energy transfer (Mohseni et al. (2008); Rebentrost (2009)) since the quantum walk can increase the search efficiency with exponentially speed up in the case of the uncharted network (Childs et al. (2003)). Also in some literature the search process in photosynthesis from the pigment antenna to the reaction center is compared with the Grover type search, it is more natural to use the algorithm of section 3.2 to explain the high efficiency of the energy transfer process.

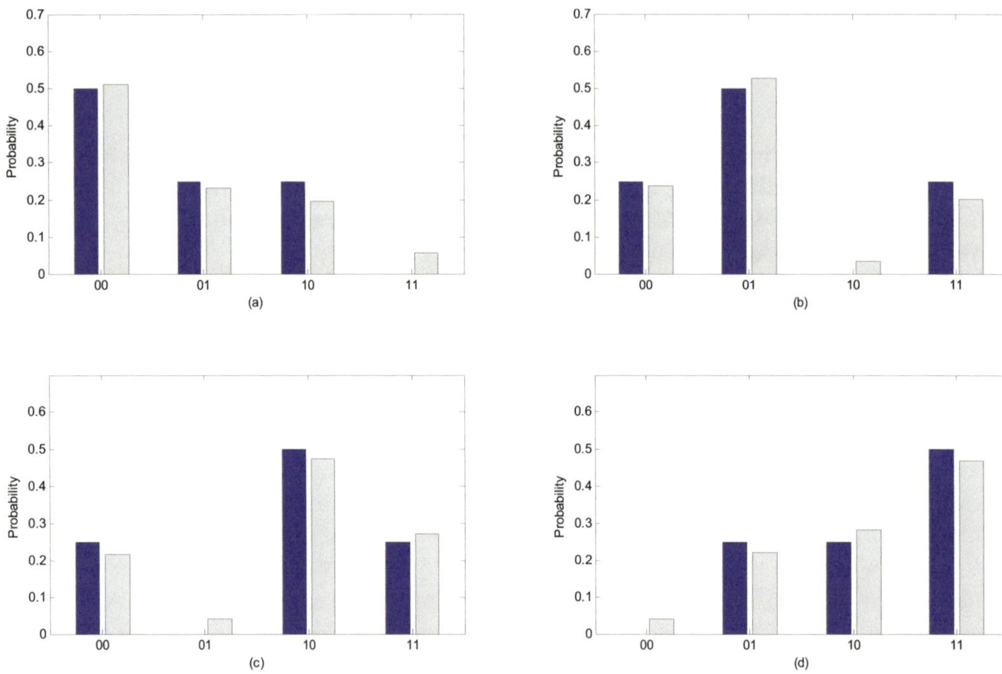

Fig. 13. Experimental results of the SKW algorithm. (a), (b), (c), (d) correspond to the cases of finding $|00\rangle_{12}$, $|01\rangle_{12}$, $|10\rangle_{12}$ and $|11\rangle_{12}$. The blue (dark) bars represent the theoretical prediction and the gray (light) bars represent the experimental analog, respectively.

5.1 Photosynthesis and quantum walk

In photosynthesis the energy is absorbed by pigments and then transferred to the reaction center where the energy is converted to the chemical energy and starts the electron transfer process. The most model of the energy transfer from the antennas to the reaction center is illustrated in the Fig. 14 (Blankenship (2002)). In the past the popular view is the excitons from the antennas hop to the reaction center, which is analogical to the classical random walk. However this is challenged by recent experiments and theory model, in which the quantum coherence is applying to the energy transfer process in order to explain the high efficiency in photosynthesis.

The first wavelike energy transfer through quantum coherence is found in FMO protein complex of purple bacteria at the temperature of 77K (Engel et al. (2007)) and soon the long lived quantum coherence in photosynthetic complexes is observed at physiological temperature (Panitchayangkoon et al. (2010)).

The theory model of the energy transfer in photosynthesis is using the quantum walk (Mohseni et al. (2008); Rebentrost (2009)), at most of the time the array of the pigment can be treated as a graph network of quantum walk (Fig. 15), in the figure the red sites is just as the exits of the Fig. 10 and the gray sites act as the entrance.

Another astonishing result is the assist of the environment to the quantum walk transport in photosynthetic energy transfer, if we know that environment is the main source of the decoherence of quantum systems and the decoherence is the main obstacle to build a quantum computer that surpass the classical computer. In contrast the interaction of the free Hamiltonian of the protein complex with the thermal fluctuations in the environment leads to an increase of the energy transfer efficiency from about 70% to 99% (Mohseni et al. (2008)).

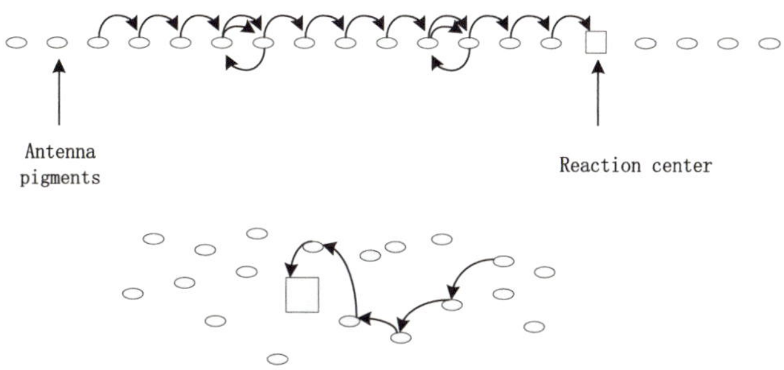

Fig. 14. Antenna organization models. The circle represents the antennas and the rectangle acts as the reaction center. The top schematic is the one dimensional array and the bottom schematic is the three dimensional array model. Of course the three dimensional model is more close to the actual case. The schematics come from the book written by Robert E. Blankenship. (Blankenship (2002)).

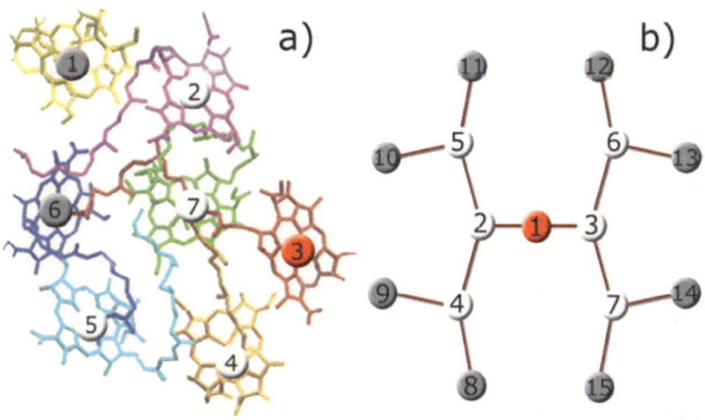

Fig. 15. a) chlorophyll molecules Fenna-Matthews-Olson (FMO) protein complex, this is investigated widely for its simple structure compared with the chlorophyll molecules in higher plant and algae. b) artificial systems described by a tight-binding Hamiltonian. Here is a four generation binary tree. In particular, an exponential speed up in reaching certain target sites (red) in these structures has been proposed in the context of quantum walk algorithms. (The gray sites represent initial states for the quantum transport.) (Rebentrost (2009)).

5.2 Biomimetic application in solar energy

Energy is a crucial problem for human since the fossil fuels are being exhausted. A commonly accepted alternative energy consuming way is to use the solar energy directly, since it can be got continuously. However the efficiency of utilizing the solar energy now is still very low. On the other hand the efficiency of the energy transfer in the photosynthesis is very high: more than 90% sometimes upon to 99%. If the energy transfer efficiency in the solar cell achieve to the same as in photosynthesis then the conversion efficiency of solar cell will double up. This will give an exciting perspective to the future of the energy utilization if we can understand the principle of the energy transfer in photosynthesis. Hitherto many groups have committed to build an artificial photosynthesis system, but so far no results successful enough have been obtained. Although many of them claim to solve the puzzler of the energy in the earth, from

a scientific view we cannot conclude when we can see the hydrogen emerge from the water extensively under the shine of the sun.
It is not necessary to list the benefit of the solar energy since there are so many eyes searching them. The only task for us is to make the principle of the photosynthesis clear so we can utilize it as we will do.

6. Conclusions and future directions

Quantum walk is another approach to design a quantum algorithm surpassing the classical algorithms, hitherto many scientists have made commitment to build a quantum computer. Apart from the search problem, there are many problems that can not be solved by classical computer efficiently, but can be solved by quantum algorithms in a relative short time. Quantum walk is not just the artificial tool for the search algorithm, but is also likely to be the tool for nature. All of these are instilling confidence for us to solve the intractable problems we have met.
However, the main obstacle of the quantum walk based algorithms including the search algorithm is the physical implementation since the decoherence occurs almost everywhere and every time. Thus in the future an important investigation is overcoming the decoherence or realizing the coherent manipulation of the quantum bits and quantum systems for relative long time in particular case. There are many physical systems proposed to implement the quantum computer and the quantum walk, but which is the practical one is still unknown.
Quantum walk has been realized in various physical systems, first in NMR based computer (Du et al. (2003))for continuous time quantum walk and then coined quantum walk (Ryan et al. (2005)). Other successful physical systems include waveguide lattices (Perets et al. (2008)), trapped ions (Schmitz et al. (2009); Zähringer et al. (2010)), photon systems (Broome et al. (2010); Schreiber et al. (2010)) and optical lattices (Karski et al. (2009)). But the number of steps is still very small. Maybe the photons in waveguide lattice is a particular system since more than one hundred steps can be performed in it for the continuous quantum walk, though it is not convenient to modulate the walker. Anyway it is a great progress to realize the quantum walk in physical systems, based on which various search algorithms may be carried out.

7. References

Aharonov, Y. ; Davidovich, L. & Zagury, N. (1993). Quantum random walks, *Phys. Rev. A* , 48, 1687.

Ambainis, A. (2003). Quantum walks and their algorithmic applications, *International Journal of Quantum Information* , 1, 507-518.

Ambainis, A.; Kempe, J. & Rivosh, A. (2005). Coins Make Quantum Walks Faster, *Proceedings of the 16th annual ACM-SIAM symposium on Discrete algorithms* , pp. 1099 - 1108 , 0-89871-585-7, Vancouver, British Columbia, 2005, Society for Industrial and Applied Mathematics. Philadelphia.

Ambainis, A. (2007). Quantum walk algorithm for element distinctness, *SIAM Journal on Computing* , 37(1), 210-239.

Blankenship, R. E. (2002). *Molecular Mechanisms of Photosynthesis*, Wiley-Blackwell, 978-0632043217, Oxford/ Malden.

Baugh, J. et al., (2007). 'Special issue on quntum information and quantum computing', *Phys. in Can.* 63, No.4.

Broome, M. A.; Fedrzzi, A.; Lanyon, B. P.; Kassal, I.; Apspuru-Guzik, A. & White, A. G. (2010). Discrete Single-Photon Quantum Walks with Tunable Decoherence, *Phys. Rev. Lett.* 104, 153602.

Childs, A. M. ; Cleve, R. ; Deotto, E.; Farhi, E.; Gutmann, S. & Speilman, D. A. (2003). Exponential algorithmic speedup by quantum walk, *Proceedings of the thirty-fifth annual ACM symposium on Theory of computing* , pp. 59-68, 1-58113-674-9, San Diego, CA, USA, 2003, ACM, New York.

Childs, A. M. & Goldstone, J. (2004). Spatial search by quantum walk, *Phys. Rev. A* , 70, 022314.

Chandrashekar, C.; Srikanth, R. & Laflamme, R. (2008). Optimizing the discrete time quantum walk using a SU(2) coin, *Phys.Rev. A* 77, 032326.

Du, J. F.; Li, H.; Xu, X. D.; Shi, M. J.; Wu, J. H.; Zhou, X. Y.; & Han, R. D. (2003). Experimental implementation of the quantum random-walk algorithm, *Phys. Rev. A* , 67, 042316.

Douglas, B. L. & Wang J. B. (2009). Efficient quantum circuit implementation of quantum walks, *Phys. Rev. A* , 79, 052335.

Engel, G. S. ; Calhoun, T. R.; Read, E. L.; Ahn, T. K.; Mančal, T.; Cheng, Y. C.; Blankenship, R. E.; & Fleming, G. R. (2007). Evidence for wavelike energy transfer through quantum coherence in photosynthetic systems, *Nature*, 446, 782.

Farhi, E. & Gutmann, S. (1998). Quantum computation and decision trees, *Phys. Rev. A* , 58, 915-928.

Grover, L. K. (1997). Quantum Mechanics Helps in Searching for a Needle in a Haystack, *Phys. Rev. Lett.* , 79, 325-328.

Hilley, M.; Reitzner, D. & Bužek, V. (2009). Searching via walking: How to find a marked subgraph of a graph using quantum walks, *arXiv*, arXiv:0911.1102v1.

Kempe, J. (2003). Quantum random walks - an introductory overview, *Contemporary Physics* , 44 (4), 307-327.

Khaneja, N.; Reiss, T.; Kehlet, C.; Schulte-Herbrüggen, T. & S. Glaser. (2005). Optimal control of coupled spin dynamics: design of NMR pulse sequences by gradient ascent algorithms, *J. Magn. Reson.* 172, 296;

Kendon, V. M.; (2006). A random walk approach to quantum algorithms, *Phil. Trans. R. Soc. A* , 364, 3407-3422.

Kendon, V. & Maloyer, O. (2007). Optimal computation with noisy quantum walks, *Quantum Information School of Physics & Astronomy University of Leeds Leeds LS2 9JT* .

Karski, M.; Förster, L.; Choi, J. M.; Steffen, A.; Alt, W. & Meschede, D. (2009). Quantum Walk in Position Space with Single Optically Trapped Atoms, *Science* 325, 174-177.

Lu, D.; Zhu, J.; Zou, P.; Peng, X.; Yu, Y.; Zhang, S.; Chen, Q. & Du, J. (2010). Experimental implementation of a quantum random-walk search algorithm using strongly dipolar coupled spins, *Phys. Rev. A* 81,022308.

Mohseni, M. ; Rebentrost, P. ; Lloyd, S. & Aspuru-Guzik, A. (2008). Environment-assisted quantum walks in photosynthetic energy transfer, *J. Chem. Phys.*, 129, 174106.

Pérez Delgado, C. A. (2007). Quantum Cellular Automata: Theory and Applications, *A thesis for the degree of Doctor of Philosophy in Computer Science* ,p61.

Perets, H. B.; Lahini, Y.; Pozzi, F.; Sorel, M.; Morandotti, R. & Silberberg, Y. (2008). Realization of Quantum Walks with Negligible Decoherence in Waveguide Lattices, *Phys. Rev. Lett.* 100, 170506.

Potoček, V.; Gábris, A.; Kiss, T. & Jex, I. (2009). Optimized quantum random-walk search algorithms on the hypercube, *Phys. Rev. A* 79, 012325.

Panitchayangkoon, G. ; Hayes, D.; Fransted, K. A.; Caram, J. R.; Harel, E.; Wen, J. Z.; Blankenship, R. W.; & Engel, S. (2010). Long-lived quantum coherence in photosynthetic complexes at physiological temperature, *Proc. Natl. Acad. Sci. USA* , 107, 12766-12770.

Reichl, L. E. (1998). *A Modem Course in Statistical Physics,* John Wiley & Sons, Inc., 978-0471595205, New York.

Ryan, C.; Laforest, M.; & Laflamme, R. (2005). Experimental implementation of a discrete-time quantum random walk on an NMR quantum-information processor, *Phys. Rev. A* 72, 012328.

Ryan, C.; Negrevergne, C.; Laforest, M.; Knill, E. & Laflamme, R. (2008). Liquid-state nuclear magnetic resonance as a testbed for developing quantum control methods, *Phys. Rev. A* 78, 012328.

Reitzner, D.; Hillery, M.; Feldman, E. & Bužek, V. (2009) Quantum searches on highly symmetric graphs, *Phys. Rev. A* 79, 012323.

Rebentrost,P.; Mohseni, M.; Kassal, I.; Lloyd, S. & Aspuru-Guzik, A. (2009). Environment-assisted quantum transport, *New Journal of Physics* , 11, 033003.

Suryaprakash, N. (2000). Liquid Crystals As Solvents in NMR: Spectroscopy Current Developments in Structure Determination, *Current Organic Chemistry* 4, 85-103.

Shenvi, N.; Kempe, J. & Whaley, K. (2003). Quantum random-walk search algorithm, *Phys. Rev. A* 67, 052307.

Schmitz, H.; Matjeschk, R.; Schneider, C.; Gluechert, J.; Enderlein, M.; Huber, T. & Schaetz, T. (2009). Quantum Walk of a Trapped Ion in Phase Space, *Phys. Rev. Lett.* 103, 090504.

Schreiber, A.; Cassemiro, K. N.; Potoček, V.; Gábris, A.; Mosley, P. J.; Andersson, E.; Jex, I. & Silberhorn, C. (2010). Photons Walking the Line: A Quantum Walk with Adjustable Coin Operations, *Phys. Rev. Lett.* 104, 050502.

Tulsi, A. (2008). Faster quantum-walk algorithm for the two-dimensional spatial search, *Phys. Rev. A* 78, 012310.

Zähringer, F.; Kirchmair, G.; Gerritsma, R.; Solano, E.; Blatt, R. & Roos, C. F. (2010). Realization of a Quantum Walk with One and Two Trapped Ions, *Phys. Rev. Lett.* 104, 100503.

Part 2

Search Algorithms for Image and Video Processing

6

Balancing the Spatial and Spectral Quality of Satellite Fused Images through a Search Algorithm

Consuelo Gonzalo-Martín[1] and Mario Lillo-Saavedra[2]
[1]*Dep. de Arquitectura y Tecnología de Sistemas Informáticos, Facultad de Informática, Universidad Politécnica de Madrid, Campus de Montegancedo, Boadilla del Monte, 28660*
[2]*Dep. de Mecanización y Energía, Facultad de Ingeniería Agrícola, Universidad de Concepción*
[1]*Spain*
[2]*Chile*

1. Introduction

Image fusion can be understood as the synergetic combination of information provided from several sensors or by the same sensor in different scenarios. The decrease of redundant information, while emphasizing relevant information, not only improves image-processing performance but it also facilitates their analysis and interpretation.

In the last decade, the most used image fusion strategies were based on multi-resolution analysis techniques. Their objective was to find a discrete transform that minimizes the intrinsic uncertainty associated to the joint representation of information. From this point of view, the Discrete Wavelet Transform (DWT) can be considered as the most popular approximation Garguet-Duport et al. (1996).

The DWT is a linear transformation that is very useful in the signal processing area, where one of its principal applications consists in separating data sets into distinct frequency components, which are then represented on common scales. There are different ways of calculating the DWT, among which the most important is the pyramidal algorithm of Mallat Mallat (1989).The fusion method based on Mallat algorithm Pohl & J.L.Genderen (1998); Ranchin & Wald (2000); Zhou et al. (1998) has been one of the most widely used, since it provides fused images with a high spectral quality; however, its low anisotropic nature still produces some problems for the fusion of images with a high content of borders that are not horizontal, vertical or diagonal Candès & Donoho (2000). Dutilleux (1989) has proposed a Wavelet *à trous* (with holes) algorithm. This algorithm differs from the pyramidal ones in that it presents an isotropic nature and is redundant, which implies that between two consecutive degradation levels, there is no dyadic spatial compression of the original image; but rather the size of the image is maintained. Several works, have showed that redundant DWT provides better results in determined image processing applications such as noise elimination Malfait & Roose (1997), texture classification Unser (1995); Zou & Jiang (2010), and in the case of image fusion Chibani & Houacine (2003); Nunez et al. (1999); Yang et al. (2010).

Despite the good results provided by the DWT in the image fusion field, there are several aspects that have yet to be resolved. One aspect is the precise selection of the information extracted from each of the source images; and the control of the trade-off between the spatial and spectral quality of the fused image. Indeed, it can be affirmed that multiresolution transforms with low anisotropy are not capable of intrinsically controlling this trade-off. On the other hand, it should be noted that the multidimensional versions of these transforms are built from 1-D bases. Thus the 2-D version, for example, is capable to detect discontinuities from single points, but does not favour their integration into continuous segments. Consequently these 2-D transforms cannot detect efficiently smooth discontinuities Do & Vetterli (2001). That is one of the reasons that justifies the search of new image representations, defined by bases that match image dimensionality. The appearance of new transforms, such as Curvelets Candès & Donoho (1999a), Ridgelets Candès & Donoho (1999b) and Contourlets Do & Vetterli (2005), which improves the 2-D information representation with respect to the DWT, opens a new field of research in the image fusion algorithms area. Generally speaking, it can be affirmed that these new transforms (multiresolution-multidirectional) are based on the application of a double filter bank; the first one is for stepping from a higher to a lower resolution level. The second is a directional filter bank and it allows capturing the directional features for each one of the different resolution levels. They are highly anisotropic and produce a much more efficient extraction of spatial details in different directions, which makes them especially adequate to perform the fusion process. Different published works address this issue. Choi et al. (2005) proposed the use of the Curvelet Transform, while Qiguang & Baoshu (2006) used a Contourlet transform, to fuse satellite images recorded by a panchromatic sensor and a multispectral sensor.

In order to reduce the cost involved in a double filter bank, in Lillo-Saavedra & Gonzalo (2007) a fusion method was proposed based on a new joint MultiDirectional and MultiResolution (MDMR) image representation that uses a single Directional Low Pass Filter Bank (DLPFB) defined in the frequency domain. As shown in the present paper, this new methodology has the intrinsic capacity to control the global quality (spatial-spectral) of the fused images. This control is based on the accurate tune-up of the DLPFB. The aim of this paper is to propose a method that objectively determines the design of the DLPFB. Specifically, it proposes the optimization of an objective function (OF) based on fused image quality measures, using the Simulated Annealing (SA) search algorithm.

2. Background

2.1 A MDMR representation for image analysis and synthesis

Lillo-Saavedra & Gonzalo (2007) proposed a joint MDMR representation that combines the simplicity of the Wavelet Transform, calculated using the *à trous* algorithm (WAT), with the benefits of multidirectional transforms like Contourlet Transform (CT), using a single DLPFB. Thus, at each decomposition level (θ_n), image degradation is performed applying a directional low pass filter in the frequency domain, as shown in Equation 1.

$$\text{Image}_{\theta_n}(x,y) = FFT^{-1}\left\{FFT\left\{\text{Image}_{\theta_{n-1}}(x,y)\right\}\cdot H_{\theta_n}(u,v)\right\} \qquad (1)$$

Where θ_n is the decomposition level prior to transform application and represents the directional low pass filter transfer function, applied in level n. The directional information is extracted by the difference of the directional degraded images in two consecutive levels and is stored in the transforms coefficients at each level:

$$Coef_{\theta_n}(x,y) = \text{Image}_{\theta_n}(x,y) - \text{Image}_{\theta_{n-1}}(x,y) \quad (2)$$

From Equations (1) and (2), the original image can be exactly reconstructed by Equation (3):

$$\text{Image}(\text{x},\text{y}) = \text{Image}_{\theta_k}(x,y) + \sum_{n=1}^{k} Coef_{\theta_n}(x,y) \quad (3)$$

In other words, it adds to the corresponding image at the higher decomposition level (θ_k) all the directional coefficients, ($Coef_{\theta_n}$), in a procedure analogous to the one used in WAT.

Fig.1 illustrates graphically the joint MDMR representation.

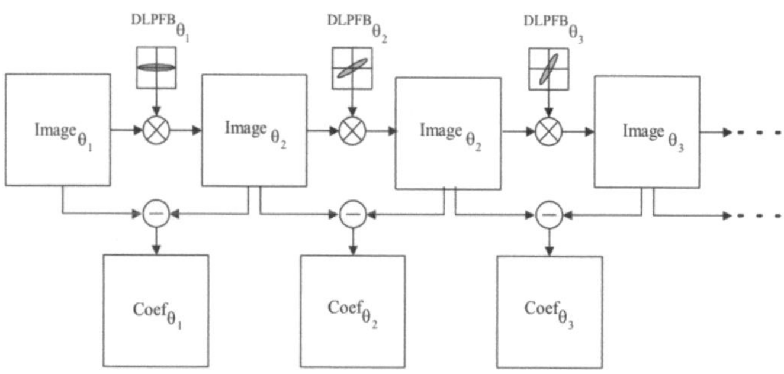

Fig. 1. Flow diagram of a MDMR image representation based on a directional low pass filter bank.

For computational reasons it is highly desirable that the directional low pass filter transfer function $H_{\theta_n}(u,v)$ could be defined as a separable function. However, Lakshmanan (2004) demonstrated that a low pass filter that is simultaneously separable and directional could not exist. But, it is possible to define a directional low pass filter as the sum of two separable filters as shown in Equation (4):

$$H_{\theta_n}(u,v) = H_1(u) \times H_2(v) - \alpha u H_1(u) \times v H_2(v) \quad (4)$$

Where α is given by the relation $(a^2 - b^2)\sin(2\theta)/(a^2 b^2)$, being θ, a and b the orientation, scale and elongation of the filter, respectively and H_1 and H_2 are defined as:

$$H_1(u) = \exp(-u^2(\frac{\cos^2\theta}{a^2} + \frac{\sin^2\theta}{b^2})) \quad (5)$$

$$H_2(v) = \exp(-v^2(\frac{\cos^2\theta}{b^2} + \frac{\sin^2\theta}{a^2})) \quad (6)$$

The most interesting characteristic of this kind of filters is not its elliptic form, but rather its directional character by which it assigns higher weights to the corresponding values in a determined direction and lower weights to its orthogonal direction. From a practical point of view, it should be also noted that the filtering results depend also strongly on the number of partitions of the frequency space (k) and the number of elements that define the filter size (m). On the other hand, given the symmetrical nature of Fourier space where the DLPFB is applied, filters must be also symmetrical.

2.2 Fusion methodology based on a MDMR representation

Similar to other fusion methods for multispectral (MULTI) and panchromatic (PAN) images, the objective of the fusion methodology investigated in this work is to coherently integrate the low frequency information from the MULTI image and the high frequency information from the PAN image, to obtain a fused image whose spatial quality would be as similar as possible to the quality of the higher resolution spatial image (PAN), while conserving the spectral characteristics of the high resolution spectral image (MULTI).
Under the previous considerations, Lillo-Saavedra & Gonzalo (2007) formalized a new images fusion methodology based on the MDMR representation described previously:

$$FUS^i(x,y) = MULTI^i_{\theta_k}(x,y) + \sum_{n=1}^{k} Coef^{PAN}_{\theta_n}(x,y) \tag{7}$$

Where $FUS^i(x,y)$ represents the i-th spectral band of the fused image, $MULTI^i_{\theta_k}(x,y)$ represents the ith band of the MULTI image degraded in k directions, and $Coef^{PAN}_{\theta_n}(x,y)$ represents the PAN image coefficients (Equation (2) and Fig.1).
The described methodology presents two relevant features: its high anisotropy and the control of the inherent compromise between spatial and spectral quality of the fused image; in particular, and as it will be showed, it is possible to obtain fused image with an equalized trade-off between both qualities. In this sense, it is important to note that the values of the filter parameters (a and b) determine the geometry of the low pass filters that conform DLPFB and therefore the information of the image that will retain the coefficients, and each of the degraded images, which is determinant of the final quality of the fused image. A sensitivity analysis of the spatial and spectral quality of the fused images against these parameters has been performed in Gonzalo & Lillo-Saavedra (2008). From this study, it was concluded that the potential of the proposed fusion methodology would be strengthened if a filter parameters tune-up method would be available.

2.3 Quality measure of fused images

In the literature, it can be found some quality indices, which measure fused images quality from different perspectives Vijayaraj et al. (2006); Wang & Bovik (2002); Zhou et al. (1998). In this chapter, the fused images quality have been measured using spectral ERGAS (Erreur Relative Globale Adimensionnelle de Synthèse, Wald (2002) and spatial ERGAS Lillo-Saavedra et al. (2005) quality indexes. The original definition of the ERGAS index was proposed by Wald (2000) through the Equation (8):

$$ERGAS_{spectral} = 100\frac{h}{l}\sqrt{\frac{1}{N_{Bands}}\sum_{i=1}^{N_{Bands}}\left(\frac{(RMSE_{spectral}(Band^i))^2}{(MULTI^i)^2}\right)} \tag{8}$$

Where h and l represent the spatial resolution of the PAN and MULTI images, respectively; N_{Bands} is the number of bands of the fused image; $MULTI^i$ is the mean radiance value of the ith band of the MULTI image. The $RMSE$ (Root Mean Square Error) is evaluated through Equation (9):

$$RMSE_{spectral}\left(Band^i\right) = \frac{1}{NP}\sqrt{\sum_{j=1}^{NP}\left(MULTI^i(j) - FUS^i(j)\right)^2} \tag{9}$$

being NP the number of pixels of the fused image. It is clear, from its definition, that low ERGAS index values represent high quality of the fused images. Although the original ERGAS index was defined as a global quality index. In Lillo-Saavedra et al. (2005), it is showed that their behaviour is rather that of a spectral quality index. It is in this sense that the Wald-ERGAS index will be called $ERGAS_{spectral}$ in this chapter. A new index was proposed Lillo-Saavedra et al. (2005) with the objective of evaluating the distance between the PAN image and the FUS image (spatial quality). This index has been named spatial ERGAS, since it is based in the same concept that the original ERGAS. In its definition, a spatial $RMSE$ has been included, which is defined as in Equation (10):

$$RMSE_{spatial}\left(Band^{i}\right) = \frac{1}{NP}\sqrt{\sum_{j=1}^{NP}\left(PAN^{i}(j) - FUS^{i}(j)\right)^{2}} \tag{10}$$

Where PAN^i is the image obtained by adjusting the histogram of the original PAN image to the histogram of the ith band of the FUS image. In this way the spectral differences between the PAN and FUS images are minimized. Therefore, replacing $RMSE_{spectral}$ by $RMSE_{spatial}$ and $MULTI^i$ by PAN^i in the Equation (8), next expression is obtained:

$$ERGAS_{spatial} = 100\frac{h}{l}\sqrt{\frac{1}{N_{Bands}}\sum_{i=1}^{N_{Bands}}\left(\frac{(RMSE_{spatial}(Band^{i}))^{2}}{(PAN^{i})^{2}}\right)} \tag{11}$$

This index is able to quantify the spatial quality of fused images by measuring the PAN and FUS image distance, in the same sense of Wald-ERGAS index, discussed above, does for spectral quality.

3. Materials and methods

3.1 Data description

In this study, two scenes registered by the panchromatic and multispectral sensors on board IKONOS and QUICKBIRD satellites, respectively, have been used. Table 1 summarizes spectral and spatial characteristics of these sensors. For both two scenes, the multispectral image size was 128x128 pixels and consequently the size of PAN images are 512x512. The IKONOS scene was recorded on March 10, 2000, and it is geographically located in the Maipo Valley, near Santiago, Chile. The QUICKBIRD scene was extracted from an image recorded on August 22, 2002, and geographically corresponds to the northwest area outside of Madrid, Spain. PAN images of these scenes are presented in Fig. 2 (a) and (d), and NGB (NearIR-Green-Blue) compositions of their corresponding MULTI images in 2 (b) and (e).

	QUICKBIRD		IKONOS	
Band	Spatial Res. (m)	Spectral Res. (μm)	Spatial Res.	Spectral Res. (μm)
B1		0.450-0.520		0.445-0.516
B2	2.44	0.520-0.600	4 m	0.506-0.595
B3		0.630-0.690		0.632-0.698
B4		0.760-0.900		0.757-0.853
PAN	0.61	0.450-0.900	1 m	0.450-0.900

Table 1. Characteristics of the multispectral and panchromatic sensors on board IKONOS and QUICKBIRD platforms

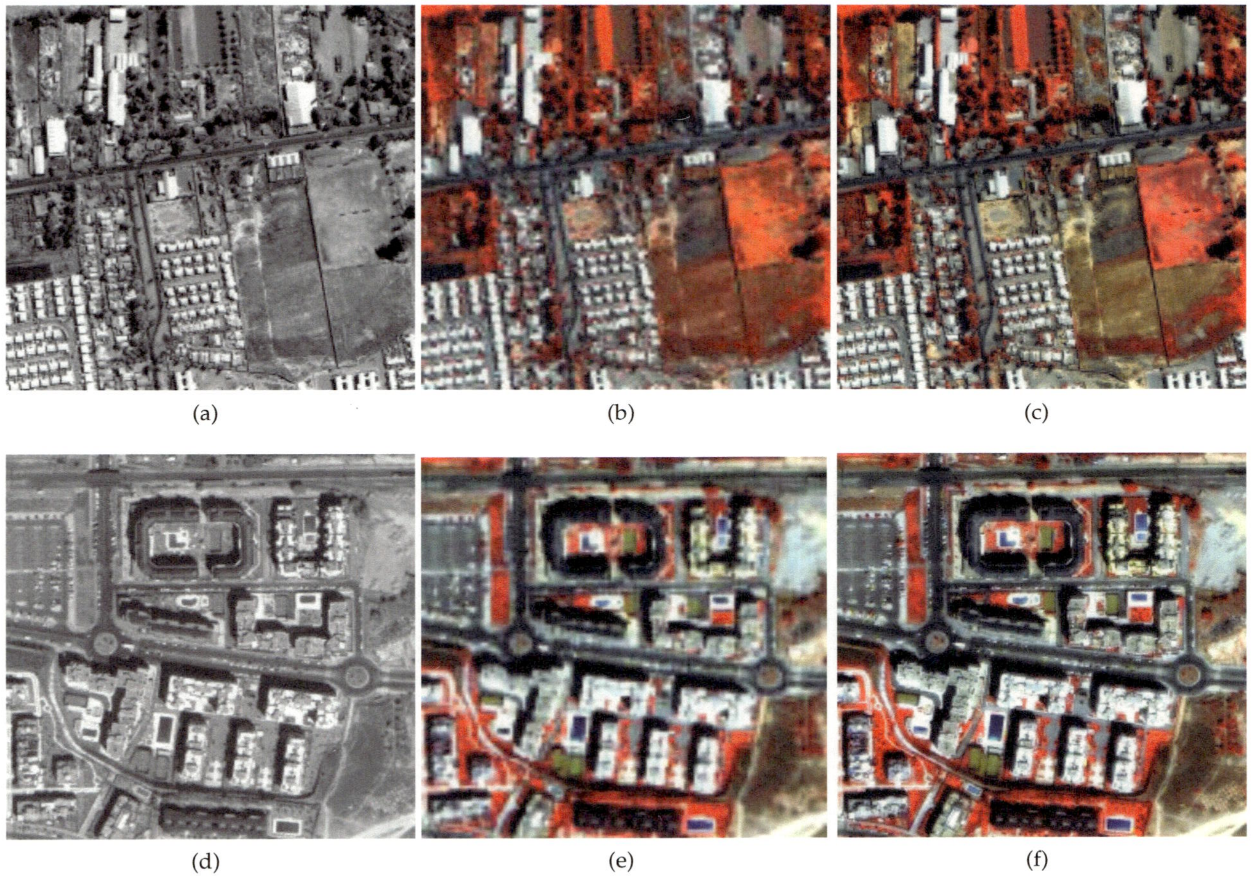

Fig. 2. Source images. First row: IKONOS scene. (a) PAN image. (b) NGB composition of MULTI image. (c) NGB composition of a FUS image. Second row: QUICKBIRD scene. (d) PAN image. (e) NGB composition of MULTI image. (f) NGB composition of a FUS image.

3.2 Search algorithm description

The search algorithm proposed in this paper is based on the SA optimization method developed by Kirkpatrick et al. (1983) and it pertains to a wide class of local search algorithms, known as Threshold Algorithms Ingber (1993). The principles of the SA optimization method is based on the physical analogy with the behavior of a set of atom nuclei, approximating to the thermodynamic equilibrium at a determined temperature, understanding a thermodynamic equilibrium as that state in which there is no energetic exchange between system components. Every time that the process iterates, the SA searches a new solution that lies in the vicinity of the actual one. Then, the difference between an objective function (OF) associated with each solution is calculated. If the difference is less than a certain threshold, then the new solution becomes the actual one and the process is repeated. In the SA algorithm is necessary a random variable that follows a certain probability function with values between 0 and infinity. The acceptance of worse solutions is governed by the following criterion:

$$rand(0,1) < e^{(OF(x_{i+1})-OF(x_i))/T} \tag{12}$$

Where T represents a parameter that receives the name of temperature and $rand(0,1)$ is a random number between 0 and 1 with an uniform probability distribution. The SA strategy begins with an initially high temperature, which provides a high probability to accept movements that worsen OF. In each iteration, the temperature is reduced, diminishing the probability of accepting worse solutions. This temperature reduction process is known as the cooling schedule and is controlled by the temperature decrease index (δ). A very small δ value implies a rapid convergence; however, this means that the search is not exhaustive, increasing the probability of getting confined at a local minimum. In contrast, with a high δ value, the search algorithm converges more slowly since it is more exploratory, increasing the probability of obtaining solutions close to the global minimum.

3.3 Definition of the OF

Even though other OFs can be defined, depending on the final fused image application, in this chapter, this function has been defined with the objective of obtaining a fused image with the spatial and spectral quality balanced. Thus the OF has been defined by the difference between spatial and spectral ERGAS indices, as formalized in Equation (13):

$$\Delta E = \left| ERGAS_{spatial} - ERGAS_{spectral} \right| \tag{13}$$

3.4 Methodology for searching filter parameters

Before carrying out a blind search for the parameters a and b using the SA algorithm, it has been considered highly recommended the study of the influence of these parameters on the indices ERGAS. For that, a high number of fused images have been generating by varying a and b from 0 to 5 and different values of k. The obtained surfaces for spatial ERGAS, spectral ERGAS and their average are represented at Fig. 3, for $k = 2^3$.

In Fig.3, it can observe that an increase in parameter values diminishes the spectral quality of fused images while increases their spatial quality and vice versa. Therefore, there is a set of a and b values that establishes a balance between spatial and spectral quality of fused images. On the other hand, it can be noted in Fig. 3 that the parameters a and b present a symmetrical behaviour with respect to the principal diagonal of the space defined by them. This symmetry has been checked for a large number of cases. As a result, this condition has been also imposed in the search space. Derived from this fact, an oriented search criterion has been established:

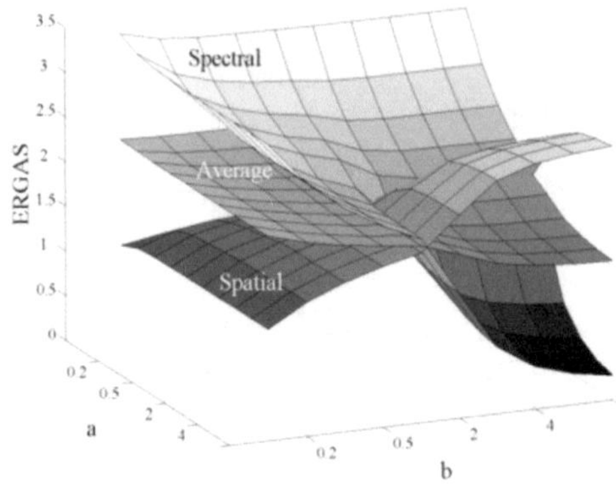

Fig. 3. Surfaces of spatial and spectral ERGAS and their average values for a fused image with $k = 2^3$

if the OF value is less than zero ($ERGAS_{spatial} < ERGAS_{spectral}$), then the spectral quality should be improved in diminishment of the spatial quality of the fused image and vice versa in the opposite case, for OF greater than zero, the spatial quality of the fused image should be increased. Introducing these considerations in the classical SA algorithm, the methodology applied for searching filter parameters can be illustrated by the flow diagram represented at Fig. 4.

As it can be saw at Fig. 4, the input to the algorithm are the two pre-processed source images: the PAN and one spectral band of the MULTI image. Then filter parameters are initialized (k, m, a_{ini} and b_{ini}) for generating an initial filter. With this first filter, a fused image (Equation 7) is obtained and an initial value of OF (Equation 13) is calculated. Next, filter parameters, a and b, should be updated according to the oriented search criterion established above. For that a and b parameters should be modified in the right direction. In this sense, the terms da and db are defined for increasing or decreasing current values of a and b as:

$$da = |\Delta E_{ini}|\, rand \tag{14}$$

$$db = |\Delta E_{ini}|\, rand \tag{15}$$

As it can observe in Equations 14 and 15, da and db take random values scaled in the ΔE_{ini} range, which decreases with the algorithm convergence.

Once the new solution ΔE_{end} is obtained from the new parameters ($a_{end} = a_{ini} \pm da$ and $b_{end} = b_{ini} \pm db$), it is compared with ΔE_{ini}, then if it is lower the new solution is accepted, in otherwise it will be accepted or discarded according to the SA acceptance criterion (Equation 12). Thus in each iteration a new fused image is obtained and a new OF solution is calculated and compared with the previous one to go to next SA iteration, after decreasing the T value through the δ parameter ($\delta < 0$).

4. Results

The methodology described above allows to determine in an objective way the a and b parameters; however, the quality of images fused using the described fusion methodology is determined also by other DLPFB parameters: filter size (m) and the number of partitions of the frequency space (k). It is noteworthy to do some considerations about these two parameters.

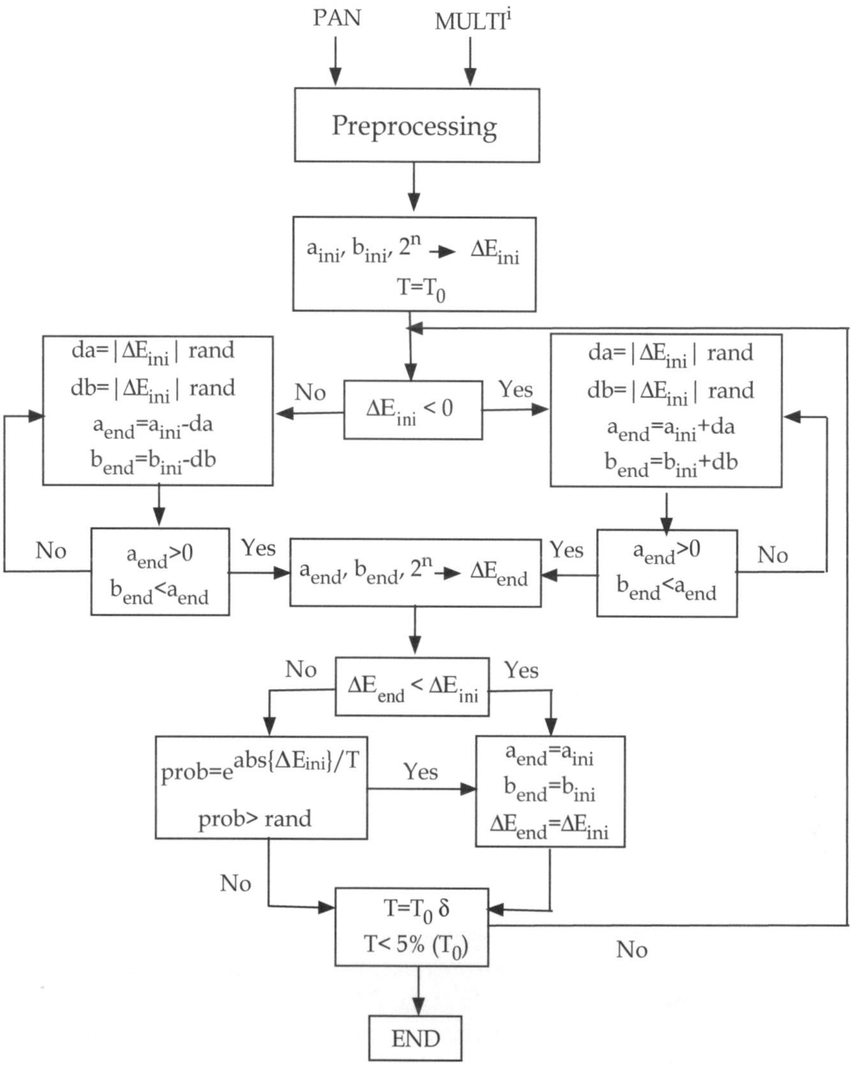

Fig. 4. Flow chart of the directed search algorithm

Experimentally, it was observed that $m = 5$ is the minimal number of samples required to define a symmetric kernel of this type of filters (Equation 4). Other kernel sizes that maintain the symmetry are $m = 11$ and $m = 21$, which present similar behaviour. However, an increase in size implies an elevated increase in computational complexity. On the other hand, empirical studies have shown that for frequency space partitions (k) varying between 2^2 and 2^6, there is a pair of values (a, b) that provides very similar spatial and spectral qualities.

Before applying the SA searching algorithm for obtaining a pair of parameter values (a and b) which provides a fused image with spatial and spectral quality balanced, for each scene, the dependence of OF on filter parameters have been investigated. For that, the two selected scenes (IKONOS and QUICKBIRD) have been fused by varying a and b (from 0 to 10), m (equal to 5, 11 and 21) and k (equal to 2^3 and 2^4). After that, objective functions have been evaluated for each set of values. Fig (5) presents a summary of OF's surfaces: the first row of

Fig. (5) corresponds to the IKONOS scene and the second row to the QUICKBIRD scene. The surfaces presented in the 1st and 2nd column correspond to the images fused with a 5-sample filter bank and a frequency space partition of 2^3 and 2^4, respectively; while the 3rd and 4th columns correspond to a 21-sample filter size with the same partitions for the frequency space. One of the most notable aspects in the surfaces shown in Fig. (5) is the presence of valleys. That means, for all analyzed cases, there is a set of pairs of parameter values, a and b, for which the objective function takes minimum values. That justifies the use of a search method based on certain rules to find the parameters that optimize the OF in few iterations.
With the goal of determining the value of the temperature decreasing factor, δ, that provides the best compromise between algorithm convergence velocity and search efficiency, in terms of fused images quality, different pairs of parameters a and b have determined through the search algorithm for δ values equal to 0.4, 0.6 and 0.8. Results indicated that δ values greater or equal to 0.8 provide the best results, since a high δ values reduce the convergence velocity, this last value has used in all experiments carried out in this study.
Different experiments have been performed, in order to analyze the convergence behaviour of the search algorithm. General speaking, it can affirm that the quality of the results obtained using the SA algorithm is independent of initial values of parameters Kirkpatrick et al. (1983). In Fig. 6, it can appreciate that for different initial MDMR filter parameter values (a_{ini} and b_{ini}), the final (ΔE) value is the same.
In order to assess the influence of the oriented search criterion proposed in this work, on the SA algorithm convergence, average values for the number of iterations required for converging have been estimated, without the search criterion and with it. Fig. 7 shows these results for the IKONOS scene. Fig. 7 (a) and 7 (b) show the evolution of ΔE, da and db without the directed search criterio and Fig. 7 (c) and 7 (d) with it. It can appreciate as the convergence is much faster when the oriented criterion is applied. It should be noted that this is a critical aspect in applications where the OF estimation implies a high computational complexity, like it is the images fusion problem.
Applying the oriented SA algorithm, for $k = 2^3$, $m = 5$ and $\delta = 0.8$, values of a and b were obtained for each scene and for each spectral band. The obtained values have summarized at Table 2. IKONOS and QUICKBIRD scenes have been fused with the parameter values included in Table 2 through the MDMR method. NGB compositions of fused images are presented in Fig.2 (c) and 2 (f), respectively. It should be noted that a visual comparison with the multispectral images (2 (b) and 2 (e)), shows a noteworthy improvement in spatial quality while maintaining spectral quality.

SCENE	B1		B2		B3		B4	
	a	b	a	b	a	b	a	b
IKONOS	0.7035	1.4081	0.8848	1.9519	0.8833	1.9199	0.8380	1.8354
QUICKBIRD	0.5670	1.7205	0.7973	1.8117	0.8240	2.0493	0.7014	1.5462

Table 2. Filter parameters determined using the oriented search algorithm

The two scenes were fused as well, using other fusion methods based on different transformations: IHS Tu et al. (2004), Wavelet-Mallat (WMT) Mallat (1989) and Wavelet-*á trous* (WAT) Nunez et al. (1999). Fig.8 presents details of two particular areas, one per scene, of original MULTI images (a) and (f), and the corresponding images fused by the four fusion methods: IHS ((b) and (g)), WMT ((c) and (h)), WAT ((d) and (i)) and MDMR((e) and (j)). A comparative visual analysis between these details indicates that the fusion methods WMT and MDMR conserve more faithfully the original images spectral content for the two scenes.

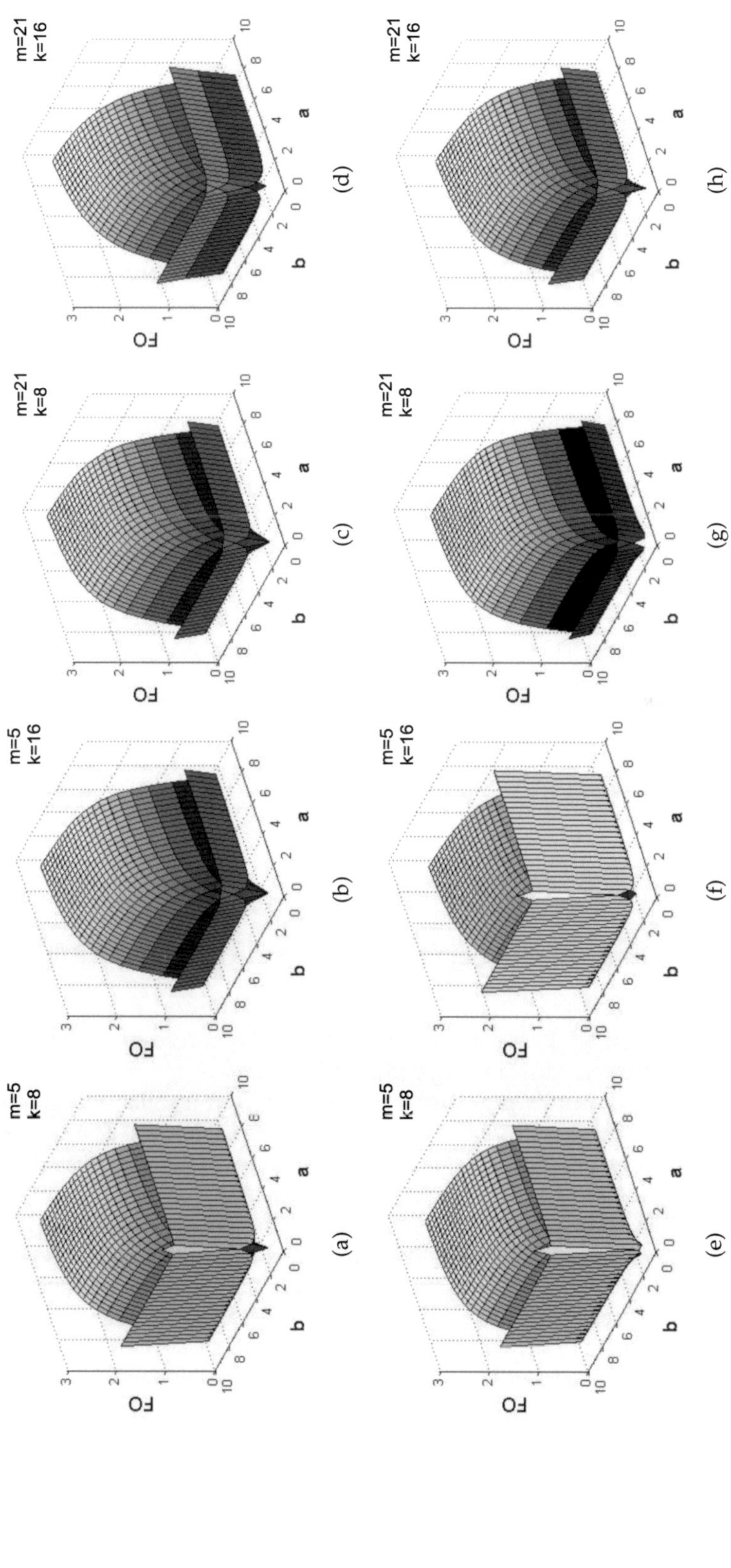

Fig. 5. OF surfaces. Row 1: IKONOS scene. Row 2: QUICKBIRD scene.

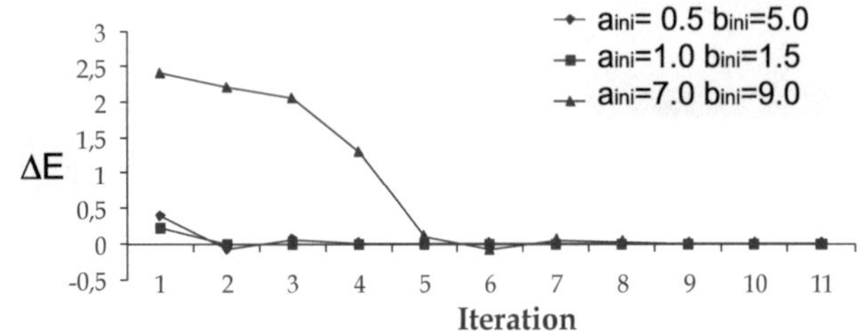

Fig. 6. Convergence of the SA search algorithm for different initial conditions of the filter bank parameters

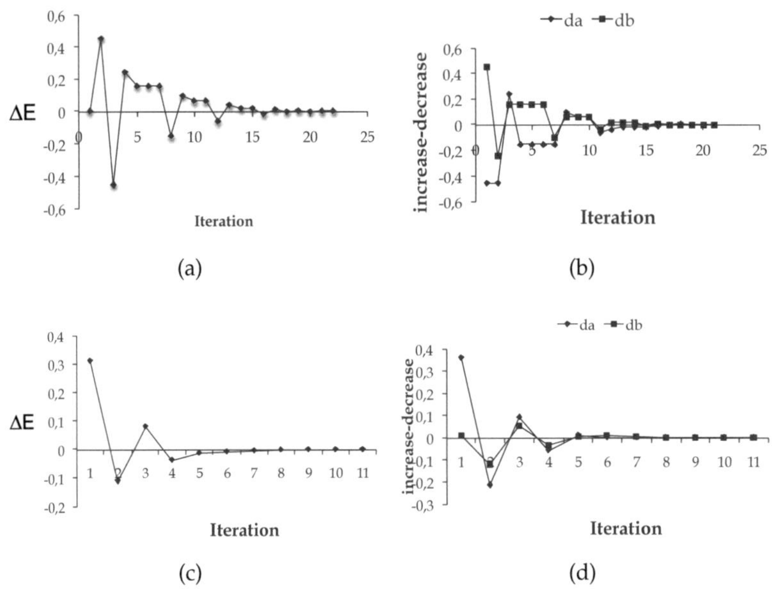

Fig. 7. Evolution of ΔE, *da* and *db* without the directed search criterio (a) and (b) and with it (c) and (d)

Moreover, the presence of artefacts that worsen spatial quality can be appreciated in Fig.8 (b), (c), (g) and (h) while they are absent in Fig.8 (d), (e), (i) and (j).

In order to quantify the results previously exposed, ERGAS (spatial and spectral) index values as well as its average and standard deviation were calculated. The two last indices represent a global quality measure and a measure of the trade-off between spatial and spectral quality, respectively. Values of indices are included in Table 3 for IKONOS scene and in 4 for QUICKBIRD scene. In these tables, it can observe that the lowest $ERGAS_{spatial}$ value, and therefore the best spatial quality, is given by the WAT method, although it does not result in a balance between spatial and spectral quality, as the value of standard deviation reflects. However, the MDMR method gives a total equilibrium between spatial and spectral quality. And additionally, this method provides fused images with the best spectral quality, since the corresponding $ERGAS_{spectral}$ values are lower than for the other methodologies.

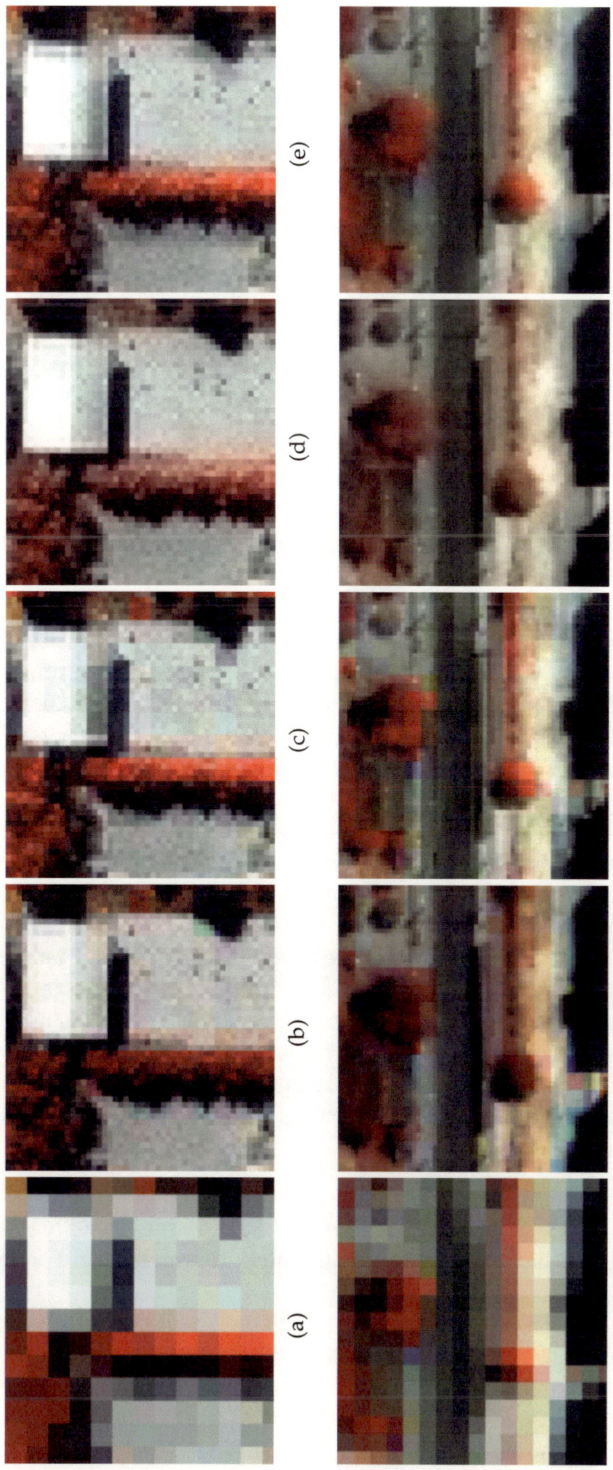

Fig. 8. Details of original MULTI images and fused images. First row: IKONOS scene. Second row: QUICKBIRD scene. Original MULTI images: (a) and (f) . Fused images: IHS method ((b) and (g)), WMT method ((c) and (h)), WAT method ((d) and (i)) and MDMR method ((e) and (j)).

FUSION METHOD	$ERGAS_{spatial}$	$ERGAS_{spectral}$	Average	St. Dev.
IHS	1.9931	2.6574	2.3252	0.6643
WMT	2.0790	2.2083	2.1436	0.1293
WAT	**1.7067**	2.3029	2.0048	0.5692
MDMR	1.9226	**1.9226**	1.9226	0.0000

Table 3. ERGAS Values for the fused IKONOS scene

FUSION METHOD	$ERGAS_{spatial}$	$ERGAS_{spectrall}$	Average	St. Dev.
IHS	1.8860	2.5938	2.2399	0.5004
WMT	2.1334	1.7731	1.9533	0.2548
WAT	**1.7079**	1.8822	1.7951	0.1233
MDMR	1.7627	**1.7627**	1.7627	0.0000

Table 4. ERGAS values for the fused QUICKBIRD scene

5. Conclusions

In this chapter, it has been proposed a search algorithm, based on the Simulating Annealing, which improves the global quality of satellite images fused through a fusion algorithm based on a joint MDMR representation.
In a first phase, the search algorithm has been implemented for carrying out an exhaustive exploration of the space defined by two parameters (elongation and scale), involved in design of the filter bank used by the fusion algorithm. The analysis of the influence of these parameters on the fused images quality has allowed establishing an oriented search criterion, which reduces significantly the number of iterations requiered for converging. This search algorithm can be applied to different functions. But, since the aim of this work is to get fused images with the spatial and spectral quality balanced, here OF has been defined as the difference of two quality indices: one spatial and one spectral.
Experimental results have proved that the convergence of the algorithm is independent on initial conditions and that the number of iterations is significatively reduced when the oriented criterion is applied.
From the qualitative and quantitative analysis of the fused images quality, it can be concluded that the MDMR fusion methodology complemented with the oriented search algorithm, which is proposed in this paper, provides fused images with a higher spectral quality than the other algorithms evaluated; and spatial quality comparable to that offered by the WAT method. Still, the most notable feature of the proposed methodology is that it provides a total balance between the two qualities, spatial and spectral, for the two kind of images used.

6. References

Candès, E. J. & Donoho, D. L. (1999a). *Curve and Surfaces*, Vanderbilt University Press., chapter Curvelets - A Surprisingly Effective Nonadaptive Representation For Objects with Edges.

Candès, E. J. & Donoho, D. L. (1999b). Ridgelets: A key to higher-dimensional intermittency?, *Philosophical Transactions of the Royal Society* 357: 2459–2509.

Candès, E. J. & Donoho, D. L. (2000). Curvelets, multiresolution representation, and scaling laws, *in* A. Aldroubi, A. Laine & M. Unser (eds), *Wavelet Applications in Signal and Image Processing VIII*, number 4119, SPIE, pp. 1–12.

Chibani, Y. & Houacine, A. (2003). Redundant versus orthogonal wavelet descomposition for multisensor image fusion, *Pattern Recognition* 36(4): 879–887.

Choi, M., Young, K. R., Nam, M. R. & Kim, H. O. (2005). Fusion of multispectral and panchromatic satellite, images using the curvelet transform, *IEEE Transactions on Geoscience and Remote Sensing Letters* 2(2): 136–140.

Do, M. N. & Vetterli, M. (2001). Pyramidal directional filter banks and curvelets, *In International Conference in Image Processing*, Vol. 3, pp. 158–161.

Do, M. N. & Vetterli, M. (2005). The contourlet transform: an efficient directional multiresolution image representation, *IEEE Transactions on Image Processing* 14(12): 2091 – 2106.

Dutilleux, P. (1989). An implementation of the algorithm à trous to compute the wavelet transform, *in* J. Combes, A. Grossmann & P. Tchanitchian (eds), *Compt-rendus du congrès ondelettes et mèthodes temps-frèquence et espace des phases*, Springer-Verlag, pp. 298–304.

Garguet-Duport, B., Girel, J., Chassery, J. & Pautou, G. (1996). The use of multiresolution analysis and wavelets transform for merging spot panchromatic and multispectral image data, *Photogrammetric Engineering and Remote Sensing* 62(9): 1057–1066.

Gonzalo, C. & Lillo-Saavedra, M. (2008). A directed search algorithm for setting the spectral-spatial quality trade-off of fused images by the wavelet à trous method, *Canadian Journal of Remote Sensing* 34(4): 367–375.

Ingber, L. (1993). Simulated annealing: practice versus theory, *Math. Comput. Modelling* 18(11): 29–57.

Kirkpatrick, S., Gelatt, C. D. & Vecchi, M. P. (1983). Optimization by simulated annealing, *Science* 4598(220): 671–680.

Lakshmanan, V. (2004). A separable filter for directional smoothing, *IEEE Transactions on Geoscience and Remote Sensing Letters* 1(3): 192–195.

Lillo-Saavedra, M. & Gonzalo, C. (2007). Multispectral images fusion by a joint multidirectional and multiresolution representation, *International Journal of Remote Sensing* 28(18): 4065–4079.

Lillo-Saavedra, M., Gonzalo, C., Arquero, A. & Martinez, E. (2005). Fusion of multispectral and panchromatic satellite sensor imagery based on tailored filtering in the fourier domain, *International Journal of Remote Sensing* 26(6): 1263–1268.

Malfait, M. & Roose, D. (1997). Wavelet-based image denoising using a markov random field a priori model, *IEEE Transactions on Image Processing* 6(4): 549–656.

Mallat, S. G. (1989). A theory for multiresolution signal decomposition: The wavelet representation, *IEEE Transactions on Pattern Analysis and Machine Intelligence* 2(7): 674–693.

Nunez, J., Otazu, X., Fors, O., Prades, A., Pala, V. & Arbiol, R. (1999). Multiresolution-based image fusion with additive wavelet decomposition, *IEEE Transactions on Geoscience and Remote Sensing* 37(3): 1024–1211.

Pohl, C. & J.L.Genderen (1998). Multisensor image fusion in remote sensing: Concepts, methods and application, *International Journal of Remote Sensing* 19(5): 823–854.

Qiguang, M. & Baoshu, W. (2006). The contourlet transform for image fusion, *in* B. V. Dasarathy (ed.), *Information Fusion: Architectures, Algorithms and Applications*, Vol. 6242, SPIE.

Ranchin, T. & Wald, L. (2000). Fusion of high spatial and spectral resolution image: The arsis concept and its implementation, *Photogrammetric Engineering and Remote Sensing* 66(1): 49–61.

Tu, T., Huang, P. S., Hung, C. & Chang, C. (2004). A fast intensity-hue-saturation fusion technique with spectral adjustment for IKONOS imagery, *IEEE Transactions on Geoscience and Remote Sensing Letter* 1(4): 309–312.

Unser, M. (1995). Texture classification and segmentation using wavelet frames, *IEEE Transactions on Image Processing* 4(11): 1549–1560.

Vijayaraj, V., O'Hara, C. G. & Younan, N. H. (2006). Quality analysis of pansharpened images, *Optical Engineering* 45(4): 88.

Wald, L. (2002). *Data Fusion: Definitions and Architectures : Fusion of Images of Different Spatial Resolutions*, Les Presses - Mines Paris.

Wang, Z. & Bovik, A. C. (2002). A universal image quality index, *IEEE Signal Processing Letters* 9(3): 81–84.

Yang, S., Wang, M., Jiao, L., Wu, R. & Wang, Z. (2010). Image fusion based on a new contourlet packet, *Information Fusion* 11(2): 78–84.

Zhou, J., Civco, D. L. & Silander, J. A. (1998). A wavelet transform method to merge landsat tm and spot panchromatic data, *International Journal of Remote Sensing* 19(4): 743–757.

Zou, H. & Jiang, J. (2010). A texture image recognition method based on the contourlet transform and biomimetic pattern recognition, *Computer Engineering and Science* 01.

7

Graph Search and its Application in Building Extraction from High Resolution Remote Sensing Imagery

Shiyong Cui[1], Qin Yan[2] and Peter Reinartz[3]
[1]*Remote Sensing Technology Institute (IMF), German Aerospace Centre (DLR)*
[2]*Chinese Academy of Surveying and Mapping*
[3]*Remote Sensing Technology Institute (IMF), German Aerospace Centre (DLR)*
[1,3]*Germany,*
[2]*China*

1. Introduction

Man-made object recognition from remotely sensed imagery is not only scientifically challenging but also of significant practical importance for spatial data acquisition and update of geographic information system databases, mapping, cartography, image interpretation, military activities and other applications, etc. In the literature, a large amount of work that has been done in the field of high resolution image understanding focuses on the development of efficient and robust algorithms to detect and extract typical man-made objects, such as buildings and roads. Most methods for building extraction can be classified into two categories: edge-driven approaches and region-driven approaches. The edge-driven approaches usually involve a procedure of bottom-up processing of image primitive features, trying to link or group the linear features corresponding to a building to obtain building boundary. In a region-driven strategy, various methods, such as artificial neural networks, support vector machines, machine learning strategies and other traditional classification schemes in pattern recognition are employed to categorize the regions derived by segmentation based on region features. The following section briefly reviews the methodologies of these two categories available in the literature.

Edge-driven methods, such as perceptual grouping and contour tracing, are widely used for building extraction in the literature. Perceptual organization (Mohan and Nevatia 1989) was used to detect and describe buildings in aerial images. There, linear features are firstly extracted and grouped into parallel lines. Parallel lines with aligned endpoints trigger the formation of a U structure. Two U structures trigger the formation of a rectangle hypothesis which is further filtered. Katartzis and Sahli (2008) proposed a method based on a stochastic image interpretation model, using a novel contour-based grouping hierarchy under the principles of perceptual organization. The BABE (Buildup Area Building Extraction) system (McKeown 1990) performed perceptual organization of lines and orthogonal corners into chains and rectangles to form building hypotheses that were further verified using shadow information. Lin and Nevatia (1998) derived the geometric relationship between building margin lines and building shadows analytically according to a general illumination model.

Zheltov et al. (2001) used the line extraction method proposed by Burns et al. (1986) and combined it with a rectangular building model to extract buildings from aerial images. Karantzalos and Paragios (2009) introduced a recognition-driven variational framework which facilitates automatic and relatively accurate multiple building extraction from aerial and satellite images.

Region-driven methods are also widely used for building extraction in the literature. Fua and Hanson (1987) first segment an image into regions, and extract edges corresponding to region boundaries, and then determine any if there was evidence of geometric structures among the edges to classify a region as a man-made object. Lee et al. (2003) proposed an approach using classification results of IKONOS multi-spectral images to provide approximate locations and shapes for candidate buildings. A fine extraction is then carried out in the corresponding panchromatic image by segmentation and squaring. Baatz and Schäpe (2000) proposed a method that combines multi-scale region segmentation with an object-oriented decision tree classifier to classify target by analysing the spectral, texture and context information. In (Matsuyama and Hwang 1985) a region segmentation method was used and the relationships between objects such as roads and houses are used to improve detection performance. Segl and Kaufmann (2001) combined supervised shape classification with unsupervised image segmentation for the detection of small buildings in suburban areas.

Although many techniques have been proposed to address the task of building detection and mapping using high resolution imagery, there are still many challenges resulting from the complexity of a scene. Most of the edge-driven approaches lack a well-founded formulation of the grouping process to derive the relationship among randomly distributed and fragmented linear features. Although many endeavors (Matsuyama and Hwang 1985, Huertas and Nevatia 1988, Venkateswar and Chellapa 1986, Mohan and Nevatia 1989, Irvin and McKeown 1989) have been made to link or group the line segments corresponding to buildings to obtain a desired building boundariy, this problem can still not be addressed robustly. Region-driven building extraction strategies, also encounter the problem of fragmentation as the region of a building may not be homogenous. There are also a number of strategies reported in the literature which combine linear feature extraction and image segmentation. These strategies offer a better solution compared to approaches that rely merely on edges or regions as the integration of complementary methods helps to overcome the drawbacks of individual methods. However, this category of methods usually can not fully utilize the complementary information of edges and regions. Therefore, most of these methods are not able to extract buildings robustly and efficiently in the presence of noise and interfering structures and it remains impossible to extract small structures.

Therefore, based on the robustness of the Hough transformation and the capabilities of graph in shape representation, we propose a robust approach for building description and extraction from high resolution remotely sensed imagery. In the literature, although there are also some graph-based approaches, most of them can not extract the exact building boundary robustly and the graph construction procedures are usually complex. Jaynes et al. (1994) proposed a method to represent feature relationships by a weighted feature relation graph. However, the construction of this relation graph requires a complex grouping strategy. Kim and Muller (1999) utilized a graph to describe the relationship of the lines, followed by the extraction of the cheapest cost in a function. Yet, their graph construction is still based on a complex grouping process. Croitoru and Doytsher (2004) used a graph approach to express building structures. A search algorithm is used to extract node sequences corresponding to a building model. However, as a model based approach, it is restricted to certain types of buildings. Sirmaçek and Ünsalan (2009) employed a scale invariant feature transformation (SIFT) and graph theoretical tools, which may fail in dense urban areas and is also restricted by building models.

2. Methodology

In practice, most building roofs in urban areas and industrial centers are rectangular or combinations of several rectangles. Therefore the extracted building polygon should be dominated by rectangles. In this sense, Hough transformation is an efficient strategy to extract perpendicular and parallel lines which comprise the structure of a building. To be more efficient and robust, the extraction scheme should incorporate region information of the building since the integration of edges and regions provides complementary information. Therefore, we propose the scheme demonstrated in Fig.1 to address the problem of building extraction with four main steps as described below.

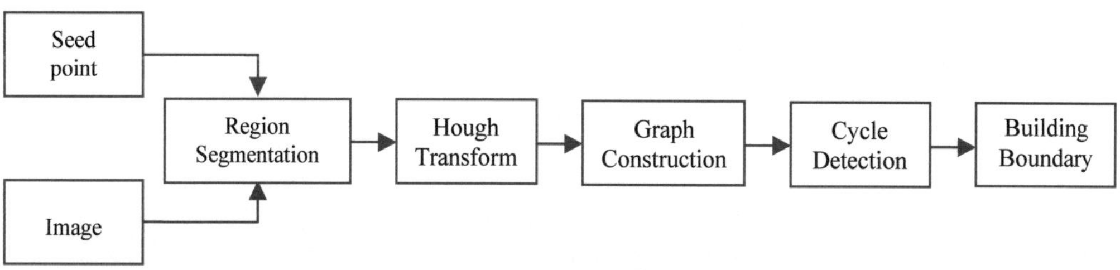

Fig. 1. Extraction workflow

2.1 Building region segmentation

In the first step, a region growing method is employed to derive the approximate building region due to its simplicity and low computational complexity, but could be replaced by other sophisticated image segmentation algorithms at a local neighborhood as used in the first experiment, such as mean shift image segmentation (Comaniciu and Meer 2002). For region growing segmentation, the user has to determine the building manually by selecting the position of the building in the image, and define a threshold used for the stop criterion. After derivation of the building region, edge detection or contour tracing is applied to get the approximate outline, which is usually needed as the input for the following Hough transformation.

2.2 Parallel and perpendicular line detection by hough transformation

The commonly used methods for straight lines extraction are based on various edge detection techniques followed by a chain code extraction process, such as the Douglas-Peuker algorithm (Douglas and Peuker 1973). Then the chain codes are segmented into line segments. Although such algorithms are straightforward for line extraction, they are of low robustness in the presence of noise or occlusions which are common in remotely sensed imagery.

To retrieve the parallel and perpendicular lines corresponding to a building efficiently, the Hough transformation provides a robust solution especially in the presence of noise. Straight line candidates are identified as local maxima in a parameter space derived by transforming each pixel in the image into a parameter space according to the following formula

$$x = \rho\cos\theta, y = \rho\sin\theta \tag{1}$$

where x and $\rho \geq 0$ are the coordinates of the pixels in image space. After transforming, each straight line parameterized by (θ, ρ) in the image space is associated with a point (θ, ρ) in the parameter space, where $\rho \geq 0$ is the distance between the line and the origin and θ $\theta \in [0, 2\pi)$ [0, 2π) is the angle of the line as can be seen in figure 2(a). Pixels lying on the same straight line in the image space correspond to curves through a common point in the parameter space. Similarly, points lying on the same curve in the parameter space correspond to lines through the same pixel in the image space. Consequently, peaks corresponding to parallel lines in the image space align vertically in the parameter space, and the distance along the horizontal axis in the parameter space between peaks corresponding to perpendicular lines in the image space is about $\pi/2$, as can be seen from figure 2(b) and figure 2(c). Parallel lines in the image space can be detected by retrieval of all the peaks with the same θ and simultaneously surpassing a threshold value which is about 30% of the maximum value in the parameter space. Lines which are perpendicular to a set of parallel lines can also be detected in the same way along the column with the horizontal coordinate $\theta_2 = \theta_1 \pm \pi/2$, where θ1 represents horizontal coordinate of these parallel lines and θ_2 is the horizontal coordinate of the lines to be detected.

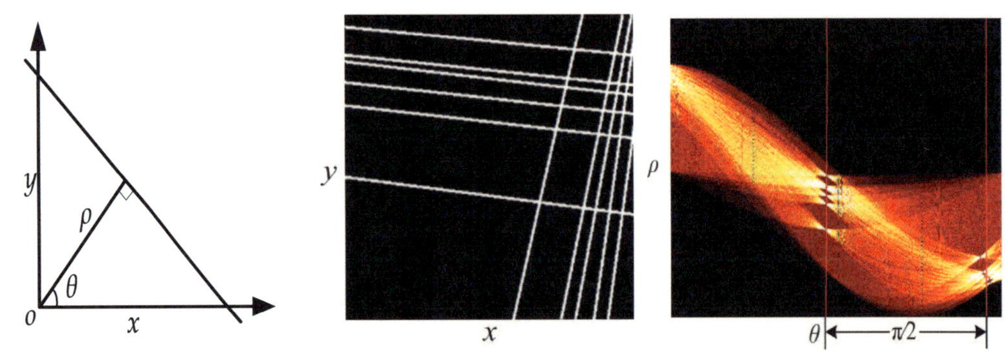

Fig. 2. Hough transformation: (a) Straight line representation in image space; (b) Test image with straight lines; (c) Parameter space, the distance between the two red lines is $\pi/2$, the horizontal coordinates of the two red lines are θ_1 and θ_2 respectively.

2.3 Construction of a building structural graph construction

The structure of a building can be intuitively represented by an undirected graph, the vertices of which represent a building corner, while the edges of the graph represent building edges connecting two corners. If all the intersections of the dominant line sets comprising the building outline are used to create an undirected graph, it will become expensive. To reduce the computational complexity, we have to eliminate certain edges which are not related to the building. It is reasonable to assume that there should be certainly a difference in the grey values between the two sides of the building edges. The average grey value of pixels within two rectangles on both sides of an edge is used to remove false edges. If the difference of the average grey value is smaller than a predefined threshold, the edge can be safely removed. According to this criterion, irrelevant edges will be eliminated. After the filtering of irrelevant edges, the remaining edges are used to construct the building structural graph.

2.4 Cycle detection

Based on the building structural graph, cycle detection is needed to derive the desired cycle corresponding to the building polygon. In the literature, the most widely used method is the backtrack algorithm. However, this category of backtrack algorithm may not be suitable for an undirected graph. We therefore adopted an effective scheme which is preferable for an undirected graph and composed of the following three steps.

Step 1. Detect a spanning tree of the graph. One approach is to initially remove all edges of the graph. Then each edge of the graph is incrementally put back to the graph. If the graph contains cycles after the return of an edge, the edge is assumed to be a chord which is defined as an edge connecting two not-adjacent nodes in a cycle. In this way, all the chords of the graph can be derived. It is worth noting that the result depends on the initial spanning tree and therefore may not be unique..

Step 2. Find fundamental cycles of the graph. Each chord derived in the previous step is associated with a fundamental cycle. If there are k chords, there will be k fundamental cycles. Each cycle contains a chord which does not exist in all the other k-1 cycles. These cycles constitute a series of fundamental cycles.

Step 3. List all the feasible unions of the fundamental cycles. All the feasible combinations of 1, 2 ... k-1 fundamental cycles are enumerated. There may be certain cases where the closed path is composed of two or more cycles. For a graph, the maximum number of cycles and chords is $G(V,E),|V|=n,|E|=e$, where n and e are the numbers of edges and vertices respectively. Accordingly, there will be $C_k^1+C_k^2+\cdots+C_k^k=2^k-1$ feasible combinations of all the cycles at most. After cycle detection, areas of all polygons corresponding to cycles are computed. The polygon with maximum area is selected as the building boundary.

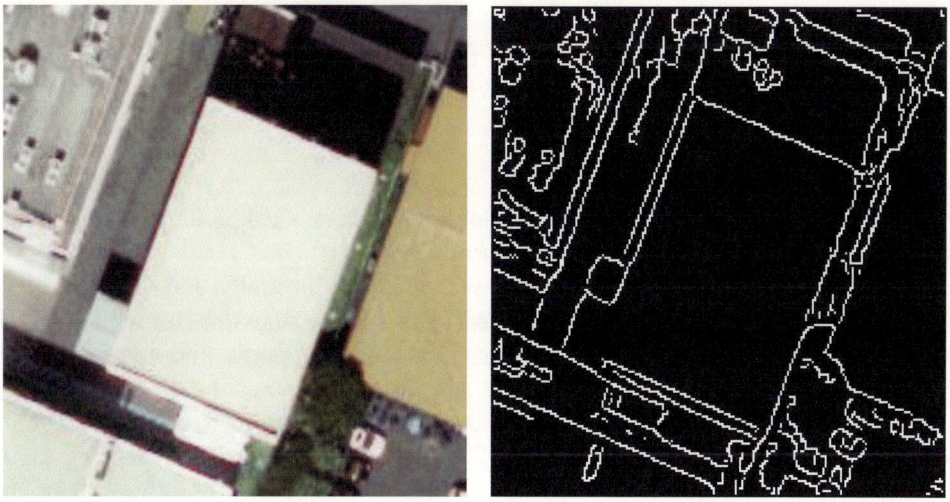

(a) (b)

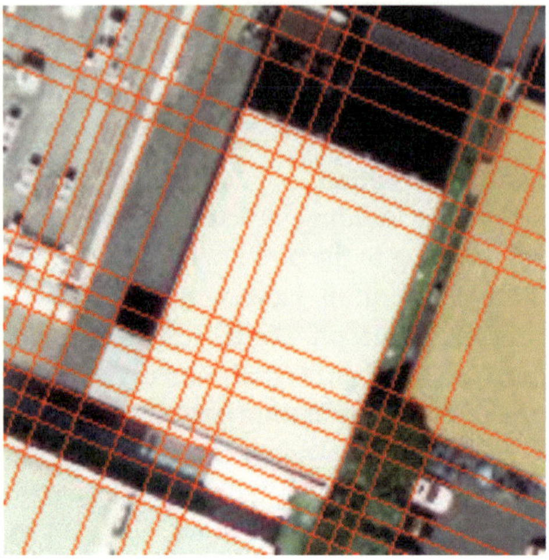

(c) (d)

Fig. 3. Comparison of line extraction results: (a) Original image; (b) Edges detected by Canny detector; (c) Straight lines extracted by chain code splitting; (d) Straight lines extracted by Hough transformation.

3. Experiments and discussion

Three experiments were carried out in the following section in a Microsoft Visual C++ 6.0 environment to validate the proposed approach using real world imagery acquired by a Leica ADS40 digital sensor in the north part of Chiba in Japan with a ground sampling distance of 0.2 meter. In that region, most buildings are flat and rectangular. The first experiment was carried out on a simple subset of this large image to demonstrate our approach and the second deals with a more complex subset. Red, green, blue bands are used as a color image in the subsequent experiments. The third experiment was carried out to evaluate the ability to extract small building structures. In the first experiment, the region segmentation of a building is achieved by mean shift image segmentation. In the second and the third experiment, the user needs to pick a seed pixel within the building, and the scheme is then carried out automatically.

3.1 First experiment

The test image shown in Fig. 3(*a*) has dimensions of 203 pixels × 198 pixels. This simple scene comprises one salient building with two subordinate wings.

The two line extraction schemes described in section 2.2 are illustrated and compared in Fig. 3. The edges shown in Fig. 3 (b) were detected by the Canny edge detector with a variance of 0.4 for the Gaussian filter. After linking of all the edge pixels into edge chains, the Douglas-Peuker algorithm with threshold of 2.5 was applied to split each chain code into approximately straight line segments followed by least square fitting to obtain straight lines shown in Fig. 3(c). The straight lines in Fig. 3(d) were detected by applying Hough transformation to the edge map in Fig. 3(b). As can be seen from the resulting straight lines, the lines extracted by the Hough transformation are much better than those extracted by the

Douglas-Peuker algorithm as there are too many spurious short line segments which not only raise computational complexity but also decrease the efficiency. However, there are still many irrelevant straight lines not corresponding to any building edges, which is the main reason to incorporate the region information as described in section 2.1.

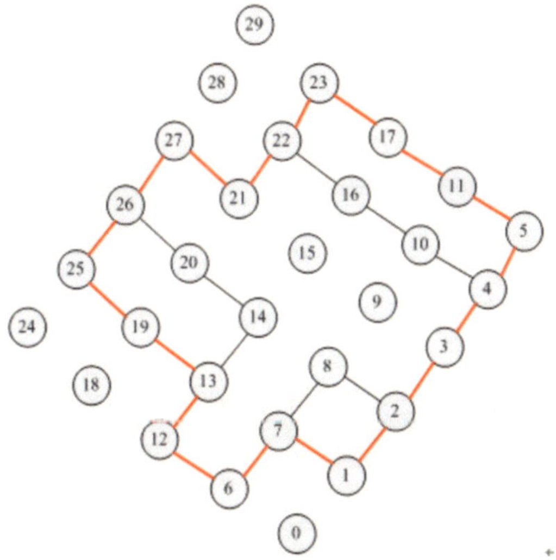

Fig. 4. Building structural graph.

To incorporate region information, image segmentation based on mean shift is applied to discriminate the building region. In this step, the building region may be segmented into different parts as a result of inhomogeneous conditions. Thus, a region merging based on grey value discrepancy is necessary when dealing with a complex scene. The result of segmentation is shown in Fig.5 (a). After segmentation, Hough transformation is applied to the boundary map of the building region to derive the straight lines corresponding to the building. As can be seen in Fig.5 (b), the resulting straight lines are much better than those in Fig. 3(d).

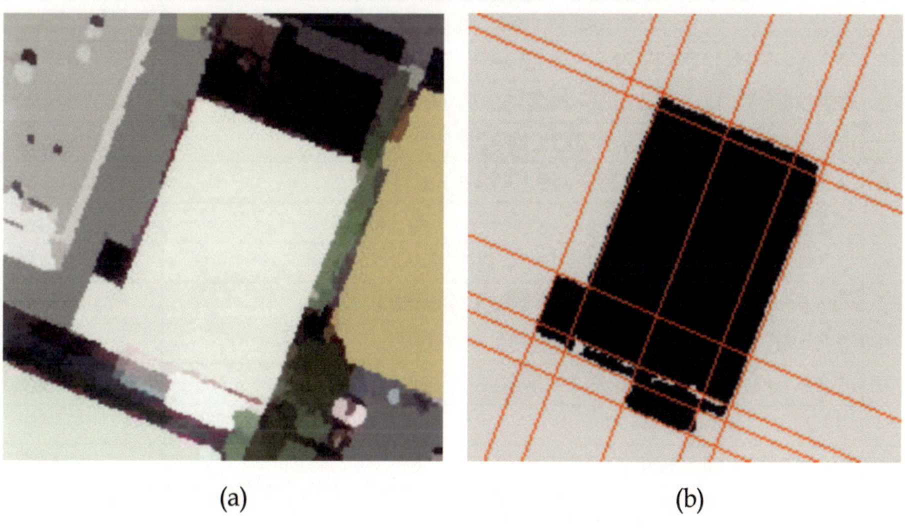

(a) (b)

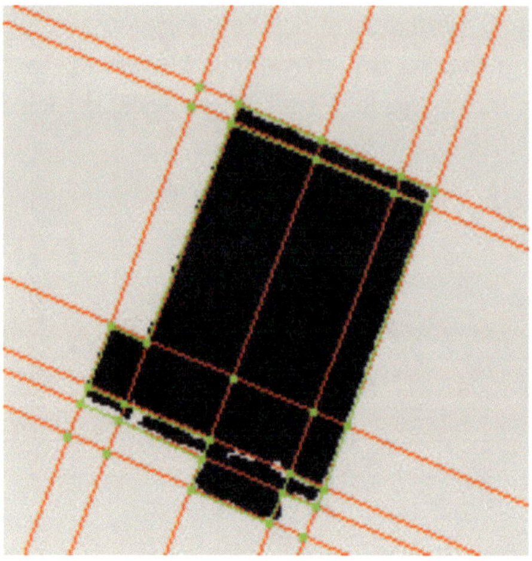

(c)

(d)

Fig. 5. (a) Segmented image using a mean shift segmentation algorithm; (b) Lines extracted using Hough transformation; (c) Green line segments are related with a building; (d) Extraction result.

To construct a building structural graph, spurious line segments which are irrelevant to any building edges have to be removed by comparing the average grey value of pixels inside two rectangles on both sides of each line segment. If the difference of the average grey value is smaller than a threshold, the edge can be safely removed. In this step, the threshold being used is 10. The width of the two rectangles perpendicular to the corresponding line segments and the threshold value are important as they determine the complexity of the graph and whether there are cycles in the graph. The remaining line segments after the removal of spurious line segments are shown and marked in green in Fig. 5(c). With these remaining line segments, a building structural graph is constructed and shown in Fig.4. The cycle marked in red in Fig.4 is the desired one and corresponds to the building outline. After

ID	Sequential vertices of each cycle	Area (m2)
1	1 2 3 4 5 11 17 23 22 21 27 26 20 14 13 12 6 7 1	10612.76
2	1 2 3 4 5 11 17 23 22 21 27 26 25 19 13 12 6 7 1	11022.41
3	1 2 3 4 10 16 22 21 27 26 20 14 13 12 6 7 1	10036.44
4	1 2 3 4 10 16 22 21 27 26 25 19 13 12 6 7 1	10446.09
5	1 2 8 7 1	112.45
6	2 3 4 5 11 17 23 22 21 27 26 20 14 13 12 6 7 8 2	10500.31
7	2 3 4 5 11 17 23 22 21 27 26 25 19 13 12 6 7 8 2	10909.96
8	2 3 4 10 16 22 21 27 26 20 14 13 12 6 7 8 2	9923.99
9	2 3 4 10 16 22 21 27 26 25 19 13 12 6 7 8 2	10333.64
10	22 23 17 11 5 4 10 16 22	576.32
11	26 25 19 13 14 20 26	409.65

Table 1. Cycles in the graph and area of each cycle

cycle detection, all the cycles contained in the building structural graph are retrieved and the sequential vertices of each cycle are listed in table 1. The cycle with maximum area was selected as the final building outline and is shown in Fig. 5(d).

3.2 Second experiment

To further test this method on buildings with complex shapes, another experiment was performed on the color image shown in Fig.6 (*a*). It has dimensions of 428 pixels × 536 pixels. The geographical location of this subset is about 35°41'05.70″ N and 140°05'33.10″ E. In this scene, there are two buildings with complex shapes which increase the difficulty of extraction.

(a) (b)

Fig. 6. Polygon approximation: (a) Experimental image subset containing six buildings; (b) Boundary derived by traditional polygon approximation.

From the results shown in Fig.6, we can see that the approximate shapes of the buildings have been identified by the region growing algorithm. Yet, the boundaries of these regions are severely fragmented. After polygon approximation illustrated in Fig. 6(b), the boundary is irregular and is not composed of straight line segments. Therefore, the Hough transformation is especially useful in such cases because it can extract straight lines even if the boundary is severely fragmented. This can be verified by the results shown in Fig. 6 and the red lines in Fig.7 are the dominant lines of the buildings, while the green line segments are the remaining lines after line filtering, which are then used to construct the structural graphs shown in Fig.8. The following step is to detect all cycles contained in the graph. The red cycles with maximum area are the final building boundaries. The sequential nodes of all cycles detected in each graph are listed in table 2. The final extraction results and some other experimental results are shown in Fig.9.

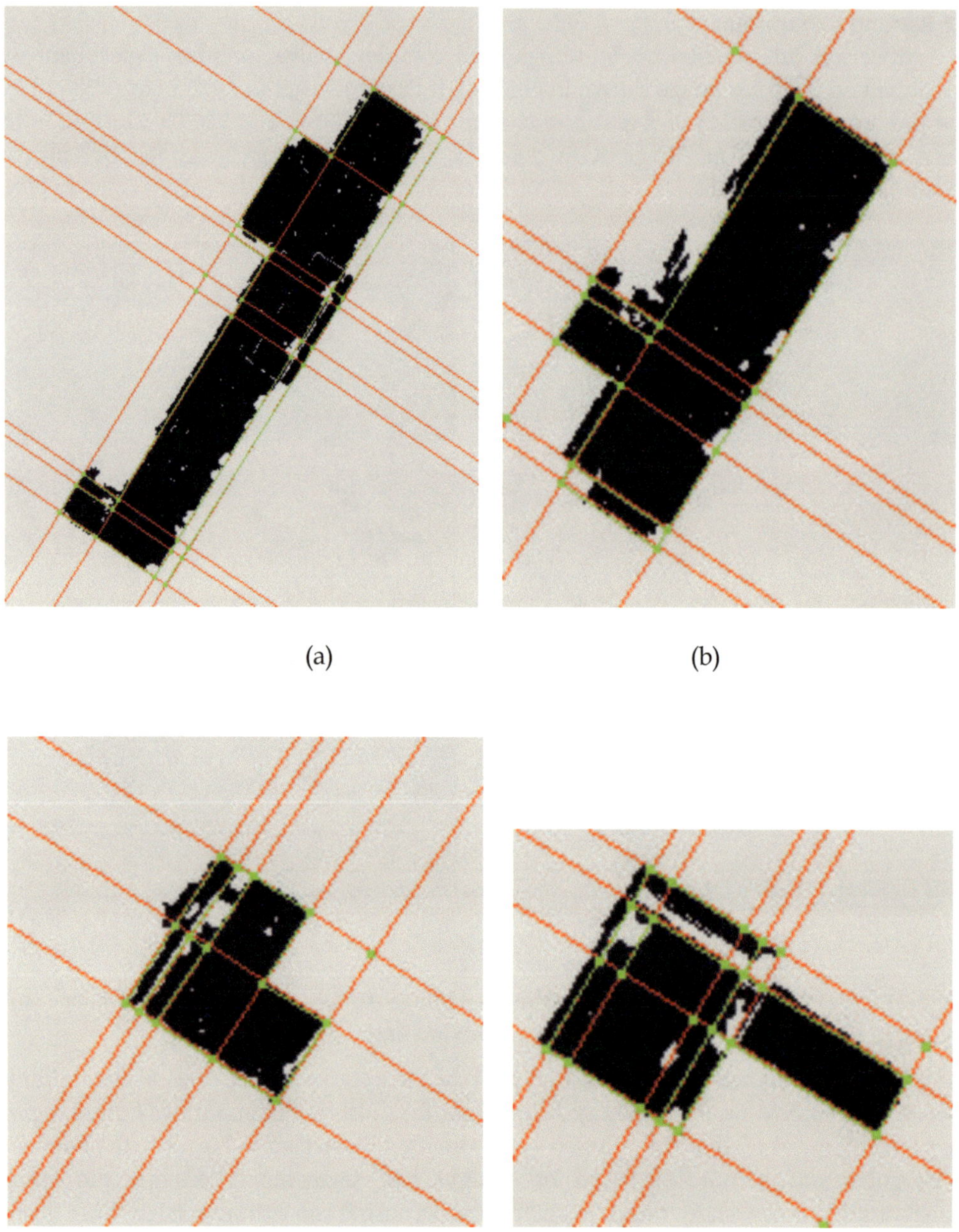

Fig. 7. Line sets of buildings A-D attained by Hough transformation.

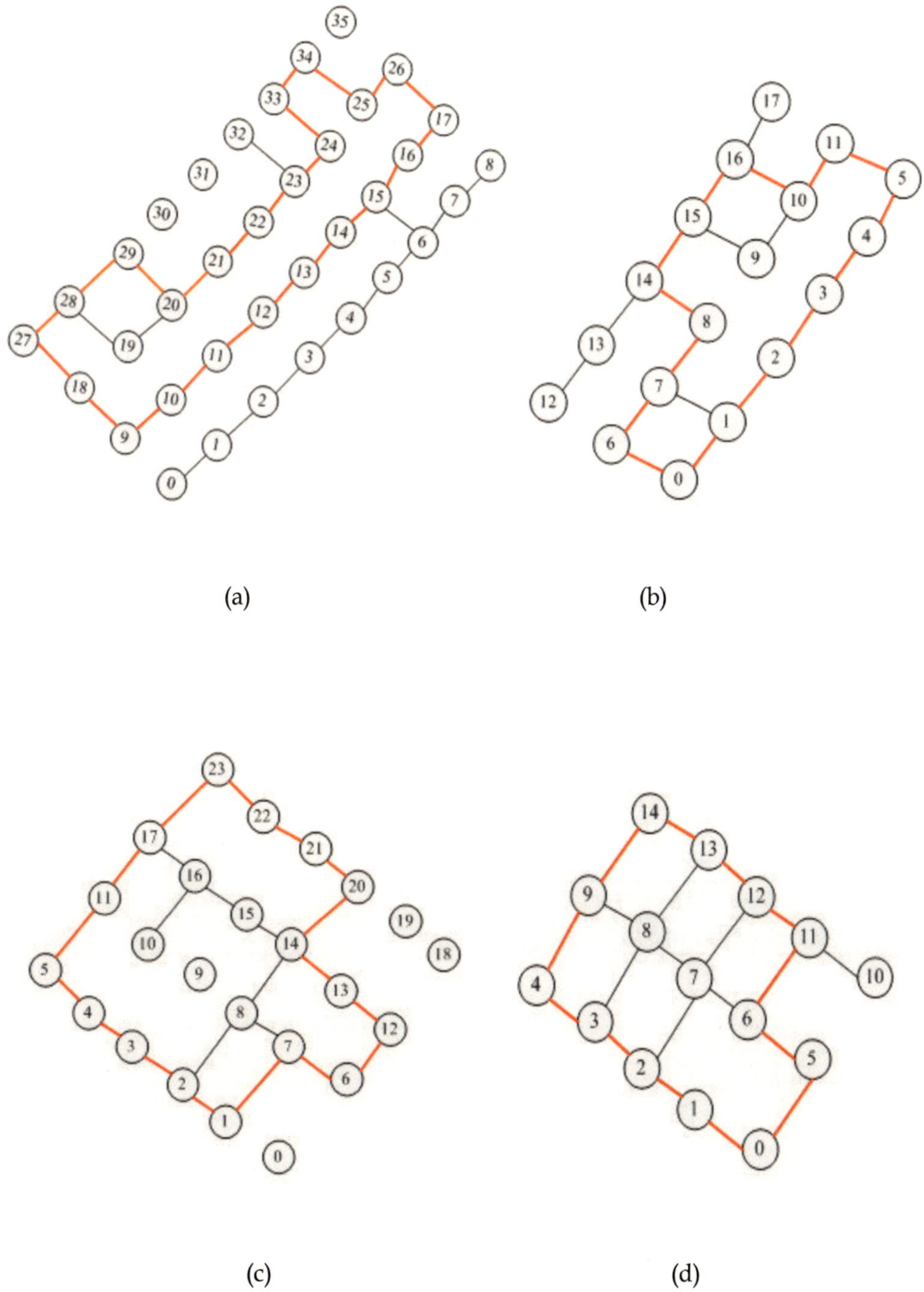

Fig. 8. Building structural graphs: (a) Building A; (b) Building B; (c) Building C; (d) Building D.

Graph	Sequential vertices of each cycles	Area (m^2)
A	20 29 28 19 20	224.60
	24 33 34 25 26 17 16 15 14 13 12 11 10 9 18 27 28 19 20 21 22 23 24	17885.71
	24 33 34 25 26 17 16 15 14 13 12 11 10 9 18 27 28 29 20 21 22 23 24	*18110.31*
B	0 1 2 3 4 5 11 10 16 15 14 8 7 6 0	*8268.05*
	0 1 7 6 0	352.94
	1 2 3 4 5 11 10 16 15 14 8 7 1	7915.11
	10 16 15 9 10	210.56
	15 9 10 11 5 4 3 2 1 0 6 7 8 14 15	8057.49
	15 9 10 11 5 4 3 2 1 7 8 14 15	7704.55
C	1 2 3 4 5 11 17 16 15 14 8 7 1	2414.44
	1 2 3 4 5 11 17 16 15 14 13 12 6 7 1	3657.76
	1 2 3 4 5 11 17 23 22 21 20 14 8 7 1	2919.79
	1 2 3 4 5 11 17 23 22 21 20 14 13 12 6 7 1	*4163.11*
	1 2 8 7 1	224.60
	2 3 4 5 11 17 16 15 14 8 2	2189.84
	2 3 4 5 11 17 16 15 14 13 12 6 7 8 2	3433.16
	2 3 4 5 11 17 23 22 21 20 14 8 2	2695.19
	2 3 4 5 11 17 23 22 21 20 14 13 12 6 7 8 2	3938.51
	6 12 13 14 8 2 1 7 6	1467.92
	6 12 13 14 8 7 6	1243.32
	17 23 22 21 20 14 13 12 6 7 1 2 8 14 15 16 17	1973.26
	17 23 22 21 20 14 13 12 6 7 8 14 15 16 17	1748.66
	17 23 22 21 20 14 15 16 17	505.35
D	0 1 2 3 4 9 14 13 12 11 6 5 0	*3293.79*
	0 1 2 7 8 3 4 9 14 13 12 11 6 5 0	3062.17
	2 7 12 11 6 5 0 1 2	2409.43
	3 8 7 2 3	231.62
	4 9 14 13 8 3 4	442.18
	4 9 14 13 8 7 2 3 4	673.80
	7 12 11 6 5 0 1 2 3 8 7	2641.04
	12 13 8 3 2 7 12	442.18
	12 13 8 7 12	210.56
	12 13 14 9 4 3 2 7 12	884.36
	12 13 14 9 4 3 8 7 12	652.74
	13 8 3 2 1 0 5 6 11 12 13	2851.61
	13 8 7 2 1 0 5 6 11 12 13	2619.99
	13 8 7 12 11 6 5 0 1 2 3 4 9 14 13	3083.22

Table 2. Cycles in each graph and area of each cycle.

Fig. 9. Final extraction result

3.3 Third experiment

To further test this method on buildings with complex shapes, another experiment was performed on the color image shown in Fig.10 (*a*). It has dimensions of 428 pixels × 536 pixels.

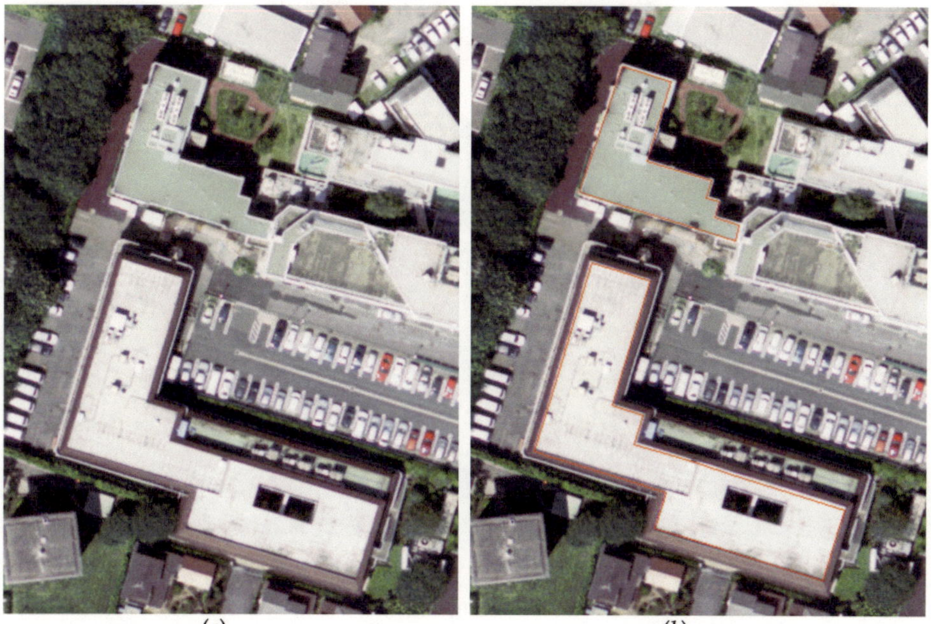

(*a*) (*b*)

Fig. 10. Polygon approximation: (*a*) Original test image with complex buildings; (*b*) Extraction results.

The geographical location of this subset is about 35°41'05.70″ N and 140°05'33.10″ E. In this scene, there are two buildings with complex shapes which increase the difficulty of extraction. Following the proposed procedure, the first step is to use region growing algorithm with a stopping threshold of 5 to identity the approximate shape of the building. Then Hough transformation is applied to detect parallel and perpendicular lines followed by graph construction. The resulting building structure graphs are shown in Fig.11. The first graph is complex because there are numerous small structures within the building. The red cycles with maximum areas are the desired cycles corresponding to building outlines. Based on the retrieved cycles, the final building outlines are extracted and shown in Fig.10 (*b*).

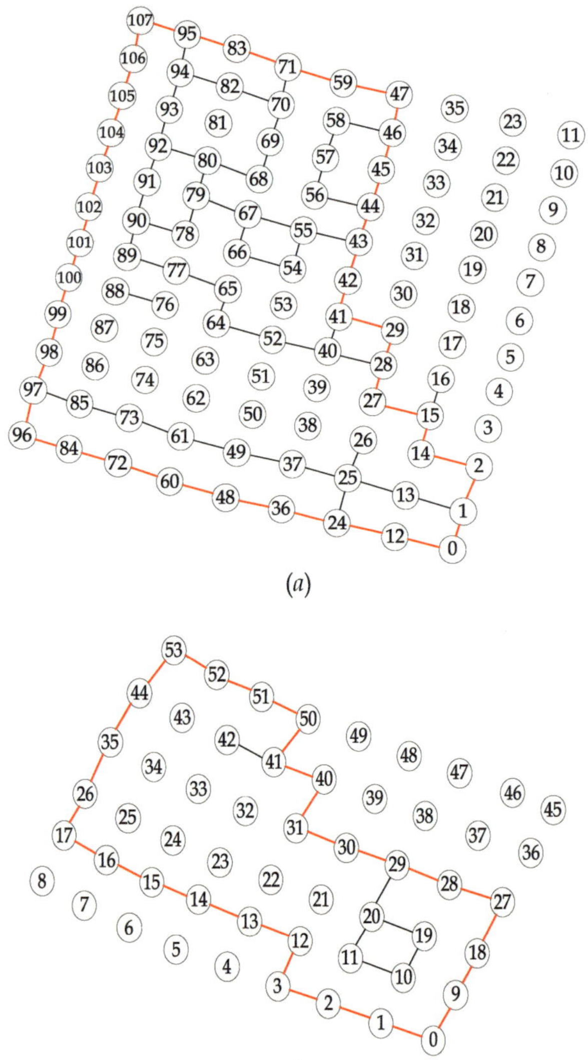

(*a*)

(*b*)

Fig. 11. Building structural graphs from figure 5: (*a*) Upper building; (*b*) Lower building.

3.3 Discussion

In the extraction process, two crucial steps, region growing and Hough transformation, determine directly the graph complexity and tell us whether the resulting graph contains cycles. The region growing method is carried out in RGB (red, green, blue) space because of its simplicity; it can be substituted with image segmentation in a local neighborhood. Another key point is that the Hough transformation is sensitive to the threshold and the width of the rectangle being used in the identification of the building related line segments. The threshold determines the number of lines in the two line sets. This parameter can be adjusted to extract short lines which are critical to extract small and complex structures, as can be seen in Fig.10 and Fig. 12. The small and complex structures in Fig. 10 and Fig. 12 are difficult to extract by traditional methods.

The computational complexity of this strategy depends on building region segmentation, graph construction and cycle detection. As our region growing is carried out over in a local neighborhood, it has low computational complexity, even when the image is very large. If image segmentation is used to identify the building region, we propose to apply segmentation within a local neighborhood around the building. The complexity of the graph construction is determined by the number of lines extracted by the Hough transformation. Most buildings are not extremely complex. Accordingly, the number of lines corresponding to a building is usually small. In the case of a complex structural graph, the cycle detection process may become time-consuming as the total number cycles in a planar graph can even be exponential in the number of vertices. In most cases, the search process takes one to two seconds on a PC equipped with an Intel Core2Dual processor with 2.0 GHz.

(a) (b)

Fig. 12. More results: (a) Small structures can be extracted; (b) Complex shape can also be extracted

4. Conclusion

In this chapter, we presented a simple but efficient and robust approach to address the task of building description and extraction. The experimental results confirm the effectiveness of this proposed approach, especially for flat rectangular building roofs.

Several advantages in this scheme have been confirmed. Firstly, it combines the robustness of the Hough transform with a graph search algorithm. Therefore, it improves the quality of line extraction and avoids a complex feature grouping process and boundary approximation. Secondly, this approach is not restricted by the shape of the building as long as the building is composed of orthogonal corners (and can be extended to nonrectangular buildings) and the extracted boundaries are regular as the shape of the building is derived by the graph search algorithm. If the boundary is curved, as shown in Fig. 6(b), the building polygon can not be used in subsequent applications. Finally, small building structures can also be extracted robustly, as shown in Fig. 10 and Fig. 12.

However, there are still some limitations to this approach which need to be improved in future research. The key step of this proposed method is the identification of building regions, for which region growing and mean shift segmentation were adopted in our case. Nevertheless, in the presence of noise, this step may fail; the following steps will not be able to extract the exact shape of the building. We consider that this step may be substituted with a clustering technique or accurate segmentation and this approach will be extended to nonrectangular building. Another drawback of this method may be that shadow is not considered. These two drawbacks will be overcome in future research.

5. Acknowledgements

The author is grateful to his colleagues, Gottfried Schwarz and Prof. Mihai Datcu, in German Aerospace Center (DLR) for their constructive comments and suggestions in writing this chapter.

6. References

Baatz, M. & Schäpe, A. (2000). Multiresolution segmentation – an optimization approach for high quality multi-scale image segmentation. *In Angewandte Geographische Informationsverarbeitung*, Strobl, A., Blaschke, T., and Greisebener, G., (Ed.), pp. 12-23. (Heidelberg: Wichmann-Verlag).

Burns, J.B.; Hanson, A.R. & Riseman, E.M. (1986). Extracting straight lines. *IEEE Transactions on Pattern Analysis and Machine Intelligence*, Vol. 8, No. 4, pp. 425-455.

Comaniciu, D. and Meer, P. (2002). Mean shift: a robust approach toward feature space analysis. *IEEE Transactions on Pattern Analysis and Machine Intelligence*, Vol. 24, No. 5, pp. 603-619.

Croitoru, A. & Doytsher, Y. (2004). Right-angle rooftop polygon extraction in regularized urban areas: cutting the corners. *The Photogrammetric Record*, Vol. 19, No. 108, pp. 311-411.

Douglas, D. & Peuker, T. 1973, Algorithms for the reduction of the number of points required to represent a digitized line or its caricature. *The Canadian Cartographer*, Vol. 10, No. 2, pp: 112-122.

Duda, R.O. & Hart, P.E. (1972). Use of the Hough transformation to detect lines and curves in pictures. *Communications of the ACM*, Vol. 15, No.1, pp. 11-15.

Fua, P. & Hanson, A.J. (1987) Using generic geometric models for intelligent shape extraction. In Proc DARPA Image Understanding Workshop, February 1987, Los Angeles, California.

Huertas, A. and Nevatia, R. (1988). Detecting buildings in aerial images. *Computer Vision, Graphics, and Image Processing*, Vol. 41, No. 2, pp. 131-152.

Irvin, R.B. & Mckeown, D.M. (1989). Methods for exploiting the relationship between buildings and their shadows in aerial imagery, *IEEE Transactions on Systems, Man, and Cybernetics*, Vol. 19, Vol. 6, pp. 1564-1575.

Jaynes, C.; Stolle, F. & Collines, R. (1994). Task driven perceptual organization for extraction of rooftop polygon. In *IEEE Workshop on Applications of Computer Vision*, pp. 152-159.

Katartzis, A. & Sahli, H. (2008). A stochastic framework for the identification of building rooftops using a single remote sensing Image. *IEEE Transactions on Geoscience and Remote Sensing*, Vol. 46, No. 1, pp. 259-271.

Kim, T. & Muller, J.P. (1999). Development of a graph-based approach fro building detection. *Image and Vision Computing*, Vol.17, No. 1, pp. 3-14.

Karantzalos, K. & Paragios, N. (2009). Recognition-driven two-dimensional competing priors toward automatic and accurate building detection. *IEEE Transactions on Geoscience and Remote Sensing*, Vol. 47, No. 1, pp. 133-144.

Lee, D.S.; Shan, J. & Bethl, J.S. (2003). Class-guided building extraction from IKONOS Imagery. *Photogrammetric Engineering and Remote Sensing*, Vol. 69, No. 2, pp. 143-150.

Lin, C. & Nevatia, R. (1998). Building detection and description from a single intensity image. *Computer Vision and Image Understanding*, Vol. 72, No. 2, pp. 101-121.

Matsuyama, T. & Hwang, V. (1985). SIGMA: A framework for image understanding: Integration of bottom-up and top-down analyses. *Proceedings of the 9th international joint conference on Artificial Intelligence*, Los Angles, California, pp. 908-915.

Mckeown, D.M. (1990). Toward automatic cartographic feature extraction. *Mapping and Spatial Modeling for Navigation*, 65, pp. 149-180 (Berlin: Springer).

Mohan, R. & Nevatia, R. (1989). Using perceptual organization to extract 3-D structures. *IEEE Transactions on Pattern Analysis and Machine Intelligence*, Vol. 11, No. 11, pp. 1121-1139.

Segl, K. & Kaufmann, K. (2001). Detection of small objects from high resolution panchromatic satellite imagery based on supervised image segmentation. *IEEE Transactions on Geoscience and Remote Sensing*, Vol. 39, No. 9, pp. 2080-2083.

Sirmaçek, B. & Ünsalan, C. (2009). Urban area and building detection using SIFT keypoints and graph theory, *IEEE Transactions on Geoscience and Remote Sensing*, Vol. 47, No. 4 pp. 1156-1167.

Venkateswar, V. & Chellapa. R. (1986). Extraction of straight lines in aerial images. *IEEE Transactions on Pattern Analysis and Machine Intelligence*, Vol. 14, No. 11, pp. 1111-1114.

Zheltov, S.U.; Sibiryakov, A.V. & Bibitchev, A.E. (2001). Building extraction at the state research institute of aviation systems (GosNIIAS). *3rd International Workshop on Automatic Extraction of Man-Made Objects from Aerial and Space Images*, Ascona, Bulkema Publishers, pp.65-74.

8

Applied Extended Associative Memories to High-Speed Search Algorithm for Image Quantization

Enrique Guzmán Ramírez[1], Miguel A. Ramírez[2] and Oleksiy Pogrebnyak[3]
[1]*Electronic and Computer Science Dept., Universidad Tecnológica de la Mixteca*
[2]*Informatic Dept., Universidad de la Sierra Juárez*
[3]*Computer Science Dept., Centro de Investigación en Computación – IPN*
México

1. Introduction

Vector quantization (VQ) has been used as an efficient and popular method in lossy image and speech compression (Gray, 1984; Nasrabadi & King, 1988; Gersho & Gray, 1992). In these areas, VQ is a technique that can produce results very close to the theoretical limits. The most widely used and simplest technique for designing vector quantizers is the LBG algorithm by Y. Linde et al. (1980). It is an iterative descent algorithm which monotonically decreases the distortion function towards a local minimum. Sometimes, it is also referred to as generalized Lloyd algorithm (GLA), since it is a vector generalization of a clustering algorithm due to Lloyd (1982).

New algorithms for VQ based on associative memories or artificial neuronal networks (ANNs) have arisen as an alternative to traditional methods. Within this approach, many VQ algorithms have been proposed. We mention some of them.

The self-organizing map (SOM) ANN, developed by Prof. Teuvo Kohonen in the early 1980s (Kohonen, 1981; Kohonen 1982), has been used with a great deal of success in creating new schemes for VQ. The SOM is a competitive-learning network. C. Amerijckx et al. (1998) proposed a lossy compression scheme for digital still images using Kohonen's neural network algorithm. They applied the SOM at both quantification and codification stages of the image compressor. At the quantification stage, the SOM algorithm creates a correspondence between the input space of stimuli, and the output space constituted of the codebook elements (codewords, or neurons) derived using the Euclidean distance. After learning the network, these codebook elements approximate the vectors in the input space in the best possible way. At the entropy coder stage, a differential entropy coder uses the topology-preserving property of the SOMs resulted from the learning process and the hypothesis that the consecutive blocks in the image are often similar. In (Amerijckx et al., 2003), the same authors proposed an image compression scheme for lossless compression using SOMs and the same principles.

Eyal Yair et al. (1992) provide a convergence analysis for the Kohonen Learning Algorithm (KLA) with respect to VQ optimality criteria and introduce a stochastic relaxation technique which produces the global minimum but is computationally expensive. By incorporating the

principles of the stochastic approach into the KLA, a new deterministic VQ design algorithm, called the soft competition scheme (SCS), is introduced. The new algorithm is an on-line method in which the codeword update is governed by a "soft" competition between the codevector, which are updated simultaneously for each presentation of a training vector.
A new VQ scheme based on competitive learning neural network and LBG vector quantization was presented by Basil and Jiang (1999). The algorithm integrates advantages presented in both LBG vector quantization and competitive learning neural networks to achieve an improved performance in comparison with their existing forms when it is applied to image compression.
Chin-Chuan Han et al. (2006; 2007) proposed an hybrid approach for VQ for obtaining the better codebook. It is modified and improved based on the centroid neural network adaptive resonance theory (CNN-ART) and the enhanced LBG (Linde-Buzo-Gray) approaches. Three modules, a neuronal net (NN) based clustering, a mean shift (MS) based refinement, and a principal component analysis (PCA) based seed assignment, are repeatedly utilized. Basically, the seed assignment module generates a new initial codebook to replace the low utilized codewords during the iteration. The NN-based clustering module clusters the training vectors using a competitive learning approach. The clustered results are refined using the mean shift operation.
A fuzzy Learning Vector Quantization (LVQ) which is based on the fuzzification of LVQ was proposed by Yong-Soo and Sung-Ihl (2007). The proposed fuzzy LVQ uses the different learning rate depending on whether classification is correct or not. When the classification is correct, it uses the combination of a function of the distance between the input vector and the prototypes of classes and a function of the number of iteration as the fuzzy learning rate. On the other hand, when the classification is not correct, it uses the combination of the fuzzy membership value and a function of the number of iteration as the fuzzy learning rate. The proposed FLVQ (fuzzy LVQ) is integrated into the supervised IAFC (Integrated Adaptive Fuzzy Clustering) neural network 5. The iris data set was used to compare the performance of the supervised IAFC neural network 5 with those of LVQ algorithm and back propagation neural network.
VQ is a process in which data to be encoded are divided into small blocks, forming vectors, which are then sequentially encoded vector by vector. The VQ process is divided in two phases: codebook design and encoding phases.
In the codebook design phase the idea is to identify a set, named codebook, of possible vectors (codewords) which are representative of the information to be encoded. The encoding phase searches for codeword with the closest match for every given input vector. The final encoding is then simply a process of sequentially listing the codeword indexes which were deemed to most closely match the vectors making up the original data.
One of the most serious problems for VQ, especially for high dimensional vectors, is the high computational complexity of searching for the closets codeword in the codebook design and encoding phases. Although quantizing high dimensional vectors rather than low dimensional vectors result in a better performance, the computation time needed for vector quantization grows exponentially with the vector dimension. This makes high dimensional vectors unsuitable for vector quantization. Thus, Given a data set (codebook) of m codewords, $\{\mathbf{c}_1, \mathbf{c}_2, ..., \mathbf{c}_i, ..., \mathbf{c}_m\}$, the problem is to find the i element that is closest to a input vector, $\mathbf{x}$, where $\mathbf{x}, \mathbf{c}_i \in \Re^d \forall i$.

In this study, to overcome the said problem an efficient high-speed search algorithm for image quantization based on Extended Associative Memories (EAM) is proposed. This new algorithm significantly reduces the computation needed without sacrificing performance.
A preliminary version of this work first appeared in (Guzmán et al., 2008). The present work is a widespread version of that one. The new results that this work includes are: 1) A mathematical analysis of the influence that each operator of our proposal has in the codebook design and encoding phase performance. 2) The results of the proposed algorithm when additional operators, **pmed** and **sum**, are used. 3) A complexity analysis of the proposed algorithm for additional operators. 4) The results that let us evaluate the influence that the proposed VQ algorithm has in the image compression performance.
The remaining sections of this work are organized as follows. In next Section, a brief theoretical background of extended associative memories is given. In Section 3 we describe our proposal, the high-speed search algorithm for image quantization based on EAM; furthermore, this sección include a complexity analysis of the proposed algorithm. Numerical simulation results obtained for the conventional image quantization techniques (LBG algorithm) and the proposed algorithm, when it uses **prom, med** and **pmed** operators, are provided and discussed in Section 4. Finally, Section 5 contains the conclusions of this study.

2. Extended associative memories model

An associative memory designed for pattern classification is an element whose fundamental purpose is to establish a relation of an input pattern $\mathbf{x} = [x_i]_n$ with the index i of a class $\mathbf{c}_i$ (see Fig. 1).

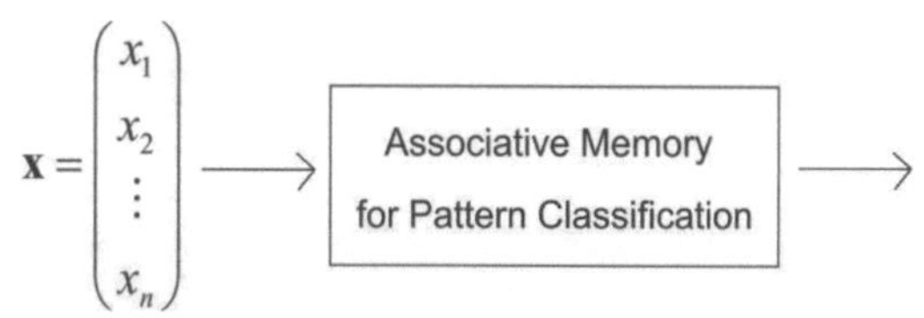

Fig. 1. Associative memory scheme for pattern classification.

Let $\{(\mathbf{x}^1, c_1), (\mathbf{x}^2, c_2), ..., (\mathbf{x}^N, c_N)\}$ be N couples of a pattern and its corresponding class index forming the fundamental set of couples composed by patterns and their corresponding class indices:

$$\{(\mathbf{x}^\mu, c_\mu); \mu = 1,2,...,N\} \tag{1}$$

where $\mathbf{x}^\mu \in \Re^n$ and $c_\mu = 1,2,...,N$. The associative memory is represented by a matrix generated from the fundamental set of couples and denoted by $\mathbf{M}$.
H. Sossa et al. (2004) proposed an associative memory model for the classification of real-valued patterns. This model, named Extended Associative Memory (EAM), is an extension of the Lernmatrix model proposed by K. Steinbuch (1961). The EAM is based on the general concept of the associative memory learning function and presents a high performance in pattern classification of real value data by its components and with altered patterns (Vázquez, 2005; Barron, 2006).

In the EAM, being an associative memory utilized for pattern classification, all the synaptic weights that belong to output *i* are accommodated at the *i*-th row of a matrix $\mathbf{M}$. The final value of this row is a function ϕ of all the patterns belonging to class *i*. The function ϕ acts as a generalizing learning mechanism that reflects the flexibility of the memory (Sossa et al., 2004).

2.1 Training stage of the EAM

The training stage of the EAM consists of evaluating function ϕ for each class. Then, the matrix $\mathbf{M}$ can be structured as:

$$\mathbf{M} = \begin{bmatrix} \boldsymbol{\varphi}_1 & \cdots & \boldsymbol{\varphi}_N \end{bmatrix}^T \tag{2}$$

where $\boldsymbol{\varphi}_i$ is the evaluation of ϕ for all patterns of *i*-th class, $i = 1,2,...,N$. The function ϕ can be evaluated in various manners. The arithmetical average operator (**prom**) is frequently used in the signals and images treatment. In (Sossa et al., 2004), the authors studied the performance of this operator and the median operator (**med**) to evaluate the function ϕ. Furthermore, in (Vázquez, 2005) the use of the average point operator (**pmed**) and sum operator (**sum**) were proposed to evaluate the function ϕ.
The goal of the training stage is to establish a relation between an input pattern $\mathbf{x} = [x_i]_n$, and the index *i* of a class c_i.
Considering that each class is composed for q patterns $\mathbf{x} = [x_i]_n$, and $\boldsymbol{\varphi}_i = [\phi_{i,1},...,\phi_{i,n}]$. Then, the training stage of the EAM, when the **prom** operator is used to evaluate the function $\boldsymbol{\varphi}_i$, is defined as:

$$\phi_{i,j} = \frac{1}{q}\sum_{l=1}^{q} x_{j,l}, \quad j = 1,...,n \tag{3}$$

The training stage of the EAM, when the **med** operator is used to evaluate the function $\boldsymbol{\varphi}_i$, is defined as:

$$\phi_{i,j} = \operatorname*{med}_{l=1}^{q} x_{j,l}, \quad j = 1,...,n \tag{4}$$

When the **pmed** operator is used to evaluate the function $\boldsymbol{\varphi}_i$, the training stage of the EAM is defined as:

$$\phi_{i,j} = \frac{\gamma_{i,j} + \lambda_{i,j}}{2}, \quad j = 1,...,n \tag{5}$$

When the **sum** operator is used to evaluate the function $\boldsymbol{\varphi}_i$, the training stage of the EAM is defined as:

$$\phi_{i,j} = \gamma_{i,j} + \lambda_{i,j} \tag{6}$$

where γ_{ij} and λ_{ij} represent the maximum and minimum vectors of the class *i* respectively. These vectors are defined as

$$\gamma_{i,j} = \bigvee_{l=1}^{q} \left(x_j^{i,l} \right) \tag{7}$$

$$\lambda_{i,j} = \bigwedge_{l=1}^{q} \left(x_j^{i,l} \right) \tag{8}$$

The operators max ($\vee$) and min ($\wedge$) perform the morphological operations on the patterns belongs to each class.

The associative memory, $\mathbf{M}$, is obtained after evaluating all functions $\boldsymbol{\varphi}_i$. In the case when N classes exist and the vectors to classify are n-dimensional, the resultant memory $\mathbf{M} = [m_{ij}]_{N\times n}$ is denoted as:

$$\mathbf{M} = \begin{bmatrix} \phi_{1,1} & \phi_{1,2} & \cdots & \phi_{1,n} \\ \phi_{2,1} & \phi_{2,2} & \cdots & \phi_{2,n} \\ \vdots & \vdots & \ddots & \vdots \\ \phi_{N,1} & \phi_{N,2} & \cdots & \phi_{N,n} \end{bmatrix} = \begin{bmatrix} m_{1,1} & m_{1,2} & \cdots & m_{1,n} \\ m_{2,1} & m_{2,2} & \cdots & m_{2,n} \\ \vdots & \vdots & \ddots & \vdots \\ m_{N,1} & m_{N,2} & \cdots & m_{N,n} \end{bmatrix} \tag{9}$$

2.2 Classification stage of the EAM

The goal of the classification stage is the generation of the class index to which an input pattern belongs.

The pattern classification by EAM is done when a pattern $\mathbf{x}^{\mu} \in \Re^n$ is presented to the memory $\mathbf{M}$ generated at the training stage. The EAM possess the feature of classifying a pattern not necessarily one of those already used to build the memory $\mathbf{M}$.

When the **prom** or **pmed** operators are used, the class to which $\mathbf{x}$ belongs is given by

$$i = \underset{l}{\mathbf{arg}} \left[\bigwedge_{l=1}^{N} \bigvee_{j=1}^{n} \left| m_{lj} - x_j \right| \right] \tag{10}$$

In this case, the operators $\vee \equiv max$ and $\wedge \equiv min$ perform morphological operations on the difference of the absolute values of the elements m_{ij} of $\mathbf{M}$ and the component x_j of the pattern $\mathbf{x}$ to be classified.

When the EAM uses the **med** operator, the class to which $\mathbf{x}$ belongs is given by

$$i = \underset{l}{\mathbf{arg}} \left[\bigwedge_{l=1}^{N} \left| \operatorname*{med}_{j=1}^{n} m_{lj} - \operatorname*{med}_{j=1}^{n} x_j \right| \right] \tag{11}$$

In this case, the operator $\wedge \equiv min$ performs a morphological erosion over the absolute difference of the median of the elements m_{ij} of $\mathbf{M}$ and the median of the component x_j of the pattern $\mathbf{x}$ to be classified.

When the **sum** operator is used, the recovery matrix, $\mathbf{r} = [r_{ij}]_{N\times n}$, must be generated. The components of the recovery matrix can be computed of two forms:

$$r_{ij} = x_j + \gamma_{l,j} \tag{12}$$

$$r_{ij} = x_j + \lambda_{l,j} \tag{13}$$

Then, the class to which $\mathbf{x}$ belongs is given by

$$i = \underset{l}{\mathbf{arg}}\left[\bigwedge_{l=1}^{N}\bigvee_{j=1}^{n}\left|m_{lj} - r_{lj}\right|\right] \tag{14}$$

In this case, the operators $\vee \equiv max$ and $\wedge \equiv min$ perform morphological operations on the difference of the absolute values of the elements m_{ij} of $\mathbf{M}$ and the component r_{ij} of the recovery matrix.

The **Theorem 1** and **Corollaries 1-5** from (Sossa et al., 2004) govern the conditions that must be satisfied to obtain a perfect pattern classification; either the pattern may be from the fundamental set of couples or be an altered version of the pattern. Here we reproduce them.

Theorem 1. Let $d_i = \bigvee_{\mathbf{x}\text{ class } i} d(\mathbf{x},\boldsymbol{\varphi}_i)$ and $\mathbf{R}_i = \{\mathbf{x} : d(\mathbf{x},\boldsymbol{\varphi}_i) \le d_i\}$ be hyper cubes centred at $\boldsymbol{\varphi}_i$ and semi-sides d_i, $i = 1,\ldots,N$. If $d(\boldsymbol{\varphi}_i,\boldsymbol{\varphi}_j) > 2\,\mathbf{max}\{d_i, d_j\}$ then:

i. $R_i \cap R_j = \varnothing,\ 1 \le i,j \le N,\ i \ne j.$

ii. $\mathbf{x} \in R_i$ implies $d(\mathbf{x},\boldsymbol{\varphi}_i) \le d(\mathbf{x},\boldsymbol{\varphi}_j)$.

iii. $\mathbf{x} \in R_j$ implies $d(\mathbf{x},\boldsymbol{\varphi}_j) \le d(\mathbf{x},\boldsymbol{\varphi}_i)$.

Corollary 1. If the conditions of Theorem 1 hold for all $1 \le i,j \le m,\ i \ne j$ then:

i. $R_i \cap R_j = \varnothing,\ 1 \le i,j \le N,\ i \ne j.$

ii. If $\mathbf{x} \in R_i$ then $d(\mathbf{x},\boldsymbol{\varphi}_i) \le d(\mathbf{x},\boldsymbol{\varphi}_j),\ 1 \le i,j \le N,\ i \ne j.$

Corollary 2. Perfect classification of the fundamental set of patterns is immediate due to any fundamental pattern $\mathbf{x}$, by constructions, belongs to its corresponding region R_i and if the conditions of Theorem 1 hold, then $d(\mathbf{x},\boldsymbol{\varphi}_i) \le d(\mathbf{x},\boldsymbol{\varphi}_j),\ 1 \le j \le N,\ i \ne j$. Thus the memory assigns the fundamental pattern $\mathbf{x}$ to class *i* as is due.

Corollary 3. If $\tilde{\mathbf{x}}$ is an altered version of fundamental pattern $\mathbf{x} \in R_i$, $\tilde{\mathbf{x}}$ is correctly classified if $\tilde{\mathbf{x}} \in R_i$.

Corollary 4. The attraction basin of *i*-th class is at least R_i and the convergence of correct classification happens in one step.

Corollary 5. Let $\mathbf{x}$ be a pattern to be classified. If $\mathbf{x} \notin R_i$ and $\mathbf{x} \notin R_j$ then it must be classified at the class for which:

i. $i = \underset{l}{\arg}\left[\bigwedge_{l=1}^{N}\bigvee_{j=1}^{n}\left|m_{lj} - x_j\right|\right]$ **prom** and **pmed** operators.

ii. $i = \underset{l}{\arg}\left[\bigwedge_{l=1}^{N}\left|\operatorname*{med}_{j=1}^{n} m_{lj} - \operatorname*{med}_{j=1}^{n} x_j\right|\right]$ **med** operator.

iii. $i = \underset{l}{\arg}\left[\bigwedge_{l=1}^{N}\bigvee_{j=1}^{n}\left|m_{lj} - r_{lj}\right|\right]$ sum operator.

3. Image quantization based on extended associative memories

In this section the image quantization algorithm based on EAM is described. Our proposal uses the EAM in both codebook generation and in the encoding phase. In codebook generation, applying the learning stage of the EAM on a codebook generated by the LBG algorithm a new codebook, named EAM-codebook, is obtained. In encoding phase, we propose a High-Speed Search Algorithm Applied to Image Quantization based on EAM; the VQ process is performed by means of the recalling stage of EAM using as associative memory the EAM-codebook. This process generates a set of the class indices to which each input vector belongs.

3.1 Basic notations and preliminary definitions

Vector quantization can be viewed as a mapping **Q**, from a n-dimensional vector space R^n into a finite subset **C** of R^n

$$Q: R^n \rightarrow C \tag{15}$$

where $C = \{\mathbf{y}^i : i = 1, 2, \ldots, N\}$ is the set of reconstruction vectors and N is the number of vectors in C. Thus,

i. $\bigcup_{i=1}^{N} \mathbf{y}^i = C,$

ii. $\mathbf{y}^i \bigcap \mathbf{y}^j = \varnothing, \ \forall i, j, i \neq j.$

Each $\mathbf{y}^i$, in C is called a *codeword* and C is called the *codebook* for the vector quantizer. For every source vector $\mathbf{x}$, a codeword $\mathbf{y}^i$, in C is selected as the representation for $\mathbf{x}$. This process is called the *quantization phase* (or the *codebook search phase)* of the vector quantizer, denoted by $Q(\mathbf{x}) = \mathbf{y}^\mathbf{i}$. Then, the codeword $\mathbf{y}^i$, is represented by some symbols (normally the address of the codeword in the codebook) and transmitted through the channel. This process is called the *encoding phase* of the vector quantizer.

On the other side of the channel, the received symbols are used to select the codewords from the codebook to reproduce the source signals. This process is called the *decoding phase* of the vector quantizer. The average number of bits required to represent the symbols in the encoding phase is the *rate* of the quantizer, and the average quantization error between input source signals and their reproduction codewords is the *distortion* of the vector quantizer. Increasing the number of codewords in the codebook can decrease the distortion of a vector quantizer and, normally, will increase the rate also. One major concern for vector quantizer design is the trade-off between distortion and rate.

On the other hand, both codebook generation and encoding phases of the proposed VQ algorithm make use of individual blocks of the image, which must be converted to vectors. Let the image be represented by a matrix, $\mathbf{A} = [a_{ij}]_{hi \times wi}$, where *hi* is the image height and *wi* is the image width; and *a* represents the *ij*-th pixel value: $a \in \{0, 1, 2, \ldots, 2^L - 1\}$, where L is the number of bits necessary to represent the value of a pixel.

Now, we define the *image block* and *image vector* terms.

Definition 1, image block (**ib**). Let $\mathbf{A} = \lfloor a_{ij} \rfloor$ be a $hi \times wi$ matrix representing an image, and let $\mathbf{ib} = \lfloor ib_{ij} \rfloor$ be a $d \times d$ matrix. The **ib** matrix is defined as a image block of the **A** matrix if the **ib** matrix is a subgroup of the **A** matrix such that

$$ib_{ij} = a_{\delta_i \tau_j} \tag{16}$$

where $i, j = 1,2,...,d$, $\delta = 1, d+1, 2d+1,..., h-d+1$, $\tau = 1, d+1, 2d+1,..., w-d+1$ and $a_{\delta_i \tau_j}$ represents the value of the pixel determined by the coordinates ($\delta+i$, $\tau+j$), where (δ, τ) and ($\delta+d$, $\tau+d$) are the beginning and the end of the image block, respectively.

Definition 2, image vector (**iv**). Let $\mathbf{ib} = [ib_{ij}]$ be an image sub-block and let $\mathbf{iv} = [iv_i]$ be a vector of size *d*. The *i*-th row of the **ib** matrix is said to be an image vector **iv** such that

$$iv_i = \left[ib_{i1}, ib_{i2}, ..., ib_{id} \right] \tag{17}$$

where $i = 1,2,3,..., d$. From each imageblock, *d* image vectors can be obtained:

$$\mathbf{iv}^{\mu} = \left[ib_{\mu 1}, ib_{\mu 2}, ..., ib_{\mu d} \right] \tag{18}$$

where $\mu = 1,2,3,..., d$.

A image block can be represented as a vector $\mathbf{x} = [x_j]_n$; thus, **ib** can be defined as a set of *d* row image vectors $\mathbf{iv} = [iv_j]_d$: $\{\mathbf{iv}^1, \mathbf{iv}^2, ..., \mathbf{iv}^d\}$, where, $iv_j^i = ib_{ij} | i, j = 1,2,...,d$; then

$$\mathbf{x} = \{\mathbf{iv}^i : i = 1,2,..d\} \tag{19}$$

where, $x_p = iv_j^i | i, j = 1,2,...,d$, $p = 1,2,...,n$, $n = d \times d$.

Finally, the new image representation is defined as

$$\mathbf{A} = X = \{\mathbf{x}^i : i = 1,2,..., M\} \tag{20}$$

where, $M = (hi / d)(wi / d)$.

In both EAM-codebook generation and encoding phases the new image representation is used.

3.2 Codebook generation

In this phase, an associative network is generated applying the learning stage of the EAM between a codebook generated by the LBG algorithm and a training set. This associative network is named EAM-codebook and establishes a relation between training set and the LBG codebook.

The codebook generation based on the LBG algorithm and the EAM is fundamental in obtaining a fast search algorithm for image VQ.

The EAM-codebook is computed in three steps:

Step 1. *LBG codebook generation.* This step applied the LBG algorithm on the image blocks (training set), $X = \{\mathbf{x}^i : i = 1, 2,..., M\}$, to generate an initial codebook: $C = \mathbf{y}^i : i = 1, 2,..., N$. This codebook is formed by a set of *n*-dimensional vectors $\mathbf{y} = [y_j]$, named *codeword.*

The Fig 2 shows the scheme of the LBG algorithm, where, $i = 1,..., n$, $\mu = 1,..., N$, $s_1, s_2, ..., s_N$ can have different value and $s_1 + s_2 + ... + s_N = M$.

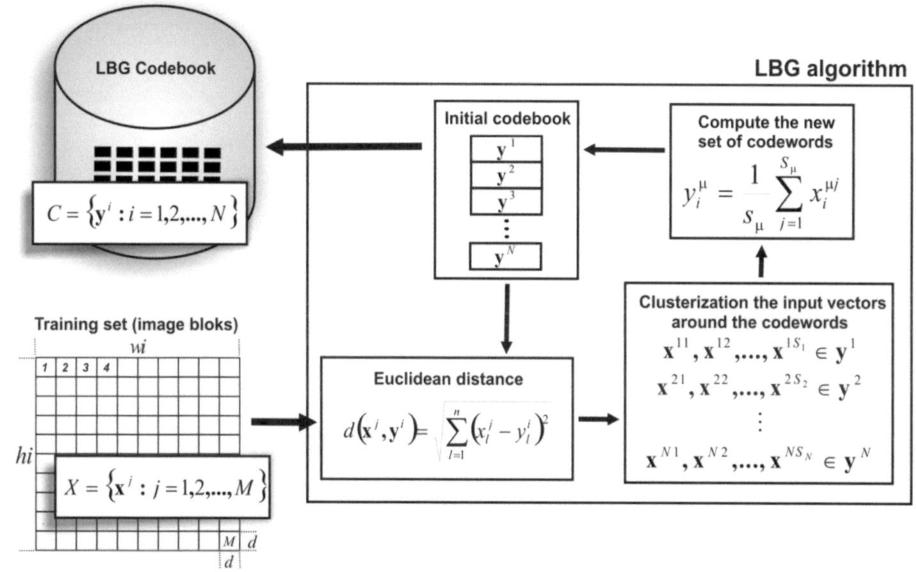

Fig. 2. LBG codebook generation.

Step 2. *Definition of the fundamental set of couples.* This step uses the codebook generated in the previous step and the training set.

This step designs a **Q** mapping and assigns an index i to each n-dimensional input pattern $\mathbf{x}=(x_1,x_2,\ldots,x_n)$, with $\mathbf{Q}(\mathbf{x})=\mathbf{y}^i=(y_{i1},y_{i2},\ldots,y_{in})$. The **Q** mapping is designed to map $\mathbf{x}$ to $\mathbf{y}^i$ with $\mathbf{y}^i$ satisfying the following condition:

$$d(\mathbf{x},\mathbf{y}^i)=\min_j d(\mathbf{x},\mathbf{y}^j) \text{ for } j=1,2,3,\ldots,N \tag{21}$$

where $d(\mathbf{x},\mathbf{y}^j)$ is the distortion of representing the input pattern $\mathbf{x}$ by the codeword $\mathbf{y}^j$, measured by Euclidean distance.

Each codeword $\mathbf{y}^i$ represents a class (existing N classes), then a set of M indices that indicates to which class, $\mathbf{y}^i$, each input pattern $\mathbf{x}$ belongs is generated. Let us to denote this set of indices as $H=\{h_i : i=1,2,\ldots,M\}$. This step also generates a set of N indices that indicates the number of input patterns that integrate to each class. This set is denoted as $B=\{b_i : i=1,2,\ldots,N\}$.

Based on the sets H and B and considering that the set of input patterns is integrated from M image blocks, $X=\{\mathbf{x}^i : i=1,2,\ldots,M\}$, the fundamental set of couples is formed

$$\begin{matrix} \mathbf{x}^{h_{11}} \in c_1 & \mathbf{x}^{h_{21}} \in c_2 & \cdots & \mathbf{x}^{h_{M1}} \in c_N \\ \mathbf{x}^{h_{12}} \in c_1 & \mathbf{x}^{h_{22}} \in c_2 & \cdots & \mathbf{x}^{h_{M2}} \in c_N \\ \vdots & \vdots & \ddots & \vdots \\ \mathbf{x}^{h_{1b_1}} \in c_1 & \mathbf{x}^{h_{2b_2}} \in c_2 & \cdots & \mathbf{x}^{h_{Mb_N}} \in c_N \end{matrix} \tag{22}$$

where, $b_1,b_2,\ldots,b_N$ can have different value and $b_1+b_2+\ldots+b_N=M$.

The Fig. 3 shows the definition of the fundamental set of couples.

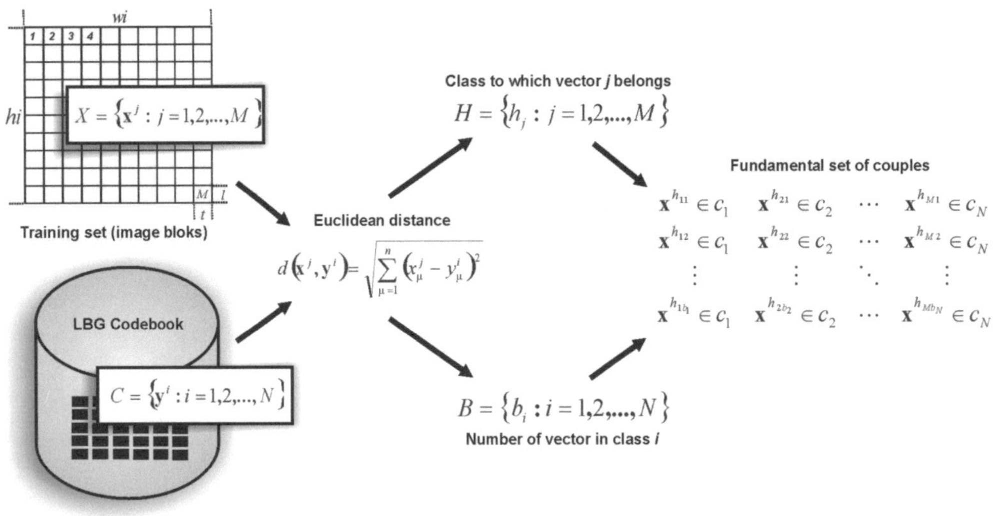

Fig. 3. Definition of the fundamental set of couples.

Step 3. *Generation of a new codebook based on EAM.* The goal of the third step is to generate the EAM-codebook.

Finding an optimal solution of the feature vector quantization problem necessitates a training process which involves learning the probability distribution of the input data. For this purpose, the training stage of the EAM is applied on the fundamental set of couples, denoted by the equation (22).

Considering that each class can group $b_1, b_2, \ldots, b_N$ input vectors, $\mathbf{x} = [x_i]_n$, the generalizing learning mechanism of the EAM is defined by the expressions (3), (4), (5) and (6) for the operators **prom, med, pmed** and **sum** respectively

$$m_{uv} = \frac{1}{q} \sum_{g=1}^{q} x_v^g$$

$$m_{uv} = \operatorname*{med}_{g=1}^{q} x_v^g$$

$$m_{uv} = \frac{\bigvee_{g=1}^{q} x_v^{u,g} + \bigwedge_{g=1}^{q} x_v^{u,g}}{2}$$

$$m_{uv} = \bigvee_{g=1}^{q} x_v^{u,g} + \bigwedge_{g=1}^{q} x_v^{u,g}$$

where q can take the value of $b_1, b_2, ..., b_N$, $v = 1, ..., n$, and $u = 1, 2, ..., N$.
The result of this step is an associative network that establishes a relation between the q input vectors and the class to which they belong.
Since N classes exist and the input vectors that integrate them are n-dimensional, then the associative network is represented by a matrix $\mathbf{M} = [m_{uv}]_{N\times n}$, which is the EAM-codebook:

$$\text{EAM-codebook} = \mathbf{M} = \begin{bmatrix} m_{11} & m_{12} & \cdots & m_{1n} \\ m_{21} & m_{22} & \cdots & m_{1n} \\ \vdots & \vdots & \ddots & \vdots \\ m_{N1} & m_{N2} & \cdots & m_{Nn} \end{bmatrix} = [m_{uv}]_{N\times n} \tag{23}$$

The column $(m_{u,1}, m_{u,2}, ..., m_{u,n})$ of $\mathbf{M}$ represents the centroid of the class u, $u = 1,2,..., N$.

That is, the synaptic weight, m_{uv}, is a function ϕ of all elements belonging to class u. These synaptic weights determine the behaviour of the net.

3.3 High-speed search algorithm for image quantization based on EAM

In the encoding phase of VQ process each input pattern is replaced by the codeword index that presents the nearest matching based on the similarity criterion between input patterns and codewords. In our proposal, this criterion has been codified in the associative memory (EAM-codebook).
The EAM-codebook generation is based on the EAM training stage. Therefore, using the EAM classification stage, the index class to which each input vector belongs is obtained; at the end of this step the image VQ process is completed.
In a general case, when N classes exist, the input vectors, $\mathbf{x}$, are n-dimensional and the **prom** or **pmed** operator is used to generate the memory $\mathbf{M}$, the index class to which an input vector belongs is determined using the morphologic operators *max* and *min*

$$\text{index class} = \arg_h \left[\bigwedge_{h=1}^{N} \bigvee_{j=1}^{n} \left| m_{hj} - x_j \right| \right]$$

The morphologic operation $\bigvee_{j=1}^{n} \left| m_{hj} - x_j \right| \equiv d(\mathbf{x}, m_h)$ is the metrics that indicates the distance between each row of $\mathbf{M}$ and the feature vector $\mathbf{x}$, that is to say, the degree of belonging of the feature vector $\mathbf{x}$ with each one of the N classes; that is

$$d(\mathbf{x}, m_h) = (|m_{h1} - x_1|) \vee (|m_{h2} - x_2|) \vee \ldots \vee (|m_{hn} - x_n|) \tag{24}$$

On the other hand, when the **med** operator is used to generate the memory $\mathbf{M}$, the region to which a feature vector $\mathbf{x}$ belongs is determined using the median and the morphologic operator *min.*

$$\text{index class} = \mathbf{arg}_h \left[\bigwedge_{h=1}^{N} \left| \operatorname{med}_{j=1}^{n} m_{hj} - \operatorname{med}_{j=1}^{n} x_j \right| \right]$$

Here, $\left|\operatorname*{med}_{j=1}^{n} m_{hj} - \operatorname*{med}_{j=1}^{n} x_j\right| \equiv d(\mathbf{x},m_h)$ is a metric that indicates the degree of belonging of the feature vector **x** to each one of the N classes.

Considering that $m_{h1}, m_{h2},..., m_{hn}$ and $x_1, x_2,..., x_n$ are sets of finite values in either ascending or descending order, the median has two cases: if n is an odd number, then the median is the value defined as $m_{h((n+1)/2)}$ and $x_{(n+1)/2}$; if n is an even number, then the median is the value defined as $\left(m_{h(n/2)} + m_{h((n/2)+1)}\right)/2$ and $\left(x_{n/2} + x_{(n/2)+1}\right)/2$, then:

$$\begin{aligned} d(\mathbf{x},m_h) &= \left|m_{h((n+1)/2)} - x_{(n+1)/2}\right| \\ d(\mathbf{x},m_h) &= \left|\left(m_{h(n/2)} + m_{h((n/2)+1)}\right)/2 - \left(x_{n/2} + x_{(n/2)+1}\right)/2\right| \end{aligned} \tag{25}$$

The computation of $d(\mathbf{x},m_h)$ is simpler when the **prom** operator is used because the values of $\mathbf{x}$ and m_h have not to be ordered, this fact implies the highest processing speed. On the other hand, when the **med** operator is used, the extreme values of the set do not have important effects on the results.

The result of $d(\mathbf{x},m_h)$ computation for three cases, **prom**, **med** and **pmed** operators, is a column vector where each element indicates the degree of belonging of the input vector, $\mathbf{x}$, with each one of the N classes

$$\begin{bmatrix} d(\mathbf{x},m_1) \\ d(\mathbf{x},m_2) \\ \vdots \\ d(\mathbf{x},m_N) \end{bmatrix} \tag{26}$$

Finally, to establish which class belongs to a new input vector, the operator *min* is applied to the vector in the expression (26). The class is indicated by the index of the row of $\mathbf{M}$ that presents the nearest matching with the input vector $\mathbf{x}$.

$$\text{index class} = \arg_h\left[\bigwedge_{h=1}^{N} d(\mathbf{x},m_h)\right] \tag{27}$$

The VQ process finishes when all the inputs vectors (image blocks) have been replaced by the index class to which it belongs.

In most of the data processing, the proposed algorithm makes use of morphological operations that is, sums and comparisons. Therefore, the proposed algorithm offered a high processing speed. The Fig. 4 shows the structure of the associative memory that implements the high-speed search algorithm.

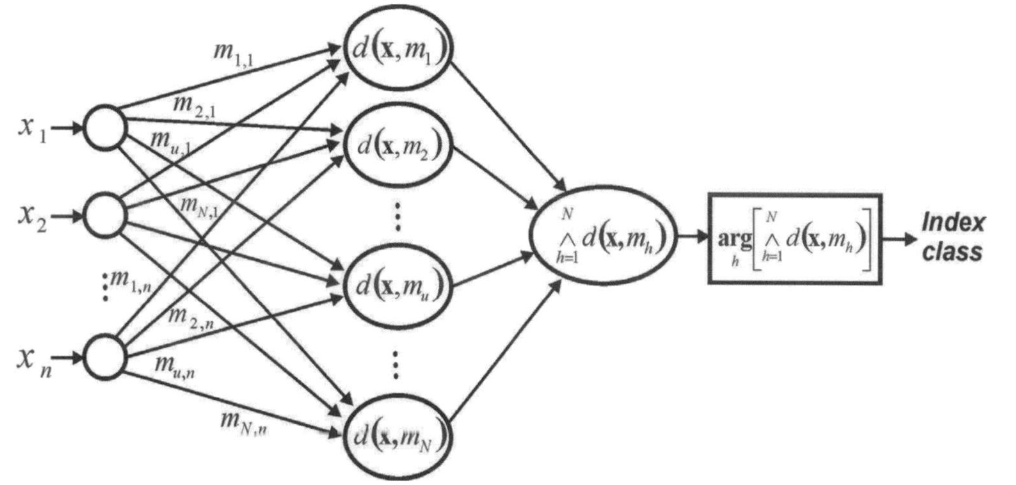

Fig. 4. Structure of the High-speed search algorithm based on EAM.

3.4 Complexity of the high-speed search algorithm

In this subsection, we analyze both the time and space complexity of the proposed algorithm. The algorithm complexity is measured by two parameters: the *time* complexity, or how many steps need the algorithm to solve the problem, and the *space* complexity, or how much memory it requires. To compute these parameters, we will use the pseudocodes of the **prom, med** and **pmed** operators that our algorithm uses to quantify a input vector (see Algorithm 1).

3.4.1 Time complexity

In order to measure the algorithm time complexity, we first obtain the run time based on the number of elementary operations (EO) that our proposal realizes to classify a input vector.

For **prom** and **pmed** operators, we consider pseudocode from Algorithm 1(a), thus in the *worst case*, the conditions of lines 9 and 16 will always be true. Therefore, the lines 10, 17 and 18 will be executed in all iterations, and then the internal loops realize the following number of EO:

$$\left(\sum_{j=1}^{n}(9+3)\right)+3=12\left(\sum_{j=1}^{n}1\right)+3=12n+3$$

$$\left(\sum_{l=1}^{N}(5+3)\right)+3=8\left(\sum_{l=1}^{N}1\right)+3=8N+3$$

(a)

```
// prom and pmed operators
subroutine prom()
variables
   x,k,j,l,aux: integer
   arg[N]='0': integer
begin
   for k←1 to N [operations k=k+1] do
      for j←1 to n [operations j=j+1]) do
         aux=abs(prom_codebook[k][j]-x[j]);
         if (aux>arg[k]) then
            arg[k]=aux;
         end_if
      end_for
   end_for
   aux=max(x);
   for l←1 to N [operations l=l+1] do
      if(arg[l]<aux)
         aux=arg[l];
         index=l;
      end_if
   end_for
end_subroutine
```

(b)

```
   // med operator
01 | subroutine med()
02 | variables
03 |    z,aux,w,aux2,index: integer
04 |    median: float
05 | begin
   // Arranges the vector input elements
06 |    for z←1 to n [operations z=z+1] do
07 |       aux=x[z];
08 |       w=z-1;
09 |       while (w>=0 && x[w]>aux) do
10 |          x[w+1]=x[w];
11 |          w=w-1;
12 |       end_while
13 |       x[w+1]=aux;
14 |    end_for
   // Compute the median
15 |   if (n%2==0) then
16 |      median=(x[n/2]+x[(n/2)-1])/2;
17 |   else
18 |      median=x[n/2];
19 |   end_if
   // Compute an element of M
20 |    aux2=max(x);
21 |    for k←1 to N [operations k=k+1] do
22 |       aux=abs(med_codebook[k]-median);
23 |       if(aux<aux2)
24 |          aux2=aux;
25 |          index=k;
26 |       end_if
27 |    end_for
28 | end_subroutine
```

Algorithm 1. Pseudocodes of the high-speed search algorithm: (a) **prom** and **pmed** operators, (b) **med** operator.

The next loop will repeat $12n+3$ EO at each iteration:

$$\left(\sum_{k=1}^{N}(12n+3)+3\right)+3=\left(\sum_{k=1}^{N}12n+6\right)+3=N(12n+6)+3=12Nn+6N+3$$

Thus, the equation (28) defines the total number of EO that the algorithm realizes.

$$T(n)=(12Nn+6N+3)+(8N+3)+1=12Nn+14N+7 \tag{28}$$

where N is a codebook size and n is a pattern dimension.

Now, for **med** operator, we consider the *worst case* of the pseudocode from Algorithm 1(b), thus, the conditions of lines 15 and 23 will always be true and the "while loop" will be executed z times in each iteration. From Algorithm 1(b), we can distinguish 3 phases: "arranges the vector input elements", "compute the median" and "compute an element of **M**".

The "arranges the vector input elements" phase realizes the following number of EO:

$$\left(\sum_{z=1}^{n}(7+3)\right)+3=10\left(\sum_{z=1}^{n}1\right)+3=10n+3,\ \text{without "while loop"}$$

$$\frac{n(n+1)}{2}(12) = 6n(n+1) = 6n^2 + 6n, \text{ only the "while loop"}$$

The "compute the median" phase realizes 10 EO and the "compute an element of $\mathbf{M}$ " phase realizes the following number of EO:

$$\left(\sum_{k=1}^{N}(7+3)+3\right)+1 = 10\sum_{k=1}^{N}1+4 = 10N+4$$

Finally, the equation (29) defines the total number of EO that the algorithm realizes.

$$T(n) = \left((10n+3)+\left(6n^2+6n\right)\right)+(10)+(10N+4) = 6n^2+16n+10N+17 \quad (29)$$

Also, we analyze the number and type of arithmetical operations used by our algorithm during the VQ process of an image. Then, for **prom** and **pmed** operators, we consider the pseudocode from Algorithm 1(a); furthermore, we know that this process is applied to image of $hi \times wi$ size. Thus, the number of operations that our algorithm, with **prom** or **pmed** operators, needs to quantify the image depends on the image size, the codebook size N and the pattern dimension n

$$\left(\frac{hi \times wi}{n}\right)\left[Nn(op2)+N(op1)\right] \quad (30)$$

where *op1*=1 comparison and *op2*=1 sum and 1 comparison; $(hi \times wi)/n$ is the number of patterns to quantify.

$Nn(op2)$ is the number and type of arithmetical operations used to perform a morphological dilation over the absolute difference of the EAM-codebook elements and the input pattern components; $N(op1)$ is the number and type of arithmetical operations used to perform a morphological erosion over the result of the previous process.

Now, for **med** operator, we consider pseudocode from Algorithm 1(b). Thus, the number of operations that our algorithm, with **med** operator, needs to quantify the image depends on the image size, the codebook size N, the pattern dimension n and the computation of the median

$$\left(\frac{hi \times wi}{n}\right)\left[n(op1)+(op2)+N(op3)\right] \quad (31)$$

where *op1* = 2 sums and 2 comparisons, *op2* = 2 sums, 1 comparison and 3 shift, *op2* = 1 sum and 1 comparison.

$n(op1)$ is the number and type of arithmetical operations used to arranges the vector input elements; $(op2)$ is the number and type of arithmetical operations used to compute the median and $N(op3)$ is the number and type of arithmetical operations used to compute an element of $\mathbf{M}$.

3.4.2 Space complexity

The algorithm space complexity is determined by the amount of memory required for its execution. To quantify an image of $hi \times wi$ size, which contains $M = (hi \times wi)/n$ n-dimensional patterns, the proposed algorithm implementation for **prom** and **pmed** operators, requires two vectors $\text{arg}[N]$ and $\text{indexes}[M]$, and one matrix $\text{prom\_codebook}[N][n]$. Thus, the number of memory units (*mu*) required for this process is:

$$mu\_\text{arg} + mu\_\text{indexes} + mu\_\text{prom\_codebook} = N{+}M{+}N(n) = M{+}N(n{+}1) \tag{32}$$

When the **med** operator is used, our algoritm only requires two vector $\text{indexes}[M]$ and $\text{med\_codebook}[N]$. Thus, the number of *mu* required is:

$$mu\_\text{indexes} + mu\_\text{med\_codebook} = M{+}N \tag{33}$$

For grayscale image (8 bits/pixel), the variables arg, prom_codebook and med_codebook are declared type *byte*, whereas the variable indexes depends on the codebook size, thus, if $N \le 256$ then indexes is type *byte* and if $N > 256$ then indexes is type *short* (16 bit integer signed numbers).
Then the total number of bytes required by the implementation of the algorithm with **prom** or **pmed** operatos is:

$$\begin{array}{l} M + N(n+1) \;\text{ if }\; N \le 256 \\ 2M + N(n+1) \;\text{ if }\; N > 256 \end{array} \tag{34}$$

and, the total number of bytes required by the implementation of the algorithm with **med** operato is:

$$\begin{array}{l} M + N \;\text{ if }\; N \le 256 \\ 2M + N \;\text{ if }\; N > 256 \end{array} \tag{35}$$

The number of memory units depends on the image size, codebook size and the codeword size chosen for the VQ process.

4. Experimental results

This section presents the experimental results obtained when our proposal is applied to an image quantization process. First, we show the proposed algorithm performance when it is using the **prom**, **med** and **pmed** operators. Then, we compare the proposed algorithm performance with the traditional LBG algorithm. The evaluated parameters are, the distortion generated on the reconstructed image and the influence that the VQ process has in the image compression when diverse codification methods are used. Finally, we analyze the number and type of operations and the amount of memory used by the proposed algorithm and the traditional LBG algorithm. For this purpose, a set of standard test images of size 512×512 pixels and 256 gray levels (Fig. 5) was used in simulations.
In order to measure the performance of both our proposal and LBG algorithm, we used a popular objective performance criterion named peak signal-to-noise ratio (PSNR), which is defined as

Fig. 5. Set of test images: (a) Lena, (b) Peppers, (c) Elaine, (d) Man, (e) Barbara, (f) Baboon.

$$PSNR = 10\log_{10}\left(\frac{\left(2^n - 1\right)^2}{\frac{1}{M}\sum_{i=1}^{M}\left(p_i - \tilde{p}_i\right)^2}\right) \tag{36}$$

where n is the number of bits per pixel, M is the number of pixels in the image, p_i is the i-th pixel in the original image, and $\widetilde{p}_i$ is the i-th pixel in the reconstructed image.

The first experiment has the purpose to determine the performance that the algorithm proposed has with each of the operators (**prom**, **med** and **pmed**) when it is applied on the test images. The table 1 includes the distortion that each operator adds to the images during the quantization process when different sizes of codebook are used; the results show that the **prom** operator generates the minor distortion when the algorithm is applied on the test images.

In this experiment a codebook was generated for each test image to determine which image presents the best performance when it is used as training set; the best results were obtained when the image Lena was used to generate the EAM-codebook.

To minimize the distortion generated in the quantification process of images that were not used to obtain the EAM-codebook, it is possible to use an evolutionary method that allows adding information of new images to the book. This aspect is the subject of future work based on paper where the authors proposed the design of an evolutionary codebook using morphological associative memories (Guzmán et al., 2007).

The second experiment has the objective to compare the distortions that both the proposed algorithm (with **prom** operator) and LBG algorithm (the most widely quantization method used) add to the original image. For this purpose, the codebook was generated using the image Lena as the training set and the results were obtained using different sizes of the codebook. Then, VQ was applied to the set of the test images in order to determine the behavior of the algorithms with the patterns that do not belong to the training set. Table 2 shows the results of this experiment.

From Table 2, we can make the following observations: 1) the results obtained show that the proposed method is competitive with the LBG algorithm in the PSNR parameter; 2) the proposed algorithm replaced an input pattern by the index of the codeword that presents the nearest matching, not necessarily one of those already used to built the **M** memory. This property allows our algorithm to quantify efficiently the images that have not been used in the generation of the EAM-codebook.

In the third experiment, the performance of diverse standard coding methods applied to the quantified image with the proposed algorithm was evaluated. These methods included statistical modeling techniques, such as arithmetical, Huffman, range, Burrows Wheeler transformation, PPM, and dictionary techniques, LZ77 and LZP. The purpose of the third experiment is to analyze the proposed algorithm performance in image compression. For this purpose, a coder that includes our algorithm and diverse entropy coding techniques was developed. Table 3 shows the compression results obtained from applying the coder on test images expressed as bit per pixel (bpp).

Operator	Images	Proposed algorithm			
		Codebook size			
		64	128	256	512
		PSNR	PSNR	PSNR	PSNR
prom	Lena	26.4166	27.4702	28.3959	29.2524
	Peppers	25.2016	26.0691	26.5467	27.0489
	Elaine	28.3715	29.1042	29.6899	30.1218
	Man	23.2950	23.9506	24.5434	25.0942
	Barbara	21.3870	21.7271	22.0764	22.4347
	Baboon	18.1937	18.5259	18.8603	19.1508
med	Lena	18.2766	18.4610	18.5554	19.6281
	Peppers	18.1225	18.2008	17.9674	18.6897
	Elaine	18.8188	19.1405	19.1743	20.6147
	Man	17.5697	17.7426	17.7681	18.3887
	Barbara	17.0985	17.1972	17.1063	17.8108
	Baboon	14.5220	14.7361	14.5346	15.0243
pmed	Lena	24.5133	26.4137	27.6557	28.7976
	Peppers	23.5998	25.0989	26.1539	26.8024
	Elaine	25.6682	27.4973	28.7723	29.6578
	Man	22.0482	23.3018	24.3623	24.9216
	Barbara	20.8122	21.5167	22.0609	22.4012
	Baboon	18.1270	18.5977	18.9179	19.2329

Table 1. Proposed algorithm performance with **prom**, **med** and **pmed** operators (the image Lena was used to generate the codebook).

Images	LBG Algorithm				Proposed algorithm (prom operator)			
	Codebook size				Codebook size			
	64	128	256	512	64	128	256	512
	PSNR	PSNR	PSNR	PSNR	PSNR	PSNR	PSNR	PSNR
Lena	27.1448	28.2131	29.0855	29.9825	26.4166	27.4702	28.3959	29.2524
Peppers	26.3830	27.1805	27.6496	28.2132	25.2016	26.0691	26.5467	27.0489
Elaine	28.9191	29.6845	30.3035	30.7453	28.3715	29.1042	29.6899	30.1218
Man	24.2034	24.9395	25.4963	26.0266	23.2950	23.9506	24.5434	25.0942
Barbara	21.8144	22.2457	22.6960	23.1359	21.3870	21.7271	22.0764	22.4347
Baboon	18.8927	19.3438	19.6829	20.0105	18.1937	18.5259	18.8603	19.1508

Table 2. Performance comparison of the proposed algorithm and the LBG algorithm.

Images	Entropy encoding technique	LBG Algorithm				Proposed algorithm (prom)			
		Codebook size				Codebook size			
		64 bpp	128 bpp	256 bpp	512 bpp	64 bpp	128 bpp	256 bpp	512 bpp
Elaine	PPM	0.168	0.216	0.290	0.394	0.174	0.225	0.304	0.410
	SZIP	0.179	0.227	0.301	0.403	0.185	0.237	0.316	0.417
	Burrown	0.190	0.236	0.313	0.419	0.191	0.245	0.328	0.433
	LZP	0.191	0.239	0.312	0.452	0.197	0.248	0.328	0.470
	LZ77	0.211	0.268	0.352	0.520	0.218	0.279	0.366	0.538
	Range	0.285	0.340	0.409	0.624	0.284	0.340	0.410	0.621
Peppers	PPM	0.185	0.234	0.307	0.414	0.194	0.245	0.323	0.429
	SZIP	0.196	0.243	0.317	0.415	0.206	0.255	0.333	0.431
	Burrown	0.267	0.254	0.329	0.429	0.215	0.264	0.346	0.446
	LZP	0.207	0.254	0.326	0.473	0.218	0.267	0.342	0.492
	LZ77	0.225	0.279	0.363	0.523	0.237	0.292	0.379	0.546
	Range	0.313	0.364	0.429	0.636	0.310	0.363	0.430	0.635
Lena	PPM	0.209	0.262	0.339	0.462	0.214	0.269	0.348	0.470
	SZIP	0.217	0.269	0.347	0.464	0.224	0.276	0.356	0.472
	Burrown	0.225	0.276	0.359	0.475	0.227	0.284	0.368	0.483
	LZP	0.227	0.276	0.354	0.522	0.234	0.284	0.364	0.532
	LZ77	0.241	0.300	0.386	0.563	0.248	0.308	0.397	0.575
	Range	0.332	0.392	0.459	0.661	0.330	0.388	0.457	0.657
Barbara	PPM	0.229	0.292	0.366	0.474	0.228	0.291	0.374	0.488
	SZIP	0.246	0.307	0.379	0.480	0.244	0.306	0.387	0.491
	Burrown	0.251	0.312	0.389	0.490	0.251	0.311	0.398	0.503
	LZP	0.257	0.315	0.387	0.541	0.258	0.316	0.397	0.559
	LZ77	0.265	0.329	0.408	0.575	0.270	0.331	0.415	0.597
	Range	0.333	0.394	0.463	0.660	0.325	0.385	0.455	0.656
Man	PPM	0.240	0.307	0.386	0.493	0.244	0.312	0.393	0.499
	SZIP	0.255	0.320	0.395	0.493	0.259	0.325	0.402	0.499
	Burrown	0.259	0.322	0.402	0.502	0.261	0.328	0.410	0.507
	LZP	0.271	0.334	0.410	0.569	0.276	0.340	0.418	0.575
	LZ77	0.284	0.351	0.428	0.605	0.289	0.357	0.433	0.612
	Range	0.328	0.389	0.452	0.651	0.326	0.387	0.452	0.650
Baboon	PPM	0.284	0.356	0.443	0.536	0.281	0.360	0.449	0.544
	SZIP	0.302	0.371	0.450	0.536	0.299	0.375	0.455	0.542
	Burrown	0.301	0.373	0.473	0.547	0.298	0.376	0.477	0.552
	LZP	0.317	0.388	0.470	0.619	0.315	0.393	0.478	0.628
	LZ77	0.322	0.391	0.470	0.651	0.322	0.390	0.471	0.664
	Range	0.336	0.402	0.470	0.663	0.328	0.397	0.470	0.664

Table 3. Compression results obtained from applying several entropy encoding technique on the information generated from the proposed algorithm.

Images	Entropy encoding technique	Proposed algorithm (med) Codebook size				Proposed algorithm (pmed) Codebook size			
		64 bpp	128 bpp	256 bpp	512 bpp	64 bpp	128 bpp	256 bpp	512 bpp
Elaine	PPM	0.238	0.280	0.315	0.372	0.181	0.230	0.296	0.391
	SZIP	0.254	0.297	0.331	0.382	0.193	0.242	0.309	0.399
	Burrown	0.258	0.298	0.337	0.392	0.201	0.250	0.320	0.413
	LZP	0.269	0.311	0.345	0.429	0.207	0.255	0.322	0.449
	LZ77	0.289	0.332	0.366	0.498	0.226	0.281	0.355	0.515
	Range	0.324	0.360	0.387	0.559	0.277	0.330	0.396	0.603
Peppers	PPM	0.232	0.274	0.308	0.344	0.198	0.242	0.309	0.412
	SZIP	0.245	0.287	0.322	0.354	0.209	0.252	0.320	0.413
	Burrown	0.250	0.292	0.330	0.360	0.216	0.260	0.330	0.424
	LZP	0.259	0.301	0.333	0.398	0.223	0.266	0.331	0.474
	LZ77	0.275	0.320	0.358	0.473	0.241	0.289	0.362	0.527
	Range	0.327	0.362	0.392	0.560	0.302	0.349	0.411	0.619
Lena	PPM	0.254	0.300	0.330	0.363	0.214	0.267	0.339	0.452
	SZIP	0.271	0.315	0.345	0.372	0.223	0.274	0.345	0.451
	Burrown	0.277	0.320	0.351	0.385	0.230	0.281	0.355	0.461
	LZP	0.283	0.327	0.355	0.419	0.234	0.283	0.356	0.512
	LZ77	0.292	0.339	0.370	0.487	0.248	0.305	0.382	0.559
	Range	0.338	0.375	0.398	0.560	0.314	0.371	0.436	0.641
Barbara	PPM	0.266	0.310	0.340	0.374	0.236	0.292	0.364	0.473
	SZIP	0.283	0.324	0.356	0.384	0.252	0.307	0.376	0.477
	Burrown	0.285	0.328	0.361	0.395	0.253	0.313	0.384	0.489
	LZP	0.299	0.341	0.371	0.437	0.266	0.318	0.388	0.545
	LZ77	0.303	0.346	0.376	0.501	0.276	0.331	0.401	0.585
	Range	0.334	0.370	0.396	0.558	0.322	0.377	0.440	0.644
Man	PPM	0.261	0.307	0.335	0.373	0.245	0.305	0.378	0.488
	SZIP	0.280	0.324	0.351	0.381	0.259	0.318	0.390	0.489
	Burrown	0.279	0.323	0.355	0.385	0.330	0.321	0.395	0.499
	LZP	0.300	0.344	0.370	0.436	0.274	0.333	0.404	0.565
	LZ77	0.301	0.345	0.373	0.500	0.288	0.347	0.418	0.604
	Range	0.323	0.361	0.385	0.556	0.320	0.376	0.438	0.641
Baboon	PPM	0.313	0.353	0.381	0.416	0.286	0.359	0.446	0.542
	SZIP	0.331	0.368	0.394	0.421	0.303	0.374	0.454	0.541
	Burrown	0.405	0.367	0.397	0.424	0.301	0.373	0.462	0.552
	LZP	0.350	0.391	0.418	0.488	0.320	0.392	0.476	0.627
	LZ77	0.339	0.373	0.397	0.544	0.324	0.388	0.470	0.662
	Range	0.334	0.368	0.392	0.560	0.330	0.395	0.469	0.663

Table 3. Compression results obtained from applying several entropy encoding technique on the information generated from the proposed algorithm (continuation).

These results show that when these coding methods are applied on the results obtained by our algorithm, the entropy coding technique that offers the best results in compression ratio is the PPM coding. The PPM is an adaptive statistical method; its operation is based on partial equalization of chains, that is, the PPM coding predicts the value of an element based on the sequence of previous elements.

Furthermore, these results show that the proposed algorithm remains competitive with the algorithm LBG in the compression parameter.

Finally, based on results obtained in section 3.4 and the study for LBG algorithm presented in (Guzmán et al., 2008), a complexity analysis of both algorithms was realized. Table 4 summarizes computation complexities of the encoding phase of both LBG and proposed algorithm in terms of the type and average number of operations per pixels. This experiment was performed for n = 16 and 64, which are the most popular pattern dimensions. With regard to time complexity, this Table shows that the proposed algorithm provides considerable improvement over the LBG algorithm. Table 4 also shows that the memory required by our algorithm is smaller than the memory needed by the LBG when a VQ process is performed.

Algorithm	**Pattern dimension** (n)	**Codebook size** (N)	**Required memory** (bytes)	**Average number of operations per pixel**				
				CMP	±	×	**SQRT**	**Shift**
LBG	16	128	41088	8	387	129	8.06	-
		256	49280	16	771	257	16.06	-
		512	65664	32	1539	513	32.06	-
	64	128	41472	2	387	129	2.015	-
		256	74240	4	771	257	4.015	-
		512	139776	8	1539	513	8.015	-
Our proposal with **prom** and **pmed** operators	16	128	18560	136	128	-	-	-
		256	20736	272	256	-	-	-
		512	41472	544	512	-	-	-
	64	128	12416	130	128	-	-	-
		256	20736	260	256	-	-	-
		512	37376	520	512	-	-	-
Our proposal with **med** operator	16	128	16512	10.062	10.125	-	-	0.1875
		256	16640	18.062	18.125	-	-	0.1875
		512	33280	34.062	34.125	-	-	0.1875
	64	128	4224	4.015	4.031	-	-	0.0468
		256	4352	6.015	6.031	-	-	0.0468
		512	8704	10.015	10.031	-	-	0.0468

Table 4. Computation complexities of the encoding phase of both proposed algorithm and the LBG algorithm.

5. Conclusions

In the present work, we have proposed the use of extended associative memories in a high-speed search algorithm applied to image quantization. With the purpose of evaluating the influence that the proposed VQ algorithm has in the image compression, it was integrated in a codec where the codification stage includes to several standard codification methods. The compression ratio and the signal to noise ratio obtained by our proposal show that the rate of compression and the decoding quality remain competitive with respect to the LBG algorithm.

Furthermore, the EAM has the property of substituting the input pattern by the class index that present the nearest match, without taking care that they have not been used in the construction of the associative memory. Our Algorithm inherited this property. This property allows our algorithm to quantify efficiently images that have not been used in the generation of the EAM-codebook, this is the reason it obtains good results in the decoding quality parameter.

Finally, in most of the data processing, the proposed algorithm makes use of the morphological operations, that is to say, its operation is based on maximums or minimums of sums, it uses only the operations of sums and comparisons. Therefore, the proposed algorithm offers a high processing speed in the search process of the encoding phase. Thus, with respect to traditional VQ algorithms, the main advantages offered by the proposed algorithm are, a high processing speed and low demand of resources (system memory).

For these reasons, we can conclude that our proposal provides a considerable improvement over the LBG algorithm.

6. References

Amerijckx, C., Verleysen, M., Thissen, P. and Legat, J.-D. (1998). Image Compression by Self-Organized Kohonen Map. *IEEE Transactions on Neural Networks*, Vol. 9, No 3, pp. 503-507, ISSN 1045-9227.

Amerijckx, C., Legat, J.-D. and Verleysen, M. (2003). Image Compression using Self-Organizing Maps. *Systems Analysis Modelling Simulation, Taylor & Francis Ltd.*, Vol. 43, No. 11, pp. 1529-1543, ISSN 0232-9298.

Barron, R. (2006). Associative Memories and Morphological Neural Networks for Patterns Recall. Ph.D. dissertation, Center for Computing Research of National Polytechnic Institute, México.

Basil, G. and Jiang, J. (1999). An Improvement on Competitive Learning Neural Network by LBG Vector Quantization. Proceedings of IEEE International Conference on Multimedia Computing and Systems, Vol 1, pp 244-249, ISBN 978-1-4244-3756-6, Florence, Italy.

Chin-Chuan, H., Ying-Nong, C., Chih-Chung, L., Cheng-Tzu, W. and Kuo-Chin, F. (2006). A Novel Approach for Vector Quantization Using a Neural Network, Mean Shift, and Principal Component Analysis. Proceedings of *IEEE Intelligent Vehicles Symposium*, pp 244-249, ISBN 4-901122-86-X, Tokyo, Japon.

Chin-Chuan, H., Ying-Nong, C., Chih-Chung, L. and Cheng-Tzu W. (2007). A Novel Approach for Vector Quantization Using a Neural Network, Mean Shift, and Principal Component Analysis-based seed re-initialization. *Signal Processing, Journal.* Elsevier. Vol. 87, Issue 5, pp 799-810, ISSN 0165-1684.

Gersho, A. and Gray, R. M. (1992). *Vector Quantization and Signal Compression.* Kluwer Academic, ISBN 0-7923-9181-0, Norwell, Massachusetts USA.

Gray, R. M. (1984). Vector Quantization. *IEEE ASSP Magazine,* Vol 1, pp. 4-9, ISSN 0740-7467.

Guzmán, E., Oleksiy, P. and Yánez, C. (2007). Design of an Evolutionary Codebook Based on Morphological Associative Memories. *Proceeding of the 6th Mexican International Conference on Artificial Intelligence,* LNAI 4827, Springer, Vol. 4827/2007, pp. 601-611, ISSN 0302-9743, Aguascalientes, México.

Guzmán, E., Oleksiy, P., Sánchez, L. and Yánez, C. (2008). A Fast Search Algorithm for Vector Quantization based on Associative Memories. *Proceeding of the 13th Iberoamerican congress on Pattern Recognition,* LNCS 5197, Springer, Vol. 5197/2008, pp. 487-495, ISSN 0302-9743, Havana, Cuba.

Kohonen, T. (1980). Automatic formation of topological maps of patterns in a self-organizing system., *Proceedings of 2nd Scandinavian Conference on Image Analysis,* pp. 214-220, Helsinki, Finland.

Kohonen T. (1982). Self-organizing formation of topologically correct feature maps. *Biological Cybernetics,* Vol. 43 No. 1, pp. 59-69, ISSN 0340-1200.

Linde, Y., Buzo, A. and Gray R. (1980). An Algorithm for Vector Quantizer Design. *IEEE Trans. on Communications,* Vol 28, No. 1, pp. 84-95, ISSN 0090-6778.

Lloyd, L. P. (1982). Least Squares Quantization in PCM. *IEEE Trans. Inform. Theory,* Vol. IT-28, No. 2, pp. 129-137, ISSN 0018-9448.

Nasrabadi, N. M. and King, R. A. (1988). Image Coding Using Vector Quantization: A Review. *IEEE Trans.on Communications,* Vol. 36, No. 8, pp. 957-971, ISSN 0090-6778.

Sossa, H., Barrón, R. and Vázquez, A. (2004). Real-valued Patterns Classification based on Extended Associative Memory, *Proceedings of IEEE 15th Mexican International Conference on Computer Science,* pp. 213-219, ISBN 0-7695-2160-6, Colima, México.

Steinbuch, K. (1961). Die Lernmatrix, Kybernetik, Vol. 1 No. 1, pp. 26-45, ISSN 0340-1200.

Vázquez, R. (2005). Objects recognition in presence of traslapes by means of associative memories and invariants descriptions. Master dissertation, Center for Research in Computing of National Polytechnic Institute, México.

Yair, E., Zeger, K. and Gersho, A. (1992). Competitive Learning and Soft Competition for Vector Quantizer Design. *IEEE Transaction on Signal Processing,* Vol. 40, No. 2, pp. 294-309, ISSN 1053-587X.

Yong-Soo, K. and Sung-Ihl K. (2007) Fuzzy Neural Network Model Using a Fuzzy Learning Vector Quantization with the Relative Distance. *Proceedings of IEEE 7th International Conference on Hybrid Intelligent Systems*, pp. 90-94, ISBN 978-0-7695-2946-2, Kaiserslautern, Germany.

9

Search Algorithms and Recognition of Small Details and Fine Structures of Images in Computer Vision Systems

S.V. Sai, I.S. Sai and N.Yu.Sorokin
Pacific National University
Russia

1. Introduction

Search algorithms and object recognition in digital images are used in various systems of technical vision. Such systems include: vision systems of robots, the system of recognition and identification of fingerprint, authentication system for stamp on a document and many others. Description of known search algorithms and the recognition of objects in images is well represented in the literature, for example, in (Gonzalez & Woods, 2002) and (Pratt, 2001). Review of the literature shows that in most cases, problems of recognition take into account such characteristics of the object as its geometric shape and distribution of luminosity over the entire area of the object. As a criterion of recognition the standard deviation is commonly used. Spectral characteristics, the numerical moments, color characteristics, segmentation, etc. are used in addition to the basic attributes. Wavelet analysis and fractal recognition are the latest methods (Potapov et al., 2008) in image processing and pattern recognition.

Algorithms for searching small details and fine structures are used in detection and analysis of the quality of images. The accuracy of search and recognition of fine details is affected by the distortions arising during the digital compression and transmission of image signals through a noisy communication channel with interference. The peak signal-to-noise ratio (PSNR) is considered nowadays the most popular criterion of noisy images (Pratt, 2001). According to this criterion the normalized root-mean-square deviation of color coordinates is calculated and the averaging is carried out at all pixels of the image. Thus, the closer the noisy image to the original, the bigger the PSNR value and therefore the better its quality we have. However this and other similar metrics (e.g., MSE) allow for estimating only root-mean-square difference between images, therefore the best results from the metrics point of view are not always correspond to the best visual perception. For instance, the noisy image containing fine details with low contrast can have high PSNR value even when the details are not visible on the background noise.

A number of leading firms suggest hardware and software for the objective analysis of dynamic image quality. For example, Tektronix – PQA 300 analyzer, Snell & Wilcox – Mosalina software, Pixelmetrix – DVStation device (Glasman, 2004). Principles of image quality estimation in these devices are various. For example, PQA 300 analyzer measures image quality on algorithm of "Just Noticeable Difference – JND", developed by Sarnoff

Corporation. PQA 300 analyzer carries out a series of measurements for each test sequence of images and forms common PQR estimation on the basis of JND measurements which is close to subjective estimations. To make objective analysis of image quality Snell & Wilcox firm offers a PAR method - Picture Appraisal Rating. PAR technology systems control artefacts created by compression under MPEG-2 standard. The Pixelmetrix analyzer estimates a series of images and determines definition and visibility errors of block structure and PSNR in luminosity and chromaticity signals. Works (Wang & Bovik, 2002) and (Wang et. al., 2004) propose objective methods for measuring image quality using a universal index (UQI) and on the basis of structural similarity (SSIM).

The review of objective methods of measurements shows that high contrast images are usually used in test tables, while distortions of fine details with low contrast, which are most common after a digital compression, are not taken into account. It is necessary to note that there exists a lack of practical objective methods of measurement of quality of real images: analyzers state an integrated rating of distortions as a whole and do not allow for estimating authentically distortion of local fine structures of images.

The investigation results and methods of the distortions analysis of fine details of real images after application of JPEG, JPEG-2000 and MPEG-4 compression are given in authors works (Sai, 2006) and (Sai, 2007). Results of the present work are the development in the field of objective criterions in the search systems and recognition of fine details and fine structures of the image.

2. Search algorithms

Fine details of image can be classified by the following attributes: a "dot object," a "thin line," a "texture fragment". Search algorithms of the dots and lines are simple (Gonzalez & Woods, 2002). The most common search algorithm is processing the images with a sliding mask. For example, for the mask size 3 x 3 pixels the processing is a linear combination of the mask coefficients with the luminance values of image pixels, covered with the mask. The response of each image point is defined by:

$$R = \sum_{i=1}^{9} w_i Y_i \,, \tag{1}$$

where w_i is the mask value, Y_i is the luminance value of pixel.

Examples of masks used to identify the bright dots or the thin lines of images are presented on Fig. 1. For identifying dark dots or lines the mask coefficients should be inversed.

-1	-1	-1
-1	8	-1
-1	-1	-1

-1	-1	-1
2	2	2
-1	-1	-1

-1	2	-1
-1	2	-1
-1	2	-1

2	-1	-1
-1	2	-1
-1	-1	2

Fig. 1. Examples of mask for identifying dots and thin lines

In order to detect the dot or the line with thickness of one pixel, one should compute the response (1) for the selected mask and compare the response value with the threshold value:

$$|R| \geq T. \tag{2}$$

If the condition (2) is fulfilled the decision on identifying the dot or the thin line in the block size 3 x 3 is taken. The coefficients of the mask corresponding to the position of the dot or the thin line are selected in such a way that the total value of all coefficients is equal to zero. It is obvious that for blocks with a constant luminosity the value $R = 0$. The value R will be maximal for blocks containing dots or thin lines on the background elements with the same luminosity. The threshold T is chosen on the basis of a given contrast of the dot or the thin line on the background luminosity.

Consider features of the described algorithm.

1. The search algorithm is quite simple to implement. 2. The search algorithm provides good detection accuracy of fine details at the equal background luminosity and at the equal luminosity of the thin line elements or texture. 3. For real images the background luminosity values of pixels or object may change, that reduces the detection accuracy. 4. The fine details can be masked by noise and may not be detected by the criterion (2) while sending image signals through a noisy channel. 5. In the case of impulsive noise the disturbance can be detected as a dot object. 6. The algorithm takes into account only the luminosity component of the image. 7. The algorithm does not take into account the peculiarities of contrast sensitivity of vision.

The authors propose a modified algorithm for searching and detection of fine details of color digital images. The main idea of the algorithm is a transformation of primary *RGB* signals into equal color space. Such a transformation makes possible to take into account the peculiarities of visual perception of color contrast fine details during the runtime of the search algorithm.

Consider the features of the transformation of digital *RGB* signals. It is well known that the uniform color spaces, e.g. $L^*u^*v^*$, $L^*a^*b^*$ and $W^*U^*V^*$ (Novakovsky, 1988), are frequently used to evaluate the color differences between big details of the static image. In such systems the area of dispersion of color coordinates transforms from ellipsoid to sphere with the fixed radius for the whole color space. In this case the threshold size is equal to mean perceptible color difference and keeps constant value independently of the object color coordinates.

For the analyses the equal color space $W^*U^*V^*$ was selected. Color coordinates of the pixel in the $W^*U^*V^*$ (Wyszecki) system (Wyszecki, 1975) are defined as follows:

$$W^* = 25Y^{1/3} - 17;$$

$$U^* = 13W^*(u - u_0);$$

$$V^* = 13W^*(v - v_0),$$

where Y is the luminance, changed from 1 to 100, W^* - is the brightness index, U^* and V^* are the chromaticity indices, u and v are the chromaticity coordinates in Mac-Adam diagram (Mac Adam, 1974); $u_0 = 0.201$ and $v_0 = 0.307$ are the chromaticity coordinates of basic white color. The transformation from *RGB* system to the Y, u and v coordinates is done using the well-known matrix transformations (Pratt, 2001).

The transformation into the equal color space allows for estimating the color differences of the big image details using the minimum perceptible color difference (MPCD). These values are almost equal through the whole color space (Krivosheev & Kustarev, 1990). Here the error of the color rendering is determined by the MPCD value using the following equation:

$$\varepsilon = 3\sqrt{(\Delta W^*)^2 + (\Delta U^*)^2 + (\Delta V^*)^2}\,, \tag{3}$$

where ΔW^*, ΔU^* and ΔV^* are the difference values of color coordinates of two images. Equation (3) can be used for estimation of the color contrast of a big detail relative to the background. Threshold values on brightness and chromaticity indices depend on the size of image details, background color coordinates, time period of object presentation and noise level. Therefore the equation (3) will not be objective for the analysis of color transfer distortions of fine details.

Works (Sai, 2002) and (Sai, 2003) propose to use the normalized value of the color contrast for estimating the color transfer distortions of fine details:

$$\Delta\overline{K} = 3\sqrt{(\Delta\overline{W}^*)^2 + (\Delta\overline{U}^*)^2 + (\Delta\overline{V}^*)^2}\,, \tag{4}$$

where $\Delta\overline{W}^* = (W^*_{\max} - W^*_{\min}) / \Delta W^*_{th}$; $\Delta\overline{U}^* = (U^*_{\max} - U^*_{\min}) / \Delta U^*_{th}$ and $\Delta\overline{V}^* = (V^*_{\max} - V^*_{\min}) / \Delta V^*_{th}$ are the normalized to the thresholds contrast values of the image with fine details and ΔW^*_{th}, ΔU^*_{th} and ΔV^*_{th} are the thresholds according to brightness and chromaticity indices for fine details. These threshold values are obtained experimentally (Sai, 2003) for fine details with sizes not exceeding one pixel. From the experimental data, for fine details of the test table located on a grey background threshold values are approximately $\Delta W^*_{th} \approx 6$ MPCD and $\Delta U^*_{th} \approx \Delta V^*_{th} \approx 72$ MPCD.

Search algorithms (Sai & Sorokin, 2008) and (Sai & Sorokin, 2009) of fine details divides the image into the blocks of size 3 x 3 pixels. After this, the recognition of the image blocks using special binary masks is performed. These masks have the following attributes: a "dot object", a "thin line", a "texture fragment". This work also describes the search algorithm with sliding window size 3 x 3 pixels.

Consider the modified search algorithm.

At the first step the values $(W^*_{\max}, U^*_{\max}, V^*_{\max})$ and $(W^*_{\min}, U^*_{\min}, V^*_{\min})$ are computed along with the value of normalized color contrast (4) for a window. Next, the following condition is checked:

$$\Delta\overline{K}_{\min} < \Delta\overline{K}_n < \Delta\overline{K}_{\max}\,, \tag{5}$$

where $\Delta\overline{K}_{\min} \geq 1$ and $\Delta\overline{K}_{\max}$ are pre-defined minimal and maximal contrast values, n – number of the current block. Obviously, the maximal contrast value corresponds to the bright white detail on the black background of the image. Using Y_{max}=*100* in equation (4) we obtain $\Delta\overline{K}_{\max} \approx 19$. Note, that the definition of values $\Delta\overline{K}_{\min}$ and $\Delta\overline{K}_{\max}$ depends upon the search task. For example, if we search the fine details with low contrast the equation (5) can be defined as:

$$1 < \Delta\overline{K}_n < 4\,.$$

If the condition (5) is fulfilled the decision is made that the nth block of the image contains small details identified by an eye. If the condition (5) is not fulfilled this block is excluded from further analysis. Next, the window position is changed by one pixel (vertically or horizontally) and the first step is repeated.

At the second step the image of the block with small details is converted to the binary form. For each pixel of the block the following conditions are checked:

$$\sqrt[3]{\left(\frac{W_i^* - W_{\max}^*}{\Delta W_{th}^*}\right)^2 + \left(\frac{U_i^* - U_{\max}^*}{\Delta U_{th}^*}\right)^2 + \left(\frac{V_i^* - V_{\max}^*}{\Delta V_{th}^*}\right)^2} \le T_n \tag{6}$$

$$\sqrt[3]{\left(\frac{W_i^* - W_{\min}^*}{\Delta W_{th}^*}\right)^2 + \left(\frac{U_i^* - U_{\min}^*}{\Delta U_{th}^*}\right)^2 + \left(\frac{V_i^* - V_{\min}^*}{\Delta V_{th}^*}\right)^2} \le T_n\,, \tag{7}$$

where $i=1\ldots9$ is the pixel number in the block and T_n – threshold value. If the condition (6) is fulfilled the decision on membership of the pixel to the maximal value is taken. If the condition (7) is fulfilled the decision on membership of the pixel to the minimal value is taken. Next, the levels of one and zero are assigned to the maximal and minimal values accordingly.

The threshold value is dependent on $\Delta\overline{K}_n$ and always satisfies $T_n \le 1$. If the contrast of the block belongs to $1 < \Delta\overline{K}_n < 10$, the threshold value is equal to $T_n = 0.1 \cdot \Delta\overline{K}_n$, otherwise for $\Delta\overline{K}_n \ge 10$ we set $T_n = 1$.

At the third step the binary image of the block is compared to the binary mask from the defined set. Figures of the binary masks coincide with those defined on Fig. 1, but the value w_i is set to one for the white pixel and to zero for the dark pixel, accordingly.

The binary block of the image is compared to the binary image of the jth mask with the help of a simple equation:

$$M_k = \sum_{i=1}^{9} (Ib_{n,j} - w_{k,j})\,. \tag{8}$$

The decision is made that the given block refers to the image of the jth mask in case if the computed value (8) is equal to zero. The decision about exclusion of the current block from the analysis is made if the value (8) is not equal to zero for all masks.

The same is done if the texture elements must be detected. Fig. 2 shows different examples of binary masks for the case when the number of bright pixels is equal to five.

1	0	1
0	1	0
1	0	1

0	1	1
1	0	0
0	1	1

1	1	1
0	1	0
0	1	0

0	1	1
0	0	1
1	1	0

Fig. 2. Examples of binary masks for identifying texture elements

The distinctive feature of the algorithm is that the thresholds of visual perception of fine details contrast of the image depend on the average brightness of the analyzed block. In particular, the contrast change on light blocks of the image will be more visible than on dark ones.

The given condition can be taken into account with the help of adjusting coefficients during the computation of the thresholds. For example, for the brightness threshold:

$$\Delta W_{th}^{*} = k_{W^*} \cdot \Delta W_{th}^{*}, \tag{9}$$

where $k_{W^*} \approx 1$ for the grey blocks ($70 < W^* < 90$), $k_{W^*} < 1$ for the light blocks ($W^* \geq 90$) and $k_{W^*} > 1$ for the dark blocks ($W^* \leq 70$).

Thus, the offered search algorithm allows for allocating fine details in the image for the further analysis and recognition. Compared with the classical search algorithm the developed algorithm has the following advantages. 1. The algorithm takes into account the properties of the visual perception of contrast of small details. 2. The algorithm allows for searching the color details with a given contrast. 3. Application of sliding window and binary blocks improve the accuracy of search and detection. 4. The algorithm allows for selection the texture elements from the image.

Results of experiments show that search algorithm works quite well in the processing of test images without noise. The presence of noise leads to "diffusion" of the values of pixels color coordinates in the *RGB* image signals; that reduces the accuracy of search and recognition of fine details with low contrast.

Let's consider the application of the described algorithm in the systems of search and recognition of fine details in the noisy images. The following assumptions are used in order to analyze the noise influence on the image definition reduction: 1) Interaction of signals and noise is additive. 2) Density distribution law of stationary noise probabilities is close to the normal law. 3) Noise in *RGB* signals of the decoded image is not correlative. Such assumptions are widely used in the engineering computations of noise-immune TV systems. They permit to simplify the analysis with the admissible errors.

Noise in the system results in "diffusion" of both objects color coordinates and background in the decoded image. Thus a point in *RGB* space is transformed into ellipsoid with semi axis. Their values are proportional to root-mean-square noise levels ($\sigma_R, \sigma_G, \sigma_B$). During the transformation $\{R_i G_i B_i\} \rightarrow \{W_i^* U_i^* V_i^*\}$ the values of equal color space coordinates become random variables with root-mean-square deviations ($\sigma_{W^*}, \sigma_{U^*}, \sigma_{V^*}$). Works (Sai, 2007) and (Sai, 2003) present the probability analysis of such transformation and obtain a criterion that describes when the fine detail will be recognized against the background noise. This criterion is formulated as:

$$\Delta \overline{K} \geq 3\sqrt{(\sigma_{W^*})^2 + (\sigma_{U^*})^2 + (\sigma_{V^*})^2}, \tag{10}$$

where $\Delta \overline{K}$ is normalized contrast (4) of the block with fine details; $\sigma_{W^*}, \sigma_{U^*}, \sigma_{V^*}$ - are normalized to visual perception thresholds root-mean-square deviations of noise values. Note, that this criterion uses a simple "three sigma" rule:

$$\sigma_{\Sigma} = \sqrt{(\sigma_{W^*})^2 + (\sigma_{U^*})^2 + (\sigma_{V^*})^2},$$

where σ_{Σ} is a total root-mean-square value computed for all image blocks that contain fine details.

Therefore, the low level of color contrast interval should be changed in order to take into account the influence of noise in the search algorithm. In this case the pre-defied value $\Delta \overline{K}_{\min}$ should satisfy the following condition:

$$\Delta\overline{K}_{\min} \geq 1 \text{ and } \Delta\overline{K}_{\min} \geq 3\sigma_{\Sigma} . \tag{11}$$

Thus, the search algorithm is able to detect the fine details only with high contrast if the noise level in the image is high. If $\sigma_{\Sigma} < 1/3$, then the image noise will be imperceptible or hardly noticeable for an eye during the observation of fine details with the lowest contrast. This permits to identify the fine details even with low contrast $\Delta\overline{K} \approx 1...2$.
Proposed algorithm can be applied in automated search and object detection systems or in the computer vision systems. Consider the features of such applications.
Computer vision systems may not take into account the features of human eye perception. In this case the foto and video sensor properties should be considered: sensitivity and the dynamic signal range. Today's foto and video sensors have high sensitivity and dynamic range properties; this enables to receive digital signal with a big number of quantization levels. For example, MT9V sensors from Micron have digital *RGB* output from 10-bit ADC. Digital TV systems require 8 bit per one color channel; that corresponds to the digital interval 255/1. Along with this, threshold will be equal to one.
Therefore, during the computation of color contrast in search algorithm the transformation from *RGB* to equal color space is not necessary. The RGB space can be used directly, or it can be transformed to luminance and chromaticity system, e.g., YC_RC_B. The widely used model is defined by CCIR 601-2 (ITU-R BT.601) recommendations. The components are computed as follows:

$$\begin{aligned} Y &= 0{,}299R + 0{,}587G + 0{,}114B; \\ C_R &= 0{,}5R - 0{,}419G - 0{,}081B; \\ C_B &= -0{,}169R - 0{,}331G + 0{,}5B. \end{aligned} \tag{12}$$

Let's consider the search algorithm of fine details in the selected color space. At the first stage the contrast value in the sliding widow size 3 x 3 is computed:

$$\Delta\overline{K}_n = \sqrt{(\Delta\overline{Y})^2 + (\Delta\overline{C}_R)^2 + (\Delta\overline{C}_B)^2} , \tag{13}$$

where $\Delta\overline{Y} = (Y_{\max} - Y_{\min}) / \Delta Y$, $\Delta\overline{C}_R = (C_{R\max} - C_{R\min}) / \Delta C$ and $\Delta\overline{C}_B = (C_{B\max} - C_{B\min}) / \Delta C$ are the luminance and chromaticity contrast values of fine details, ΔY and ΔC are the luminance and chromaticity thresholds of the computer vision system. The values of thresholds of the system depend on the precision of *RGB* signals and on the noise level. If the noise level is quite low, the values of thresholds will be defined by the least significant bit of each Y, C_R and C_B signal, i.e. $\Delta Y = \Delta C = 1$.
Now let's define the upper border of the interval for the contrast values of the 8-bit Y, C_R and C_B signals. Value $Y_{\max} = 255$ is obtained by plugging the maximal values of the digital RGB signals into equation (12). Therefore, the maximal contrast value (13) is then $\Delta\overline{K}_{\max} = 255$ and the interval for the contrast is

$$\Delta\overline{K}_{\min} < \Delta\overline{K}_n < 255 . \tag{14}$$

The value of the low bound is selected using the noise level of the system like (11), where the total noise value is defined as

$$\sigma_{\Sigma} = \sqrt{(\sigma_Y)^2 + (\sigma_{C_R})^2 + (\sigma_{C_B})^2},$$

$\sigma_Y, \sigma_{C_R}, \sigma_{C_B}$ - are root-mean-square deviations of noise values in the luminance and chromaticity channels. After selection of contrast interval for a block and check for the condition (5), the search of fine details is processed using equations (6)-(9).

Thus, the differences are in the selected color space and defined thresholds. In particular, during the transformation to binary form of the block instead of conditions (6) and (7) the following conditions will be applied:

$$\sqrt{(Y_i - Y_{\max})^2 + (C_{Ri} - C_{R\max})^2 + (C_{Bi} - C_{B\max})^2} \le T_n, \tag{15}$$

$$\sqrt{(Y_i - Y_{\min})^2 + (C_{Ri} - C_{R\min})^2 + (C_{Bi} - C_{B\min})^2} \le T_n, \tag{16}$$

where the constant threshold value T_n is selected greater than zero and is independent of contrast value $\Delta \overline{K}_n$. For example, during the analyses of fine details only on luminance and using $T_n = 1$ the condition (15) is changed to $|Y_i - Y_{\max}| \le 1$. This means, that the pixel has level of "one" if its luminance differs from maximal value not greater than by least significant bit. For the correct application of search algorithm in the noisy system the threshold should be selected as $T_n \ge 3\sigma_{\Sigma}$.

3. Algorithms for analyses and recognition

Previous section was devoted to the search algorithms of fine details of images using the following attributes: "dot object," "thin line," "texture fragment". The fine details detected and identified in the source image can be used for the further analyses and recognition.

The common task of search for objects and their recognition can be divided into the following steps: formation of object properties; forming the source image of the object; search for the object in the test image using the defined properties; object recognition and identification.

Small details can form a part of properties of the bigger objects while solving the recognition and identification tasks. Such bigger objects can be, e.g., stamp on the document or a fingerprint. In the task of analyzing image quality the investigation object is the distortions of fine details. These distortions arise after image compression or image transfer through the noisy channels.

Thus, one has to compare the properties of the fine details in the reference and investigated images using the defined criteria during the object recognition or distortion analyses. Such properties of the fine detail can be: attitude, form, brightness, chromaticity, contrast. For the binary images only attitude and form of the object are necessary.

Consider the well-known method (Wang at. al., 2004) of the grayscale image quality analyses - Structural Similarity Index SSIM. In this method distortions are estimated using a sliding window size 8 x 8 pixel. Suppose x and y are two nonnegative image signals, which have been aligned with each other (blocks from two images). The SSIM value is computed as:

$$SSIM(x, y) = l(x, y) \cdot c(x, y) \cdot s(x, y), \tag{17}$$

where $l(x,y)$ – luminance comparison function, $c(x,y)$ – contrast comparison function and $s(x,y)$ – structure comparison function. These functions are defined as follows:

$$l(x,y) = \frac{2\mu_x\mu_y + C_1}{\mu_x^2 + \mu_y^2 + C_1},$$

$$c(x,y) = \frac{2\sigma_x\sigma_y + C_2}{\sigma_x^2 + \sigma_y^2 + C_2}, \tag{18}$$

$$c(x,y) = \frac{\sigma_{xy} + C_3}{\sigma_x\sigma_y + C_3},$$

where μ_x and μ_y are mean intensities, C_1, C_2, C_3 are constants, $\sigma_x, \sigma_y, \sigma_{xy}$ are standard deviations and correlation coefficient in the analyzed blocks of image, accordingly. The following equations define those parameters (from (Wang at. al., 2004)):

$$\mu_x = \frac{1}{N}\sum_{i=1}^{N} Y_{i(x)}\ ;\ \mu_y = \frac{1}{N}\sum_{i=1}^{N} Y_{i(y)} \tag{19}$$

$$\sigma_x = \sqrt{\frac{1}{N-1}\sum_{i=1}^{N}(Y_{i(x)} - \mu_x)^2}\ ;\ \sigma_y = \sqrt{\frac{1}{N-1}\sum_{i=1}^{N}(Y_{i(y)} - \mu_y)^2} \tag{20}$$

$$\sigma_{xy} = \frac{1}{N-1}\sum_{i=1}^{N}(Y_{i(x)} - \mu_x)\cdot(Y_{i(y)} - \mu_y) \tag{21}$$

With the windows size 8 x 8 pixel parameter $N=64$. Constants are defined as:

$$C_1 = (K_1L)^2\ ;\ C_2 = (K_2L)^2\ ;\ C_3 = C_2 / 2, \tag{22}$$

where $L=255$ – dynamic rage of the pixels values for the grayscale image, $K_1=0.01$ and $K_2=0.03$ – defined parameters. Note, that equation (18) uses the property of human visual system (HVS): HVS is sensitive to the relative luminance change, and not the absolute luminance change.

After computing SSIM value (17) for each block, the integral value is calculated:

$$MSSIM(X,Y) = \frac{1}{M}\sum_{i=1}^{M} SSIM(x_i, y_i), \tag{23}$$

where M is a number of analyzed blocks in the image. Results presented in (Wang at. al., 2004) showed quite good correspondence between estimation (23) and subjective quality estimations for the JPEG and JPEG2000 standards. Along with this, the deviation of such estimation is much lower compared to PSNR, JND and UQI methods.

To our opinion SSIM method has the following drawbacks: 1. SSIM computations and estimation involve only the luminance of the image, this means that the distortions can not be estimated using the chromaticity component of the image. 2. SSIM computation is done using 8 x 8 pixel block, it does not provide the estimation of distortions of fine detail with particular form. 3. SSIM method uses common properties of HVS without counting the definite thresholds of the visual perception of fine details contrast.

Consider an alternative method of distortion analyses of fine details of the image.

At the first step the position of the fine details with particular form in the reference image is located. With this purpose the search algorithm of fine details (described in section 2) on the reference image is carried out. After the execution of search algorithm the coordinates of the objects will correspond to the 3 x 3 block numbers, where those fine details were detected.

At the second step for each found j^{th} block the deviation of the maximal value of color coordinates is computed:

$$\tilde{\varepsilon}_j = \max_N \left(\sqrt{\left(\Delta\tilde{W}_i^*\right)^2 + \left(\Delta\tilde{U}_i^*\right)^2 + \left(\Delta\tilde{V}_i^*\right)^2} \right), \tag{24}$$

where $i=1\ldots N$, $N=9$ is the number of elements in the block and

$$\Delta\tilde{W}_i^* = 3(W_i^* - \tilde{W}_i^*) / \Delta W_{th}^*,$$
$$\Delta\tilde{U}_i^* = 3(U_i^* - \tilde{U}_i^*) / \Delta U_{th}^*,$$
$$\Delta\tilde{V}_i^* = 3(V_i^* - \tilde{V}_i^*) / \Delta V_{th}^*$$

are the normalized to thresholds deviations on brightness and on chromaticity for each pixel of reference ($W_i^* U_i^* V_i^*$) and corrupted ($\tilde{W}_i^* \tilde{U}_i^* \tilde{V}_i^*$) blocks.

In particular if the block is analyzed only on brightness the expression (24) will be transformed into:

$$\tilde{\varepsilon}_{j(W^*)} = \max_N \left(3\left|W_i^* - \tilde{W}_i^*\right| / \Delta W_{th}^* \right), \tag{25}$$

where $\tilde{W}_i^*$ is the value of brightness of the ith pixel in the image block after the compression. If the block is analyzed on chromaticity we obtain:

$$\tilde{\varepsilon}_{j(U^*,V^*)} = \max_N \left(\sqrt{\left(\Delta\tilde{U}_i^*\right)^2 + \left(\Delta\tilde{V}_i^*\right)^2} \right). \tag{26}$$

Equation (26) determines the maximal error of color transfer of fine details in the block.

Here it is necessary to note that in the compression standards the most complete information on fine details is contained in the brightness component. Therefore, a separate calculation of the errors on brightness and chromaticity is justified.

At the third step the average values of deviation on brightness and on chromaticity for all image blocks are calculated:

$$\bar{\varepsilon}_{W^*} = \frac{1}{M}\sum_{j=1}^{M} \tilde{\varepsilon}_{j(W^*)}; \quad \bar{\varepsilon}_{U^*,V^*} = \frac{1}{M}\sum_{j=1}^{M} \tilde{\varepsilon}_{j(U^*,V^*)}; \quad \bar{\varepsilon}_{\Sigma} = \bar{\varepsilon}_{W^*} + \bar{\varepsilon}_{U^*,V^*}, \tag{27}$$

where M is the number of blocks in the image, which contain fine details found by the search algorithm.

At the final step the quality rating of fine details for transfer and reproduction in the analyzed image is established using the error value (27).

The ten-point scale of quality (Sai, 2007), used in Adobe Photoshop 5.0 system, during the realization of JPEG compression algorithm is chosen. Experimental results of research of the error dependences for other test images have shown that for support of a high quality rating ($R \geq 7$) the average value of the coordinates deviation of fine details on brightness should not exceed the threshold value, i.e.,

$$\bar{\varepsilon}_{\Sigma} < 1.0 . \quad (28)$$

In difference to MSSIM (23) the proposed method estimates the distortions of fine details by the number of normalized visual thresholds. Thus, if the criterion (28) is fulfilled then the following decision is made: for the fine details the contrast change is imperceptible for an eye.

Experimental results showed that the objective criterion (28) is in good correlation with the subjective quality estimation not only for the JPEG standard, but also for other lossy compression algorithms applied to static images.

Let's consider the algorithm of recognition and identification of fine details in the computer vision system. The recognition properties of fine details are: attitude, contrast and form.

At the first step the search of fine details on the reference image is carried out (algorithm is described in section 2). In equation (13) of this algorithm thresholds of sensitivity for luminance and for chromaticity are used.

After the execution of search algorithm the coordinates of the objects will correspond to the 3 x 3 block numbers, where those fine details were detected. Forms of the detected details correspond to the binary masks. In particular, forms of binary masks correspond to masks depicted on Fig. 3, if the search properties are position and orientation of dark lines on the white background.

1	1	0
1	0	1
0	1	1

1	1	1
0	0	0
1	1	1

1	0	1
1	0	1
1	0	1

0	1	1
1	0	1
1	1	0

Fig. 3. Examples of binary masks for identifying thin lines

At the second step the comparison of fine details color coordinates is processed for the reference and analyzed images. For each found j^{th} block the deviation of the maximal value of color coordinates is computed (like in (24)):

$$\tilde{\varepsilon}_j = \max_N \left(\sqrt{\left(\Delta\tilde{Y}_i\right)^2 + \left(\Delta\tilde{C}_{Ri}\right)^2 + \left(\Delta\tilde{C}_{Bi}\right)^2} \right), \quad (29)$$

where

$$\Delta\tilde{Y}_i = (Y_i - \tilde{Y}_i) / \Delta Y;$$
$$\Delta\tilde{C}_{Ri} = (C_{Ri} - \tilde{C}_{Ri}) / \Delta C;$$
$$\Delta\tilde{C}_{Bi} = (C_{Bi} - \tilde{C}_{Bi}) / \Delta C$$

are the normalized to thresholds deviations on brightness and on chromaticity for each pixel of reference ($Y_i C_{Ri} C_{Bi}$) and analyzed ($\tilde{Y}_i \tilde{C}_{Ri} \tilde{C}_{Bi}$) blocks.
Next, the error value is compared to the defied threshold T:

$$\tilde{\varepsilon}_j < T \,, \tag{30}$$

where T depends on the noise level and like in (11) is selected equal to at least $3\sigma_\Sigma$. Obviously, bigger noise in the analyzed image corresponds to the worse recognition results.
If the criterion (30) is fulfilled then the following decision is made: the fine detail in the jth block is recognized and the next block can be processed. Otherwise, the block is not recognized.
The probability of the complete object depends on the total number of blocks with fine details. For our algorithm is can be defined as:

$$P_r = N_r / N_\Sigma \,, \tag{31}$$

where N_r is the number of recognized blocks and N_Σ is the total number of blocks.
The probability value will be quite high if the deviation of color coordinates of fine details are below their thresholds. It must be noted, that the probability of recognition depends on the accuracy of matching reference and analyzed objects.
For the real images the luminance and the object contrast can significantly differ from the reference object. In this case, some blocks with fine details may not be recognized using criterion (30). The following algorithm can be applied, if the recognition properties are only attitude and form of fine details. This algorithm is based on the previously described.
At the first step the coordinates of the blocks with fine details in the reference image are obtained using the search algorithm.
At the second step the blocks in the analyzed image are processed as follows. For each selected block j size 3 x 3 pixel the transformation to binary form is carried out like in (15) and (16):

$$\sqrt{\left(\tilde{Y}_i - \tilde{Y}_{\max}\right)^2 + \left(\tilde{C}_{Ri} - \tilde{C}_{R\max}\right)^2 + \left(\tilde{C}_{Bi} - \tilde{C}_{B\max}\right)^2} <= T_n \,, \tag{32}$$

$$\sqrt{\left(\tilde{Y}_i - \tilde{Y}_{\min}\right)^2 + \left(\tilde{C}_{Ri} - \tilde{C}_{R\min}\right)^2 + \left(\tilde{C}_{Bi} - \tilde{C}_{B\min}\right)^2} <= T_n \,. \tag{33}$$

After that the jth binary block of the analyzed image is compared to the binary image of the kth mask:

$$M_k = \sum_{i=1}^{9} (Ib_{j,i} - w_{k,i}) \,. \tag{34}$$

The decision is made that the given j^{th} block refers to the image of the kth mask in case if the computed value (34) is equal to zero. Thus, the analyzed j^{th} block has fine details identical to the jth block from the reference image.

At the last step the probability of recognition is computed using equation (31).
Therefore, the proposed algorithm allows for recognition and identification of fine details using their attitude and form independent of their luminance and chromaticity.
Some examples of practical applications of algorithms are presented in the next section.

4. Examples of algorithms applications

The developed algorithms of search and recognition of fine details can be applied in different computer vision systems. For example, consider two systems: the first is a system of distortion analysis of fine details of noisy images; the second is a system of search and recognition of fine details in images of stamp.
Consider the efficiency of algorithms application in the first system.
The peak signal-to-noise ratio (PSNR) is considered nowadays the most popular criterion of noisy images (Pratt, 2001). According to this criterion the normalized root-mean-square deviation of color coordinates is calculated and the averaging is carried out at all pixels of the image. The ratio of the maximal amplitude (A) of the signal to the root-mean-square deviation in logarithmic scale defines PSNR value:

$$\mathrm{PSNR} = 20\lg \frac{A}{\sqrt{\frac{1}{N_x \cdot N_y} \sum_{i=1}^{N_x} \sum_{j=1}^{N_y} \Delta C_{i,j}}}, \tag{35}$$

where $\Delta C_{i,j} = (R_{i,j} - \tilde{R}_{i,j})^2 + (G_{i,j} - \tilde{G}_{i,j})^2 + (B_{i,j} - \tilde{B}_{i,j})^2$; R, G, B are the color signals without noise, $\tilde{R}, \tilde{G}, \tilde{B}$ are the color signals with noise and $N_x \cdot N_y$ is the number of pixels in the image.
Thus, the closer the noisy image to the original, the bigger the PSNR value (35) and therefore the better its quality we have. However this and other similar metrics allow for estimating only root-mean-square difference between images, therefore the best results from the metrics point of view are not always correspond to the best visual perception.
Filtering algorithms of noisy images are well investigated and described in literature, e.g., (Hamza et. al., 2002). They are usually specializing on suppression of a particular kind of noise. Meanwhile there are no universal filters that could detect and suppress all kinds of noise. However many kinds of noise can be rather well approximated using model of Gaussian noise. And therefore the majority of algorithms are focused on suppression of this kind of noise.
The basic problem at noise filtering is not to spoil sharpness of details borders of the image, and also not to lose the fine details that are comparable on amplitude with noise. One more complication is the rating of noise suppression quality. As a rule, the quality is estimated as follows: the artificial noise is imposed on the original image, and then the resulted image is filtered with the help of the chosen algorithm and compared to the initial image with the help of the chosen metrics. Thus, the closer the filtered image to the original, the bigger PSNR value is obtained and that is considered the quality of the filtering algorithm. As it has been pointed above, the PSNR value allows for estimating only the root-mean-square difference between images, and therefore the best results from the point of view of the metrics (also other than PSNR) do not always correspond to the best visual perception.

Let's consider the applications of the proposed algorithms for the quality estimation of fine details in the noisy images. At the beginning the search algorithm of fine details is performed using on the images without noise. The equations (3)-(8) are used, where the condition (5) is changed to:

$$\Delta \bar{K}_n > 1 . \tag{36}$$

If the normalized contrast satisfies condition (36) for blocks 3 x 3, then the decision is made that the fine details or the texture elements of big details are present in the image block.
The common criterion, when the fine details with contrast $\Delta \bar{K}_n$ will be detected by an eye on the background noise, is formulated as:

$$\Delta \bar{K} \geq 3\sqrt{(\bar{\sigma}_{W^*})^2 + (\bar{\sigma}_{U^*})^2 + (\bar{\sigma}_{V^*})^2} , \tag{37}$$

where $\bar{\sigma}_{W^*}, \bar{\sigma}_{U^*}, \bar{\sigma}_{V^*}$ are normalized to visual perception thresholds root-mean-square deviation values of noise.
Let's define criterion when the image noise will be imperceptible or hardly noticeable for an eye during the observation of fine details with the lowest contrast $\Delta \bar{K}_n \approx 1$:

$$\bar{\sigma}_{\Sigma} = \sqrt{(\bar{\sigma}_{W^*})^2 + (\bar{\sigma}_{U^*})^2 + (\bar{\sigma}_{V^*})^2} \leq 1/3 , \tag{38}$$

where $\bar{\sigma}_{\Sigma}$ is a total root-mean-square value computed for all image blocks that contain fine details. The root-mean-square deviation values are computed as, e.g., for brightness:

$$\bar{\sigma}_{W^*} = \max_M \left(\frac{1}{W^*_{th} \cdot N} \sum_{i=0}^{N-1} \left| W^*_{j,i} - \tilde{W}^*_{j,i} \right| \right) , \tag{39}$$

where $N=9$ is a number of elements in the block, $j=1 \ldots M$ and M is a number of blocks. Values $\bar{\sigma}_{U^*}$ and $\bar{\sigma}_{V^*}$ are computed similar to (39). Note, that in contrast to formulas (24) and (25) in (39), at first, we compute the mean value of the noise in the block and then select the maximum.
Thus, for estimating the noisiness of the fine details we should search for these details and then estimate the value $\bar{\sigma}_{\Sigma}$ using criterion (39). If this criterion is fulfilled the decision is made that: for the fine details the contrast change is imperceptible for an eye, and the presence of noise in the *RGB* channels does not impair the image quality.
Main differences of the new criterion (39) from the PSNR are:

1. new algorithm analyzes distortions over the part of the image: it covers only image fragments that contain the fine details;
2. root-mean-square difference between the source and noisy images is defined by the value $\bar{\sigma}_{\Sigma}$ which is estimated by the number of normalized thresholds of an eye.

Therefore, the proposed criterion (39) is more objective because it takes into account the features of the visual perception of the contrast distortions of fine details.
A program analyzer is implemented in order to investigate the efficiency of the quality estimation of fine details representation. As the additive noise models the fluctuation Gaussian noise and impulsive noise were selected.

Fig.4 shows examples of the test images "Lena" with different levels of the impulsive noise.

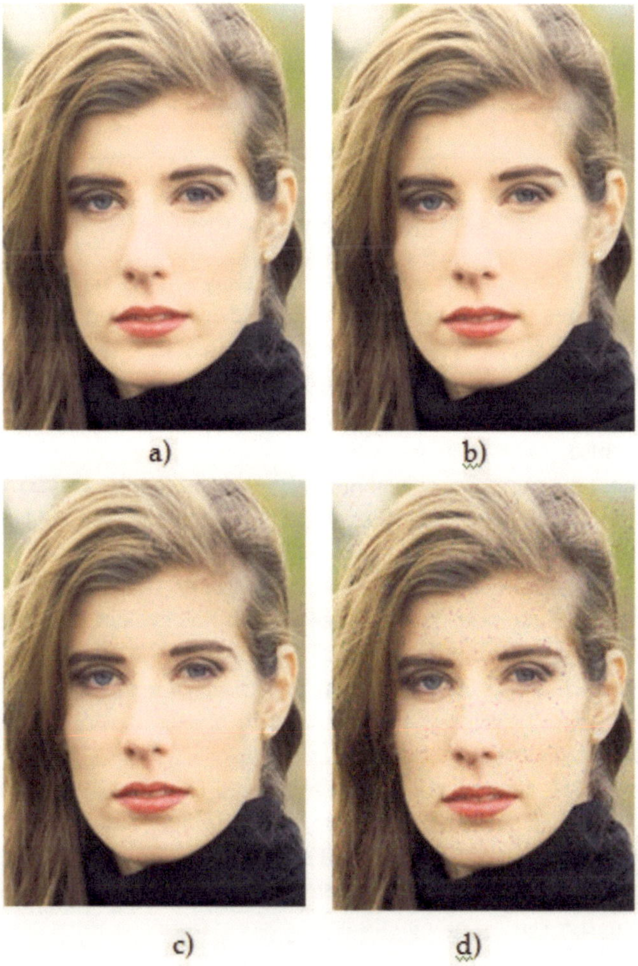

Fig. 4. Test image "Lena" with impulsive noise: a) original image; b) $P_{err} = 1 \cdot 10^{-3}$; c) $P_{err} = 1 \cdot 10^{-2}$; d) $P_{err} = 5 \cdot 10^{-2}$

Table 1 contains the experimental dependencies of $\bar{\sigma}_{\Sigma}$ and PSNR from root-mean-square noise value (σ) for the test images "Lena". Here the root-mean-square value of the Gaussian noise was set as a ratio to the maximum amplitude (A) of the signal. The following assumption was used: $\sigma \approx \sigma_R \approx \sigma_G \approx \sigma_B$.

σ	0.5	1.0	1.5	2.0	3.0
$\bar{\sigma}_{\Sigma}$	0.08	0.13	0.19	0.29	0.43
PSNR	46.67	43.96	42.27	41.03	39.32

Table 1. Dependencies of $\bar{\sigma}_{\Sigma}$ and PSNR (in dB) from σ (in %)

Table 2 presents the experimental dependencies of $\bar{\sigma}_{\Sigma}$ and PSNR from the error probability value P_{err} of the image transfer. The value P_{err} was set as a ratio of the number of error bytes to the whole number of bytes in the image when the impulsive noise was modeled.

P_{err}	$5\cdot10^{-4}$	$1\cdot10^{-3}$	$5\cdot10^{-3}$	$1\cdot10^{-2}$	$5\cdot10^{-2}$
$\bar{\sigma}_{\Sigma}$	0.24	0.30	0.43	0.58	0.72
PSNR	64.82	61.78	54.48	51.03	43.98

Table 2. Dependencies of $\bar{\sigma}_{\Sigma}$ and PSNR (in dB) from P_{err}

Experimental results of the quality analysis of the noisy images have shown that the PSNR estimation gives different results for fluctuation and impulsive noise. Data from Tables 1 and 2 together with the subjective estimations show that the "good" image quality is: for Gaussian noise with *PSNR>40* dB, and for impulsive noise with *PSNR>60* dB.
Therefore, the PSNR criterion is not objective for quality analysis of the images with different types of noise.
Proposed criterion (39) is more objective and gives adequate results compared to the subjective estimations independently from types of the noise. This is confirmed with the experimental results.
Consider the efficiency of developed algorithms application in the automated authentication system for stamp on a document. Two images exist in this system: a reference stamp image and a test image of a stamp on a document. For the authentication of stamp: 1) a "stamp" object should be detected and extracted from the image of a document, 2) extracted object should be aligned with the reference image, and 3) object should be identified using the defined properties.
Suppose that the initial steps of the search algorithm are already done and the "stamp" object is precisely aligned with the reference stamp image. Along with this, two stamps should be compared for the purpose of identification of the object.
In a simple case two images can be compared using the root-mean-square deviation of the pixels. This value in the YC_RC_B color space is:

$$\Delta_{\mathrm{RMS}} = \frac{1}{N_x \cdot N_y} \sum_{i=1}^{N_x} \sum_{j=1}^{N_y} \sqrt{\left(Y_{i,j} - \tilde{Y}_{i,j}\right)^2 + \left(C_{Ri,j} - \tilde{C}_{Rj}\right)^2 + \left(C_{Bi,j} - \tilde{C}_{Bj}\right)^2}\,, \tag{40}$$

where YC_RC_B and $\tilde{Y}\tilde{C}_R\tilde{C}_B$ are pixel coordinates for luminosity and chromaticity of the reference and analyzed images.
Obviously, that such an integral comparison does not allow for estimating the originality of stamp for the following reasons: 1) the image of the original stamp can differ from one document to another by luminance and contrast. 2) Some parts of the stamp can be poorly printed or even be absent on the image. 3) The original document has additional dots coming from the signature or text of a document under the stamp.
Note that normally the fake stamps are of high quality level and differ from the original stamp insignificantly. Thus, the task of comparison and identification of image stamp with reference stamp is complex (Sai, 2009).

Using the developed algorithms of search and recognition of fine details we propose the following algorithm of stamp authentication.
The following properties are selected for the recognition of fine details: attitude, orientation of thin lines and texture structures. The preprocessing of reference and analyzed stamp images must be carried out:

1. Covert the images from color to grayscale system.
2. Transfer the images into the binary form.
3. Obtain the contour images using Sobel operator.
4. Filter the contour images for smoothing the edges.
5. Make contour details more definite using the Zong Sun algorithm.

Fig. 5 shows an example of reference stamp image during the preprocessing steps.

Fig. 5. Stamp image after the preprocessing: a) original image, b) binary image, c) contour image, d) image with definite contour details

Thus, the reference and analyzed stamps are obtained in a form of thin lines and texture elements after the preprocessing step. Next, the search algorithm of fine details is applied to these two images. As the images are in a binary form, obtain the blocks size 3 x 3 pixels corresponding to k^{th} mask (like in equation (8)):

$$M_k = \sum_{i=1}^{9}(Ib_{n,i} - w_{k,i}) \quad (41)$$

The decision is made that the given block refers to the image of the kth mask in case if the computed value (41) is equal to zero. Next, check the image of the nth block of analyzed image:

$$\Delta_n = \sum_{i=1}^{9}(Ib_{n,i} - \tilde{I}b_{n,i}); \quad (42)$$

where $Ib_{n,i}$ and $\tilde{I}b_{n,i}$ are binary pixel values in the reference and analyzed image blocks.
The decision is made that the reference $Ib_{n,i}$ and analyzed $\tilde{I}b_{n,i}$ image blocks are identical in case if the computed value (42) is equal to zero. After this the probability of recognition is computer using (31). The system authenticates the stamp if the probability value is equal to one. Otherwise, the system outputs the numbers of blocks that are not identical for the further analyses.
Image blocks may not be identical for the following reasons:

1. Some parts of the stamp can be poorly printed or even be absent in the image.
2. The analyzed document has additional dots coming from the signature or text of a document under the stamp.
3. The superposition errors of two stamps – the reference and the analyzed one.

Coming from the research results the probability of recognition P_r will be strictly less than one due to the reduced errors. Also the probability value will be $P_r < 1$ if we would test two equal stamps and one image will be rotated for an arbitrary angle. So the described algorithm allows the selection from the analyzed stamp image only those fragments that differ from the reference image.
Taking into account the high quality of fake stamp images we could conclude that there exist no software method to identify either the given fragment belongs to the fake image or the difference has other factors. For example, the absence of some points in the analyzed block can be identified as a fake or as the absence of points due to the low quality of the stamp image. At the end stage only the human expert can make a decision.
For the effective expert work the following functions are implemented in the interactive search and identification software system:

1. Marking all non-identical blocks of analyzed stamp image with the color markers size 3 x 3 pixels. The block is marked if the value (42) is not equal to zero.
2. Selection of the marked block into the separate window using a mouse pointer. New window consists of two selected image fragments (of the reference and analyzed stamps) in tone gradation. Two images are magnified in order to increase the visual quality analyses.

3. Error value (42) is presented for the human expert to identify the conformance of the analyzed image with the reference.

Thus, the expert can visually check each "suspicious" fragment and make a decision about the genuineness of the stamp image.

Image blocks may not be identical for the following reasons: 1. some parts of the stamp can be poorly printed or even be absent on the image. 2. The analyzed document has additional dots coming from the signature or text of a document under the stamp. After recognition of the non-identical blocks they can be analyzed and corrected using interpolation and filtering methods. If the correction process does not lead to the positive result, the system decides that the stamp on a document is a fake.

5. Conclusions

The research results of the developed search and recognition algorithms have shown that these algorithms can be applied efficiently in the image quality analyses systems and different purpose computer vision systems.

Main features of the developed algorithms for search and recognition of fine details are:

1. Search algorithm uses sliding windows size 3 x 3 pixels; this allows for detecting the fine details of image.
2. The contrast thresholds of human visual perception or computer vision system are used for the computation of contrast for the block with fine details and during its transformation to binary form.
3. Distortions of fine details are estimated using the number of normalized visual thresholds in the quality estimation system. This makes possible to take objective decisions about the presence of fine details in the corrupted image or about the visibility of distortions.

Results of this work show that the high quality reproduction of fine details and fine structures of images is necessary not only for the digital TV systems but also in automated search and recognition systems.

6. References

Gonzalez, R.S. & Woods, R.E. (2002). *Digital Image Processing*. ISBN 0201180758. Prentice Hall. New Jersey.

Glasman, K. (2004). MPEG-2 and Measurements. 625, No. 1, pp. 34-46, ISSN 0869-7914.

Hamza, A.B, Krim, H. & Unal, G.B. (2002): Unifying Probabilistic and Variational Estimation. *IEEE Signal Processing Magazine*, vol. 19, No. 5, pp. 37-47, ISSN 1053-5888.

Krivosheev, M.I. & Kustarev, A.K. (1990). *Color Measurements*. Energoatom, Moscow, ISBN 5-283-00545-3.

Mac Adam, D.L. (1974). Uniform Color Scales. *JOSA*, Vol. 64, pp. 1691-1702.

Novakovsky, S.V. (1988). *Color in Color TV*. Radio and communication, Moscow, ISBN 525600090X.

Pratt, W.K. (2001) *Digital Image Processing*. ISBN 0471374075. Wiley.

Potapov, A.A., Gulyaev, Yu.V., Nikitov, S.A., Pakhomov, A.A. & German V.A. (2008). *The Modern Methods of Image Processing*. Institute of Radio Engineering and Electronics RAS. ISBN 9785922108416. M.: FIZMATLIT.

Sai, S.V. (2002). Definition Analysis of Color Static Images in Equal Contrast Space. *Digital signals processing*, No. 1, pp. 6-9, ISSN 1684-2634.

Sai, S.V. (2003). *The Quality of Transmission and Reproduction of Fine Details in Color Television Images*. Dalnauka, Vladivostok, ISBN 5-8044-0345-1.

Sai, S.V. (2006). Quality Analysis of MPEG-4 Video Images. *Pattern Recognition and Image Analysis*, Vol. 16, No. 1, pp. 50-51, ISSN 1054-6618.

Sai, S.V. (2007) *Methods of the Definition Analysis of Fine Details of Images*. in Vision Systems: Applications, G. Obinata and A. Dutta, Eds., ISBN 9783902613011. Vienna: I-Tech Education and Publishing, pp. 279-296.

Sai, S.V. & Sorokin, N.Yu. (2008). Search Algorithm and the Distortion analysis of Fine Details of Real Images. *Proceedings of the 1st International Workshop on Image Mining Theory and Applications IMTA 2008*, pp. 58-64, ISBN 978-989-8111-25-8, Madeira, Portugal, January 2008, INTTICC, Funchal, Portugal.

Sai, S.V. & Sorokin,N.Yu. (2009) Search Algorithm and the Distortion Analysis of Fine Details of Real Images. *Pattern Recognition and Image Analysis*, Vol. 19, No. 2, pp. 257-261, ISSN 1054-6618.

Sai, I.S. (2009) Efficiency of Search Algorithms for the Impression of a Seal in the Document Image. Bulletin of Pacific National University. Vol. 15, No. 4, pp.53-60, ISSN 1996-3440.

Wang, Z. & Bovik, A.C (2002). A Universal Image Quality Index. *IEEE Signal Processing Letters*, Vol. 9, pp. 81-84, ISSN 1070-9908.

Wang, Z., Bovik, A.C., Sheikh, H.R. & Simoncelli, E.P. (2004). Image Quality Assessment: From Error Visibility to Structural Similarity. *IEEE Trans. Image Process.*, Vol. 13, No. 4, pp. 600-612, ISSN 1057-7149.

Wyszecki, G. (1975). Uniform Color Scales: CIE 1964 U*V*W* Conversion of OSA Committee Selection. *JOSA*, Vol. 65, pp. 456-460.

10

Enhanced Efficient Diamond Search Algorithm for Fast Block Motion Estimation

Yasser Ismail and Magdy A. Bayoumi
The Center for Advanced Computer Studies, University of Louisiana at Lafayette
USA

1. Introduction

Although the conventional *FS* algorithm achieves the best quality amongst various Motion Estimation (*ME*) algorithms and it is straightforward and has been successfully implemented on *VLSI* chips [1], its computational complexity is very high. In contrast, real time and portable multimedia devices require ultra computationally efficient video codec designs that will allow for a robust and reliable video quality. Many sub-optimal but faster *ME* techniques have been proposed to tackle the previous computational complexity problem. One technique is based on simplifying or easing the matching criteria (*SAD*) based on spatial and/or temporal Macro Blocks' (*MB*) features. Partial Distortion Elimination algorithm (*PDE*) and Successive Elimination Algorithm (*SEA*) [2] are examples of such techniques. Another technique is based on reducing the number of search points in the search area [3]. Although this technique reduces the computational complexity, there will be degradation in *PSNR*. New Three Step Search (*N3SS*) [4], Four Step Search (*FSS*) [5], Predictive Motion Vector Field Adaptive Search Technique (*PMVFAST*) [6], Hexagon Based Search (*HEXBS*) [7], Diamond Search (*DS*) [8], and Cross Diamond Search (*CDS*) [9] are examples for such techniques.

In this chapter, a new simple and efficient fast *MDS* is developed for higher complexity reduction than *DS* without further *PSNR* and bit-rate degradation compared to *FS*. *DS* is the most accurate suboptimal *ME* algorithm among others. This is why it was chosen to be implemented in the reference software of the standard H.264. The proposed *MDS* algorithm uses a mixed flavor approach of the previous two techniques. A computationally efficient set of stop search algorithms that skip the unnecessary operations both internally within the *MB* and externally between *MB*s utilizing accurate adaptive threshold models for reducing computations with no significant degradation in *PSNR* compared to the *FS* algorithm. Internal *SAD* operations are minimized using *DISS*. *DESS* algorithm is used to eliminate the irrelevant candidate pixels in the search area. Moreover, we are proposing to enhance the mechanism of the *DS* algorithm using zero and center bias properties. A set of adaptive and accurate thresholds that early terminate the search or select between Small Diamond Search Pattern (*SDSP*) or Large Diamond Search Pattern (*LDSP*) results in an additional computational saving. It is worth mentioning that some related work of this chapter was published in [11].

Coming up in section 2, details on the proposed modified search algorithm are explained. Following that, in section 3 comparisons are made between the proposed *MDS* and other fast motion estimation algorithms. Finally, we draw conclusion in section 4.

2. The proposed modified diamond search

It is well known that the motion field of consecutive frames in a video sequence is smooth and gentle. This means that the optimum Global Motion Vectors (*GMVs*) are located at or very close to the search center most of the time. Fig.1 illustrates the distribution of the optimum *GMVs* using *FS* with a spiral search pattern for six video sequences that contain different motion activities (low, medium, and high motion activities). It is noted that, for low motion activity video sequences, Akiyo, Coast-Guard, and News, the optimum *GMVs* are located at the search center most of the time (zero bias property). The situation is changed for the medium and high motion activity video sequences, Mobile, Foreman, and Football, at which the distance of the optimum *GMVs* from the search center will slightly increase (center bias property).

In this chapter, we use the zero bias property to reduce the computational complexity by deciding if the Initial Search Center (*ISC*) can be considered as an *GMV* or not. This will be achieved by using a dynamic *ZMP* (Zero Motion Prejudgment) threshold (T_{DESS}) which is dynamically adapted according to the change of the current block's features. We also benefit from the center bias property to reduce the computational complexity of the *DS* by dynamically selecting the appropriate diamond search pattern (either *SDSP* or *LDSP*) using a dynamic threshold T_p.

Using *SDSP* in Fig.2.a will reduce the computational complexity but will also increase the possibility of falling into local minima if it is used at the beginning of the search in a high motion or irregular video sequence. In contrast, using the *LDSP* in Fig.2.b may tackle this problem but with an increase in the computational complexity since larger number of checking points will be used. To remedy the previous problems, we adaptively select between starting with either *SDSP* or *LDSP* according to the expected motion activity of the current block. If the motion activity is low, an *SDSP* will be used. Otherwise, an *LDSP* will be used. Using the fact that there is a high correlation between neighboring blocks, the motion activity of the current block can be easily expected from the optimum *GMVs* of the previously encoded neighboring blocks so far. The threshold value in Eq.1 will be used to decide the expected motion activity of the current block.

To explain the proposed *MDS* algorithm, let the search window size be (-Δ, Δ) and the displacement with respect to the current block located at (u, v) be (x, y). The *SAD* between the current block in frame n and the candidate block in frame $n-\Psi$ is described in Eq. 2:

The new modified diamond search can be summarized as follows:

Initial step (*ZMP* decision): The $SAD_{curr}(i)$ between the current block and the candidate block i at the *ISC* will be estimated. Also, the thresholds T_{DESS} (the derivation of this threshold will be given in section 2.1.2) and T_P are calculated. If $SAD_{curr}(i) \leq T_{DESS}$, then the search will stop immediately and outputs the candidate block i located at the *ISC* position as a best matching candidate block as seen in Fig.3.a. Otherwise, go to step (i).

Step(i) (*SDSP/LDSP* decision): Using the threshold T_P, the initial used diamond pattern will be decided according to the following condition. If $T_P \leq 1$, go to step(ii). Otherwise, go to step(iii).

Step(ii) (Small Diamond Search Pattern (*SDSP*)): Four search points as in Fig.3.b will be checked one by one against the minimum *SAD* so far using the stop search procedure with both *DISS* and *DESS* techniques that will speed up the *ME* operation by eliminating unnecessary computations as will be discussed in section 2.1.1 and section 2.1.2. If all the

points in the *SDSP* didn't have any chance to hit the best matching block, then check the search point with the minimum *SAD*. If it is located at the center of *SDSP*, then safely stop the search. Otherwise, use this point as an *ISC* and repeat step ii (see Fig.3.c).
Step(iii) (Large Diamond Search Pattern (*LDSP*)): Eight points as in Fig.2.b will be checked one by one using the procedure of both the *DISS* and *DESS* techniques. If the entire candidate points in the *LDSP* are checked without hitting the best match, the search point with the minimum *SAD* will be checked. If this point is not located at the *ISC*, then start step(iii) over again and consider this point as an *ISC* for the new *LDSP*. Otherwise, if it is located at the *ISC*, an *SDSP* will be used as a final stage. If the best match is not caught by the procedure, then the point with the minimum *SAD* will be the best match as seen in Fig.3.d.
It is worth mentioning that the local minima problem, which appears in the conventional *DS* algorithm, disappears from the proposed *MDS* due to the high accuracy of estimating the motion vectors using the proposed thresholds.

3. The proposed stop search algorithms

The total computational complexity TC for any block based motion estimation technique can be expressed in Eq. 3. In this section, we reduce the computational complexity in Eq.3 by reducing the Sub, Abs, and Add operations per candidate block using smart DISS. Also we reduce the number of the search point S using smart DESS. The proposed algorithms are described in detail in the following sub sections.

3.1 Dynamic Internal Stop Search algorithm (DISS)

The main purpose of the proposed *DISS* is to reduce the computational complexity of *ME* process by reducing the *Sub*, *Abs*, and *Add* operations for each candidate block. This will consequently reduce the term $\left[l_1 \times l_2 \,.(Sub + Abs + Add)\right]$ in Eq.3. The *DISS* algorithm can be summarized in the following four steps.
Step (i): Both the current and the candidate blocks in the current and the reference frames respectively are divided into groups. Each group contains a number of row lines (2l), where $l = 0,1,2,\ldots,l_1/4$
Step (ii): Partially accumulate the *SAD* value starting at the first group in both the current and the candidate blocks.
Step (iii): compare the partially accumulated *SAD* value so far (*PSAD*) with a pre-determined dynamic threshold T_{DISS}.
Step (iv): If the accumulated *PSAD*>T_{DISS}, then stop accumulating *PSAD* for further groups and proceed to the next candidate block in the search window. Otherwise, continue accumulating *PSAD* by adding the next group of pixels to the previous *PSAD* and update the threshold accordingly.
The threshold T_{DISS} depends mainly on the normalized minimum *SAD* of the scanned blocks so far in the search window (*SADmin-curr*/$[l_1 \times l_2]$). T_{DISS} is expressed in Eq. 4.
However, sometimes some blocks are falsely skipped in the early stages of the algorithm. It was noticed experimentally that if the *PSAD* of the first group(s) for a candidate block is greater than the calculated threshold $T_{DISS}(j)$, the candidate block is skipped. Although, if we further continue accumulating the *PSAD* for the next group(s) in that block, the final accumulated *PSAD* might not exceed the threshold $T_{DISS}(j)$. This problem is avoided by

adding an accelerator parameter Ω to the threshold value in Eq.4 to control the rate of the *PSAD* skipping operation in the candidate block. The value of Ω parameter is illustrated in Eq.5:

Our exhaustive experiments reveal that the previous false skipping of *PSAD* operations is not the dominant case for all the candidate blocks. Also, these false skipping operations depend mainly on the choice of the initial group to be partially accumulated. So, the effect of the acceleration parameter Ω should be lessened with the further accumulating of *PSAD* from one group to the next one. This will be achieved by subtracting a relaxation parameter θ from the total threshold T_{DISS} in order to relax the effect of adding the accelerator parameter Ω. The value of θ is illustrated in Eq.6 where N is the total number of the groups in a block. At the last group of a block, Ω will be completely eliminated by θ and T_{DISS} will settle to the value of $SAD_{min-curr}$. The final form of the proposed *DISS* threshold is given in Eq.7.

It is worth mentioning that all the divisions and multiplications in Eq.7 can be simply replaced by shift operations to speed up the performance of the proposed algorithm.

3.2 Dynamic External Stop Search algorithm (DESS)

The main purpose of the *DESS* algorithm is to reduce the computational complexity given in Eq.3 by reducing the redundant candidate blocks in the search window that can not be considered as an optimum solution for the current block. If the previous *DISS* algorithm fails, a second level of reduction will be used. If the *PSAD* calculations of a reference block are not skipped, then the value of the $SAD_{min-curr}$ for the current block will be updated according to the value of the obtained final *PSAD* for that candidate block. If the final *PSAD* is less than the $SAD_{min-curr}$, then the value of the $SAD_{min-curr}$ is replaced by the current value of the final *PSAD*. Thereafter, we check this updated $SAD_{min-curr}$ against a pre-determined Dynamic External Stop Search threshold $T_{DESS}(i)$; where i is the index of the candidate block in the search window. If the updated $SAD_{min-curr} \le T_{DESS}(i)$, then skip all the remaining candidates in the search window and select the i block as our best candidate block.

Experimental analysis reveals that the best match block in the search window has a minimum *SAD* that is highly correlated with the minimum *SAD*s of the neighbors of the current block, i.e., blocks 1, 2, 3, and 4 in Fig.4. Therefore, the optimum minimum *SAD*s of the neighboring blocks to the current block can be used to build the function £ in the linear model of Eq.8 to form the threshold $T_{DESS}(i)$. A small matrix is required to store the minimum *SAD* values of the coded neighbor blocks so far. The function £ can be simply set to the average of the minimum *SAD*s of the neighbors surrounding the current block. Nevertheless, an improvement in the accuracy of the threshold $T_{DESS}(i)$ can be obtained by replacing the average value by the median function. Implicitly, using the median function is considered as the average of the best two neighboring blocks since it will exclude the irregular minimum *SAD* values of the neighbors to the current block from the calculations.

The proposed model in Eq.8 requires only three shift operations and one addition operation (required for the constant μ_1). If we use £ as the average, three addition operations and two shift operations will be also required. However, using the median would increase the complexity as it also requires comparison operations. Fig.5 illustrates the whole flow diagram of the proposed *DISS* and *DESS* algorithms combined together.

4. Simulation results

Our experiments have been conducted, based on the reference software JM12.4 [10], to show the effectiveness of the proposed MDS algorithm. Three main parameters are used for measuring the performance. First, the PSNR difference (ΔPSNR) of the reconstructed video which is the PSNR difference between FS and the fast ME techniques. Second, the increase in the bit-rate percentage (ΔBR%). Finally, the ME time saving percentage (METS%). ΔPSNR, ΔBR%, and METS% are measured with respect to FS. Due to lack of space, only four different video sequences, with different motion activities, are illustrated here. Motion Vector (MV) search is based on the luminance component of the block of size 16×16. The search window size is 32×32. The proposed MDS algorithm is compared against FS, N3SS, 4SS, PMVFAST, HEXBS, DS, and finally CDS algorithms. It is clear from table 1 that the speed up of the proposed MDS is significant compared with other fast ME techniques. Practically, it achieves approximately 99% and 20% saving in ME time, for high motion video sequence (Football), compared with FS and DS respectively. This is with a negligible degradation in both PSNR and bit-rate.

Fig.6 represents the average number of Absolute Difference (AB) operations per MV for Foreman video sequence. It is clear from the figure that the MDS algorithm has the lowest AB operations compared with other fast ME search techniques. This reflects the superior performance of our proposed MDS algorithm to speed up the ME process. The performance of the proposed algorithm is also measured using the Rate Distortion (RD) curves in Fig.7 (calculated at 30 frames per sec). It is clear from Fig.7 that the proposed MDS performs very close to the DS algorithm and better than CDS algorithm.

5. Tables and figures

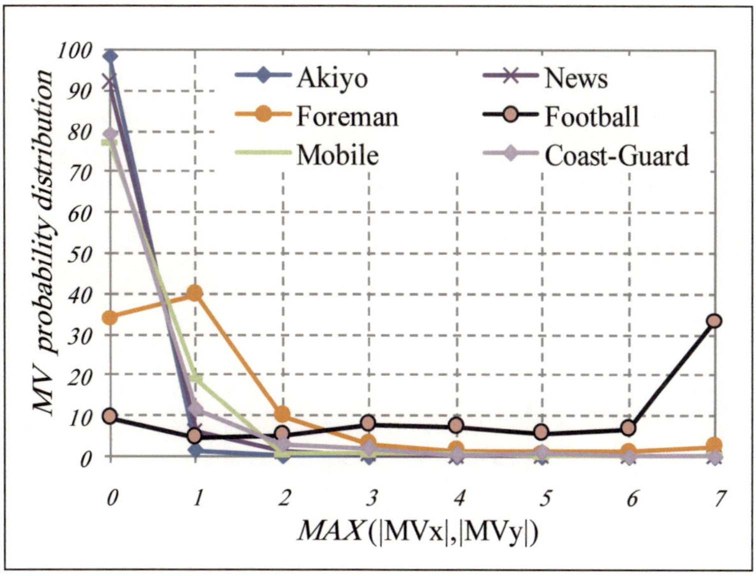

Fig. 1. Motion vector probability distribution using FS (16×16 search window size).

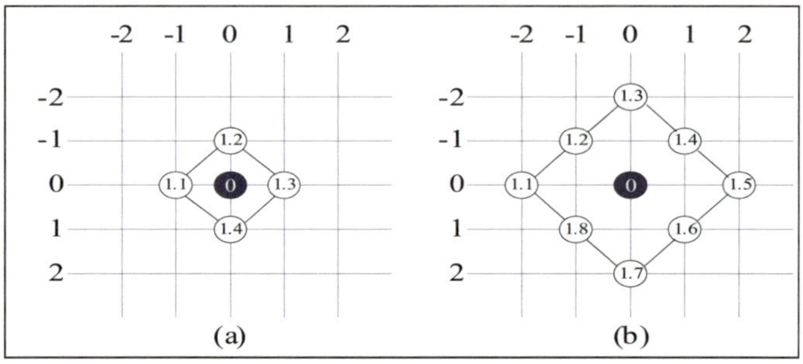

Fig. 2. Diamond Search Patterns (a) SDSP. (b) LDSP.

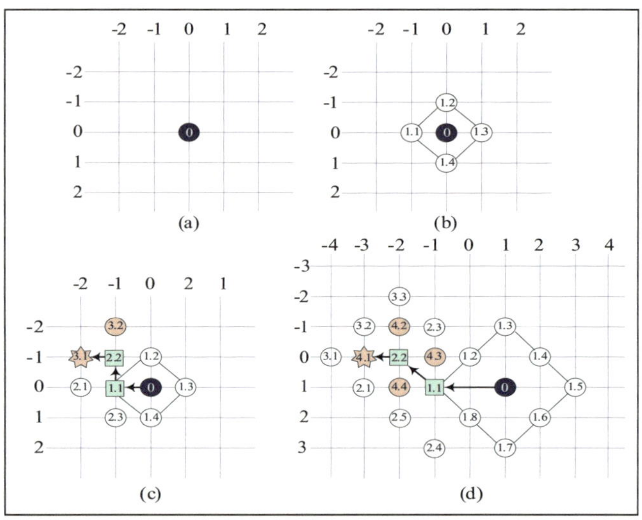

Fig. 3. Modified Diamond Search Algorithm (MDS).

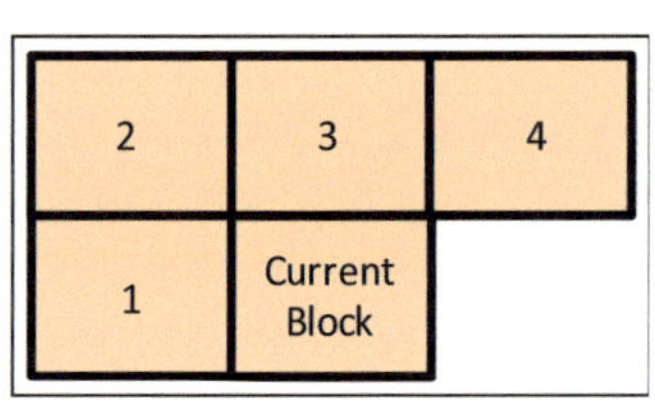

Fig. 4. Current Macro-block and its 4 neighbors used for calculating $T_{DESS}(i)$.

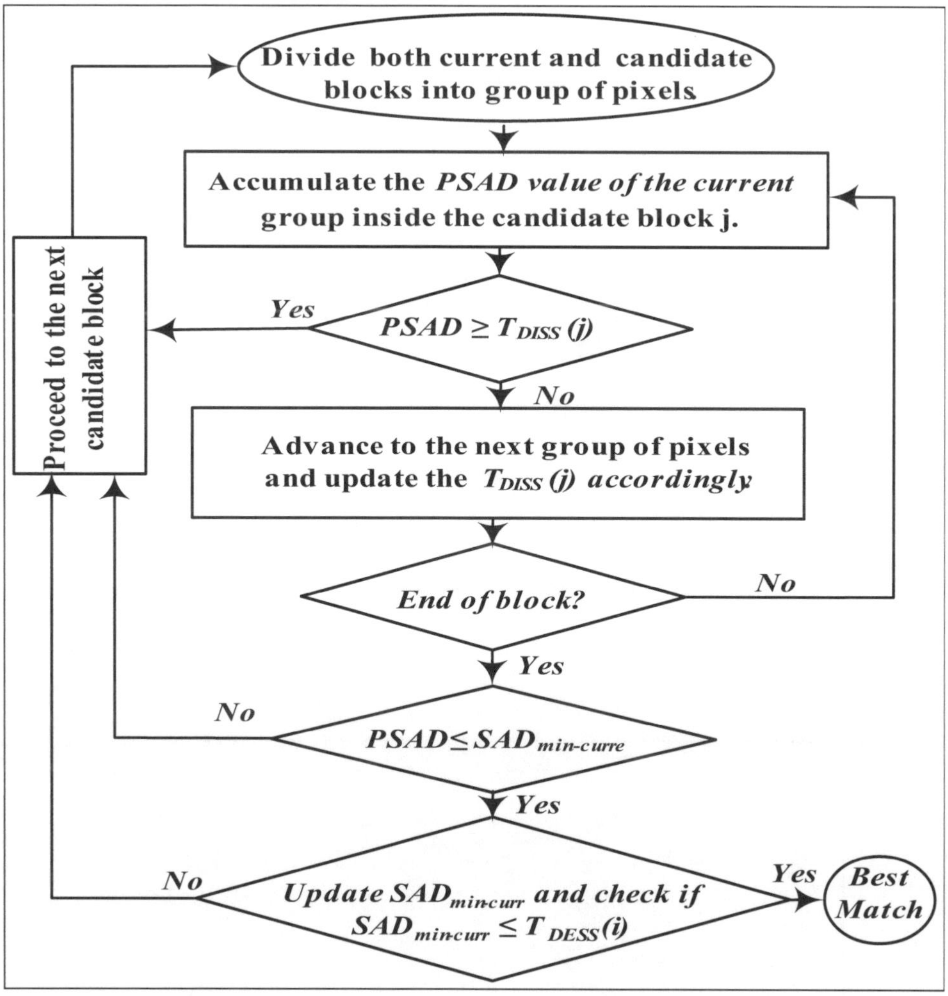

Fig. 5. The flow chart of the proposed DISS and DESS algorithms.

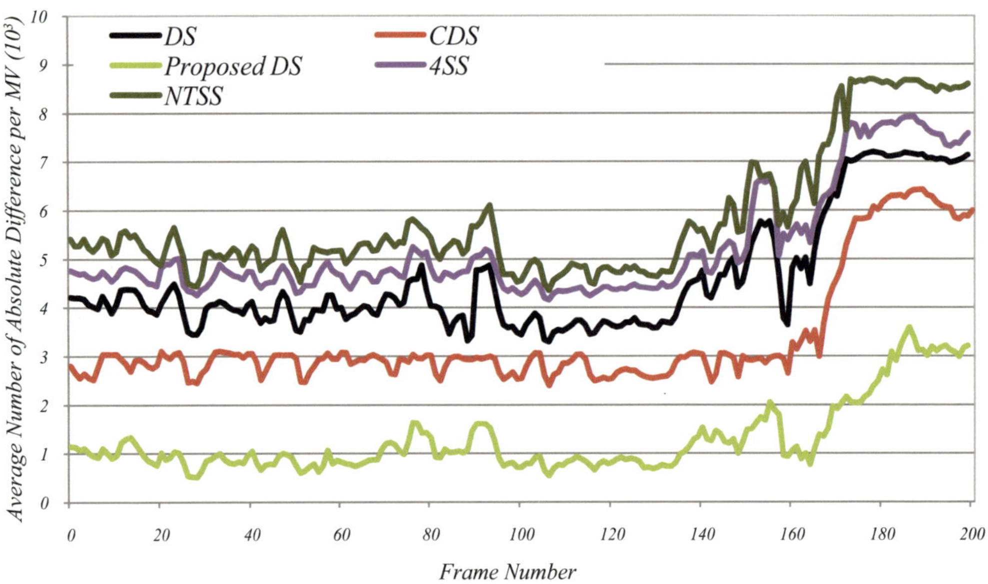

Fig. 6. The total computational complexity per MV for Foreman video sequence.

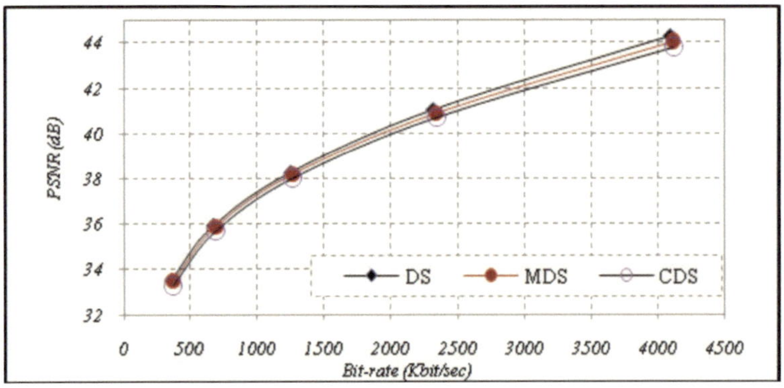

Fig. 7. Bit-rate Distortion Curves for Foreman video sequence using the proposed MDS and other fast ME techniques.

ME technique	Akiyo (QCIF)			Forman (CIF)			Coast-Guard (QCIF)			Football (CIF)		
	PSNR(dB)	BR	METS%	PSNR(dB)	BR%	METS	PSNR(dB)	BR	METS	PSNR(dB)	BR	METS
FS	38.55	28650	194.796	37.71	474840	1143.653	34.79	243900	671.30	37.10	1036980	1021.45
	ΔPSNR(dB)	BR%	METS%	ΔPSNR(dB)	BR%	METS%	ΔPSNR(dB)	BR%	METS%	ΔPSNR(dB)	BR%	METS%
N3SS [4]	-0.01	0.09	74.62	-0.4	0.81	70.04	-0.04	0.08	72.16	-0.62	0.33	65.08
4SS [5]	0.00	0.05	79.93	-0.2	0.43	74.64	-0.0[illegible]	0.06	77.23	-0.51	0.29	73.95
PMVFAST[6]	-0.06	-0.21	85.71	-0.05	-2.06	95.13	-0.01	0.05	93.83	-0.01	0.62	94.38
HEXBS [7]	0.00	0.03	95.01	-0.02	0.98	94.56	0.00	0.04	95.18	-0.03	1.44	94.62
DS [8]	-0.06	-0.31	85.73	-0.03	-1.88	82.12	0.00	0.19	87.78	-0.02	0.67	80.42
CDS [9]	-0.05	0.21	89.11	-0.05	1.98	88.63	-0.07	2.64	92.13	-0.04	2.55	84.52
MDS	-0.01	0.17	99.37	-0.03	2.32	99.15	0.00	0.29	99.43	0.00	0.06	99.34

Table 1. The performance of the proposed MDS compared with FS algorithm and the state of the art fast motion estimation techniques using QP=28

6. Equations

$$T_P = \text{Median}\{GMV_{min}(m)\}, \quad m = 1, 2, \ldots, K \tag{1}$$

Where GMV_{min} is the minimum GMVs of the neighboring blocks m and K is the number of the GMV_{min} that are used to calculate T_P. The small value of T_P is an indication that the best match is very close to the search center. A large value of T_P means that the best match block is far away from the ISC.

$$SAD = \sum_{i=0}^{N-1}\sum_{j=0}^{N-1}\left|I_n(u,v) - I_{n-\psi}(u+x, v+y)\right| \tag{2}$$

Where $-\Delta \le x, y \le \Delta$, N is the block size, and I is the pixel intensity.

$$TC = \left[l_1 \times l_2 .(Sub + Abs + Add)\right].S \tag{3}$$

Where l_1 and l_2 are the number of rows and columns of both the current block and the reference block respectively. S is the total search points in a search window of size $(-\Delta, \Delta)$. Sub, Abs, and Add are the number of subtraction, absolute value, and addition operations required for calculating the matching criteria defined by the SAD operation.

$$T_{DISS}(j) = j \times P \times \frac{SAD_{min-curr}}{l_1 \times l_2} \tag{4}$$

Where j and P are the group index and the number of pixels per group respectively. $SAD_{min-curr}$ is the minimum SAD of the scanned blocks so far in the search window.

$$\Omega = \varepsilon \times \frac{SAD_{min-curr}}{l_1 \times l_2}, \quad \varepsilon = 1, 2, \ldots, P/2 \tag{5}$$

The higher the value of Ω is, the harder it is to skip the $PSAD$ calculations for the candidate block which consequently increases the ability to find the optimal GMV. But, this defeats our target here as it might cause an increase in the non-skipped blocks and hence increasing the computational complexity.

$$\theta = \frac{(j-1) \times \Omega}{(N-1)} \tag{6}$$

$$T_{DISS}(j) = j \times P \times \frac{SAD_{min-curr}}{l_1 \times l_2} + \Omega - \frac{(j-1) \times \Omega}{(N-1)} \tag{7}$$

$$T_{DESS}(i) = \mu_1 \times £ + \mu_2 \tag{8}$$

Where the statistical function £ is defined as:

$$£ = \begin{cases} \frac{1}{N}\sum_{m=1}^{N} SAD_{min}(m) \quad \text{or,} \\ \text{Median}\{SAD_{min}(m)\}, \quad m = 1, 2, \ldots, K \end{cases} \tag{9}$$

Where K is the number of the closest neighbors coded so far, μ_1 is an accelerator parameter, and μ_2 is a constant factor set experimentally to zero. Note that this threshold is computed only once per a current block. The accelerator parameter μ_1 is set experimentally to 0.75.

7. Referring

(Yasser Ismail & Magdy A. Bayoumi, 2011).

8. Conclusion

A new *MDS* algorithm that utilizes an accurate and efficient dynamic stop search algorithm is proposed. Reduction in the complexity of *MDS* algorithm is achieved by employing an adaptive threshold to skip the unnecessary redundant internal *SAD* operations and also to skip the irrelevant blocks' operations in the search area. There is approximately 99% and 20% saving in *ME* time with negligible degradation in *PSNR* and bit-rate compared with the conventional *FS* and *DS*. This qualifies the proposed *MDS* algorithm to be applied to real time video applications such as video conferencing over wireless networks due to its superior speedup and performance.

9. References

[1] S. Goel, Y. Ismail, P. Devulapalli, J. McNeely, and M. Bayoumi, "An Efficient Data Reuse Motion Estimation Engine," IEEE Workshop on Signal Processing Systems (SIPS 06), Banff, Canada, Sept. 2006.

[2] S. Yang, L. Zhenyu, T. Ikenaga, and S. Goto, "Enhanced Strict Multilevel Successive Elimination Algorithm for Fast Motion Estimation," in IEEE International Symposium on Circuits and Systems, ISCAS'07., pp. 3659-3662, 2007.

[3] G.-L. Li and M.-J. Chen, "Fast Motion Estimation Algorithm by Finite-State Side Match for H.264 Video Coding Standard," in IEEE Asia Pacific Conference on Circuits and Systems, APCCAS'06. , pp. 414-417, 2006.

[4] R. Li, B. Zeng, and M. L. Liou, "A New Three-Step Search Algorithm For Block Motion Estimation," IEEE Trans. Circuits Syst. Video Technol., vol. 4, pp. 438-442, Aug. 1994.

[5] L. M. Po and W. C. Ma, "A Novel Four-Step Search Algorithm For Fast Block Motion Estimation," IEEE Trans. Circuits Syst. Video Technol., vol. 6, pp. 313-317, June 1996.

[6] Alexis M. Tourapis, Oscar C. Au, and Ming L. Liou, "Highly Efficient Predictive Zonal Algorithms for Fast Block-Matching Motion Estimation," IEEE Trans. Circuits Syst. Video Technol., vol. 12, NO. 10, October 2002

[7] C. Zhu, X. Lin, and L.-P. Chau, "Hexagon-Based Search Pattern For Fast Block Motion Estimation," IEEE Trans. Circuits Syst. Video Technol., vol.12, pp. 349-355, May 2002.

[8] S. Zhu and K.-K. Ma, "A New Diamond Search Algorithm For Fast Block Matching Motion Estimation," IEEE Trans. Image Processing, vol. 9, pp. 287-290, Feb. 2000.

[9] C. H. Cheung and L. M. Po, "A Novel Cross-Diamond Search Algorithm For Fast Block Motion Estimation," IEEE Trans. Circuits Syst. Video Technol., vol. 12, pp. 1168-1177, Dec. 2002.

[10] Joint Video Team, "Reference Software JM12.4," http://iphome.hhi.de/suehring/tml/download/".

[11] Yasser Ismail, Jason McNeely, Mohsen Shaaban, and Magdy A. Bayoumi, "A Generalized Fast Motion Estimation Algorithm Using External and Internal Stop Search Techniques for H.264 Video Coding Standard," IEEE International Symposium on Circuits and Systems (ISCAS), Seattle, Washington, USA, 18-21 May 2008.

11

A Novel Prediction-Based Asymmetric Fast Search Algorithm for Video Compression

Chung-Ming Kuo[1], Nai-Chung Yang[1], I-Chang Jou[1] and Chaur-Heh Hsieh[2]
[1]*Department of Information Engineering, I-Shou University Dahsu, 840, Kaohsiung,*
[2]*Dept. of Computer and Communication Engineering, Ming Chung University*
Gui-Shan, 333, Taoyuan,
Taiwan, R.O.C.

1. Introduction

The successive frames of a video sequence are highly correlated. Therefore, by reducing temporal redundancy a high compression ratio can be achieved. Motion estimation, which reduces temporal redundancy, plays an important role in video coding systems such as H.26x and MPEG-x. The block-matching algorithm (BMA) is the most popular and widely used algorithm for motion estimation due to its simplicity and reasonable performance. In BMA, an image frame is divided into non-overlapping rectangular blocks with equal or variable block sizes. The pixels in each block are assumed to have the same motion. The motion vector (MV) of a block is estimated by searching for its best match within a search window in the previous frame. The distortion between the current block and each searching block is employed as a matching criterion. The resulting MV is used to generate a motion-compensated prediction block. The motion-compensated prediction difference blocks (called residue blocks) and the MVs are encoded and then sent to the decoder. Among the various BMAs, the full search (FS) is global optimal and most straightforward algorithm because it searches the entire search window for the best matching block. However, its only drawback is a heavy computational load.

To address this drawback, many fast BMAs have been proposed in the literature since 1981, such as the three-step search (TSS) (Koga et al., 1981), cross search (Ghanbari, 1990), new three-step search (NTSS) (Li et al., 1994), block-based gradient descent search (Liu & Feig,1996), four-step search (Po & Ma, 1996), diamond search (DS) (Zhu & Ma, 2000), hexagon-based search (HEXBS) (Zhu et al., 2002), and the cross-diamond search (CDS) (Cheung & Po, 2002), etc. The primary assumption of most fast BMAs is that the block distortion is monotonic over the search range, implying that the distortion decreases monotonically as the search position moves toward the minimum distortion point. Therefore, the best match point can be found by following the distortion trend without checking all search points in the search window. Consequently, these fast BMAs use various search patterns to reduce the number of search points, thereby speeding up the search. In addition, some fast BMAs (Liu & Zaccarin, 1993; Yu et al., 2001; Bierling, 1988) speed up the search by sub-sampling the block pixels on distortion computation and/or by sub-sampling the search points in the search window. Furthermore, since there is a high correlation between a current block and its adjacent blocks in spatial and/or temporal domains, the current block's MV can be predicted by using the MVs of adjacent blocks. The Prediction Search Algorithm (PSA) (Luo et al., 1997) computes the mean value of MVs as the predicted motion vector (PMV) using 3 neighboring blocks (up, up right, left) in the current frame, and then starts the search algorithm from the location of the PMV. Xu et al. proposed a prediction scheme (Xu et al., 1999) in which four blocks in the previous frame are used to compute the PMV in order to enhance the traditional fast BMAs. The Adaptive Rood Pattern Search (ARPS) (Yao & Ma, 2002) uses only the previous MV on the left in the current frame as the PMV, while the search center and the pattern size are re-defined accordingly. C.-M. Kuo et al. use an adapted Kalman filter to predict the MV (Kuo et al., 2002), which greatly improves prediction accuracy while maintaining the trend of the MVs. In addition, a lot of similar models for fast BMAs have been proposed in recent years (Chimienti et al., 2002; Namuduri, 2004; Ahmad et al., 2006; Kuo et al., 2006 and 2009). In general, the common feature in all fast BMAs is the trade-off between quality and search speed. Increasing speed as much as possible, while preserving quality, is the major goal of all fast BMAs.

In this paper, a novel fast BMA is developed. In this new approach, we effectively use the information of the matching error as well as the center-biased characteristic in order to greatly minimize the search points while maintaining high quality. The experimental results show that the proposed method yields a very promising performance.

The remainder of this paper is organized as follows. In Section 2, we briefly describe the intrinsic problems of some traditional fast BMAs. The details of the proposed DAS are given in Section 3. In Section 4, the DAS algorithms with prediction and prejudgment (DASp & DASpb, respectively) are introduced. Section 5 comprises a discussion of the experimental results. Finally, conclusions are provided in Section 6.

2. Problem formulaton

This section addresses some important issues about conventional fast BMAs. Herein we also present a framework for the proposed method.

Issue 1: The design of search pattern is usually a tradeoff between fast (large) and small motions

In some of the earlier methods (e.g. TSS and 2Dlog) that consider the possibility of fast motion, the initial search pattern is quite large and refined by gradually decreasing the search size of the search pattern. Afterwards, most fast BMAs adopt a two-stage, or coarse-to-fine, search strategy in order to accommodate various possible video types. In the coarse-to-fine search strategy, a large pattern is first used to find the possible position quickly and then switch to a small pattern to pinpoint the precise location.

We summarize the minimum search points (MSP) needed to locate an MV for some representative fast BMAs as follows:

1. TSS checks 9 points in its first step, and then 8 points in the two subsequent steps respectively. Thus MSP of the algorithm is 25 points.
2. NTSS uses nine checking points of TSS plus eight center-biased points in its first step to favor blocks with small motion. Therefore, the MSP of NTSS is 17 points.
3. DS adopts a nine-point diamond-shaped search pattern, referred to as the large diamond search pattern (LDSP), in the coarse search stage. And then a small diamond search pattern (SDSP) containing four nearest points around the center is applied in the fine stage. The MSP of DS is 13 and therefore DS outperforms NTSS in terms of search speed.

4. HEXBS adopts a 7-point large hexagonal pattern in its first step. If the minimum block distortion (MBD) occurs at the center of the hexagonal pattern, an additional 4-point small hexagonal pattern around the center is analyzed to determine the MV. The lower bound of HEXBS is 11 points and therefore HEXBS outperforms DS in terms of search speed.
5. CDS utilizes a more compact nine-point cross-shaped pattern (CSP) in its first step. If the MBD occurs at the center of the cross-shaped pattern, the search discontinues. Thus, CDS requires at least 9 search points, and therefore CDS outperforms HEXBS, on average, in terms of search speed.

However, under current two-stage search strategy, it is very difficult to further improve the search speed. In the present study, we attempt to break the two-stage strategy to further improve search efficiency.

Issue 2: The search pattern is usually symmetric, and the magnitude of block matching error is not effectively used

For most fast BMAs, the origin of search is usually set at the center of the search window and the search occurs according to a symmetric pattern. After comparison, the new center is set at the point with the least amount of block distortion, and then generates a new symmetric pattern for the next search. This procedure continues until the conditions of convergence are satisfied. However, there are two main drawbacks in such a procedure. First, in BMA, the most important assumption is the monotonic error surface. However, the design of the symmetrical pattern assumes that the direction of convergence is equally alike in each direction with respect to the search center. Therefore, the monotonic property is not properly used. If the search direction can be correctly determined, the search speed will be further improved. Second, for most BMAs, the block matching error is used to compare and find the best match. Generally, the magnitude of matching error is not effectively used. We believe that observing the magnitude variation can provide the direction of convergence and be used to enhance search speed.

Issue 3: Prediction is very useful for large motion or frame skipping

In some applications, there exists a large motion between adjacent frames due to fast motion or frame skipping. In such cases, the center-biased characteristic is not sufficiently satisfied, and therefore using a large search pattern should be more efficient. In fact, this inference is not completely true. According to our extensive experiments, whatever search pattern is used, large or small, the number of search points increases significantly. Instead of search pattern design, the prediction scheme seems to be more appropriate for reducing such bias.

From the above discussion, we can conclude that search speed is highly dependent on the design of the search pattern, and the MSP dominates search speed. To improve search speed, the MSP must be decreased. However, under the two-stage search strategy, it is very difficult to further reduce the MSP. Therefore, we have made a break with the two-stage strategy and have adopted a very compact center-biased search pattern with a directional search strategy in our study. Although using a compact center-biased search pattern decreases the MSP, it is easier to be trapped in a local minimum. Meanwhile, the number of checking points may remarkably increase for blocks with a larger MV. Using a prediction scheme is a good solution to this problem. A prediction scheme involves estimating the MV for the current block. As previously mentioned, there are many ways to predict the MV. A better prediction scheme may result in a better performance, but improvement is noticeable even with a simple one.

Based on the above discussion, utilizing a compact center-biased search pattern to favor a small MV and incorporating it with a prediction scheme to benefit a larger MV appears to be the best strategy for achieving a fast BMA. Therefore, we propose using the DAS and DASp algorithms.

3. Directional asymmetric search

The center-biased characteristic has been reported and widely used in many studies [3, 6, 8, 12-14]. It means that most MVs are very close to zero motion. Thus, the best search strategy is to search from the center of the search window and its nearest neighbors. On the other hand, although the hypothesis of monotonic error surface is not always true, it holds true primarily in the nearby region around the minimum error point (global or local). This implies that the minimum error point can be found along the direction of the block error from the highest to the lowest point. As long as the error direction is known, only the points along the search path need to be checked. Therefore, an asymmetric search pattern is more efficient in subsequent steps.

Some key issues about DAS are addressed below.

3.1 Error direction determination

Most fast BMAs find the MBD in each step using symmetric patterns. The location of the MBD in the current step is the center of the next step until the MBD occurs at the center. Under this condition, the information regarding block distortions has not been effectively used. Thus far, for most fast BMAs, it is used only for finding the MBD. Actually, it reveals not only the MBD but also the error direction.

In our study, the error direction (or search direction) in each step is defined as the direction from the location of the maximum block distortion toward the minimum block distortion. Herein S denotes a search pattern, $BD(k)$ denotes the block distortion of the search point k, and $k \in S$ is a point in S. The search direction for a specific step is defined as:

$$\vec{d} = \overrightarrow{(\arg \underset{k \in S}{Max}(BD(k)))\ \ (\arg \underset{k \in S}{Min}(BD(k)))} \tag{1}$$

As shown in Fig 1., the arrowheads designate the positions of the MBD and the arrow tails indicate the positions of the maximum block distortion. The search direction provides a very good clue regarding the approach of the final MV.

3.2 Proper search pattern selection

As shown in Fig. 1., the proposed DAS consists of 13 possible search patterns, 12 directional patterns and 1 initial pattern. In the first step, a compact 5-point cross pattern is selected, as the white circles in Fig. 1 (e), that is, S = {the white circles in Fig. 1 (e)}. If the MBD occurs at the center, the search discontinues; otherwise, subsequent steps are conducted and the search direction is determined by Eq. (1). According to the definition in Eq. (1), there are eight possible directions, but there are 12 directional patterns due to the different locations of the MBD. Once the search direction is obtained, the corresponding directional pattern will be used in the next step.

For each step that follows, three additional points (the orange circles in each directional pattern as shown in Fig. 1) are checked and the search direction is determined by Eq. (1) but with a different S, which contains 4 points, that is, S={the 3 additional points plus the MBD point in the previous step}. Regardless of the number of checking points, the search direction is determined in the same way and both have eight possible directions.

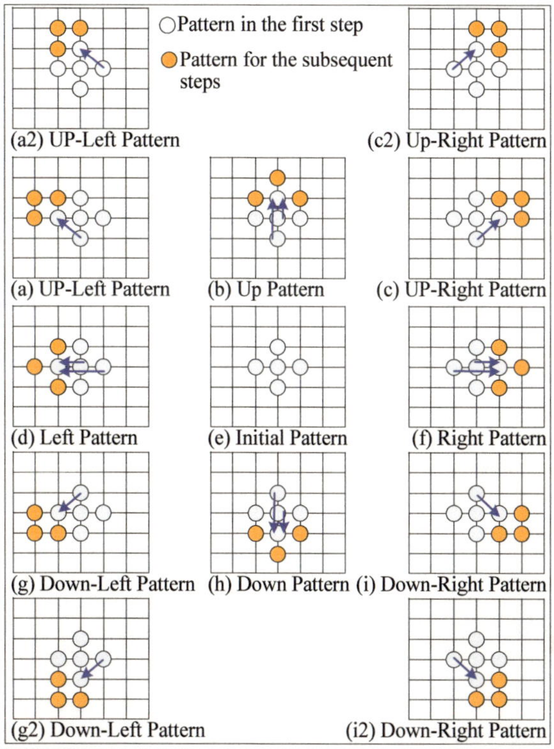

Fig. 1. Search patterns of DAS

3.3 Summary of DAS

The proposed DAS looks complicated but the underlying mechanism is quite easy. A flowchart of the DAS is shown in Fig. 3 and is summarized as follows:

Step 1. The initial cross-pattern (the white circles in Fig. 1 (e)) is centered at the origin of the search window.

Step 2. The block distortions of the 5 checking points of the cross-pattern are calculated. If the location of the MBD occurs at the center, the search discontinues and the MV is set at the center. If not, we proceed to step 3.

Step 3. Set the location of the MBD as the new center, find the error direction and select the proper search pattern for the next step accordingly.

Step 4. According to the selected pattern, three additional points (the orange circles) are checked, some of which may have already been checked. If the location of the MBD remains unchanged, the search discontinues, and the MV is set at the location of the MBD. If not, revert to step 3.

For each fast BMA, the MSP is the minimum number of checking points needed to locate the MV for a block. The lower the MSP of a fast BMA, the faster the search speed. Therefore, we have adopted a very compact 5-point cross pattern in the first step of DAS to reduce the MSP and to favor blocks with a small MV.

Fig. 2 illustrates the proposed DAS and compares it to some well-known fast BMAs. It took 16 checking points to locate the MV for DAS in this case. The required checking points for other fast BMAs are: TSS (25), NTSS (22), DS (22), CDS (24), and HEXBS (17). Obviously, DAS is the fastest algorithm in this case. Moreover, it is true in most cases and is confirmed by the experimental results of this study.

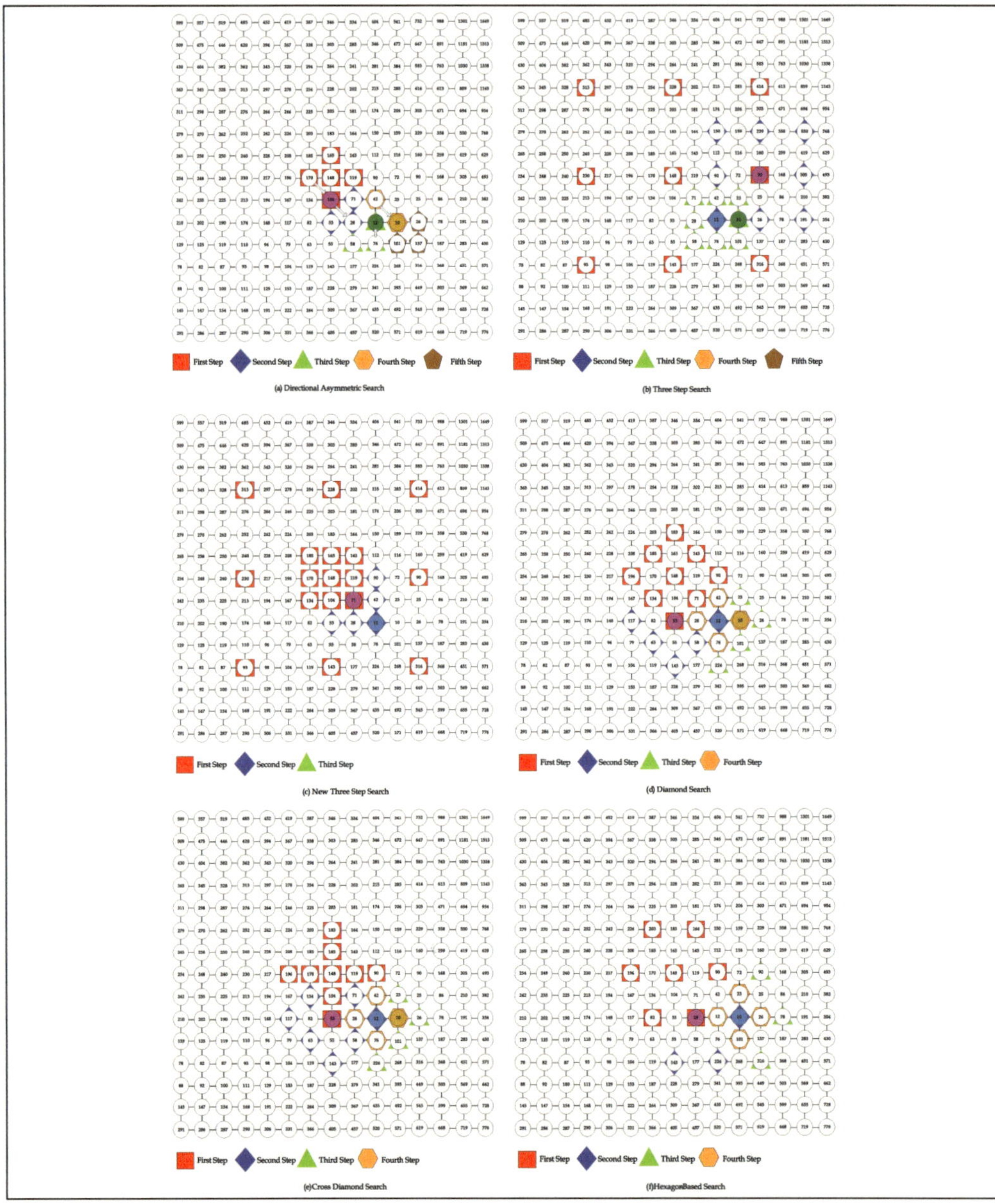

Fig. 2. A practical search example for various fast BMAs (a) DAS (b) TSS (c) NTSS (d) DS (e) CDS (f) HEXB Selected from Foreman sequence, frame 12, block 214, MV(+3,+2), block size: 16×16, search window: ±7. The number in each circle indicates the mean square error of that block.

4. Directional asymmetric search with prediction (DASP)

4.1 Prediction sheme

The DAS can be viewed as an enhanced center-biased algorithm requiring only a few checking points to locate the MV for blocks with a small MV. However, the checking points increase as the value of the MV increases. The larger the MV, the more checking points are required. Although the DAS requires a lower number of checking points compared to other fast BMAs, even in the case of a large MV, we believe this situation should be carefully addressed. A good solution for this situation is to use a prediction scheme. The initial search can start from either the PMV point or the original center point according to their block distortions.

As mentioned in Section 1, there are many ways to predict the MV for the current block [12-19]. Any kind of prediction scheme can be incorporated into the DAS. Although better prediction schemes may yield better results, we have selected the simplest one; namely, the motion vector of the previous block on the left in current frame is selected as the PMV for current block. In simulations, we will show that the prediction scheme achieves very promising performance without extra computational burdens.

The prediction scheme is incorporated into our DAS as follows and the flowchart of DASp is shown inFig. 3:

1. If the current block is a left-most block, the PMV is set to be (0, 0); otherwise the PMV is set as the MV of the previous block on the left.
2. Compute the block distortions for the position of the PMV and the center of the search window, respectively.
3. Select the position with the smaller block distortion as the search center, and start the DAS in Section 3.3 from Step 2.

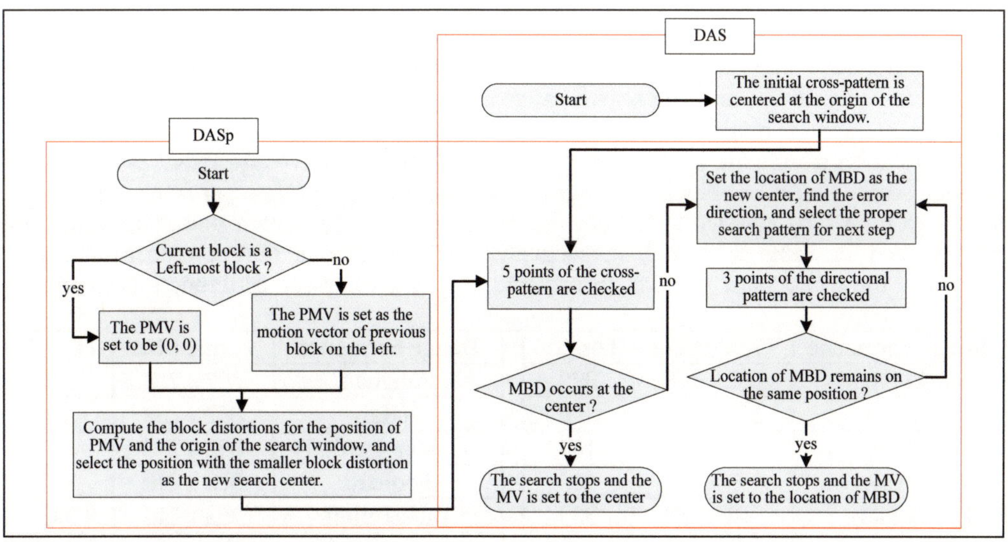

Fig. 3. Flow chart of DAS and DASp

4.2 Best-match prejudgment

According to our observations, for many stationary or quasi-stationary blocks the distortion of the best match block is close to zero. Since we found a block with a very small block distortion in our search, it was deemed unnecessary to check other points because they would not significantly improve performance, even though blocks with lower distortions may exist. We define T_{best} as the best match threshold. If the block distortion of a particular point is smaller than the T_{best} at any time during the search, the search discontinues, and that point is regarded as the best match point. Our Best-match prejudgment is different from the Zero-Motion prejudgment [14] in that the Zero-Motion prejudgment only checks the center of the search window. If the value of the block distortion is smaller than a predefined threshold, the search discontinues. Nevertheless, this situation happens not only in the zero-motion position but also in other positions, especially when a prediction scheme is incorporated. Therefore, our Best-match prejudgment reduces more checking points compared to the Zero-Motion prejudgment. With the Best-match prejudgment, the MSP of the DAS is reduced from 5 points to 1 point.

5. Experimental results and discussion

In our simulations, the FS and several famous fast BMAs are compared with the proposed DAS, DASp (DAS with prediction scheme), and DASpb (DAS with prediction scheme and the Best-match prejudgment). The fast BMAs include TSS, NTSS, DS, CDS, HEXBS, ARPS, and ARPSz (ARPS with the Zero-Motion prejudgment). To ensure a more valid comparison, these fast BMAs are classified into 3 groups as follows:

Group 1→ TSS, NTSS, DS, HEXBS, CDS, DAS

Group 2→Prediction-Based: DASp, ARPS

Group 3→Prediction-Based with prejudgment: DASpb, ARPSz

We will demonstrate the efficiency of the search pattern and search strategy either with or without prediction and prejudgment.

As shown in Table 1, nineteen popular video sequences are used in our simulations. These sequences cover a wide range of motion content and have various formats. In all simulations, the Mean Square Error (MSE) is used to measure block distortion with the block size being 16×16, and the search range ±7 pixels. The Best-match threshold T_{best} for DASpb and the Zero-motion threshold for ARPSz are all set at 1 for a fair comparison.

The simulation results are given in five aspects, which are 1) average PSNR per frame, 2) average search points per block, 3) speed-up ratio, 4) average runtime per frame, 5) runtime speed-up ratio. The average PSNR per frame and the average search points per block are summarized in Table 2, and 3, respectively. For the sake of easy comparison, Fig. 4 illustrates the contents of Table 3. In order to clearly present the differences between the

Image Sequence	Frame Size	Length	Image Sequence	Frame Size	Length
Akiyo	352 x 288	300	Foreman	352 x 288	300
Bream	352 x 288	300	Stefan	352 x 288	90
Claire	352 x 288	100	Flower_garden	352 x 240	100
Miss_America	352 x 288	100	Football	352 x 240	210
Mobile	352 x 288	300	TableTennis	352 x 240	300
Mother_daughter	352 x 288	300	Grandma	176 x 144	300
News	352 x 288	300	Silent	176 x 144	300
Paris	352 x 288	300	Suzie	176 x 144	150
Salesman	352 x 288	200	Carphone	176 x 144	300
Coastguard	352 x 288	300			

Table 1. Test sequences

simulated BMAs, the FS is not shown in Fig. 4. Table 4 shows the speed-up ratio, which is the ratio of search points per block of FS to that of other methods. In addition, the average runtime per frame is summarized in Table 5. Because the simulation is conducted on a computer under the Windows XP and the Windows XP is a multitasking operating system, under which many threads are running simultaneously sharing the CPU time, it is very hard to precisely measure the CPU time consumed by a process. Therefore, we conducted the simulation 5 times and then the mean values are shown. Fig. 6 shows the runtime speed-up ratio, which is the ratio of average runtime per frame of FS to that of other methods. The proposed methods are highlighted in Table 2, 3, 4, 5 and 6 with underlining and italics.

By observing Group 1 in Table 3, in most test sequences we can easily find that the average search points per block for each algorithm are close to the MSP of its own, especially for those sequences with small-motion content (i.e. Akiyo, Claire, News, Paris, and Grandma). The results show that the value of average search points for fast BMAs strongly depends on the selected search pattern, and using a large pattern is inefficient for sequences with small-motion content. For simplicity sake, we have used the Akiyo sequence as an example. Fig.5 gives the frame-wise comparison on the performance index of "average search points per block" for the first 300 frames and it clearly confirms our points. On the other hand, for those sequences with large-motion content, such as Coastguard, Foreman, Stefan, Flower garden, and Football, the value of average search points increases remarkably no matter which algorithms are used, except for the constant FS and TSS. However, the proposed DAS

Algorithm / Image Sequence			Group 1						Group 2		Group 3	
		FS	TSS	NTSS	DS	HEXBS	CDS	*DAS*	ARPS	*DASp*	ARPSz	*DASpb*
Akiyo	(CIF)	42.93	42.72	42.92	42.90	42.51	42.89	**42.89**	42.88	**42.89**	42.88	**42.89**
Bream	(CIF)	32.83	30.73	31.99	31.96	31.19	31.88	**31.45**	32.14	**32.35**	32.20	**32.31**
Claire	(CIF)	41.32	41.22	41.30	41.30	40.99	41.26	**41.26**	41.23	**41.27**	41.27	**41.27**
Miss_America	(CIF)	39.16	38.68	39.09	38.83	38.35	39.05	**39.04**	38.96	**38.88**	38.96	**38.88**
Mobile	(CIF)	25.16	24.86	25.13	25.08	24.82	25.10	**25.09**	24.98	**25.09**	24.99	**25.09**
Mother_daughter	(CIF)	40.34	40.12	40.26	40.23	40.04	40.20	**40.13**	39.99	**40.22**	40.07	**40.22**
News	(CIF)	37.06	36.81	36.90	36.87	36.70	36.85	**36.73**	36.68	**36.77**	36.68	**36.77**
Paris	(CIF)	32.13	31.91	32.05	32.02	31.86	31.99	**31.92**	31.52	**31.95**	31.52	**31.95**
Salesman	(CIF)	35.70	35.53	35.67	35.61	35.53	35.66	**35.66**	35.61	**35.63**	35.61	**35.63**
Coastguard	(CIF)	*30.80*	*30.46*	*30.74*	*30.72*	*30.66*	*30.72*	***30.65***	*30.74*	***30.76***	*30.74*	***30.76***
Foreman	(CIF)	*31.48*	*30.81*	*31.16*	*31.02*	*30.46*	*31.00*	***30.78***	*31.01*	***31.10***	*31.01*	***31.10***
Stefan	(CIF)	*24.84*	*24.30*	*24.29*	*23.57*	*23.43*	*23.48*	***22.99***	*24.35*	***24.38***	*24.35*	***24.38***
Flower_garden	(SIF)	*25.38*	*24.06*	*25.13*	*25.09*	*24.44*	*25.12*	***24.79***	*24.19*	***25.06***	*24.19*	***25.06***
Football	(SIF)	*25.22*	*24.68*	*24.89*	*24.72*	*24.52*	*24.69*	***24.42***	*24.69*	***24.66***	*24.69*	***24.66***
TableTennis	(SIF)	28.32	25.26	27.59	27.94	27.39	27.91	**27.35**	27.06	**27.68**	27.06	**27.68**
Grandma	(QCIF)	42.35	42.34	42.34	42.34	42.32	42.34	**42.34**	42.25	**42.34**	42.28	**42.34**
Silent	(QCIF)	35.64	35.57	35.58	35.56	35.42	35.53	**35.45**	35.39	**35.48**	35.41	**35.48**
Suzie	(QCIF)	36.58	36.38	36.55	36.50	36.16	36.43	**36.41**	36.43	**36.42**	36.43	**36.42**
Carphone	(QCIF)	32.51	32.17	32.30	32.26	31.94	32.19	**32.13**	31.93	**32.14**	31.93	**32.14**
Total Average		33.67	33.08	33.47	33.40	33.09	33.38	**33.24**	33.26	**33.42**	33.28	**33.42**

Table 2. Average PSNR per frame (dB)

is still the fastest. This indicates that the two-stage (coarse-to-fine) search strategy requires more search points due to its larger MSP. The Coastguard sequence is another example. Fig.6 gives the frame-wise comparison on the performance index of "average search points per block" for the first 300 frames. It clearly shows that the proposed DAS requires the least amount of search points among all the BMAs in Group 1 for almost all frames. An exception is frames 69 to 73, where HEXBS is the fastest one. Nevertheless, by observing Group 1 in Table 2, we found that the PSNR of the proposed DAS reveals a little degradation for the large-motion sequences mentioned above. Moreover, Fig. 7 shows the average magnitude of MV per block calculated by FS. It can be seen that the average magnitude values of frames 69 to 73 are much larger than on other frames. Meanwhile, the PSNRs of the proposed DAS are worst in these frames. Compared with the motion estimation algorithms with large search pattern, the results strongly indicate that using only small patterns can easily be trapped into local minimum especially for large-motion sequences, and therefore we should carefully address this disadvantage.

Algorithm (MSP) / Image Sequence			Group 1						Group 2		Group 3	
		FS (255)	**TSS** (25)	**NTSS** (17)	**DS** (13)	**HEXBS** (11)	**CDS** (9)	***DAS*** (5)	**ARPS** (5)	***DASp*** (5)	**ARPSz** (1)	***DASpb*** (1)
Akiyo	(CIF)	225	25.00	17.13	13.08	11.04	9.12	**5.12**	5.35	**5.07**	2.70	**2.60**
Bream	(CIF)	225	25.00	21.29	16.80	13.47	13.15	**8.91**	8.91	**6.16**	5.84	**3.56**
Claire	(CIF)	225	25.00	17.54	13.30	11.16	9.47	**5.35**	6.22	**5.26**	4.53	**4.20**
Miss_America	(CIF)	225	25.00	21.48	17.53	12.81	12.44	**8.01**	8.78	**6.73**	8.97	**6.73**
Mobile	(CIF)	225	25.00	19.65	14.30	11.56	11.01	**7.56**	7.94	**5.54**	7.95	**5.52**
Mother_daughter	(CIF)	225	25.00	19.62	14.59	11.83	11.36	**6.64**	7.60	**6.28**	7.06	**5.99**
News	(CIF)	225	25.00	17.80	13.67	11.38	10.07	**5.79**	6.22	**5.58**	4.29	**3.77**
Paris	(CIF)	225	25.00	17.63	13.47	11.26	9.72	**5.58**	6.06	**5.43**	5.18	**4.62**
Salesman	(CIF)	225	25.00	18.09	13.60	11.29	9.87	**6.07**	6.56	**5.48**	6.58	**5.48**
Coastguard	(CIF)	*225*	*25.00*	*21.24*	*17.52*	*13.68*	*16.62*	***10.04***	*8.64*	***6.45***	*9.24*	***6.45***
Foreman	(CIF)	*225*	*25.00*	*23.04*	*18.40*	*13.78*	*16.79*	***10.86***	*9.31*	***7.56***	*9.73*	***7.53***
Stefan	(CIF)	*225*	*25.00*	*24.18*	*17.99*	*13.96*	*16.75*	***10.70***	*8.66*	***6.95***	*9.20*	***6.95***
Flower_garden	(SIF)	*225*	*25.00*	*23.42*	*18.26*	*14.20*	*16.47*	***10.53***	*9.35*	***6.75***	*9.77*	***6.68***
Football	(SIF)	*225*	*25.00*	*25.77*	*20.87*	*15.24*	*20.30*	***13.32***	*10.86*	***9.92***	*11.46*	***9.92***
TableTennis	(SIF)	225	25.00	20.53	16.53	13.11	14.18	**8.50**	8.18	**6.47**	8.54	**6.47**
Grandma	(QCIF)	225	25.00	17.73	13.46	11.25	9.73	**5.40**	6.27	**5.40**	6.02	**5.19**
Silent	(QCIF)	225	25.00	17.86	13.65	11.35	10.04	**5.79**	6.65	**5.68**	4.08	**3.49**
Suzie	(QCIF)	225	25.00	18.76	14.23	11.61	10.87	**6.55**	7.19	**6.02**	5.83	**4.96**
Carphone	(QCIF)	225	25.00	19.71	15.07	12.03	12.06	**7.41**	8.52	**6.84**	8.08	**6.41**
Total Average		225	25.00	20.13	15.60	12.42	12.63	**7.80**	7.75	**6.29**	7.11	**5.61**

Table 3. Average search points per block

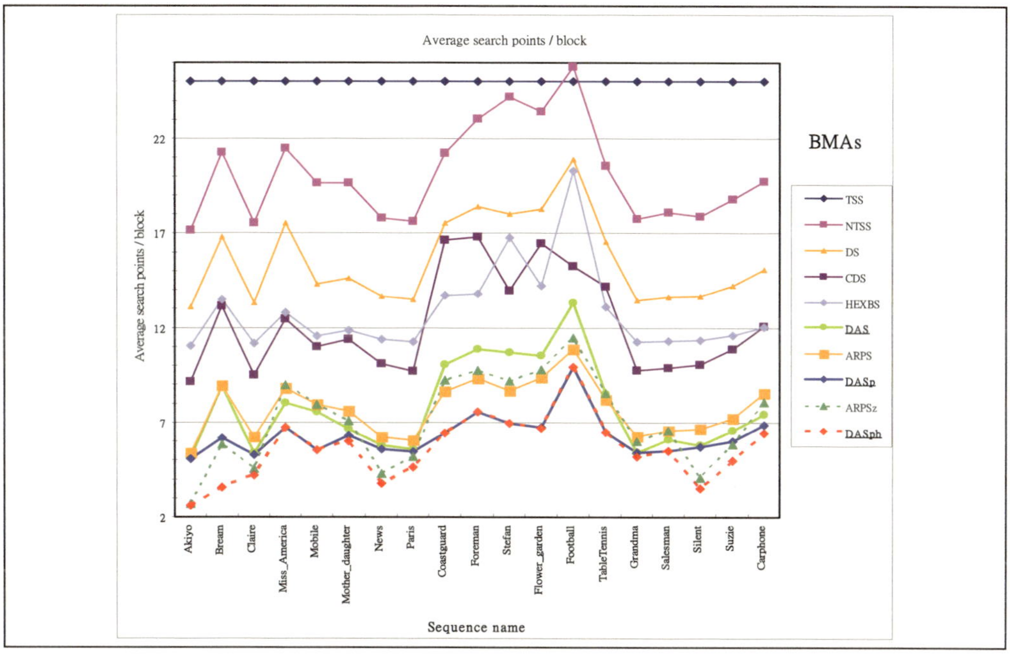

Fig. 4. Average search points per block for all test sequences

Algorithm / Image Sequence			Group 1						Group 2		Group 3	
		FS	TSS	NTSS	DS	HEXBS	CDS	*DAS*	ARPS	*DASp*	ARPSz	*DASpb*
Akiyo	(CIF)	1.00	9.00	13.13	17.20	20.38	24.67	**43.95**	42.06	**44.38**	83.33	**86.54**
Bream	(CIF)	1.00	9.00	10.57	13.39	16.70	17.11	**25.25**	25.25	**36.53**	38.53	**63.20**
Claire	(CIF)	1.00	9.00	12.83	16.92	20.16	23.76	**42.06**	36.17	**42.78**	49.67	**53.57**
Miss_America	(CIF)	1.00	9.00	10.47	12.84	17.56	18.09	**28.09**	25.63	**33.43**	25.08	**33.43**
Mobile	(CIF)	1.00	9.00	11.45	15.73	19.46	20.44	**29.76**	28.34	**40.61**	28.30	**40.76**
Mother_daughter	(CIF)	1.00	9.00	11.47	15.42	19.02	19.81	**33.89**	29.61	**35.83**	31.87	**37.56**
News	(CIF)	1.00	9.00	12.64	16.46	19.77	22.34	**38.86**	36.17	**40.32**	52.45	**59.68**
Paris	(CIF)	1.00	9.00	12.76	16.70	19.98	23.15	**40.32**	37.13	**41.44**	43.44	**48.70**
Salesman	(CIF)	1.00	9.00	12.44	16.54	19.93	22.80	**37.07**	34.30	**41.06**	34.19	**41.06**
Coastguard	(CIF)	*1.00*	*9.00*	*10.59*	*12.84*	*16.45*	*13.54*	**22.41**	*26.04*	**34.88**	*24.35*	**34.88**
Foreman	(CIF)	*1.00*	*9.00*	*9.77*	*12.23*	*16.33*	*13.40*	**20.72**	*24.17*	**29.76**	*23.12*	**29.88**
Stefan	(CIF)	*1.00*	*9.00*	*9.31*	*12.51*	*16.12*	*13.43*	**21.03**	*25.98*	**32.37**	*24.46*	**32.37**
Flower_garden	(SIF)	*1.00*	*9.00*	*9.61*	*12.32*	*15.85*	*13.66*	**21.37**	*24.06*	**33.33**	*23.03*	**33.68**
Football	(SIF)	*1.00*	*9.00*	*8.73*	*10.78*	*14.76*	*11.08*	**16.89**	*20.72*	**22.68**	*19.63*	**22.68**
TableTennis	(SIF)	1.00	9.00	10.96	13.61	17.16	15.87	**26.47**	27.51	**34.78**	26.35	**34.78**
Grandma	(QCIF)	1.00	9.00	12.69	16.72	20.00	23.12	**41.67**	35.89	**41.67**	37.38	**43.35**
Silent	(QCIF)	1.00	9.00	12.60	16.48	19.82	22.41	**38.86**	33.83	**39.61**	55.15	**64.47**
Suzie	(QCIF)	1.00	9.00	11.99	15.81	19.38	20.70	**34.35**	31.29	**37.38**	38.59	**45.36**
Carphone	(QCIF)	1.00	9.00	11.42	14.93	18.70	18.66	**30.36**	26.41	**32.89**	27.85	**35.10**
Total Average		1.00	9.00	11.34	14.71	18.29	18.84	**31.23**	30.03	**36.62**	36.15	**44.27**

Table 4. Speed-up ratio with respect to FS

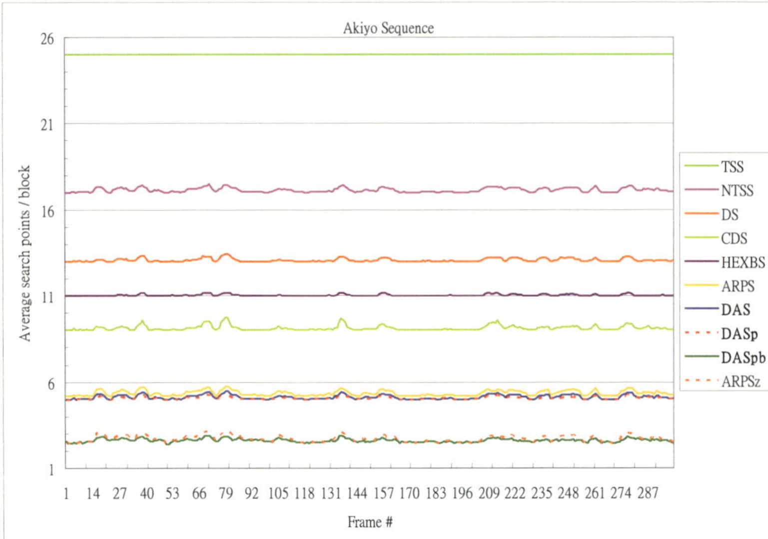

Fig. 5. Frame-wise average search points comparison between various BMAs on CIF sequence "Akiyo"

Image Sequence \ Algorithm			Group 1						Group 2		Group 3	
		FS	**TSS)**	**NTSS**	**DS**	**HEXBS**	**CDS**	***DAS***	**ARPS**	***DASp***	**ARPSz**	***DASpb***
Akiyo	(CIF)	295.98	33.58	23.71	18.52	15.79	13.26	**7.56**	7.92	**7.62**	4.39	**4.26**
Bream	(CIF)	295.85	34.29	29.14	23.77	19.12	18.49	**12.87**	13.35	**8.88**	8.84	**5.52**
Claire	(CIF)	297.08	34.06	24.24	18.47	15.62	13.51	**7.63**	9.14	**7.81**	6.79	**6.31**
Miss_America	(CIF)	295.71	34.05	29.30	24.14	17.84	17.12	**12.41**	12.58	**10.00**	13.06	**9.46**
Mobile	(CIF)	296.07	34.18	27.02	20.26	16.61	15.58	**11.18**	12.07	**8.13**	12.11	**8.22**
Mother_daughter	(CIF)	295.47	34.19	27.23	20.84	16.98	16.08	**9.78**	11.28	**9.17**	10.56	**8.68**
News	(CIF)	295.32	34.34	24.50	19.30	16.22	14.32	**8.54**	9.12	**8.15**	6.51	**5.83**
Paris	(CIF)	295.59	34.06	24.24	19.01	15.87	13.91	**8.41**	9.01	**8.15**	7.76	**7.04**
Salesman	(CIF)	295.86	34.13	24.78	18.92	16.03	14.51	**9.33**	9.60	**8.20**	9.85	**7.82**
Coastguard	(CIF)	*296.43*	*34.46*	*29.05*	*24.41*	*19.36*	*22.98*	**14.52**	*12.10*	*9.65*	*13.24*	*9.79*
Foreman	(CIF)	*296.24*	*34.26*	*31.74*	*25.79*	*19.65*	*23.81*	**15.74**	*13.39*	***11.07***	*14.03*	***11.19***
Stefan	(CIF)	*297.65*	*34.15*	*32.98*	*25.12*	*19.87*	*23.93*	**14.90**	*12.19*	***10.47***	*13.39*	***10.38***
Flower_garden	(SIF)	*246.64*	*28.37*	*26.24*	*21.08*	*16.32*	*19.26*	**12.52**	*10.93*	*8.42*	*11.39*	*8.08*
Football	(SIF)	*246.52*	*28.57*	*29.71*	*23.89*	*17.99*	*23.60*	**15.93**	*13.07*	***12.33***	*13.78*	***11.91***
TableTennis	(SIF)	246.84	28.88	23.63	19.23	15.68	16.78	**10.45**	9.95	**8.14**	10.21	**8.46**
Grandma	(QCIF)	74.99	8.31	10.91	5.98	5.11	3.90	**1.54**	2.09	**1.75**	1.85	**1.80**
Silent	(QCIF)	75.49	8.97	5.59	4.19	2.52	2.74	**2.54**	3.29	**2.16**	2.10	**1.92**
Suzie	(QCIF)	75.18	8.87	5.89	3.57	3.48	3.60	**1.98**	1.65	**1.84**	2.54	**1.31**
Carphone	(QCIF)	75.29	8.43	7.28	8.12	6.76	6.52	**2.62**	3.90	**2.41**	3.41	**2.41**
Note: the frame size is different for different formats												

Table 5. Average runtime per frame (ms)

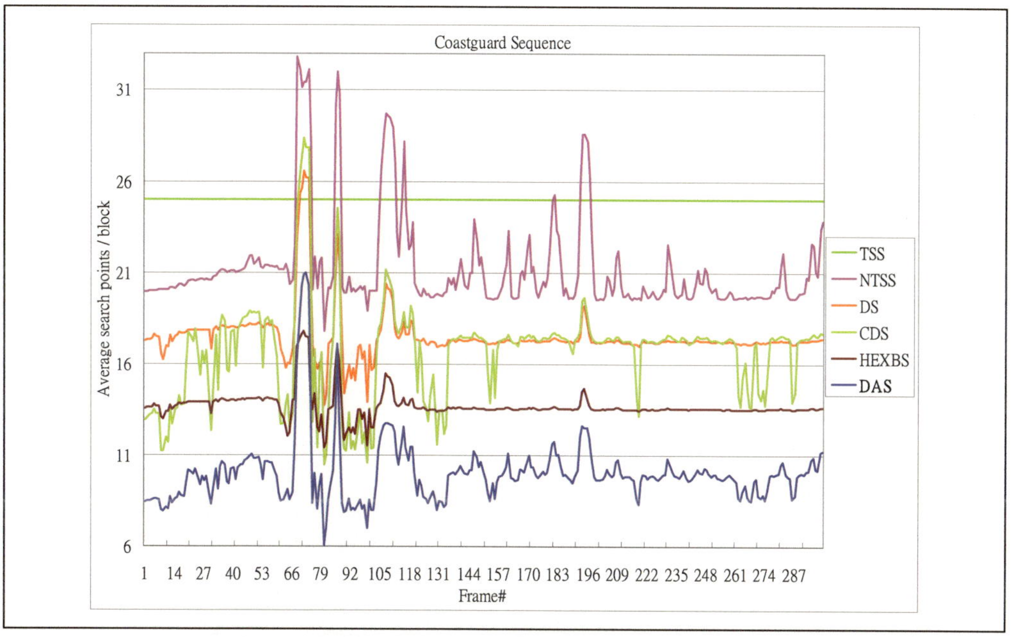

Fig. 6. Frame-wise average search points comparison between various BMAs on CIF sequence "Coastguard"

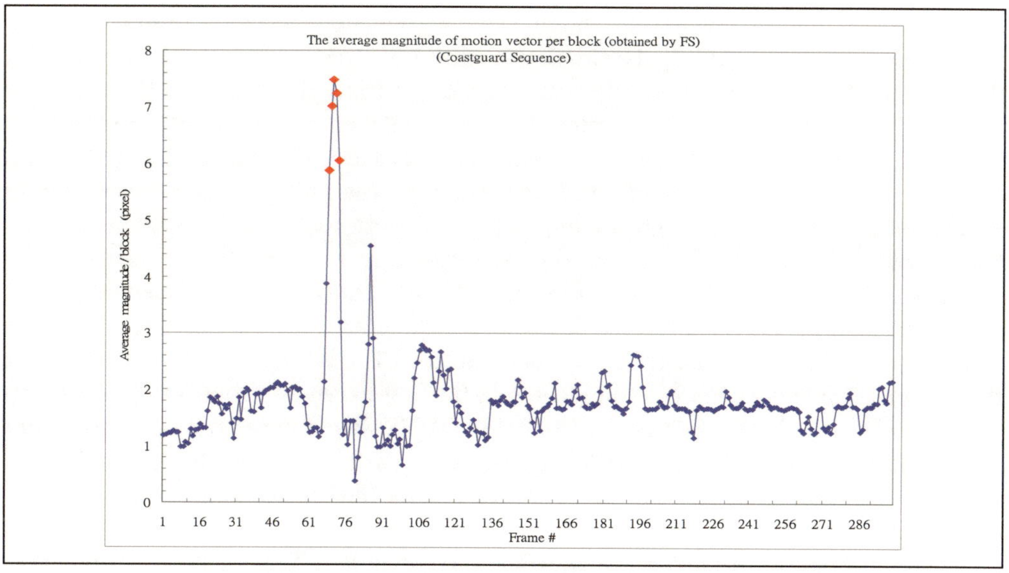

Fig. 7. The average magnitude of motion vector per block for Coastguard Sequence

Algorithm / Image Sequence			Group 1						Group 2		Group 3	
		FS	TSS	NTSS	DS	HEXBS	CDS	*DAS*	ARPS	*DASp*	ARPSz	*DASpb*
Akiyo	(CIF)	1.00	8.81	12.48	15.99	18.74	22.32	**39.15**	37.37	**38.86**	67.47	**69.45**
Bream	(CIF)	1.00	8.63	10.15	12.45	15.47	16.00	**22.99**	22.16	**33.33**	33.48	**53.61**
Claire	(CIF)	1.00	8.72	12.26	16.08	19.02	21.99	**38.94**	32.49	**38.02**	43.73	**47.10**
Miss_America	(CIF)	1.00	8.68	10.09	12.25	16.58	17.27	**23.84**	23.50	**29.58**	22.64	**31.26**
Mobile	(CIF)	1.00	8.66	10.96	14.61	17.83	19.01	**26.49**	24.54	**36.42**	24.46	**36.04**
Mother_daughter	(CIF)	1.00	8.64	10.85	14.18	17.40	18.38	**30.20**	26.20	**32.22**	27.97	**34.03**
News	(CIF)	1.00	8.60	12.06	15.30	18.21	20.62	**34.56**	32.38	**36.25**	45.35	**50.65**
Paris	(CIF)	1.00	8.68	12.20	15.55	18.62	21.24	**35.13**	32.82	**36.25**	38.10	**41.98**
Salesman	(CIF)	1.00	8.67	11.94	15.64	18.46	20.39	**31.71**	30.83	**36.08**	30.04	**37.86**
Coastguard	(CIF)	*1.00*	*8.60*	*10.21*	*12.14*	*15.31*	*12.90*	**20.41**	*24.50*	**30.72**	*22.39*	**30.29**
Foreman	(CIF)	*1.00*	*8.65*	*9.33*	*11.49*	*15.08*	*12.44*	**18.82**	*22.12*	**26.77**	*21.12*	**26.47**
Stefan	(CIF)	*1.00*	*8.72*	*9.03*	*11.85*	*14.98*	*12.44*	**19.98**	*24.41*	**28.42**	*22.23*	**28.66**
Flower_garden	(SIF)	*1.00*	*8.69*	*9.40*	*11.70*	*15.12*	*12.81*	**19.70**	*22.57*	**29.30**	*21.66*	**30.53**
Football	(SIF)	*1.00*	*8.63*	*8.30*	*10.32*	*13.70*	*10.45*	**15.47**	*18.86*	**19.99**	*17.89*	**20.70**
TableTennis	(SIF)	1.00	8.55	10.45	12.83	15.74	14.71	**23.63**	24.81	**30.31**	24.17	**29.19**
Grandma	(QCIF)	1.00	9.02	6.87	12.53	14.67	19.23	**48.56**	35.85	**42.95**	40.51	**41.75**
Silent	(QCIF)	1.00	8.41	13.50	18.00	29.91	27.53	**29.67**	22.96	**34.98**	35.87	**39.25**
Suzie	(QCIF)	1.00	8.47	12.76	21.07	21.61	20.90	**37.87**	45.53	**40.95**	29.55	**57.52**
Carphone	(QCIF)	1.00	8.94	10.35	9.27	11.15	11.54	**28.77**	19.29	**31.30**	22.06	**31.21**
Total Average		1.00	8.67	10.69	13.86	17.24	17.48	28.73	27.54	33.30	31.09	38.82

Table 6. Runtime speed-up ratio with respect to FS

To compensate the bias due to fast motion, using a prediction scheme is a useful solution. This viewpoint is confirmed by the simulation results of DASp. With a prediction scheme, the DASp performs quite well in both search speed and PSNR. Fig. 8 gives a closer view of the Coastguard sequence and indicates that the prediction scheme greatly reduces the search points needed for each frame, especially for frames 69 to 73. In addition, Fig. 9 shows PSNR performance for frames 69 to 73. As expected, the prediction scheme effectively compensates the bias and thus greatly improves PSNR performance. It is worth mentioning that the prediction scheme does not need to be very accurate. In our study, we use only the previous block to predict the MV in the current block. However, it effectively improved PSNR performance. Furthermore, the Best-match prejudgment is quite useful for sequences with a stationary background. The Best-match threshold T_{best} is used to control the results of the Best-match prejudgment. With a higher T_{best}, the Best-match prejudgment eliminates the need for more search points, but may degrade the PSNR. In our experiments, we set a very low value (T_{best}=1) for the Best-match threshold in order to preserve high estimation accuracy (high PSNR). What is the best value of T_{best} for the tradeoff between search speed and PSNR performance is beyond the scope of this paper. Nevertheless, even with such a low value, the speed-up ratio is still significant. As shown in Table 4, the DASpb almost doubles the search speed of the DASp for Akiyo without degrading PSNR.

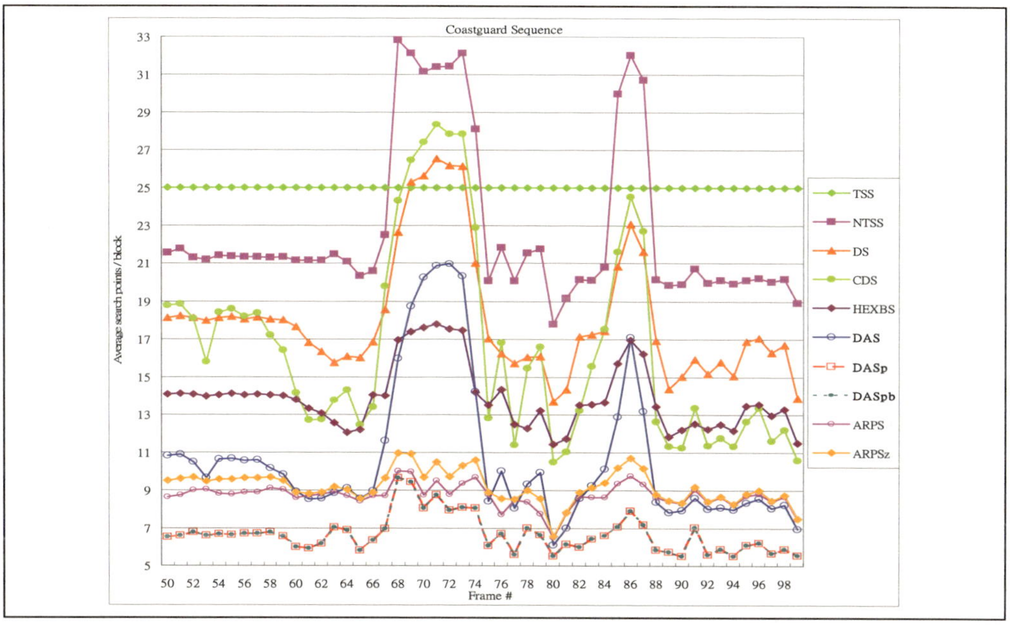

Fig. 8. Average search points / block for frame #50 to #100 of Coastguard sequence

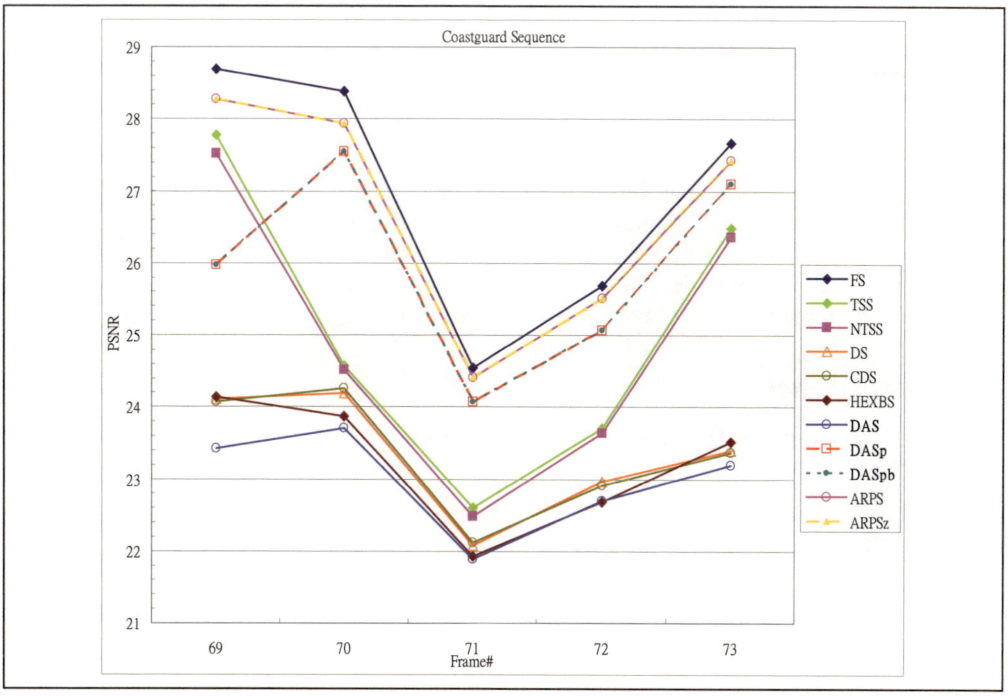

Fig. 9. The PSNR for frame #69 to #73 of Coastguard sequence

From the viewpoint of PSNR performance, Table 2 shows that the PSNR of the proposed DAS is approximately close to the average PSNR in Group 1. Furthermore, for both the DASp and DASpb, the PSNR values significantly improve, especially in fast motion sequences. In other words, for most sequences, we should enhance the property of center-bias even for those with fast motion. However, to avoid being trapped in a local minimum due to a small search pattern, the prediction of search center can effectively address this problem. For the sequences of Coastguard, Foreman, Stefan, Flower garden, and Football, Table 3 shows that the DASp improves the PSNR performance significantly. In Table 4 it can be seen that the search points for these sequences are almost the same as those sequences with a small motion. By using Best-match prejudgment, we can filter out the stationary background, thus improving search speed. Since the threshold is very low, performance degradation is minimal.

Finally, in terms of search speed, we can see from Table 3 that our methods outperform all other methods for all test sequences in the same group and the proposed DASpb has the best search speed among all BMAs with negligible degradation in the PSNR. Furthermore, the actual runtime in Table 5. confirmed the theoretical search speed in Table 3 and the runtime speed-up ratio in Table 6 roughly corresponds to the theoretical speed-up ratio in Table 4.

6. Conclusion

In this paper, we have proposed a novel fast block-matching algorithm for motion estimation. We explored the relationship between block distortions and search patterns and came up with a rule for determining search direction. With a known search direction, asymmetric search patterns are developed, and the search points on the outside of the direction were disregarded. Since the unnecessary search points are eliminated, the search speed is greatly improved.

In our study, we adopted a very compact center-biased initial pattern to minimize the required MSP. Nevertheless, it is easier to become trapped in a local minimum. We introduced a prediction scheme to address this disadvantage. The prediction scheme effectively and efficiently improves both the PSNR and search speed, especially for those sequences with fast motion (e.g. Coastguard, Foreman, Stefan, Flower garden and Football). In addition, the Best-match prejudgment was also incorporated to profit stationary and quasi-stationary blocks. The experimental results have verified our points and demonstrated the superiority of our methods. The authors would like to express their sincere thanks to the anonymous reviewers for their invaluable comments and suggestions.

7. Acknowledgement

This work was supported by the National Science Counsel of Republic of China Granted NSC 99-2221-E-214 -055.

8. References

Koga, T.; Iinuma, K.; Hirano, A.; Iijima, Y. & lshiguro, T. (1981). Motion-compensated interframe coding for video conferencing, *in Proc. Nat. Telecommunication Conf. , New Orleans*, LA, pp. G5.3.1-G5.3.5.

Ghanbari, M. (1990). The cross-search algorithm for motion estimation, *IEEE Trans. Commun.*, Vol. 38, No. 7, pp. 950-953, ISSN : 0090-6778.

Li, R.; Zeng,B. & Liou, M. L. (1994). A new three-step search algorithm for block motion estimation, *IEEE Trans. Circuits Syst. Video Technol.* , Vol. 4, No. 4, pp. 438-442, ISSN: 1051-8215.

Liu, L. K. & Feig, E. (1996). A block-based gradient descent search algorithm for block motion estimation in video coding, *IEEE Trans. Circuits Syst. Video Technol.* , Vol. 6, No. 4, pp. 419-422, ISSN : 1051-8215.

Po, L. M. & Ma, W. C. (1996). A novel four-step search algorithm for fast block motion estimation, *IEEE Trans. Circuits Syst. Video Technol.* , Vol. 6, No. 3, pp. 313-317, ISSN: 1051-8215.

Zhu, S. & Ma, K. K. (2000). A new diamond search algorithm for fast block-matching motion estimation, *IEEE Trans. Image Process.* , Vol. 9, No. 2, pp. 287-290, ISSN: 1057-7149.

Zhu, C.; Lin, X. & Chau, L. P. (2002). Hexagon-based search pattern for fast block motion estimation, *IEEE Trans. Circuits Syst. Video Technol.* , Vol. 12, No. 5, pp. 349-355, ISSN : 1051-8215.

Cheung, C. H. & Po, L. M. (2002). A novel cross-diamond search algorithm for fast block motion estimation, *IEEE Trans. Circuits Syst. Video Technol.* , Vol. 12, No. 12, pp. 1168-1177, ISSN : 1051-8215.

Liu, B. & Zaccarin, A. (1993). New fast algorithms for the estimation of block motion vectors, *IEEE Trans. Circuits Syst. Video Technol.* , Vol. 3, No. 2, pp. 148-157, ISSN : 1051-8215.

Yu, Y.; Zhou, J. & Chen, C. W. (2001). A novel fast block motion estimation algorithm based on combined subsamplings on pixels and search candidates, *J. Vis. Commun. Image Represent.* , Vol. 12, No. 1, pp. 96-105, ISSN: 1047-3203.

Bierling, M. (1988). Displacement estimation by hierarchical block matching, *in Proc. SPIE Conf. On Vis. Commun. And Image Proc*, ISSN: 1018-8770.

Luo, L.; Zou, C.; Gao, X. & He, Z. (1997). A new prediction search algorithm for block motion estimation in video coding, *IEEE Trans. Consum. Electron.*, Vol. 43, No.1, pp. 56-61, ISSN : 0098-3063.

Xu, J. B.; Po, L. M. & Cheung, C. K. (1999). Adaptive motion tracking block matching algorithms for video coding, *IEEE Trans. Circuits Syst. Video Technol.*, Vol. 9, No.7, ISSN : 1051-8215.

Yao, N. & Ma, K. K. (2002). Adaptive rood pattern search for fast block-matching motion estimation, *IEEE Trans. Image Process.* , Vol. 11, No. 12, pp. 1442-1449, ISSN : 1057-7149.

Kuo, C. M.; Chao, C. P. & Hsieh, C. H. (2002) A new motion estimation algorithm for video coding using adaptive kalman filter, *Real-Time Imaging*, Vol. 8, No. 5, pp. 387-398, ISSN 1077-2014.

Chimienti, A.; Ferraris, C. & Pau, D. (2002). A complexity-bounded motion estimation algorithm, *IEEE Trans. Image Process.* , Vol. 11, No. 4, pp. 387-392, ISSN : 1057-7149.

Namuduri, K. R. (2004). Motion estimation using spatio-temporal contextual information, *IEEE Trans. Circuits Syst. Video Technol.* , Vol. 14, No. 8, pp. 1111-1115, ISSN : 1051-8215.

Ahmad, I.; Zheng, W.; Luo, J. & Liou, M. (2006). A fast adaptive motion estimation algorithm, *IEEE Trans. Circuits Syst. Video Technol.*, Vol. 16, No. 3, pp. 420-438, ISSN: 1051-8215.

Kuo, C. M.; Chung, S. C. & Shih, P. Y. (2006). Kalman filtering based rate-constrained motion estimation for very low bit rate video coding, *IEEE Trans. Circuits Syst. Video Technol.*, Vol. 16, No. 1, pp. 3-18, ISSN : 1051-8215.

Kuo, C. M.; Kuan, Y. H.; Hsieh, C. H. & Lee Y. H. (2009). A novel prediction-based directional asymmetric search algorithm for fast block-matching motion estimation, *IEEE Trans. Circuits Syst. Video Technol.*, Vol. 19, No. 6, pp. 893-899, ISSN : 1051-8215.

12

Block Based Motion Vector Estimation Using FUHS16, UHDS16 and UHDS8 Algorithms for Video Sequence

S. S. S. Ranjit
Universiti Teknikal Malaysia Melaka (UTeM)
Malaysia

1. Introduction

1. Fast Unrestricted Hexagon Search (FUHS16) algorithm

In this section a short description about the Fast Unrestricted Hexagon Search (FUHS16) algorithm for motion estimation development based on some of the existing algorithms that have been discussed and simulated. Comparison of the performance among techniques is conducted as part of experimental result preparation.

FUHS16 algorithm is developed based on 16 × 16 pixels in a block size and two different models of hexagon sizes are applied to perform the motion vector search. Figure 1 shows how a single frame is extracted into required block size, where in FUHS16 algorithm each frame size is represented by 176 × 144 pixels. This means, that each frame will have 9 blocks horizontally and 11 blocks vertically. Hence, there are 99 extracted blocks in a video frame.

Assumed has the following parameters i = *horizontal (9 blocks),*
j = *vertical (11 blocks),*
$i = 1: (r / bsize)$,
$j = 1: (c / bsize)$,

where, r = 144, c = 176.

B = *Block,*
CF = *current_frame,*
BZ = *Block_Size*

Eq. (1) shows the formula to extract the video frame into 16 × 16 block size.

$$B=CF(1+BZ^*(i-1):BZ^*i,1+BZ^*(j-1):BZ^*j) \quad (1)$$

2. Fast unrestricted hexagon search algorithm search procedure

In the first step, large hexagon search shape with seven checking points are used to perform the search for the best-matched motion vector from the inner large hexagon search shape. If the best-matched motion vector is found at the center of large hexagon, the large hexagon search shape switches to small hexagon search shape that includes four checking points for the focused inner search.

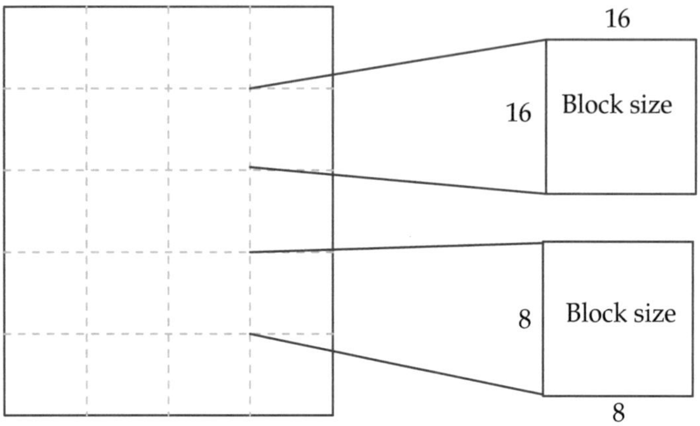

Fig. 1. Extraction 16 × 16 and 8 × 8 Pixels Block Size from Single Frame

These four checking points are compared in order to determine the final best-matched motion vector coordinate. Otherwise, the search continues around the point with the smallest MAD by using the same large hexagon search shape. This process continues till the large hexagon search shape moves along the direction of decreasing distortion. It is noted that a small hexagon search shape is applied in the final step after the decreasing distortion reaches optimum of the motion vector for large hexagon search shape. Then the small hexagon search shape will focus on the final search for the best-matched motion vector coordinate.

The proposed FUHS16 algorithm can be described further in the following three steps.

i. Starting

The large hexagon search shape with seven checking points are centered at (+8, +8) and it is assumed as (0, 0). We name this as the predefined search window in the motion field. If the smallest MAD point with best-matched motion vector is found to be at the center of the large hexagon, we will proceed to Step (iii); otherwise Step (ii) will be proceed.

ii. Searching

Since the MAD point in the previous search step is not located at the center, a new large hexagon search shape is formed to perform new checking. It confines of seven checking points. Now the new MAD point is identified. If the MAD point is located at the center of newly to form large hexagon search shape, we proceed to Step (iii); otherwise, this step is repeated continuously till the next smallest MAD is again found at the center of large hexagon search shape.

iii. Ending

For the final search, large hexagon search shape determines the best-matched motion vector which is located at the center inner large hexagon search shape. After this, it will then switch to the small hexagon search shape to perform the final best-matched motion vector coordinate, MAD search point. The four points in the small hexagon search shape are evaluated to compare with the current MAD point. The MAD point is the final solution of best-matched motion vector coordinate location.

From the above procedure, it can be easily derived that the total number of search points per frame are,

$$N_{FUHS16(m_x,m_y)} = (LHS + SHS) + 3n, \tag{2}$$

Where, (m_x, m_y) = final best-matched motion vector coordinate,

n = number of execution of Step (ii),
LHS = Large hexagon shape search points,
SHS = Small hexagon shape search points.

In Figure 2, the motion vector is predicted at MAD_4 after emerging 3 hexagon search shape. Based on the Equation 2, the $N_{FUHS(m_x m_y)} = 7 + 3(3) + 4 = 20$. The FUHS16 needs 20 search points to predict final best-matched motion vector at MAD_4.

MAD_0 is the starting search point in the large hexagon search shape, center at coordinate (+8, +8) - it is then assumed as coordinate (0, 0). The outer six points in the large hexagon search shape are evaluated to compare to the optimal MAD in the first search. If the optimal MAD is found to be at the center, then small hexagon search shape will take place to focus on the fine resolution search to predict the optimum motion vector in that area.

If the smallest MAD is found at one of the outer search point of large hexagon search shape, then three new search points are emerged to form a new large hexagon search shape as shows in Figure 2. The current optimal MAD is known as MAD_1 and is positioned at the center of newly form large hexagon search shape. The current coordinate of MAD_1 is at (+7, +10). All the points in the large hexagon search shape are again evaluated to predict the optimal MAD in the second search.

In the second search, the optimal MAD is MAD_2 which is located at one the six outer search points. Again three new search points are emerged to form a new large hexagon search shape and repositioned MAD_2 to be at the center of newly formed large hexagon search shape. The newly form large hexagon search shape is centered at coordinate (+6, +12). All the search points surrounding the large hexagon search shape are evaluated again to predict the optimal MAD.

In the third search, MAD_3 is found at the outer search point of large hexagon search shape. Three new search points are emerged to form a new large hexagon search shape and MAD_3 is repositioned at the newly form large hexagons search shape. The new coordinate of MAD_3 is (+7, +14).

All the points surrounding the MAD_3 are evaluated again (assigned with number 2) and the optimal MAD is located at MAD_3 which is at the center of the large hexagon search shape. Then the small hexagon search shape will take place surrounding MAD_3 to conduct fine resolution search at the inner search. All the four points in the small hexagon search shape are evaluated again to find the best-matched motion in that block. So, the MAD_4 is the optimal MAD found in the fine resolution search and is coordinated at (+8, +15).

The final coordinate is considered the best-matched motion vector coordinate in the block of the current frame. This process is repeated in every single frame to predict the best-matched motion estimation of a current frame.

The preliminary development of FUHS16 technique is described in this section. The FUHS16 technique is then used as a baseline to enhance or develop our next algorithm. The FUHS16 algorithm is simulated to obtain the motion vector estimation search point, performance analysis compare to the other superior algorithms. The obtained results are analysed and the algorithm has been improved with some changes. These changes will be further discussed in next section.

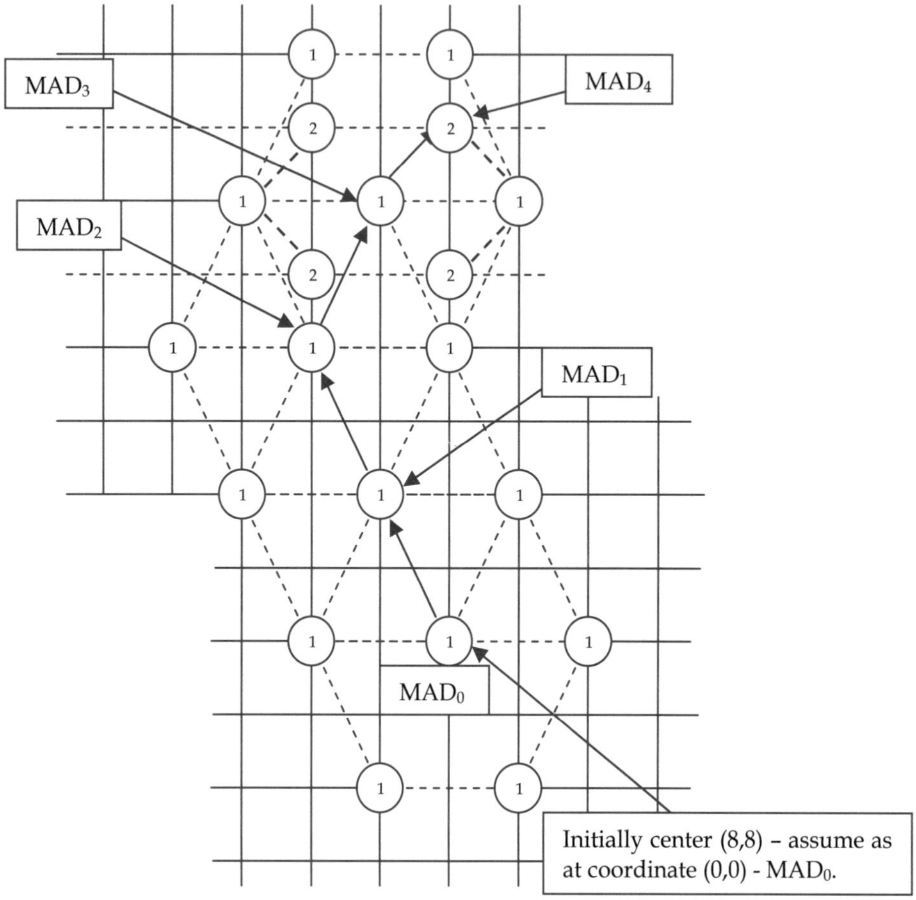

Fig. 2. Hexagon 3 new check points are formed and evaluated as new candidates to predict the motion vectors

3. Unrestricted Hexagon Diamond Search (UHDS16) algorithm

This section starts with some modifications from the FUHS16 algorithm. In this section, the UHDS16 technique is introduced. This technique is developed to have unrestricted search. To achieve this, a simple and efficient fast block-matching algorithm based on hexagon-diamond search shape is proposed. UHDS16 is designed uniquely with a large hexagon shape and shrink diamond search step (SDSS). Large hexagon is more unique to identify the motion vector in the small region of large hexagon shape. Finally, the shrink diamond search step is to locate the best-matched motion vector in the large hexagon small region. Experimental results show that the proposed UHDS16 algorithm significantly produces smaller computation complexity.

The speed and accuracy of the rood pattern based search algorithm are highly related to the size of the pattern. First step of the proposed method permits the algorithm to adapt itself to the content of motion. In most cases, adjacent blocks belong to the same moving object that has similar motions. Therefore, it is reasonable to predict the motion of current blocks from motion vectors of adjacent blocks.

UHDS16 is designed to have repetitive search in the small region of large hexagon search shape. The large hexagon search shape is to locate the best motion vector before switching to shrink diamond search step for the final best-matched motion vector coordinate.
The UHDS algorithms are implemented using two different block sizes. Initially, the UHDS16 algorithm is developed using the 16 × 16 block size with search windows 15 × 15 and then the same technique and ideology is used for 8 × 8 block size with search windows size 7 × 7. The difference between UHDS16 algorithm and UHDS8 algorithm is the block size.
Figure 1 illustrates the extraction of 8 × 8 pixels block size from a single frame. The FUHS16 algorithm block extraction procedure is applied in the UHDS8 algorithm. This means, that each frame will have 18 blocks horizontally and 22 blocks vertically.

4. Unrestricted Hexagon Diamond Search (UHDS16) and (UHDS8) algorithm search procedure

Based on the switching strategy with two different shape searches in Figure 3, we develop the following search methodology as depicted in Figure 4.
The UHDS algorithm employs two search procedures as depicted in Figure 3. Large hexagon is assigned with a signed number '1'. The hexagon shape procedure is to locate the final best-matched motion vector coordinate in the search area. The coarse hexagon shape continues to search till the motion vector found in the hexagon area is an optimal MAD point. This is then followed by the shrink diamond shape which checks all four points with number assigned with '2' in Figure 3. The four search points are evaluated and compared to the center point in order to locate the final best-matched motion vector coordinate.
Figure 4 describes the basics of the UHDS16 and UHDS8 search algorithm. The number of search points needed for UHDS16 and UHDS8 algorithm is 12. The large hexagon is confined with seven outer search points, while the SDSS is confined with five search points.

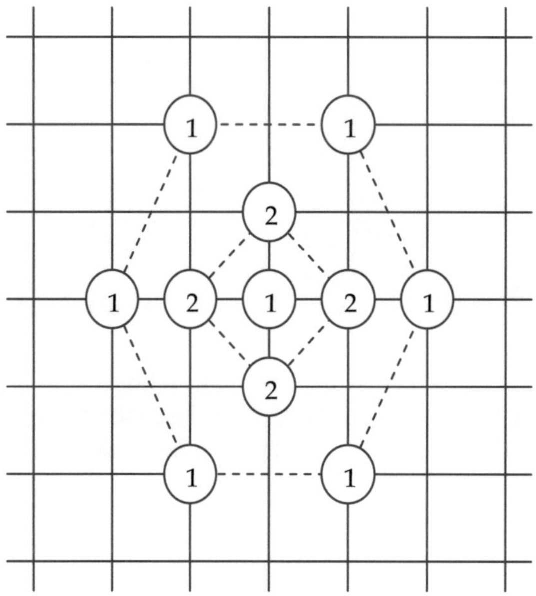

Fig. 3. Hexagon-Diamond Search Modelling Shape

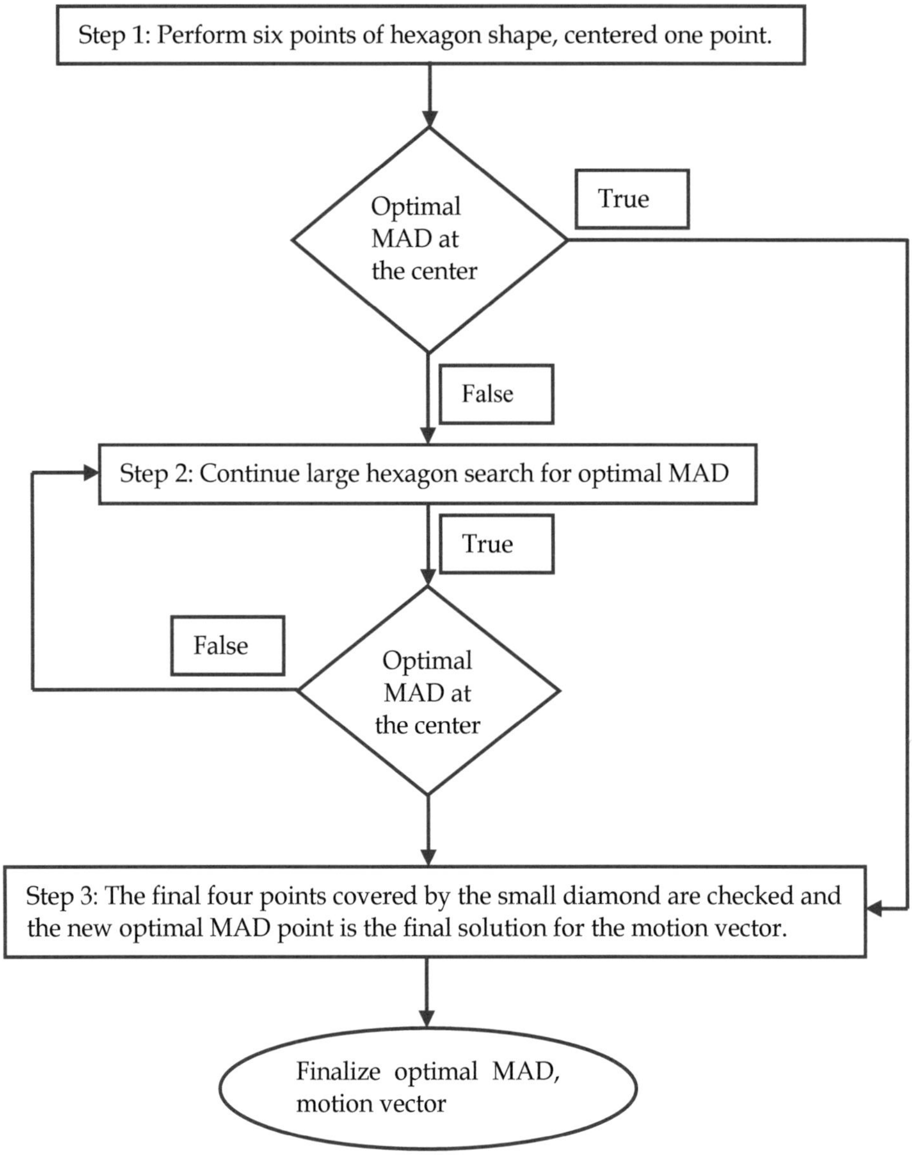

Fig. 4. Motion Estimation Search Procedure of Unrestricted Hexagon Diamond Search Algorithm

In the first step, seven checking points of the hexagon, within the search window around the motion vector predictor are compared to obtain the best motion vector. MAD is positioned at the center (0, 0) and served as a reference point to determine the final best motion vector in the SDSS. If the MAD point is found to be at the center of the hexagon search, then the hexagon search is switched to the small diamond search pattern for the final motion vector.

In the second step, MAD is the motion vector found by comparing the motion vector at step one MAD. If the MAD point is not located at the center and has best motion vector compared to the center one in step one, a new hexagon is formed and current MAD point

becomes the center. All the six points surrounding MAD points will be compared again to relocate the best motion vector before switching to the small diamond search step.
In the third step, SDSS will finalize the best motion vector and make comparison to determine the greatest motion vector amongst the four MAD points. Otherwise, the second step is repeated until the best optimal MAD distortion and best motion vector are found.

5. Peak Signal-to-Noise Ratio

The PSNR is a method used for objective quality comparison between two values for different reconstructed images. It gives one measure of quality which is applied in image processing perspective. PSNR analysis uses a standard mathematical model to measure the difference between two images in video sequence. It is commonly used in the development and analysis of algorithms, and comparing image quality between different compression systems. The PSNR Equation (3) is mostly used as a measure of quality of reconstruction within the compression of images. The peak in PSNR refers to the maximum pixel value. The following formula is used to calculate the PSNR value:

$$PSNR = 10\log_{10}\frac{255 * 255}{MSD\_pred}, \tag{3}$$

The PSNR measured usually is in decibels (dB). The higher the PSNR, the better quality will be produced for a compressed or reconstructed image.
Where

$$MSD\_pred = \frac{\sum_{M,N}\left[I_1(m,n) - I_2(m,n)\right]^2}{N \times N}. \tag{4}$$

$I_1(m,n)$ = pred_frame,

$I_2(m,n)$ = current_frame,

$N \times N$ = block pixels.

Equation (4) describes the cumulative squared error between the compressed and the reference image. If the value of Equation (4) is low, then the squared error accumulated will be low.

5. Experimental result and discussion for FUHS16, UHDS16 and UHDS8 algorithm

This section describes about the experimental results for FUHS16, UHDS16, and UHDS8 algorithms. Each algorithm is conducted using ten different video sequences with size of 176 × 144 pixels. Each video sequence is represented with ten video frames for simulation purposes. The experimental results are measured using the MATLAB and described accordingly based on quality performance in terms of PSNR points, computational complexity in terms of search points and elapsed processing time for each algorithm.

5.1 Results for FUHS16 and UHDS16 algorithm

In this section, results for FUHS16 and UHDS16 algorithm are presented. The presented figures represent the original frame and predicted frame of "Claire" - Slow Motion (Lee et al., 2005), "News" - Slow Motion (Wu et al., 2010), "Mother" - Slow Motion (Yang et al., 2007), "Salesman" - Large Motion (Shilpa et al., 2010), "Container" - Slow Motion (Wu et al., 2010), "Coastguard" - Large Motion (Wu et al., 2010), "Foreman" - Medial Motion (Wang et al., 2010), "Table Tennis" - Large Motion (Chen et al., 2002), "Akiyo" - Slow Motion (Wang et al., 2008) and "Hall" - Slow Motion (Wu et al., 2010). Each of these video sequences have

Original Frame
Claire
Predicted Frame

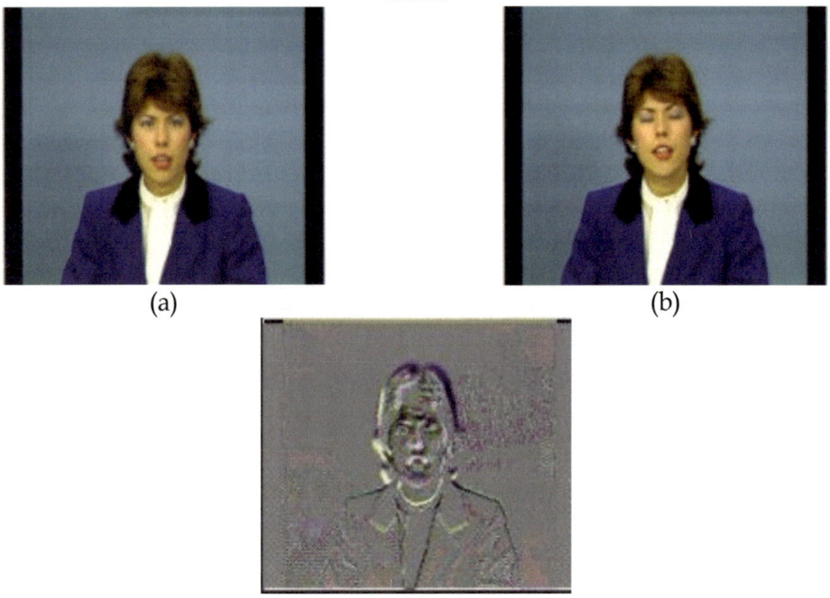

Fig. 5.1. (a) Claire Original Frame; (b) Claire Predicted Frame and (c) Claire Frame Difference

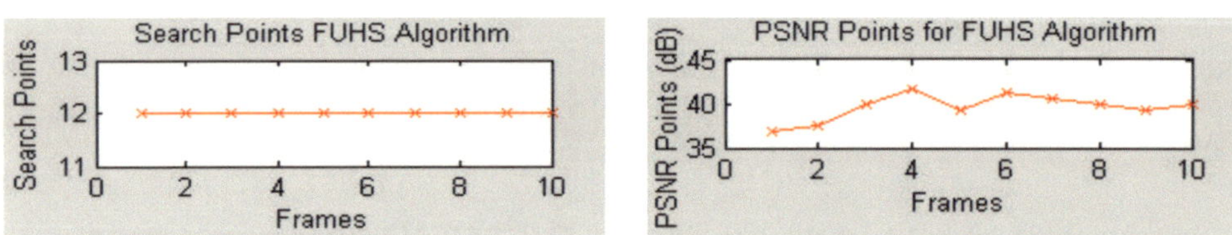

MV = 8, 8

MV = (9,5) (10,7)(8,6)

Fig. 5.2. Search Points and PSNR Points for FUHS16 Algorithm (Claire)

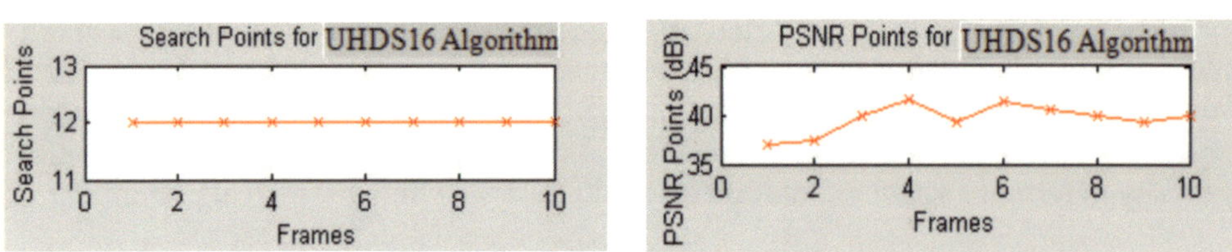

MV = 8, 8

MV = (9,6) (10,10) (8,7)

Fig. 5.3. Search Points and PSNR Points for UHDS16 Algorithm (Claire)

News

(a)

(b)

(c)

Fig. 5.4. (a) News Original Frame; (b) News Predicted Frame and (c) News Frame Difference

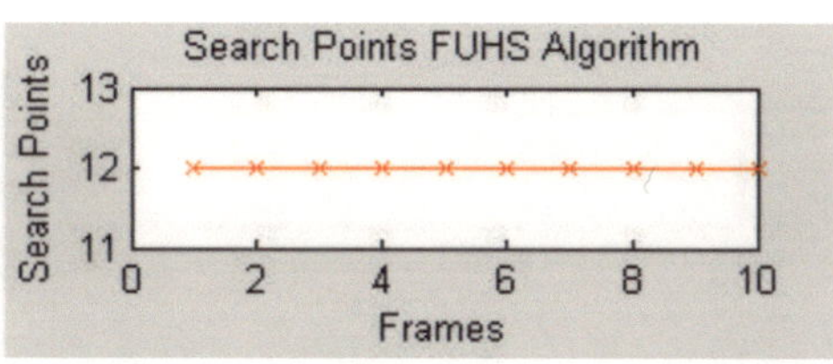

MV = (8,8)

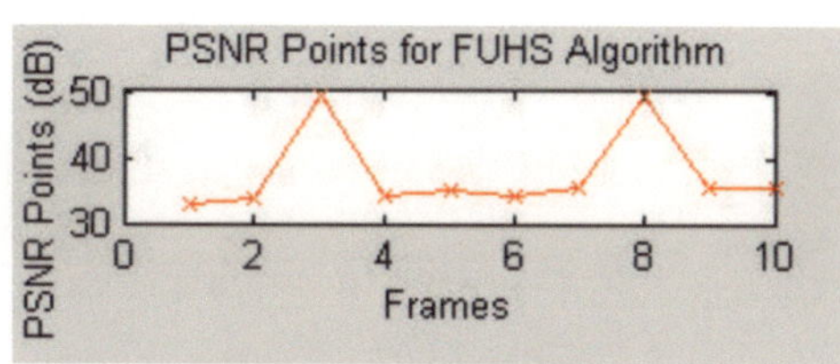

MV = (10,6)(10,7)(9,7)

Fig. 5.5. Search Points and PSNR Points for FUHS16 Algorithm (News)

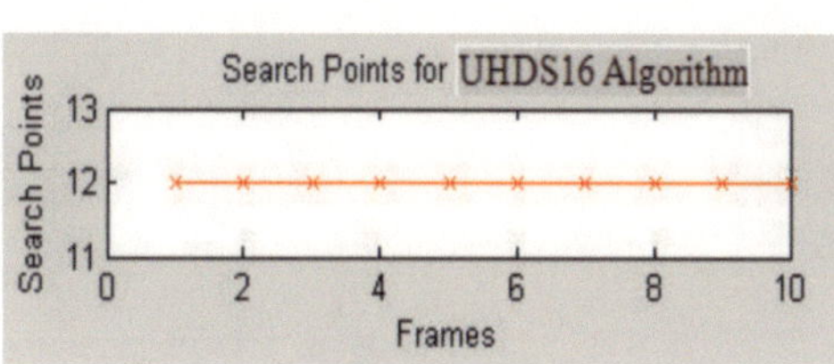

MV = (8,8)

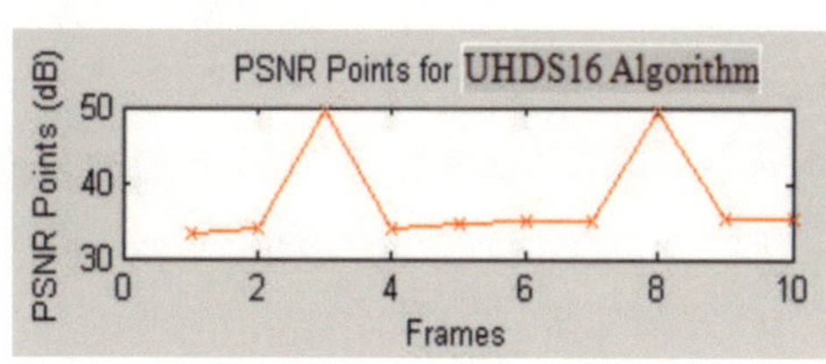

MV = (11,6) (8,9) (10,7)

Fig. 5.6. Search Points and PSNR Points for UHDS16 Algorithm (News)

Mother

(a)

(b)

(c)

Fig. 5.7. (a) Mother Original Frame; (b) Mother Predicted Frame and (c) Mother Frame Difference

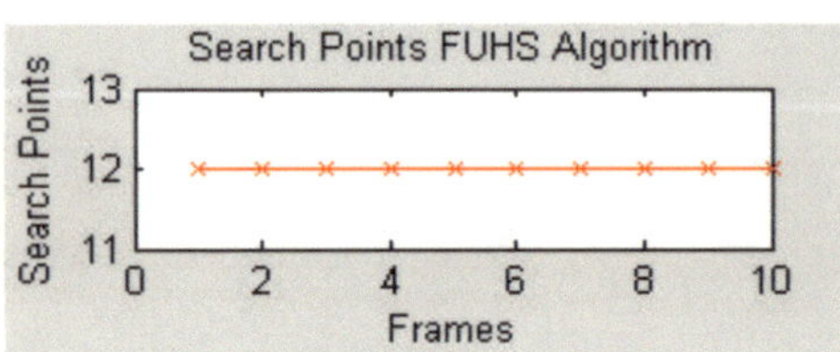

MV = (8,8)

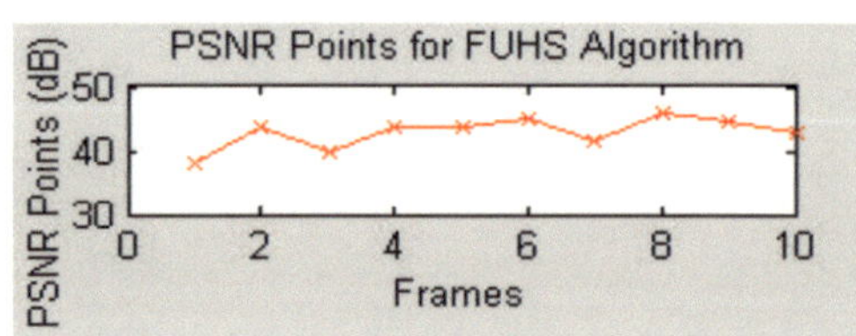

MV = (8,6)(10,7)(7,7)

Fig. 5.8. Search Points and PSNR Points for FUHS16 Algorithm (Mother)

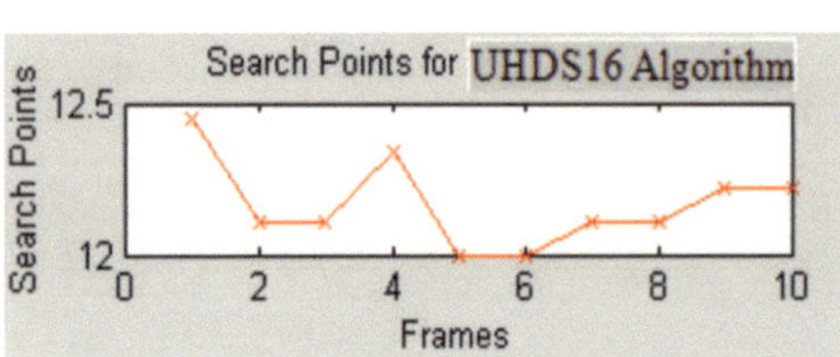

MV = (8,8)

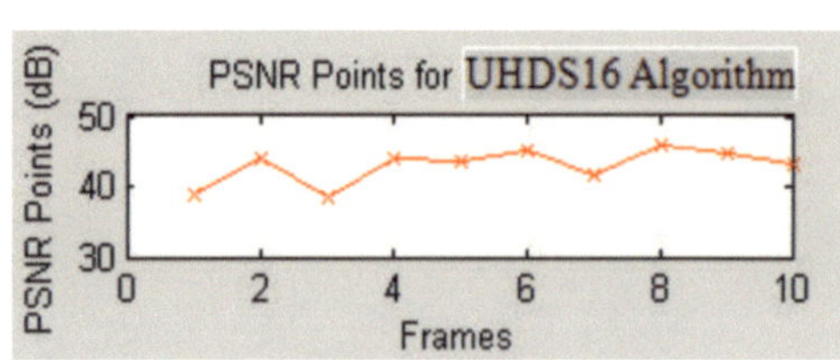

MV = (8,6) (7,6) (7,7)

Fig. 5.9. Search Points and PSNR Points for UHDS16 Algorithm (Mother)

Salesman

(a)

(b)

(c)

Fig. 5.10. (a) Salesman Original Frame; (b) Salesman Predicted Frame and (c) Salesman Frame Difference

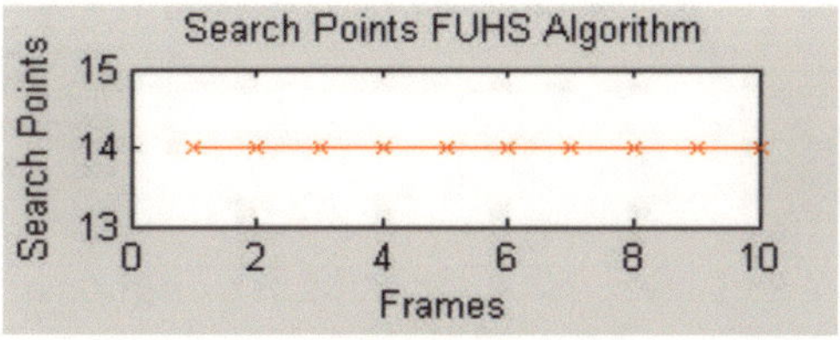

MV = (8,8)

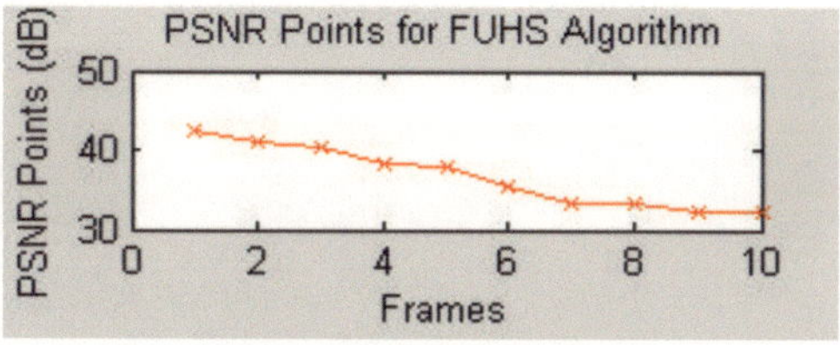

MV =(9,5) (10,7) (8,6)

Fig. 5.11. Search Points and PSNR Points for FUHS16 Algorithm (Salesman)

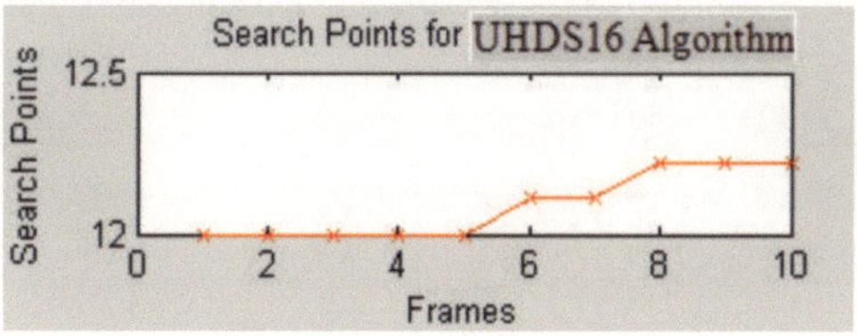

MV = (8,8)

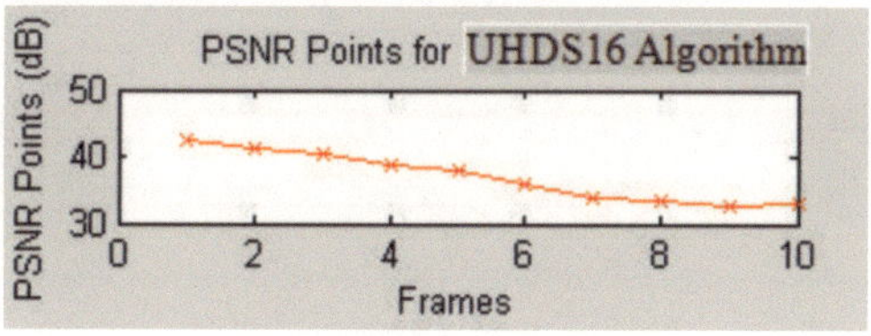

MV =(9,5) (10,6) (8,6)

Fig. 5.12. Search Points and PSNR Points for UHDS16 Algorithm (Foreman)

Container

(a)

(b)

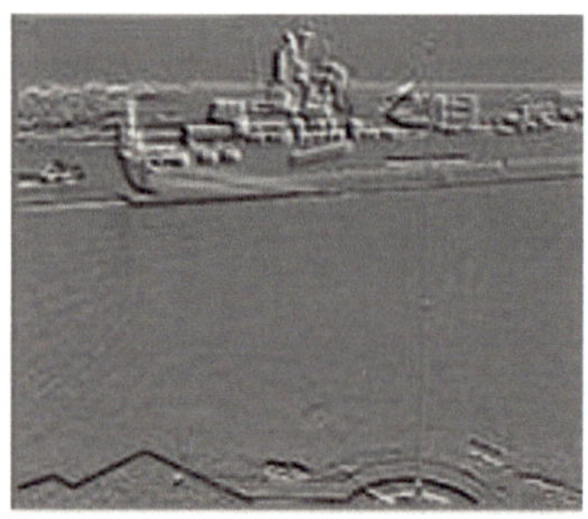

(c)

Fig. 5.13. (a) Container Original Frame; (b) Container Predicted Frame and (c) Container Frame Difference

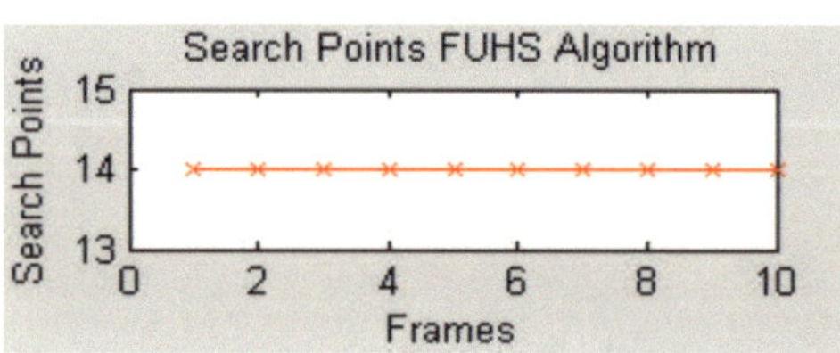

MV = (8,8)

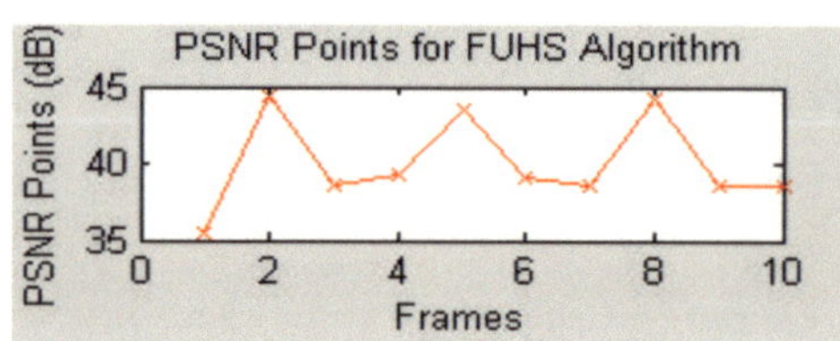

MV = (9,6) (10,7) (8,7)

Fig. 5.14. Search Points and PSNR Points for FUHS16 Algorithm (Container)

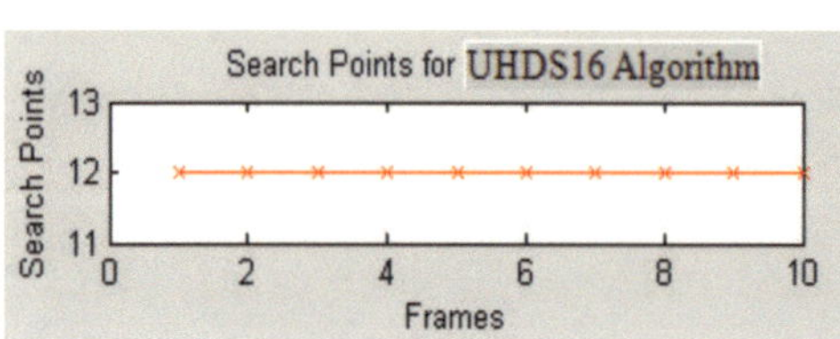

MV = (8,8)

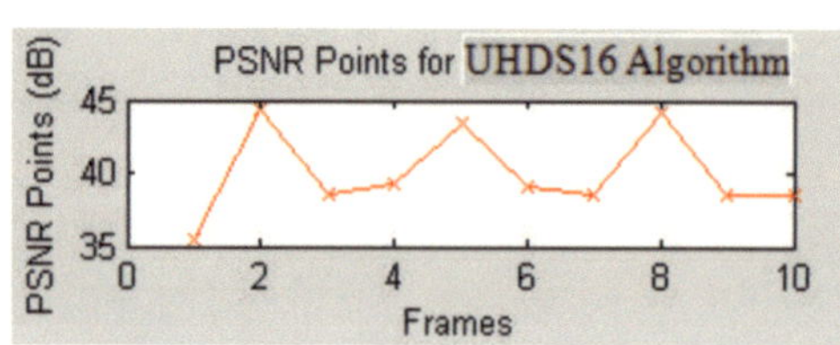

MV = (9,6) (10,6) (8,7)

Fig. 5.15. Search Points and PSNR Points for UHDS16 Algorithm (Container)

Coastguard

(a)

(b)

(c)

Fig. 5.16. (a) Coastguard Original Frame; (b) Coastguard Predicted Frame and (c) Coastguard Frame Difference

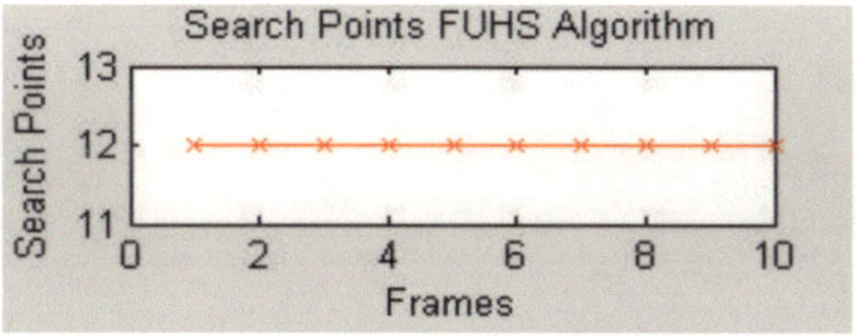

MV = (8,8)

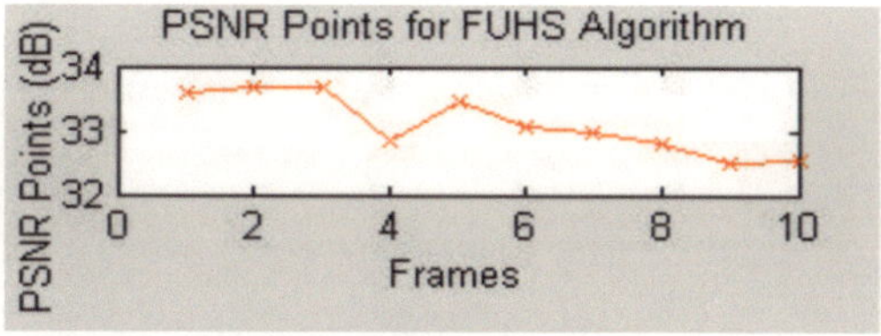

MV = (9,5)(10,7)(8,6)

Fig. 5.17. Search Points and PSNR Points for FUHS16 Algorithm (Coastguard)

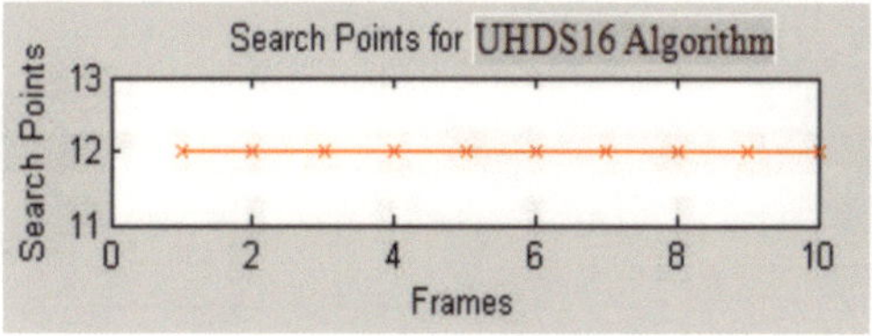

MV = (8,8)

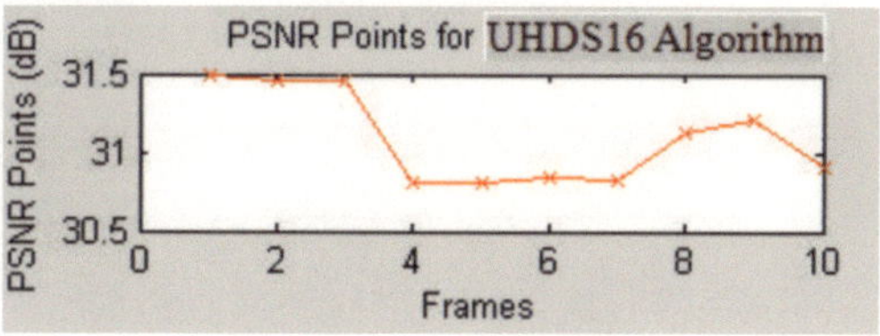

MV = (9,5)(10,7)(8,6)

Fig. 5.18. Search Points and PSNR Points for UHDS16 Algorithm (Coastguard)

Foreman

(a)

(b)

(c)

Fig. 5.19. (a) Foreman Original Frame; (b) Foreman Predicted Frame and (c) Foreman Frame Difference

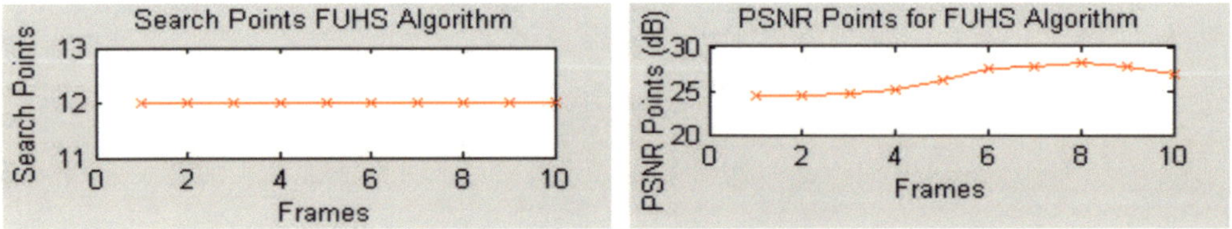

MV = (8,8)

MV= (8,6) (10,7) (7,7)

Fig. 5.20. Search Points and PSNR Points for FUHS16 Algorithm (Foreman)

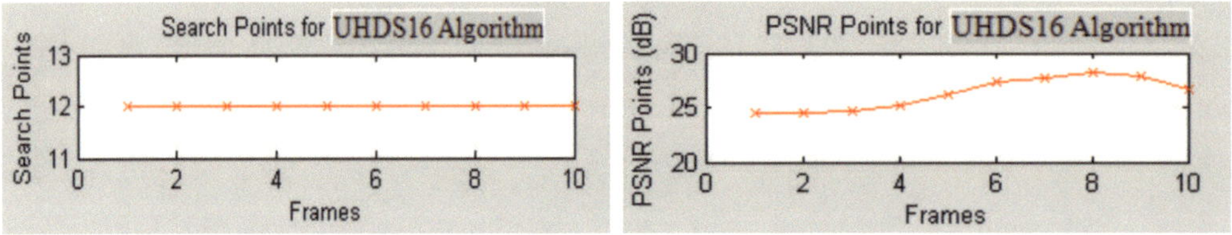

MV = (8,8)

MV= (8,6) (10,7) (7,7)

Fig. 5.21. Search Points and PSNR Points for UHDS16 Algorithm (Foreman)

Table Tennis

(a)

(b)

(c)

Fig. 5.22. (a) Table Tennis Original Frame; (b) Table Tennis Predicted Frame and (c) Table Tennis Frame Difference

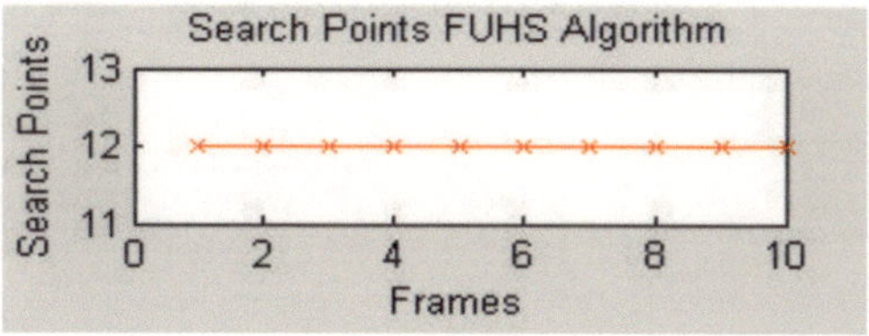

MV = (8,8)

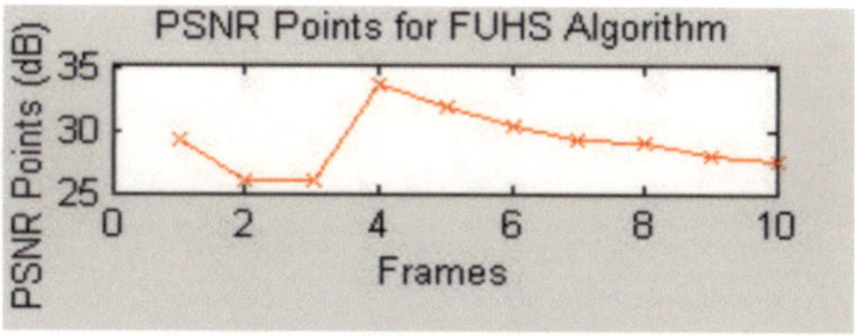

MV = (10,7) (10,7) (9,8)

Fig. 5.23. Search Points and PSNR Points for FUHS16 Algorithm (Table Tennis)

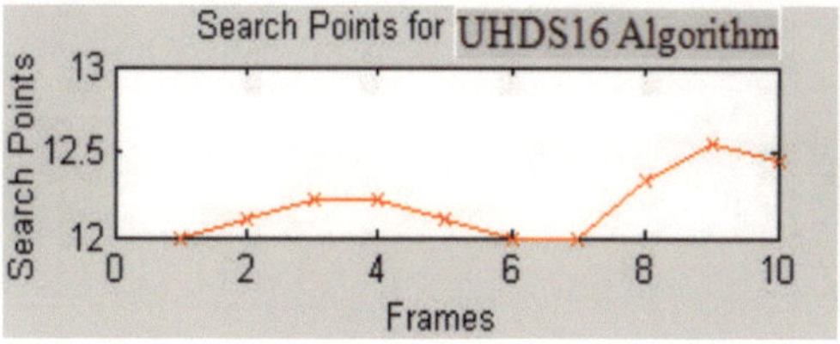

MV = (8,8)

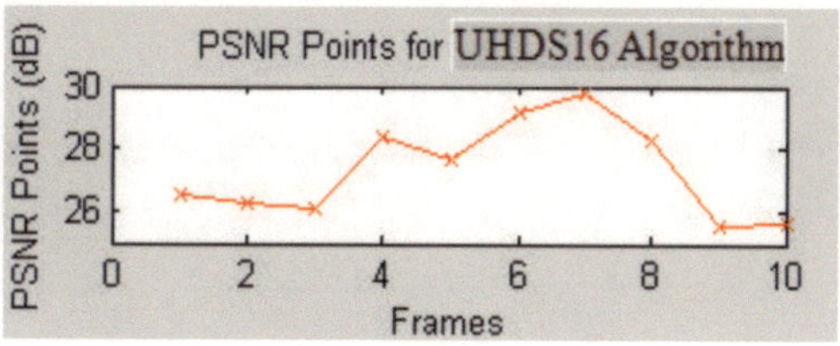

MV = (5,14) (5,14) (4,15)

Fig. 5.24. Search Points and PSNR Points for UHDS16 Algorithm (Table Tennis)

Akiyo

(a)

(b)

(c)

Fig. 5.25. (a) Akiyo Original Frame; (b) Akiyo Predicted Frame and (c) Akiyo Frame Difference

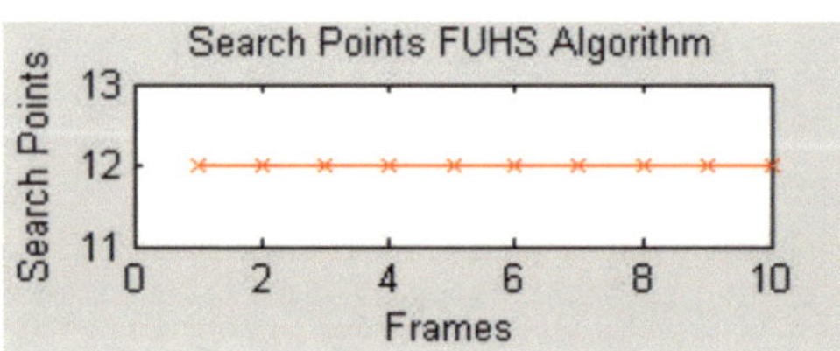

MV = (8,8)

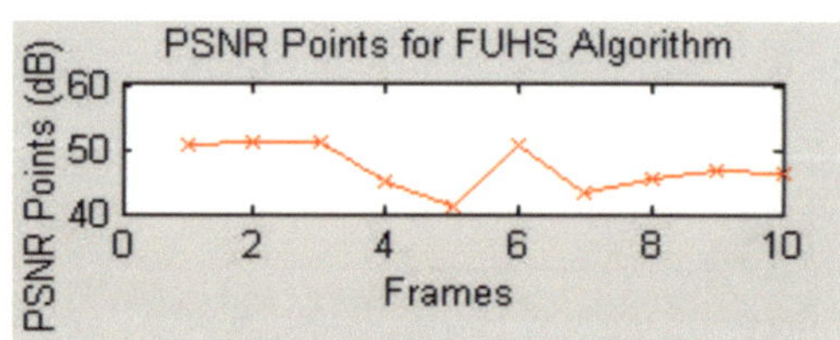

MV = (9,6) (10,7) (8,7)

Fig. 5.26. Search Points and PSNR Points for FUHS16 Algorithm (Akiyo)

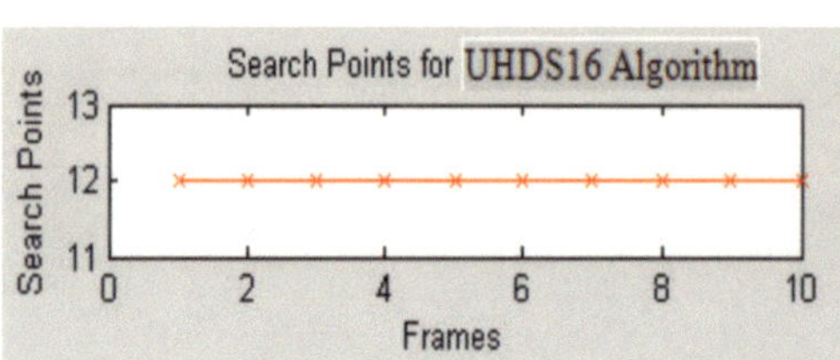

MV = (8,8)

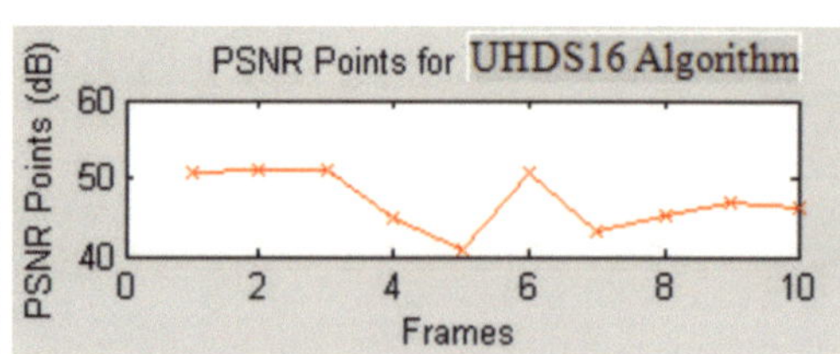

MV = (9,6) (10,7) (8,7)

Fig. 5.27. Search Points and PSNR Points for UHDS16 Algorithm (Akiyo)

Hall

(a)

(b)

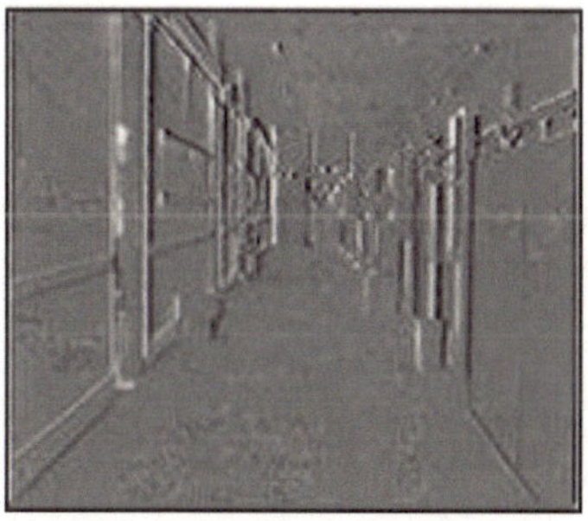

(c)

Fig. 5.28. (a) Hall Original Frame; (b) Hall Predicted Frame and (c) Hall Frame Difference

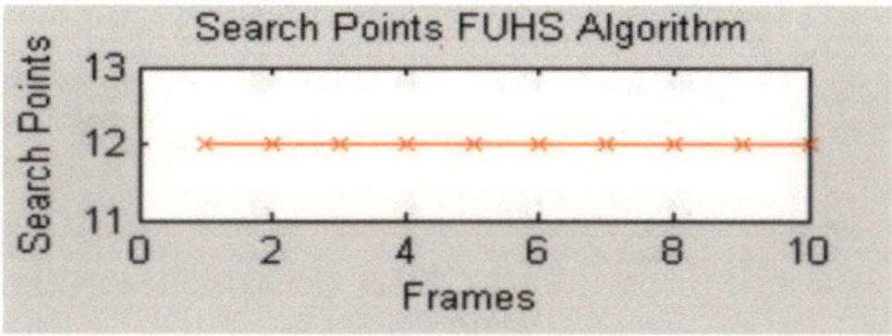

MV = (8,8)

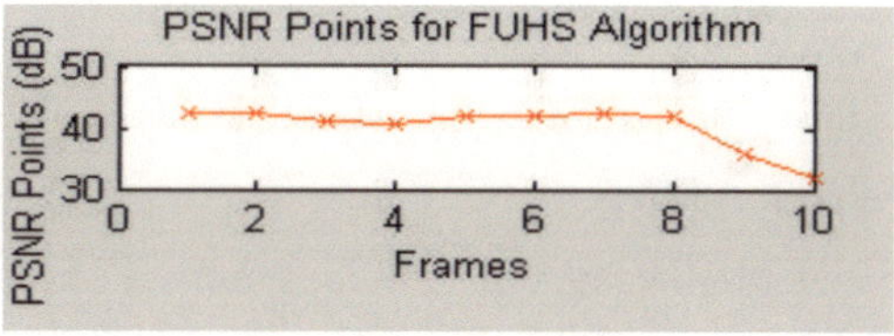

MV = (9,6) (10,7) (8,7)

Fig. 5.29. Search Points and PSNR Points for FUHS16 Algorithm (Hall)

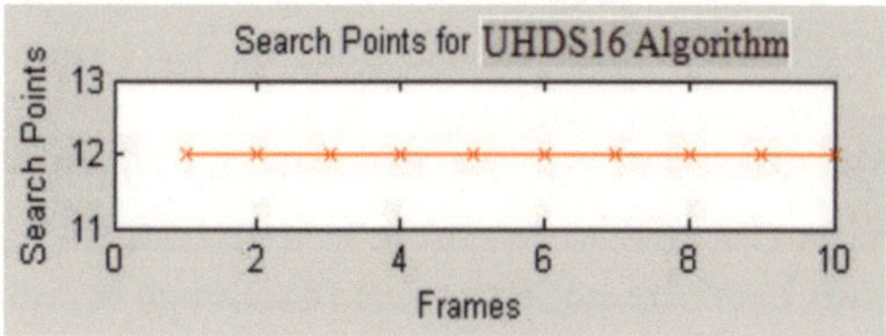

MV = (8,8)

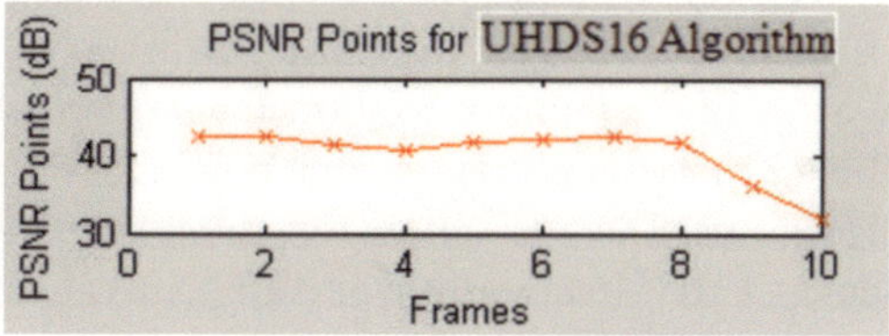

MV = (9,6) (10,7) (8,7)

Fig. 5.30. Search Points and PSNR Points for UHDS16 Algorithm (Hall)

300 raw video frames, the video format of Quarter Common Intermediate Format (QCIF) and can be categories into different motion varying from small to large. Based on the presented results, original frame and predicted frame is not similar to the matched frame. This is to reveal that there is object translation between the original frame and predicted frame.
The motion vector coordinates shown are for ten video frames that have been conducted in FUHS16 and UHDS16 algorithm. Based on each vector coordinate, the motion represents the object translation between two frames. The first coordinate shows the first search of large hexagon shape, second vector coordinate represents the repetitive search of large hexagon shape and the best-matched motion vector coordinate represent the search for small hexagon shape. The repetitive search of large hexagon search is to gauge for the best-matched zero motion in the large hexagon region. While the small hexagon shape will finalized the best-matched motion vector coordinate among the four search points in the small region.
The results shown in Table 1 are the average PSNR points for FS, NTSS, TSS, DS, HEXBS, FUHS16 and UHDS16 algorithms. The average PSNR points values for all ten video sequences. These results are used for analysis purposes and for further improvement.

Average PSNR Points (dB)							
Algorithms	FS	TSS	NTSS	DS	HEXBS	FUHS16	UHDS16
Claire	39.93	38.91	38.91	39.04	39.20	39.23	39.89
News	37.65	36.95	37.26	37.34	37.35	37.21	37.57
Mother	43.21	42.70	42.70	42.79	42.75	42.70	42.92
Salesman	37.20	36.40	36.55	36.74	36.66	36.57	37.07
Container	40.02	40.02	40.02	40.02	40.02	40.02	40.02
Coastguard	33.11	31.00	31.03	31.09	31.03	31.00	33.11
Foreman	26.40	24.25	24.78	24.46	25.76	25.74	26.28
Tennis	32.47	26.39	28.00	27.52	28.95	29.26	29.07
Akiyo	47.06	47.06	47.06	47.06	47.05	47.05	47.06
Hall	40.30	40.29	40.30	40.30	40.29	40.29	40.30

Table 1. Average PSNR Points

Based on the average PSNR points, FUHS16 and UHDS16 algorithms produces similar PSNR points compared with the other algorithms. However, UHDS16 algorithm shows significant improvement in measuring the average PSNR point's compares with FUHS16 algorithm.
UHDS16 algorithm has outperformed all the other algorithms except for the FS algorithm in terms of PSNR point measurement. The overall average PSNR point's difference between UHDS16 and FS algorithm is approximately 0.31 dB. The importance to calculate the overall average PSNR points is to show the individual comparison of each algorithm.
Table 2 presents average search points for FS, TSS, NTSS, DS, HEXBS, FUHS16 and UHDS16 algorithms. The average search points calculated are for 990 blocks for ten video frames. As shown, FUHS16 algorithm and UHDS16 algorithm have the same number of average search points as HEXBS algorithm to obtain the similar algorithm performance with all the other algorithms. FUHS16 algorithm and UHDS16 algorithm have approximately improved 2 search points (17 percent) in terms of motion vector search points compared with DS algorithm. FS algorithm requires 213 extra search points (94.7 percent), TSS requires 13 extr

Average Search Points							
Algorithms	FS	TSS	NTSS	DS	HEXBS	FUHS16	UHDS16
Claire	225	25	27	14	12	12	12
News	225	25	25	14	12	12	12
Mother	225	25	25	14	12	12	12
Salesman	225	25	25	14	12	12	12
Container	225	25	25	14	12	12	12
Coastguard	225	25	25	14	12	12	12
Foreman	225	25	25	14	12	12	12
Tennis	225	25	28	14	12	12	12
Akiyo	225	25	25	14	12	12	12
Hall	225	25	26	14	12	12	12

Table 2. Average Search Points

a search points (52 percent) and NTSS requires 16 extra search points (57.1 percent) to gauge the similar motion vector coordinate as FUHS16 algorithm and UHDS16 algorithm.

Based on average PSNR points and average search points, FUHS16 algorithm and UHDS16 algorithm maintains the similar PSNR point's quality even though the search points are reduced 94.7 percent compare with FS algorithm. This also shows that reducing the search points can still maintain the similar performance and quality compare with the other algorithms. And, reducing the search points also reduces the computational complexity in terms of the MAD calculation (search points) and increases the best-matched motion vector coordinate estimation performances.

Table 3 shows the average elapsed processing time taken for FS, TSS, NTSS, DS, HEXBS, FUHS16 and UHDS16 algorithms. Based on the presented result, UHDS16 algorithm has the lowest average elapsed processing time compared with all the other algorithms. FUHS16 algorithm saved a small relative average elapsed processing time compared with HEXBS algorithm and DS algorithm. UHDS16 algorithm and FUHS16 algorithm approximately saved 14 percent, 23 percent and 55 percent of average elapsed processing time compared with NTSS, TSS and FS algorithms respectively. The result for UHDS16 algorithm shows, even though the search points are reduced and repetitive search pattern is developed, the average elapsed processing time still can be reduced.

Average Elapsed Processing Time (Sec)							
Algorithms	FS	TSS	NTSS	DS	HEXBS	FUHS16	UHDS16
Claire	3.28	1.86	1.70	1.63	1.55	1.53	1.47
News	3.14	1.84	1.77	1.63	1.58	1.61	1.45
Mother	3.58	2.01	1.71	1.68	1.59	1.62	1.38
Salesman	3.38	1.88	1.74	1.62	1.61	1.61	1.48
Container	2.86	2.02	1.92	1.72	1.70	1.64	1.53
Coastguard	3.23	1.81	1.77	1.64	1.62	1.64	1.46
Foreman	3.42	1.84	1.77	1.70	1.68	1.69	1.49
Tennis	3.61	2.00	1.74	1.70	1.59	1.49	1.43
Akiyo	3.48	1.81	1.61	1.59	1.57	1.57	1.46
Hall	2.96	2.08	1.79	1.65	1.55	1.54	1.43

Table 3. Average Elapsed Processing Time

5.2 Results for UHDS8 Algorithm

In order to evaluate the performance of UHDS8 algorithm, the UHDS8 algorithm is compared with the FS, TSS, NTSS, DS, and HEXBS algorithms in terms of the average PSNR points, computation complexity in terms of average search points and average elapsed processing time.

Original Frame Predicted Frame

Claire

(a)

(b)

(c)

Fig. 5.31. (a) Claire Original Frame; (b) Claire Predicted Frame and (c) Claire Frame Difference

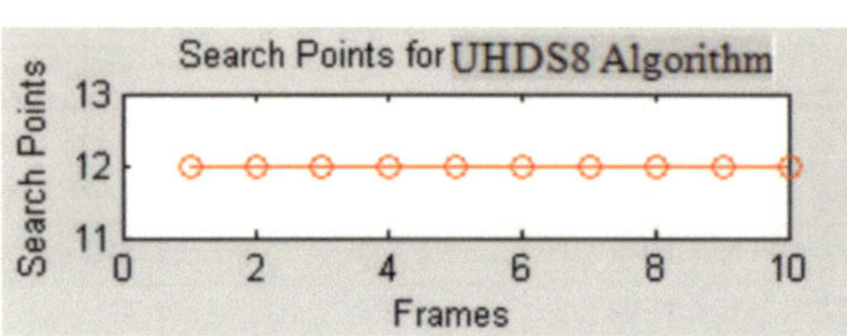

MV = (4,4)

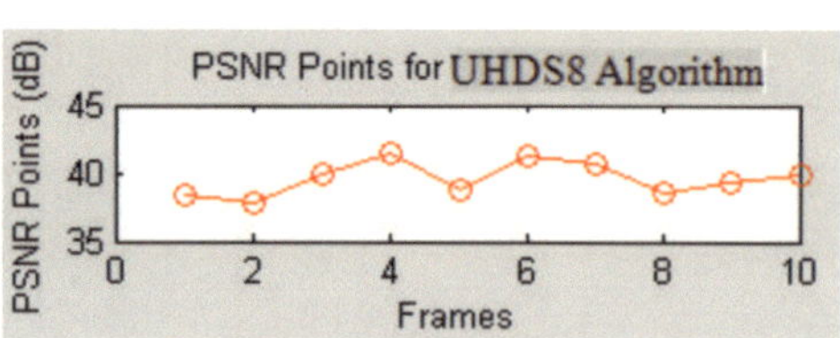

MV = (5,2) (6,4) (4,3)

Fig. 5.32. Search Points and PSNR Points for UHDS8 Algorithm (Claire)

News

(a)

(b)

(c)

Fig. 5.33. (a) News Original Frame; (b) News Predicted Frame and (c) News Frame Difference

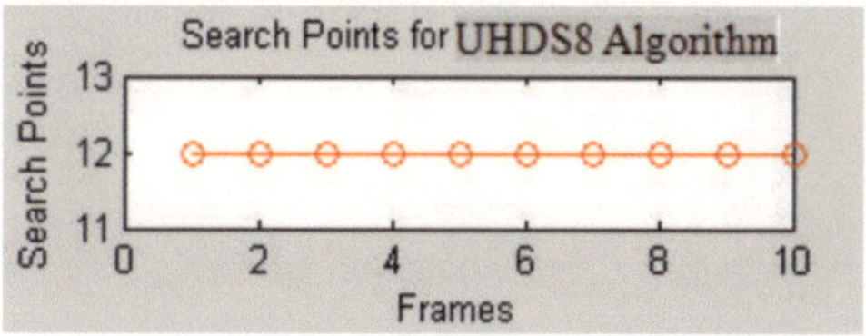

MV = (4,4)

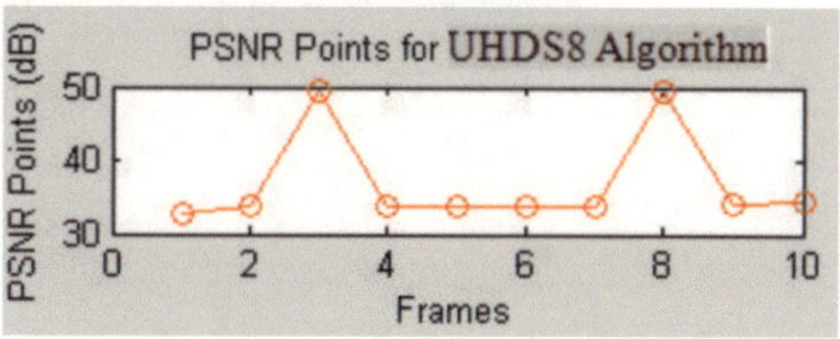

MV = (5,2) (5,2) (2,4)

Fig. 5.34. Search Points and PSNR Points for UHDS8 Algorithm (News)

Mother

(a)

(b)

(c)

Fig. 5.35. (a) Mother Original Frame; (b) Mother Predicted Frame and (c) Mother Frame Difference

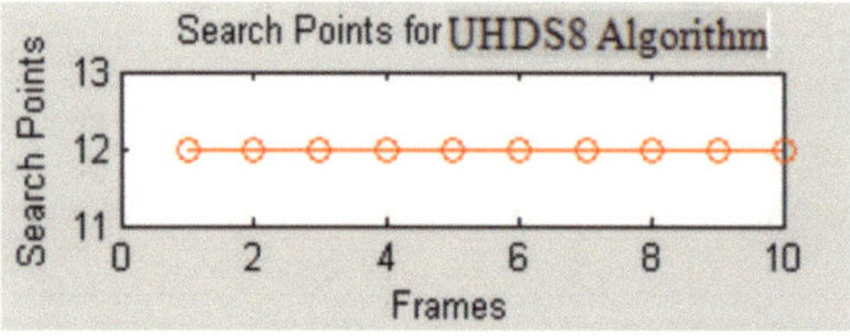

MV = (4,4)

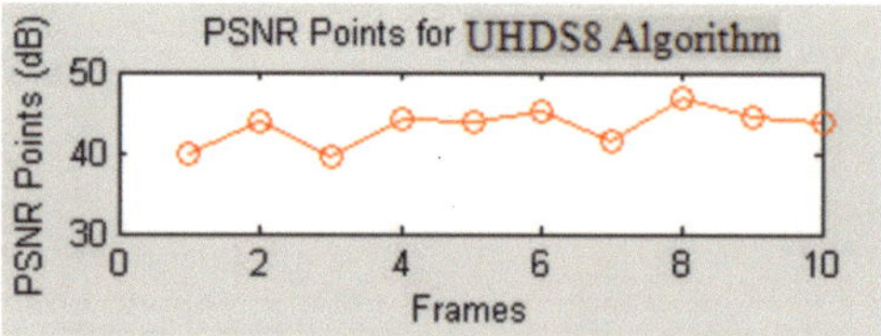

MV = (4,2) (3,2) (3,3)

Fig. 5.36. Search Points and PSNR Points for UHDS8 Algorithm (Mother)

Salesman

(a)

(b)

(c)

Fig. 5.37. (a) Salesman Original Frame; (b) Salesman Predicted Frame and (c) Salesman Frame Difference

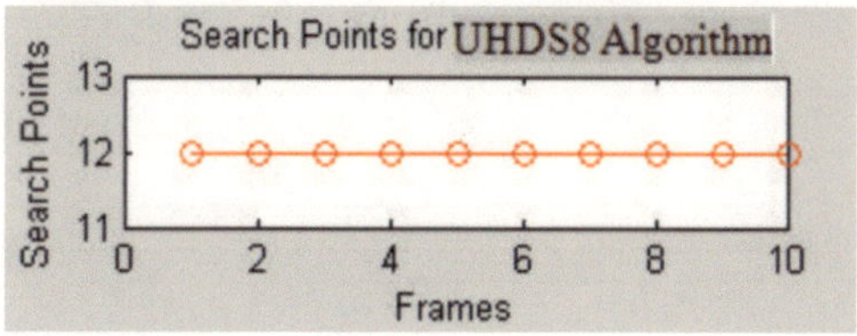

MV = (4,4)

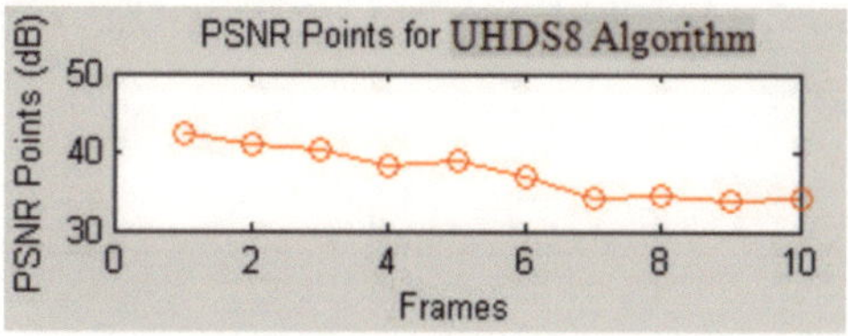

MV = (5,2) (5,2) (2,4)

Fig. 5.38. Search Points and PSNR Points for UHDS8 Algorithm (Salesman)

Container

(a)

(b)

(c)

Fig. 5.39. (a) Container Original Frame; (b) Container Predicted Frame and (c) Container Frame Difference

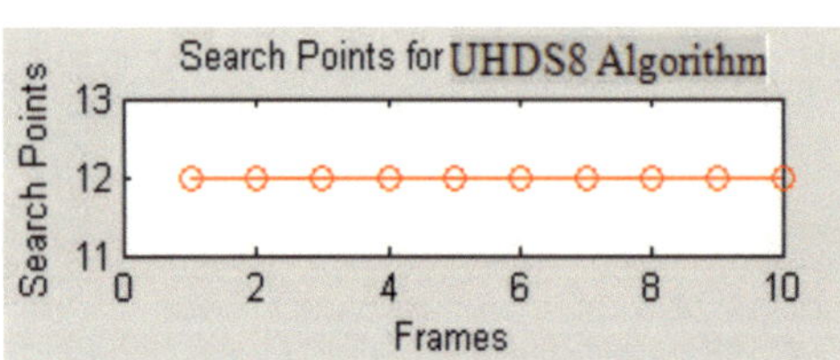

MV = (4,4)

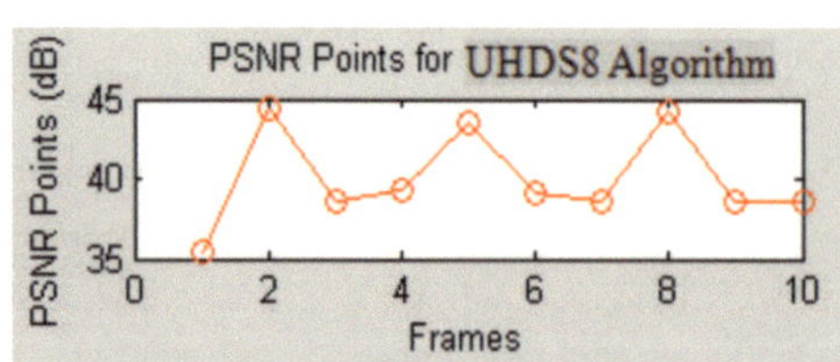

MV = (5,2) (5,3) (4,3)

Fig. 5.40. Search Points and PSNR Points for UHDS8 Algorithm (Container)

Coastguard

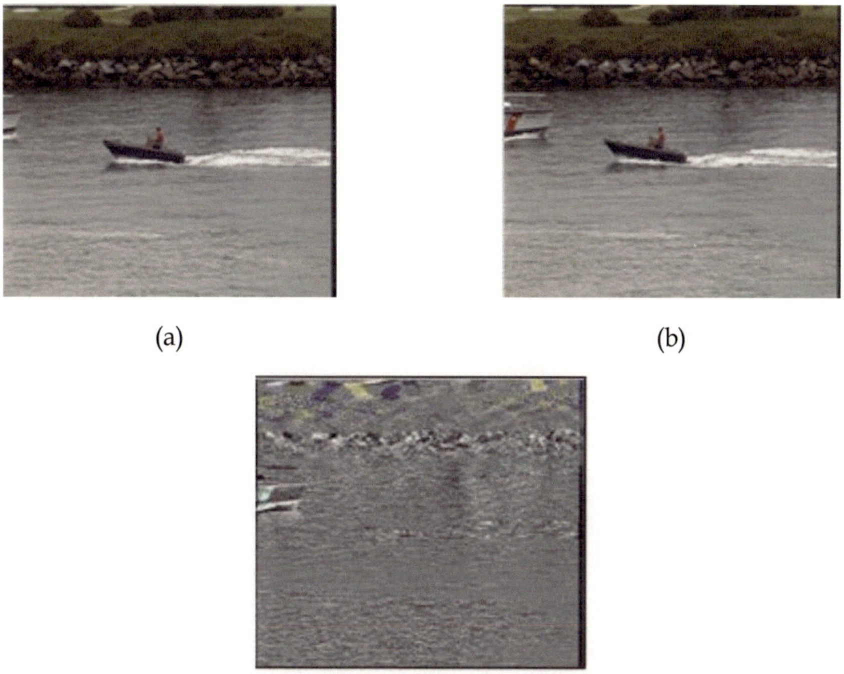

(a) (b)

(c)

Fig. 5.41. (a) Coastguard Original Frame; (b) Coastguard Predicted Frame and (c) Coastguard Frame Difference

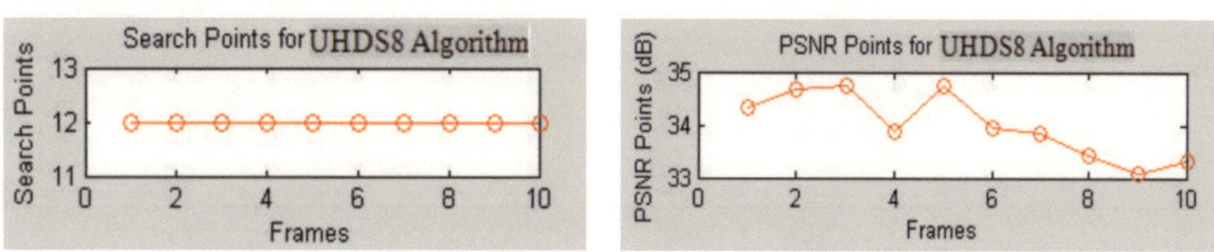

MV = (4,4) MV = (5,2) (6,4) (4,3)

Fig. 5.42. Search Points and PSNR Points for UHDS8 Algorithm (Coastguard)

Foreman

(a)

(b)

(c)

Fig. 5.43. (a) Foreman Original Frame; (b) Foreman Predicted Frame and (c) Foreman Frame Difference

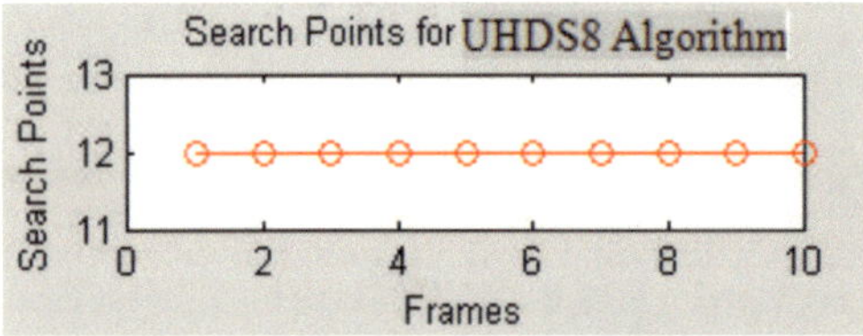

MV = (4,4)

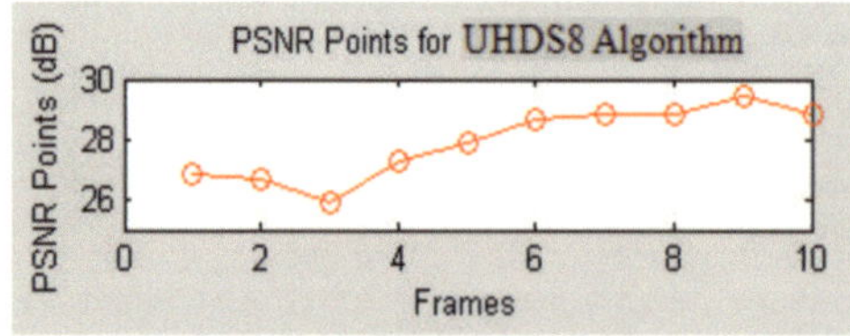

MV= (4,3) (5,-5) (3,4)

Fig. 5.44. Search Points and PSNR Points for UHDS8 Algorithm (Foreman)

Table Tennis

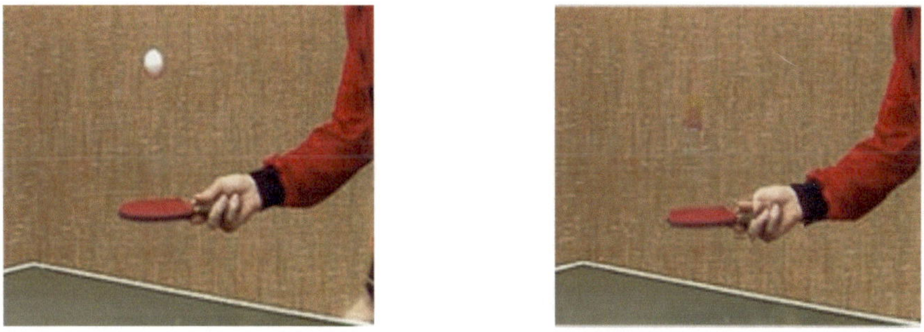

(a) (b)

(c)

Fig. 5.45. (a) Table Tennis Original Frame; (b) Table Tennis Predicted Frame and (c) Table Tennis Frame Difference

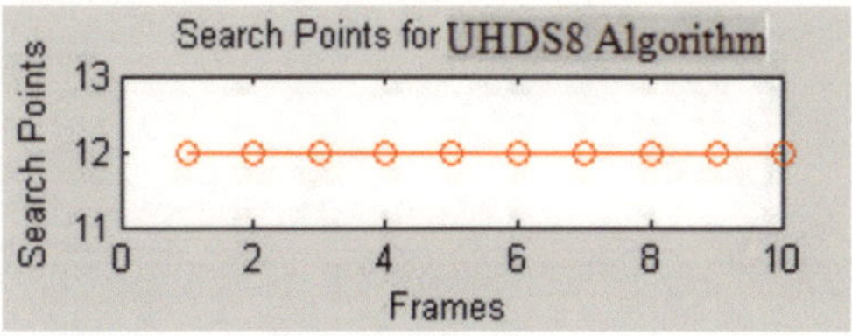

MV = (4,4)

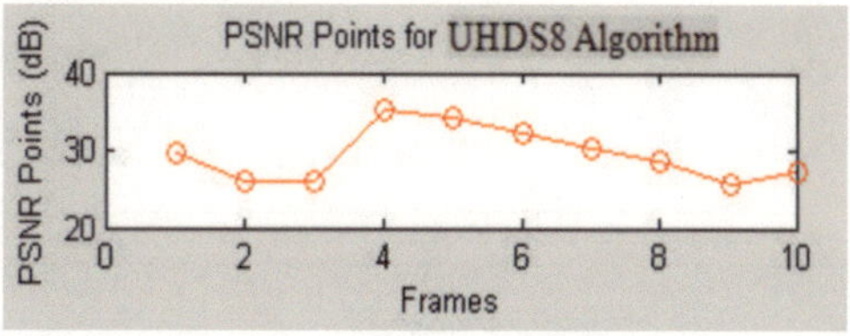

MV = (5,2) (5,2) (2,4)

Fig. 5.46. Search Points and PSNR Points for UHDS8 Algorithm (Table Tennis)

Akiyo

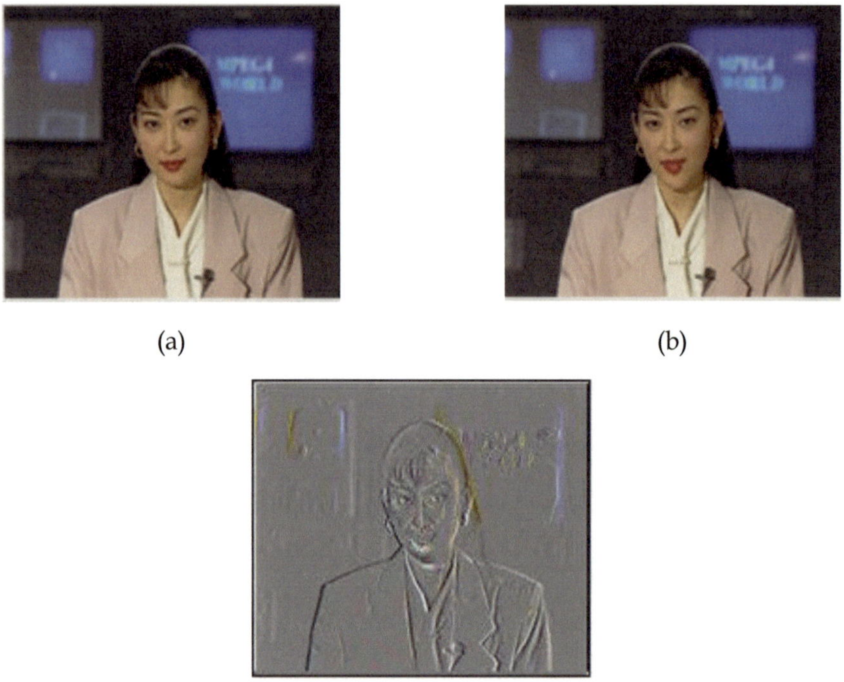

(a) (b)

(c)

Fig. 5.47. (a) Akiyo Original Frame; (b) Akiyo Predicted Frame and (c) Akiyo Frame Difference

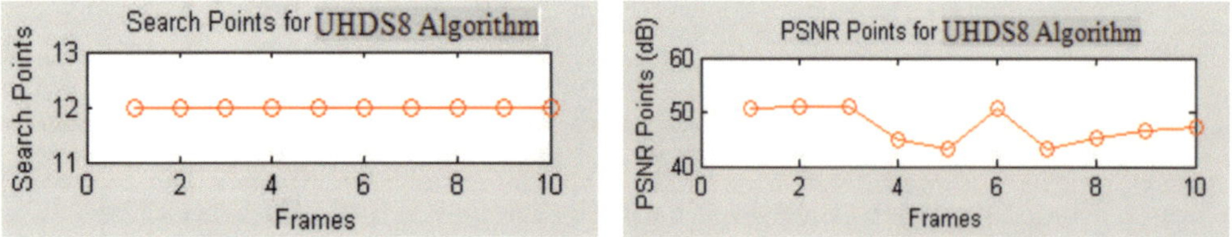

MV = (4,4) MV = (5,2) (6,4) (3,6)

Fig. 5.48. Search Points and PSNR Points for UHDS8 Algorithm (Akiyo)

Hall

(a)

(b)

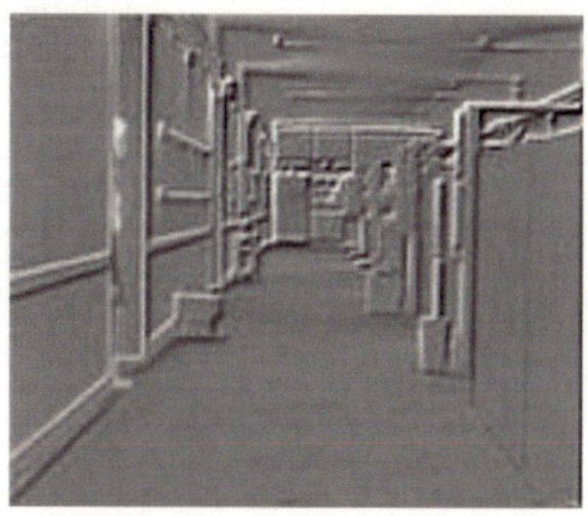

(c)

Fig. 5.49. (a) Hall Original Frame; (b) Hall Predicted Frame and (c) Hall Frame Difference

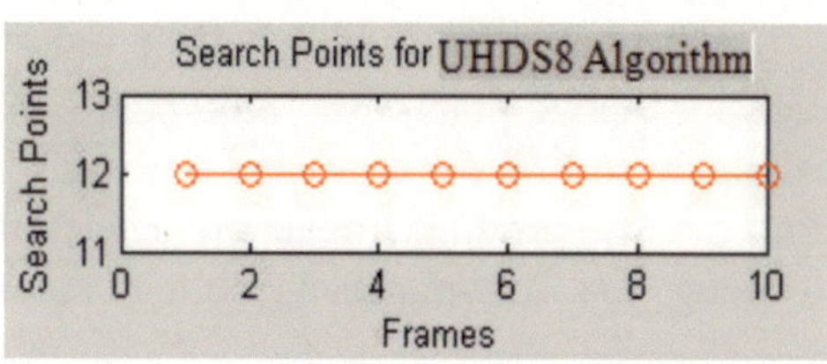

MV = (4,4)

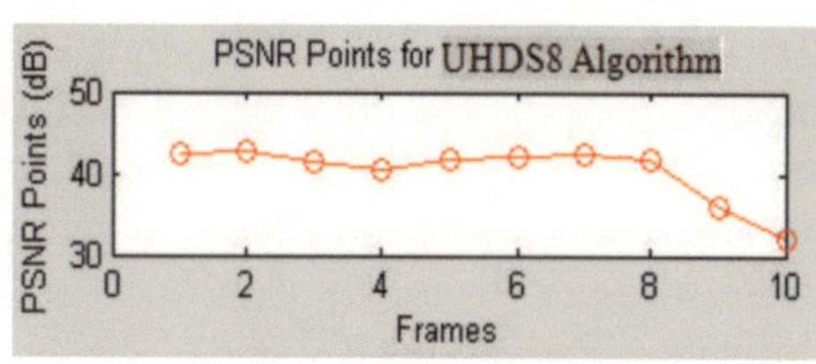

MV = (4,2) (5,4) (4,3)

Fig. 5.50. Search Points and PSNR Points for UHDS8 Algorithm (Hall)

In this section, the proposed UHDS8 algorithm is compared with the popular FS, NTSS, TSS, DS, HEXBS and FUHS8 algorithms. In the first stage, ten video frames from each video sequence are used to simulate the coded algorithm. The results using UHDS8 algorithm and all the other algorithms are shown in Table 4 for average PSNR points, Table 5 for average search points and Table 6 for average elapsed processing time.

Average PSNR Point (dB)						
Algorithms	FS	NTSS	TSS	DS	HEXBS	UHDS8
Claire	40.46	38.91	38.91	39.47	39.48	39.76
News	38.47	37.46	36.95	37.69	37.72	37.73
Mother	43.88	42.72	42.69	42.89	43.22	43.29
Salesman	38.11	36.83	36.40	36.80	36.82	37.48
Container	40.03	40.02	40.02	40.02	40.02	40.03
Coastguard	33.95	31.16	30.10	31.16	32.98	33.94
Foreman	28.40	25.06	24.25	25.01	27.65	27.96
Tennis	32.64	27.10	26.40	28. 60	29.05	29.15
Akiyo	47.48	47.06	47.06	47.25	47.28	47.42
Hall	40.45	40.34	40.29	40.30	40.31	40.31

Table 4. Average PSNR Points

Table 4 shows the average PSNR points for FS, TSS, NTSS, DS, HEXBS, FUHS8 and UHDS8 algorithms. The FS algorithm has the most promising result among all the developed algorithms. This is because FS algorithm does brute search among all the search points. In Table 5.4, the average PSNR points shows that the UHDS8 algorithm improves the average PSNR points compared with the NTSS, TSS, DS, HEXBS, and FUHS8 algorithms. Analysis shows "Claire" video sequence have improved 0.13 dB of average PSNR point's compared with HEXBS algorithm and DS algorithm. While, "Coastguard" have improved approximately 3 dB of average PSNR point's compared with TSS, NTSS and DS algorithms. "Akiyo" and "Container" video sequences produces the similar average PSNR point's compared with all the other algorithms. The average PSNR points for "Salesman" and "Tennis" video sequences also improved approximately to 0.55 dB compared with all the other algorithms. This shows that UHDS8 algorithm can also produce similar average PSNR points compared with FS algorithm while locating the best-matched motion vector coordinate.

Based on the ten video sequences overall average PSNR points, UHDS8 algorithm and FUHS8 algorithm have slightly improved the performance compared with the NTSS, TSS, DS and HEXBS algorithms. The overall average PSNR points analysis shows that UHDS8 algorithm have outperformed all the other algorithms except for FS algorithm. The overall average PSNR point's difference between UHDS8 algorithm and FS algorithm is approximately 0.68 dB.

Referring to the Table 5, FUHS8, UHDS8 and HEXBS algorithms have the lowest average search points compared with all the other algorithms. FS and TSS algorithms have 49 and 25 fixed search points respectively. Meanwhile NTSS algorithm search point ranging from 25 to 33 and DS algorithm has 14 search points.

Based on the average search points obtained from Table 5, FS algorithm needs to perform extra numbers of MAD calculations in order to determine the optimal MAD point. This will lead to extra usage of memory and consume 52 percent of extra processing time to predict the similar image as UHDS8 algorithm. UHDS8 algorithm reduces search points and elapsed processing time to perform all the MAD calculations in order to estimate the MAD point.

Hence, this shows that UHDS8 algorithm have the ability to reduce the elapsed processing time while maintaining the global optimal point properties of the image. Besides that, the UHDS8 algorithm approximately can save up to 37 search points compared with FS algorithm, 2 search points compared with DS algorithm, 13 search points compared with TSS algorithm and 21 search points compared with NTSS algorithm. This shows that the UHDS8 algorithm requires less MAD calculation and save memory approximately up to 75.5 percent compared with all the other algorithms.

Table 6 shows the elapsed processing time compared with FS algorithm. UHDS8 algorithm has the lowest average elapsed processing time compared with TSS, NTSS, DS, and HEXBS algorithms. Thus, Table 6 reveals that UHDS8 algorithm approximately has saved 40 percent of processing time compared with FS algorithm. Meanwhile, TSS, NTSS, DS and HEXBS algorithms approximately saved 21 percent, 19 percent and 29 percent average elapsed processing time respectively.

Average search points						
Algorithms	FS	TSS	NTSS	DS	HEXBS	UHDS8
Claire	49	25	26.99	14.70	12	12
News	49	25	25.55	14.27	12	12
Mother	49	25	26.42	14.90	12	12
Salesman	49	25	25.16	14.20	12	12
Container	49	25	25.06	14.00	12	12
Coastguard	49	25	25.00	14.00	12	12
Foreman	49	25	25.37	14.22	12	12
Tennis	49	25	26.81	14.36	12	12
Akiyo	49	25	25.00	14.01	12	12
Hall	49	25	25.78	14.00	12	12

Table 5. Average Search Points

This shows that FS algorithm approximately consumes 31 percent extra computational complexity in terms of search points compared with UHDS8 algorithm. Even though the average elapsed processing time produced by UHDS8 algorithm is almost similar as FUHS8 algorithm, but UHDS8 algorithm average elapsed processing time is slightly faster. UHDS8 algorithm approximately saved 3 percent of average elapsed processing time compared with UHDS8 algorithm. TSS algorithm and NTSS algorithm shows increment of 14 percent and 18 percent average elapsed processing time respectively.

Average Elapsed Processing Time (Sec)						
Algorithms	FS	TSS	NTSS	DS	HEXBS	UHDS8
Claire	2.84	1.86	1.65	1.53	1.34	1.21
News	2.77	1.75	1.63	1.59	1.37	1.19
Mother	2.92	1.91	1.71	1.67	1.37	1.12
Salesman	2.72	1.82	1.68	1.59	1.39	1.22
Container	2.93	1.94	1.82	1.65	1.47	1.28
Coastguard	3.01	1.89	1.80	1.67	1.42	1.22
Foreman	2.99	1.86	1.66	1.59	1.41	1.19
Tennis	3.11	1.81	1.61	1.52	1.35	1.23
Akiyo	2.97	1.80	1.59	1.54	1.32	1.17
Hall	2.89	1.98	1.69	1.55	1.36	1.20

Table 6. Average Elapsed Processing Time

6. Conclusion

Motion vector estimation is the processes which generates the motion vectors to determine how each motion compensated prediction frame is created from the previous frame. Motion estimation is basically extracting the difference between the reference frame compared with the current frame. Motion vectors are typically used to compress the frame by storing the changes in the current frame. The vectors are used to detect and track the motion and to find the information required in the current frame. In this thesis, the previously developed algorithms were investigated and new algorithms were to design to compare the performance with the discussed algorithms.

Five most widely known motion estimation algorithms such as the full search, three step search, new three step search, diamond search and hexagon based search algorithms were explicated. All of these algorithms are reported to be the baseline algorithms in block-matching motion estimation algorithm development. These algorithms are studied to understand the basis of block-matching motion estimation. The motion vector is determined using the motion estimation block prediction. The knowledge is used to develop the proposed algorithm.

The motion estimation technique is developed to detect the motion in the video sequences. Each of the video sequence applied in the proposed algorithms have motion varies from slow to fast. All the discussed algorithms are simulated using all the different type's video motion. The purpose of testing each algorithm with different kind of motions is to test the algorithms robustness. This also will explain that each algorithm is suitable to perform motion vector estimation based on different type of motions.

Based on this research and the findings of this study with baseline models, FUHS16 algorithm is selected as the basic algorithm for the proposed algorithm. Other proposed algorithms are used for comparison with all the superior algorithms. Fewer search points, less computational complexity and time savings was consequently proposed.

Validation of results involved three categories which are image PSNR points, computational complexity in terms of search points and elapsed processing time. In this thesis, the proposed algorithms are developed to have similar result as FS algorithm while out performing the other TSS, NTSS, DS and HEXBS algorithms. Additionally, measuring the PSNR points of each proposed algorithm is to determine the efficiency of the proposed algorithm. Based on the accumulated results, the proposed algorithms which are FUHS16, FUHS8, UHDS16 and UHDS8 have improved the search point efficiency and effectively have saved the elapsed processing time. This leads to lesser computational complexity when motion estimation prediction is done.

The proposed algorithm shows favorable characteristics for use in a real-world system. The PSNR point's measurements are similar or equal to that achieved using FS algorithm motion estimation block. Furthermore, the PSNR points measurement achieved by the proposed algorithm has outperformed the TSS, NTSS, DS and HEXBS algorithms. As in section 5.2, the UHDS8 algorithm has very close PSNR points measurement as compared with FS algorithm. Besides that, UHDS8 algorithm has also saved 94.7 percent of the computational complexity in terms of search points. The UHDS8 algorithm has also saved approximately 57 percent of the elapsed processing time to estimate the best-matched block compared with the FS algorithm. The numbers of memory accesses required during operation were also reduced.

7. References

Chen, M. J., Chu, M. C., and Pan, C. W. (2002). Efficient motion-estimation algorithm for reduced frame-rate. *IEEE Transactions on Circuit and Systems for Video Technology*, 12(4), 269 - 275.

Lee, J. K. & Chung, K. D. (2005). Conversion Scheme DCT-Domain Transcoding of MPEG-2 to H.264/AVC. *International conference on image analysis and processing*, pp. 551-558, 3617, Italy, September, 2005, Springerlink, Cagliari.

Shilpa, P. M. & Sanjay, N. T. (2010). Fast Motion Estimation Using Modified Orthogonal Search Algorithm for Video Compression. *Journal of Signal, Image and Video Processing*, 4(1), 123-128.

Wang, P., Zheng, Z. & Li L. (2008). A video watermarking scheme based on motion vectors and mode selection. *International Conference on Computer Science and Software Engineering*, 5, 233-237.

Wu, H., Mark C., and Robert K. (2010). A study of video motion and scene complexity. [Online]. Available: ftp://ftp.cs.wpi.edu/pub/techreports/pdf/06-19.pdf [2010, July 14].

Yang, K. C., Clark C. G., Pankaj K. D. & Khaled El-M. (2007). Perceptual Temporal Quality Metric for Compressed Video. *Journal Multimedia*, Vol.9, No. 7, 1528-1535.

Part 3

Search Algorithms for Engineering Applications

13

Multiple Access Network Optimization Aspects via Swarm Search Algorithms

Taufik Abrão[1], Lucas Hiera Dias Sampaio[2], Mario Lemes Proença Jr.[3], Bruno Augusto Angélico[4] and Paul Jean E. Jeszensky[5]

[1,2,3]*State University of Londrina (UEL), Londrina, PR*
[4]*Federal University of Technology (UTFPR), Cornélio Procópio, PR*
[5]*Polytechnic School of University of Sao Paulo (EPUSP), São Paulo, SP*
Brazil

1. Introduction

In the current telecommunication scenario, companies must deal with spectrum scarcity, power consumption issues, increasing throughput demand, and quality of service (QoS) requirements, including high performance (in terms of bit error rate (BER)) with guarantees of delivering the target information rate per user-class, maximum allowed delay, and so on. In these situations, many optimization problems arise, such as multiuser detection and resource allocation.

A lot of innovative algorithms conception and research efforts have been spent in order to satisfy the new services requirements, such as growing capacity, availability, mobility, and multiclass services (i.e., multirate users) with different quality of service (QoS). Hence, inspired by this scenario, a different optimization approach based on heuristic procedures has been investigated.

Particle swarm optimization (PSO) was developed after some researchers have analyzed the birds behavior and discerning that the advantage obtained through their group life could be explored as a tool for a heuristic search. Considering this new concept of interaction among individuals, J. Kennedy and R. Eberhart developed a new heuristic search based on a particle swarm Kennedy & Eberhart (1995). The PSO principle is the movement of a group of particles, randomly distributed in the search space, each one with its own position and velocity. The position of each particle is modified by the application of velocity in order to reach a better performance. The interaction among particles is inserted in the calculation of particle velocity.

In a multiple access DS/CDMA system, a conventional detector by itself may not provide a desirable performance and quality of service, once the system capacity is strongly affected by multiple access interference (MAI). The capacity of a DS/CDMA system in multipath channels is limited mainly by the MAI, self-interference (SI), near-far effect (NFR) and fading. The conventional receiver for multipath channels (Rake receiver) explores the path diversity in order to reduce fading impairment; however, it is not able to mitigate neither the MAI nor the near-far effect Moshavi (1996); Verdú (1998). In this context, multiuser detection (MUD) emerged as a solution to overcome the MAI. The best performance is acquired by the optimum multiuser detection (OMUD), which is based on the log-likelihood function (LLF), but results in a non-deterministic polynomial-time hard (NP-hard) complexity Verdú (1989). After the Verdu's revolutionary work, a great variety of suboptimal approaches have been proposed, such as (non-)linear multiuser detectors Castoldi (2002); Verdú (1998) and heuristic multiuser detectors Ergün & Hacioglu (2000); Juntti et al. (1997).

Heuristic methods have been proposed for solving the MUD problem, obtaining near-optimum performance at cost of polynomial computational complexity Abrão et al. (2009); Ergün & Hacioglu (2000). Examples of heuristic multiuser detection (HEUR-MUD) methods include: evolutionary programming (EP), specially the genetic algorithm (GA) Ciriaco et al. (2006); Ergün & Hacioglu (2000), particle swarm optimization (PSO) Khan et al. (2006); Oliveira et al. (2006); Zhao et al. (2006) and, sometimes included in this classification, the deterministic local search (LS) methods Lim & Venkatesh (2003); Oliveira et al. (2009), which has been shown very attractive performance $\times$ complexity trade-offs for low order modulation formats. High-order modulation HEUR-MUD in SISO or MIMO systems were previously addressed in Khan et al. (2006); Oliveira et al. (2008); Zhao et al. (2006). In Oliveira et al. (2008), PSO was applied to near-optimum asynchronous 16−QAM DS/CDMA multiuser detection problem under SISO multipath channels. Previous results on literature Abrão et al. (2009); Oliveira et al. (2006) suggest that evolutionary algorithms and particle swarm optimization have similar performance, and that a simple local search heuristic optimization is enough to solve the MUD problem with low-order modulation Oliveira et al. (2009). However for high-order modulation formats, the LS-MUD does not achieve good performances due to a lack of search diversity, whereas the PSO-MUD has been shown to be more efficient for solving the optimization problem under M-QAM modulation Oliveira et al. (2008). Firstly, in this chapter the multiuser detection optimization problem is treated under a heuristic perspective. A wide analysis is carried out considering multiple access systems under BPSK, QPSK and 16-QAM modulation formats, and diversity exploration as well.

A second optimization problem treated in this chapter refers to the resources allocation in wireless multiple access networks. In order to satisfy consumers necessities while keeping companies' profits, the resource allocation issues associated to these networks must be examined, mainly spectrum and power[1] allocation schemes. Thus, many researchers have been seeking resource allocation algorithms that could be easily applied to multiple access networks with high performance guarantee, i.e. low complexity combined with high solution quality. The application of heuristic optimization to the power allocation in CDMA systems was discussed in Elkamchouchi et al. (2007); Moustafa et al. (2000). In Moustafa et al. (2000; 2001a), a genetic approach, named genetic algorithm for mobiles equilibrium (GAME), was considered in order to control two main resources in a wireless network: bit rate and corresponding transmitting power level from mobile terminals. The basic idea is that all the mobile terminals have to harmonize their rate and power according to their location, QoS, and density. However, due to the centralized nature of the power-rate allocation problem and the complexity aspects, the GAME algorithm is suitable to be implemented in the base station only, which forwards the controlling signals to the mobile terminals.

Another heuristic approach that solve efficiently the power allocation problem, while resulting in lower computational complexity than genetic schemes, involves the swarm intelligence principle. In Elkamchouchi et al. (2007), particle swarm optimization (PSO) algorithm was used to solve the power allocation problem, while in Zielinski et al. (2009)

[1] Power allocation procedures imply in battery autonomy improvement.

the power control scheme with PSO was associated with parallel interference cancelation multiuser detector.

On the other hand, from an analytical perspective, the classical power allocation problem in wireless networks, posed two decades ago, has been analyzed and investigated over the years and many deterministic (semi-)analytical algorithms were proposed to solve this specific problem. One of these algorithms proposed by Foschini and Miljanic Foschini & Miljanic (1993) have been considered the foundation of many well-known distributed power control algorithms (DPCA).

More recently, many researchers have proposed new algorithms to solve the resource allocation problem in wireless networks. A distributed power control algorithm for the downlink of multiclass wireless networks was proposed in Lee et al. (2005). Also, under specific scenario of interference-limited networks, a power allocation algorithm to achieve global optimality in weighted throughput maximization based on multiplicative linear fractional programming (MLFP) was proposed in Li Ping Qian (2009). Moreover, in Dai et al. (2009) the goal is to maximize the fairness between users in the uplink of CDMA systems, satisfying different QoS requirements. In Gross et al. (2010) the Verhulst mathematical model, initially designed to describe population growth of biological species with food and physical space restriction, was adapted to a single rate DS/CDMA system DPCA. The work was the first to propose a Verhulst equilibrium equation adaptation to resource allocation problems in DS/CDMA networks.

In this chapter, optimization procedures based on particle swarm intelligence are investigated in details, aiming to efficiently solve the rate allocation problem (throughput maximization) with power constraint in multiclass DS/CDMA wireless networks, which show different QoS requirements, related to different user classes, making the resource allocation optimization procedure a more challenging task.

The chapter is organized in the following manner: in Section 2 the multiuser detection problem is treated under a guided search perspective, while in Section 3 a second class of optimization problem, namely the power and rate allocation problem in multi-class QoS multiple access networks is analyzed under the same heuristic optimization principle. In each multiple access network optimization context, after system model description, figures of merit are presented and a suitable swarm algorithm version is developed, with emphasis in the optimization of PSO′ input parameters. Afterward, extensive numerical results for both problems are discussed for realistic networks operation scenarios. Finally, the main conclusions are offered in Section 4.

2. Multiuser detection problem

This section focuses on the DS/CDMA multiuser problem. A single-cell asynchronous multiple access DS/CDMA system model is described for Rayleigh channels, considering different modulation schemes, such as binary/quadrature phase shift keying (BPSK/QPSK) and 16-quadrature amplitude modulation (16-QAM), and single or multiple antennas at the base station receiver. After describing the conventional detection approach with a maximum ratio combining (MRC) rule, the OMuD and the PSO-MuD are described. The model is generic enough to allow describing additive white Gaussian noise (AWGN) and Rayleigh flat channels, other modulation formats and single-antenna receiver.

2.1 DS/CDMA

The base-band transmitted signal of the kth user is described as Proakis (1989)

$$s_k(t) = \sqrt{\frac{\mathcal{E}_k}{T}} \sum_{i=-\infty}^{\infty} d_k^{(i)} g_k(t - iT), \tag{1}$$

where $\mathcal{E}_k$ is the symbol energy, and T is the symbol duration. Each symbol $d_k^{(i)}$, $k = 1, \ldots, K$ is taken independently and with equal probability from a complex alphabet set $\mathcal{A}$ of cardinality $M = 2^m$ in a squared constellation, i.e., $d_k^{(i)} \in \mathcal{A} \subset \mathbb{C}$, where $\mathbb{C}$ is the set of complex numbers. Fig. 1 shows the modulation formats considered, while Fig. 2 sketches the K base-band DS/CDMA transmitters.

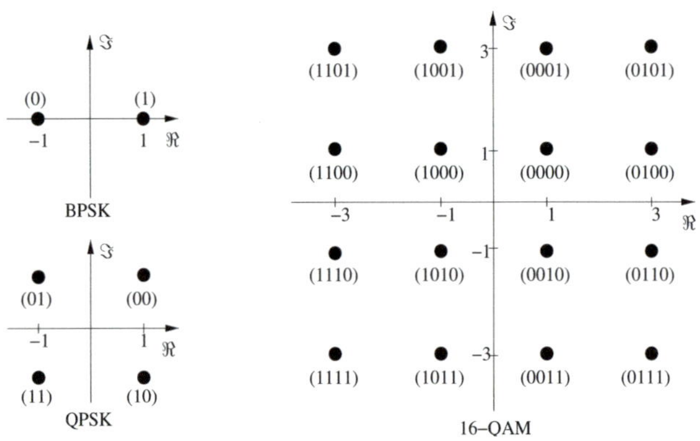

Fig. 1. Three modulation formats with Gray mapping.

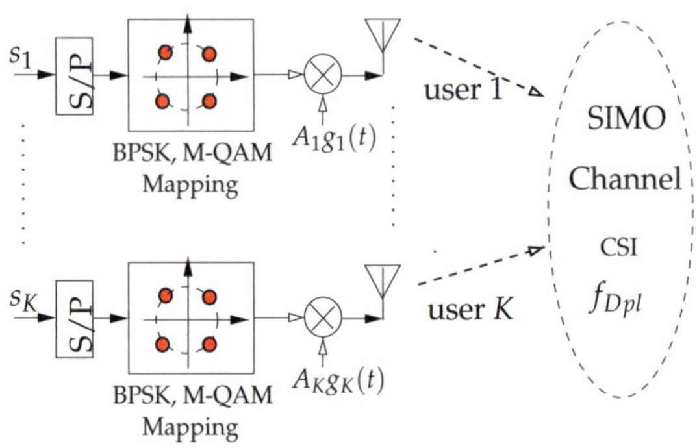

Fig. 2. Uplink base-band DS/CDMA transmission model with K users.

The normalized spreading sequence for the k-th user is given by

$$g_k(t) = \frac{1}{\sqrt{N}} \sum_{n=0}^{N-1} a_k(n) p(t - nT_c), \qquad 0 \leq t \leq T, \tag{2}$$

where $a_k(n)$ is a random sequence with N chips assuming the values $\{\pm 1\}$, $p(t)$ is the pulse shaping, assumed rectangular with unitary amplitude and duration T_c, with T_c being the chip interval. The processing gain is given by $N = T/T_c$.

The equivalent base-band received signal at qth receive antenna, $q = 1, 2, \ldots, Q$, containing I symbols for each user in multipath fading channel can be expressed by

$$r_q(t) = \sum_{i=0}^{I-1} \sum_{k=1}^{K} \sum_{\ell=1}^{L} A_k d_k^{(i)} g_k(t - nT - \tau_{q,k,\ell})\, h_{q,k,\ell}^{(i)} e^{j\varphi_{q,k,\ell}} + \eta_q(t), \tag{3}$$

with $A_k = \sqrt{\frac{\mathcal{E}_k}{T}}$, L being the number of channel paths, admitted equal for all K users, $\tau_{q,k,\ell}$ is the total delay[2] for the signal of the kth user, ℓth path at qth receive antenna, $e^{j\varphi_{q,k,\ell}}$ is the respective received phase carrier; $\eta_q(t)$ is the additive white Gaussian noise with bilateral power spectral density equal to $N_0/2$, and $h_{q,k,\ell}^{(i)}$ is the complex channel coefficient for the ith symbol, defined as

$$h_{q,k,\ell}^{(i)} = \gamma_{q,k,\ell}^{(i)} e^{j\theta_{q,k,\ell}^{(i)}}, \tag{4}$$

where the channel gain (modulo) $\gamma_{q,k,\ell}^{(i)}$ is characterized by a Rayleigh distribution and the phase $\theta_{q,k,\ell}^{(i)}$ by the uniform distribution $\mathcal{U}[0, 2\pi]$.

Generally, a slow and frequency selective channel[3] is assumed. The expression in (3) is quite general and includes some special and important cases: if $Q = 1$, a SISO system is obtained; if $L = 1$, the channel becomes non-selective (flat) Rayleigh; if $h_{q,k,\ell}^{(i)} = 1$, it results in the AWGN channel. Moreover, if $|\tau_{q,k,\ell}| \leq \epsilon_\tau$, with $\epsilon_\tau \in [0; 3T_c]$, a quasi-synchronous DS/CDMA system can be characterized.

At the base station, the received signal is submitted to a matched filter bank (CD), with $D \leq L$ branches (fingers) per antenna of each user. When $D \geq 1$, CD is known as Rake receiver. Assuming perfect phase estimation (carrier phase), after despreading the resultant signal is given by

$$\begin{aligned} y_{q,k,\ell}^{(i)} &= \frac{1}{T} \int_{nT}^{(i+1)T} r_q(t) g_k(t - \tau_{q,k,\ell}) dt \\ &= A_k h_{q,k,\ell}^{(i)} d_k^{(i)} + SI_{q,k,\ell}^{(i)} + I_{q,k,\ell}^{(i)} + \widetilde{\eta}_{q,k,\ell}^{(i)}. \end{aligned} \tag{5}$$

The first term is the signal of interest, the second corresponds to the self-interference (SI), the third to the multiple-access interference (MAI) and the last one corresponds to the filtered AWGN.

Considering a maximal ratio combining (MRC) rule with diversity order equal to DQ for each user, the $M-$level complex decision variable is given by

$$\zeta_k^{(i)} = \sum_{q=1}^{Q} \sum_{\ell=1}^{D} y_{q,k,\ell}^{(i)} \cdot \mathrm{w}_{q,k,\ell}^{(i)}, \quad k = 1, \ldots, K \tag{6}$$

where the MRC weights $\mathrm{w}_{q,k,\ell}^{(i)} = \widehat{\gamma}_{q,k,\ell}^{(i)} e^{-j\widehat{\theta}_{q,k,\ell}^{(i)}}$, with $\widehat{\gamma}_{q,k,l}^{(i)}$ and $\widehat{\theta}_{q,k,\ell}^{(i)}$ been a channel amplitude and phase estimation, respectively.

[2] Considering the asynchronism among the users and random delays for different paths.

[3] Slow channel: channel coefficients were admitted constant along the symbol period T; and frequency selective condition is hold: $\frac{1}{T_c} >> (\Delta B)_c$, the coherence bandwidth of the channel.

After that, at each symbol interval, decisions are made on the in-phase and quadrature components[4] of $\zeta_k^{(i)}$ by scaling it into the constellation limits obtaining $\breve{\zeta}_k^{(i)}$, and choosing the complex symbol with minimum Euclidean distance regarding the scaled decision variable. Alternatively, this procedure can be replaced by separate $\sqrt{M}-$level quantizers $\mathtt{qtz}$ acting on the in-phase and quadrature terms separately, such that

$$\hat{d}_k^{(i),\text{CD}} = \underset{\mathcal{A}_{\text{real}}}{\mathtt{qtz}}\left(\Re\left\{\breve{\zeta}_k^{(i)}\right\}\right) + j\,\underset{\mathcal{A}_{\text{imag}}}{\mathtt{qtz}}\left(\Im\left\{\breve{\zeta}_k^{(i)}\right\}\right), \tag{7}$$

for $k = 1, \ldots, K$, been $\mathcal{A}_{\text{real}}$ and $\mathcal{A}_{\text{imag}}$ the real and imaginary value sets, respectively, from the complex alphabet set $\mathcal{A}$, and $\Re\{\cdot\}$ and $\Im\{\cdot\}$ representing the real and imaginary operators, respectively. Fig. 3 illustrates the general system structure.

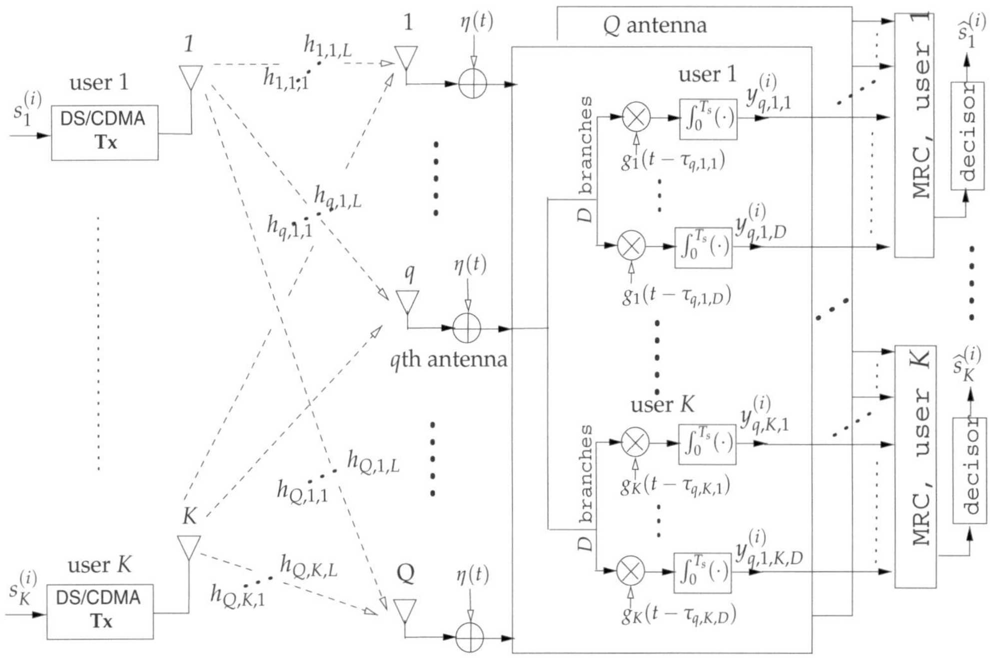

Fig. 3. Uplink base-band DS/CDMA system model: K users transmitters, SIMO channel and Conventional (Rake) receiver with Q multiple receive antennas.

2.2 Optimum detection

The OMuD estimates the symbols for all K users by choosing the symbol combination associated with the minimal distance metric among all possible symbol combinations in the $M = 2^m$ constellation points Verdú (1998).

In the asynchronous multipath channel scenario considered in this chapter, the one-shot asynchronous channel approach is adopted, where a configuration with K asynchronous users, I symbols and D branches is equivalent to a synchronous scenario with KID virtual users.

---
[4] Note that, for BPSK, only the in-phase term is presented.

Furthermore, in order to avoid handling complex-valued variables in high-order squared modulation formats, henceforward the alphabet set is re-arranged as $\mathcal{A}_{\text{real}} = \mathcal{A}_{\text{imag}} = \mathcal{Y} \subset \mathbb{Z}$ of cardinality $\sqrt{M}$, e.g., 16−QAM ($m = 4$): $d_k^{(i)} \in \mathcal{Y} = \{\pm 1, \pm 3\}$.
The OMUD is based on the maximum likelihood criterion that chooses the vector of symbols $\underline{\mathbf{d}}_p$, formally defined in (12), which maximizes the metric

$$\underline{\mathbf{d}}^{\text{opt}} = \arg \max_{\underline{\mathbf{d}}_p \in \mathcal{Y}^{2KID}} \left\{ \Omega\left(\underline{\mathbf{d}}_p\right) \right\}, \tag{8}$$

where, in a SIMO channel, the single-objective function is generally written as a combination of the LLFs from all receive antennas, given by

$$\Omega\left(\underline{\mathbf{d}}_p\right) = \sum_{q=1}^{Q} \Omega_q\left(\underline{\mathbf{d}}_p\right). \tag{9}$$

In a more general case considered herein, namely K asynchronous users in a SIMO multipath Rayleigh channel with diversity $D \leq L$, the LLF can be defined as a decoupled optimization problem with only real-valued variables, such that

$$\Omega_q(\underline{\mathbf{d}}_p) = 2\underline{\mathbf{d}}_p^\top \mathbf{W}_q^\top \underline{\mathbf{y}}_q - \underline{\mathbf{d}}_p^\top \mathbf{W}_q \underline{\mathbf{R}} \mathbf{W}_q^\top \underline{\mathbf{d}}_p, \tag{10}$$

with definitions

$$\underline{\mathbf{d}}_p \triangleq \begin{bmatrix} \Re\{\mathbf{d}_p\} \\ \Im\{\mathbf{d}_p\} \end{bmatrix}; \quad \mathbf{W}_q \triangleq \begin{bmatrix} \Re\{\mathbf{AH}\} & -\Im\{\mathbf{AH}\} \\ \Im\{\mathbf{AH}\} & \Re\{\mathbf{AH}\} \end{bmatrix}; \quad \underline{\mathbf{y}}_q \triangleq \begin{bmatrix} \Re\{\mathbf{y}_q\} \\ \Im\{\mathbf{y}_q\} \end{bmatrix}; \quad \underline{\mathbf{R}} \triangleq \begin{bmatrix} \mathbf{R} & \mathbf{0} \\ \mathbf{0} & \mathbf{R} \end{bmatrix}, \tag{11}$$

where $\underline{\mathbf{y}}_q \in \mathbb{R}^{2KID\times 1}$, $\mathbf{W}_q \in \mathbb{R}^{2KID\times 2KID}$, $\underline{\mathbf{d}}_p \in \mathcal{Y}^{2KID\times 1}$, $\underline{\mathbf{R}} \in \mathbb{R}^{2KID\times 2KID}$. The vector $\mathbf{d}_p \in \mathcal{Y}^{KID\times 1}$ in Eq. (11) is defined as

$$\mathbf{d}_p = [(\underbrace{d_1^{(1)} \cdots d_1^{(1)}}_{D\,\text{times}}) \cdots (\underbrace{d_K^{(1)} \cdots d_K^{(1)}}_{D\,\text{times}}) \cdots (\underbrace{d_1^{(I)} \cdots d_1^{(I)}}_{D\,\text{times}}) \cdots (\underbrace{d_K^{(I)} \cdots d_K^{(I)}}_{D\,\text{times}})]^\top. \tag{12}$$

In addition, the $\mathbf{y}_q \in \mathbb{C}^{KID\times 1}$ is the despread signal in Eq. (6) for a given q, in a vector notation, described as

$$\underline{\mathbf{y}}_q [(y_{q,1,1}^{(1)} \cdots y_{q,1,D}^{(1)}) \cdots (y_{q,K,1}^{(1)} \cdots y_{q,K,D}^{(1)}) \cdots (y_{q,1,1}^{(I)} \cdots y_{q,1,D}^{(I)}) \cdots (y_{q,K,1}^{(I)} \cdots y_{q,K,D}^{(I)})] \tag{13}$$

Matrices $\mathbf{H}$ and $\mathbf{A}$ are the coefficients and amplitudes diagonal matrices, respectively, and $\mathbf{R}$ represents the block-tridiagonal, block-Toeplitz cross-correlation matrix, composed by the sub-matrices $\mathbf{R}[1]$ and $\mathbf{R}[0]$, such that Verdú (1998)

$$\mathbf{R} = \begin{bmatrix} \mathbf{R}[0] & \mathbf{R}[1]^\top & \mathbf{0} & \ldots & \mathbf{0} & \mathbf{0} \\ \mathbf{R}[1] & \mathbf{R}[0] & \mathbf{R}[1]^\top & \ldots & \mathbf{0} & \mathbf{0} \\ \mathbf{0} & \mathbf{R}[1] & \mathbf{R}[0] & \ldots & \mathbf{0} & \mathbf{0} \\ \cdots & \cdots & \cdots & \cdots & \cdots & \cdots \\ \mathbf{0} & \mathbf{0} & \mathbf{0} & \ldots & \mathbf{R}[1] & \mathbf{R}[0] \end{bmatrix}, \tag{14}$$

with $\mathbf{R}[0]$ and $\mathbf{R}[1]$ being KD matrices with elements

$$\underline{\rho_{a,b}}[0] = \begin{cases} 1, & \text{if } (k=u) \text{ and } (\ell = l) \\ \rho^q_{k,\ell,u,l}, & \text{if } (k<u) \text{ or } (k=u, \ell < l) \\ \rho^q_{u,l,k,\ell}, & \text{if } (k>u) \text{ or } (k=u, \ell > l), \end{cases}$$

$$\underline{\rho_{a,b}}[1] = \begin{cases} 0, & \text{if } k \geq u \\ \rho^q_{u,l,k,\ell}, & \text{if } k < u \end{cases}, \tag{15}$$

where $a = (k-1)D + \ell$, $b = (u-1)D + l$ and $k, u = 1, 2, \ldots, K$; $\ell, l = 1, 2, \ldots, D$; the cross-correlation element between the kth user, ℓth path and uth user, dth path, at qth receive antenna is defined by:

$$\rho^q_{k,\ell,u,d} = \frac{1}{T}\int_0^T g_k(t - \tau_{q,k,\ell}) g_u(t - \tau_{q,u,d}) dt. \tag{16}$$

The evaluation in (8) can be extended along the whole message, where all symbols of the transmitted vector for all K users are jointly detected, namely vector maximum-likelihood (ML) approach, or the decisions can be taken considering the optimal single symbol detection of all K multiuser signals (symbol ML approach). In the synchronous case, the symbol ML approach with $I = 1$ is considered, whereas in the asynchronous case the vector ML approach is adopted with $I = 7$ (I must be, at least, equal to three ($I \geq 3$)).
The vector $\underline{\mathbf{d}}_p$ in (11) belongs to a discrete set with size depending on M, K, I and D. Hence, the optimization problem posed by (8) can be solved directly using a $m-$dimensional ($m = \log_2 M$) search method. Therefore, the associated combinatorial problem strictly requires an exhaustive search in $\mathcal{A}^{KID}$ possibilities of $\mathbf{d}$, or equivalently an exhaustive search in $\mathcal{Y}^{2KID}$ possibilities of $\underline{\mathbf{d}}_p$ for the decoupled optimization problem with only real-valued variables. As a result, the maximum likelihood detector has a complexity that increases exponentially with the modulation order, number of users, symbols and branches, becoming prohibitive even for moderate product values $m\,K\,I\,D$, i.e., even for a BPSK modulation format, medium system loading (K/N), small number of symbols I and realistic values for the D Rake fingers (around 4 to 6).

2.3 Discrete swarm optimization algorithm

A discrete or, in several cases, binary PSO Kennedy & Eberhart (1997) is considered in this chapter. Such scheme is suitable to deal with digital information detection/decoding. Hence, binary PSO is adopted herein. The particle selection for evolving is based on the highest fitness values obtained through (10) and (9).
Accordingly, each candidate-vector defined like $\mathbf{d}_i$ has its binary representation, $\mathbf{b}_p[\mathtt{t}]$, of size mKI, used for the velocity calculation, and the pth PSO particle position at instant (iteration) $\mathtt{t}$ is represented by the $mKI \times 1$ binary vector

$$\mathbf{b}_p[\mathtt{t}] = [\mathbf{b}^1_p\, \mathbf{b}^2_p\, \cdots\, \mathbf{b}^r_p\, \cdots\, \mathbf{b}^{KI}_p]; \qquad \text{with} \quad \mathbf{b}^r_p = \left[b^r_{p,1} \cdots b^r_{p,v} \cdots b^r_{p,m}\right]; \; b^r_{p,v} \in \{0, 1\}, \tag{17}$$

where each binary vector $\mathbf{b}^r_p$ is associated with one $d^{(i)}_k$ symbol in Eq. (12). Each particle has a velocity, which is calculated and updated according to

$$\mathbf{v}_p[\mathtt{t}+1] = \omega \cdot \mathbf{v}_p[\mathtt{t}] + \phi_1 \cdot \mathbf{U}_{p_1}[\mathtt{t}](\mathbf{b}^{\text{best}}_p[\mathtt{t}] - \mathbf{b}_p[\mathtt{t}]) + \phi_2 \cdot \mathbf{U}_{p_2}[\mathtt{t}](\mathbf{b}^{\text{best}}_g[\mathtt{t}] - \mathbf{b}_p[\mathtt{t}]), \tag{18}$$

where ω is the inertial weight; $\mathbf{U}_{p_1}[\mathtt{t}]$ and $\mathbf{U}_{p_2}[\mathtt{t}]$ are diagonal matrices with dimension mKI, whose elements are random variables with uniform distribution $\mathcal{U} \in [0,1]$; $\mathbf{b}_g^{\text{best}}[\mathtt{t}]$ and $\mathbf{b}_p^{\text{best}}[\mathtt{t}]$ are the best global position and the best local positions found until the $\mathtt{t}$th iteration, respectively; ϕ_1 and ϕ_2 are weight factors (acceleration coefficients) regarding the best individual and the best global positions influences in the velocity update, respectively.
For MUD optimization with binary representation, each element of $\mathbf{b}_p[\mathtt{t}]$ in (18) just assumes "0" or "1" values. Hence, a discrete mode for the position choice is carried out inserting a probabilistic decision step based on threshold, depending on the velocity. Several functions have this characteristic, such as the sigmoid function Kennedy & Eberhart (1997)

$$S(v_{p,\nu}^r[\mathtt{t}]) = \frac{1}{1+e^{-v_{p,\nu}^r[\mathtt{t}]}}, \tag{19}$$

where $v_{p,\nu}^r[\mathtt{t}]$ is the rth element of the pth particle velocity vector, $\mathbf{v}_p^r = \left[v_{p,1}^r \cdots v_{p,\nu}^r \cdots v_{p,m}^r\right]$, and the selection of the future particle position is obtained through the statement

$$\begin{aligned} &\text{if} \quad \mathrm{u}_{p,\nu}^r[\mathtt{t}] < S(v_{p,\nu}^r[\mathtt{t}]), \quad && b_{p,\nu}^r[\mathtt{t}+1] = 1; \\ &\text{otherwise,} && b_{p,\nu}^r[\mathtt{t}+1] = 0, \end{aligned} \tag{20}$$

where $b_{p,\nu}^r[\mathtt{t}]$ is an element of $\mathbf{b}_p[\mathtt{t}]$ (see Eq. (17)), and $\mathrm{u}_{p,\nu}^r[\mathtt{t}]$ is a random variable with uniform distribution $\mathcal{U} \in [0,1]$.
After obtaining a new particle position $\mathbf{b}_p[\mathtt{t}+1]$, it is mapped back into its correspondent symbol vector $\mathbf{d}_p[\mathtt{t}+1]$, and further in the real form $\underline{\mathbf{d}}_p[\mathtt{t}+1]$, for the evaluation of the objective function in (9).
In order to obtain further diversity for the search universe, the $V_{\max}$ factor is added to the PSO model, Eq. (18), being responsible for limiting the velocity in the range $[\pm V_{\max}]$. The insertion of this factor in the velocity calculation enables the algorithm to escape from possible local optima. The likelihood of a bit change increases as the particle velocity crosses the limits established by $[\pm V_{\max}]$, as shown in Table 1.

Table 1. Minimum bit change probability as a function of $V_{\max}$.

$V_{\max}$	1	2	3	4	5
$1 - S(V_{\max})$	0.269	0.119	0.047	0.018	0.007

Population size $\mathcal{P}$ is typically in the range of 10 to 40 Eberhart & Shi (2001). However, based on Oliveira et al. (2006), it is set to

$$\mathcal{P} = 10\left\lfloor 0.3454\left(\sqrt{\pi(mKI-1)}+2\right)\right\rfloor. \tag{21}$$

Algorithm 1 describes the pseudo-code for the PSO implementation.

2.4 Parameters optimization for PSO-MuD

The PSO-MUD parameters optimization is carried out using Monte-Carlo simulation Jeruchim et al. (1992). Such an optimization is directly related to the complexity × performance trade-off of the algorithm. A wide analysis with BPSK, QPSK and 16-QAM modulation schemes, and diversity exploration is carried out.

Algorithm 1 SOO Discrete PSO Algorithm for the MUD Problem

Input: $\mathbf{d}^{\text{CD}}, \mathcal{P}, G, \omega, \phi_1, \phi_2, V_{\max}$; **Output:** $\mathbf{d}^{\text{PSO}}$
begin
1. initialize first population: $\mathtt{t} = 0$;
   $\mathbf{B}[0] = \mathbf{b}^{\text{CD}} \cup \widetilde{\mathbf{B}}$, where $\widetilde{\mathbf{B}}$ contains $(\mathcal{P} - 1)$ particles randomly generated;
   $\mathbf{b}_p^{\text{best}}[0] = \mathbf{b}_p[0]$ and $\mathbf{b}_g^{\text{best}}[0] = \mathbf{b}^{\text{CD}}$;
   $\mathbf{v}_p[0] = \mathbf{0}$: null initial velocity;
2. while $\mathtt{t} \leq G$
   a. calculate $\Omega(\underline{\mathbf{d}}_p[\mathtt{t}]), \forall \mathbf{b}_p[\mathtt{t}] \in \mathbf{B}[\mathtt{t}]$ using (9);
   b. update velocity $\mathbf{v}_p[\mathtt{t}],\ p = 1, \ldots, \mathcal{P}$, through (18);
   c. update best positions:
      for $p = 1, \ldots, \mathcal{P}$
         if $\Omega(\underline{\mathbf{d}}_p[\mathtt{t}]) > \Omega(\underline{\mathbf{d}}_p^{\text{best}}[\mathtt{t}])$, $\mathbf{b}_p^{\text{best}}[\mathtt{t}+1] \leftarrow \mathbf{b}_p[\mathtt{t}]$
         else $\mathbf{b}_p^{\text{best}}[\mathtt{t}+1] \leftarrow \mathbf{b}_p^{\text{best}}[\mathtt{t}]$
      end
      if $\exists\ \mathbf{b}_p[\mathtt{t}]$ such that $\left[\Omega(\underline{\mathbf{d}}_p[\mathtt{t}]) > \Omega(\underline{\mathbf{d}}_g^{\text{best}}[\mathtt{t}])\right] \wedge$
      $\left[\Omega(\underline{\mathbf{d}}_p[\mathtt{t}]) \geq \Omega(\underline{\mathbf{d}}_j[\mathtt{t}]), j \neq p\right]$,
         $\mathbf{b}_g^{\text{best}}[\mathtt{t}+1] \leftarrow \mathbf{b}_p[\mathtt{t}]$
      else $\mathbf{b}_g^{\text{best}}[\mathtt{t}+1] \leftarrow \mathbf{b}_g^{\text{best}}[\mathtt{t}]$
   d. Evolve to a new swarm population $\mathbf{B}[\mathtt{t}+1]$, using (20);
   e. set $\mathtt{t} = \mathtt{t} + 1$.
   end
3. $\mathbf{b}^{\text{PSO}} = \mathbf{b}_g^{\text{best}}[G]$; $\mathbf{b}^{\text{PSO}} \overset{\text{map}}{\longrightarrow} \mathbf{d}^{\text{PSO}}$.
end

- -

$\mathbf{d}^{\text{CD}}$: CD output.
$\mathcal{P}$: Population size.
G: number of swarm iterations.
For each $\underline{\mathbf{d}}_p[\mathtt{t}]$ there is a $\mathbf{b}_p[\mathtt{t}]$ associated.

A first analysis of the PSO parameters gives raise to the following behaviors: ω is responsible for creating an inertia of the particles, inducing them to keep the movement towards the last directions of their velocities; ϕ_1 aims to guide the particles to each individual best position, inserting diversification in the search; ϕ_2 leads all particles towards the best global position, hence intensifying the search and reducing the convergence time; $V_{\max}$ inserts perturbation limits in the movement of the particles, allowing more or less diversification in the algorithm. The optimization process for the initial velocity of the particles achieves similar results for three different conditions: null, random and CD output as initial velocity. Hence, it is adopted here, for simplicity, null initial velocity, i.e., $\mathbf{v}[0] = \mathbf{0}$.

In Oliveira et al. (2006), the best performance $\times$ complexity trade-off for BPSK PSO-MUD algorithm was obtained setting $V_{\max} = 4$. Herein, simulations carried out varying $V_{\max}$ for different modulations and diversity exploration accomplish this value as a good alternative. This optimization process is quite similar for systems with QPSK and 16-QAM modulation formats.

2.4.1 ω optimization

It is worth noting that a relatively larger value for ω is helpful for global optimum, and lesser influenced by the best global and local positions, while a relatively smaller value for ω is helpful for course convergence, i.e., smaller inertial weight encourages the local exploration Eberhart & Shi (2001); Shi & Eberhart (1998) as the particles are more attracted towards $\mathbf{b}_p^{\text{best}}[\mathtt{t}]$ and $\mathbf{b}_g^{\text{best}}[\mathtt{t}]$.

Fig. 4 shows the convergence of the PSO scheme for different values of ω considering BPSK modulation and flat channel. It is evident that the best performance $\times$ complexity trade-off is accomplished with $\omega = 1$.

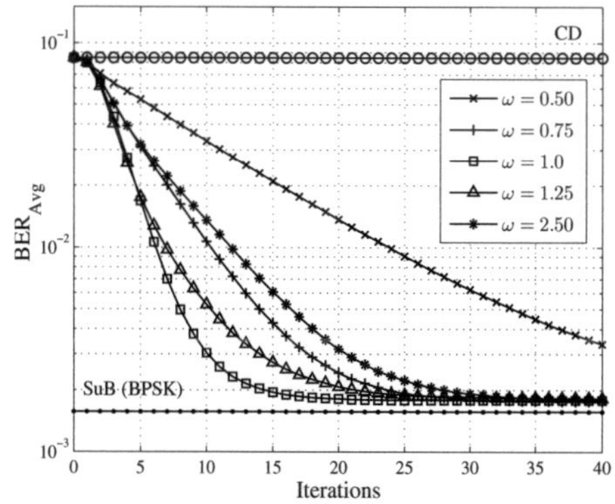

Fig. 4. ω optimization under Rayleigh flat channels with BPSK modulation, $E_b/N_0 = 22$ dB, $K = 15$, $\phi_1 = 2$, $\phi_2 = 10$ and $V_{\max} = 4$.

Many research' papers have been reported new PSO procedures and strategies in order to improve its performance and reduce its complexity. For instance, in Chatterjee & Siarry (2006) the authors have been discussed adaptive nonlinear inertia weight in order to improve PSO convergence. However, the current analysis indicates that no further specialized strategy is necessary, since the conventional PSO works well to solve the MUD DS/CDMA problem in several practical scenarios.

The optimization of the inertial weight, ω, achieves analogous results for QPSK and 16-QAM modulation schemes, where $\omega = 1$ also achieves the best performance $\times$ complexity trade-off (results not shown). In the next Subsection, a special attention is given for ϕ_1 and ϕ_2 input parameter optimization, since their values impact deeply in the PSO performance, also varying for each order modulation.

2.4.2 ϕ_1 and ϕ_2 optimization

For BPSK modulation and Rayleigh flat channels, the performance improvement expected by ϕ_1 increment is not evident, and its value can be reduced without performance losses, as can be seen in Fig. 5. Therefore, a good choice seems to be $\phi_1 = 2$, achieving a reasonable convergence rate.

Fig. 6.(a) illustrates different convergence performances achieved with $\phi_1 = 2$ and $\phi_2 \in [1; 15]$ for medium system loading and medium-high E_b/N_0. Even for high system loading, the PSO performance is quite similar for different values of ϕ_2, as observed in Fig. 6.(b). Hence, considering the performance $\times$ complexity trade-off, a reasonable choice for ϕ_2 under Rayleigh flat channels is $\phi_2 = 10$.

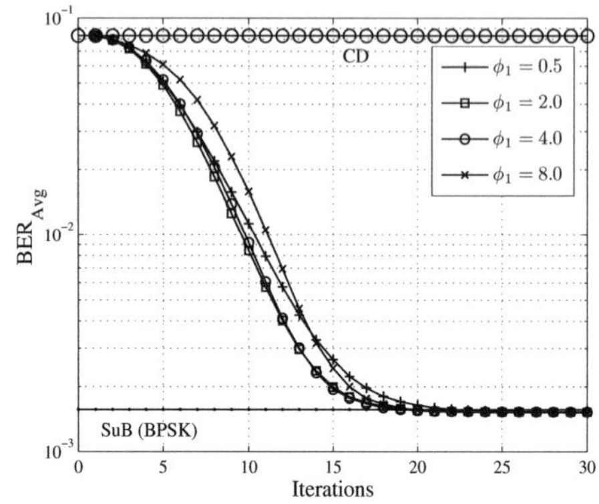

Fig. 5. ϕ_1 optimization in Rayleigh flat channels with BPSK modulation, $E_b/N_0 = 22$ dB, $K = 15$, $\phi_2 = 10$ (fixed), $V_{\max} = 4$, and $\omega = 1$.

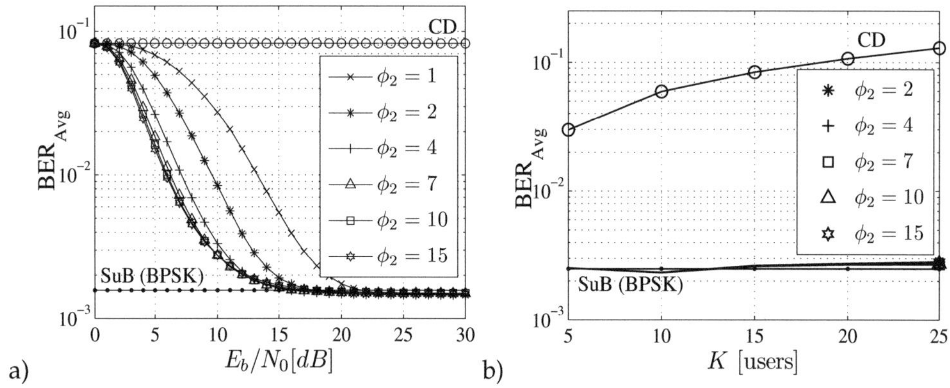

Fig. 6. ϕ_2 optimization in Rayleigh flat channels with BPSK modulation, $V_{\max} = 4$, $\omega = 1$, and $\phi_1 = 2$ (fixed); a) convergence performance with $E_b/N_0 = 22$ dB and $K = 15$; b) average BER $\times$ K with $E_b/N_0 = 20$ dB, $G = 30$ iterations.

Different results from BPSK are achieved when a QPSK modulation scheme is adopted. Note in Fig. 7 that low values of ϕ_2 and high values ϕ_1 delay the convergence, the inverse results in lack of diversity. Hence, the best performance $\times$ complexity is achieved with $\phi_1 = \phi_2 = 4$.

Under 16-QAM modulation, the PSO-MUD requires more intensification, once the search becomes more complex due to each symbol maps to 4 bits. Fig. 8 shows the convergence curves for different values of ϕ_1 and ϕ_2, where it is clear that the performance gap is more evident with an increasing number of users and E_b/N_0. Analyzing this result, the chosen values are $\phi_1 = 6$ and $\phi_2 = 1$.

The best range for the acceleration coefficients under resolvable multipath channels ($L \geq 2$) for MuD SISO DS/CDMA problem seems $\phi_1 = 2$ and $\phi_2 \in [12; 15]$, as indicated by the simulation results shown in Fig. 9. For medium system loading and SNR, Fig. 9 indicates that the best values for acceleration coefficients are $\phi_1 = 2$ and $\phi_2 = 15$, allowing the combination of fast convergence and near-optimum performance achievement.

The optimized input parameters for PSO-MUD vary regarding the system and channel scenario conditions. Monte-Carlo simulations exhibited in Section 2.5 adopt the values

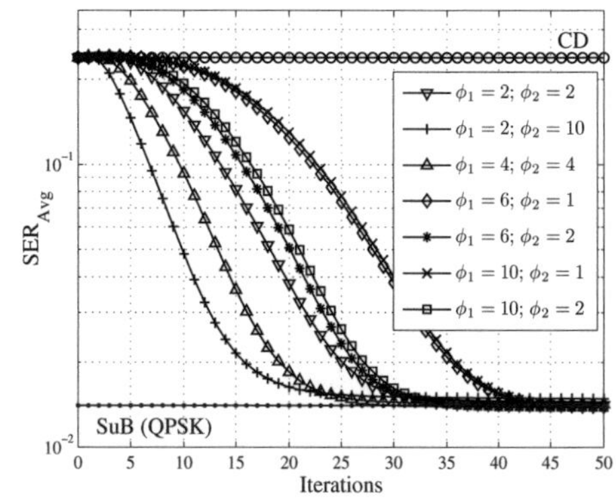

Fig. 7. ϕ_1 and ϕ_2 optimization under flat Rayleigh channels for QPSK modulation, $E_b/N_0 = 22$ dB, $K = 15$, $\omega = 1$ and $V_{max} = 4$.

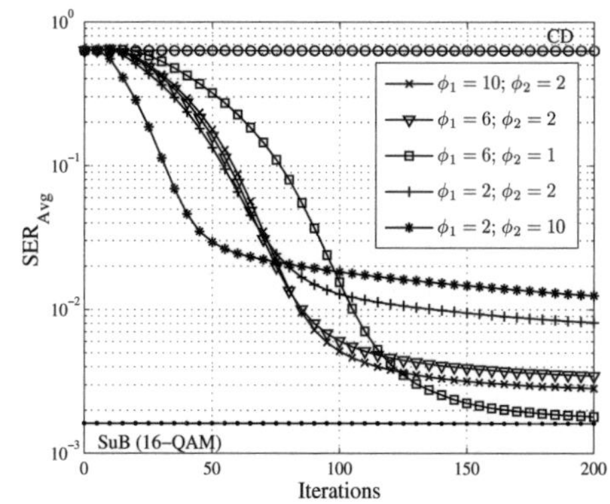

Fig. 8. ϕ_1 and ϕ_2 optimization under flat Rayleigh channels for 16-QAM modulation, $E_b/N_0 = 30$ dB, $K = 15$, $\omega = 1$ and $V_{max} = 4$.

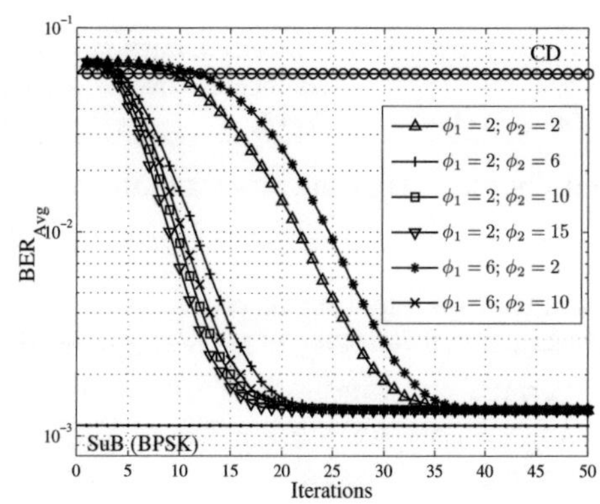

Fig. 9. ϕ_1 and ϕ_2 optimization under Rayleigh channels with path diversity ($L = D = 2$) for BPSK modulation, $E_b/N_0 = 22$ dB, $K = 15$, $\omega = 1$, $V_{max} = 4$.

Channel & Modulation	$\mathcal{L}$ range	ω	ϕ_1	ϕ_2	V_{max}
Flat Rayleigh BPSK	[0.16; 1.00]	1	2	10	4
Flat Rayleigh QPSK	[0.16; 1.00]	1	4	4	4
Flat Rayleigh 16-QAM	[0.03; 0.50]	1	6	1	4
Diversity Rayleigh BPSK	[0.03; 0.50]	1	2	15	4

Table 2. Optimized parameters for asynchronous PSO-MUD.

presented in Table 2 as the optimized input PSO parameters for the MuD problem. Loading system $\mathcal{L}$ range indicates the boundaries for $\frac{K}{N}$ which the input PSO parameters optimization was carried out. For system operation characterized by spatial diversity ($Q > 1$ receive antennas), the PSO-MUD behaviour, in terms of convergence speed and quality of solution, is very similar to that presented under multipath diversity.

2.5 Numerical results with optimized parameters for MuD problem

Numerical performance results are obtained using Monte-Carlo simulations, with optimized PSO parameters for different loading, E_b/N_0, near-far effect, modulation, diversity exploitation and errors in the channel coefficients estimation. The results obtained are compared with theoretical single-user bound (SuB), according to Appendix A, since the OMUD computational complexity results prohibitive. The adopted PSO-MUD parameters, as well as system and channel conditions employed in Monte-Carlo simulations are summarized in Table 3.

Parameter	Adopted Values
DS/CDMA System	
# Rx antennas	$Q = 1, 2, 3$
Spreading Sequences	Random, $N = 31$
modulation	BPSK, QPSK and 16−QAM
# mobile users	$K \in [5; 31]$
Received SNR	$E_b/N_0 \in [0; 30]$ dB
PSO-MUD Parameters	
Population size, $\mathcal{P}$	Eq. (21)
acceleration coefficients	$\phi_1 \in [2; 6]$; $\phi_2 \in [1; 10]$
inertia weight	$\omega = 1$
Maximal velocity	$V_{max} = 4$
Rayleigh Channel	
Channel state info. (CSI)	perfectly known at Rx coefficient error estimates
Number of paths	$L = 1, 2, 3$

Table 3. System, channel and PSO-MUD parameters for fading channels performance analysis.

Fig. 10 presents the performance as a function of received E_b/N_0 for two different near-far ratio scenarios under flat Rayleigh channel. Fig. 10.(a) was obtained for perfect power control, whereas Fig. 10.(b) was generated considering half users with $NFR = +6$ dB. Here, the BER_{Avg} performance is calculated only for the weaker users. Note the performance of the PSO-MUD is almost constant despite of the $NFR = +6$ dB for half of the users, illustrating the robustness of the PSO-MUD against unbalanced powers in flat fading channels.

Regarding channel diversity, two assumptions are considered when there are more than one antenna at receiver (Spatial Diversity): first, the average received power is equal for

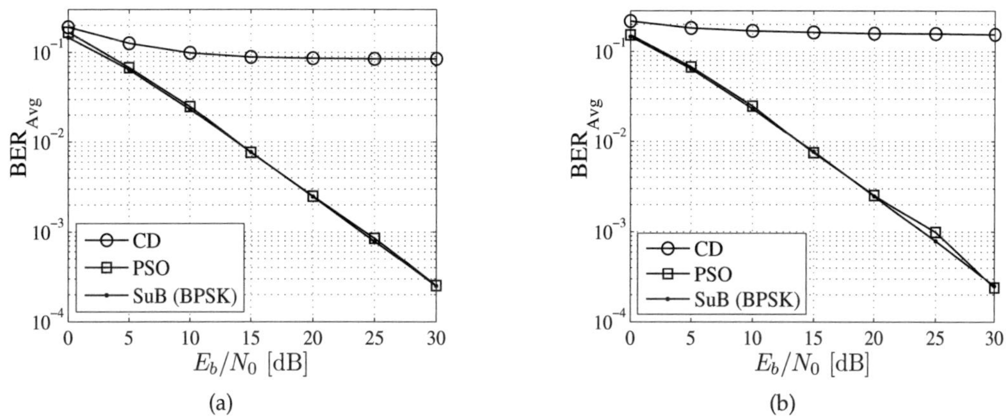

Fig. 10. Average BER$_{Avg}\times E_b/N_0$ for flat Rayleigh channel with $K = 15$: (a) perfect power control; (b) $NFR = +6$ dB for 7 users. In scenario (b), the performance is calculated only for the weaker users.

all antennas; and second, the SNR at the receiver input is defined as the received SNR per antenna. Therefore, there is a power gain of 3 dB when adopted $Q = 2$, 6 dB with $Q = 3$, and so on. The effect of increasing the number of receive antennas in the convergence curves is shown in Fig. 11, where PSO-MUD works on systems with $Q = 1,\ 2$ and 3 antennas. A delay in the PSO-MUD convergence is observed when more antennas are added to the receiver, caused by the larger gap that it has to surpass. Furthermore, PSO-MUD achieves the SuB performance for all the three cases.

The exploitation of the path diversity also improves the system capacity. Fig. 11 shows the BER$_{Avg}$ convergence of PSO-MUD for different of paths, $L = 1,\ 2$ and 3, when the detector explores fully the path diversity, i.e., the number of fingers of conventional detector is equal the number of copies of signal received, $D = L$. The power delay profile considered is exponential, with mean paths energy as shown in Table 4 Proakis (1989). It is worth mentioning that the mean received energy is equal for the three conditions, i.e., the resultant improvement with increasing number of paths is due the diversity gain only.

Param.	PD-1	PD-2		PD-3		
Path, ℓ	1	1	2	1	2	3
τ_ℓ	0	0	T_c	0	T_c	$2T_c$
$\mathbb{E}[\gamma_\ell^2]$	1.0000	0.8320	0.1680	0.8047	0.1625	0.0328

Table 4. Three power-delay profiles for different Rayleigh fading channels used in Monte-Carlo simulations.

Note there is a performance gain with the exploration of such diversity, verified in both the Rake receiver and PSO-MUD. The PSO-MUD performance is close to SuB in all cases, exhibiting its capability of exploring path diversity and dealing with SI as well. In addition, the convergence aspects are kept for all conditions.

The PSO-MUD single-objective function, Eq. (9), takes into account the channel coefficient estimation of each user, and imperfect channel estimation degrades its performance. In order to raise a quantitative characterization of such aspect, the PSO-MUD is evaluate under channel

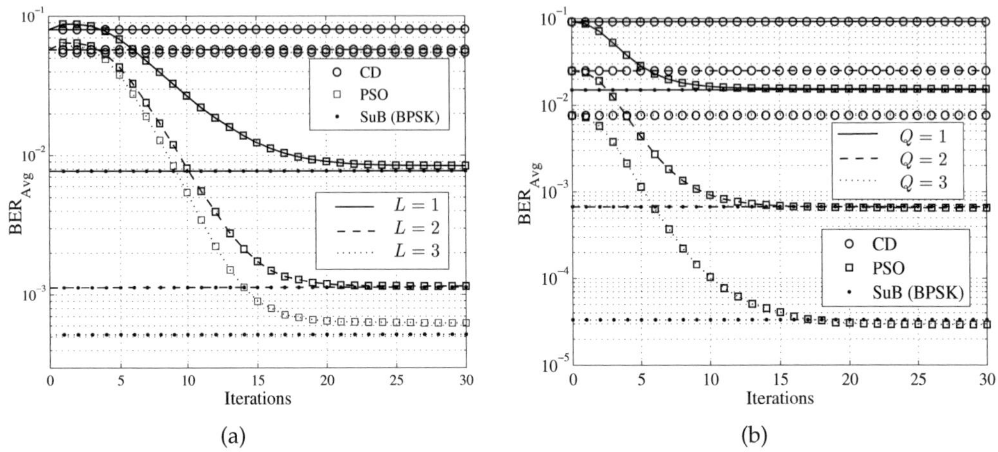

Fig. 11. Convergence performance of PSO-MUD, with $K = 15$, $E_b/N_0 = 15$, BPSK modulation, (a) under asynchronous multipath slow Rayleigh channels and $I = 3$, for $L = 1$, 2 and 3 paths; and (b) synchronous flat Rayleigh channel, $I = 1$ and $Q = 1, 2, 3$ antennas.

error estimation, which are modeled through the continuous uniform distributions $\mathcal{U}[1 \pm \epsilon]$ centralized on the true values of the coefficients, resulting

$$\widehat{\gamma}_{k,\ell}^{(i)} = \mathcal{U}[1 \pm \epsilon_\gamma] \times \gamma_{k,\ell}^{(i)}; \quad \widehat{\theta}_{k,\ell}^{(i)} = \mathcal{U}[1 \pm \epsilon_\theta] \times \theta_{k,\ell}^{(i)}, \tag{22}$$

where ϵ_γ and ϵ_θ are the maximum module and phase normalized errors for the channel coefficients, respectively. For a low-moderate SNR and medium system loading ($\mathcal{L} = 15/31$), Fig. 12 shows the performance degradation of the PSO-MUD considering BPSK modulation, $L = 1$ and $L = 2$ paths or $Q = 1$ and $Q = 2$ antennas, with estimation errors of order of 10% or 25%, i.e., $\epsilon_\gamma = \epsilon_\theta = 0.10$ or $\epsilon_\gamma = \epsilon_\theta = 0.25$, respectively. Note that PSO-MUD reaches the SuB in both conditions with perfect channel estimation, and the improvement is more evident when the diversity gain increases. However, note that, with spatial diversity, the gain is higher, since the average energy is equally distributed among antennas, while for path diversity is considered a realistic exponential power-delay profile. Moreover, there is a SNR gain of +3 dB in the E_b/N_0 for each additional receive antenna. Although there is a general performance degradation when the error in channel coefficient estimation increases, PSO-MUD still achieves much better performance than the CD under any error estimation condition, being more evident for larger number of antennas.

As expected from previous results for flat Rayleigh channel, Fig. 13 shows the performance degradation CD for path ($L = 1$ and $L = 2$) and spatial ($Q = 1$ and $Q = 2$) diversity as function of number of users K. It is evident that the PSO-MUD performance is superior when diversity is exploited. As can be seen, independently of the loading and number of paths, PSO-MUD always accomplishes a much better performance.

In the new generations of wireless systems, beyond spatial and path diversity, the high-order modulation is also explored. Hence, since PSO-MUD must work efficiently for other modulation constellation, Fig. 14 shows the convergence for three different modulations: (a) BPSK, (b) QPSK, and (c) 16-QAM. It is worth mentioning, as presented in Table 2, that the PSO-MUD optimized parameters is specific for each modulation format.

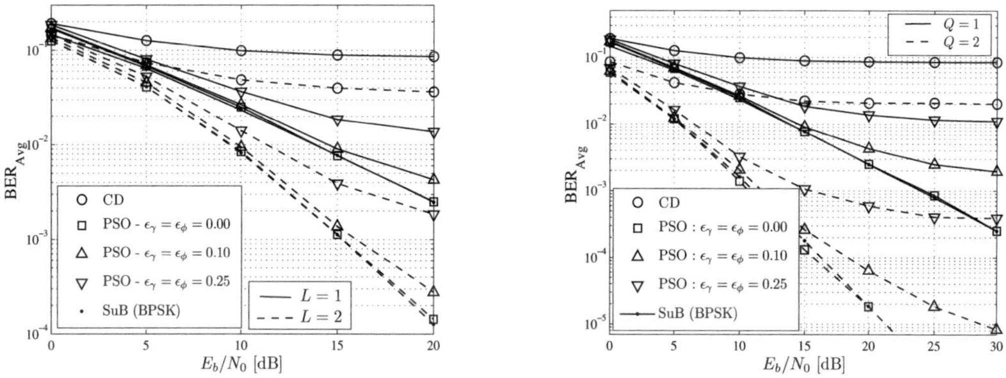

(a) (b)

Fig. 12. Performance of PSO-MUD with $K = 15$, BPSK modulation and error in the channel estimation, for a system with (a) path and (b) spatial diversity.

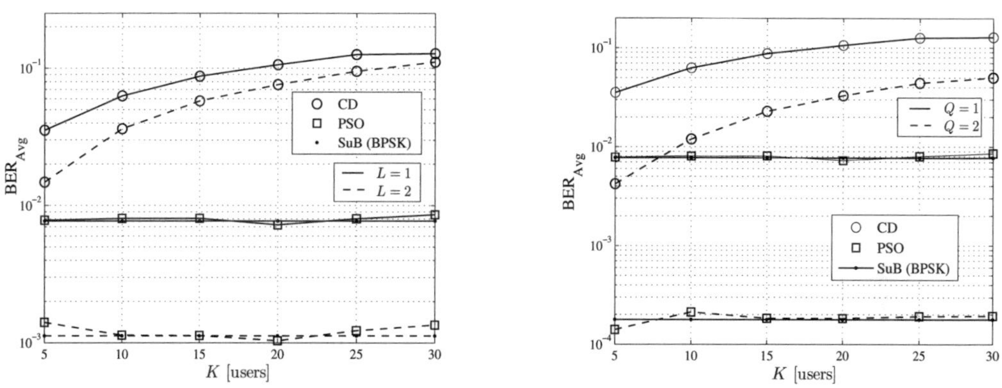

(a) (b)

Fig. 13. Performance of PSO-MUD with $E_b/N_0 = 15$ dB and BPSK modulation, for a system with (a) path and (b) spatial diversity.

Similar results are obtained for E_b/N_0 curves in QPSK and 16-QAM cases. Nevertheless, Fig. 15 shows that for 16-QAM modulation with $\phi_1 = 6$, $\phi_2 = 1$, the PSO-MUD performance degradation is quite slight in the range ($0 < \mathcal{L} \leq 0.5$), but the performance is hardly degraded in medium to high loading scenarios.

3. Resource allocation problem

This Section discusses the rate resource allocation with power constraint in multiple access multi-class networks under heuristic optimization perspective. Multirate users associated with different types of traffic are aggregated to distinct user' classes, with the assurance of minimum target rate allocation per user and QoS. Therein, single-objective optimization (SOO) methodology under swarm intelligence approach was carried out aiming to achieve newsworthy performance-complexity tradeoffs. The results are promising in terms of sum

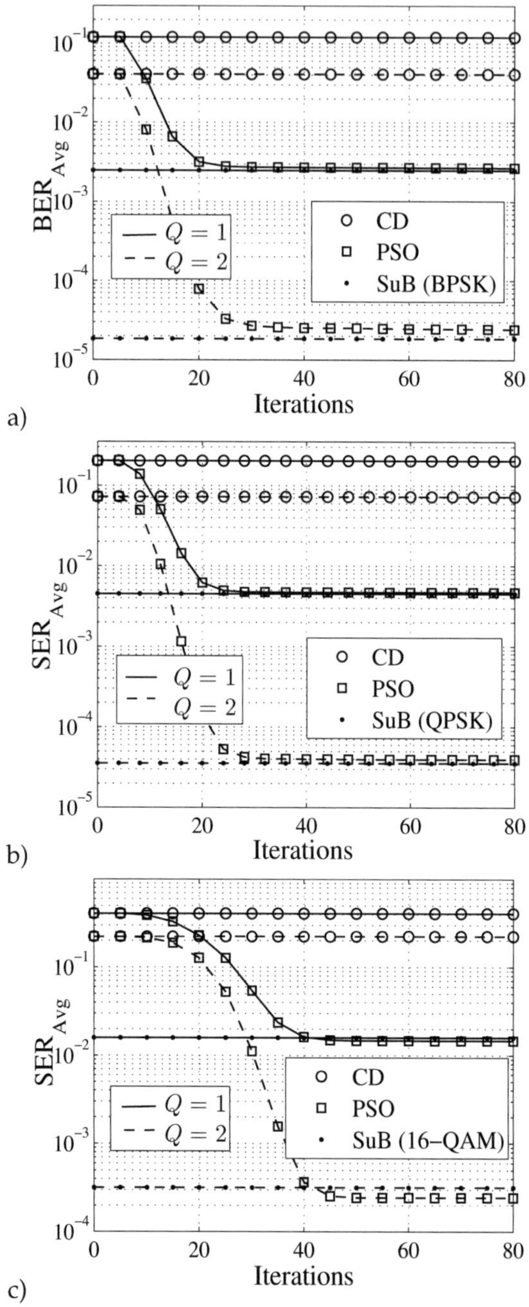

Fig. 14. Convergence of PSO-MUD under flat Rayleigh channel, $E_b/N_0 = 20$ dB, and a) $K = 24$ users with BPSK modulation, b) $K = 12$ users with QPSK modulation and c) $K = 6$ users with 16-QAM modulation

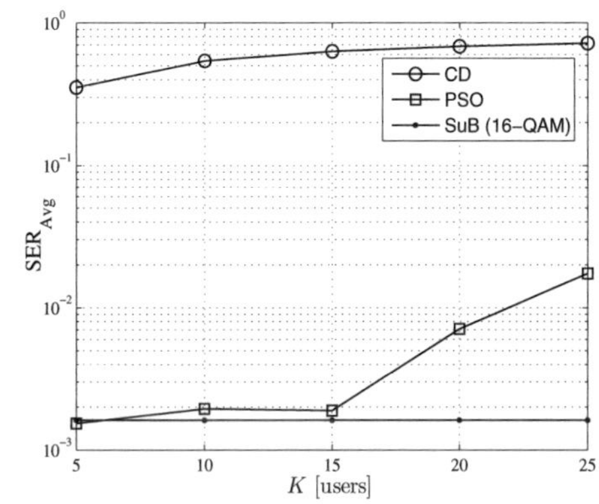

Fig. 15. PSO-MUD and CD performance degradation × system loading under flat Rayleigh channel. 16-QAM modulation and $\phi_1 = 6, \phi_2 = 1$.

rate maximization while simultaneously minimizing the total power allocated to each multirate mobile terminal.

3.1 Power-rate allocation problem

In a multiple access system, such as DS/CDMA, the power control problem is of great importance in order to achieve relevant system capacity[5] and throughput. The power allocation issue can be solved by finding the best vector that contains the minimum power to be assigned in the next time slot to each active user, in order to achieve the minimum quality of service (QoS) through the minimum carrier to interference ratio (CIR) allowable.

In multirate multiple access wireless communications networks, the bit error rate (BER) is often used as a QoS measure and, since the BER is directly linked to the signal to interference plus noise ratio (SINR), this parameter can be used as the QoS measurement. Hence, associating the SINR to the CIR at iteration t results:

$$\delta_i[t] = \frac{R_c}{R_i[t]} \times \Gamma_i[t], \qquad t = 0, 1, \ldots \mathcal{G} \tag{23}$$

where $\delta_i[t]$ is the SINR of user i at the tth iteration, R_c is the chip rate and approximately equal to the system's spreading bandwidth; $R_i[t]$ is the data rate for user i, $\Gamma_i[t]$ is the CIR for user i at iteration t, and $\mathcal{G}$ is the maximal number of iterations.

In multirate DS/CDMA systems with multiple processing gains (MPG), where each user class has a different processing gain $\mathsf{G} > 1$, defined as a function of the chip rate by

$$\mathsf{G}_i^\ell = \frac{R_c}{R_i^\ell}, \qquad \ell = 1, 2, \ldots, L, \tag{24}$$

where L is the number of total user's classes defined in the system (voice, data, video). Hence, in MPG-DS/CDMA multiple access systems, the SINR and CIR for the ℓth user's class are related to the processing gain of that service class: $\delta_i^\ell = \mathsf{G}_i^\ell \times \Gamma_i$.

From (23), the data rate for user i at iteration n can be calculated as:

$$R_i[t] = \frac{R_c}{\delta_i[t]} \times \Gamma_i[t], \qquad t = 0, 1, \ldots, \mathcal{G} \tag{25}$$

[5] In this chapter the term capacity is employed to express the total number of active users in the system.

The CIR for the ith user can be calculated as Elmusrati & Koivo (2003); Gross et al. (2010):

$$\Gamma_i[t] = \frac{p_i[t]g_{ii}[t]}{\sum_{\substack{j=1\\j\neq i}}^{K} p_j[t]g_{ij}[t] + \sigma^2}, \qquad i = 1, \ldots, K \tag{26}$$

where $p_i[t]$ is the power allocated to the ith user at iteration t and is bounded by $P_{\max}$, the channel gain (including path loss, fading and shadowing effects) between user j and user (or base station) i is identified by g_{ij}, K is the number of active users in the system (considering all user's classes), and $\sigma_i^2 = \sigma_j^2 = \sigma^2$ is the average power of the additive white Gaussian noise (AWGN) at the input of ith receiver, admitted identical for all users. Therefore, in DS/CDMA multirate systems the CIR relation to achieve the target rate can be calculated to each user class as follows Elmusrati et al. (2008):

$$\Gamma_{\min}^{\ell} = \frac{R_{\min}^{\ell}\delta^*}{R_c}, \qquad \ell = 1, \ldots, L \tag{27}$$

where $\Gamma_{\min}^{\ell}$ and $R_{\min}^{\ell}$ is the minimum CIR and minimum user rate[6] associated to the ℓth user class, respectively, δ^* is the minimum (or target) signal to noise ratio (SNR) to achieve minimum acceptable BER (or QoS). Besides, the power allocated to the kth user belonging to the ℓth class at nth iteration is

$$p_k^{\ell}[t], \qquad k = 1, \ldots, K_{\ell}; \quad \ell = 1, \ldots, L. \tag{28}$$

Hence, the total number of active users in the system is given by $K = K_1 \cup \ldots \cup K_{\ell} \cup \ldots \cup K_L$. Note that indexes associated to the K users are obtained by concatenation of ascending rates from different user's classes. Thus, K_1 identifies the lowest user's rate class, and K_L the highest.

The $K \times K$ channel gain matrix, considering path loss, shadowing and fading effects, between user j and user i (or base station) is given by

$$\mathbf{G} = \begin{bmatrix} g_{11} & g_{12} & \cdots & g_{1K} \\ g_{21} & g_{22} & \cdots & g_{2K} \\ \vdots & \vdots & \ddots & \vdots \\ g_{K1} & g_{K2} & \cdots & g_{KK} \end{bmatrix}, \tag{29}$$

which could be assumed static or even dynamically changing over the optimization window (T time slots).

Assuming multirate user classes, the classical power control problem can be adapted to achieve the target rates for each user, simply using the Shannon capacity relation between minimum CIR and target rate in each user class, resulting in

$$\Gamma_{k,\min}^{\ell} = 2^{\frac{R_{k,\min}^{\ell}}{R_c}} - 1 = 2^{r_{k,\min}^{\ell}} - 1 \tag{30}$$

[6] Or target rate, for single (fixed) rate systems.

where $r_{i,\min}^{\ell}$ is the normalized minimum capacity for the kth user from ℓth user class, expressed by bits/sec/Hz. This equation can be obtained directly from the Shannon capacity equation

$$r_{i,\min}(\mathbf{p}) = \log_2\left[1 + \Gamma_{i,\min}(\mathbf{p})\right] \tag{31}$$

Now, considering a $K \times K$ interference matrix $\mathbf{D}$, with

$$D_{ij} = \begin{cases} 0, & i = j; \\ \dfrac{\Gamma_{i,\min} g_{ji}}{g_{ii}}, & i \neq j; \end{cases} \tag{32}$$

where $\Gamma_{i,\min}$ can be obtained from (27), taking into account each rate class requirement and the column vector $\mathbf{u} = [u_1, u_2, \ldots, u_K]^T$, with elements

$$u_i = \frac{\Gamma_{i,\min}\sigma_i^2}{g_{ii}}, \tag{33}$$

the analytical optimal power vector allocation $\mathbf{p}^* = [p_1, p_2, \ldots, p_K]^T$ can be obtained simply by matrix inversion as:

$$\mathbf{p}^* = (\mathbf{I} - \mathbf{D})^{-1}\mathbf{u} \tag{34}$$

if and only if the maximum eigenvalue of $\mathbf{D}$ is smaller than 1 Seneta (1981); $\mathbf{I}$ is the $K \times K$ identity matrix. In this situation, the power control problem shows a feasible solution.

3.1.1 Fixed-rate power allocation criterion

The classical power allocation problem is extended to incorporate multi but fixed rate criterion in order to guarantee the target data rate per user class[7] while minimizing the total power consumption of mobile terminals. Mathematically, the optimization problem is expressed by:

$$\begin{aligned} \min \quad & \mathbf{p} = \left[p_1^1 \ldots p_{K_1}^1, \ldots, p_1^{\ell} \ldots p_{K_\ell}^{\ell}, \ldots, p_1^L \ldots p_{K_L}^L\right] \\ \text{s.t.} \quad & 0 < p_k^{\ell} \leq P_{\max} \\ & R^{\ell} = R_{\min}^{\ell}, \qquad \forall k \in K_{\ell}, \text{ and } \forall\, \ell = 1, 2, \ldots, L \end{aligned} \tag{35}$$

Under multirate environment, and in order to achieve the QoS to each user class, the recursive resource allocation update must be adapted to reach an equilibrium. Particularly, for power updating process, $\lim_{n\to\infty} p_i[n] = p_i^*$ when the power allocated to each user satisfies the target rate constraint given in (35). Hence, the recursive equation must be rewritten considering SINR per user class, via (23), in order to incorporate multirate scenario. The minimum CIR per user class is obtained directly by (27). In this way, considering the relation between CIR and SINR in a multirate DS/CDMA context, the following equation is employed in order to iteratively solve optimization problem of (35):

$$\begin{aligned} \delta_i[n] &= \mathrm{G}_i^{\ell} \times \Gamma_i[n] \\ &= \mathrm{G}_i^{\ell} \times \frac{p_i[n] g_{ii}[n]}{\sum\limits_{\substack{j=1 \\ j\neq i}}^{K} p_j[n] g_{ij}[n] + \sigma^2}, i = 1, \ldots, K \end{aligned} \tag{36}$$

[7] As a consequence, assure the QoS for each user.

where G_i is the spreading factor for the ith user:

$$\mathrm{G}_i = \frac{R_c}{R_i^\ell} \tag{37}$$

For all users from the same user class transmitting at the minimum (of fixed) rate per class, the spreading factor is given by:

$$\mathrm{G}_i = \frac{R_c}{R_{i,\min}^\ell} \tag{38}$$

Note that the CIR of ith user at the nth iteration is weighted by spreading factor; so the corresponding SINR is inversely proportional to the actual (minimum) rate of the ith user of the ℓth class.

Therefore, the single-objective optimization problem in (35) can be slightly modified as:

$$\begin{aligned} J_1(\mathbf{p}) = \min \ & \sum_{k=1}^{K} p_k \\ \text{s.t.} \ & \delta_k \geq \delta_k^*, \quad 0 < p_k^\ell \leq P_{\max}, \quad \text{and} \quad R^\ell = R_{\min}^\ell \\ & \forall k \in K_\ell, \text{ and } \forall\, \ell = 1, 2, \ldots, L \end{aligned} \tag{39}$$

or alternatively, the min-max version of (39) could be obtained:

$$\begin{aligned} J_1(\mathbf{p}) = \min \ & \max_{k=1,\ldots,K} p_k \\ \text{s.t.} \ & \delta_k \geq \delta_k^*, \quad 0 < p_k^\ell \leq P_{\max}, \quad \text{and} \quad R^\ell = R_{\min}^\ell \\ & \forall k \in K_\ell, \text{ and } \forall\, \ell = 1, 2, \ldots, L \end{aligned} \tag{40}$$

Based on the work of Moustafa et al. (2000), and further results of Elkamchouchi et al. (2007), the above single-objective function could be modified in order to incorporate the near-far aspect; hence the following maximization cost function could be employed as an alternative:

$$\begin{aligned} J_1(\mathbf{p}) = \max \ & \frac{1}{K} \sum_{k=1}^{K} \mathcal{F}_k^{\text{th}} \left(1 - \frac{p_k}{P_{\max}}\right) + \frac{\rho}{\sigma_{\text{rp}}} \\ \text{s.t.} \ & \delta_k \geq \delta_k^*, \quad 0 < p_k^\ell \leq P_{\max}, \quad \text{and} \quad R^\ell = R_{\min}^\ell \\ & \forall k \in K_\ell, \text{ and } \forall\, \ell = 1, 2, \ldots, L \end{aligned} \tag{41}$$

where the term $\frac{\rho}{\sigma_{rp}^2}$ gives credit to the solutions with small standard deviation of the normalized (by the inverse of rate factor, G^ℓ) received power distribution:

$$\sigma_{\text{rp}}^2 = \text{var}\left(\mathrm{G}^1 p_1 g_{11}, \mathrm{G}^1 p_2 g_{22}, \ldots, \mathrm{G}^\ell p_k g_{kk}, \ldots, \mathrm{G}^L p_k g_{KK}\right), \tag{42}$$

i.e. the more close the normalized received power values are with other (i.e., small variance of normalized received power vector), the bigger this term. For single-rate DS/CDMA systems, $\mathrm{G}^1 = \ldots = \mathrm{G}^\ell = \ldots = \mathrm{G}^L$.

It is worth to note that since the variance of the normalized received power vector, σ_{rp}^2, normally assumes very small values, the coefficient ρ just also take very small values in order to the ratio $\rho/\sigma_{\rm rp}$ achieves a similar order of magnitude of the first term in (41), and will be determined as a function of the number of users, K, and cell geometry (basically, the cell radius). Hence, the term $\rho/\sigma_{\rm rp}$ has an effective influence in minimizing the near-far effect on CDMA systems, and at the same time it has a non-zero value for all swarm particles Elkamchouchi et al. (2007). Besides, the threshold function in (41) is defined as:

$$\mathcal{F}_k^{th} = \begin{cases} 1, & \delta_k \geq \delta^* \\ 0, & \text{otherwise} \end{cases}$$

with the SINR for the kth user, δ_k, given by (36), and the term $1 - \frac{p_k}{P_{\max}}$ gives credit to solutions that use minimum power and punishes others using high levels Moustafa et al. (2000; 2001a;b).

3.1.2 Throughput maximization for multirate systems under power constraint

The aiming herein is to incorporate multirate criterion with throughput maximization for users with different QoS, while the power consumption constraint at mobile terminals is bounded by a specific value at each user. As a result, the optimization problem can be formulated as a special case of generalized linear fractional programming (GLFP) Phuong & Tuy (2003). So, the following optimization problem can be posed

$$\begin{aligned} \max \quad & \prod_{i=1}^{K} \left[\frac{f_i(\mathbf{p})}{g_i(\mathbf{p})}\right]^{w_i} \qquad (43) \\ \text{s.t.} \quad & 0 < p_i^\ell \leq P_{\max}; \\ & \frac{f_i(\mathbf{p})}{g_i(\mathbf{p})} \geq 2^{r_{i,\min}^\ell}, \qquad \forall i \in K_\ell, \text{ and } \forall\, \ell = 1, 2, \cdots L \end{aligned}$$

where $r_{i,\min}^\ell \geq 0$ is the minimum normalized (by CDMA system bandwidth, R_c) data rate requirement of ith link, including the zero-rate constraint case; and $w_i > 0$ is the priory weight for the ith user to transmit with minimum data rate and QoS guarantees, assumed normalized, so that $\sum_{i=1}^K w_i = 1$. Moreover, note that the second constraint in (43) is obtained directly from (30), (26), and (23), where the minimum data rate constraints was transformed into minimum SINR constraints through Shannon capacity equation

$$R_i = R_c \log_2 \left[1 + \theta^{\text{BER}_i} \mathrm{G}_i^\ell \times p_i g_{ii} \times \left(\sum_{j \neq i}^{K} p_j g_{ij} + \sigma^2\right)^{-1}\right], \qquad (44)$$

for $i = 1, \ldots, K$, with $\theta^{\text{BER}_i} = -\frac{1.5}{\log(5\,\text{BER}_i)}$, BER_i is the maximal allowed bit error rate for user i,

$$f_i(\mathbf{p}) = \theta^{\text{BER}_i} \mathrm{G}_i^\ell \times p_i g_{ii} + \sum_{\substack{j=1 \\ j \neq i}}^{K} p_j g_{ij} + \sigma^2, \text{ and } \quad g_i(\mathbf{p}) = \sum_{\substack{j=1 \\ j \neq i}}^{K} p_j g_{ij} + \sigma^2 \qquad (45)$$

for $i = 1, \ldots, K$. The objective function in (43) is a product of exponentiated linear fractional functions, and the function $\Pi_{i=1}^K (z_i)^{w_i}$ is an increasing function on K-dimensional nonnegative real domain Li Ping Qian (2009). Furthermore, the optimization problem (43) can be rewritten using the basic property of the logarithmic function, resulting in

$$\begin{aligned} J(\mathbf{p}) = \max \sum_{i=1}^{K} w_i \left[\log_2 f_i(\mathbf{p}) - \log_2 g_i(\mathbf{p})\right] &= \max \sum_{i=1}^{K} w_i \left[\widetilde{f}_i(\mathbf{p}) - \widetilde{g}_i(\mathbf{p})\right] \\ \text{s.t.} \; 0 < p_i^{\ell} \leq P_{\max}; & \\ \widetilde{f}_i(\mathbf{p}) - \widetilde{g}_i(\mathbf{p}) \geq r_{i,\min}^{\ell}, & \quad \forall i \in K_{\ell}, \; \ell = 1, 2, \cdots L \end{aligned} \tag{46}$$

3.1.3 Quality of solution × convergence speed

The quality of solution achieved by any iterative resource allocation procedure could be measured by how close to the optimum solution is the found solution, and can be quantified by means of the normalized mean squared error (NMSE) when equilibrium is reached. For power allocation problem, the NMSE definition is given by

$$NSE[t] = \mathbb{E}\left[\frac{\|\mathbf{p}[t] - \mathbf{p}^*\|^2}{\|\mathbf{p}^*\|^2}\right], \tag{47}$$

where $\|\cdot\|^2$ denotes the squared Euclidean distance to the origin, and $\mathbb{E}[\cdot]$ the expectation operator.

3.2 Continuous PSO algorithm for resource allocation wireless networks

In this section, a different approach for throughput maximization under power constraint problems, described by (46) will be considered using swarm intelligence optimization method Kennedy & Eberhart (2001). Single-objective optimization (SOO) approach was adopted. The convexation of the original multi-class throughput maximization problem, obtained in (46), is employed hereafter as cost function for the PSO.

The problem described in (46) indicated an optimization developed in the $\mathbb{R}$ set. Hence, in the PSO strategy, each candidate power-vector defined as $\mathbf{b}_p[t]$, of size[8] K, is used for the velocity calculation of next iteration

$$\mathbf{v}_p[t+1] = \omega[t] \cdot \mathbf{v}_p[t] + \phi_1 \cdot \mathbf{U}_{p_1}[t](\mathbf{b}_p^{\text{best}}[t] - \mathbf{b}_p[t]) + \phi_2 \cdot \mathbf{U}_{p_2}[t](\mathbf{b}_g^{\text{best}}[t] - \mathbf{b}_p[t]) \tag{48}$$

where $\omega[t]$ is the inertia weight of the previous velocity in the present speed calculation; $\mathbf{U}_{p_1}[t]$ and $\mathbf{U}_{p_2}[t]$ are diagonal matrices with dimension K, and elements are random variables with uniform distribution $\sim \mathcal{U} \in [0,1]$, generated for the pth particle at iteration $t = 1, 2, \ldots, \mathcal{G}$; $\mathbf{b}_g^{\text{best}}[t]$ and $\mathbf{b}_p^{\text{best}}[t]$ are the best global position and the best local positions found until the tth iteration, respectively; ϕ_1 and ϕ_2 are acceleration coefficients regarding the best particles and the best global positions influences in the velocity update, respectively.

The particle(s) selection for evolving under power-multirate adaptation strategy is based on the lowest fitness values satisfying the constraints in (46). The pth particle's position at iteration t is a power candidate-vector $\mathbf{b}_p[t]$ of size $K \times 1$. The position of each particle is updated using the new velocity vector (48) for that particle

$$\mathbf{b}_p[t+1] = \mathbf{b}_p[t] + \mathbf{v}_p[t+1], \qquad i = 1, \ldots, \mathcal{P} \tag{49}$$

[8] Remember, as defined previously, for multirate power optimization problem: $K = K_1 \cup \ldots \cup K_{\ell} \cup \ldots \cup K_L$.

The PSO algorithm consists of repeated application of the update velocity and position update equations. A pseudo-code for the single-objective continuous PSO power-multirate allocation problem is presented in Algorithm 2.

Algorithm 2 SOO Continuous PSO Algorithm for the Power-Multirate Allocation Problem

Input: $\mathcal{P}, \mathcal{G}, \omega, \phi_1, \phi_2, V_{\max}$; **Output:** $\mathbf{p}^*$
begin
1. initialize first population: $t = 0$;
   $\mathbf{B}[0] \sim \mathcal{U}[P_{\min}; P_{\max}]$
   $\mathbf{b}_p^{\text{best}}[0] = \mathbf{b}_p[0]$ and $\mathbf{b}_g^{\text{best}}[0] = \mathbf{P}_{\max}$;
   $\mathbf{v}_p[0] = \mathbf{0}$: null initial velocity;
2. while $n \leq N$
   a. calculate $J(\mathbf{b}_p[t]), \forall \mathbf{b}_p[t] \in \mathbf{B}[t]$ using (46);
   b. update velocity $\mathbf{v}_p[t],\ p = 1, \ldots, \mathcal{P}$, through (48);
   c. update best positions:
      for $p = 1, \ldots, \mathcal{P}$
         if $J(\mathbf{b}_p[t]) < J(\mathbf{b}_p^{\text{best}}[t]) \wedge R_p[t] \geq r_{p,\min}$,
            $\mathbf{b}_p^{\text{best}}[t+1] \leftarrow \mathbf{b}_p[t]$
         else $\mathbf{b}_p^{\text{best}}[t+1] \leftarrow \mathbf{b}_p^{\text{best}}[t]$
      end
      if $\exists\ \mathbf{b}_p[t]$ such that $\left[J(\mathbf{b}_p[t]) < J(\mathbf{b}_g^{\text{best}}[t])\right] \wedge R_p[t] \geq r_{p,\min}$
         $\wedge \left[J(\mathbf{b}_p[t]) \leq J(\mathbf{b}'_p[n]),\ \forall p' \neq p\right]$,
         $\mathbf{b}_g^{\text{best}}[t+1] \leftarrow \mathbf{b}_p[t]$
      else $\mathbf{b}_g^{\text{best}}[t+1] \leftarrow \mathbf{b}_g^{\text{best}}[t]$
   d. Evolve to a new swarm population $\mathbf{B}[t+1]$, using (46);
   e. set $t = t + 1$.
   end
3. $\mathbf{p}^* = \mathbf{b}_g^{\text{best}}[\mathcal{G}]$.
end

- -

$\mathcal{P}$: population size.
$\mathbf{B} = [\mathbf{b}_1, \ldots, \mathbf{b}_p, \ldots, \mathbf{b}_{\mathcal{P}}]$ particle population matrix, dimension $K \times \mathcal{P}$.
$\mathcal{G}$: maximum number of swarm iterations.
$\mathbf{P}_{\max}$: maximum power vector considering each mobile terminal rate class.

In order to reduce the likelihood that the particle might leave the search universe, maximum velocity $V_{\max}$ factor is added to the PSO model (48), which will be responsible for limiting the velocity in the range $[\pm V_{\max}]$. The adjustment of velocity allows the particle to move in a continuous but constrained subspace, been simply accomplished by

$$v_p[t] = \min\left\{V_{\max};\ \max\left\{-V_{\max};\ v_p[t]\right\}\right\} \tag{50}$$

From (50) it's clear that if $|v_p[t]|$ exceeds a positive constant value $V_{\max}$ specified by the user, the pth particle' velocity is assigned to be $\text{sign}(v_p[t])V_{\max}$, i.e. particles velocity on each of $K-$dimension is clamped to a maximum magnitude $V_{\max}$. If the search space could be defined by the bounds $[P_{\min}; P_{\max}]$, then the value of $V_{\max}$ will be typically set so that $V_{\max} = \tau(P_{\max} - P_{\min})$, where $0.1 \leq \tau \leq 1.0$, please refer to Chapter 1 within the definition of reference Nedjah & Mourelle (2006).

To elaborate further about the inertia weight it can be noted that a relatively larger value of w is helpful for global optimum, and lesser influenced by the best global and local positions[9], while a relatively smaller value for w is helpful for convergence, i.e., smaller inertial weight encourages the local exploration as the particles are more attracted towards $\mathbf{b}_p^{\text{best}}$ and $\mathbf{b}_g^{\text{best}}$ Eberhart & Shi (2001); Shi & Eberhart (1998).
Hence, in order to achieve a balance between global and local search abilities, a linear inertia weight decreasing with the algorithm evolving, having good global search capability at beginning and good local search capability latter, was adopted herein

$$w[n] = (w_{\text{initial}} - w_{\text{final}}) \cdot \left(\frac{N-n}{N}\right)^m + w_{\text{final}} \tag{51}$$

where w_{initial} and w_{final} is the initial and final weight inertia, respectively, $w_{\text{initial}} > w_{\text{final}}$, N is the maximum number of iterations, and $m \in [0.6; 1.4]$ is the nonlinear modulation index Chatterjee & Siarry (2006).

3.2.1 PSO Parameters optimization for resource allocation problem

For power-rate resource allocation problem, simulation experiments were carried out in order to determine the suitable values for the PSO input parameters, such as acceleration coefficients, ϕ_1 and ϕ_2, maximal velocity factor, V_{max}, weight inertia, ω, and population size, $\mathcal{P}$, regarding the throughput multirate optimization problem.
Under discrete optimization problems, such as DS/CDMA multiuser detection, it is known that fast PSO convergence without losing certain exploration and exploitation capabilities could be obtained increasing the parameter ϕ_2 Oliveira et al. (2006) while holding ϕ_1 into the low range values. However, for the continuous optimization problem investigated herein, numerical results presented in Section 3.3.1 indicate that after an enough number of iterations ($\mathcal{G}$) for convergence, the maximization of cost function were obtained within low values for both acceleration coefficients.
The V_{max} factor is then optimized. The diversity increases as the particle velocity crosses the limits established by $[\pm V_{\text{max}}]$. The range of V_{max} determines the maximum change one particle can take during iteration. Without inertial weight ($w = 1$), Eberhart and Shi Eberhart & Shi (2001) found that the maximum allowed velocity V_{max} is best set around 10 to 20% of the dynamic range of each particle dimension. The appropriate choose of V_{max} avoids particles flying out of meaningful solution space. Herein, for multirate DS/CDMA rate allocation problem, a non exhaustive search has indicated that the better performance$\times$complexity trade-off was obtained setting the maximal velocity factor value to $V_{\text{max}} = 0.2 \times (P_{\text{max}} - P_{\text{min}})$.
For the inertial weight, ω, simulation results has confirmed that high values imply in fast convergence, but this means a lack of search diversity, and the algorithm can easily be trapped in some local optimum, whereas a small value for ω results in a slow convergence due to excessive changes around a very small search space. In this work, it was adopted a variable ω, as described in (51), but with $m = 1$, and initial and final weight inertia setting up to $w_{\text{initial}} = 1$ and $w_{\text{final}} = 0.01$. Hence, the initial and final maximal velocity excursion values

[9] Analogous to the idea of the phenomenon that it is difficult to diverge heavier objects in their flight trajectory than the lighter ones.

were bounded through the initial and final linear inertia weight multiplied by $V_{\rm m}$, adopted as a percentage of the maximal and minimal power difference values

$$w_{\rm initial} \times V_{\rm max} = 0.2\,(P_{\rm max} - P_{\rm min}), \qquad \text{and} \qquad w_{\rm final} \times V_{\rm max} = 0.002\,(P_{\rm max} - P_{\rm min}) \quad (52)$$

Finally, stopping criterion can be the maximum number of iterations (velocity changes allowed for each particle) or reaching the minimum error threshold, e.g.,

$$\left| \frac{J[t] - J[t-1]}{J[t]} \right| < \epsilon_{\rm stop} \quad (53)$$

where typically $\epsilon_{\rm stop} \in [0.001; 0.01]$.
Alternately, the convergence test can be evaluated through the computation of the average percent of success[10], taken over T runs to achieve the global optimum, and considering a fixed number of iterations N. A test is considered 100% successful if the following relation holds:

$$|J[\mathcal{G}] - J[\mathbf{p}^*]| < \epsilon_1 J[\mathbf{p}^*] + \epsilon_2 \quad (54)$$

where, $J[\mathbf{p}^*]$ is the global optimum of the objective function under consideration, $J[\mathcal{G}]$ is the optimum of the objective function obtained by the algorithm after N iterations, and ϵ_1, ϵ_2 are accuracy coefficients, usually in the range $[10^{-6}; 10^{-2}]$. In this study it was assumed that $TR = 100$ trials and $\epsilon_1 = \epsilon_2 = 10^{-2}$.

3.3 Numerical results

In order to validate the proposed swarm optimization approach in solving resource allocation problems on multiple access CDMA wireless networks, simulations were carried out with system parameters indicated in Table 5. In all simulation results discussed in this section, it was assumed a retangular multicell geometry with a number of base station (BS) equal to 4 and mobile terminals (mt) uniformly distributed over $25Km^2$ area. Besides, the initial rate assignment for all multirate users was admitted discretely and uniformly distributed over three chip rate submultiple, $R_{\rm min} = [\frac{1}{128}; \frac{1}{32}; \frac{1}{16}]R_c$ [bps].
A number of mobile terminals ranging from $K = 5$ to 250 was considered, which experiment slow fading channels, i.e., the following relation is always satisfied

$$T_{\rm slot} < (\Delta t)_c \quad (55)$$

where $T_{\rm slot} = R_{\rm slot}^{-1}$ is the time slot duration, $R_{\rm slot}$ is the transmitted power vector update rate, and $(\Delta t)_c$ is the coherence time of the channel[11]. This condition is part of the SINR estimation process, and it implies that each power updating accomplished by the DPCA happens with rate of $R_{\rm slot}$, assumed here equal to 1500 updates per second.
The optimization process $J(\mathbf{p})$ in (46) should converge to the optimum point before each channel gain g_{ij} experiments significant changing. Note that satisfying (55) the gain matrices remain approximately static during one convergence process interval, i.e., 666.7μs.
In all of the simulations the entries values for the QoS targets were fixed in $\delta^* = 4$ dB, the adopted receiver noise power for all users is $P_n = -63$ dBm, and the gain matrix $\mathbf{G}$ have intermediate values between those used in Uykan & Koivo (2004.) and Elmusrati et al. (2008).

[10] In terms of the PSO algorithm achieves full convergence.

[11] Corresponds to the time interval in which the channel characteristics do not suffer expressive variations.

Parameters	Adopted Values
DS/CDMA Power-Rate Allocation System	
Noise Power	$P_n = -63$ [dBm]
Chip rate	$R_c = 3.84 \times 10^6$
Min. Signal-noise ratio	$SNR_{\min} = 4$ dB
Max. power per user	$P_{\max} \in [30, 35]$ [dBm]
Min. Power per user	$P_{\min} = SNR_{\min} + P_n$ [dBm]
Time slot duration	$T_{\text{slot}} = 666.7\mu$s or $R_{\text{slot}} = 1500$ slots/s
# mobile terminals	$K \in [5, 250]$
# base station	BS $= 4$
Cell geometry	rectangular, with $x_{\text{cell}} = y_{\text{cell}} = 5$ Km
Mobile term. distrib.	$\sim \mathcal{U}[x_{\text{cell}}, y_{\text{cell}}]$
Fading Channel Type	
Path loss	$\propto d^{-2}$
Shadowing	uncorrelated log-normal, $\sigma^2 = 6$ dB
Fading	Rice: [0.6; 0.4]
Max. Doppler freq.	$f_{D\max} = 11.1$ Hz
Time selectivity	slow
User Types	
# user classes	$L = 3$ (voice, video, data)
User classes Rates	$R_{\min} = [\frac{1}{128}; \frac{1}{32}; \frac{1}{16}]R_c$ [bps]
User classes BER	$\theta^{\text{BER}} = [5 \times 10^{-3}; 5 \times 10^{-5}; 5 \times 10^{-8}]$
Swarm Power-Rate Algorithm	
Accel. Coefs.	$\phi_1 = 1$ $\phi_2 = 2$
Max. veloc. factor	$V_{\text{m}} = 0.2 \times (P_{\max} - P_{\min})$
Weight inertia (linear decay)	$w_{\text{initial}} = 1$; $w_{\text{final}} = 0.01$
Population Size	$\mathcal{P} = K + 2$
Max. # iterations	$\mathcal{G} \in [500, 2000]$
Simulation Parameter	
Trials number	$TR = 1000$ samples

Table 5. Multirate DS/CDMA system parameters

Finally, the PSO resource allocation performance analysis was characterized considering static channels condition. In this scenario, the channel coefficients remain constant during all the convergence process (N iterations), i.e., for a time interval equal or bigger than T_{slot}. However, the extension of the presented numerical results to dynamic channels is straightforward.

3.3.1 Numerical results for the multirate SOO throughput maximization

A parameters analysis was done in order to determine the best combination of ϕ_1 and ϕ_2 parameters under multirate SOO throughput maximization problem. Simulations were carried out using the same configuration, i.e., channel conditions, number of users in the system, users QoS requirements and users services classes.

Table 6 and Fig. 16 illustrate the different solution qualities in terms of cost function value, when different values for ϕ_1 and ϕ_2 are combined in a system with $K = 5$ users. The average cost function values where taken as the average over 1000 trials. Furthermore, the cost function values showed in Table 6 were obtained at the 1000th iteration. User's rates were assigned following just one class rate: $R_{\min} = \frac{1}{128} R_c$ [bps].

From Table 6 and Fig. 16 it is clear that for $K = 5$ users the parameters $\phi_1 = 2$ and $\phi_2 = 1$ result in an average cost function value higher than other configurations at the 1000th iteration. Thus, the use of this parameters for a small system loading is the best in terms of rate-power

(ϕ_1, ϕ_2)	(1,2)	(2,1)	(2,2)	(4,2)	(2,8)	(8,2)
$J[\mathcal{G}]$	4.2866	4.3131	4.2833	4.3063	4.2532	4.3091

$\mathcal{G} = 1000$ Its, average value taken over 1000 trials.

Table 6. Acceleration coefficients choice for $K = 5$ users, single-rate problem.

allocation optimization problem. It is worth to note that the differences between the results shown in Table 6 are equivalent to a sum rate difference raging from $\Delta\Sigma_R = 60$ kbps to $\Delta\Sigma_R =$ 670 kbps, Fig. 16.

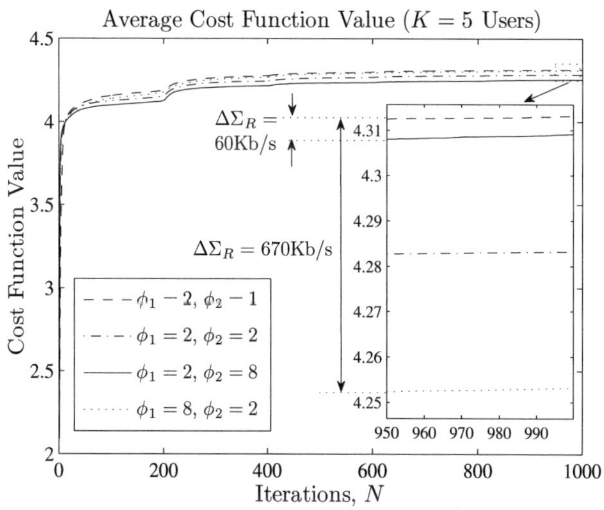

Fig. 16. Cost function evolution through 1000 iterations, averaged over 1000 realizations. $K = 5$ users under the same channel conditions for different ϕ_1 and ϕ_2 parameters.

Figures 17.a) and 17.b) show typical sum rate and sum power allocation evolution through iterations with $K = 20$ users, $\phi_1 = 2$ and $\phi_2 = 1$ and population size $M = K + 2$. Observe that the power allocation updates after $\approx$ 385th iteration are almost insignificant in terms of sum rate values. This happens due to the small increments on each user rate, ranging from 1 to 10 Kbps, when compared to the system throughput.

The proposed algorithm has been found robust under a high number of multirate active users in the system. Figures 18.a) and 18.b) show typical sum rate and sum power allocation evolution through iterations for $K = 100$ users. As expected, the algorithm needs more iterations to achieve convergence (around 500 iterations), regarding to $K = 20$ users case, but the gain in terms of throughput increasing combined to power reduction after optimization is significant.

Additionally, a small increase in the maximum power per user, i.e. from 30dBm to 35dBm, allows the algorithm to easily find a solution to the throughput optimization problem for a huge system loading, i.e 250 multirate users in a $25Km^2$ rectangular cell geometry. Figures 19.a) and 19.b show a typical sum power and sum rate evolution through iterations for $K = 250$ users. Observe that the algorithm achieves convergence around 750 iterations, which implies that convergence speed, in terms of iterations, grows with the number of active users in the system.

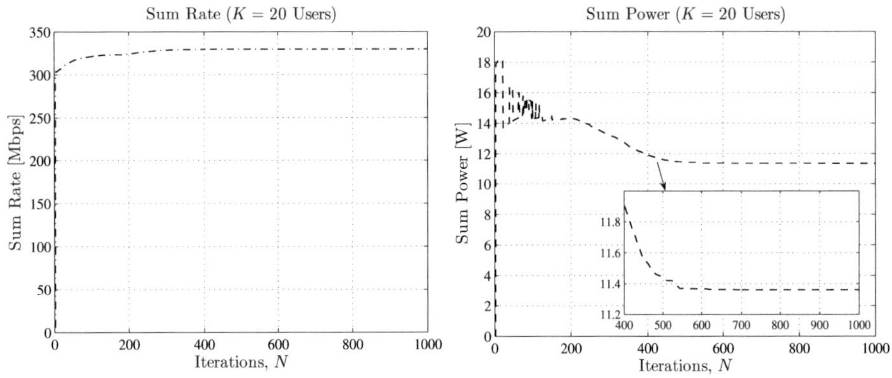

Fig. 17. Typical a) sum rate and b) sum power evolution with $\phi_1 = 1, \phi_2 = 2$, and $K = 20$ users.

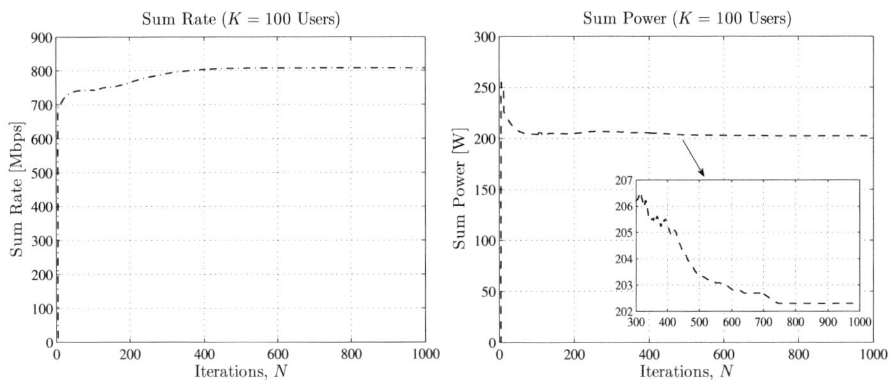

Fig. 18. Typical a) sum rate and b) sum power evolution with $\phi_1 = 1, \phi_2 = 2$, and $K = 100$ users.

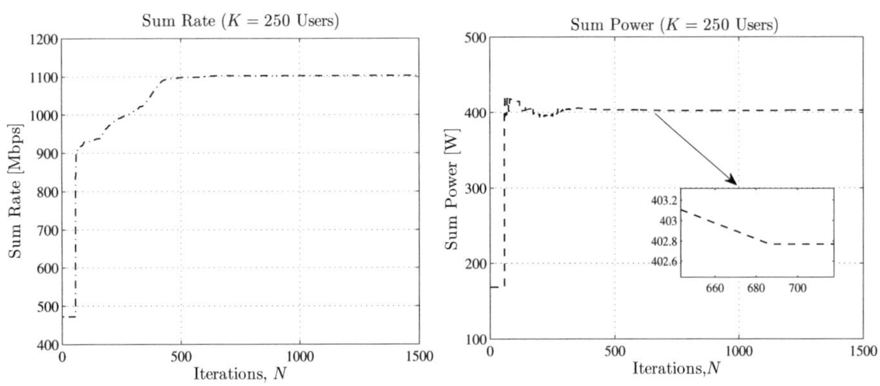

Fig. 19. Typical a) sum rate and b) sum power evolution with, $\phi_1 = 1, \phi_2 = 2$, $P_{\max} = 35$dBm per user, and $K = 250$ users.

3.3.2 Numerical results for the multirate fixed-rate power minimization

In the following subsections there will be discussed aspects of parameters optimization for the obtained simulation results, also presented herein.

3.3.2.1 Convergence aspects: ϕ_1 and ϕ_2 optimization

Simulation experiments were carried out in order to determine a good choice for acceleration coefficients ϕ_1 and ϕ_2 regarding the power multirate optimization problem. Table 7 illustrates different solution qualities in terms of the NMSE, when different values for ϕ_1 and ϕ_2 are combining in a system with different number of users K. Systems with single-rate and multi-rate as well were considered. The NMSE values where taken as the average over 100 trials. Besides, the NMSE convergence values were taken after $N = 800$ iterations for single-rate (SR) systems with $K = 25$ users, and $N = 1000$ iterations for multi-rate (MR) systems with $K = 10$ users. User's rates were randomly assigned following three classes rate: $R_{\min} = [\frac{1}{128}; \frac{1}{32}; \frac{1}{16}]R_c$ [bps].

Note that for multi-rate scenarios the optimal acceleration coefficient values change. Hence, considering the solution quality, it was found $\phi_1 = 1.2$ and $\phi_2 = 0.6$ for single-rate power optimization problem, and $\phi_1 = 2$ and $\phi_2 = 2$ for multi-rate systems high dimensional ($K \geq 10$) power optimization. For $K < 10$ the best convergence $\times$ solution quality trade-off was achieved with $\phi_1 = 1$ and $\phi_2 = 2$.

(ϕ_1, ϕ_2)	$(1.2, 0.6)$	$(2,2)$	$(6,2)$	$(8,2)$	$(1,2)$	$(0.8,2)$
$NMSE_{\text{SR}}$	$10^{-1.5}$	$10^{-1.2}$	$10^{0.75}$	$10^{2.25}$	10^{-1}	$10^{-0.9}$
$NMSE_{\text{MR}}$	$10^{0.9}$	$10^{-1.3}$	10^{2}	$10^{2.1}$	$10^{-0.8}$	10^{-1}

SR: $N = 800$ Its; $K = 25$ users; MR: $N = 1000$ Its; $K = 10$ users

Table 7. Coarse optimization results for ϕ_1 and ϕ_2 parameters considering single-rate (SR) and multi-rate (MR) systems.

Results have shown that the algorithm achieves convergence to the optimal (analytical) solution for a wide range of number of users, cell geometries and channel conditions. Figure 20 shows the P_g^{best} vector evolution through the 800 iterations for two different acceleration coefficient configurations under $K = 5$ users. The algorithm reaches convergence around 550-600 iterations for the left graphs and 350-375 iterations under $\phi_1 = 1.0$, $\phi_2 = 2.0$ (right). Simulations revealed that increasing ϕ_2 or reducing $\phi_1 < 1.0$ causes the non-convergence of the algorithms. Additionally, parameters $\phi_1 = 1.0$ and $\phi_2 = 2.0$ result in an $\approx 45\%$ faster convergence when compared to parameters $\phi_1 = 2.0$, $\phi_2 = 2.0$. In the other hand the NMSE and the normalized square error (NSE)[12] for faster convergence is higher than for the slower convergence parameters.

Additionally, for low-medium system loading ($K < 10$ users) further simulations revealed that parameters $\phi_1 = 1.0$ and $\phi_2 = 2.0$ result in an $\approx 45\%$ faster convergence when compared to parameters $\phi_1 = 2.0$, $\phi_2 = 2.0$. However, when $K > 13$, Figure 21 shows that the best values for the local and global acceleration factors are $\phi_1 = 1$ and $\phi_2 = 2$, while for $K \leq 13$ the best combination confirms the values $\phi_1 = 2$ and $\phi_2 = 2$. Besides, the NSE for $K > 20$ users is almost constant, increasing slowly (low slope) when compared with the NMSE slope for the range $5 \leq K \leq 20$.

[12] Or instantaneous NMSE.

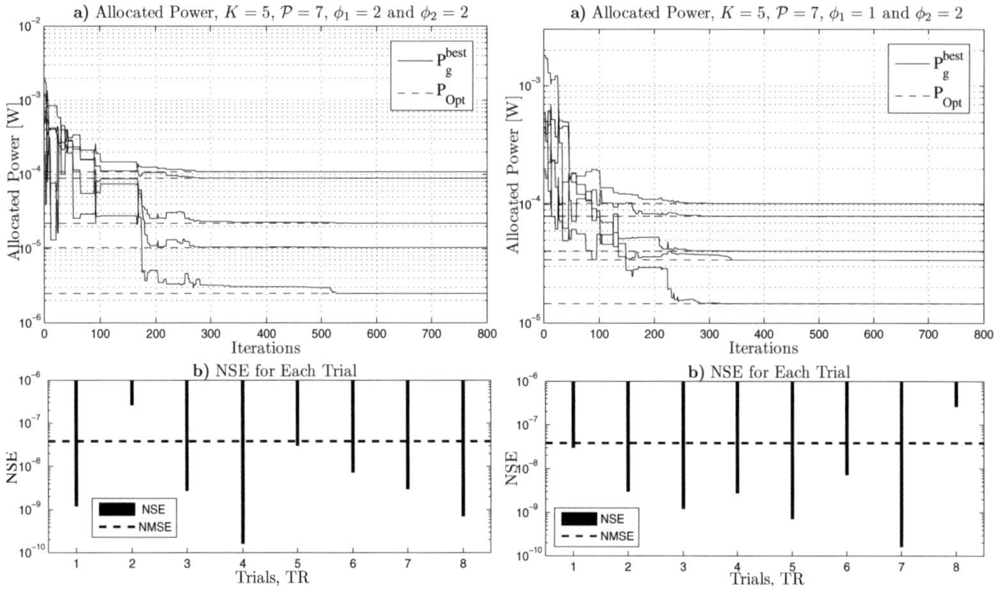

Fig. 20. Typical power convergence (**a**), NSE and NMSE (**b**). Random P_{initial} and channel realization for $K = 5$ users swarm power optimization. Same channel conditions throughout the $T = 10$ trials. Swarm population size, $M = K + 2$. Multi-rate case. Left) $\phi_1 = \phi_2 = 2$; Right) $\phi_1 = 1.0, \phi_2 = 2.0$

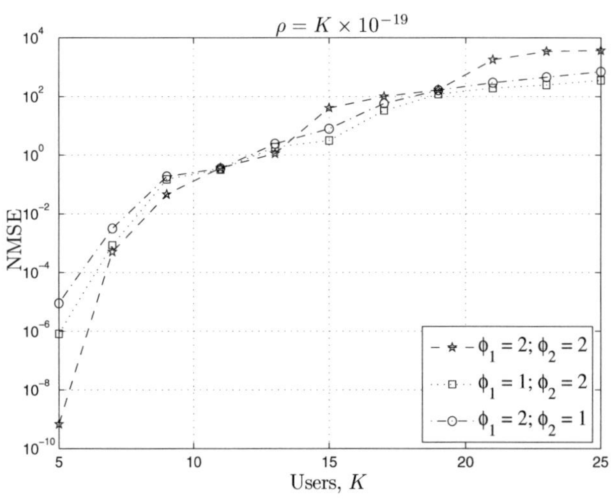

Fig. 21. Average $NMSE$ over 100 samples, $K \in [5, 25]$ for different ϕ_1 and ϕ_2. Multi-rate scenarios. $N = 1000$ iterations.

On the other hand, in terms of convergence test, as defined by eq. (54), and assuming $\epsilon_1 = \epsilon_2 = 10^{-2}$, Table 8 shows that the PSO algorithm achieves faster convergence (under this criterium) with $\phi_1 = 1$ and $\phi_2 = 2$ for any $K \in [5, 20]$ users.

K multirate users	5	10	15	20
$\mathcal{G}$ Iterations	500	600	1000	1800
$\phi_1 = 1, \phi_2 = 2$	108	301	420	488
$\phi_1 = 2, \phi_2 = 1$	127	479	526	696
$\phi_1 = 2, \phi_2 = 2$	263	591	697	757

Table 8. Convergence Results in Multirate Scenario, under (54) and $\epsilon_1 = \epsilon_2 = 10^{-2}$.

In conclusion, the numerical results for the power minimization with randomly user's rate assignment problem have revealed for high system loading that the best acceleration coefficient values lie on $\phi_1 = 1$ and $\phi_2 = 2$, in terms of convergence and solution quality trade-off. For low system loading the parameters choice $\phi_1 = 2$ and $\phi_2 = 2$ results in the best solution quality.

3.3.2.2 Power allocation overhead regards to ϕ_1 and ϕ_2

In order to corroborate the best values choice for the acceleration factors, Figure 22 shows the total system power allocation under typical channel situations, i.e., deep fading, as a function of number of multirate users, parameterized by ϕ_1 and ϕ_2. The algorithm performance in terms of minimal total power consumption for $K > 13$ is achieved with $\phi_1 = 1.0$ and $\phi_2 = 2.0$. As already mentioned, other combinations of ϕ_1 and ϕ_2 results in higher total power consumption.

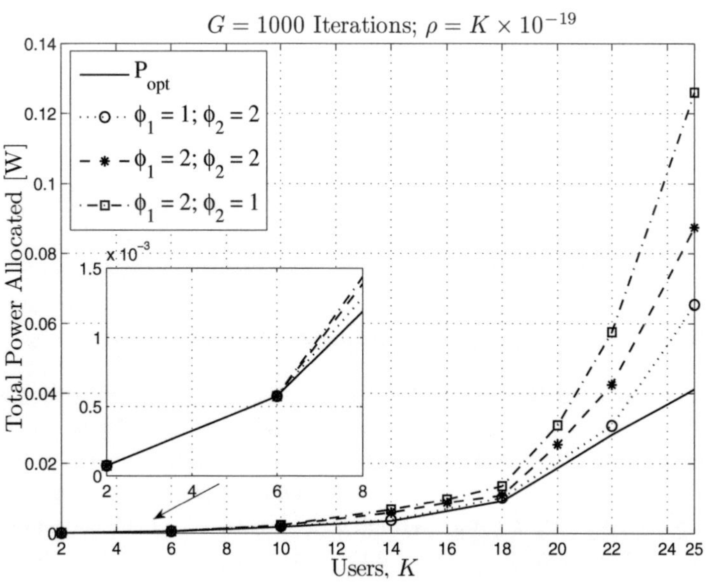

Fig. 22. System power allocation for different ϕ_1 and ϕ_2 parameters. $K \in [2, 25]$, 1000 iterations limit, Single Rate case with $R_{\min} = \frac{1}{128} R_c$.

3.3.2.3 ρ Optimization

The parameter ρ in cost function (41), was set as a function of the number of users K, such that $\rho = K \times 10^{-19}$. This relation was found based on the value suggested in Elkamchouchi et al. (2007) and adapted for the power-rate allocation problem through an non-exhaustive search. For different number of users, Figure 23 indicates the evolution of the standard deviation of the hypothetical received power vector, σ_{rp}, given by the PSO solution at the Nth iteration multiplied by the respective channel gain, $\mathbf{p}_{\text{g}}^{\text{best}}\,\text{diag}(\mathbf{G})$. The σ_{rp} results of Figure 23 were obtained averaging over 1000 initial swarm population (admitted uniformly distributed over $[P_{\text{min}}; P_{\text{max}}]$) and a single channel realization. Hence the σ_{rp} values give us a good idea about the received power disparities (near-far reduction) when the swarm optimization evolves. As a consequence, the ρ values and its direct dependence (increasing) with the number of users could be established.

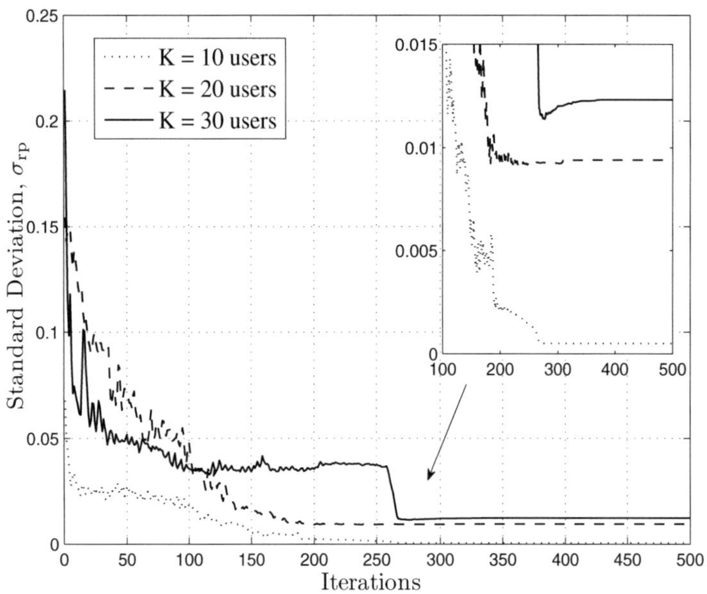

Fig. 23. Average standard deviation curves of the hypothetical received power vector, σ_{rp}, as a function of the number of iteration. Average over 1000 initial swarm population (admitted uniformly distributed over $[P_{\text{min}}; P_{\text{max}}]$), and single channel realization.

Figure 24 shows how hard is to solve the power allocation problem associated to the cost function in (41) on the $\mathbb{R}^K$ space. In this particular channel condition, the optimal power allocation solution and the cost function global maximum are not the same points. This happens due to the presence of users with poor channel conditions, e.g. user far away from the base station combined to deep fading channel. In this cases it is better drop the users (outage) under bad channel conditions than rise the total system power consumption to keep those users active on the system.

4. Conclusions

This chapter discusses the application of search heuristic approaches in solving different optimization problem that arise in multiple access wireless communication networks.

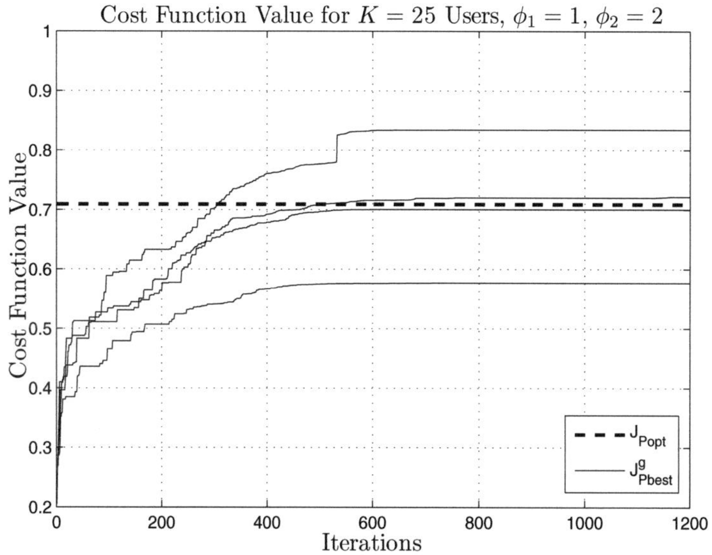

Fig. 24. Global best cost function evolution and optimal cost function value in four different samples with $\phi_1 = 1$ and $\phi_2 = 2$ parameters, $K = 25$ users, 1200 iterations limit, $\rho = K \times 10^{-19}$ and under the same channel conditions.

Specially, two optimization aspects of multiple access networks are deeply treated: multiuser detection, and simultaneous power and information rate allocation. To facing either NP optimization problem arising in multiuser detection or intrinsic non-feasibility power-rate allocation problem that appear in several practical scenarios, a discrete and continuous PSO algorithm versions are adopted and completely characterized. In both cases, the input parameters, specially the weight factors (acceleration coefficients), are optimized for each considered scenario. For both problems, extensive numerical results demonstrated the effectiveness of the proposed heuristic search approach.

Under multipath channels, different order modulations formats and antenna diversity, the PSO algorithm shown to be efficient for SISO/SIMO MuD asynchronous DS-CDMA problem, even under the increasing of number of multipath, system loading (MAI), NFR and/or SNR. Under a variety of analyzed realistic scenarios, the performance achieved by PSO-MuD always was near-optimal but with much lower complexity when compared to the OMuD, even under moderate channel errors estimation. In all evaluated system conditions, PSO-MuD resulted in small degradation performance if those errors are confined to 10% of the true instantaneous values.

Furthermore, under realistic and practical systems conditions, the PSO-MuD results in much less computational complexity than OMuD. The PSO-MuD, when compared to the CD receiver, is able to reach a much better performance with an affordable computational complexity. This manageable complexity depends on the hardware resources available and the system requirements such as minimum throughput, maximum admitted symbol-error-rate, and so on.

Besides, the PSO-MuD DS-CDMA accomplishes a flexible performance complexity trade-off solutions, showing to be appropriate for low and high-order modulation formats, asynchronous system, as well as multipath channels and spatial diversity scenarios. The

increasing system loading slightly deteriorates the performance of the swarm multiuser detector, but only under higher-order modulation. In all other scenarios, PSO-MuD presents complete robustness against MAI increasing.
For resource allocation optimization problem, numerical results indicated that searching for the global optimum over a high dimension power-rate allocation problem is a hard task. The search universe is denoted as $\mathbb{R}^K$ and constrained by power, rate and SNR ranges. Since the search space is continuous one can concludes that there is an infinite number of solutions, even if all these solutions are constrained.
The simulations results revealed that the proposed PSO approach can be easily applied to the throughput maximization problem under power consumption constraint in a large multirate system loading and realistic fading channel conditions. The algorithm has been found robust under a high number of active users in the systems, namely $K \geq 200$, while held the efficient searching feature and quality solutions. Those features make the PSO resource allocation approach a strong candidate to be implemented in real multiple access networks.
Further work and directions include a) the discretization of the search space aiming to reduce the problem dimension and, as a consequence, the complexity order; b) the application of the heuristic optimization techniques to solve resource allocation problems under a multi-objective optimization perspective; and c) the analysis of power and rate allocation problems under dynamic channels condition.

5. References

Abrão, T., de Oliveira, L. D., Ciriaco, F., Angélico, B. A., Jeszensky, P. J. E. & Palacio, F. J. C. (2009). S/mimo mc-cdma heuristic multiuser detectors based on single-objective optimization, *Wireless Personal Communications* .

Castoldi, P. (2002). *Multiuser Detection in CDMA Mobile Terminals*, Artech House, London, UK.

Chatterjee, A. & Siarry, P. (2006). Nonlinear inertia weight variation for dynamic adaptation in particle swarm optimization, *Computers & Operations Research* 33(3): 859–871.

Ciriaco, F., Abrão, T. & Jeszensky, P. J. E. (2006). Ds/cdma multiuser detection with evolutionary algorithms, *Journal Of Universal Computer Science* 12(4): 450–480.

Dai, J., Ye, Z. & Xu, X. (2009). Power allocation for maximizing the minimum rate with qos constraints, *Vehicular Technology, IEEE Transactions on* 58(9): 4989 –4996.

Eberhart, R. & Shi, Y. (2001). Particle swarm optimization: developments, applications and resources, *Proceedings of the 2001 Congress on Evolutionary Computation*, Vol. 1, pp. 81–86.

Elkamchouchi, H., Elragal, H. & Makar, M. (2007). Power control in cdma system using particle swarm optimization, *24th National Radio Science Conference*, pp. 1–8.

Elmusrati, M., El-Sallabi, H. & Koivo, H. (2008). Applications of multi-objective optimization techniques in radio resource scheduling of cellular communication systems, *IEEE Transactions on Wireless Communications* 7(1): 343–353.

Elmusrati, M. & Koivo, H. (2003). Multi-objective totally distributed power and rate control for wireless communications, *The 57th IEEE Semiannual Vehicular Technology Conference, VTC'03-Spring*, Vol. 4, pp. 2216–2220.

Ergün, C. & Hacioglu, K. (2000). Multiuser detection using a genetic algorithm in cdma communications systems, *IEEE Transactions on Communications* 48: 1374–1382.

Foschini, G. & Miljanic, Z. (1993). A simple distributed autonomous power control algorithm and its convergence, *IEEE Transactions on Vehicular Technology* 42(4): 641–646.

Gross, T. J., Abrão, T. & Jeszensky, P. J. E. (2010). Distributed power control algorithm for multiple access systems based on verhulst model, In Press, Corrected Proof: –.

Jeruchim, M. C., Balaban, P. & Shanmugan, K. S. (1992). *Simulation of Communication Systems*, Plenum Press, New York.

Juntti, M. J., Schlosser, T. & Lilleberg, J. O. (1997). Genetic algorithms for multiuser detection in synchronous cdma, *Proceedings of the IEEE International Symposium on Information Theory*, p. 492.

Kennedy, J. & Eberhart, R. (1995). Particle swarm optimization, *IEEE International Conference on Neural Networks*, pp. 1942–1948.

Kennedy, J. & Eberhart, R. (1997). A discrete binary version of the particle swarm algorithm, *IEEE international conference on Systems*, pp. 4104–4108.

Kennedy, J. & Eberhart, R. C. (2001). *Swarm Intelligence*, first edn, Morgan Kaufmann.

Khan, A. A., Bashir, S., Naeem, M. & Shah, S. I. (2006). Heuristics assisted detection in high speed wireless communication systems, *IEEE Multitopic Conference*, pp. 1–5.

Lee, J.-W., Mazumdar, R. R. & Shroff, N. B. (2005). Downlink power allocation for multi-class wireless systems, *IEEE/ACM Transactions on Networking* 13(4): 854–867.

Li Ping Qian, Ying Jun Zhang, J. H. (2009). Mapel: Achieving global optimality for a non-convex wireless power control problem, *IEEE Transactions on Wireless Communications* 8(3): 1553–1563.

Lim, H. S. & Venkatesh, B. (2003). An efficient local search heuristics for asynchronous multiuser detection, *IEEE Communications Letters* 7(6): 299–301.

Moshavi, S. (1996). Multi-user detection for ds-cdma communications, *IEEE Communication Magazine* 34: 132–136.

Moustafa, M., Habib, I. & Naghshineh, M. (2000). Genetic algorithm for mobiles equilibrium, MILCOM 2000. 21st Century Military Communications Conference Proceedings.

Moustafa, M., Habib, I. & Naghshineh, M. (2001a). Wireless resource management using genetic algorithm for mobiles equilibrium, *Computer Networks* 37(5): 631–643.

Moustafa, M., Habib, I. & Naghshineh, M. (2001b). Wireless resource management using genetic algorithm for mobiles equilibrium, Sixth IEEE Symposium on Computers and Communications. Proceedings.

Nedjah, N. & Mourelle, L. M. (2006). *Swarm Intelligent Systems*, Springer, Springer-Verlag Berlin Heidelberg.

Oliveira, L. D., Abrão, T., Jeszensky, P. J. E. & Casadevall, F. (2008). Particle swarm optimization assisted multiuser detector for m-qam ds/cdma systems, *SIS'08 - IEEE Swarm Intelligence Symposium*, pp. 1–8.

Oliveira, L. D., Ciriaco, F., Abrão, T. & Jeszensky, P. J. E. (2006). Particle swarm and quantum particle swarm optimization applied to ds/cdma multiuser detection in flat rayleigh channels, *ISSSTA'06 - IEEE International Symposium on Spread Spectrum Techniques and Applications*, Manaus, Brazil, pp. 133–137.

Oliveira, L. D., Ciriaco, F., Abrão, T. & Jeszensky, P. J. E. (2009). Local search multiuser detection, *AEÜ International Journal of Electronics and Communications* 63(4): 259–270.

Phuong, N. T. H. & Tuy, H. (2003). A unified monotonic approach to generalized linear fractional programming, *Journal of Global Optimization* pp. 229–259.

Proakis, J. (1989). *Digital Communications*, McGraw-Hill.

Seneta, E. (1981). *Non-Negative Matrices and Markov Chains*, 2 edn, New York: Springer-Verlag.

Shi, Y. & Eberhart, R. C. (1998). Parameter selection in particle swarm optimization, *1998 Annual Conference on Evolutionary Programming*, San Diego, USA.

Uykan, Z. & Koivo, H. (2004.). Sigmoid-basis nonlinear power-control algorithm for mobile radio systems, *IEEE Transactions on Vehicular Technology* 53(1): 265–271.

Verdú, S. (1989). Computational complexity of optimum multiuser detection, *Algorithmica* 4(1): 303–312.

Verdú, S. (1998). *Multiuser Detection*, Cambridge University Press, New York.

Zhao, H., Long, H. & Wang, W. (2006). Pso selection of surviving nodes in qrm detection for mimo systems, *GLOBECOM - IEEE Global Telecommunications Conference*, pp. 1–5.

Zielinski, K., Weitkemper, P., Laur, R. & Kammeyer, K.-D. (2009). Optimization of power allocation for interference cancellation with particle swarm optimization, *IEEE Transactions on Evolutionary Computation* 13(1): 128–150.

14

An Efficient Harmony Search Optimization for Maintenance Planning to the Telecommunication Systems

Fouzi Harrou and Abdelkader Zeblah
[1]*University of Bourgogne, Institute of Automotive and Transport Engineering (ISAT), 49rue Mademoiselle Bourgeois, 58000 Nevers,*
[2]*University Of Sidi Bel Abbes, Engineering Faculty,*
[1]*France*
[2]*Algeria*

1. Introduction

A necessary precondition for high production is availability of the technical equipment. In addition, reliability engineers have to build a reliable and efficient production system. The system reliability affects essentially the reliability of its equipments. This characteristic is a function of equipment age on system's operation life. In this work, we consider series-parallel systems. To keep the desired levels of availability, strongly performs a preventive maintenance actions to components are best than breakdown maintenance. This suggestion is supported by a number of case studies demonstrating the benefits of PM in (Gude et al, 1993). In this case, the task is to specify how PM activity should be scheduled. One of the commonly used PM policies is called periodic PM, which specifies that systems are maintained at integer multiple of some fixed period. Another PM is called sequential PM, in which the system is maintained at a sequence of interval that have unequal lengths. The first kind of PM is more convenient to schedule. Contrary the second is more realistic when the system require more frequent maintenance at it age. A common assumption used in both these PM is that minimal repair is conducted on system if it fails between successive PM activities. In other words, minimal repairs do not change the hazard function or the effective age of the system.

Traditionally PM models assume that the system after PM is either as good as new state in this case is called perfect PM or simply replacement, as bad as old state the same as minimal repair, where he only restores the function of the system, this concept is well understood in the literature (Brown et al, 1983). The more realistic assumption is that the system after PM not return at zero age and remains between as good as new and as bed as old. This kind of PM is called imperfect PM. The case when equipment fails (damage), a corrective maintenance (CM) is performed which returns equipment to operating condition, in fact specially, the task of preventive maintenance actions served to adjust the virtual age of equipment. Our particular interest is under investigation to present an harmony search algorithm which determines the optimal intervals of PM actions to minimize maintenance-cost rate or maximize mission reliability.

1.1 Summuray of previous work

Several years ago, much work was reported on policy optimization of preliminary planned PM actions with minimal repair as in (Zhao, 2003), (Borgonovo et al, 2000). Most of these researches are based on two popular approaches to determine the optimal intervals for a PM sequence. The first is reliability-based method and the second is optimization method.
In the first one the PM is performed whenever the system availability or the hazard function of the system reaches a predetermined level and the optimal PM intervals will be selected. The second is finding the optimal intervals as a decision variable in the optimization problem. (Lin et al 2000) presents an algorithm to determine the optimal intervals based on the reliability-based method and in there models the effective age reduction and hazard function are combined. (Levitin et al, 2000) present a genetic algorithm which determine a minimal cost plan of the selecting PM actions which provides the required levels of power system reliability. A list of possible PM actions available for each MSS, are used. Each PM action is associated with cost and reduction age coefficient of its implementation.

1.2 Approach and outlines

The proposed approach is based on the optimization method using harmony search algorithm, which determines the intervals sequence of PM actions to minimize the maintenance-cost subject to availability or (reliability) constraints. The goal of the proposed approach is to know when, where, to which component and what kind of available PM actions among the set of available PM actions should be implemented. To evaluate the reliability and the effect of PM actions of series-parallel MSS, UGF method is applied. It's proved to be effective at solving problem of MSS redundancy and maintenance in (Monga et al, 1997), (Levitin et al, 1999) and (Ushakov et al, 2002).

2. Preventive maintenance

It has been shown that the incorporation of the preventive maintenance has a benefit and success. Also it was observed that the impact of the decrease of component failure rate and improvement of component reliability is vital to maintain efficiency of production. The

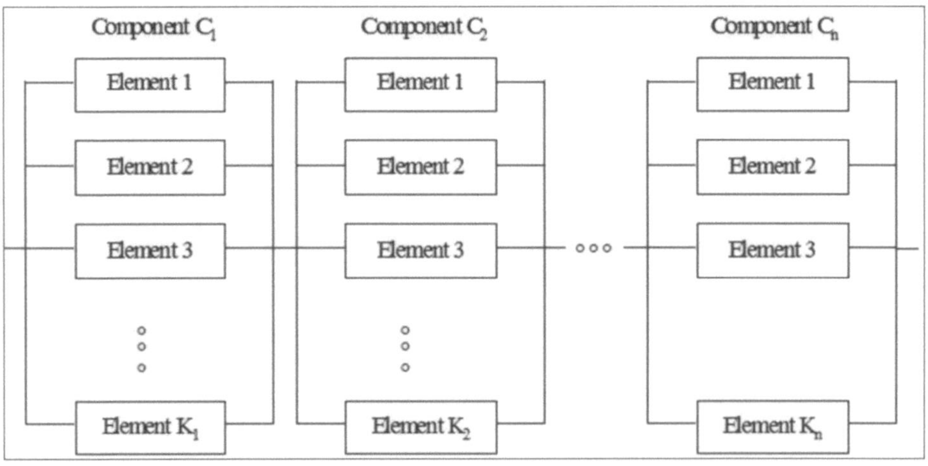

Fig. 1. Series-parallel Power System

major subject of maintenance is focused on the planning maintenance service of the power system. Such as cleaning, adjustment and inspection performed on operation's lifetime are classed as a preventive maintenance policy. However, all actions of PM not capable to reduce age component to zero age is imperfect. There are two main alternatives for modeling an imperfect PM activity. The first one assumes that PM is equivalent to minimal repair with probability p and $1-p$ is the equivalent to replacement in (Nakagawa, 1999). The second model where the imperfect PM directly analyzes how the hazard function or the effective age change after PM as in (Lin et al, 2000). The proposed model is based on reduction age concept. Let consider the series-parallel MSS system shown in figures 1.
If the component j undergoes on PM actions calendar at chronological times as follows:

$$(t_{j1}, \ldots, t_{jn}) \tag{1}$$

Based on the second model description, the effective age after i-th PM actions may be written as:

$$\tau_j(t) = \tau_j^+(t) + (t - t_{ji}) \quad \text{for } t_{ji} < t < t_{ji+1}, (1 \le i \le n) \tag{2}$$

and $\tau_j^+(t_{ji}) = \varepsilon_i \tau_j(t_{ji}) = \varepsilon_i \left(\tau_j^+(t_{ji-1}) + (t_{ji} - t_{ji-1})\right)$ where $\tau_j^+(t_{ji})$ is the age of component immediately after the i-th PM action which ranges in the interval [0, 1]. By definition, we assume that $\tau_j(0) = 0$, $t_{j0} = 0$ and ε_i is the age reduction coefficient. Two limits for PM actions is, where $\varepsilon_i = 1$ and $\varepsilon_i = 0$. In the first case the component at least be restored to "as bed as old" state which assumes that PM does not affect the effective age. In the second case the model reduce the component age to "as good as new", which means that the component age reaches zero age (replacement). In fact, all PM actions which improve the component age are imperfect. As it be mentioned and demonstrated in (Lin et al, 2000), the hazard function of component j, as function of its actual age, can be calculated as

$$h_j^* = h_j\left(\tau_j(t)\right) + h_{j0} \tag{3}$$

where $h_j(t)$ is the hazard function is defined when equipment does not undergo PM actions and h_{j0} correspond to the initial age of equipment. The reliability of the equipment j in the interval between PM actions i and $i+1$ can be written as:

$$r_j(t) = \exp\left(- \int_{\tau_j^+(t_{ji})}^{\tau_j(t)} h_j^*(x)dx \right)$$

$$= \exp\left(H_j(\tau_j^+(t_{ji})) - H_j(\tau_j(t))\right) \tag{4}$$

$H_j(\tau)$ represents the accumulative hazard function. Clearly if $t = t_{ji}$ in equation (4) the reliability reaches the maximum and is equal to 1.
The Minimal repairs are performed if MSS equipment fails between PM actions, and there cost expected in interval [0, t] can be given as

$$C_{Mj} = c_j \int_0^t h_j(x)dx \tag{5}$$

Possible equipment j, undergoes PM actions at each chronological time $t_{j1}, ..., t_{jn_j}$, in this case, the total minimal repair cost is the sum of all cost can be written as :

$$C_{Mj} = c_j \sum_{i=0}^{n_j} \int_{\tau_j^+(t_{ji})}^{\tau_j(t_{ji+1})} h_j(x)dx = c_j \sum_{i=0}^{n_j} \left(H(\tau_j(t_{ji+1})) - H_j(\tau_j^+(t_{ji})) \right) \tag{6}$$

where $t_{j0} = 0$ and $t_{jn_j+1} = T$ where T represents the lifetime.

3. Optimization problem

Let consider a power system organized with components connected in series arrangement. Each component contains different component put in parallel. Components are characterized by their nominal performance rate Ξ_j, hazard function $h_j(t)$ and associated minimal repair cost C_j. The system is composed of a number of failure prone components, such that the failure of some components leads only to a degradation of the system performance. This system is considered to have a range of performance levels from perfect working to complete failure. In fact, the system failure can lead to decreased capability to accomplish a given task, but not to complete failure. An important MSS measure is related to the ability of the system to satisfy a given demand.

When applied to electric power systems, reliability is considered as a measure of the ability of the system to meet the load demand (W), i.e., to provide an adequate supply of electrical energy (Ξ). This definition of the reliability index is widely used for power systems: see e.g., (Ross, 1993), (Murchland, 1975), (Levitin et al, 1996), (Levitin et al, 1997) and (Levitin et al, 1998). The Loss of Load Probability index (LOLP) is usually used to estimate the reliability index (Billinton et al, 1990). This index is the overall probability that the load demand will not be met. Thus, we can write R = Probab(ΞMSS≥ W) or R = 1-LOLP with LOLP = Probab(ΞMSS<W). This reliability index depends on consumer demand W.

For reparable MSS, a multi-state steady-state instantaneous availability A is used as Probab(ΞMSS ≥ W). While the multi-state instantaneous availability is formulated by equation (7):

$$A_{MSS}\{t, W\} = \sum_{\Sigma_j \geq D} P_j(t) \tag{7}$$

where ΞMSS (t) is the output performance of MSS at time t. To keep system reliability at desired level, preventive and curative maintenance can be realized on each MSS. PM actions modify components reliability and CM actions does not affect it. The effectiveness of each PM actions is defined by the age reduction coefficient ε ranging from 0 to 1. As in (Levitin et al, 2000), the structure of the system as defined by an available list of possible PM actions (v) for a given MSS. In this list each PM actions (v) is associated with the cost of its implementation $C_p(v)$, and $M(v)$ is the number of equipment affected corresponding to their age reduction $\varepsilon(v)$. Commonly the system lifetime T is divided into y unequal lengths, and each interval have duration θ_y $1 \le y \le Y$, at each end of this latter an PM action is performed. This action will be performed if the MSS reliability $R(t,w)$ becomes lower than the desirable level R_0.

Let us remark that the increase in the number of intervals increases solution precision. On the other hand, the number of intervals can be limited for technical reasons. All the PM actions performed to maintain the MSS reliability are arranged and presented by a vector V as they appear on the PM list. Each time the PM is necessary to improve the system reliability; the performed following action is defined by the next number from this vector. When the scheduled PM action v_i was insufficient to improve reliability, automatically the v_{i+1} action should be performed at the same time and so on. For a given vector V, the total number n_j and chronological times of PM action in equation (1) are determined for each component j $1 \le j \le J$. For all scheduled PM actions $v_i \in V$. The total cost of PM actions can be expressed as

$$C_p(V) = \sum_{i=1}^{N} C_p(v_i) \tag{8}$$

and the cost of minimal repair can be calculated as

$$C_M(V) = \sum_{j=1}^{J} c_j \sum_{i=0}^{n_j} \left(H(\tau_j(t_{ji+1})) - H(\tau_j^+(t_{ji})) \right) \tag{9}$$

The optimization problem can be formulated as follows: find the optimal sequence of the PM actions chosen from the list of available actions which minimizes the total maintenance cost while providing the desired MSS availability. That is,

Minimize:

$$f(V) \to C = C_p(V) + C_M(V) \tag{10}$$

Subject To:

$$A_\theta(\mathbf{V}, \mathbf{D}, \mathbf{t}) \ge R_0 \tag{11}$$

To solve this combinatorial optimization problem, it is important to have an effective and fast procedure to evaluate the availability index. Thus, a method is developed in the following section to estimate the system availability.

4. Reliability estimation based on Ushakov's method

The last few years have seen the appearance of a number of works presenting various methods of quantitative estimation of systems consisting of devices that have a range of working levels in (Reinschke, 1985) and (El-Neweihi, 1984). Usually one considers reducible systems. In general forms the series connection, the level of working is determined by the worst state observed for any one of the devices, while for parallel connection is determined by the best state. However, such the approach is not applicable for the majority of real systems.

In this paper the procedure used is based on the universal z-transform, which is a modern mathematical technique introduced in (Ushakov, 1986). This method, convenient for numerical implementation, is proved to be very effective for high dimension combinatorial problems. In the literature, the universal z-transform is also called UMGF or simply u-transform. The UMGF extends the widely known ordinary moment generating function (Ross, 1993). The UMGF of a discrete random variable Ξ is defined as a polynomial:

$$u(z) = \sum_{j=1}^{J} P_j z^{\Xi_j} \tag{12}$$

The probabilistic characteristics of the random variable Ξ can be found using the function u(z). In particular, if the discrete random variable Ξ is the MSS stationary output performance, the availability A is given by the probability $\text{Proba}(\Xi \geq W)$ which can be defined as follows:

$$\text{Proba}(\Xi \geq \text{W}) = \Phi\left(u(z)z^{-\text{W}}\right) \tag{13}$$

where Φ is a distributive operator defined by expressions (14) and (15):

$$\Phi(Pz^{\sigma-\text{W}}) = \begin{cases} P, & \text{if } \sigma \geq \text{W} \\ 0, & \text{if } \sigma < \text{W} \end{cases} \tag{14}$$

$$\Phi\left(\sum_{j=1}^{J} P_j z^{\Xi_j-\text{W}}\right) = \sum_{j=1}^{J} \Phi\left(P_j z^{\Xi_j-\text{W}}\right) \tag{15}$$

It can be easily shown that equations (14)-(15) meet condition $\text{Proba}(\Xi \geq \text{W}) = \sum_{\Xi_j \geq \text{W}} P_j$. By using the operator Φ, the coefficients of polynomial u(z) are summed for every term with $\Xi_j \geq W$, and the probability that Ξ is not less than some arbitrary value W is systematically obtained.

Consider single devices with total failures and each device i has nominal performance Ξ_i and reliability Ai. The UMGF of such an device has only two terms can be defined as:

$$u_i(z) = (1 - A_i)z^0 + A_i z^{\Xi_i} = (1 - A_i) + A_i z^{\Xi_i} \tag{16}$$

To evaluate the MSS availability of a series-parallel system, two basic composition operators are introduced. These operators determine the polynomial u(z) for a group of devices.

4.1 Parallel devices

Let consider a system device m containing Jm devices connected in parallel. The total performance of the parallel system is the sum of performances of all its devices. In power systems, the term capacity is usually used to indicate the quantitative performance measure of an device in (Chern, 1992). Examples: generating capacity for a generator, carrying capacity for an electric transmission line, etc. Therefore, the total performance of the parallel unit is the sum of capacity (performances) in (Ushakov, 1986). The u-function of MSS device m containing J_m parallel devices can be calculated by using the $\Im$ operator:

$$u_p(z) = \Im(u_1(z),\ u_2(z),\ \ldots,\ u_n(z)),\ \text{where } \Im(\Xi_1,\ \Xi_2,\ \ldots,\ \Xi_n) = \sum_{i=1}^{n} \Xi_i$$

Therefore for a pair of devices connected in parallel:

$$\Im(u_1(z),u_2(z)=\Im(\sum_{i=1}^{n}P_iz^{a_i},\sum_{j=1}^{m}Q_jz^{b_j})=\sum_{i=1}^{n}\sum_{j=1}^{m}P_iQ_jz^{a_i+b_j}$$

The parameters ai and bj are physically interpreted as the performances of the two devices. n and m are numbers of possible performance levels for these devices. Pi and Q_j are steady-state probabilities of possible performance levels for devices. One can see that the $\Im$ operator is simply a product of the individual u-functions. Thus, the device UMGF is: $u_p(z)=\prod_{j=1}^{J_m}u_j(z)$. Given the individual UMGF of devices defined in equation (11), we have: $u_p(z)=\prod_{j=1}^{J_m}(1-A_j+A_jz^{\Xi_i})$.

4.2 Series devices

When the devices are connected in series, the device with the least performance becomes the bottleneck of the system. This device therefore defines the total system productivity. To calculate the u-function for system containing n devices connected in series, the operator δ should be used: $u_s(z)=\delta(u_1(z),\ u_2(z),\ \ldots,\ u_m(z))$,where $\delta(\Xi_1,\Xi_2\ldots,\Xi_m)=\min\{\Xi_1,\Xi_2\ldots,\Xi_m\}$ so that

$$\delta(u_1(z),u_2(z))=\delta\left(\sum_{i=1}^{n}P_iz^{a_i},\sum_{j=1}^{m}Q_jz^{b_j}\right)=\sum_{i=1}^{n}\sum_{j=1}^{m}P_iQ_jz^{\min\{a_i,\,b_j\}}$$

Applying composition operators $\Im$ and δ consecutively, one can obtain the UMGF of the entire series-parallel system. To do this we must first determine the individual UMGF of each device.

4.3 Devices with total failures

Let consider the usual case where only total failures are considered and each subsystem of type *i* and version v_i has nominal performance Ξ_{iv} and availability A_{iv}. In this case, we have: Proba(Ξ = Ξ_{iv}) = A_{iv} and Proba(Ξ = W) = $1-A_{iv}$. The UMGF of such an device has only two terms can be defined as in equation (11) by $u^*_i(z)=(1-A_{iv})z^0+A_{iv}z^{\Xi_{iv}}=1-A_{iv}+A_{iv}z^{\Xi_{iv}}$. Using the $\Im$ operator, we can obtain the UMGF of the *i*-th system device containing k_i parallel devices $u_i(z)=\left(u^*_i(z)\right)^{k_i}=\left(A_{iv}z^{\Xi_{iv}}+(1-A_{iv})\right)^{k_i}$.

The UMGF of the entire system containing *n* devices connected in series is:

$$u_s(z)=\delta\begin{pmatrix}\left(A_{1v}z^{\Xi_{1v}}+(1-A_{1v})\right)^{k_1},\\ \left(A_{2v}z^{\Xi_{2v}}+(1-A_{2v})\right)^{k_2},\ldots,\\ \left(A_{nv}z^{\Xi_{nv}}+(1-A_{nv})\right)^{k_n}\end{pmatrix} \tag{17}$$

To evaluate the probability $\Pr oba(\Xi \geq W)$ for the entire system, the operator Φ is applied to equation (18):

$$\Pr oba(\Xi \geq W) = \Phi\left(u_s(z)z^{-W}\right) \tag{18}$$

5. The harmony search approach

The problem formulated is a complicated NP-hard complex problem. The total number of different solutions to be examined is very large. An exhaustive examination of the enormous number of possible solutions is not feasible given reasonable time limitations. Thus, because of the search- space size of the problem. Adopting the idea that existing evolutionary or meta-heuristic algorithms are found in the paradigm of natural processes, a new algorithm can be conceptualized from a musical performance process (say, a jazz trio) in (Geem et al, 2005) and (Mahdavi et al, 2007) involving searching for a better harmony. Musical performance seeks a best state (fantastic harmony) determined by aesthetic estimation, as the optimization process seeks a best state (global optimum: minimum cost; minimum error; maximum benefit; or maximum efficiency) determined by objective function evaluation. Aesthetic estimation is done by the set of the pitches sounded by joined instruments, as objective function evaluation is done by the set of the values produced by composed variables; the aesthetic sounds can be improved practice after practice, as the objective function values can be improved iteration by iteration in (Fesanghary et al, 2008).

Figure 2 shows the structure of the Harmony Memory (HM) that is the core part of the HS algorithm. Consider a jazz trio composed of saxophone, double bass, and guitar. There exist certain amount of preferable pitches in each musician's memory: saxophonist, {Do, Fa, Mi, Sol, Re}; double bassist, {Si, Do, Si, Re, Sol}; and guitarist, {La, Sol, Fa, Mi, Do}. If saxophonist randomly plays {Sol} out of its memory {Do, Fa, Mi, Sol, Re}, double bassist {Si} out of {Si, Do, Si, Re, Sol}, and guitarist {Do} out of {La, Sol, Fa, Mi, Do}, the new harmony (Sol, Si, Do) becomes another harmony (musically chord). And if this new harmony is better than existing worst harmony in the HM, the new harmony is included in the HM and the worst harmony is excluded from the HM (Omran, 2008). This procedure is repeated until fantastic harmony is found.

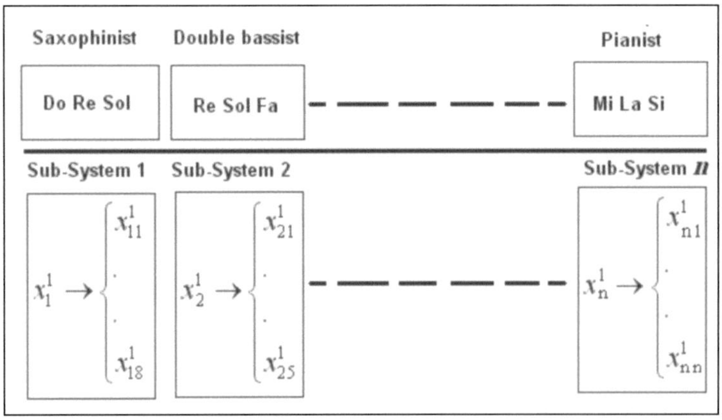

Fig. 2. Synoptic Modeling HS For Optimization

Step 1. Initialize:

Set N_istrument:=N_sybsystem {N is the integer number},
Set MHCR:=0.7{harmony memory considering rate},
Set PAR:=0.35{Pitch adjustment rate},
Set PAD {Pitch adjustment decision},
Set NI:=75{improvisation number},
Set t:=0 {*t* is the time counter},
Set Interval_t:=0 {θ is Interval time},
Set List PM_actions [L_{n1}]:= $\left[P_{n1}^{\upsilon}\right]$ {Available PM_actions},
Set PM_Action:=0 {*m* is the time counter},
For every Components (i,j) set an initial value $x_{ij}^{1} \rightarrow \left\{x_{11}^{1},...,x_{n1}^{1}\right\}$ x_{ij}^{1},
Set For All components (*1 ≤j ≤J*):
Set Effectve_age:= τj
Set $H_j(\tau_j^+) = 0$
For i:=1 to n do
Mat$_k$ (HM):= i {starting component is the first element of the **Mat** list of the k-th instrument},
The HM matrix is filled with randomly generated as the HMS.

Step 2. Improvise a New list **Mat**$_k$ until is full {this step will be repeated (n-1) times}, $x^{n\upsilon} \rightarrow \left\{x_{11}^{n\upsilon}, x_{12}^{n\upsilon},...,x_{nk}^{n\upsilon}\right\}$

2.0. y:=Interval_time+1
2.1 T:= Interval_time +t'
2.2 Effectve_age:=τj+t
2.3 New PM_action:= $x^{n\upsilon} \in \left[P_{n1}^{\upsilon}\right]$

Step 3.

Compute For j:=1 To J
$H_j(\tau_j)$ According equation (3)
End
Compute For j:=1 To J
$r_j(\tau_j)$ According equation (4)

Step 4.

Compute For j:=1 To n do {for every k-th instrument on Subsystem i }
Choose the PM_Action with probability

$$PAD\ for\ x_{ij}^{n\upsilon} \begin{cases} Yes\ If\ ran_1 \leq PAR \\ No\ If\ ran_1 \succ (1-PAR) \end{cases}$$

Then $x_{ij}^{n\upsilon} \leftarrow x_{gi}^{n\upsilon} \pm ran_i(\ )*bw$

With Cost j, corresponding to Equation (8) and (9)
Increment to the k-th instrument on the *i* subsystems
Insert PM_Action and Cost j in **MAT**$_k$ (s).

Step 5.

If R $(t,\Xi) < R_0$ increment and define the new PM_Action to perform, add the new cost to total Cost.

Recalculate the reliability r

Else Goto Step 2.

If R (t,Ξ) >= evaluate the cost of minimal repair for all components $(1 \leq j \leq J)$: and add these costs to the total cost.

Print minimal total cost to the corresponding reliability and

Stop.

6. Illustrative example

6.1 Description of the power system to be optimized

Let consider a series-parallel MSS (transmission system) consisting of three subsystem connected in series arrangment as depickted in figure.3 and 4. The system contains 13 equipments with different performance and reliabilty.

The transmission systems is composed by a emission and reception station where the signal is modeled to the analyzer series parallel components and emitted to orbital satellite. Concerning reception the series parallel system is composed by modelyzer RTID-2, 2 and 3 other amplifier TM-841, 842 and 843. Following the process and transmitted by telecom network (Linking with lines and without lines transmission). At the end the system supplies a graphique and TMAE station. The reliability of each component is defined by veibull function: $h(t) = \lambda^{\delta}\delta(\tau(t))^{\delta-1} + h_0$ MSS lifetime is 20 years. The time for possible PM_actions are spaced intervals of θ= 2.0 months. The problem is to guarantee a PM plan wich provide the system work during its lifetime with a performance, relaibility not less than Ξ0, R0 and the age reduction is the same of all components ε =0.56

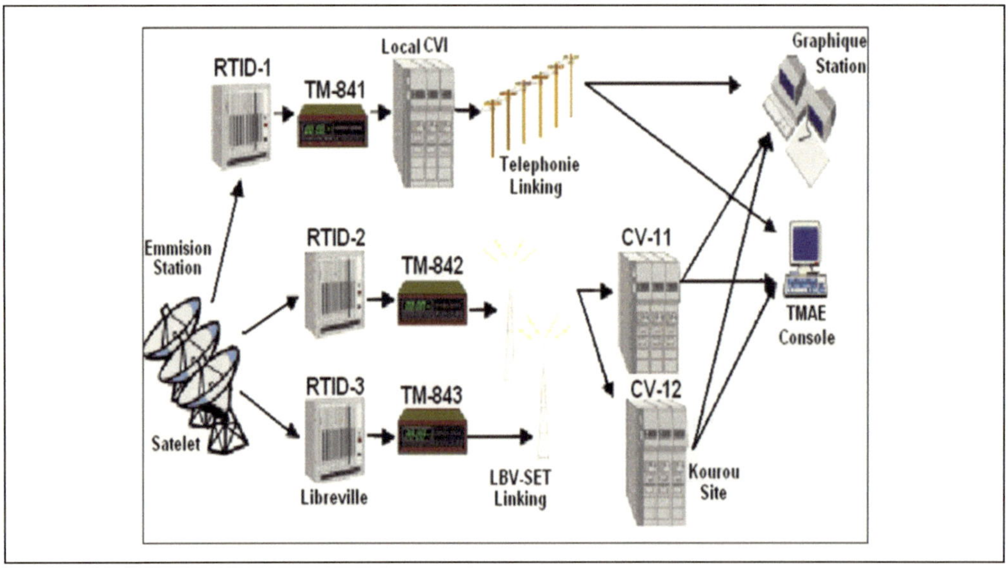

Fig. 3. Detailed Series-Parallel Transmission System

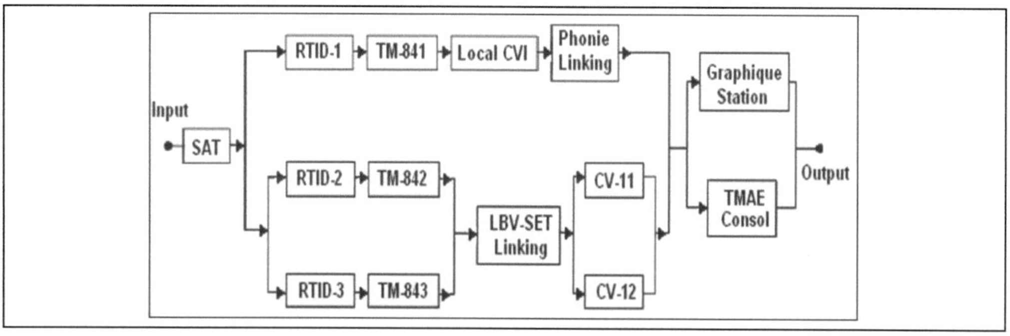

Fig. 4. Synoptic Series-Parallel Transmission System

	λ	δ	h_0	Min_Cost	Ξ %
1	0.05	1.8	0.001	1.02	40
2	0.05	1.8	0.003	0.9	80
3	0.05	1.8	0.003	0.9	80
4	0.05	1.8	0.003	0.9	80
5	0.02	1.3	0.002	0.7	70
6	0.02	1.3	0.002	0.7	70
7	0.02	1.3	0.002	0.7	70
8	0.08	1.6	0.006	0.8	85
9	0.07	1.8	0.005	0.6	89
10	0.05	1.8	0.003	0.8	90
11	0.08	1.7	0.002	0.8	90
12	0.03	1.6	0.001	0.9	95
13	0.004	1.5	0.001	0.8	87

Table 1. Parameter Of components

PM_Actions	Components	PM_Cost
1	1- SAT	10.2
2	2- RTID-1-2-3	2.9
3	2- RTID-1-2-3	4.1
4	2- RTID-1-2-3	2.2
5	3-TM-841-2-3	2.9
6	3-TM-841-2-3	4.1
7	3-TM-841-2-3	2.2
8	4-Tele-Linking	3.9
9	5-LBV-SET	4.1
10	5-LBV-SET	3.7
11	6-CV-11	5.5
12	6-CV-11	2.2
13	7- Graphique-S	3.5
14	8-TMAE	8.2

Table 2. Parameter Of Pm_Actions

t	PM_Actions	Affected Components	R (t,0.8)
12.250	2(6)	3	0.923
16.652	8	4	0.922
20.00	9	5	0.954
22.11	4	2	0.911
25.64	2	1	0.937

Table 3.The Best Pm plan By HS For R(t,0.8)>0.9

Action times	Kind of PM_Actions	Affected Components	Levels R (t,0.8)
09	4	2	0.920
07.20	2(7)	3	0.987
05.85	8	4	0.985
06.03	10	5	0.960
25.60	11	7	0.983

Table 4.The Best Pm plan By Ant Colony For R(t,0.8)>0.9

7. Conclusion

In this paper we formulated the problem of imperfect maintenance optimization for series-parallel transmission system structure. This work focused on selecting the optimal sequence of intervals to perform PM actions to improve the availability. The model analyzes cost and reliability, to construct a strategy to select the optimal maintenance intervals, formulating a complex problem. An exhaustive examination of all possible solution is not realistic, considering reasonable time limitations. Because of this, an efficient meta-heuristic can be applied (Harmony Search Algorithm) to solve the formulated problem. More specifically, the harmony search approach is a good solution for such a combinatorial problem.

8. References

Gude, D., Schmidt K.H., (1993). Preventive maintenance of advanced manufacturing systems: a laboratory experiment and its implications for human centered approach, International Journal of Human factors in Manufacturing; 3, 335-350.

Brown, M., Proschan, F., (1983). Imperfect repair. Journal of Applied probability, 20, 851-859.

Zhao, M., (2003). On preventive maintenance policy of critical reliability level for system subject to degradation, Reliability Engineering & System Safety, 79 (203), No. 3, 301-308.

Borgonovo, E., Marseguerra, M., Zio E., (2000). A Monte Carlo methodological approach to plant availability modeling with maintenance, aging and obsolescence, Reliability Engineering & System Safety; 67, No. 1, 61-73.

Lin, D., Zuo, M.J., Yam, RCM., (2000). General sequence imperfect preventive maintenance models. International Journal of reliability, Quality and safety Engineering; 7, No. 3, 253-266.

Levitin, G., Lisniaski, A., (2000). Optimization of imperfect preventive maintenance for multi-state systems, reliability Engineering and System safety 67, 193-203.

Monga, A., Toogood, R., Zuo, M.J., (1997). reliability-based design of systems considering preventive maintenance and minimal repair. International Journal of Reliability, Quality and Safety Engineering, 4, 55-71.

Levitin, G., Lisniaski, A., (1999). Optimal multistage modernization of power system subject to reliability and capacity requirements. Electric Power System Research, 50, 183-90.

Ushakov .I.A., Levitin G., Lisnianski A., (2002). Multi-state system reliability: from theory to practice. Proc. of 3 Int. Conf. on mathematical methods in reliability, MMR 2002, Trondheim, Norway, 635-638.

Nakagawa, T., (1999). Sequential imperfect preventive maintenance policies. IEEE Transactions on Reliability; 37, No. 3, 295-298.

Ross, S.M., (1993). Introduction to probability models. Academic press.

Murchland, J., (1975). Fundamental concepts and relations for reliability analysis of multi-state systems. Reliability and Fault Tree Analysis, ed. R. Barlow, J. Fussell, N. Singpurwalla. SIAM, Philadelphia.

Levitin G., Lisnianski A., Ben-Haim H., Elmakis D., (1998). Redundancy optimization for series-parallel multi-state systems, IEEE Transactions on Reliability, 47No. 2, 165-172.

Levitin, G., Lisniaski, A., Ben-haim, H., Elmakis, D., (1996). Power system structure optimization subject to reliability constraints, Electric Pôwer System Research, 40, 145-52.

Levitin, G., Lisnianski, A., Ben-Haim, H., Elmakis, D., (1997). Structure optimization of power system with different redundant elements. Electric Power Systems Research, 43, No. 1,19-27.

Billinton, R., Allan, R., (1990). Reliability evaluation of power systems. Pitman.

Reinschke, B., (1985). System of elements with many states. radio i svyaz, Moscow.

El-Neweihi, E., Proschan, F., (1984). Degradable systems: A survey of multistates system theory. Common. Statist. Theor. math., 13 No. 4.

Ushakov, I.A., (1986). Universal generating function. Sov. J. Computing System Science, 24, No. 5, 118-129.

Chern, M.S., (1992). On the Computational Complexity of Reliability redundancy Allocation in a Series System. Operations Research Letters, 11, 309-315.

Geem, Z.W., Tseng, C.L., Park, Y, (2005). Harmony Search for Generalized Orienteering Problem: Best Touring in China, Book advanced in natural computation Springer Berlin / Heidelberg, 361, 741-750.

Mahdavi, M., Fesanghary M., Damangir, E, (2007). An improved harmony search algorithm for solving optimization problems Applied Mathematics and Computation N°188, pp-1567–1579.

Fesanghary, M., Mahdavi, M., Minary-Jolandan M., Alizadeh, Y, (2008). Hybridizing harmony search algorithm with sequential quadratic programming for engineering optimization problems Comput. Methods Appl. Mech. Engrg, v197. pp:3080-3091.

Omran, M.G.H., Mahdavi, M., (2008). Global-best harmony search, Applied Mathematics and Computation N°198, 643–656.

15

Multi-Objective Optimization Methods Based on Artificial Neural Networks

Sara Carcangiu, Alessandra Fanni and Augusto Montisci
Electrical and Electronic Engineering Department, University of Cagliari, Cagliari, Italy

1. Introduction

During the last years, several optimization algorithms have been presented and widely investigated in literature, most of which based on deterministic or stochastic methods, in order to solve optimization problems with multiple objectives that conflict with each other.
Some multi-objective stochastic optimizers have been developed, based on local or global search methods, in order to solve optimal design problems. Despite the significant progress obtained in this field, there are still many open issues. In fact, both the deterministic and stochastic approaches present hard limits.
In the first case, although the number of function evaluations needed to reach the optimal solution is generally small, the risk to be trapped in local minima is very high, whereas in the second case, the probability to reach the optimal solution is higher but the computational cost could become prohibitive.
In particular, this is the case of the electromagnetic problems. Electromagnetic devices are fundamental in the modern society. They are used for storing and converting energy (Magele, 1996), manufacturing processes (Takahashi et al., 1996), magnetic resonance imaging (Gottvald et al., 1992), telecommunications, etc.
The design optimization of the electromagnetic devices is one key to enhance product quality and manufacturing efficiency. Definition of geometric boundaries to achieve specific design goals together with nonlinear behaviour of ferromagnetic materials often give rise to multimodal, non-linear, and non-derivable objective functions. For this reason, resorting to numerical approaches, such as the Finite Element Method (FEM), to evaluate objective functions in many cases is compulsory.
When the number of design parameters to be optimized is considerable, the number of objectives evaluations to be performed could be of the order of thousand and the use of numerical solution during the optimization process can be unfeasible.
Approximating techniques have been proposed as a way to overcome the time consuming numerical procedure (Alotto et al., 2001, Canova et al., 2003, Wang & Lowther, 2006). One of the most effective approximation approaches is based on Artificial Neural Networks. In fact, an alternative method to numerical evaluation consists of applying the optimization procedure to the approximation of the objective function, rather than to its numerical model (Abbass, 2003, Fieldsend & Singh, 2005, Carcangiu et al., 2008). On the other hand, the quality of the solution of the optimization problem depends on the error introduced by the approximation

model. In order to take under control such approximation error the constructive algorithm presented in (Carcangiu et al., 2009a) can be used to build the neural model.
The search algorithms presented in this chapter resort to a procedure able to solve inverse problems by inverting the NN approximation model (Cherubini et al., 2005). This procedure consists in imposing the value of the desired objective functions and by searching for the corresponding values of the design parameters.
The proposed approach allows one to look for the Pareto front solutions directly in the objectives space, rather than in the design parameters one, allowing both to uniformly sample the Pareto front, and to limit the computational load (Carcangiu et al., 2009b).
Moreover the search for the Pareto points directly in the objectives space allows one to exploit the *a priori* knowledge of the Decision Maker (DM), guiding the search towards non-dominated solutions having predefined characteristics. In the following, an *interactive* approach is proposed. The DM can impose his own fitting criterion in the objective space fixing in this way a trajectory along which the Pareto points can be searched. In such a way, sampling of the whole Pareto front is avoided, and the deterioration of the different objective functions during the search for the Pareto optimal solution is kept under control.
The remainder of this chapter is organized as follows. In the Section 2 an overview of the multi-objective optimization is given. Section 3 describes the method to construct neural models having a prefixed precision degree. In Section 4 the Neural Network Inversion procedure is illustrated. In Sections 5 and 6 the search algorithms are described. Analytical and electromagnetic applicative examples are presented in Section 7, and the results are discussed. In Section 8 conclusions are drawn.

2. Multi-objective optimization

Multi-objective Optimization Problems (MOPs) usually present a possibly uncountable set of solutions, called Pareto optimal solutions, which, when evaluated, produces vectors whose components represent trade-offs in objective space. A DM has to choose acceptable solutions by selecting one or more of these vectors.
The MOPs objective functions are designated $f_1(\underline{x})$, $f_2(\underline{x})$, ..., $f_k(\underline{x})$, where k (k>1) is the number of distinct objective functions and $\underline{x}$ is the decision vector. The objective functions form a vector function $\underline{f}(\underline{x})$ defined by $\underline{f}(\underline{x})=[f_1(\underline{x}), f_2(\underline{x}), ..., f_k(\underline{x})]^T$. The optimization problem can be formalized as follows:

$$\begin{aligned} & \min \underline{f}(\underline{x}) \\ s.t. \quad & g_j(\underline{x}) \le 0, \quad j = 1,\dots,q \\ & h_j(\underline{x}) = 0, \quad j = q+1,\dots,m \end{aligned} \tag{1}$$

where $g_j(\underline{x})$ and $h_j(\underline{x})$ define the feasible region Ω of the decision variables.
Two Euclidean spaces are considered in MOP formulation:

1. The n-dimensional space $\Re^n$ of decision variables, where each coordinate axis corresponds to a component of vector $\underline{x}$ (decision space).
2. The k-dimensional space of objective functions $\Re^k$, where each coordinate axis corresponds to a component of vector $\underline{f}(\underline{x})$ (objective function space).

Each point in the decision space represents a solution and corresponds to a certain point in the objective function space (Fig. 1).

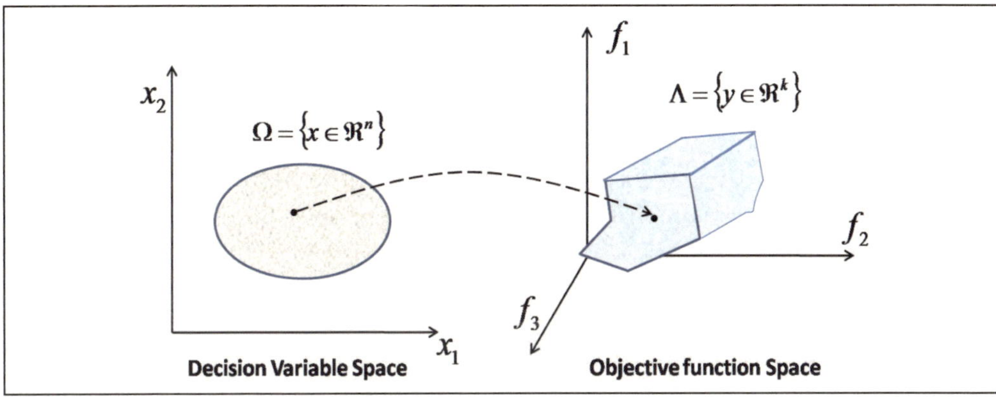

Fig. 1. Variable space mapped into the objective space.

In other words, one wishes to determine, among the set of all values satisfying (1), the particular set $\{x_1^*, x_2^*,..., x_n^*\}$ yielding optimum values for all the simultaneously considered k objective functions. The vector $\underline{x}_i^*$ is reserved to denote the ith optimal solution as MOPs often have many "optimal" solutions.

In a MOP, a solution $\underline{x}_d$ is dominated by another solution $\underline{x}_{nd}$ if $\underline{x}_{nd}$ is better than $\underline{x}_d$ on all objectives, and it will be denoted, here, by $\underline{x}_d \prec \underline{x}_{nd}$. A solution $\underline{x}_p$ is a Pareto optimal solution if no objective function can be improved without worsening at least one other objective function. Such solution is not unique, and the set of the Pareto optimal solutions are known as the Pareto front.

In the objective domain search space it is possible to identify the **Utopia** and **Nadir** points, whose components are the best and the worst values respectively of all the objective functions. The Utopia point is then defined as the ideal solution in which all the objective functions have their optimum of the problem considering each objective separately. The Utopia is usually unfeasible.

In the objectives space two regions can be distinguished: the former is the feasible region whose points correspond to existing solutions in the parameters space, the latter is the unfeasible region, which is the complementary region in the objectives space. The frontier that separates these regions is not necessarily composed by non-dominated solutions; therefore in general the Pareto Front is included in such frontier. In general, it is not easy to find an analytical expression of the line or surface that contains the Pareto optimal points, and the normal procedure consists in computing a Pareto Optimal set of points. When a sufficient number of these points have been obtained, the DM may proceed to take the final decision.

Various approaches can be used to guide the DM towards a final solution among the Pareto optimal solutions (Pareto front): *a priori*, *a posteriori*, and *interactive* approaches, which make use of some utility criteria.

In the *a priori* approaches, the DM combines the objectives into a global utility function, thus transforming the MOP into a standard scalar optimization problem, which can be solved using traditional optimization methods. Although they have been widely used in the past, *a priori* techniques suffer from various drawbacks: they do not work properly with non convex Pareto fronts; they provide a single Pareto optimal solution, which is very sensitive to the scalarization of the objectives and to the choice of the parameters (e.g., weighting

coefficients, target values, starting point) associated with the preferences of the DM. In the *a posteriori* approaches, firstly the multi objective search is performed in order to sample the Pareto front and then a fitting criterion is applied to perform the ultimate choice. The *interactive* approaches, like that proposed in this chapter, are capable to overcome the previously described drawbacks.
The performance of a MOP solver can be evaluated on the basis of different criteria: capability of finding Pareto optimal solutions; capability of uniformly sampling the Pareto front; limited computational cost. All these criterion have been considered in evaluating the performance of the algorithms presented in this chapter.

3. Neural Network approximation model

As previously mentioned, one of the most effective approximation approach is based on Artificial Neural Networks. A Neural Network (NN) suitably trained with a limited number of configurations can be successfully used in the optimization procedure, and it can evaluate the objectives values instead of the costly assessment of the numerical procedure. Indeed, it is well known that NNs are effective tools for modelling the non-linear interactions among multiple variables (Principe et al., 2000, Haykin, 1998).
In our procedure a three layers MultiLayer Perceptron (MLP) is trained to capture the functional relationship between the design parameters and the objective functions of the optimization problem. The structure of the used MLP is shown in Fig. 2.
The functional relationship is expressed as in the following:

$$\begin{cases} \underline{\underline{W}}_2 \cdot \sigma\left(\underline{\underline{W}}_1 \underline{x} + \underline{b}_1\right) + \underline{b}_2 = \underline{u} \\ \underline{x} \in D_{\underline{x}} \end{cases} \tag{2}$$

where $\underline{x}$ is the input of the network (corresponding to the design variables), $\underline{y}$ and $\underline{h}$ are the input and the output of the hidden layer, respectively, $\sigma(\cdot)$ is the hidden logistic activation function, and $\underline{u}$ is the output of the network (corresponding to the specified target). In the case of Fig. 2, the output layer has a linear activation function.

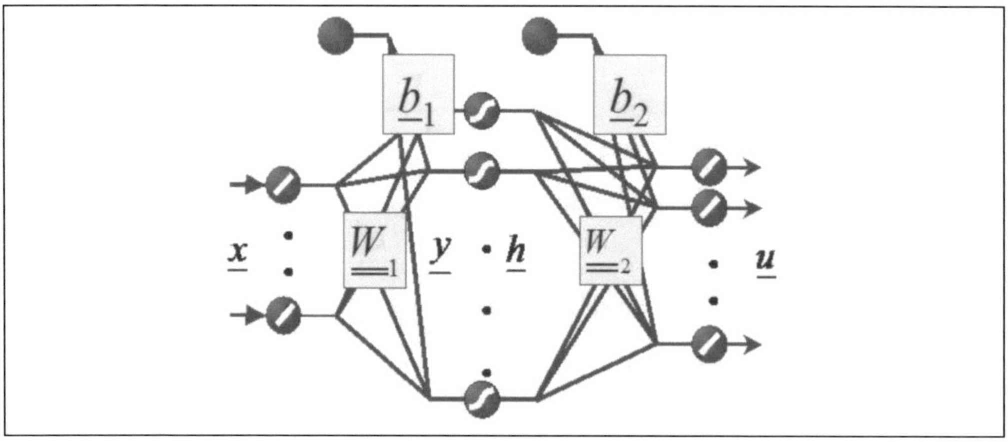

Fig. 2. MLP neural network architecture with a single hidden layer.

$\underline{\underline{W}}_1$ and $\underline{\underline{W}}_2$ are the weights of the connections between the input and hidden layers, and the hidden and the output layers, respectively, and $\underline{b}_1$ and $\underline{b}_2$ are the biases of the hidden and output layers, respectively.

The problem in synthesizing such network is to determine both the number of nodes in the unique hidden layer and the weights of the synapses between the layers. The former part of the problem is usually solved by a trial and error procedure, i.e., by training several networks of increasing or decreasing size on the same training patterns, whereas the latter part is solved by using learning algorithms based on error minimization to find the connection weights.

Recently, different interpretations for neural networks have been given, leading to approach the problem in a completely different way with regard to the classical error correction methods. In particular, a geometrical interpretation of the neural network has been proposed by some authors (Delogu et al., 2008) where each neuron behaves as a linear separator and the connection weights converging to that neuron are equal to the coefficients of the hyper-plane that defines the separation. In particular, in (Delogu et al., 2008) the authors proposed a new method to synthesize MLP networks with a single hidden layer, which are able to correctly classify whatever finite real valued training-set. The key idea of such method is to project the training set in a high-dimensional space, called feature space (Vapnik, 1998), by means of a set of step functions. The images of the two classes of training examples are always linearly separable in the feature space, therefore it is possible to define a unique output neuron that performs the definitive separation.

3.1 Synthesis of the Neural Network

In (Carcangiu et al., 2009a) the method for the synthesis of neural classifiers described in (Delogu et al., 2008) has been adapted to the synthesis of neural regressors.

In order to synthesize the MLP neural network, the function approximation problem has to be firstly converted in a classification problem. To this end, the continuous values of the function to be approximated have to be quantized. Associating a binary coding to each interval, a classification problem can be defined, where each digit is associated to an output node of the network. By choosing a coding with $\log_2 N$ bits, where N is the number of quantization levels, the minimal dimension of the output layer is obtained. The activation functions of both hidden and output nodes are step functions. The number of nodes in the hidden layer, as well as the synaptic weights of the network, will be automatically set during the training phase following the procedure in (Delogu et al., 2008).

In order to obtain a continuous approximation function, the step activation functions of the hidden nodes of the previously synthesized neural network are substituted with sigmoid functions:

$$\sigma(y_i) = \frac{1}{1+\exp(-\alpha_i y_i)}$$

where y_i is the input to the ith hidden neuron, and α_i tunes the slope of the ith sigmoid. Furthermore, the second layer of connections and the output neurons are substituted by a unique linear output neuron and the corresponding connections. The connections weights between the hidden layer and the output node have to be evaluated, in order to minimize

the mean squared error on the training set. As the output of the hidden layer and the output of the network are linearly related, the best approximation is obtained with the regression hyper-plane. The coefficients of such hyper-plane are used as connections weights of the second layer. The value of the mean squared error depends on the correlation between the output of the hidden layer and the output of the network, which in turn is affected by the slope coefficients α_i. The best values of the coefficients can be found by means of an iterative optimization procedure. In this way we can construct an MLP that is able to approximate a continuous function with a prefixed precision.
As an example, let us consider the analytical Schwefel function defined in a 1-D input space:

$$f(x) = -x \cdot \sin\left(\sqrt{x}\right) \qquad 0 \le x \le 500$$

This function presents several local minima. In Fig. 3, the normalized Schwefel function is reported (continuous line). In order to convert the function in a discrete one, N=32 intervals are chosen (see Fig. 3); hence the corresponding binary coding has 5 digits.

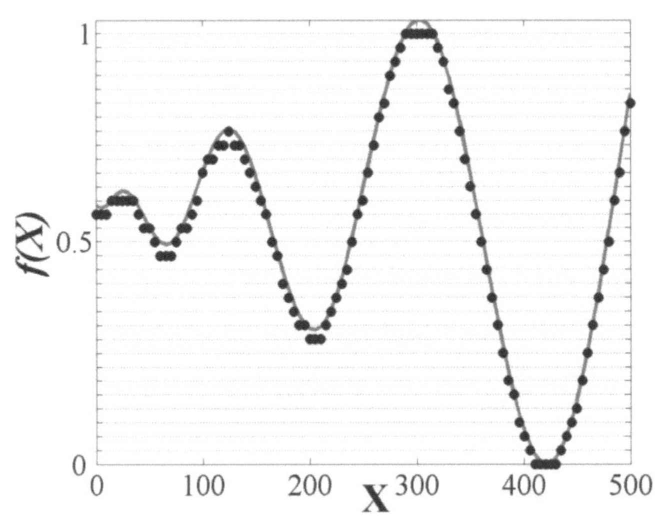

Fig. 3. **Continuous line**: Schwefel function; **dots**: the training set.

The neural network to be synthesized has one input node, corresponding to the x values, and 5 output nodes that correspond to the 5 digits of the binary coding. A training set of 100 examples is selected (see the dots in Fig. 3), and the synthesis of the network is obtained running the procedure in (Delogu et al., 2008).
In Fig. 4 a) the Schwefel function approximated by the smoothed neural model is shown, whereas in Fig. 4 b) the corresponding approximation error is reported. The values of the parameters α_i have been obtained minimizing the MSE evaluated on 500 examples.

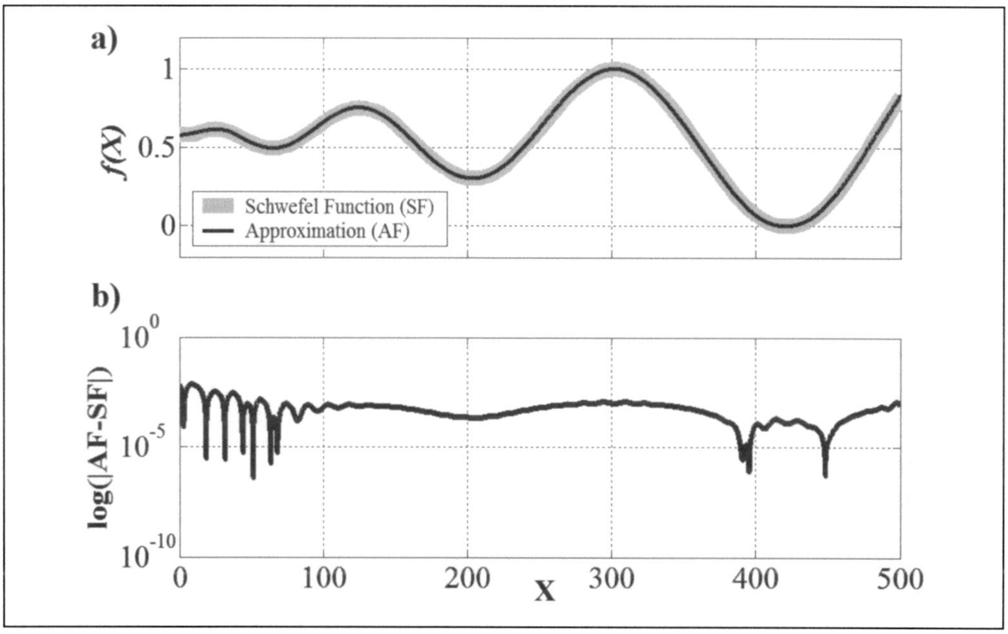

Fig. 4. a) **Continuous gray line**: Schwefel function (SF); **Continuous black line**: function approximated by the neural model (AF); b) absolute approximation error.

4. Neural Network inversion

The procedures proposed in this chapter consist in inverting the NN model of the problem. The aim of the inverting procedure is to determine the inputs that correspond to prefixed target outputs (Jensen et al., 1999, Bao-Liang Lu et al., 1999).

Referring to Fig. 5, the inversion of the MLP consists in finding a solution of the non linear neural network equations system:

$$\begin{aligned} &a)\quad \underline{\underline{W}}_1 \cdot \underline{x} + \underline{b}_1 = \underline{y} \\ &b)\quad \underline{\underline{W}}_2 \cdot \underline{h} + \underline{b}_2 = \underline{u} \\ &c)\quad \underline{h} = \sigma\left(\underline{y}\right) \end{aligned} \tag{3}$$

The non linearity is introduced by the non linear activation function of the hidden neurons.

Since non linear equations can have multiple solutions, it seems that also the direct neural network model has a built-in non-invertible character (Rico-Martinez et al., 2000).

Nevertheless, if the target of the network can be specified with a prefixed degree of error, the iterative procedure in (Cherubini et al., 2005) can be run in order to find (if it exists) a solution whose value differs from the specified target less that the error threshold imposed. If this solution does not exist, the error constraints can be relaxed until a solution is found.

By means of equation (3.a), the input domain $\boldsymbol{D}_x$ can be linearly projected into the space **Y** where the vector $\underline{y}$ is defined, obtaining the domain $\boldsymbol{D}_y$. This means that, in order to match the constraints of the input, the vector $\underline{y}$ has to belong to $\boldsymbol{D}_y$. On the other hand, by means of equation (3.b), the output domain $\boldsymbol{D}_u$ can be linearly projected into the space **H** where the

vector $\underline{h}$ is defined, obtaining the domain D_h. In order to match the constraints of the output, the vector $\underline{h}$ has to belong to D_h. The equation (3.c) states a biunivocal relationship between $\underline{y}$ and $\underline{h}$, so that the domain D_y can be projected into the space **H** throughout the hidden layer obtaining the domain D'_y. Note that, also D_h can be projected into the space **Y** throughout the hidden layer. A point, which belongs to the intersection between the two domains D_h and D'_y matches at the same time the constraints of the input and the constraints of the output, and then it is a solution of the design problem.
In literature, there are several papers that deal with projection algorithms for finding intersection points between two convex sets (Elser et al., 2007; Bauschke et al., 2002). In particular, in (Bauschke et al., 2002) the convergence of the Fienup's algorithm (Fienup, 1982) to the intersection of two convex sets has been proven. No results are present in literature, which demonstrated the convergence for non convex sets. In fact, in the majority of literature, which deals with most difficult real problems, the convergence is based almost entirely on a large body of empirical evidence, as claimed in (Elser et al., 2007).

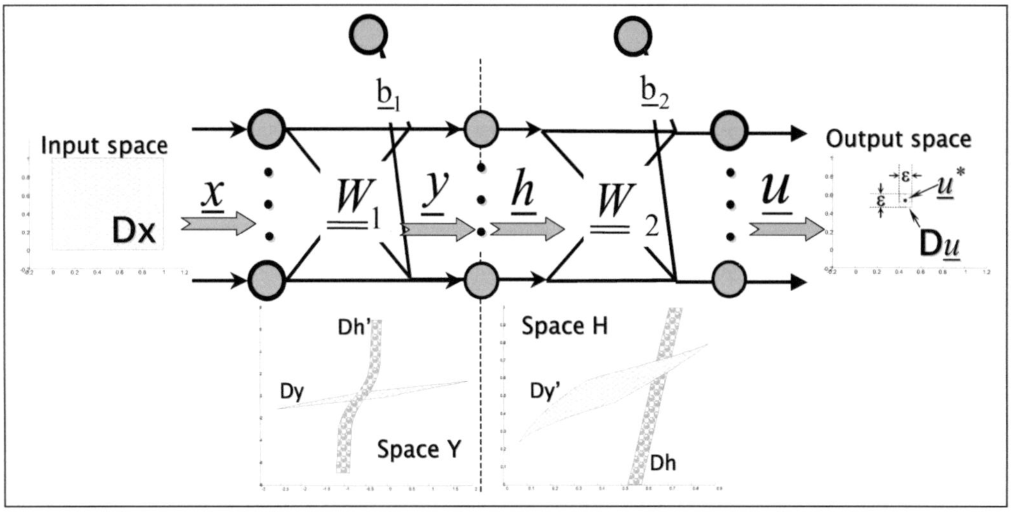

Fig. 5. MLP network structure: D_x is the input domain, D_u is the output domain, D_y and D_h are the domains of $\underline{y}$ and $\underline{h}$ respectively.

The problem of finding the intersection between non convex sets has been also dealt with in (Carcangiu et al., 2009b). Let us suppose, to fix the ideas, that the domain D_h has been projected into the space **Y** (before the hidden layer), and we are trying to find out a point of the intersection I_{yh} between the nonlinear projected domain D'_h and the linear domain D_y. Starting from a point external to a linear domain, it is easy projecting such point on the domain, namely to find the point of the domain nearest to the starting point. Projecting is more difficult in the case of nonlinear domains. The easiness to project a point on a linear domain is due to the fact that one must follow a linear path in the direction orthogonal to one plane. This is no longer valid for a nonlinear surface, because a univocal orthogonal direction does not exist, so the shortest path to reach the surface is not known a priori. In the case on study, one has difficulties on projecting points on the nonlinear domain D'_h, whereas there is no difficult if the same projection is performed in the space **H**, where the domain is linear. In order to exploit the algorithms available for linear domains, the nonlinear facets of the domain I_{yh} are approximated by means of hyperplanes. In doing this, we are aided by the fact that each coordinate of the space **Y** is related to its corresponding coordinate of the space **H** independently from the others. Therefore, we can approximate the nonlinear facets by substituting the sigmoidal functions with their first-order approximation:

$$w_1\sigma(y_1)+...+w_n\sigma(y_n) \cong w_1\left[\sigma(y_{10})+\sigma'(y_1)\cdot(y_1-y_{10})\right]+...+w_n\left[\sigma(y_{n0})+\sigma'(y_n)\cdot(y_1-y_{n0})\right] \quad (4)$$

where $\sigma(\cdot)$ is the sigmoidal function assumed for the neurons of the hidden layer, $\sigma'(\cdot)$ represents the first-order derivative of the sigmoid, $\underline{y}_0=(y_{10},\ldots,y_n)$ represents the starting point from which the projection has to be calculated. The goodness of the projection on the approximated domain depends on the precision of the approximation (4), and then on the length of the step between the starting and the projected points.

Anyway, the substitution (4) allows one to treat the domain I_{yh} as if it were linear, the starting point can be projected on the approximated domain and a new linear approximation is calculated in the arrival point.

In Fig. 6 a sequence is shown that describes how the projection procedure performs. Starting from a generic point $\underline{y}_0$ of the space **Y**, e.g. a point belonging to D_y, firstly a first order approximation of the sigmoid functions is calculated, taking the point $\underline{y}_0$ as reference point. The domain D'_{h} is transformed in the domain L_h and a point of the intersection with D_y is searched. If such point belongs also to I_{yh}, the procedure ends, otherwise the obtained point is assumed as starting point in the successive iteration.

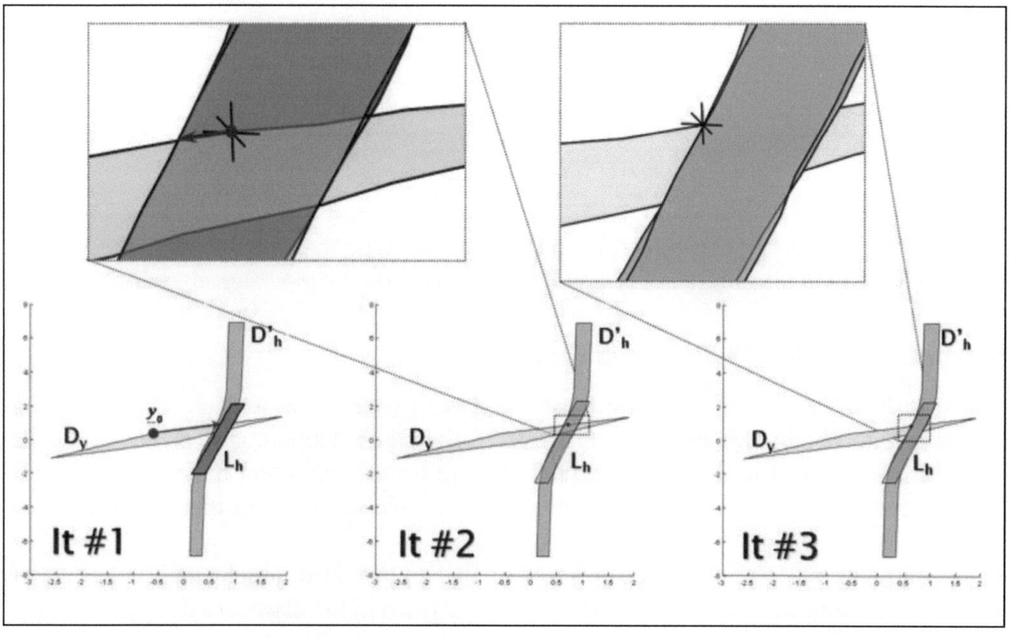

Fig. 6. Procedure for intersection searching.

The intersection between D_y and L_h could be empty, but this not implies that there isn't a solution of the inversion problem. Hence, if no point is found that belongs to the intersection between D_y and L_h, one of the two nearest points between such domains is taken as solution.

A suitable relaxation of the constraints on one or both the input and the output domains will make the intersection $\boldsymbol{I}_{yh}$ not empty and the procedure can be performed once again.
In Fig. 7, the result of the procedure applied to the neural model, which approximates the 1-D Schwefel function, is reported.
The iterative procedure converges to the optimum (circle in Fig. 7 a)). As can be noted from Fig. 7 b), the trajectory followed by the inversion algorithm, starting from a randomly chosen point, crosses a local minimum and reaches the global minimum in 14 iterations.

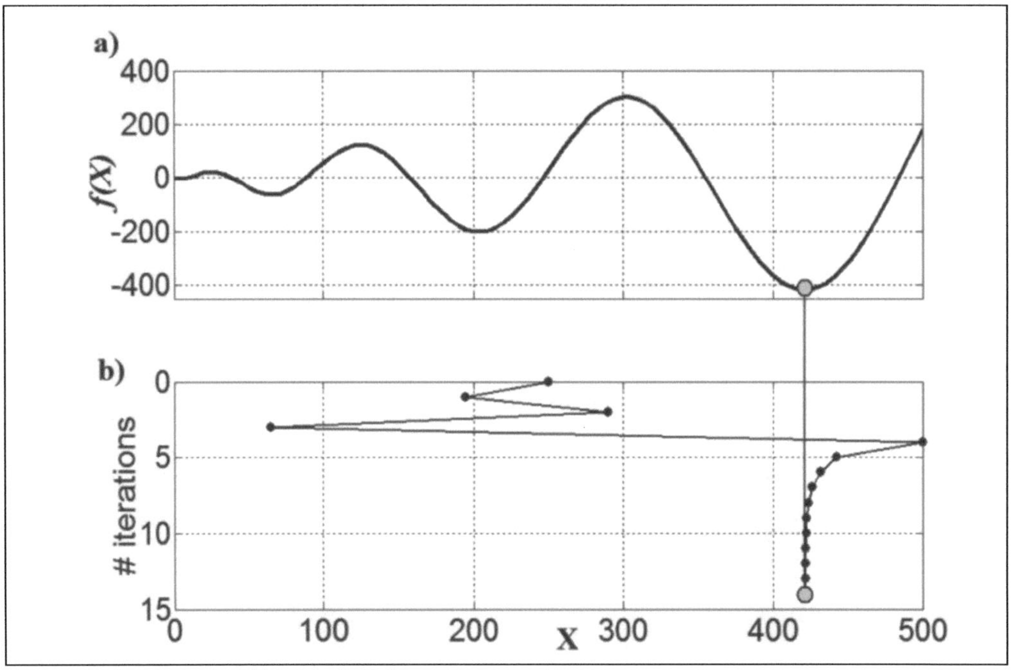

Fig. 7. a): *Continuous line*: Schwefel function approximated by the neural model; *dot*: optimal objective function value founded; b) Trajectory followed by the inversion algorithm.

5. Sampling of the whole Pareto Front (IN-MO)

Using an MLP to describe the relationship between parameters and objective functions allows one to obtain two advantages: reducing the computational cost of function calls, which is the main obstacle to use some search strategies; exploiting the neural model in order to search the Pareto points directly in the objective space rather than in the decision space.
In the following, a search algorithm is described that allows us to sample the frontier (with a user-defined sampling step) starting from whatever point in the objectives domain. In Fig. 8, this method is illustrated for a problem with two objectives to be maximized.
Starting from a feasible point in the objective space, one can move toward the utopia point until an unfeasible solution is reached, which means that the frontier has been reached. Starting from this first point (0) one can start to sample the frontier. Firstly, the desired sampling step Δ of the frontier is set. Then, a circle is ideally drawn with centre placed on

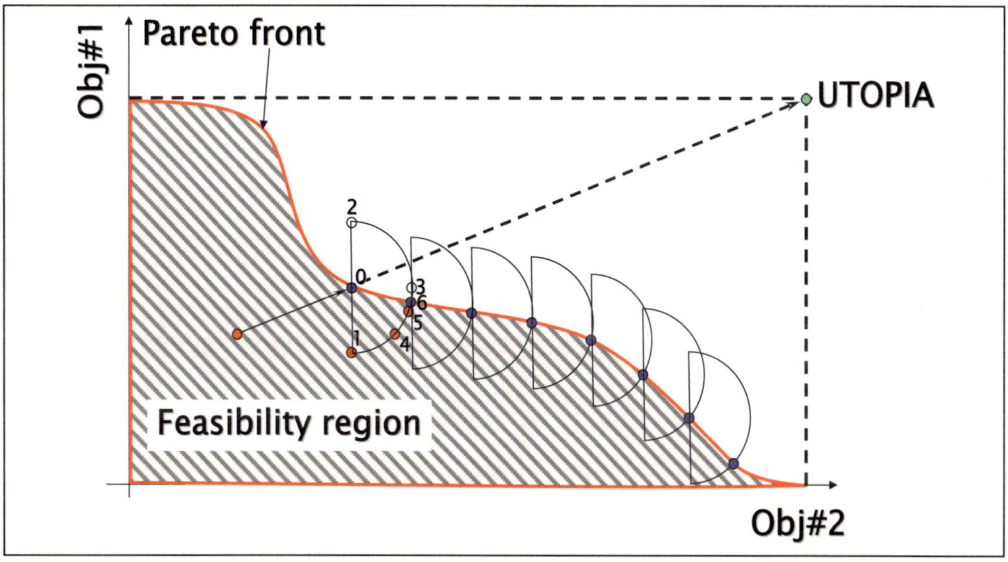

Fig. 8. Sampling of the Pareto front with IN-MO algorithm.

the first point (0) and radius equal to the sampling step. Two points (1) and (2) can be identified on the opposite sides of the circle: one in the feasibility region (1), and one in the non feasibility region (2). In a polar coordinates system with origin in the point (0), these points have coordinates:

$$p(1)=\begin{cases} r=\Delta \\ \theta=-\pi/2 \end{cases} \qquad p(2)=\begin{cases} r=\Delta \\ \theta=\pi/2 \end{cases}$$

By means of, e.g., a bisection method, the intersection between the circle and the Pareto front (point 6) is reached. The new point becomes the centre of a new circle and the procedure is iterated until the whole frontier is reconstructed.

Once the frontier is available, a control on the dominance allows one to select the subset of frontier points that belong to the Pareto Front. The final choice is taken *a posteriori* by the decision maker on the basis of a fitness criterion.

6. Strategy-Driven Search Algorithm (SD-MO)

The large majority of approaches to a MOP consist of two stages: firstly a multiobjective search is performed in order to obtain a set of optimal solutions called Pareto front or non-dominated solutions, and then a fitting criterion is applied to perform the ultimate choice. Hence, the selection of a single solution from the set of non-dominated solutions is an *a posteriori* operation and the final solution consists of the optimal point that best fits the requirements of the decision maker.

Instead, in the approach here proposed, the usually unfeasible utopia solution is evaluated and then a strategy is assumed in order to iteratively improve the values of the objective functions with respect to a starting feasible solution, until an unfeasible solution is reached. Said strategy corresponds to a trajectory in the objective space (see Fig. 9), and the aim of the procedure is to find the intersection between such trajectory and the Pareto front. The choice of that trajectory is left to the DM.

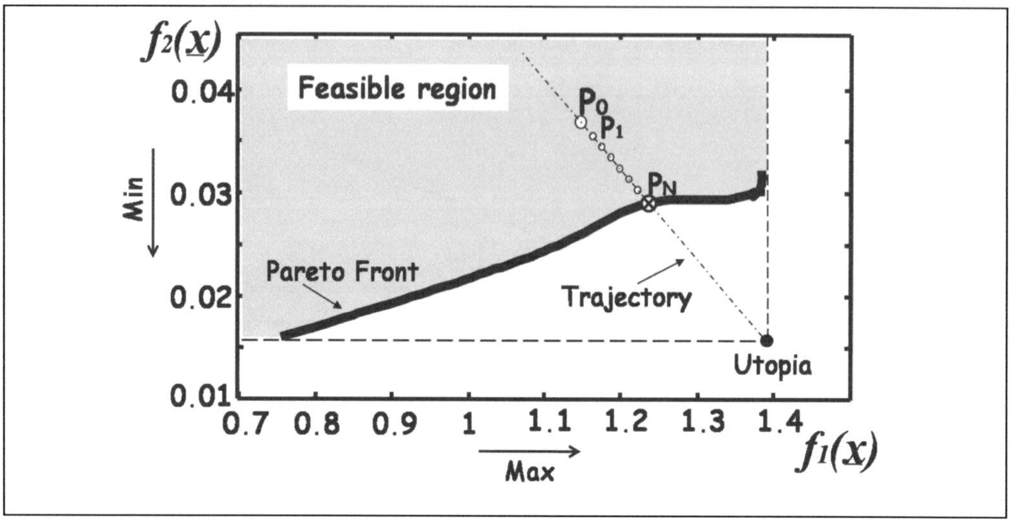

Fig. 9. Pareto front and search trajectory for a MOP.

Thanks to the NN inversion algorithm, such trajectory can be run along directly in the objective space rather than in the decision space. Starting from an initial feasible point P_0 on the trajectory (see Fig. 9) the algorithm iteratively move towards the utopia point until the unfeasible region is reached.

In this way, both the *a posteriori* information consisting in the feasibility of the found point and the *a priori* knowledge, imposed by the DM, are used to guide the search towards the desired non-dominated solution.

In order to find a frontier solution that belongs to the given trajectory, the proposed procedure implements a two-phases method.

In the first phase a starting point is searched, which belongs both to the feasible region and to the trajectory. Generally, such point will be dominated (i.e., it will not belong to the Pareto front).

The second phase consists in searching a frontier point, by following the trajectory.

Firstly, let us suppose the trajectory be a straight line. In the following subsection, the extension to the case of piecewise linear trajectory is given. Let

$$f_K = \underline{m}^T \cdot \underline{f}_{1,\ldots,K-1} + n \tag{5}$$

be the linear trajectory in the objective space, where K is the dimension of the objectives space, $\underline{f}_{1,\ldots,K-1}$ is the vector of all the objectives but the K-th, $\underline{m}$ and n are the coefficients of the linear trajectory, carried on the K-th objective function f_K. The values of objective functions in (5) can be expressed as a function of the parameters of the MLP neural network model:

$$\underline{W}_{2,K}^T \cdot \underline{h} + b_{2,K} = \underline{m}^T \cdot \left(\underline{\underline{W}}_{2,(1\ldots K-1)} \cdot \underline{h} + \underline{b}_{2,(1\ldots K-1)} \right) + n \tag{6}$$

where $\underline{\mathbf{W}}_{2,K}$ is the K-th column of $\underline{\underline{W}}_2$, and $b_{2,K}$ is the K-th element of $\underline{b}_2$. By re-ordering the equation (6), the following equation is obtained:

$$\left(\underline{W}_{2,K}^{T} - \underline{m}^{T} \cdot \underline{\underline{W}}_{2,(1\ldots K-1)}\right) \cdot \underline{h} + \left(b_{2,K} - \underline{m}^{T} \cdot \underline{b}_{2,(1\ldots K-1)}\right) = n \tag{7}$$

The equation (7) represents a constraint for a new MLP neural network represented in Fig. 10. That network has only one output, the same input and hidden layers of the MLP in (3), and the same connections weights $\underline{\underline{W}}_1$ and $\underline{b}_1$, whereas the connections weights between hidden and output layers and the output bias are respectively equal to:

$$\begin{aligned} \underline{A} &= \underline{W}_{2,K} - \underline{\underline{W}}_{2,(1\ldots K-1)}^{T} \cdot \underline{m} \\ \beta &= b_{2,K} - \underline{m}^{T} \cdot \underline{b}_{2,(1\ldots K-1)} \end{aligned} \tag{8}$$

Note that the parameters $\underline{A}$ and β are known as they are expressed in terms of the parameters of the neural model in (3) and in terms of the coefficients of the linear trajectory, which are imposed by the DM. Thanks to the equations in (8), the first phase of the procedure can be solved by inverting the one-output neural network in Fig. 10.

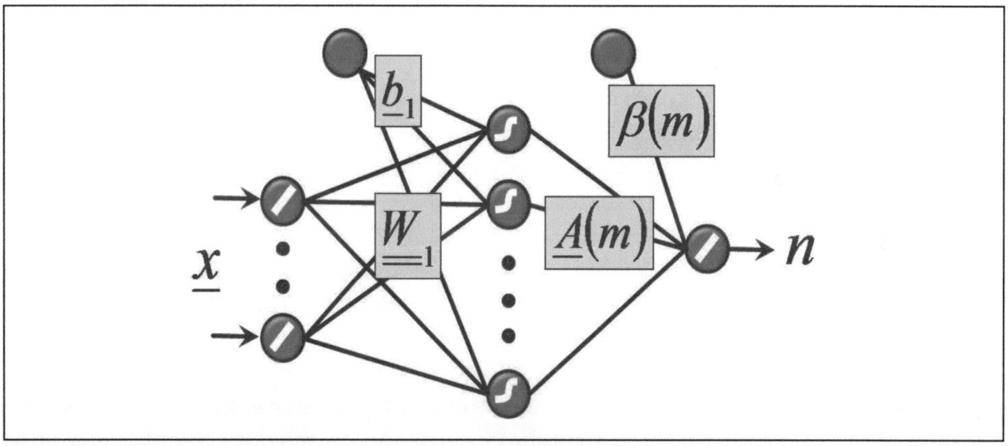

Fig. 10. NN for the search of the trajectory in the objective space.

Using as target output the value of the coefficient n, a corresponding input $\underline{x}$ is obtained. Then, by forwarding the obtained input $\underline{x}$ through the neural model in (3), a point P_0=$P_0(\underline{f})$ in the objective space is found, which surely lies on the trajectory (see Fig. 9). Once the point P_0 has been found, a step is performed on the linear trajectory towards the utopia point, and the endpoint of the step is assumed as target output in the inversion of the neural model in (3). If the inversion process leads to a feasible configuration, the procedure is iterated until the inversion process does not converge. The last visited feasible point P_N is assumed as belonging to the frontier of the feasible region. The step size is chosen according to the desired approximation of the final solution P_N to the frontier of the feasible region.
Such frontier point could not belong to the Pareto front depending on whether it is placed on a concave portion of the feasible region, or because the Pareto front is discontinuous (see Fig. 11, referring to the analytical problem reported in (Deb et al., 2005), which is discontinuous and non-convex).

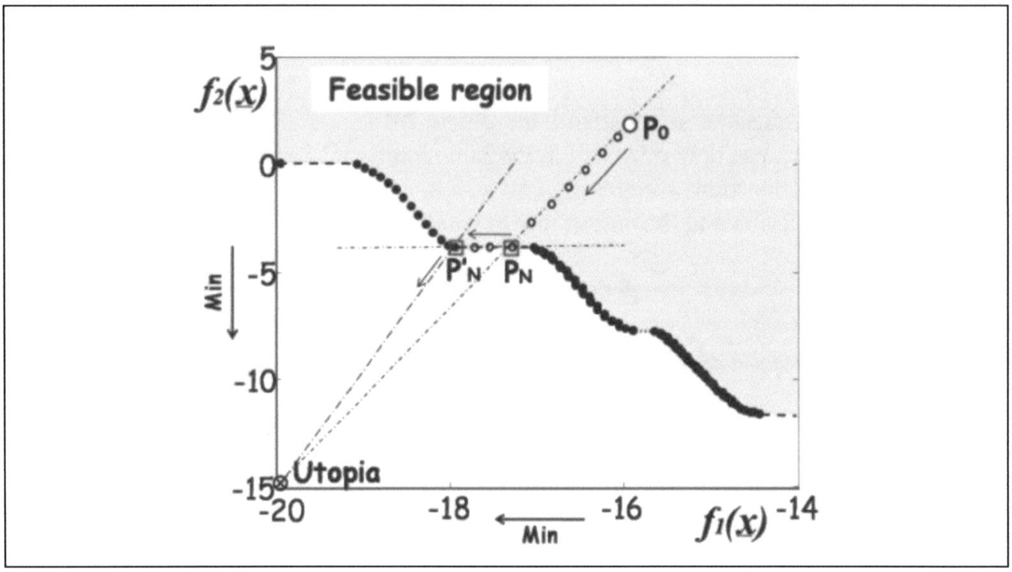

Fig. 11. Pareto front (•) and search trajectory (- ·-) for the Kursawe analytical problem (Deb et al., 2005).

For this reason, a strategy has been implemented to verify if the final point P_N belongs to the Pareto front rather than simply to the frontier of the feasible region. To this end, starting from P_N, one at a time, we try to improve the value of each objective, leaving the remaining ones at the values corresponding to the frontier point.

If this search gives positive result, P_N is substituted by the new dominating point (P'_N in Fig. 11). As in general also P'_N could not belong to the Pareto front, the decision maker has to define a new linear trajectory along which to search a new frontier point.

6.1 Piecewise linear trajectory

A piecewise linear trajectory formalizes a possible strategy introduced by the DM. By assuming an enough fine segmentation of the piecewise linear trajectory, a continuous curve can be also well approximated.

As an example, in Fig. 12, referring to the electromagnetic problem reported in (Di Barba & Mognaschi, 2005), a piecewise linear trajectory is chosen (U_0, U_1, U_2...).

Following the linear trajectory U_0-U_1, the two objectives deteriorate at the same rate, but the DM could be interested in introducing further constraints, e.g., on the maximum deterioration of objective function f_1, hence the new linear trajectory U_1-U_2 is followed whenever that constraint is violated. The new trajectory deteriorates only f_2. When f_2 deteriorates too much, the new trajectory U_2-U_3 is adopted.

Each segment of the trajectory represents a linear strategy where the current utopia point is represented by its non-dominated end point (U_0, U_1, U_2,... in Fig. 12). If the final point P_N^0 belongs to the segment $\overline{U_0U_1}$, the procedure terminates and P_N^0 is the searched frontier point, otherwise U_1 is assumed as new utopia point and the linear trajectory U_1-U_2 is assumed as new strategy. The procedure is iterated for all the segments until a solution is found that lies in the current segment of the piecewise linear trajectory (P_N^2 in Fig. 12).

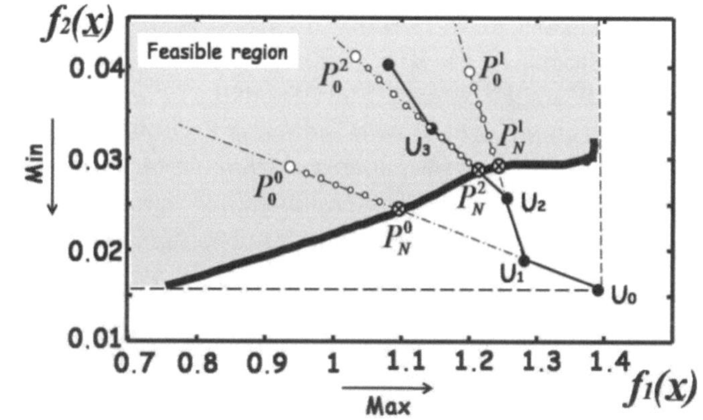

Fig. 12. Piecewise linear trajectory strategy (-•-) applied to the magnetic pole problem (Di Barba & Mognaschi, 2005).

7. Application and results

In order to evaluate the performance of the proposed approaches, both analytical and electromagnetic benchmarks have been used. The first two examples are electromagnetic problems for which the Pareto front has been sampled using the procedure presented in Section 5. One of such examples has been used to test the optimization strategy described in Section 6, together with an analytical problem.

7.1 High field superconducting dipole magnet

The dipole magnet (Fig. 13) consists of a pair of identical saddle-shaped coils of rectangular cross section (chequered area in Fig. 13). A circular shape iron yoke (dashed) is used to improve the field quality and intensity over the bore cross-section. An outer cylinder made of austenitic steel encloses the whole dipole assembly and provides pre-compression at cryogenic temperature due to the differential contraction.

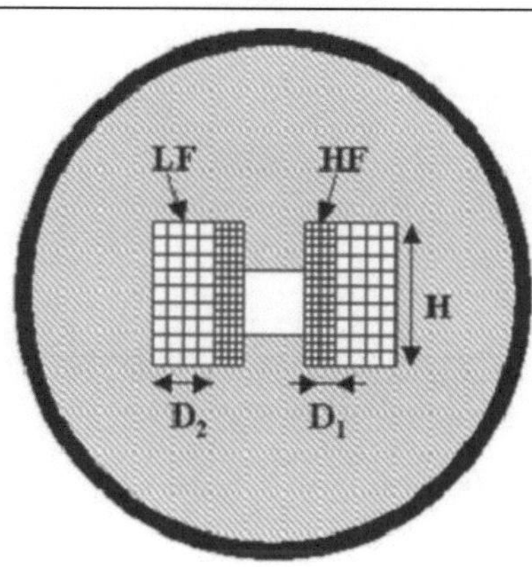

Fig. 13. Dipole assembly (Portone et al., 2006).

Each coil is made of a High Field (HF) section and a Low Field (LF) section. All conductors carry the same operating current, all turns being in series. The HF grade differs from the LF grade in the outer dimensions of the superconducting strands, resulting in a different current density between HF and LF sections. The HF and the LF sections together constitute the winding pack. The design problem consists in finding the optimal values of the HF and LF winding areas, therefore reducing the superconducting cable, in order to have a 12.5 T magnetic field value in the dipole axis. The multiobjective optimization problem can be stated as the minimization of the cost of the superconducting coils, while the prescribed magnetic field value can be considered as a constraint or as objective function to be maximized. The design variables of the MOP are reported in Fig. 13: the width D_1 of the HF section, the width D_2 of the LF section, and the height H of the winding pack.

This benchmark is a three parameters-two objectives problem, in which the design parameters are D_1, D_2, and H (see Fig. 13), and the objectives are the magnetic induction **B** and the total winding pack area ***A***. The neural network model has 3 input neurons, 12 hidden neurons, and 2 output neurons, corresponding to *B* and *A*. The training, validation and test sets consist of 2448, 306, and 306 couples of input-output patterns.

When the learning phase ends, the MSE in the validation set is equal to 2.9e-006. The maximum distance between a point analytically calculated and the corresponding point approximated by the neural model is 0.0564. In this case, the sampling step Δ has been set equal to 0.01, which corresponds to the denormalized steps ΔB=0.39 T, and ΔA=0.003 m^2.

In Fig. 14 the Pareto front obtained with the search algorithm is presented. The point corresponding to the actual design parameters in (Portone et al., 2006) is indicated with a circle.

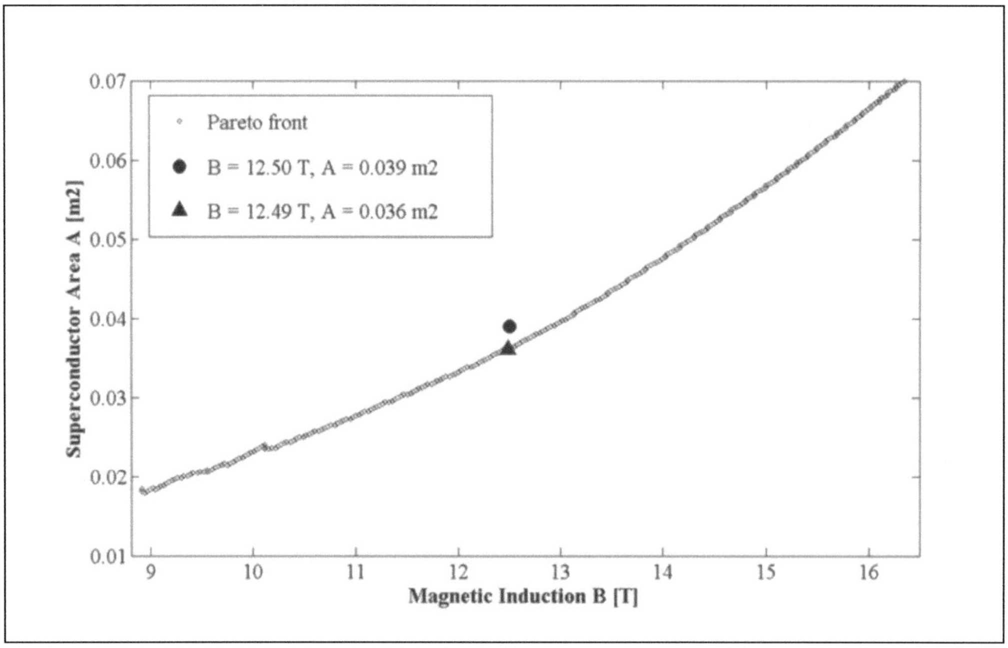

Fig. 14. Pareto front for the dipole magnet.

The closest point of the sampled Pareto front (triangle in Fig. 14) corresponds to the following design parameters: B= 12.489 T; A= 0.036 m^2; D_1=0.0289 m; D_2=0.1838 m; H=0.1696 m. A saving of about 8% in the superconducting material is obtained, with a magnetic field variation less than 1%.

7.2 Optimal electromagnetic devices design (IN-MO algorithm)

The optimal shape design of a magnetic pole is considered (Di Barba & Mognaschi, 2005) to critically evaluate the suitability of the proposed algorithm in the field of electromagnetic devices design.

In Fig. 15, the model of the device is shown. Because of the symmetry with respect to the x-axis, only a half of the magnetic pole rectilinear section has been modeled. The current density is uniform in the winding and is zero elsewhere. The non-linear permeability of the ferromagnetic material is taken into account.

As far as the inverse problem is concerned, four design variables y_1, y_2, x_3, x_4 are selected. The feasible region of the design variables is defined by the conditions of both geometric congruency and non-saturation of the material.

Two objective functions are defined:

- f_1 is the maximum component of magnetic induction in the y-axis direction along the air gap midline, to be maximized;
- f_2 is the average component of magnetic induction in the x-axis direction in the winding, to be minimized.

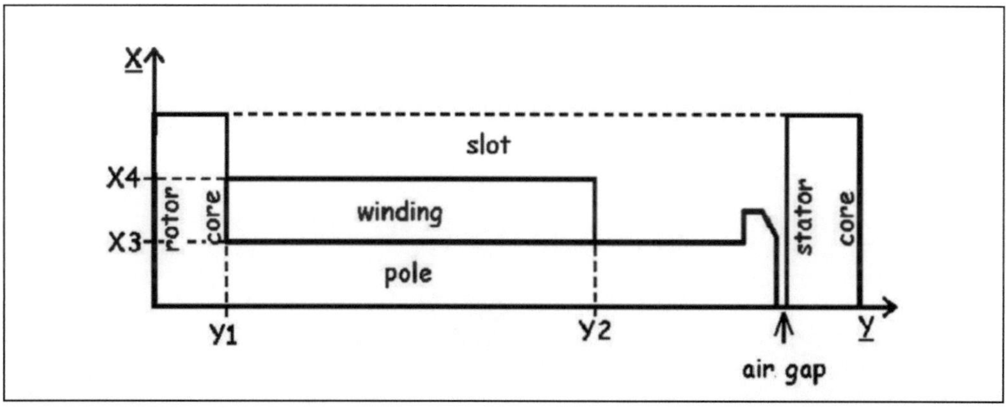

Fig. 15. Magnetic Pole.

The neural model has 4 inputs corresponding to the design variables, whose values are normalized in the range [-1 , 1]. The hidden layer has 40 neurons, having hyperbolic tangent activation function. The output layer has two neurons, corresponding to the objective functions. Also the output values are normalized in the same interval of the inputs. The neural network is trained to associate the input vector of the design variables to the corresponding values of the objective function. To this end a set of input-output pairs is selected, and the network is modified in order to minimize the difference between the expected output and that one calculated with the network. The training examples are calculated by means of FEM simulations.

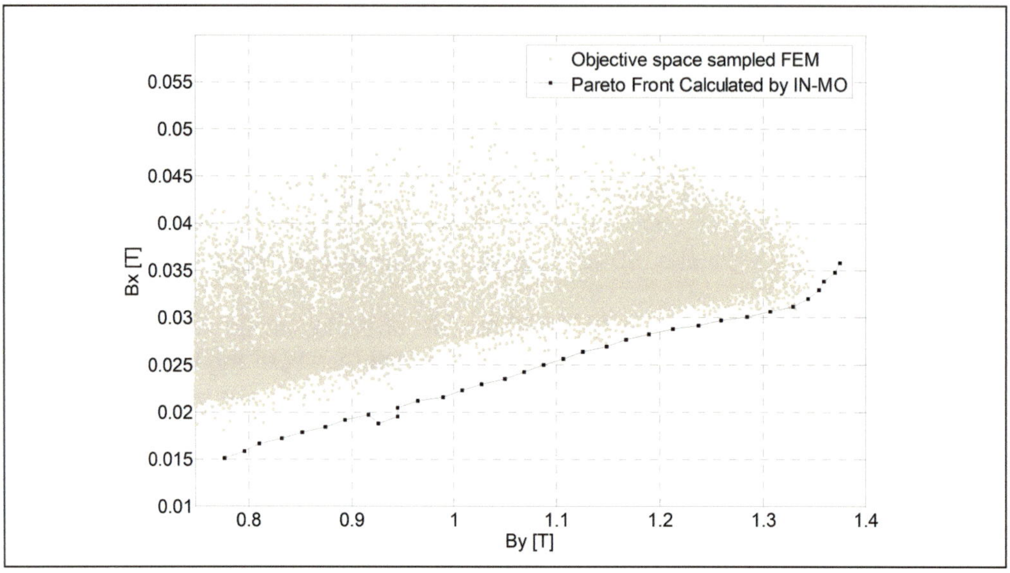

Fig. 16. Magnetic pole: approximated Pareto front.

Fig. 16 shows a random sampling of the objectives space and the Pareto front with 34 sample points obtained by means of the procedure proposed in Section 5.

It has to be highlighted that, the approximation of the Pareto front mostly depends on the accuracy of the neural approximation model, which is known a priori. This is a considerable advantage, especially in engineering problems.

7.3 Analytical test for the SD-MO algorithm

The Kursawe function is a three parameters-two objectives problem (Deb et al., 2005), where the two cost functions to be minimized are stated as:

$$\min\begin{cases} f_1(x_1,x_2,x_3)=\sum_{i=1}^{2}\left(-10\cdot e^{-0.2\cdot\sqrt{x_i^2+x_{i+1}^2}}\right) \\ f_2(x_1,x_2,x_3)=\sum_{i=1}^{3}\left(\left|x_i\right|^{0.8}+5\cdot\sin\left(x_i\right)^3\right) \end{cases} \tag{9}$$

where: $-5 \le x_1, x_2, x_3 \le 5$.

The MLP neural network model has 3 input neurons, corresponding to the values x_1, x_2, and x_3, 50 hidden neurons, and 2 output neurons, corresponding to f_1 and f_2.

In Fig. 11, the analytically calculated Pareto front is reported. As the Pareto front is discontinuous and non convex, the trajectory chosen by the DM could intersect the frontier of the feasible region in a point (P_N) that does not belong to the Pareto front. The proposed procedure looks for points dominating P_N, moving along the Cartesian coordinates in the objective space, as described in Section 6, and is able to automatically find a new point P_N', which belongs to the Pareto front. A further search is then performed along the new trajectory from P_N' to the utopia point. As can be seen from Fig. 11, no other dominating points do exist, and the procedure stops.

7.4 Optimal electromagnetic devices design (SD-MO algorithm)

As in Section 7.2, in the following the optimal shape design of a magnetic pole (Di Barba & Mognaschi, 2005) has been considered in order to test the computational performance of the SD-MO algorithm.

Note that, the computational cost of the algorithms proposed in literature (Konak et al., 2006, Zitzler & Thiele, 1999) for MOPs exponentially grows with the number of objectives. Conversely, the aim of the SD-MO algorithm is to find a unique solution that both is a Pareto point and fulfills the requirements imposed by the DM. The computational cost of the algorithm is independent from the number of objectives, but only depends on the dimension of the sampling step chosen to follow the trajectory.

As an example, in Fig. 17, a possible piecewise linear trajectory is reported, which formalizes the strategy introduced by the DM. The algorithm starts using as strategy the linear trajectory U_0-U_1. A starting point P_0^0 is found, which lies on this trajectory. Then, a number of steps are performed moving on the trajectory until the frontier of the feasibility region is intersected in the point P_N^0. Such point does not belong to the segment $\overline{U_0U_1}$ of the trajectory, hence U_1 is assumed as new utopia point for the new linear strategy U_1-U_2.

A new starting point P_0^1 is found and the algorithm, moving towards U_1, intersects the frontier in the point P_N^1, which does not belong to the segment $\overline{U_1U_2}$. Finally, the linear trajectory U_2-U_3 is assumed as new strategy, with U_2 as utopia point. In this case, the search terminates in the point P_N^2, which belongs both to the frontier of the feasible region and to the segment $\overline{U_2U_3}$ of the strategy.

This point represents the non-dominated solution of the MOP.

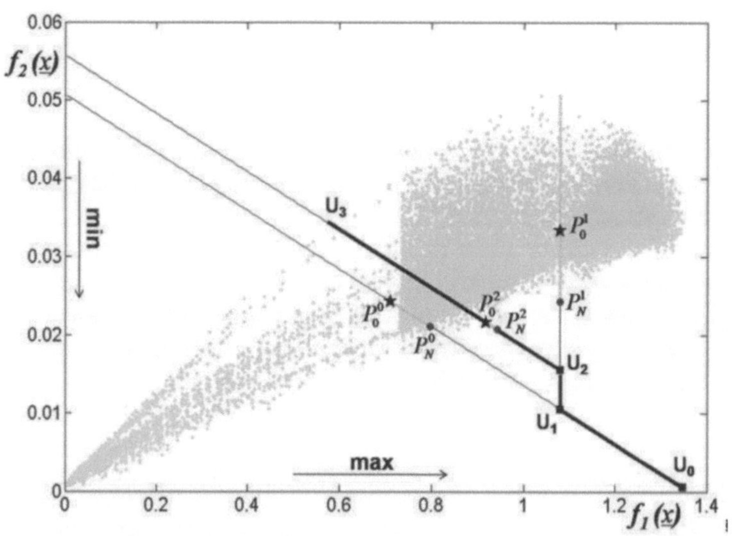

Fig. 17. Piecewise linear trajectory strategy (-•-) applied to magnetic pole problem.

Table I reports the found Pareto optimal solution. The approximated solution given by the neural model has been recalculated using FEM analysis. The error introduced by the approximation model is negligible. Fig. 12 reports the magnetic field distribution in the pole.

Design Parameters				NN Values		FEM Values	
y_1 [m]	y_2 [m]	x_3 [m]	x_4 [m]	f_1 [T]	f_2 [T]	f_1 [T]	f_2 [T]
7.63	14.93	14.49	14.45	0.942	0.02	0.893	0.02

Table 1. Pareto optimal solution of the Magnetic Pole.

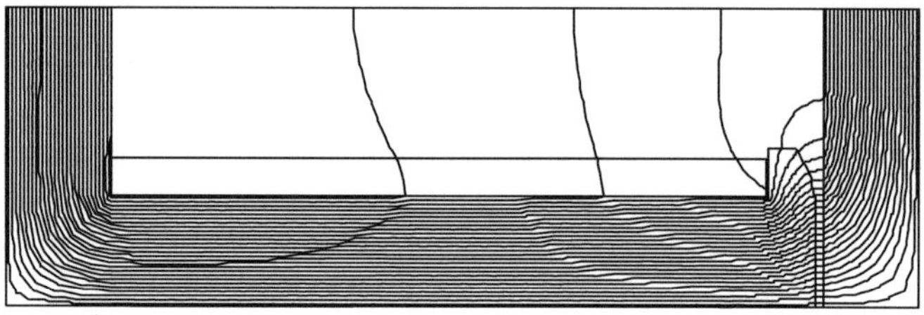

Fig. 12. Magnetic field distribution in the pole.

8. Conclusions

The optimal design of electromagnetic devices is of crucial importance in the modern industry. On the other hand, Multi-Objective Optimization reflects much better than the Single-Objective one the job of the designer, because the best project represents always the best compromise among conflicting exigencies. The performance of an approach that implements a Multi-Objective Optimization is evaluated on the basis of capability of finding Pareto optimal solutions; capability of uniformly sampling the Pareto front; limited computational cost. In this chapter some techniques have been described and the performances are evaluated with some analytical and electromagnetic benchmarks retrieved from the literature.

The capability of finding Pareto solutions has been enhanced by modelling the problem by means of neural networks synthesized by a constructive algorithm that takes under control the approximation error.

A technique that allows one to invert neural networks permits to perform the Pareto points search directly in the objective space. In this way the Pareto front can be uniformly sampled.

The use of neural models of the problem at hand together with an interactive search method, allows one to greatly reduce the computational cost of optimization.

The obtained results confirm the suitability of using the proposed methods in order to find Pareto optimal solutions in all the studied cases.

9. References

Abbass, H.A. (2003). Pareto neuro-evolution: constructing ensemble of neural networks using multi-objective optimization, *Proceedings of CEC'03*, n. 3, pp. 2074 - 2080

Alotto, P. & Nervi, M. A. (2001). An efficient algorithm for the optimization of problems with several local minima, *International Journal for Numerical Methods in Eng.*, n. 50, pp. 847-868

Bao-Liang Lu, Kita, H. & Nishikawa, Y. (1999). Inverting feedforward neural networks using linear and nonlinear programming, *IEEE Transactions on Neural Networks*, vol. 10, no. 6, pp. 1271 - 1290

Bauschke, H.H., Combettes, P.L. & Luke, D.R. (2002). Phase retrieval, error reduction algorithm, and Fienup variants: a view from convex optimization, *Journal of the Optical Society of America A.*, Vol. 19 No. 7, pp. 1334-45

Canova A., Gruosso G. & Repetto M. (2003). Magnetic design optimization and objective function approximation, *IEEE Transactions on Magnetics*, Vol 39, no. 5, pp. 2154-2162

Carcangiu, S., Fanni, A. & Montisci, A. (2008). Multiobjective Tabu Search Algorithms for Optimal Design of Electromagnetic Devices, *IEEE Transactions on Magnetics*, Vol 44, no. 6, pp. 970-973

Carcangiu, S., Fanni, A. & Montisci, A. (2009). A constructive algorithm of neural approximation models for optimization problems, *The International Journal for Computation and Mathematics in Electrical and Electronic Engineering* (COMPEL), vol. 28-5; pp. 1276-1289, ISSN: 0332-1649

Carcangiu, S., Fanni, A. & Montisci, A. (2009). Multi Objective Optimization Algorithm Based on Neural Networks Inversion, *Lecture Notes In Computer Science*, vol. 5517; pp. 744-751, Springer-Verlag, ISBN:978-3-642-02477-1, Berlin, Heidelberg

Cherubini, D., Fanni, A., Montisci, A. & Testoni, P. (2005). Inversion of MLP neural network for direct solution of inverse problems, *IEEE Transactions on Magnetics*, vol. 41, no. 5, pp. 1784-1787

Deb, K., Thiele, L., Laumanns, M. & Zitler, E. (2005). Scalable test problems for evolutionary multi-objective optimization, *TIK-Technical Report.*, no. 122

Delogu, R., Fanni, A., Montisci, A. (2008). Geometrical synthesis of MLP neural networks, *Neurocomputing*, Vol. 71, Issue 4-6, pp. 919-930

Di Barba, P. & Mognaschi, M.E. (2005). Recent Experiences of Multiobjective Optimisation in Electromagnetics: a Comparison of Methods, *The International Journal for Computation and Mathematics in Electrical and Electronic Engineering* (COMPEL), vol. 24, no. 3, pp. 921-930, ISSN: 0332-1649

Elser, V., Rankenburg, I. & Thibault, P. (2007). Searching with iterated maps, *Proceedings of the National Academy of Sciences*, Vol. 104 No. 2, pp. 418-23

Fieldsend, J.E.& Singh, S. (2005). Pareto evolutionary neural networks, *IEEE Transactions on Neural Networks*, vol. 12, no. 2, pp. 338 - 354

Fienup, J.R. (1982). Phase retrieval algorithms: a comparison, *Applied Optics*, Vol. 21, pp. 2758-69

Gottvald, A., Preis, K., Magele, C., Biro, O. & Savini, A. (1992). Global optimization methods for computational electromagnetic, *IEEE Transactions on Magnetics*, Vol. 28 No. 2, pp. 1537 - 1540

Haykin, S. (1998). *Neural Networks: A Comprehensive Foundation, 2nd edition*, Prentice Hall PTR , ISBN:0132733501, Upper Saddle River, NJ, USA

Jensen, C.A., Reed, R.D., Marks, R.J., II, El-Sharkawi, M.A., Jae-Byung Jung, Miyamoto, R.T., Anderson, G.M. & Eggen, C.J. (1999). Inversion of feedforward neural networks: algorithms and applications, *Proceedings of the IEEE*, Vol. 87 No. 9, pp. 1536 - 1549

Konak A., Coit D.W. & Smith A.E. (2006). Multi-Objective Optimization Using Genetic Algorithms: A Tutorial, *Reliability Engineering and System Safety*, Vol. 91, pp. 992-1007

Magele Ch. (1996). TEAM Benchmark Problem 22, available at: www-igte.tu-graz.ac.at/team

Portone, A., Salpietro, E., Bottura, L., Bruzzone, P., Fietz, W., Heller, R., Rifflet, J.-M., Lucas, J., Toral, F., Raff, S. & Testoni, P. (2006). Conceptual Design of the 12.5 T Superconducting EFDA Dipole, *IEEE Trans. on Appl. Superc.*, vol. 16, pp. 1312-1315

Principe J. C., Euliano N. R. & Lefebvre W. C. (2000). *Neural and Adaptive Systems*, J. Wiley & Sons, Inc.

Rico-Martinez R., Adomaitis R. A. & Kevrekidis I. G. (2000). Noninvertibility in neural networks, Computers & Chemical Engineering, Vol. 24, pp. 2417 2433

Takahashi N., Muramatsu K., Natsumeda M., Ohashi K., Miyata K. & Sayama K. (1996). Solution of problem 25 (Optimization of die press model), *Proceedings of ICEF'96*, pp. 383–386

Vapnik V. N. (1998). *Statistical Learning Theory*, Wiley, New York

Wang, L. & Lowther, D.A. (2006). Selection of approximation models for electromagnetic device optimization, *IEEE Transactions on Magnetics*, Vol. 42 No. 4, pp. 1227-30

Zitzler E. & Thiele L. (1999). Multiobjective evolutionary algorithms: A comparative case study and the strength Pareto approach, *IEEE Transactions on Evolutionary Computation*, Vol. 3, pp. 257-271

16

A Fast Harmony Search Algorithm for Unimodal Optimization with Application to Power System Economic Dispatch

Abderrahim Belmadani, Lahouaria Benasla and Mostefa Rahli
Laboratoire d'Optimisation des Réseaux Electrique (LORE)
University of Sciences and Technology of Oran,
Algeria

1. Introduction

Evolutionary algorithms are general-purpose stochastic search methods simulating natural selection and biological evolution. They differ from other optimization methods in the fact maintaining a population of potential solutions to a problem, and not just one solution. Generally, these algorithms work as follows: a population of individuals is randomly initialized where each individual represents a potential solution to the problem. The quality of each solution is evaluated using a fitness function. A selection process is applied during each iteration in order to form a new solution population. This procedure is repeated until convergence is reached. The best solution found is expected to be a near-optimum solution.

HSA that was recently proposed by Greem and al (Greem et al, 2001) is an evolutionary algorithm imitating the improvisation process of musicians. This process is constituted of three steps, in the original HSA, with a fourth step added in the improved version (Geem, 2006). In order to improve the fine-tuning characteristic of HSA, Mahdavi and al developed an Improved Harmony Search Algorithm (IHSA) that differs from original HSA in the fact that some parameters (pitch adjusting rate "PAR" and bandwidth "bw") are adjusted during the improvisation process (Mahdavi et al, 2007). Omran and al proposed another version of HSA named Global-best Harmony Search Algorithm (GHSA), which borrows concepts from swarm intelligence to enhance the performance of HSA (Omran & Mahdavi, 2008). GHSA is an IHSA version with the pitch-adjustment modified such that the new harmony can mimic the best harmony in the Harmony Memory (HM).

In this paper, we propose a Fast version of HSA for the optimization of unimodal quadratic functions. The results (optimum solution and number of improvisations) of HSA, IHSA, GHSA and FHSA are compared for some convex functions (De Jong's function and rotated hyper-ellipsoid function) then for Economic Dispatch (ED).

The ED problem is one of the important optimization problems in power system. Generally, the cost function of each generator is approximately represented by a quadratic function (Wallach & Even, 1986) with a need of a real time response from the optimization system (Rahli & Pirotte, 1999). Therefore, we investigate the effectiveness and the accuracy of different versions of HSA and our proposed version.

2. Economic dispatch

Economic dispatch is the important component of power system optimization. It is defined as the minimization of the combination of the power generation, which minimizes the total cost while satisfying the power balance relation (Benasla et al, 2008)[a]. The problem of economic dispatch can be formulated as minimization of the cost function subjected to the equality and inequality constraints (Benasla et al, 2008)[b].
In power stations, every generator has its input/output curve. It has the fuel input as a function of the power output. But if the ordinates are multiplied by the cost of \$/Btu, the result gives the fuel cost per hour as a function of power output (Wallach & Even, 1986).
In the practical cases, the fuel cost of generator i may be represented as a quadratic function of real power generation:

$$F_i(P_{Gi}) = a_i P_{Gi}^2 + b_i P_{Gi} + c_i \tag{1}$$

The objective function for the entire power system can then be written as the sum of the quadratic cost model at each generator.
This objective function will minimize the total system costs.

$$\text{Min}\left\{F = \sum_{i=1}^{ng} F_i(P_{Gi})\right\} \tag{2}$$

Where F is the total fuel cost of the system, P_{Gi} real power output, ng is the number of generators including the slack bus a_i, b_i and c_i are the cost coefficients of the i-th unit.
Constraints

1. Power balance constraints. The total power generation must cover the total demand P_{ch} and the real power loss in the transmission lines P_L. Hence

$$\sum_{i=1}^{ng} P_{Gi} - P_L - P_{ch} = 0 \tag{3}$$

2. Generation capacity constraints. For stable operation, the generator outputs are restricted by lower and upper limits as follows:

$$P_{Gimin} \le P_{Gi} \le P_{Gimax} \tag{4}$$

3. The Harmony Search Algorithms

The HSA is inspired from the musical process of searching for a perfect state of harmony (Greem et al, 2001). All Harmony Search versions consider the optimization problem defined as:

$$\text{Max or Min } f(x^j) \quad j = 1,\dots,p$$

Subject to: $$x^j_{min} \le x^j \le x^j_{max}$$

The optimization process is directed by four parameters (belmadani et al, 2009):

1. Harmony Memory Size (HMS) is the number of solution vectors stored in HM.
2. Harmony Memory Considering Rate (HMCR) is the probability of choosing one value from HM and (1-HMCR) is the probability of randomly choosing one new feasible value.
3. Pitch Adjusting Rate (PAR) is the probability of choosing a neighboring value of that chosen from HM.
4. Distance bandwidth (bw) defines the neighborhood of a value as [$x^j \pm bw \times U(0,1)$]. U(0,1) is a uniform distribution between 0 and 1.

Another intuitively important parameter is the Number of Iterations (NI) which is the stop criterion of the three previous versions of HSA.

HSA works as follows:

Step 1. Initialize the problem and HSA parameters.
Step 2. Initialize HM by randomly generated (improvised) harmonies.
Step 3. Improvise a new harmony as follows:

for j=1 to p do
if $U(0,1) > HMCR$ then $\quad x^j = x^j_{min} + (x^j_{max} - x^j_{min}) \times U(0,1)$
else (*Memory consideration*)
begin
$x^j = x_i^{\,j}$ where $i \approx U(1,HMS)$
if $U(0,1) \le PAR$ then (*pitch adjustment*)
begin
$x^j = x^j \pm bw \times U(0,1)$
endif
endif
done

Step 4. If the New Harmony (NH) is better than the Worst Harmony (WH) in HM then replace WH by NH.
Step 5. Reiter Steps 3 and 4 until satisfaction of the stop criterion.

The IHSA dynamically updates PAR and bw in improvisation step (Step 3). These two parameters change dynamically with generation number as follows:

$$PAR = PAR_{min} + \frac{PAR_{max} - PAR_{min}}{NI} \times gn \quad \text{and} \quad bw = bw_{max} \times e^{\left(\frac{Ln\left(\frac{bw_{min}}{bw_{max}}\right)}{NI} \times gn\right)}$$

where
PAR_{min} : minimum pitch adjusting rate
PAR_{max} : maximum pitch adjusting rate
NI : number of iterations
gn : generation number
bw_{min} : minimum bandwidth and bw_{max} : maximum bandwidth

The GHSA modifies the pitch adjustment step of the IHSA as follows:

if $U(0,1) \leq PAR$ then (*pitch adjustment*)
begin
$x^j = x^k_{best}$
endif

where best is the index of the best harmony in the HM and $k \approx U(1,p)$. This pitch adjustment is inspired by the concept of swarm intelligence in Particle Swarm Optimization. The position of a particle is influenced by the best position visited by itself and the best particle in the swarm.

3.1 Proposed method

The new version of HSA, proposed in this paper, is inspired by the concept of reactive search (Battiti et al, 2007) where parameter tuning, which is usually performed offline by the researcher, becomes an integral part of the search algorithm, ensuring flexibility without human intervention. The "learning" component is implemented as a reactive feedback scheme that uses the past history of the search to increase its efficiency and efficacy.
The new approach, called Fast Harmony Search Algorithm (FHSA), introduces a prohibition step between step 4 and step 5 as shown in figure 1. It consists in defining a permanent prohibition of the search space (bounds adjustment) to prevent the system from going back on its track.

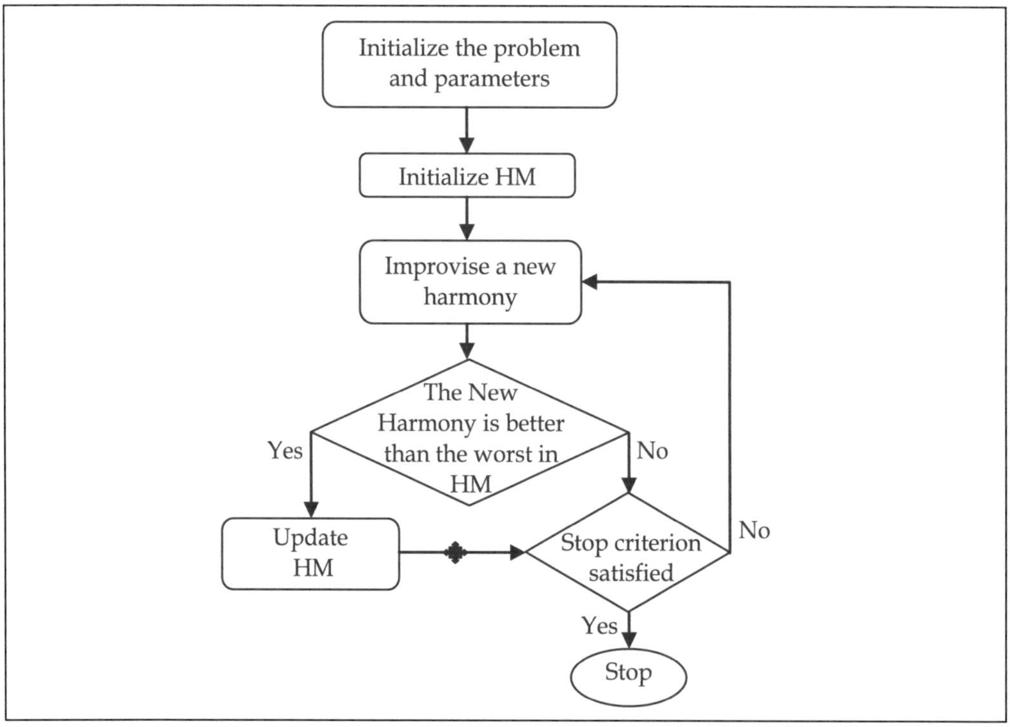

Fig. 1. Optimization procedure of HSA (✦ FHSA bounds adjustment point.)

This prohibition excludes any considered "none interesting" region from the search by adjusting the upper and/or lower bound of each decision variable and is performed as follows:

for j=1 to p do
if $f(x^j+\delta)<f(x^j)$ then $x^j_{min}=x^j+\delta$
else
if $f(x^j-\delta)<f(x^j)$ then $x^j_{max}=x^j-\delta$
else
$x^j_{max}=x^j$ and $x^j_{min}=x^j$
endif
done

The stop criterion becomes:

if $(x^j_{max}-x^j_{min})\le\varepsilon \quad j=1,\ldots,p$ then STOP endif

where δ is a real number "small enough" and ε is the precision term.
Since the search space of each variable is reduced then bw must be adjusted in accordance with this reduction. So it becomes:

$$bw=\frac{\left(x^j_{max}-x^j_{min}\right)}{c}$$

Where c is an integer, generally taken as a multiple of 10.

3.2 Examples

In order to demonstrate the performance of the FHSA, we compare it's results with those of HSA, IHSA and GHSA on these two convex and unimodal functions:
De Jong's function: It is also known as sphere model. It is continuous, convex, unimodal and defined as:

$$f_1(x)=\sum_{j=1}^{p}\left(x^j\right)^2$$
$$\text{where } x^j_{min}\le x^j\le x^j_{max} \qquad j=1,\ldots,p$$

Rotated hyper-ellipsoid function: It is continuous, convex, unimodal and defined as:

$$f_2(x)=\sum_{i=1}^{p}\left(\sum_{j=1}^{i}\left(x^j\right)\right)^2$$
$$\text{where } x^j_{min}\le x^j\le x^j_{max} \qquad j=1,\ldots,p$$

These two functions have the same optimum: $\begin{cases} f^*(x^j)=0, \\ x^j=0 \quad \text{for} \quad j=1,\ldots,p \end{cases}$

HSA, IHSA and GHSA were allowed to run for 500,000 iterations with a value of HMS=10 and HMCR=0.95. The other parameters were adjusted to obtain the best possible solution. For FHSA, the new parameters δ and ε were set to:

$$\delta = \frac{(x^j_{max} - x^j_{min})}{50} \quad \text{and} \quad \varepsilon = 10^{-14}$$

For HSA: $bw = \frac{(x^j_{max} - x^j_{min})}{10^6}$

For IHSA: $bw_{min} = \frac{(x^j_{max} - x^j_{min})}{10^9}$, $bw_{max} = \frac{(x^j_{max} - x^j_{min})}{10^4}$

For both IHSA and GHSA: PAR_{min}=0.01 and PAR_{max}=0.99

We first take a basic case where the space dimension (number of variables P) is set to 30 and the upper bound of each variable is set to 10^3 (figure 2 and figure 6). Then we explore the effect of increasing the space dimension (figure 3 and figure 7). Figure 4 and figure 8 represent the effect of increasing the upper bounds (x^j_{max}). Finally the effect of increasing space dimension and upper bounds is shown in figure 5 and figure 9. The lower bound is set for all cases to x^j_{min}=0. The results of the optimal solution and computing time are grouped in Table 1 and Table 2. For FHSA a column is added to represent the Number of Function Evaluations (NFE) needed by the algorithm to satisfy the stop criterion. The computational results are obtained using an Intel Pentium Dual CPU @ 1.80 GHz and TURBO PASCAL compiler.

		P=30, x^j_{max} =10^3	P=100, x^j_{max} =10^3	P=30, x^j_{max} =10^6	P=100, x^j_{max} =10^6
HSA	optimum	5.53E-7	5244.57	0.55	5.24E9
	time (s)	12.610	40.484	12.672	40.594
IHSA	optimum	1,01E-11	7904.41	1.01E-5	7.90E9
	time (s)	13.469	43.531	13.453	43.422
GHSA	optimum	83.63E-3	14.26	80977.46	1.43E7
	time (s)	13.016	42.297	12.796	42.266
FHSA	optimum	1.36E-28	1.10E-27	3.03E-28	1.24E-27
	time (s)	0.110	0.656	0.125	0.750
	NFE	1237	1204	1315	1437

Table 1. Optimal solution and time of execution for De Jong's function

		P=30, x^j_{max} =10^3	P=100, x^j_{max}=10^3	P=30, x^j_{max} =10^6	P=100, x^j_{max} =10^6
HSA	optimum	0.48	5.49E9	48.40E4	5.49E15
	time (s)	24.469	230.547	29.406	230.546
IHSA	optimum	10.48	7.61E9	1.05E7	7.61E15
	time (s)	31.359	244.329	31.343	244.360
GHSA	optimum	264.73	7.67E7	2.65E8	7.67E13
	time (s)	29.578	232.235	29.656	233.641
FHSA	optimum	1.48E-25	1.31E-20	1.18E-25	8.31E-21
	time (s)	6.078	93.719	7.110	111.937
	NFE	41,202	23,133	47,896	29,388

Table 2. Optimal solution and time of execution for Rotated hyper-ellipsoid function

These results show clearly that FHSA is more stable for higher dimensions and higher search spaces than the three previous versions. Moreover, it performed better than its predecessors in a lower time. The rate of convergence of HSA, IHSA and GHSA is slow, requiring a relatively greater number of function evaluations to obtain the optimal solution than the FHSA. The time for the FHSA decreases slightly because the number of function evaluations is reduced by the reduction of the search space. Moreover, defining a permanent prohibition of the search space contributes to the minimization of the size of HM, so there is no need of a large HMS.

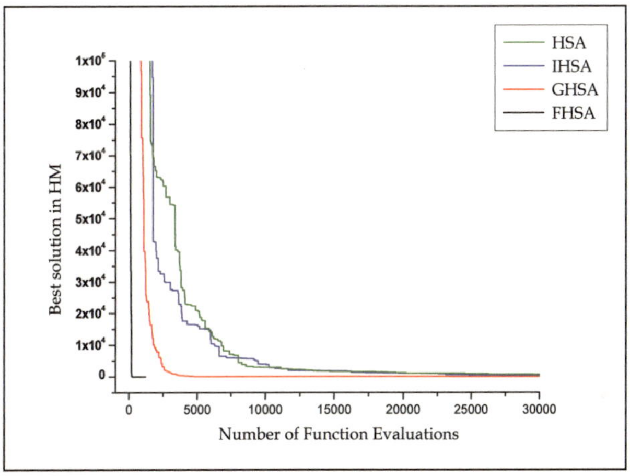

Fig. 2. Optimization of $f_1(x)$ with P=30 and $x^j_{max}=10^3$

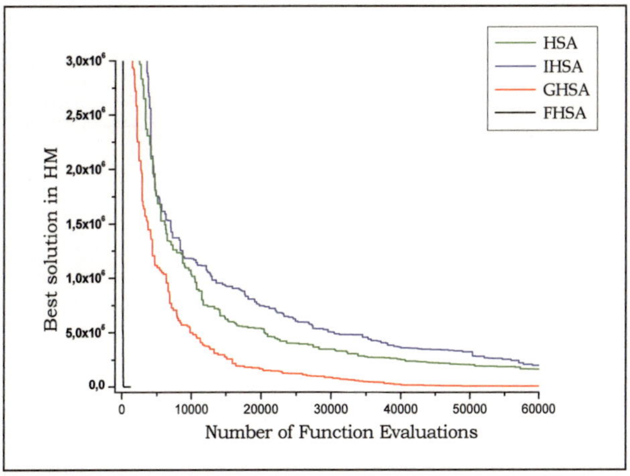

Fig. 3. Optimization of $f_1(x)$ with P=100 and $x^j_{max}=10^3$

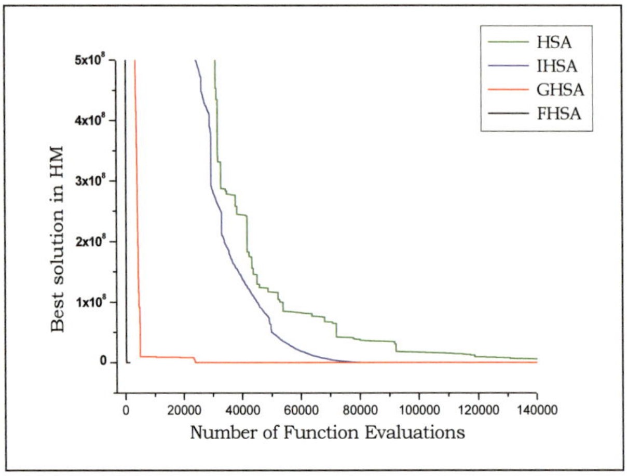

Fig. 4. Optimization of $f_1(x)$ with P=30 and $x^j_{max}=10^6$

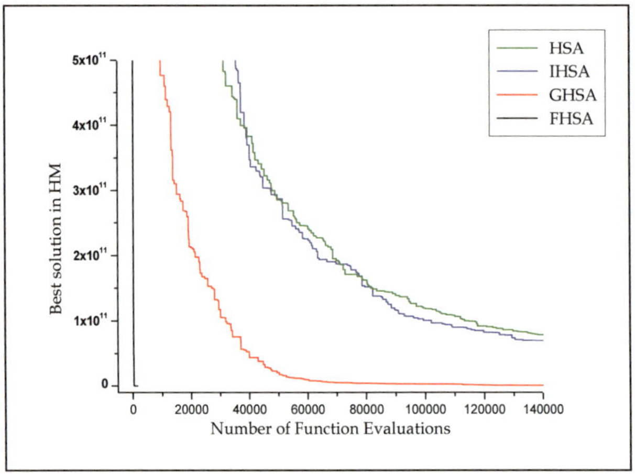

Fig. 5. Optimization of $f_1(x)$ with P=100 and $x^j_{max}=10^6$

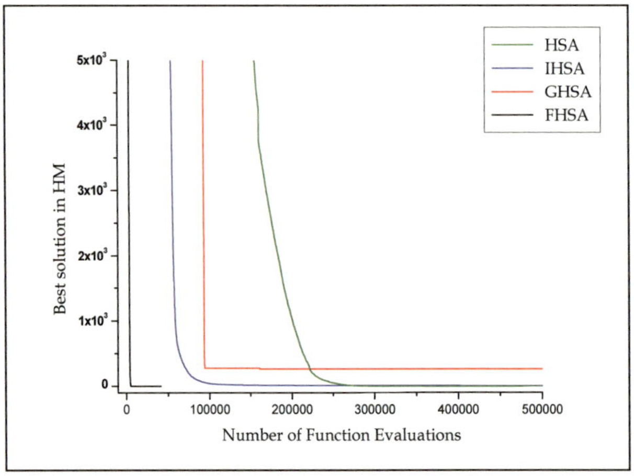

Fig. 6. Optimization of $f_2(x)$ with P=30 and $x^j_{max}=10^3$

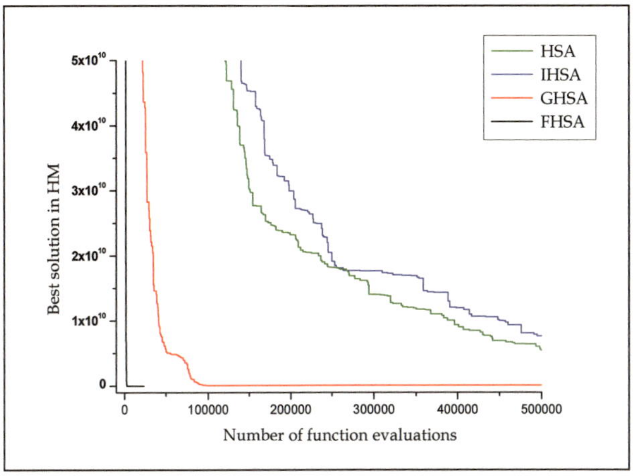

Fig. 7. Optimization of $f_2(x)$ with P=100 and $x^j_{max} = 10^3$

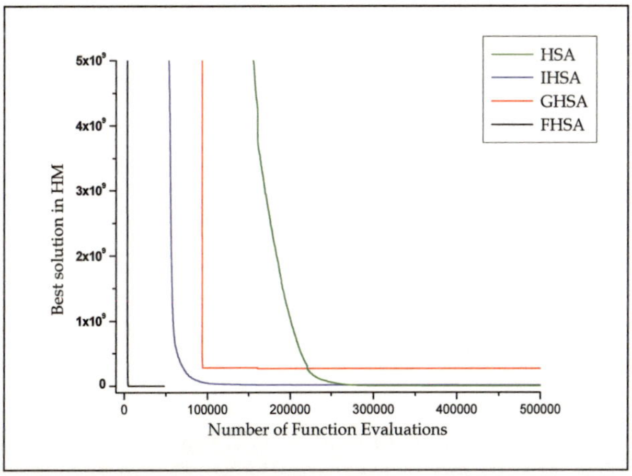

Fig. 8. Optimization of $f_2(x)$ with P=30 and $x^j_{max} = 10^6$

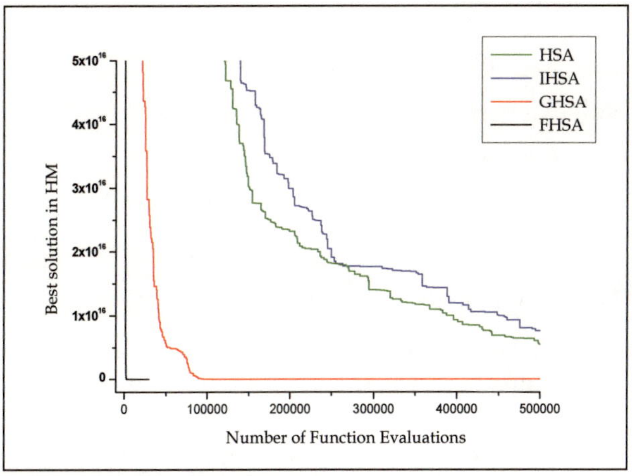

Fig. 9. Optimization of $f_2(x)$ with P=100 and $x^j_{max} = 10^6$

We have shown that the reduction of the search space contributes extensively to the effectiveness of the optimization process by Harmony Search. While knowing that Harmony Search Algorithm was originally inspired from the improvisation process of a group of musicians, the so called "reduction of the search space" might be considered as a manifestation of the experience of a performer.

Indeed, an experienced player can perceive during a concert that a pitch higher and/or lower than the actual may lead not into good harmony (music). He will, then, decide to avoid playing those pitches. This reality is implemented in FHSA as the reduction of the search space which affects directly the Harmony Memory and its Considering Rate HMCR.

The Harmony Memory Considering Rate is a major and dominant parameter in the optimization process by Harmony Search. Its role is to insure that good harmonies (good values of decision variables) are considered as elements of the new solution vectors. If this rate is too low, only few elite harmonies are selected and it may converge too slowly. If this rate is extremely high (near 1), the pitches in the harmony memory are mostly used, and other ones are not explored well, leading not into good solutions. Therefore, typically, HMCR is taken in the interval [0.7, 0.95] (Yang, 2009).

The central component of the optimization process by Harmony Search is the pitch adjustment which has parameters such as distance bandwidth bw and pitch adjusting rate PAR. As the pitch adjustment in music means changing the frequency, it means generating a slightly different value in the HS algorithm (Geem et al., 2001).

Pitch adjustment is similar to the mutation operator in genetic algorithms. We can assign a pitch adjusting rate to control the degree of the adjustment.

A low pitch adjusting rate with a narrow bandwidth can slow down the convergence of HS because of the limitation in the exploration of only a small subspace of the whole search space. On the other hand, a very high pitch-adjusting rate with a wide bandwidth may cause the solution to scatter around some potential optima as in a random search. Thus, in most applications, PAR is usually taken in the interval [0.1 , 0.5] (Yang, 2009).

In this section we investigate the effect of HMCR on the optimization process of HSA, IHSA, GHSA and FHSA. As an example, we use the De Jong's function with the four cases of increasing the search space and/or the space dimension. The four cases are:

CASE 1. P=30 and $x^j_{max}=10^3$

CASE 2. P=100 and $x^j_{max}=10^3$

CASE 3. P=30 and $x^j_{max}=10^6$

CASE 4. P=100 and $x^j_{max}=10^6$

For each case we apply the four versions of Harmony Search Algorithm with different values of HMCR. The values chosen are:

HMCR =0.95, HMCR=0.9, HMCR=0.8 and HMCR=0.7.

We do not investigate the PAR effect because it is dynamically adjusted in IHSA and GHSA. For HSA and FHSA, we maintain this parameter set to the mean value PAR=0.5.

The results are shown in the tables 3 to 6 and detailed in figure 10 to figure 25. The stop criterion of HSA, IHSA and GHSA is a maximum number of iterations NI=500,000 and the size of HM is set to HMS=10.

The other parameters are taken as follow:

HSA: PAR=0.5, $bw = \frac{(x^j_{max} - x^j_{min})}{10^6}$

IHSA: $PAR_{min} = 0.01$, $PAR_{max} = 0.99$, $bw_{min} = \frac{(x^j_{max} - x^j_{min})}{10^9}$, $bw_{max} = \frac{(x^j_{max} - x^j_{min})}{10^4}$

GHSA: $PAR_{min} = 0.01$, $PAR_{max} = 0.99$

FHSA : HMS=2, PAR =0.5, $\delta = \frac{(x^j_{max} - x^j_{min})}{50}$, $\varepsilon = 10^{-14}$

The results show a greater stability of FHSA to the diminution of HMCR.

The curves of figures 10 to 21 contain constant areas which frequency is conversely proportional to the value of HMCR. These constancies mean that the optimization process is slowed down by the diminution of HMCR. Consequently, we can conclude that the three previous version of the Harmony search algorithm are essentially based on the pitch adjustment component.

Like its predecessors, FHSA is affected by the diminution of HMCR (figures 22 to 25) but in a different way. The fact of randomly generating new solutions contributes strongly to the reduction of the search space giving rise to the acceleration of the optimization process. Taking a value of HMCR 5% lower reduce to about 50% the Number of function Evaluations needed by the algorithm to stop. However, greater values of HMCR offer a better precision of the optimal solution.

HSA (PAR=0.5)	P=30, $x^j_{max}=10^3$	P=100, $x^j_{max}=10^3$	P=30, $x^j_{max}=10^6$	P=100, $x^j_{max}=10^6$
HMCR=0.95	1.60E-6	6064.92	1.60	6.07E9
HMCR=0.9	3.66	596 187.99	3.66E6	5.96E11
HMCR=0.8	1 863.71	3.05E6	1.86E9	3.05E12
HMCR=0.7	83 644.48	6.73E6	8.36E10	6.73E12

Table 3. Results of optimization by HSA with different values of HMCR

IHSA	P=30, $x^j_{max}=10^3$	P=100, $x^j_{max}=10^3$	P=30, $x^j_{max}=10^6$	P=100, $x^j_{max}=10^6$
HMCR=0.95	1.026E-11	8 106.56	1.03E-5	8.11E9
HMCR=0.9	7.83	720 922.93	7.83E6	7.21E11
HMCR=0.8	2 123.89	3.66E6	2.12E9	3.66E12
HMCR=0.7	132 335.77	6.64E6	1.32E11	6.64E12

Table 4. Results of optimization by IHSA with different values of HMCR

GHSA	P=30, x^j_{max} =10^3	P=100, x^j_{max} =10^3	P=30, x^j_{max} =10^6	P=100, x^j_{max} =10^6
HMCR=0.95	2.76E-5	61.63	5609.54	6.16E7
HMCR=0.9	2.76E-5	107 227.36	27.57	1.07E11
HMCR=0.8	1.33	2.35E6	1.39E6	2.35E12
HMCR=0.7	20 075.84	4.78E6	2.01E10	4.78E12

Table 5. Results of optimization by GHSA with different values of HMCR

FHSA (PAR=0.5)		P=30, x^j_{max} =10^3	P=100, x^j_{max} =10^3	P=30, x^j_{max} =10^6	P=100, x^j_{max} =10^6
HMCR=0.95	optimum	3.20E-28	8.95E-28	3.11E-28	7.90E-28
	NFE	1095	1489	1209	1671
HMCR=0.9	optimum	3.66E-28	9.68E-28	1.75E-28	1.08E-27
	NFE	528	623	601	686
HMCR=0.8	optimum	3.18E-28	1.06E-27	2.21E-28	1.18E-27
	NFE	277	316	318	342
HMCR=0.7	optimum	2.96E-28	1.10E-27	3.10E-28	1.14E-27
	NFE	199	204	232	235

Table 6. Results of optimization by FHSA with different values of HMCR

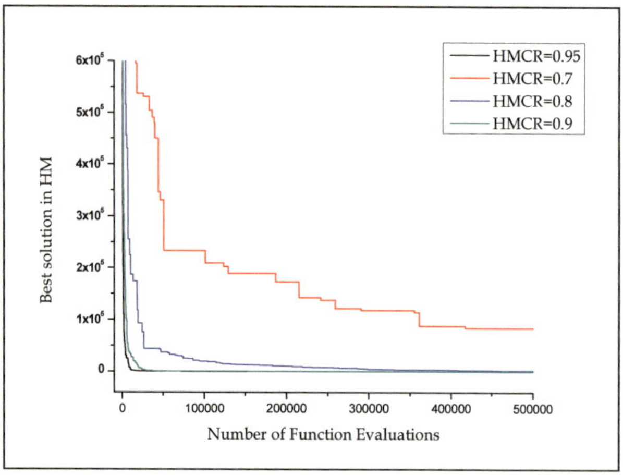

Fig. 10. Detailed results of HSA -CASE 1-

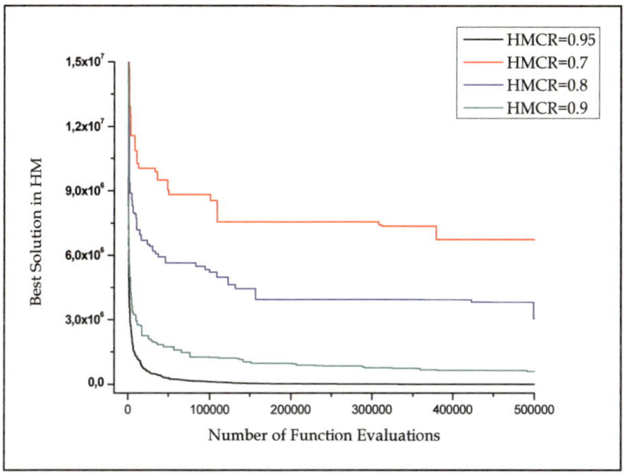

Fig. 11. Detailed results of HSA -CASE 2-

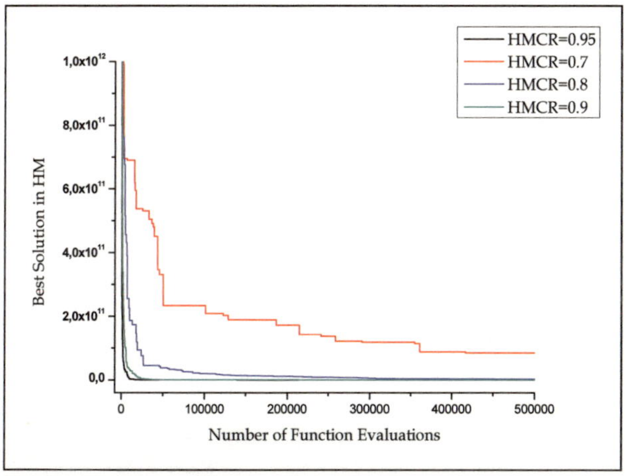

Fig. 12. Detailed results of HSA -CASE 3-

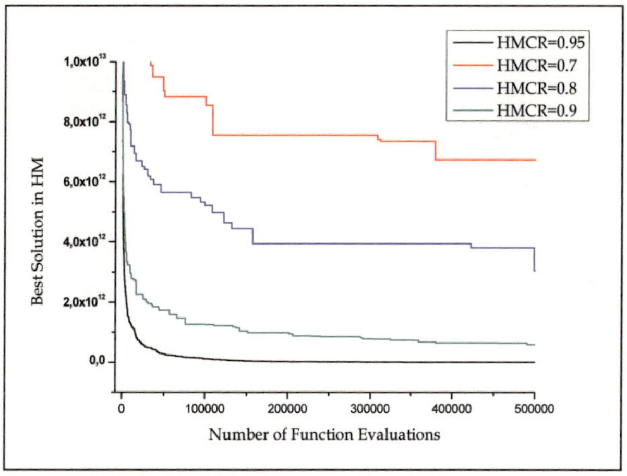

Fig. 13. Detailed results of HSA -CASE 4-

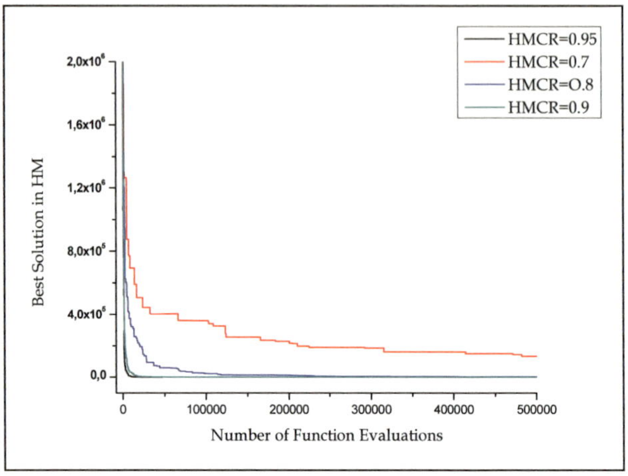

Fig. 14. Detailed results of IHSA -CASE 1-

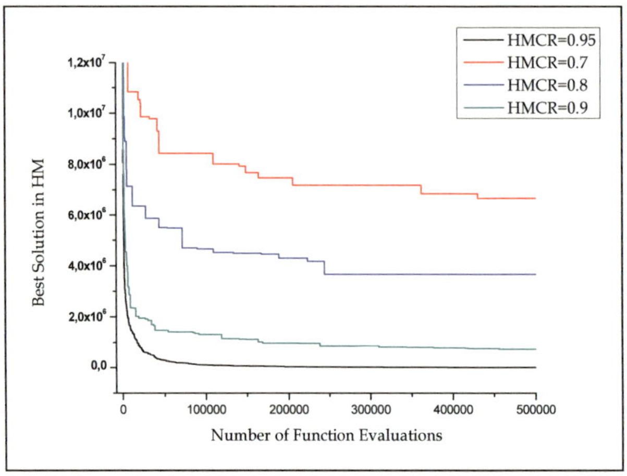

Fig. 15. Detailed results of IHSA -CASE 2-

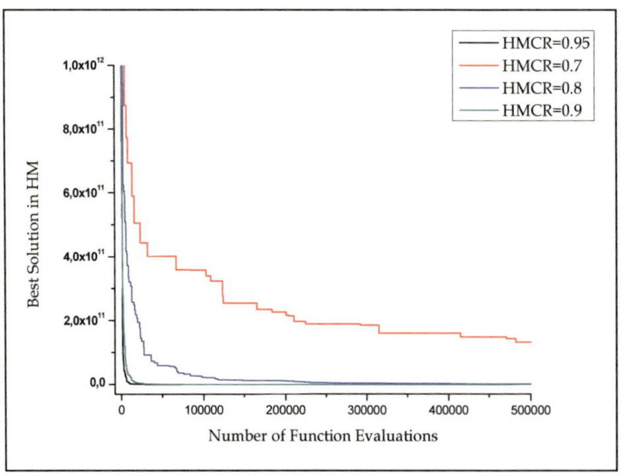

Fig. 16. Detailed results of IHSA -CASE 3-

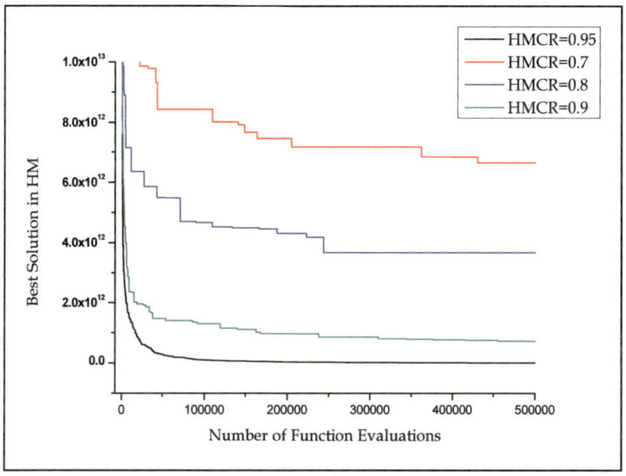

Fig. 17. Detailed results of IHSA -CASE 4-

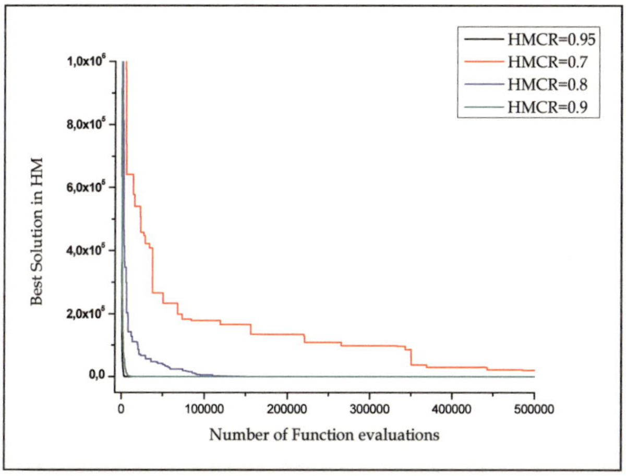

Fig. 18. Detailed results of GHSA -CASE 1-

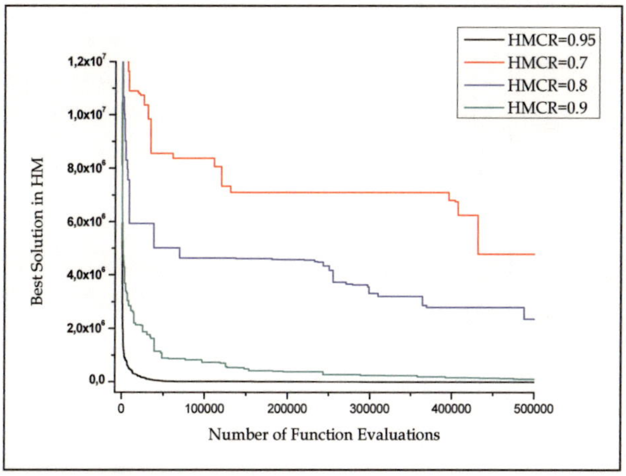

Fig. 19. Detailed results of GHSA -CASE 2-

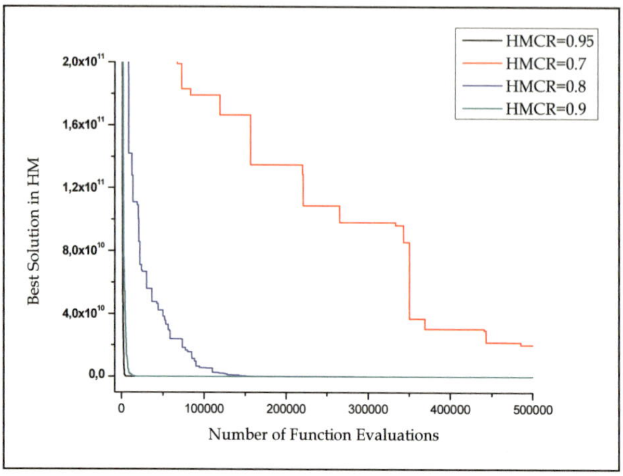

Fig. 20. Detailed results of GHSA -CASE 3-

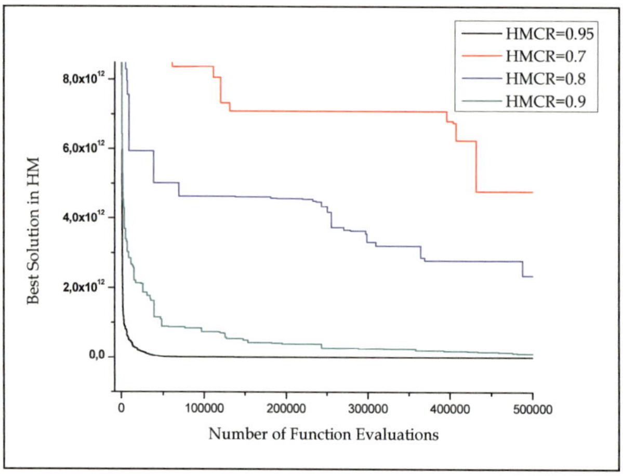

Fig. 21. Detailed results of GHSA -CASE 4-

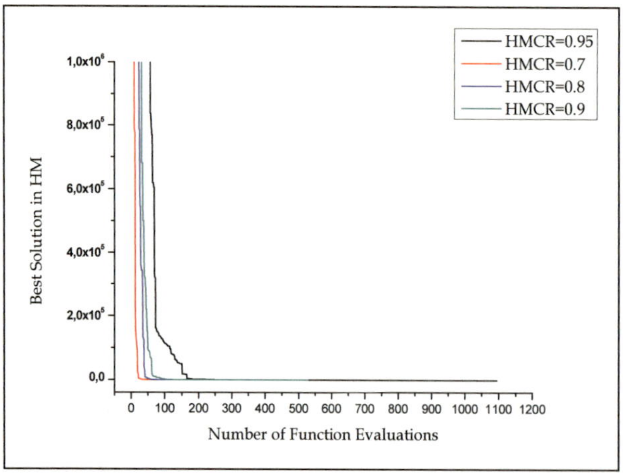

Fig. 22. Detailed results of FHSA -CASE 1-

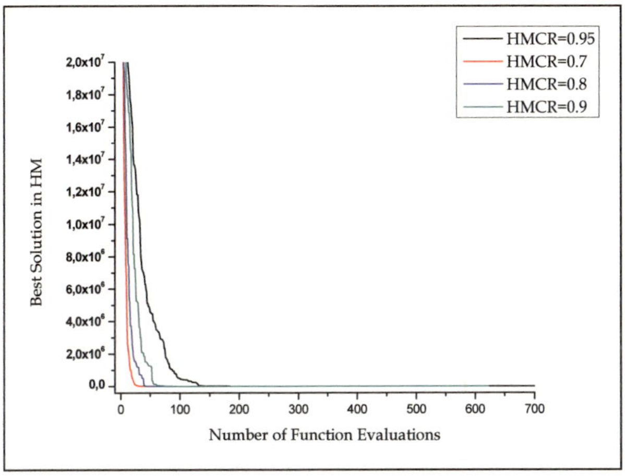

Fig. 23. Detailed results of FHSA -CASE 2-

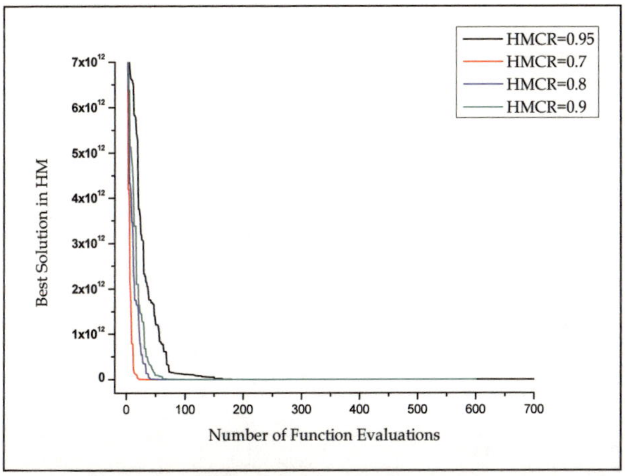

Fig. 24. Detailed results of FHSA -CASE 3-

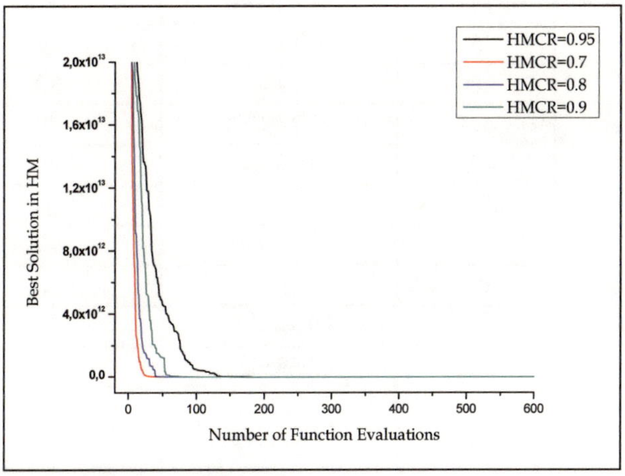

Fig. 25. Detailed results of FHSA -CASE 4-

4. Application

The proposed algorithm is applied to IEEE-118. The system has 54 thermal units. Generators characteristics, that is, cost coefficients and generation limits, are taken from Matpower web site (Zimmerman et al., accessed on 2008) and its detailed data are given in Wallach's book (Wallach & Even, 1986). The generators characteristics, power generation limits and generator cost parameters are given in table 7 and table 8. The computational results are obtained using an Intel Pentium Dual CPU @ 1.80 GHz and TURBO PASCAL compiler.

Gen	1	4	6	8	10	12	15	18	19	24	25	26	27	31	32	34	36	40
Type	#1	#1	#1	#1	#2	#3	#1	#1	#1	#1	#4	#5	#1	#6	#1	#1	#1	#1
Gen	42	46	49	54	55	56	59	61	62	65	66	69	70	72	73	74	76	77
Type	#1	#7	#8	#9	#1	#1	#10	#11	#1	#12	#13	#14	#1	#1	#1	#1	#1	#1
Gen	80	85	87	89	90	91	92	99	100	103	104	105	107	110	111	112	113	116
Type	#15	#1	#16	#17	#1	#1	#1	#1	#18	#19	#1	#1	#1	#1	#20	#1	#1	#1

Table 7. Characteristic of 54 Generators of network 118 - bus

Type	$P_{Gi\min}$ (MW)	$P_{Gi\max}$ (MW)	a_i (\$/MW².hr)	b_i (\$/MW.hr)	c_i (\$/hr)
#1	10	100	0.01	40	0.0
#2	55	550	0.0222222	20	0.0
#3	18.5	185	0.117647	20	0.0
#4	32	320	0.0454545	20	0.0
#5	41.4	414	0.0318471	20	0.0
#6	10.7	107	1.42857	20	0.0
#7	11.9	119	0.526316	20	0.0
#8	30.4	304	0.0490196	20	0.0
#9	14.8	148	0.208333	20	0.0
#10	26	255	0.0645161	20	0.0
#11	26	260	0.0625	20	0.0
#12	49.1	491	0.0255754	20	0.0
#13	49.1	492	0.0255102	20	0.0
#14	80.5	805.2	0.0193648	20	0.0
#15	57.7	577	0.0209644	20	0.0
#16	10.4	104	2.5	20	0.0
#17	70.7	707	0.01644745	20	0.0
#18	35.2	352	0.0396825	20	0.0
#19	14	140	0.25	20	0.0
#20	13.6	136	0.277778	20	0.0

Table 8. Power generation limits and generator cost parameters of networks 118-bus system

In order to demonstrate the performance of the proposed Algorithm, a comparison emerges between FHSA applied to the ED and other optimization methods, as it is shown in table 9 and figure 26. The parameters of the algorithms are taken as follow

FHSA: $PAR = 0.7, HMCR = 0.95, \varepsilon = 10^{-15}$ and $\delta = \frac{P_{Gimax} - P_{Gimin}}{5.10^7}$

HSA: $PAR = 0.7$ and $bw = 3$.

IHSA: $PAR_{min} = 0.01, PAR_{max} = 0.99$, $bw_{min} = 10^{-3}$ and $bw_{max} = 10^{+3}$

GHSA: $PAR_{min} = 0.001, PAR_{max} = 0.999$

HSA, IHSA and GHSA were allowed to run for 50,000 iterations with these common parameters: $HMCR = 0.95, HMS = 10$.

Method\Results	Fuel cost ($/h)	Time (s)
Mathpower	130 005.080	600.000
HSA	129 643.652	15.766
IHSA	129 626.923	13.657
GHSA	129 766.680	4.766
FHSA	129 620.166	1.090

Table 9. Comparison of FHSA with other methods

Figure 26 plot total fuel cost with respect of function evaluations. We can say that the proposed algorithm is performing well in the solution of Economic Dispatch problem regarding the difference between the results of the FHSA and the other methods. Even if HSA, IHSA, GHSA are performing well in fuel cost and computing time compared to Matpower method, FHSA is doing better.

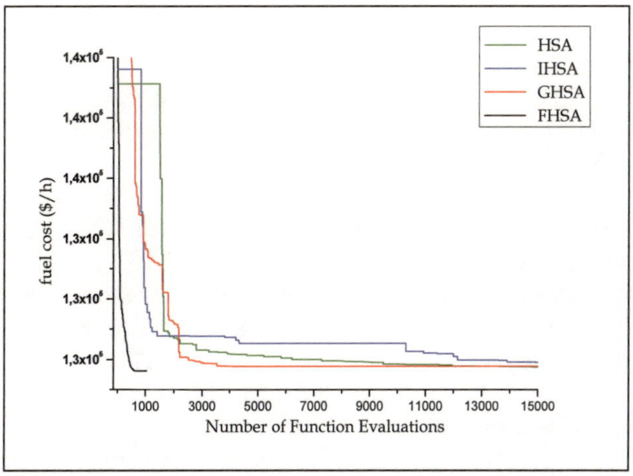

Fig. 26. Fuel cost

5. Conclusion

In this paper, a new Fast and efficient method based on Harmony Search Algorithm (FHSA) for optimizing unimodal functions is proposed. The performance of FHSA is investigated

and compared with HSA, IHSA and GHSA for the optimization of De Jong's function and Rotated hyper-ellipsoid function. Numerical results reveal that the optimization process of HSA, IHSA and GHSA is influenced by the increase of the space dimension and the search space. Thanks to space search reduction, FHSA can find optimum solutions with reduced number of function evaluations. Moreover, the optimization process of FHSA is less sensitive to the diminution of HMCR. Satisfactory results are obtained by adapting FHSA to Economic Dispatch problem and found that the results are better than those obtained by the previous versions of HSA and Matpower.
The stability of the FHSA to the increase of the space dimension and the search space compensates its disadvantage of being applicable only to unimodal functions as is the case of many optimization problems.

6. References

Battiti, R.; Brunato, M. & Mascia, F., Reactive Search and Intelligent Optimization. *Technical Report Università di Trento DIT-07-049*, available from: *http://reactive-search.org*.

Belmadani, A. ; Benasla, L. & Rahli, M. (2009). Etude d'un Dispatching Economique Environnemental par la méthode Harmony Search. *ACTA Electrotehnica*, Vol 50, N°1, (March 2009) 44-48, ISSN: 1841-3323.

Benasla, L. ; Rahli, M. ; Belmadani, A. & Benyahia, M.(2008). Nouvelle formulation du problème du dispatching économique-environnemental en tenant compte des pertes transmises. *Revue internationale de génie électrique RS série RIGE*, Vol. 11, N° 1, 69-86, ISSN: 2103-3641, 1295-490X, doi:10.3166/rige.11.69-86.

Benasla, L.; Belmadani, A. & Rahli, M. (2008). Hooke-Jeeves' Method Applied to a New Economic Dispatch Problem Formulation. *Journal of Information Science and Engineering JISE*, Vol. 24, No. 3, (May 2008) 907-917, ISSN: 1016-2364.

Geem, Z. W. (2006). Improved Harmony Search from Ensemble of Music Players. *International Conference on Knowledge-Based Intelligent Information and Engineering Systems*,Vol 4253, pp. 86-93,ISBN: 978-3-540-46542-3, Bournemouth, England (9-11 October 2006), Springer-verlag, berlin Germany.

Geem, Z. W.; Kim, J.H. & Loganathan, G. V. (2001). A New Heuristic Optimization Algorithm: Harmony Search. *SIMULATION*, Vol. 76, No. 2, (1 February2001) 60-68, ISSN: 0037-5497.

Mahdavi, M.; Fesanghary, M. & Damangir, E. (2007). An improved harmony search algorithm for solving optimization problems. *Applied Mathematics and Computation*, vol. 188, no2, (15 May 2007)1567-1579, ISSN: 0096-3003.

Omran, M.G. & Mahdavi, M. (2008). Global-best harmony search. *Applied Mathematics and Computation*, Vol. 198, No. 2, (1 May 2008) 643-656, ISSN: 0096-3003.

Rahli, M. & Pirotte, P. (1999). Economic dispatch using SUMT method under minimization power losses. *Electric Power System Research Journal*, n°52, Issue 1, (1 October 1999) 61-64, ISSN: 0378-7796.

Wallach, Y. & Even, R. (1986). *Calculations and programs for power systems network*, Englewood Cliffs, Prentice-Hall.

Yang, X.S. (2009). Harmony Search as a Metaheuristic Algorithm in *Music-Inspired Harmony Search Algorithm, Theory and applications SCI 191*, Zong Woo Geem (Ed.), 1-14, Springer-Verlag, ISBN 978-3-642-00184-0, Berlin Germany.

Zimmerman, R.D.; Murillo-Sánchez, C.E. & Gan, D. M. A Matlab Power System Simulation Package. *Version 2.0*, available from: *http://www.pserc.cornell.edu/matpower*.

17

On the Recursive Minimal Residual Method with Application in Adaptive Filtering

Noor Atinah Ahmad
Universiti Sains Malaysia
Malaysia

1. Introduction

Adaptive filters have become an integral part of adaptive signal processing and applied in diverse fields such as digital communications, speech recognition, control systems, radar and biomedical engineering. Since the adaptive filtering problem can be conveniently formulated as a stochastic quadratic minimization problem, a wide variety of adaptive filtering algorithms is derived based on numerical methods in unconstrained optimization theory. The class of iterative solvers for the adaptive filtering problem may be classified into the following categories:

1. Stochastic gradient algorithm
2. Stochastic conjugate gradient based algorithm
3. Direction set based algorithm

While stochastic gradient method offers the easiest and reliable method, its performance is proven to be poor when the eigenvalue spread of the autocorrelation matrix is large. Conjugate gradient based method (Boray & Srinath, 1992, Chang & Wilson, 2000, Dien & Bhaya, 2006) has been shown to give much better performance, however other issues arise. Finding the best estimate for gradient and search directions in the absence of the full knowledge of the autocorrelation matrix, and, in the presence of noise in the system is still an open question. Noisy estimates of gradient can easily lead to loss of conjugacy among search directions which may cause instability of the algorithm. A more recent advances can be found in (Chen, 1998) which involves a class of direction set based algorithm. The method generates a set of conjugate search directions using the method due to (Powell, 1964) and (Zangwill, 1967). This class of algorithm is very promosing in that it allows for lower complexity variants which is of much improved performance compared to the celebrated Least Mean Square algorithm.

This chapter describes the current development in a class of search algorithm for adaptive filtering which is based on the minimal residual (MR) method. The algorithms are related to the 3 classifications above in one way or another which will be described in detailed in this chapter.

The development of MR based adaptive filtering algorithms involves modification of the standard MR method for iterative solution of a system of linear equation $\Phi\mathbf{x} = \mathbf{p}$. In the standard method, the approximate solution is updated along the current residual vector $\mathbf{r}^{(k)} = \mathbf{p} - \Phi\mathbf{x}^{(k)}$, and, the stepsize is chosen so that the residual norm squared $\left\|\mathbf{p} - \Phi\mathbf{x}^{(k+1)}\right\|_2^2$

is minimized. By doing so, an orthogonality condition $\tilde{\mathbf{r}}^{(k)T}\left(\Phi\mathbf{r}^{(k)}\right)=0$, where $\tilde{\mathbf{r}}^{(k)}=\mathbf{p}-\Phi\mathbf{x}^{(k+1)}$, is imposed, giving rise to conjugation of successive gradients. When the matrix Φ is positive definite, the method can be shown to converge to the solution of the system.

The standard MR method may also be performed using direction of search other than the residual vector. Suppose $\mathbf{d}^{(k)}$ is the k th direction of search which is not necessarily equal to $\mathbf{r}^{(k)}$. The MR update equations take the form

$$\begin{aligned}\alpha_k &= \frac{\mathbf{r}^{(k)T}\mathbf{b}^{(k)}}{\mathbf{b}^{(k)T}\mathbf{b}^{(k)}} \\ \mathbf{x}^{(k+1)} &= \mathbf{x}^{(k)}+\alpha_k\mathbf{d}^{(k)}\end{aligned} \tag{1}$$

where $\mathbf{b}^{(k)}=\Phi\mathbf{d}^{(k)}$. The iteration in (1) guarantees $\mathbf{r}^{(k+1)T}\mathbf{b}^{(k)}=\left(\mathbf{p}-\Phi\mathbf{x}^{(k+1)}\right)^T\mathbf{b}^{(k)}=0$, i.e., (1) represents an orthogonal projection onto the subspace $span\left\{\mathbf{b}^{(k)}\right\}\approx span\left\{\Phi\mathbf{d}^{(k)}\right\}$. For a direction of search $\mathbf{d}^{(k)}$, we no longer insist pairwise conjugation of successive residuals. Instead, the conjugacy condition $\mathbf{r}^{(k+1)T}\left(\Phi\mathbf{d}^{(k)}\right)=0$ is imposed, i.e., we insist the new residual to be conjugated with the search direction $\mathbf{d}^{(k)}$.

For adaptive filtering problem, the MR method is applied on the recursive normal equation $\Phi_n\mathbf{x}=\mathbf{p}_n$, where Φ_n and $\mathbf{p}_n$ are the autocorrelation matrix and cross correlation vector of the problem repectively, at the n th state. As a direct consequence, the resulting MR based algorithm will involve recursively updated residual and search direction which are updated at every state n. Two forms of MR based algorithms are presented in this chapter:

1. MR based algorithm with recursive residuals as the search direction
2. MR based algorithms with search directions fixed along the Euclidean unit vectors.

Choosing the current residual as the search direction leads to a stochastic gradient method where successive gradients are forced to be conjugated with respect to the current autocorrelation matrix of the adaptive least squares problem. As a result, we obtain a method whose convergence properties is very much similar and comparable to the conjugate gradient based methods. In other words, we achieve superior convergence rate compared to the standard stochastic gradient method. The superior convergence is achieved with a slightly reduced complexity compared to conjugate gradient based algorithms because the MR based method does not require the computation of conjugate directions.

However, using residuals as search direction has its drawbacks. One of which is that it tends to produce higher misadjustment when the problem is ill conditioned. This problem is greatly improved when search directions are fixed along the Euclidean directions. Two different forms of MR based methods are considered,

Method 1: MR iterations are performed along N Euclidean directions independently, where N denotes the filter order as well as the dimension of the problem.

Method 2: MR projections are performed along the Euclidean directions cyclically.

Method 1 and Method 2 are in fact closely related. While Method 1 solves the auxilliary system using a direct method, Method 2 implements Gauss-Seidel type iterations. Both methods are shown theoretically to be globally convergent.

Other specific issues pertaining to computational complexity, misadjustment and sensitivity to eigenvalue spread is also discussed. Detailed simulation using several different configuration of the adaptive filtering problem will be provided to highlight these issues.

2. Recursive implementation of the MR method in adaptive filtering

Before we discuss the algorithm, let us review the mathematical formulation for the adaptive filtering problem. For simplicity, we confine our discussion to the linear adaptive filtering problem. In almost all adaptive filtering problem, three fundamental signals are required,

i. the input signal,
ii. the desired signal
iii. the output signal from an adaptive filter model.

For linear adaptive filtering, we assume the adaptive filter model in the form of a linear model. The objective of an adaptive filtering process is to adapt the model coefficients so as to minimize a certain error criteria which is called the cost function. The most common form for the cost function is a least squares cost function. Its popularity is due to a simple reason; the function has a single global minimum.

A linear adaptive filtering problem is the following minimization problem,

$$\min_{\mathbf{x}\in R^N} J_n(\mathbf{x}) = \sum_{i=m}^{n} \lambda^{n-i}\left(\mathbf{a}_i^T\mathbf{x} - s(i)\right)^2, \tag{2}$$

where $s(i)\in R$ is the desired signal, and, $y(i)=\mathbf{a}_i^T\mathbf{x}$ is the filter output at the i th sample instant. An example of an adaptive filtering system is depicted in Fig. 1.

For a transversal finite impulse response (FIR) adaptive filter, vectors $\mathbf{a}_i \in R^N$ are formed by the input $u(i)$, such that $\mathbf{a}_i = \left[u(i) \;\; u(i-1) \;\; \cdots \;\; u(i-N+1)\right]^T$, and vector $\mathbf{x}\in R^N$ is an estimate of the filter coefficient vector. The quantity $e_i = \mathbf{a}_i^T\mathbf{x} - s(i)$ is the error signal and $\mathbf{x}$

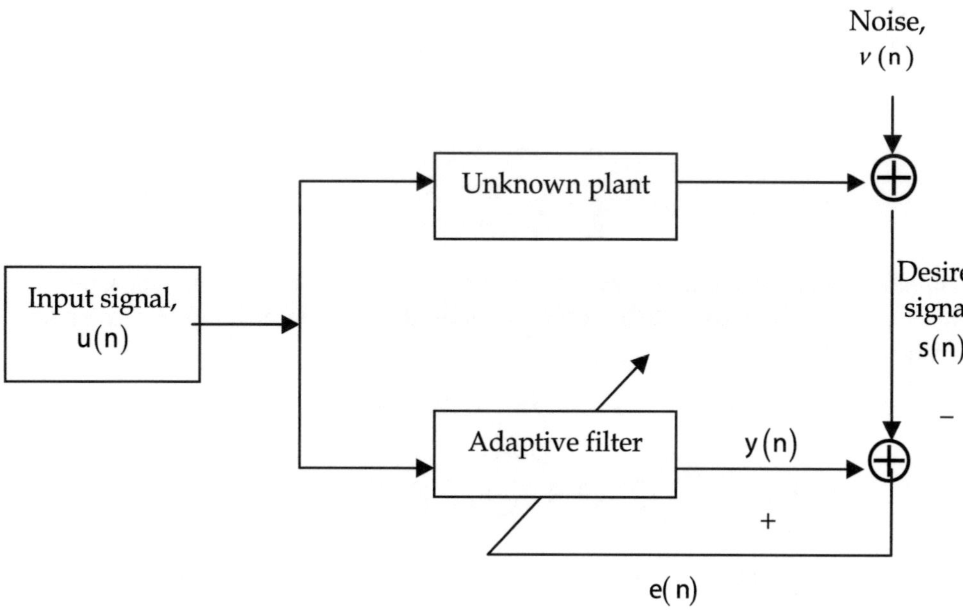

Fig. 1. Basic configuration for adaptive system identification

is updated by minimizing the sum of squared error cost function $J_n(\mathbf{x})$. The constant weight $\lambda \in [0,1]$ is known as the forgetting factor and its role is to give more emphasis/weight on the more recent signals.

For every system update, the adaptive least squares cost function is mathematically equivalent to the standard least squares problem. Consequently, the mathematical treatment of the problem is also similar. However, the time variation of $J_n(\mathbf{x})$ requires certain modification to take place. An advantage of the adaptive filtering problem is that system updating involves a rank-one update of the data matrix. This allows for the required modifications to be represented by simple recursive formulas to update the cost function. Similar to the standard least squares problem, the adaptive least squares problem (2) can also be recast in the form of adaptive normal equations. With definitions

$$\mathbf{A}_n = \left[\sqrt{\lambda^{n-m}}\mathbf{a}_m \quad \mathbf{a}_{m+1} \quad \cdots \quad \mathbf{a}_n \right]^T, \quad 0 \le m < n$$

and,

$$\mathbf{p}_n = \mathbf{A}_n^T \left[\sqrt{\lambda^{n-m}} s(m), s(m+1), \ldots, s(n) \right]^T,$$

the minimization problem in (2) can be shown to be equivalent to solving the normal equation

$$\Phi_n \mathbf{x} = \mathbf{p}_n \tag{3}$$

where $\Phi_n = \mathbf{A}_n^T \mathbf{A}_n$. The data matrix $\mathbf{A}_n$ is rank-one updated during each system update and this leads to the following recursive formulas for Φ_n and $\mathbf{p}_n$ (Haykin, 1991),

$$\Phi_n = \lambda \Phi_{n-1} + \mathbf{a}_n \mathbf{a}_n^T, \tag{4}$$

$$\mathbf{p}_n = \lambda \mathbf{p}_{n-1} + \mathbf{a}_n s(n). \tag{5}$$

The minimal residual method may be applied to the normal equation (2), where the approximations to the coefficient vector $\mathbf{x}$ after the nth sample update is updated according to

$$\begin{aligned} \alpha_k &= \frac{\mathbf{r}^{(k)T}\mathbf{b}^{(k)}}{\mathbf{b}^{(k)T}\mathbf{b}^{(k)}} \\ \mathbf{x}^{(k+1)} &= \mathbf{x}^{(k)} + \alpha_k \mathbf{d}^{(k)} \end{aligned} \tag{6}$$

where $\mathbf{d}^{(k)}$ is the kth direction of search and $\mathbf{b}^{(k)} = \Phi_k \mathbf{d}^{(k)}$. By (6), the orthogonality condition $\mathbf{r}^{(k+1)T}\left(\Phi \mathbf{d}^{(k)}\right) = 0$ no longer holds since $\mathbf{r}^{(k+1)}$ is the residual vector at the next sample update. Instead, the orthogonal condition $\tilde{\mathbf{r}}^T\left(\Phi \mathbf{d}^{(k)}\right) = 0$ is imposed, where $\tilde{\mathbf{r}}^{(k)} = \mathbf{p}_k - \Phi_k \mathbf{x}^{(k+1)}$. A relationship between $\mathbf{r}^{(k+1)}$ and $\tilde{\mathbf{r}}^{(k)}$ can be observed below,

$$\begin{aligned}\mathbf{r}^{(k+1)} &= \mathbf{p}_{k+1} - \Phi_{k+1}\mathbf{x}^{(k+1)} \\ &= \lambda\left(\mathbf{r}^{(k)} - \alpha_k \Phi_k \mathbf{r}^{(k)}\right) + \mathbf{a}_{k+1}e_{k+1} \\ &= \lambda\tilde{\mathbf{r}}^{(k)} + \mathbf{a}_{k+1}e_{k+1},\end{aligned} \tag{7}$$

where recursive formulas in (4) and (5) are used to simplify (7).
By construction of the MR method, α_k is chosen so that $\left(\tilde{\mathbf{r}}^{(k+1)}, \Phi_k \mathbf{d}^{(k)}\right) = 0$. Therefore, we have,

$$\left(\mathbf{r}^{(k+1)}, \Phi_k \mathbf{d}^{(k)}\right) = \lambda\left(\tilde{\mathbf{r}}^{(k+1)}, \Phi_k \mathbf{d}^{(k)}\right) + e_{k+1}\left(\mathbf{a}_{k+1}, \Phi_k \mathbf{d}^{(k)}\right) = e_{k+1}\left(\mathbf{a}_{k+1}, \Phi_k \mathbf{d}^{(k)}\right). \tag{8}$$

Assuming, $\mathbf{d}_k$ is a descent direction, (8) implies that, as $e_{k+1} \to 0$, the behaviour of the stochastic MR based adaptive filtering algorithm approaches that of its deterministic counterpart.

3. Recursive minimal residual method as a form of stochastic gradient method

When the search direction is set to be the residual vector, the MR method reduces to a gradient descent method. For adaptive filtering application, since the gradient is only available as a stochastic gradient estimation, the method becomes a form of a stochastic gradient method. What is unique about the MR based stochastic gradient method is in the computation of step size α_k, chosen so that the orthogonality condition

$$\left(\tilde{\mathbf{r}}^{(k+1)}, \Phi_k \mathbf{r}^{(k)}\right) = 0, \tag{9}$$

is satisfied . In other stochastic gradient method, the step size is a predetermined value which is chosen to be a number inside the open interval $(0, 2/\lambda_{\max})$, where $\lambda_{\max}$ denotes the maximum eigenvalue of the autocorrelation matrix Φ_k. This choice guarantees global convergence of stochastic gradient method

3.1 The Stochastic Pairwise Conjugate Gradient based algorithm (SPCG)

The Stochastic Pairwise Conjugate Gradient based algorithm (SPCG) (Ahmad, 2008) is the first implementation of stochastic gradient method with MR step size. It was developed based on the idea in (Schraudolph & Graepel, 2002), where it was noted that the orthogonality condition $\left(\tilde{\mathbf{r}}^{(k+1)}, \Phi_k \mathbf{r}^{(k)}\right) = 0$, also implies pairwise conjugation of succesive gradients. It is well known that conjugate gradient method out performs gradient based method in most applications. Henceforth, by insisting pairwise conjugation of successive gradients, we will achieve a stochastic gradient method which performs comparable to the conjugate gradient based methods.

The SPCG algorithm is summarized in Table 1. As shown in Table 1, the computational complexity of the SPCG algorithm is $O(N^2)$ which is still rather high for most practical application. The lower complexity versions are described in the next section

	$\times/\div$	$+/-$
Initialization:	(if $m=1$)	
(1a) $\mathbf{X}_m = \mathbf{a}_m\mathbf{a}_m^T$	1	
(1b) $\Phi_m, \mathbf{p}_m, \mathbf{x}^{(0)} = \mathbf{0} \in R^N$	-	
(1c) $\mathbf{r}^{(m)} = \mathbf{p}_m - \Phi_m\mathbf{x}^{(0)}$,	-	
(1d) $\mathbf{b}^{(m)} = \Phi_m\mathbf{r}^{(m)}$	1	
For $k = m+1,\ldots,N$		
(2) $\alpha^{(k)} = \dfrac{\mathbf{r}^{(k)T}\mathbf{b}^{(k)}}{\mathbf{b}^{(k)T}\mathbf{b}^{(k)}}$	$2N+1$	$2(N-1)$
(3) $\mathbf{x}^{(k+1)} = \mathbf{x}^{(k)} + \alpha^{(k)}\mathbf{r}^{(k)}$	N	N
New sample update: $\mathbf{a}_k \rightarrow \mathbf{a}_{k+1}$,		
(4a) $\mathbf{X}_{k+1}(2:N,2:N) = \mathbf{X}_k(1:N-1,1:N-1)$	-	
(4b) $\mathbf{X}_{k+1}(1,:) = u(n)\mathbf{a}_{k+1}^T$	N	
(4c) $\mathbf{X}_{k+1}(:,1) = \mathbf{X}_{k+1}(1,:)^T$	-	
(5) $\Phi_{k+1} = \lambda\Phi_k + \mathbf{X}_{k+1}$	$\frac{1}{2}N(N+1)$	$\frac{1}{2}N(N+1)$ (considering symmetry)
(6) $e_{k+1} = \mathbf{a}_{k+1}^T\mathbf{x}^{(k+1)} - s(k+1)$	N	$2N-1$
(7) $\mathbf{r}^{(k+1)} = \lambda\mathbf{r}^{(k)} - \alpha\lambda\mathbf{b}^{(k)} + \mathbf{a}_{k+1}e_{k+1}$	$3N+1$	$2N$
(8) $\mathbf{b}^{(k+1)} = \Phi_{k+1}\mathbf{r}^{(k+1)}$	N^2	$N(N-1)$
EndFor		
Total	$\frac{3}{2}N^2 + \frac{17}{2}N + 4$	$\frac{1}{2}(3N^2 + 13N - 3)$
(if $\lambda=1$)	$N^2 + 7N + 3$	

Table 1. The SPCG algorithm and calculation of the computational complexity

3.2 Low complexity SPCG

The computational complexity of the SPCG algorithm is of $O(N^2)$, mainly due to the matrix-vector multiplication to compute $\mathbf{b}^{(k)} = \Phi_k \mathbf{r}^{(k)}$. Lower complexity versions of SPCG algorithm introduced here are formed by making lower complexity approximation for $\mathbf{b}^{(k)} = \Phi_k \mathbf{r}^{(k)}$ as follows,

$$\begin{aligned} \varepsilon_k &= \mathbf{a}_k^T \mathbf{r}^{(k)}, \\ \hat{\mathbf{b}}^{(k)} &= \lambda \hat{\mathbf{b}}^{(k-1)} + \varepsilon_k \mathbf{r}^{(k)}. \end{aligned} \tag{10}$$

The approximation above requires $3N$ multiplications instead of N^2 multiplication in the original version.

Naturally, with the approximations introduced by (10), the conjugacy condition (9) is no longer fulfilled exactly. Instead, the stepsize α_k is calculated based on a slightly modified conjugacy (orthogonality) condition, which is $\tilde{\mathbf{r}}^{(k)T}\left(\hat{\mathbf{b}}^{(k)}\right) = 0$. From geometrical point of view (see Fig. 2), this new orthogonality condition will still result in an improvement to $\left\|\mathbf{r}^{(k)}\right\|_2^2$. However the rate of convergence may be a bit compromised. This observation is verified in Theorem 1.

Theorem 1: Convergence of Low complexity SPCG

Let $\upsilon_k = \left\|\mathbf{r}^{(k)}\right\|_2^2 - \left\|\tilde{\mathbf{r}}^{(k)}\right\|_2^2$ be the improvement factor in the low complexity SPCG iteration after the k th sample update. Then,

i. $\upsilon_k \geq 0$ for $k = 1, 2, \ldots$

ii. The iterations result in slow convergence when the angle between $\mathbf{r}^{(k)}$ and $\hat{\mathbf{b}}^{(k)}$ is close to $\pi/2$.

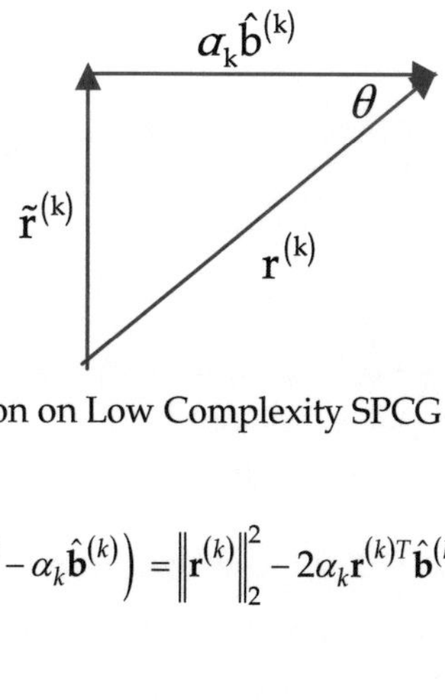

Fig. 2. Geometrical interpretation on Low Complexity SPCG iteration

Proof:

i. $\left\|\tilde{\mathbf{r}}^{(k)}\right\|_2^2 = \left(\mathbf{r}^{(k)} - \alpha_k \hat{\mathbf{b}}^{(k)}\right)^T \left(\mathbf{r}^{(k)} - \alpha_k \hat{\mathbf{b}}^{(k)}\right) = \left\|\mathbf{r}^{(k)}\right\|_2^2 - 2\alpha_k \mathbf{r}^{(k)T} \hat{\mathbf{b}}^{(k)} + \alpha_k^2 \left\|\hat{\mathbf{b}}^{(k)}\right\|_2^2.$

Substituting for α_k gives

$$\upsilon_k = \left\|\mathbf{r}^{(k)}\right\|_2^2 - \left\|\tilde{\mathbf{r}}^{(k)}\right\|_2^2 = \frac{\left(\mathbf{r}^{(k)T}\hat{\mathbf{b}}^{(k)}\right)^2}{\left\|\hat{\mathbf{b}}^{(k)}\right\|_2^2} \geq 0.$$

ii. $\dfrac{\left\|\tilde{\mathbf{r}}^{(k)}\right\|_2^2}{\left\|\mathbf{r}^{(k)}\right\|_2^2} = 1 - \dfrac{\left(\mathbf{r}^{(k)T}\hat{\mathbf{b}}^{(k)}\right)^2}{\left\|\mathbf{r}^{(k)}\right\|_2^2\left\|\hat{\mathbf{b}}^{(k)}\right\|_2^2} = 1 - \cos^2\theta_k$,

where $\theta_k = \dfrac{\mathbf{r}^{(k)T}\hat{\mathbf{b}}^{(k)}}{\left\|\mathbf{r}^{(k)}\right\|_2\left\|\hat{\mathbf{b}}^{(k)}\right\|}$, is the angle between $\mathbf{r}^{(k)}$ and $\hat{\mathbf{b}}^{(k)}$. When $\theta_k \approx \pi/2$, υ_k is small, hence resulting in slow convergence.

Slow convergence observed in the case of Theorem 1 part (ii) can be remedied by restarting the algorithm with exact values of $\hat{\mathbf{b}}^{(k)}$. Note that, when exact values of $\hat{\mathbf{b}}^{(k)}$ is used, we will obtain the improvement factor corresponds to the SPCG algorithm, i.e.,

$$\upsilon_k = \frac{\left(\mathbf{r}^{(k)T}\mathbf{b}^{(k)}\right)^2}{\left\|\mathbf{b}^{(k)}\right\|_2^2} = \frac{\mathbf{r}^{(k)T}\Phi_k\mathbf{r}^{(k)}}{\left\|\Phi_k\mathbf{r}^{(k)}\right\|_2^2}.$$

Thus, restarting will result in a convergence rate comparable to the original SPCG algorithm.

Introducing restart will automatically increase the computational complexity of the algorithm because the autocorrelation matrix and the cross-correlation vector need to be updated during each sample update. However, if restarting is performed after every N sample updates at least, this will keep the number of multiplications at $O(N)$ per sample update. The autocorrelation matrix and the cross-correlation vector can be updated for every block of M according to

$$\Phi_{(k+1)M} = \lambda\Phi_{kM} + \tilde{\Phi}_{(k+1)M}, \qquad \mathbf{p}_{(k+1)M} = \lambda\mathbf{p}_{kM} + \tilde{\mathbf{p}}_{(k+1)M} \tag{11}$$

where $\tilde{\Phi}_{(k+1)M} = \sum_{j=1}^{M}\mathbf{a}_{kM+j}\mathbf{a}_{kM+j}^T$, $\quad \tilde{\mathbf{p}}_{(k+1)N} = \sum_{j=1}^{M}\mathbf{a}_{kM+j}s_{kM+j}$.

(Choose $M \geq N$ to keep the number of multiplications $O(N)$ per sample update, at most).

3.3 Simulation results

Simulations are based on an adaptive system identification configuration shown in Fig. 1. The unknown plant is a finite impulse response filter of order 10. A white Gaussian input signal of variance $\sigma^2 = 1$ is passed through a colouring filter with frequency response $H(z) = \dfrac{\sqrt{1-\alpha^2}}{1-\alpha z^{-1}}$ (Farhang-Bouroujeny, 1999), where $|\alpha| < 1$. The parameter α controls the eigenvalue spread, or the spectral condition number of the input autocorrelation matrix, where $\alpha = 0$ gives uncorrelated sequence (white) with eigenvalue spread ≈ 1. The performance of the algorithm is studied based on the propogation of the ensemble average of the mean error norm $\left\|\mathbf{x}^{(k)} - \mathbf{x}^*\right\|_2^2$, where $\mathbf{x}^*$ is the Wiener solution. The ensemble average is formed by 200 independent runs.

In the first part of our simulation (see Fig. 3), we demonstrate the superior performance of the MR based stochastic gradient method, i.e., the SPCG algorihm compared to the well-known stochastic gradient algorithm, that is, the Least Mean Square (LMS) algorithm. In addition, we also show that the SPCG algorithm is comparable in performance compared to a conjugate gradient based adaptive filtering algorithm (referred to as the CG-CLF algorithm (Dien & Bhaya, 2006). The SPCG algorithm is also shown to be more superior when the eigenvalue spread is high (with $\alpha = 0.5$) (see Fig. 4). Increased eigenvalue spread also results in a slight increase in the magnitude of the weight error norm, which implies an increase in misadjustment. Infact our simulation shows that this problem is evident in LMS and CG-CLF as well.

In the second part of this simulation (Fig. 5 and Fig. 6), we investigate the effect of. In the simulation with lower complexity approximations (10). As expected, periodic restarting of the algorithm is required in order to achieve convergence rate comparable to the original version. It is interesting to see that the low complexity approximation (with restart) results in a slightly better misadjustment compared to the original SPCG.

4. Recursive MR method with euclidean search direction

Consider minimizing the squared norm residual $\|\mathbf{r}\|_2^2 = \|\mathbf{p} - \Phi\mathbf{x}\|_2^2$ by applying the MR iterations along N Euclidean directions simultaneously and independently, thus

$$\mathbf{x}^{(k+1)} = \mathbf{x}^{(k)} + \sum_{i=1}^{N} \Psi_k^{(i)} \mathbf{e}_i = \mathbf{x}^{(k)} + \Psi_k, \tag{12}$$

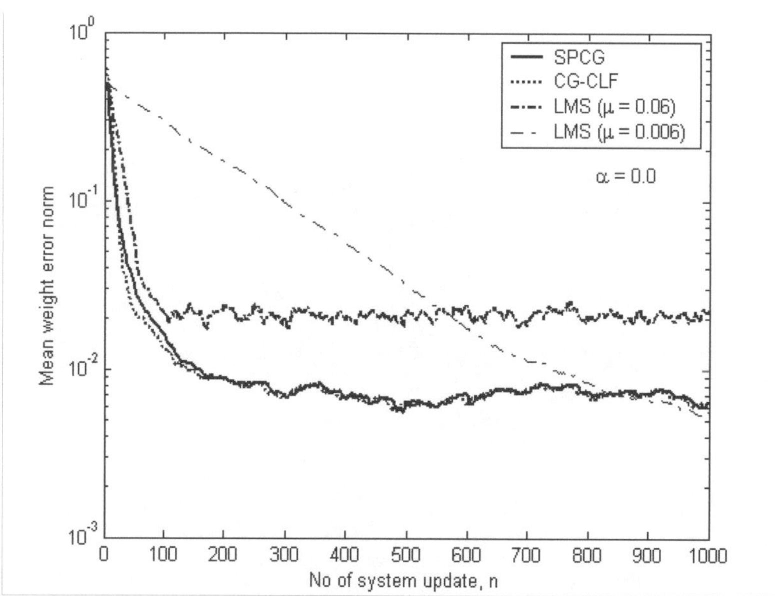

Fig. 3. Comparative performance between SPCG, LMS and CG-CLF for high eigenvalue spread. The LMS weight error norm is produced for two different stepsizes, $\mu = 0.06$ and $\mu = 0.006$.

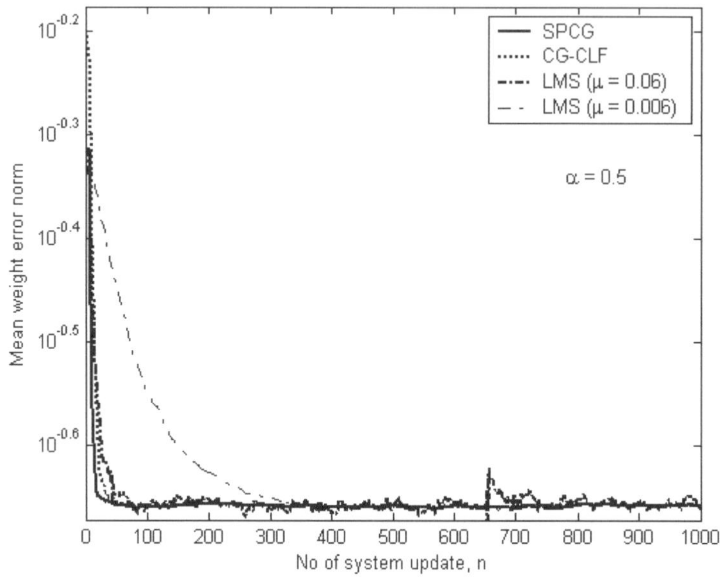

Fig. 4. Comparative performance between SPCG, LMS and CG-CLF for high eigenvalue spread.

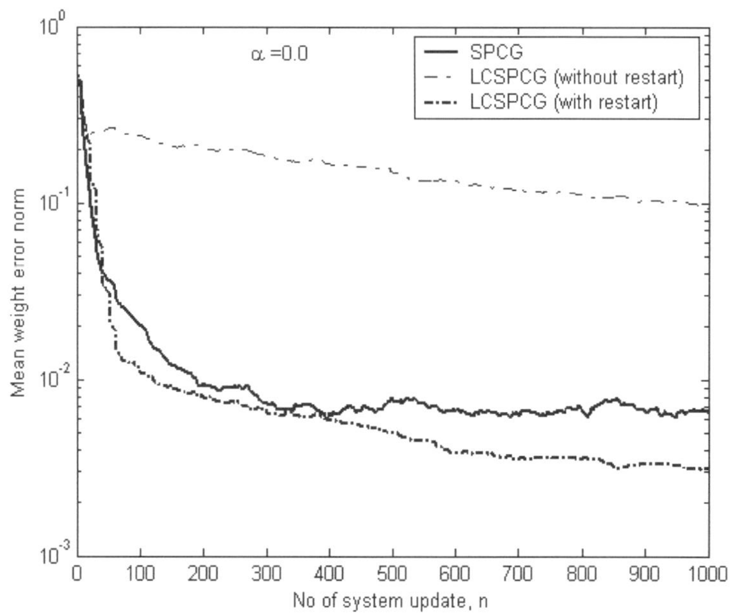

Fig. 5. Low complexity approximation requiring restart in order to achieve performance comparable to SPCG (small eigenvalue spread)

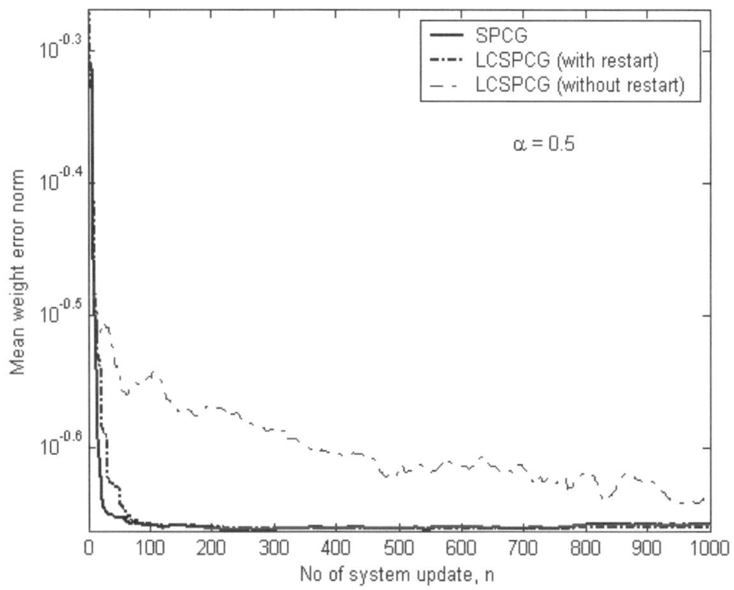

Fig. 6. Low complexity approximation compared to SPCG with large eigenvalue spread.

where $\Psi_k^{(i)}$ is the i th entry of the $N \times 1$ vector Ψ_k, and, $\mathbf{e}_i = \begin{bmatrix} 0 & 0 & \cdots & 1 & \cdots & 0 \end{bmatrix}^T$, with 1 appearing in the i th place. The stepsizes $\Psi_k^{(i)}$ are calculated by insisting that $\mathbf{r}^{(k+1)T}\Phi\mathbf{e}_i = 0$, for all $i = 1,\ldots,n$. For a symmetric $n \times n$ matrix Φ, the procedure above gives rise to a system of linear equations in $\Psi_k^{(i)}$ of the form

$$\Phi^2 \Psi_k = \Phi \mathbf{r}_k , \tag{13}$$

which solves as

$$\Psi_k = \Phi^{-1} \mathbf{r}_k \tag{14}$$

In other words,

$$\mathbf{r}_{k+1} = \mathbf{b} - \Phi\left(\mathbf{x}_k + \Phi^{-1}\mathbf{r}_k\right) = \mathbf{r}_k - \mathbf{r}_k = \mathbf{0} . \tag{15}$$

Eqn (15) implies that the procedure described above results in finite termination to the exact solution after a single step.

4.1 Simultaneous update: The auxiliary equation

Applying the procedure above on the adaptive least squares normal equation (3), leads to the auxiliary normal equation

$$\Phi_k^2 \Psi_k = \Phi_k \mathbf{r}^{(k)} . \tag{16}$$

Rather than solving it directly, we adopt an alternative procedure as follows. First consider the equivalent equation,

$$\Psi_k^T \Phi_k^2 \Psi_k = \Psi_k^T \Phi_k \mathbf{r}^{(k)} . \tag{17}$$

Now, we split $\mathbf{Q}_k = \Phi_k^2$ as,

$$\mathbf{Q}_k = \Phi_k^2 = \mathbf{L}_k + \mathbf{D}_k + \mathbf{U}_k , \tag{18}$$

where $\mathbf{D}_k$ is a diagonal matrix consisting of the main diagonal of $\mathbf{Q}_k$, and, matrices $\mathbf{L}_k$ and $\mathbf{U}_k$ are the strict lower and upper triangular parts of $\mathbf{Q}_k$ respectively. This procedure transfoms the alternative auxilliary equation to

$$\Psi_k^T \mathbf{L}_k \Psi_k + \Psi_k^T \mathbf{D}_k \Psi_k + \Psi_k^T \mathbf{U}_k \Psi_k = \Phi_k \mathbf{r}^{(k)} .$$

Consider the value of $\Psi_k^T \mathbf{L}_k \Psi_k$:
It is straightforward to see that the entries of $\mathbf{L}_k \Psi_k$ are given as

$$\left[\mathbf{L}_k \Psi_k\right]_1 = 0 , \tag{19}$$

$$\left[\mathbf{L}_k \Psi_k\right]_i = \sum_{j=2}^{i-1} \Psi_k^{(j)} \left(\Phi_k^{(i)T} \Phi_k^{(j)} \right) = \sum_{j=2}^{i-1} \Psi_k^{(j)} \mathbf{Q}_k^{(i,j)} , i = 2,\dots,N \tag{20}$$

where $\mathbf{Q}_k^{(i,j)}$ is the entry of $\mathbf{Q}_k$ in the i th row and j th column. Thus

$$\Psi_k^T \mathbf{L}_k \Psi_k = \sum_{i=2}^{N} \Psi_k^{(i)} \sum_{j=1}^{i-1} \Psi_k^{(j)} \mathbf{Q}_k^{(i,j)} .$$

Switching the order of summation leads to,

$$\begin{aligned} \Psi_k^T \mathbf{L}_k \Psi_k &= \sum_{i=2}^{N} \Psi_k^{(i)} \sum_{j=1}^{i-1} \Psi_k^{(j)} \mathbf{Q}_k^{(i,j)} \\ &= \sum_{j=1}^{N-1} \Psi_k^{(j)} \sum_{i=j}^{N} \Psi_k^{(i)} \mathbf{Q}_k^{(i,j)} \\ &= \sum_{j=1}^{N-1} \Psi_k^{(j)} \sum_{i=j}^{N} \Psi_k^{(i)} \mathbf{Q}_k^{(j,i)} = \Psi_k^T \mathbf{U}_k \Psi_k . \end{aligned} \tag{21}$$

The last line of (21) is obtained by using the fact that $\mathbf{Q}_k = \Phi_k^2$ is symmetric. Using (18), we are now able to write (17) as

$$\Psi_k^T \left(\mathbf{D}_k + 2\mathbf{L}_k \right) \Psi_k = \Psi_k^T \Phi_k \mathbf{r}^{(k)} , \tag{22}$$

Hence, the solution to the auxilliary equation is also the solution to

$$\left(\mathbf{D}_k + 2\mathbf{L}_k \right) \Psi_k = \Phi_k \mathbf{r}^{(k)} \tag{23}$$

or equivalently,

$$\left(\mathbf{D}_k + 2\mathbf{U}_k \right) \Psi_k = \Phi_k \mathbf{r}^{(k)} \tag{24}$$

By reducing (16) to (23) or (24), we have in fact reduced the problem to a lower/upper triangular system which can be solved by forward/back substitution.

4.2 Cyclic updates: Gauss-seidel iterations

An alternative MR based method is derived by performing MR iterations along the Euclidean directions cyclically. In other words, the current weight vector is updated as follows,

$$\mathbf{x}^{(k+1)} = \mathbf{x}^{(k)} + \Psi_k,$$

where the i th components of the stepsize vector Σ_k, namely $\Sigma_k^{(i)}$, is the minimizer of $\left\|\mathbf{p}_k - \Phi_k\left(\mathbf{x}_i^{(k)} + \Psi^{(i)}\mathbf{e}_i\right)\right\|_2^2$, i.e.,

$$\Psi_k^{(i)} = \frac{\mathbf{r}_{i-1}^{(k)T}\Phi_k^{(i)}}{\left(\Phi_k^{(i)}\right)^T\left(\Phi_k^{(i)}\right)}, \qquad i = 1,\dots,N$$

with

$$\mathbf{r}_i^{(k)} = \mathbf{r}_{i-1}^{(k)} - \Psi_k^{(i)}\Phi_k^{(i)},$$

$$\Phi_k^{(i)} \text{ - the } i \text{ th row of } \Phi_k.$$

The choice of $\Psi_k^{(i)}$ guarantees

$$\mathbf{r}_i^{(k)T}\left(\Phi_k\mathbf{e}_i\right) = \mathbf{r}_i^{(k)T}\Phi_k^{(i)} = 0. \tag{25}$$

Note that, by this construction,

$$\mathbf{r}_i^{(k)} = \mathbf{r}^{(k)} - \sum_{j=1}^{i}\Psi_k^{(j)}\Phi_k^{(j)},$$

and, applying (25) gives,

$$\begin{aligned}\mathbf{r}_i^{(k)T}\Phi_k^{(i)} = 0 &= \mathbf{r}^{(k)T}\Phi_k^{(i)} - \left(\sum_{j=1}^{i}\Psi_k^{(j)}\Phi_k^{(j)}\right)^T\Phi_k^{(i)} \\ &= \mathbf{r}^{(k)T}\Phi_k^{(i)} - \sum_{j=1}^{i}\Psi_k^{(j)}\left(\Phi_k^{(j)T}\Phi_k^{(i)}\right).\end{aligned}$$

Thus,

$$\Psi_k^{(1)} = \frac{\mathbf{r}^{(k)T}\Phi_k^{(1)}}{\left\|\Phi_k^{(1)}\right\|_2^2}. \tag{26}$$

For $i = 2,\dots,N$,

$$\Psi_k^{(i)} = \left\{ \Phi_k^{(i)T} \left(\mathbf{r}^{(k)} - \sum_{j=1}^{i-1} \Psi_k^{(j)} \Phi_k^{(j)} \right) \right\} \Big/ \left\| \Phi_k^{(i)} \right\|_2^2 . \tag{27}$$

Eqns. (26) and (27) can be written in the compact matrix form as

$$\mathbf{D}_k \Psi_k = \Phi_k \mathbf{r}^{(k)} - \mathbf{L}_k \Psi_k , \tag{28}$$

where $\mathbf{D}_k$ and $\mathbf{L}_k$ are defined as in (18). The form of (28) resembles the iteration procedure of the Gauss-Seidel method applied on the transformed auxilliary equation (17), but with $\Psi_{k-1} = \mathbf{0}$. The equivalent equation for the Gauss-Seidel method would be

$$\mathbf{D}_k \Psi_k = \Phi_k \mathbf{r}^{(k)} - \mathbf{L}_k \Psi_k - \mathbf{U}_k \Psi_{k-1} . \tag{30}$$

4.3 Simulation results

We use the same adaptive filtering configuration to study the performance of MR based algorithm with euclidean direction of search. We compare the two algorithms with the SPCG algorithm to study their performance with respect to eigenvalue spread. When the eigenvalue spread is small (Fig. 7), the SPCG results in lower misadjustment compared to the MR methods with Euclidean direction search. However, for large eigenvalue spread (Fig. 8), SPCG shows a significant increased in misadjustment while the other MR methods appear unaffected by the increased in eigenvalue spread.

5. Future developments

In this chapter we have described two different types of recursive MR method for adaptive filtering. The methods defer by the choice of search directions. The first method is a stochastic gradient method with a stepsize determined using the MR stepsize formula that guarantees conjugacy of successive gradients. In the second method, search directions are chosen to be N Euclidean unit vectors in R^N , with two different approaches in performing projections onto the row space of Φ .

Here's a summary of the performance of these methods:

i. The SPCG algorithm is proven to be superior compared to the traditional least mean square stochastic gradient method. We have also described a procedure to modify the SPCG algorithm so as to achieve complexity comparable to LMS algorithm.

ii. A common problem in most gradient based algorithm which is also evident in the SPCG algorithm is the poor performance when eigenvalue spread of the autocorrelation matrix is high. This problem is removed when the search direction is switched towards the Euclidean directions. Our results clearly show that the performance of recursive MR methods are unaffected by the increase in eigenvalue spread.

The two key issues that will be the focus of our research in the efforts to bring further improvements to the recursive MR methods are i) providing low complexity variants, ii) improving misadjustments especially when the eigenvalue spread of the problem is high. Research and investigations on block implementations of these algorithms are currently under way. We are also looking at a class of potential new preconditioners for the adaptive least squares problem in general. These preconditioners are in the form of recursive incomplete QR factorization preconditioners based on different orthogonalization techniques such as Gram-Schmidt, Givens rotations and Householder method.

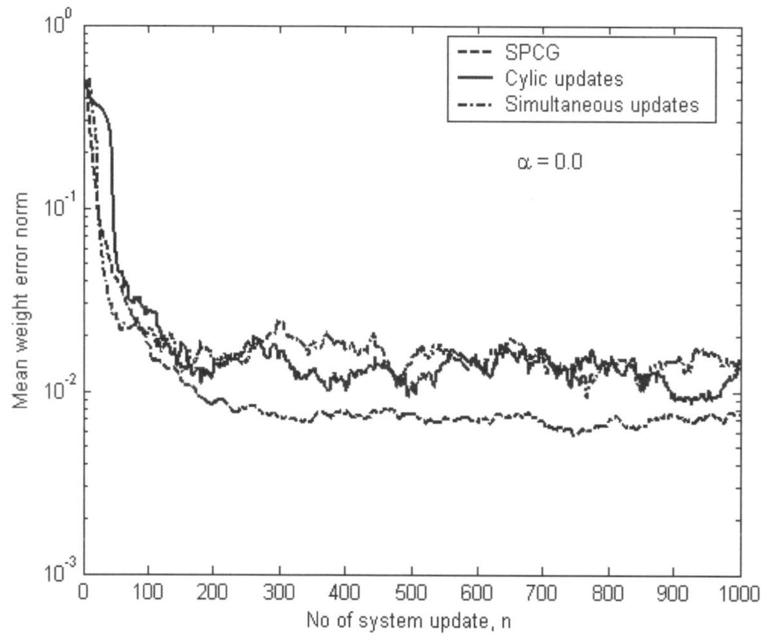

Fig. 7. SPCG compares with MR based algorithms with Euclidean direction of search (small eigenvalue spread)

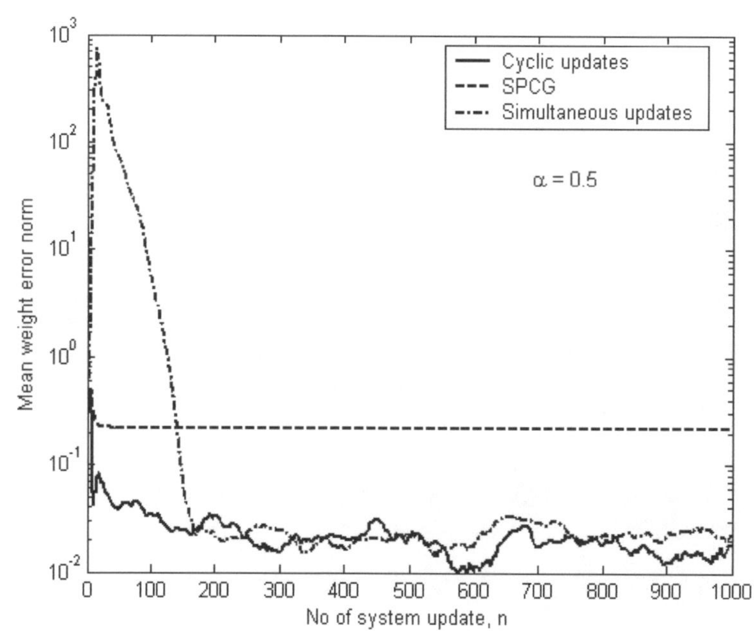

Fig. 8. SPCG compares with MR based algorithms with Euclidean direction of search (large eigenvalue spread)

6. References

Ahmad, N.A. (2008) A globally convergent stochastic pairwise conjugate gradient based adaptive filtering algorithm, *IEEE Signal Process. Lett.*, vol. 15, pp. 914-917.

Boray, G.K. & Srinath, M.D. (1992), Conjugate gradient techniques for adaptive filtering, *IEEE Trans. Circuits Syst. I, Fundam. Theory Appl.*, vol 39, no. 1, pp. 1-10.

Chang, P.S and Wilson, A.N. (2000), Analysis of conjugate gradient algorithms for adaptive filtering, *IEEE Trans. Signal Process.*, vol 48, no.2, pp. 409-418.

Chen, M. Q. (1998). A Direction set based algorithm for least squares problems in adaptive signal processing. *Linear Algebra and its Applications*, 284: 73-94.

Diene, O. and Bhaya, A. (2006), Adaptive filtering algorithms designed using control Liapunov functions, *IEEE Signal Process. Lett.*, vol 13, no. 4, pp. 224-227.

Farhang-Boroujeny, B. (1999), *Adaptive Filters: Theory and Applications*, John Wiley &Sons.

Haykin, S. (1991), *Adaptive Filter Theory*, Englewood Cliffs, NJ: Prentice-Hall.

Powell, M. J. D. (1964), An efficient method for finding the minimum of a function of several variables without calculating derivatives, Comput. J. 7 155-162.

Schraudolph, N. & Graepel, T. (2002), Towards stochastic conjugate gradient method, *Proc. 9th Int. Conf. Neural Processing, Singapore 2002.*

Zangwill, W. (1967). Minimizing a function without calculating derivatives, Comput. J. 10 293-296.

18

A Search Algorithm for Intertransaction Association Rules

Dan Ungureanu
Politehnica University of Bucharest
Romania

1. Introduction

The problem analysed in this chapter is the discovery of interesting relations between variables in large databases.
The databases are considered to contain transactions that each contain one or more items from a discrete set of items. The relations between the items are expressed in the form of association rules. The problem of searching for association rules has been denoted in the research literature as association rule mining.
The initial association rule mining problem ignored any correlation between the transactions and searched for associations only between items inside a transaction (this case is called case intratransaction association rules mining). To search for associations between items across several transactions ordered on a dimension (usually time or space), intertransaction association rule mining has been used.
We use the stock market database example to differentiate between intra- and inter-transaction analysis. If the database contains the price for each stock at the end of the trading day, an intratransaction association rule might be "If stock prices for companies A and B go up for one day, there is a probability of over c% that the price for company C will also go up the same day". However, analysts might be more interested in rules like "If stock prices for companies A and B go up for one day, there is a probability of over c% that the price for company C will go up two days later." This rule describes a relationship between items from different transactions, and it can be discovered only by using intertransaction analysis.
The main part of association rules mining has been determined to be finding the frequent itemsets.
A search algorithm that finds frequent intertransaction itemsets called InterTraSM will be presented, exemplified and analyzed in this chapter. It was first introduced in (Ungureanu & Boicea, 2008). This algorithm is an extension for the intertransactional case of the SmartMiner algorithm presented in (Zou et al., 2002). InterTraSM focuses on mining maximal frequent itemsets (MFI) - itemsets that are not a subset of any other frequent itemset. Once the MFI have obtained all the frequent itemsets can easily be derived, and they can then be counted for support in a single scan of the database.
The remainder of this chapter is organized as follows.

- Section 2 contains a formal definition for the problem of intertransaction association rules mining.

- Section 3 briefly describes other algorithms used for finding frequent intertransaction itemsets.
- Section 4 introduces the InterTraSM algorithm for searching frequent intertransaction itemsets. It also contains a detailed example of its application, and an analysis of its complexity.
- Section 5 presents an implementation of the InterTraSM algorithm, the experimental results obtained regarding its execution time, and a comparison with the performances of the algorithms from Section 3.
- Section 6 concludes the chapter and proposes future research in this area.

2. Problem description

We consider I to be a set of literals $\{a_1, a_2, \ldots, a_n\}$, also called items.
In the original association rule mining problem a transaction T was defined as a set of items such that $T \subset I$.
A database DB (also called transaction database or transactional database) was defined as a set of transactions with unique transaction IDs $\{T_1, T_2, \ldots, T_n\}$.
An association rule was defined as an implication of the form $X \rightarrow Y$, where X and Y are distinct subsets of I ($X \subset I, Y \subset I, X \cap Y = \emptyset$).
The two main measures used to characterize association rules are support and confidence.
A rule $X \rightarrow Y$ has support s in a database DB if s% of the transactions from DB contain $X \cup Y$.
A rule $X \rightarrow Y$ has confidence c in a database DB if c% of the transactions from DB that contain X also contain Y.
The initial approach to association rule mining only considered rules between items from the same transaction.
In practice though the transactions usually have some additional information attached to them, like the time when they occurred, the customers that purchased the items, or the geographical location.
In order to characterize such contexts of when / where the transactions occurred, dimensional attributes have been introduced. They can be of any kind, as long as they can be associated with the transactions from the database in a meaningful way.
In this paper we consider only the case when there is a single dimensional attribute which has an ordinal domain. Furthermore, the domain of the attribute can be divided into equal-sized intervals, such that at most one transaction from the transaction database is associated with each interval, and that each transaction can be associated with an interval.
Let d_f be the first interval and d_l be the last interval from the domain that have an associated transaction. Then, without loss of generality, we can denote the first interval with 0 and the intervals that follow it with 1, 2, 3 and so on. We consider l to be the number of interval d_l.
We denote with D the domain of the attribute and with Dom(D) the set of intervals $\{0, 1, 2, \ldots, l\}$.
So for the intertransaction case we introduce the following
Definition *Transactional database*. A transactional database is a database that contains transactions of the form $t = (d, T)$, where $d \in dom(D)$ and $T \subset I$.
In practice we are not interested in associations between items from transactions for which the distance between the associated intervals is unlimited. The running time of an algorithm that searches for such associations can be prohibitive, and also the practical use of such associations is limited at best. The goal of our research is used to find previously unknown

correlations between items, but the idea is that there might be an intrinsic relation between the data that would come into light. Such a relation would ensure that future transactions from the same domain would exhibit the same properties. This would mean that we can use the discovered associations to take useful actions related to the domain.

Research has therefore been focused on searching for associations between items from transactions for which the distance between the associated intervals has a maximum value w – we will also call this value the maximum span of the intertransaction association rules.

Definition *Sliding window.* A sliding window W in a transactional database T represents a set of continuous intervals from the domain D, such that there exists in T a transaction associated to the first interval from W. Each interval is called a subwindow of the sliding window, and they are numbered corresponding to their temporal order $d_0, d_1, \ldots, d_w$. We also use the notation W[0], W[1], …, W[w] for the intervals of W and we say that w is the size of the sliding window.

Definition *Megatransaction.* Let T be a transactional database, let I be the set of items $\{a_1, a_2, \ldots, a_n\}$ and let W be a sliding window with size w. A *megatransaction* M associated with the sliding window W is the set of all elements denoted with a_i^j, such that a_i belongs to the transaction associated with the interval W[j], for each corresponding value of $1 \le i \le n$, $0 \le j \le w$.

The items from a megatransaction will be called from now on *extended items.*

We denote with E the set of all the possible extended items $\{a_1^0, a_1^1, \ldots, a_1^w, a_2^0, \ldots, a_n^w\}$.

We call an *intratransaction itemset* a set of items $A \subset I$.

We call an *intertransaction itemset* a set of extended items $B \subset E$ such that B contains at least one extended item of the form e_i^0.

Definition *Intertransaction association rule.* An intertransaction association rule has the form $X \rightarrow Y$ where:

i. $X, Y \subset E$

ii. X contains at least one extended item of the form e_i^0, $1 \le i \le n$.

iii. Y contains at least one extended item of the form e_i^j, $1 \le i \le n$, $j > 0$.

iv. $X \cap Y = \varnothing$

Let N be the total number of transactions, T_{XY} be the set of transactions that contain the set $X \cup Y$ and T_X be the set of transactions that contain X.

Then the support of the rule is $s = |T_{XY}| \,/\, N$ and the confidence of the rule is $c = |T_{XY}| \,/\, |T_X|$.

The research in this domain has been focused on finding association rules whose support and confidence are above some specified minimum thresholds. The support threshold indicates that the two itemsets appear together in the transactional database often enough so we can benefit in practice from finding an association between them, and the confidence threshold indicates a minimum degree of confidence for the association between the two itemsets.

The problem of searching for intertransaction association rules has been divided into two parts:

- finding the intertransaction itemsets that have the support above a specified minimum threshold (this itemsets are said to be frequent)
- finding the association rules

The second problem takes much less computational time than the first one, so it presents little interest for research. A solution has been discussed for example in (Tung et al., 2003). Our work (like most of the research in this area) has therefore focused on developing an algorithm for the first problem.

3. Related work

Several algorithms for finding frequent intertransaction itemsets have been previously introduced, and some of them are presented in this chapter. Many of the algorithms for searching intertransaction association rules (including our algorithm InterTraSM that will be presented in the next chapter) are extensions for the intertransaction case of algorithms developed for searching intratransaction association rules.

3.1 E-Apriori, EH-Apriori

The classic algorithm for searching (intratransaction) association rules is Apriori, introduced in (Agrawal & Srikant, 1994). It uses the following fact: if an itemset that has k elements (also called a k-itemset) is frequent, then all its subsets, (k-1) itemsets, must also be frequent.
The algorithm first determines all the frequent 1 - itemsets (all the frequent items in this case) by counting the support of all the items.
Then, for each k>=2, the algorithms knows that the frequent itemsets must have all their subsets also frequent. The algorithm uses each combination of two itemsets with k-1 elements to see if their reunion is a k-itemset for which all the subsets with k-1 elements are frequent itemsets. For all the k-itemsets that verify this property (these itemsets are called candidate itemsets) their support is counted in a single pass through the database.
The algorithm stops when for a given k no frequent k-itemsets are found.
In order to ensure that the same frequent itemset is not discovered multiple times (starting from different initial items) the algorithm assumes there is a lexical ordering between the items, and at any given steps it tries to add to the current itemset only items that are "greater" (using the lexical ordering) than the last added item.
The E-Apriori (Extended Apriori) algorithm for the intertransaction case, introduced in (Lu et al., 2000), is an extension of the Apriori algorithm so it uses intertransaction itemsets containing extended items. A lexical order is given for the intratransaction items, and for all the extended items from the same interval the lexical order for the corresponding intratransaction items is used. It is also said that all the extended items from interval (i+1) are "greater" than all the extended items from interval i.
It has been observed that the time for obtaining the frequent 2-itemsets has a big impact on the total running time, due to the fact that there are a large number of frequent 1-itemsets, which leads to a large number of candidate 2-itemsets which have to be analized.
The EH-Apriori (Extended Hash Apriori) , also introduced in (Lu et al., 2000), uses a hashing technique to reduce the number of candidate 2-itemsets. As the support of the frequent extended items is computed, each possible 2-extended itemset is mapped to a hash table. Each bucket from the hash table indicates how many extended itemsets has been hashed to it.

3.2 FITI

Another algorithm for searching intertransaction association rules, initially introduced in (Tung et al., 2003) is called FITI (First Intra Then Inter).
FITI uses the property that given a frequent intertransaction itemset, any subset for which the same interval is associated to all the extended items must correspond to a frequent intratransaction itemset. Using this property the algorithm first determines all the frequent intratransaction itemsets, and using them determines next all the frequent intertransaction itemsets – hence the name of the algorithm.
We briefly describe the three phases of the FITI algorithm:

1. Find the frequent intratransaction itemsets (using any algorithm for intratransaction association rule mining, like Apriori). The itemsets will be stored in a special data structure called FILT (Frequent-Itemsets Linked Table). This consists of a hash table of itemsets where the nodes are linked with multiple types of connections. Each frequent itemset is associated a unique ID.
2. The database is transformed into a set of encoded frequent-itemsets tables (FIT tables). The number of FIT tables is the maximum size of the frequent intratransaction itemsets discovered in phase 1, and each table corresponds to a particular size (from 1 to the maximum value). For any FIT table, corresponding to a size denoted with k, the records have the form {d_i, $IDset_i$} where d_i represents a value of the dimensional attribute (an interval), and $IDset_i$ represents the set of IDs (defined in phase 1) of frequent intratransaction itemsets with size k that are found in the transaction associated with d_i.
3. The frequent intertransaction itemsets are discovered using a level-wise process similar to the one used in Apriori: all the candidates with k elements are determined, their support is computed during one pass through the database and then using the frequent itemsets with k elements we go on to compute all the candidates with (k+1) elements.

For the discovery of frequent itemsets with two items FITI uses a hashing approach similar to the one used in EH-Apriori.

For k>=2, the algorithm defines two kinds of combining two itemsets with k elements in order to generate a candidate itemset with (k+1) elements:

a. an intratransaction join is performed between two itemsets who have (k-1) of their items identical, and the items that are different belong to the same interval of the sliding window
b. a cross-transaction join is performed between two itemsets who have (k-1) of their items identical, and the items that are different belong to different intervals I1 and I2 of the sliding window. In order not to generate the same itemsets through both intratransaction and cross-transaction joins, the following restriction are placed for cross-transaction joins:

- the first itemset must not have any items associated to interval I2 or any items associated to any interval after I1
- the second itemset must not have any items associated to interval I1 or any items associated to any interval after I2
- any interval must have associated at most one extended item in both itemsets

3.3 ITP-Miner

The ITP-Miner algorithm, initially introduced in (Lee & Wang, 2007), tries to avoid the breadth first search approach of Apriori-like algorithms. In order to realize only one pass through the database the algorithm uses a special data structure called dimensional attribute list (dat-list) to store the dimensional attributes (the corresponding intervals in fact) associated to a frequent itemset. For a given frequent itemset A, if the megatransactions in which A appears start at the intervals $t_1, t_2, \ldots, t_n$ then the associated dat-list is $A(t_1, t_2, \ldots, t_n)$. The algorithm also assumes a lexical ordering of the intratransaction items, which leads to an ordering of the extended items in the way described for the E-Apriori and EH-Apriori algorithms. A convention is used that the extended items in a frequent itemset from a dat-list are stored in increasing order (using the ordering previously described).

The algorithm uses a structure called ITP-Tree that is a search tree that has dat-lists as nodes. The parent node of a dat-list $a(t_1, t_2, \ldots, t_n)$ is the dat list $b(u_1, u_2, \ldots, u_m)$ where b is obtained from a by removing the last extended item and m>=n. The root of an ITP-Tree is the empty itemset ∅ and the nodes on the same depth level are ordered in increasing order depending on the extended items from the itemset.

The algorithm starts with determining the frequent items and their dat-lists, and for determining the frequent itemsets with more than one element it doesn't read the database again, but it works with the already determined dat-lists.

A join between two frequent itemsets $\{u_0(0), u_1(i_1), \ldots, u_{k-1}(i_{k-1})\}$ and $\{v_0(0), v_1(j_1), \ldots, v_{k-1}(j_{k-1})\}$ is deemed possible if the first (k-1) extended items are identical and $u_{k-1}(i_{k-1}) < v_{k-1}(j_{k-1})$ using the given order relation. The unified itemset is then $\{u_0(0), u_1(i_1), \ldots, u_{k-1}(i_{k-1}), v_{k-1}(j_{k-1})\}$- so it is the same principle of generating candidate itemsets as the one used for Apriori-like algorithms, only a DFS search is used instead of a BFS-search.

The dat-list for a candidate itemset has for the set of dimensional attributes the intersection of the sets of dimensional attributes from the two itemsets used to generate it. The size of this set determines the support of the candidate itemset, and in this way it is determined if the itemset is frequent.

The following pruning strategies are used by ITP-Miner to reduce the size of the search space:

- pruning of infrequent itemsets with 2 elements: a hash table is used to check if a pair of frequent items can generate a frequent 2-itemset before the join is performed. A hash table H2 is created while finding the frequent items and their dat-lists
- pruning of infrequent itemsets with k elements: before performing a join of 2 frequent itemsets with (k-1) elements, the hash table H2 is used to check if the two extended items that differ might represent a frequent itemsets with 2 elements (once again the property that any subset of a frequent itemset must also be frequent is used here)

3.4 EFP-Growth

We will now summarize the EFP-Growth algorithm, initially presented in (Luhr et al., 2007). The algorithm uses the pattern-growth property and it is an adaptation for the intertransaction case of the FP-Growth algorithm described in (Han et al., 2000). The algorithm uses an EFP-Tree (Extended Frequent Pattern Tree) which is an adaptation for the intertransaction case of the FP-Tree used in the FP-Growth algorithm.

The EFP-Tree is composed of intraitem nodes ordered by descending frequency, and each node can have zero or one interitem subtree which is a FP-Tree where the frequency ordering of the interitems is conditioned on the intraitem parent node.

The construction of the EFP-Tree is done in three passes over the database.

The frequency of the extended items is computed in the first pass and the frequent intraitems and interitems are found.

In the second pass the intraitem tree is built and for each transaction the infrequent intraitems are removed and the frequent items are sorted in decreasing order of frequency. Also the conditional frequencies for the interitems are computed (the frequencies only in the transactions in which the intraitems appear).

In the third pass the interitem sub-trees are build.

The trees are build by passing through each transaction of the database, and for each item encountered by going one step lower in the tree (or creating a new descendent node with the new item if it doesn't exist) and increasing the support with 1. When the first interitem is reached the processing passes to the interitem subtree corresponding to the current intraitem node.

After the EFP-Tree is built the algorithm computes the association rules using the pattern growth property. A divide and conquer strategy is used to construct trees conditioned on known frequent base rules and to take the dot product of the frequent items in the conditional tree and the conditional base itemset to produce new rules, which in turn will become the conditional base for the new set of rules to be mined.
The algorithm uses two types of conditional trees:

- a conditional EFP-Tree that is used to find the intraitems and interitems that can be used to extend the present intraitem rule suffix
- a FP-Tree of the interitems inherited by the conditional base

4. The InterTraSM algorithm

4.1 Theoretical presentation

We will present in this chapter the InterTraSM algorithm for mining intertransaction association rules, which was first introduced in (Ungureanu & Boicea, 2008). The algorithm is an adaptation for the intertransaction case of the SmartMiner algorithm for finding (intratransaction) association rules, which was introduced in (Zou et al., 2002).
The InterTraSM algorithm (like the SmartMiner algorithm which it extends) searches for maximal frequent itemsets (itemset which are frequent, but for which no superset of them is also frequent) using a depth first search. Then all the frequent itemsets are derived from the maximal frequent itemsets (MFI).
The algorithms consists of a series of steps, each of which is applied to a node of a search tree. We will describe next what data is available for each node and how that data is processed.
We identify a node with X:Y, where X (the head) is the current set of extended items that has been discovered to form a frequent itemset, and Y (the tail) is the set of extended items that still has to be explored to find all the maximal frequent itemsets that contain X is a subset.
The starting node of the algorithm is identified by $\varnothing$:E (the empty set and the set of all possible extended items).
As in the SmartMiner algorithm, we also use some additional data attached to each node to help our algorithm:

- we define the transaction set T(X) to represent all the transactions from the database that contain the itemset X. For the starting node (where X is the empty set) the transaction set is the entire database, and we will show how T(X) is obtained for each subsequent node
- if we denote with M the known frequent itemsets (the itemsets determined to be frequent before we start processing of the current node) and with N = X : Y the current node, then the tail information of M to N is the parts from Y (the tail of the node) that can be inferred from M. For the processing of a given node the algorithm we use the tail information for the frequent itemsets discovered previously.

The entry data for a node consists then of:

- the transaction set T(X)
- the tail Y
- the tail information for the node that has been obtained so far (also called global tail information, or Ginf). This information is passed from the parent node, and it contains the itemsets that have been previously discovered to be frequent in T(X)

The exit data for a node consists of:

- the updated global tail information Ginf
- the local maximal frequent itemsets discovered are the node and its descendants

The data processing at the level of a node from the search tree is described below:

1. count the support for each item from Y in the transaction set T(X)
2. remove the infrequent items from Y
3. while Y has at least one element
   4. if there is an item in Ginf with the size equal to the length of the tail, the itemset containing all the items from the tail has already found to be frequent in previous processing steps, so we can skip to step 12
   5. select an item a_i from Y
   6. the head of the next state S_{i+1} will be $X_{i+1} = X \cup \{a_i\}$
   7. the tail of the next state S_{i+1} will be $Y_{i+1} = Y \setminus \{a_i\}$
   8. the global tail information for S_{i+1} is computed by projecting on Y_{i+1} the itemsets that contain a_i
   9. recursively call the algorithm for the node $N_{i+1} = X_{i+1} : Y_{i+1}$
      The returned values will be Mfi_i the local maximal frequent itemsets found at the node N_{i+1}. The global tail information Ginf is updated to include Mfi_i and then it is projected on the remaining tail. The members subsumed by Mfi_i are marked as deleted
   10. $Y = Y_{i+1}$
11. end while
12. $Mfi = \cup (a_i Mfi_i)$
13. return Mfi and the current updated value of Ginf

The InterTraSM algorithm uses extended items instead of the intratransaction items used by SmartMiner. Also for the first level nodes we select while starting from the root node we choose only extended items which have 0 as the associated interval – because each intertransaction association rule must contain at least one extended item with interval 0 in the head of the rule.

We next analyse the complexity of the InterTraSM algorithm.

We consider the following variables that affect the complexity of the algorithm:

- |D| - the number of intervals for the domain D. This is equal to the number of intertransactions from the database
- W – the size of the sliding window
- |L1| - the number of frequent intratransaction items

The processing for a node from the search tree is divided in the following parts:

1. Determining the support in T(X) for each element from Y
   The number of megatransaction from T(X) is limited to |D| and the number of elements from Y is limited to |L1|xW, so the number of operations for this step is O(|D|x|L1|xW).
2. Preparing the entry data for each sub-node, calling each sub-node recursively (without taking into account the processing inside the sub-nodes) and computing the exit data using the data returned by the subnode – the complexity is O(|L1|xW).

We conclude that the maximum complexity for a node is O(|D|x|L1|xW), but the maximum average complexity on all nodes will be lower since both the number of transactions in T(X) and the number of items in Y decrease while we descend into the search tree.

4.2 An example

We will next present a detailed example of the execution steps of the algorithm.

We consider first a set of items {a, b, c, d}.

We consider next the following transactional database: with 5 transactions:

T0	a,b
T1	a,c
T2	c
T3	a,b
T4	c,d

We consider the maximum span of the intertransaction association rules we want to discover to be 1 (so the size of the sliding window will be w=1).
We will work then with the following 5 megatransactions:
M0: a^0, b^0, a^1, c^1
M1: a^0, c^0, c^1
M2: c^0, a^1, b^1
M3: a^0, b^0, c^1, d^1
M4: c^0, d^0
The minimum support threshold for the rules we want to discover is s=0.4 (40%).
We have E = {a^0, b^0, c^0, d^0, a^1, b^1, c^1, d^1}
The entry node N0 of the algorithm has X = , Y = E, Ginf = ∅ and
T(X) = {M0, M1, M2, M3, M4}.
We start by computing the support for each item from Y in T(X) (step 1 for node N0)
We find that $s(a^0)=3$, $s(b^0)=2$, $s(c^0)=3$, $s(d^0)=1$, $s(a^1)=2$, $s(b^1)=1$, $s(c^1)=3$, $s(d^1)=1$.
The frequent extended items are the ones who have the support value at least 2 (40% of the total transactions).
When we remove the infrequent items (step 2 for node N0) we remain with {a^0, b^0, c^0, a^1, c^1}.
We select a^0 to be X1 - the head of the next node N1, and the tail Y1 will be {b^0, c^0, a^1, c^1}. Ginf will be ∅ and T(X1) = {M0, M1, M3}.
We call the algorithm recursively for node N1.
We compute the support for the items from Y1 in T(X1) (step 1 for node N1)
We find that $s(b^0)=2$, $s(c^0)=1$, $s(a^1)=1$, $s(c^1)=3$.
When we remove the infrequent items (step 2 for node N1) we remain with { b^0, c^1}
We next select b^0 to be X2 - the head of the next node N2, the tail Y2 will be { c^1}, Ginf = ∅ and T(X2) = {M0, M3}. We call the algorithm recursively for node N2.
We compute the support for the items from Y2 in T(X2) (step 1 for node N2)
We find that $s(c^1)=2$. Since there is only one element in the tail and it is frequent we can only select c^1 as the head for the next node N3 and the tail will be empty, so N3 will return ∅ as MFI. No more items remain in the tail to be processed, so the node N2 will return MFI = {c^1}
After N2 returns, the Ginf for N1 will be updated to be {c^1}.
Since the remaining value of the tail is {c^1}, according to step 4 for N1 we can skip to step 12.
The node N1 will return MFI= {b^0c^1}
After node N1 returns, the Ginf for node N0 is updated to {b^0c^1}
We next return to step 3 and we select another item from the remaining tail {b^0, c^0, a^1, c^1}
We select item b^0 to be X4, Y4 will be {c^0, a^1, c^1}, Ginf for node N4 will be the projection of Ginf on Y4 - {c^1}, T(X4) = {M0, M3}.
We next call the algorithm recursively for node N4.
We compute the support for the items from Y4 in T(X4) (step 1 for node N4)
We find that $s(c^0)=0$, $s(a^1)=1$, $s(c^1)=2$.
When we remove the infrequent items (step 2 for node N4) we remain with {c^1}.
According to step 4 we can skip to step 12.

The node N4 will return MFI = ∅
We next return to step 3 and we select another item from the remaining tail $\{c^0, a^1, c^1\}$.
We select item c^0 to be X5, Y5 will be $\{a^1, c^1\}$. Ginf for node N5 will be the projection of Ginf on Y5 - $\{c^1\}$. T(X5) = {M1, M2,M4}.
When call the algorithm recursively for node N5, no frequent items are found in the tail.
We next return to step 3 and we select another item from the remaining tail $\{a^1, c^1\}$.
We select item a^1 to be X6, Y6 will be $\{c^1\}$. Ginf for node N6 will be the projection of Ginf on Y6 - $\{c^1\}$. T(X6) = {M1, M3}.
When call the algorithm recursively for node N6, no frequent items are found in the tail.
We then return to step 3, but since the condition in step 4 is verified we go to step 12.
Node N0 returns MFI = $\{a^0b^0c^1, c^0, a^1\}$.
So the exit data of the algorithm, the maximal frequent itemsets are MFI = $\{a^0b^0c^1, c^0, a^1\}$.

5. Experiments and results

We have developed an implementation of the algorithm in C, using a structure similar to that from the SmartMiner algorithm. We used C in order to better control the memory usage and execution speed of the algorithm.
The traditional form of input data for algorithms that search for frequent itemsets is a series of transactions containing items and having associated domain intervals. We have instead used an orthogonal view of the input data. We have first determined the frequent items, and then for each frequent item we have used a bitset containing one bit for each megatransaction from the database. The bit is 1 if the item appears in the megatransaction and 0 if it does not appear.
The program was benchmarked under a Windows XP operating system, on a PC with Intel Pentium 4 processor with a speed of 3GHz and memory of 1GB. The code has been written and compiled using Visual Studio 2003.
We have used both real and artificial data to test the performance of our algorithm.
The real data consists of two datasets, WINNER and LOSER, similar to those described in (Lee & Wang, 2007). They have been obtained from the values of 10 stock exchange indices for the trading days between January 1, 1991 to December 31, 2005: ASX All Ordinaries Index (ASX), CAC40 Index (CAC), DAX Index (DAX), Dow Jones Index (DOW), FTSE 100 INDEX (FTS), Hang Seng Index (HSI), NASDAQ Index (NDQ), Nikkei 225 Index (NKY), Swiss Market Index (SMI) and Singapore ST Index (STI). In the WINNER set a transaction for a trading day contains the stock indices whose value rises for the day, while in the LOSER set a transaction for a trading day contains the stock indices whose value falls for the day.
For both the WINNER and LOSER datasets we have used the sliding window size to be 4 (the maximum span of the intertransaction association rules). We have varied the minimum support threshold value from 4% to 12% and the results are presented in Fig. 1 and Fig. 2.
The same data sets (obtained from the same stock indices for the same period) were also used to evaluate the ITP-Miner algorithm in (Lee & Wang, 2007). The same sliding window size was used and the minimum support varied between the same values, while the program was run on a processor with similar properties to the one we used using Microsoft Visual C++ 6.0. We have observed a difference of an order of magnitude between the execution times, especially larger when the minimum support threshold decreases (and there are more frequent itemsets to be found). For example for the LOSER data set when the minimum support threshold is set at 4% InterTraSM takes less than 6 seconds, while the authors reported that ITP-Miner takes about 100 seconds.

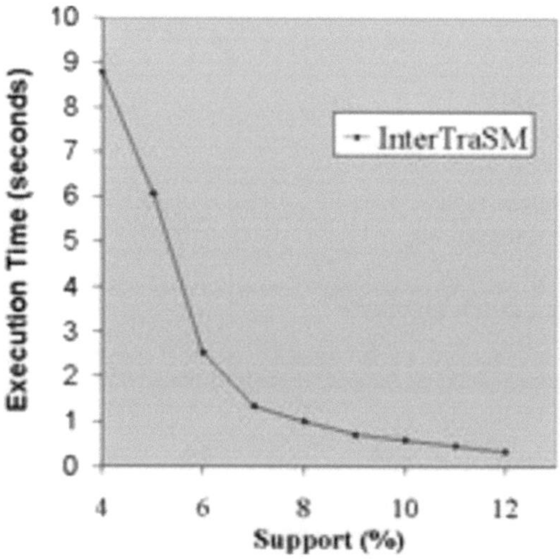

Fig. 1. Execution time vs minimum support, WINNER data set, w=4

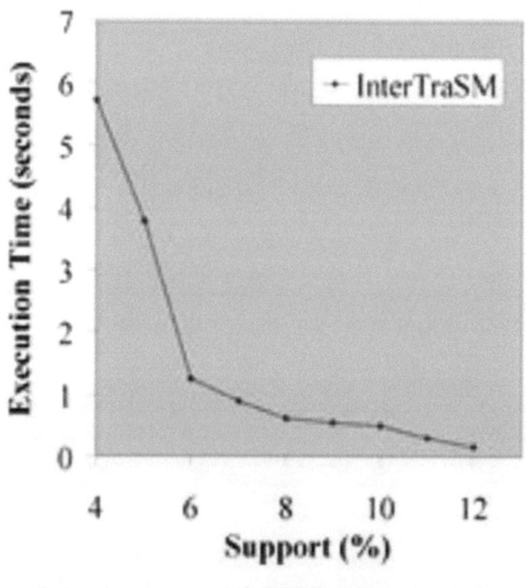

Fig. 2. Execution time vs minimum support, LOSER data set, w=4

The synthetic data was created using the generator described in (Luhr et al., 2007), gracefully provided to us by its authors.

The generation of data is a process with two steps:

- first a set of candidate frequent intertransaction itemsets is created
- then this set is used to populate with items the transactions from the dataset

We have generated two artificial datasets, representing sparse and dense data. This was the same method used in (Luhr et al., 2007) to evaluate the performances of the FITI and EFP-Tree algorithms.

The characteristics of the artificial data created are influenced by some parameters that guide the generation process. These parameters have the following values for the two artificial datasets we produced:

Parameter name	Sparse dataset	Dense dataset
Number of intratransactions	500	200
Size of the intertransaction pool	50	200
Average length of intratransactions	5	25
Maximum length of intratransactions	10	50
Average length of intertransactions	5	8
Maximum length of intertransactions	10	20
Maximum number of unique items	500	100
Maximum interval span of intertransactions	4	6

Table 1. Values of parameters used in the generation of the synthetic data sets

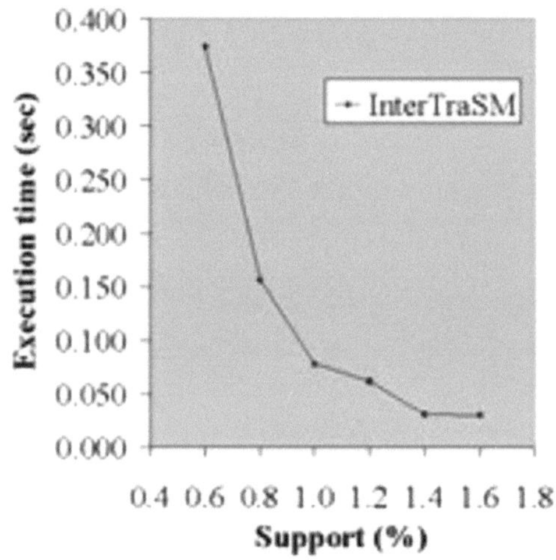

Fig. 3. Execution time vs minimum support, sparse data set, w=4

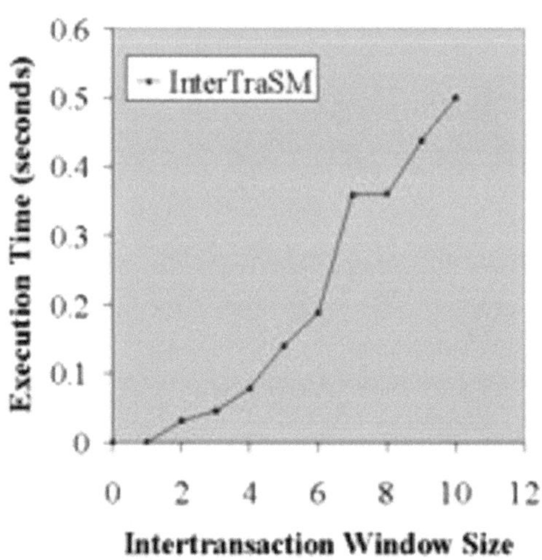

Fig. 4. Execution time vs sliding window size, sparse data set, minsup = 1%

We have compared the performance of InterTraSM and the performance of EFP-Growth for synthetic data sets created with the same parameters by the same generator (probably not identical data sets since the actual generation is random, but the data sets have the same characteristics).

For the synthetic sparse data set:

- we have varied the minimum support threshold from 1.6% to 0.6%, with the sliding window size set to 4 – the results are in Fig. 3.
- we have varied the sliding window size from w=0 to w=10 while we have kept a fixed minimum support threshold of 1% - the results are in Fig. 4.

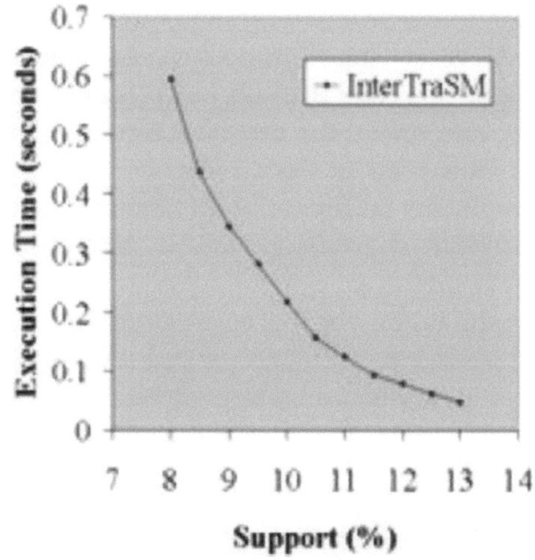

Fig. 5. Execution time vs minimum support, dense data set, w=6

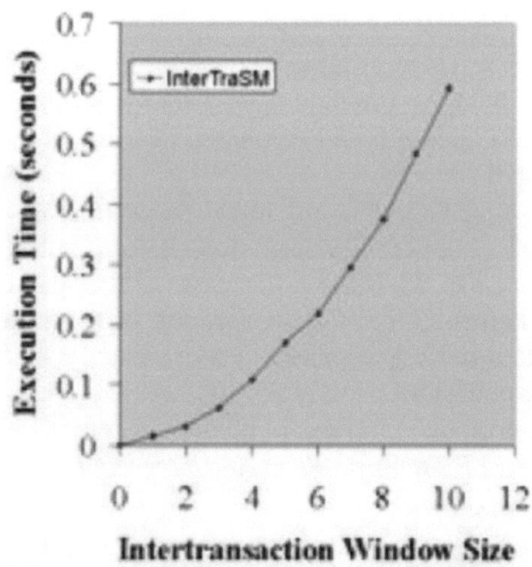

Fig. 6. Execution time vs sliding window size, dense data set, minsup = 10%

For the synthetic dense data set:

- we have varied the minimum support threshold from 13% to 8%, with the sliding window size set to 6 – the results are in Fig. 5.
- we have varied the sliding window size from w=0 to w=10 while we have kept a fixed minimum support threshold of 10% - the results are in Fig. 6.

Since the execution times observed here are all under 1 second and the execution times reported in (Luhr et al, 2007) on a similar processor have values of tens or evens hundreds of seconds, even considering for the different implementation environments we can conclude that InterTraSM generally performs at least an order of magnitude better than EFP-Growth.

6. Conclusion

We have approached in this paper the issue of searching for intertransaction association rules. We have presented the theoretical description of the problem and we have discussed the differences from the classical (intratransaction) association rule mining. We have presented some previous algorithms and then we have focused on InterTraSM - which uses a depth first search strategy and unlike the previous algorithms introduced it searches for maximal frequent itemsets. This reduces the number of support counting operations that need to be performed. Experiments performed with similar data and on similar processors with the ones used in previous algorithms show a difference of at least an order of magnitude in favour of InterTraSM.

In the future the algorithm should be applied on more real data sets and the performance should be measured. Also some interestingness measures for intertransaction association rules should be applied and the results should be analysed.

7. References

Agrawal, R. & Srikant, R. (1994). Fast algorithms for mining association rules, *Proceedings of the 20th International Conference on Very Large Databases (VLDB)*, pp. 487-499, Santiago, Chile, September 1994, Morgan Kaufmann

Han, J.; Pei, J. & Yin, Y. (2000). Mining frequent patterns without candidate generation, *Proceedings of the 2000 ACM SIGMOD International Conference on Management of Data*, pp. 1-12, Dallas, United States, May 2000, ACM

Lee, A.J.T. & Wang, C-S. (2007). An efficient algorithm for mining frequent inter-transaction patterns. *Information Sciences: an International Journal*, Vol. 177, Issue 17, (September 2007), pp. 3453-3476

Lu, H.; Feng, L. & Han, J. (2000). Beyond intra-transaction association analysis: mining multi-dimensional inter-transaction association rules. *ACM Transactions on Information Systems*, Vol. 18, Issue 4, (October 2000), pp. 423-454

Luhr, S.; West, G. & Venkatesh, S. (2007). Recognition of emergent human behaviour in a smart home: A data mining approach. *Pervasive and Mobile Computing*, Vol. 3, Issue 2, (March 2007), pp. 95-116

Tung, A.K.H.; Lu, H.; Feng, L. & Han, J. (2003). Efficient mining of intertransaction association rules. *IEEE Transactions on Knowledge and Data Engineering*, Vol. 15, Issue 1, (January 2003), pp. 43-56

Ungureanu, D. & Boicea, A. (2008). Intertrasm - a depth first search algorithm for mining intertransaction association rules, *ICSOFT 2008 - Proceedings of the Third International Conference on Software and Data Technologies*, pp. 148-153, Porto, Portugal, July 2008, INSTICC Press 2008

Zou, Q.; Chu, W. & Lu, B. (2002). SmartMiner: a depth first algorithm guided by tail information for mining maximal frequent itemsets, *Proceedings of the 2002 IEEE International Conference on Data Mining*, pp. 570-577, Maebashi City, Japan, December 2002, IEEE Computer Society

19

Finding Conceptual Document Clusters Based on Top-*N* Formal Concept Search: Pruning Mechanism and Empirical Effectiveness

Yoshiaki OKUBO and Makoto HARAGUCHI
IST, Hokkaido University
JAPAN

1. Introduction

We often rely on the *World Wide Web* as useful and rich resources of information and knowledge. A large number of web pages (documents) are on the Internet and we can easily browse and enjoy them anytime. It is, however, not so easy to efficiently find useful pages because of the hugeness of the Web space. For example, *Google*, a popular information retrieval (*IR*) engine, often gets a number of web pages with the order of hundred thousands for a given keyword set.

In general, an information retrieval system shows us an ordered list of web pages, where the ordering is determined by its own ranking mechanism. Then, only some of the higher-ranked pages in the list are actually browsed and the others are discarded as less important ones, because the list contains a large number of pages. Thus, web pages with lower ranks are usually invisible for us even if they are similar to higher-ranked ones. In this sense, we might be missing many useful pages or documents. Therefore, if we can make such hidden significant pages visible, our chance to obtain valuable information and knowledge on the Web can be enhanced. Extracting *clusters* each of which consists of similar (web) documents would be a promising approach to realizing it.

Although several clustering methods for web documents have already been investigated (e. g. (Vakali et al., 2004)), most of them adopt traditional *hierarchical* or *partitional* approaches. That is, the whole set of documents is divided into k clusters, where the number of clusters, k, is given as a parameter. As is well-known, however, providing an adequate value for k is quite difficult. This fact has motivated us to investigate a new clustering method, a *pinpoint extraction of Top-N nice clusters* (Haraguchi & Okubo, 2010; 2006b; Okubo et al., 2005; Okubo & Haraguchi, 2003).

As has been pointed out (e. g. (Hotho et al., 2003)), a meaningful cluster should have a clear explanation of what the conceptual meaning of the cluster is. Agreeing with that, we have made an informal constraint on clusters to be extracted (Haraguchi & Okubo, 2007; 2006a):

> *The notion of relevance or interestingness depends only on a conceptual class of documents, not dependent on particular instances of documents. Then the clusters we have to find must be concepts of documents that can be definable by means of feature terms.*

This kind of clusters has been originally formalized in (Haraguchi & Okubo, 2007; 2006a) with the notion of *Formal Concept Analysis* (Ganter & Wille, 1999). A *formal concept* (*FC* in short) in our case is defined as a pair of *closed sets* of documents X and feature terms Y, where the former is called the *extent* and the latter the *intent* of the concept. Such a concept means each document in X shares all the feature terms in Y and such a document never exists any more. Thus, a set of documents as the extent of an *FC* corresponds to a conceptual cluster of documents which is definable by the feature terms shared with the documents. We call this kind of cluster an *FC-cluster*.
In general, we can extract a huge number of *FC*-clusters for a given document set. In order to obtain meaningful *FC*s, we try to extract only Top-N *FC*s in the sense that their intents retain a certain degree of quality (constraint on intents by a lower threshold δ) and their extents are evaluated as in the top N (preference on extents). In (Haraguchi & Okubo, 2007; 2006a), it has been formalized as *Top-N δ-Valid FC Problem*.
In this chapter, we precisely present an algorithm for efficiently extracting Top-N *FC*s. It is based on a *maximum clique algorithm* (Balas & Yu, 1986) and can be viewed as an improved version of our previous algorithm (Haraguchi & Okubo, 2007; 2006a). The point is to *safely* and *completely* exclude duplications of extents already obtained. We show useful theoretical properties for the task with their proofs. Several pruning rules based on these properties are incorporated in our improved algorithm. The *safeness* and *completeness* of the pruning rules are also discussed with theoretical proofs. Our experimental results show that it can extract Top-N *FC*s with practical times for a real dataset. Moreover, since the exact correspondence between the notion of *closed itemsets* (Pasquier et al., 1999) and *FC*s can be observed, our improved algorithm is compared with several excellent closed itemset miners in computation times. The experimental results also show that our algorithm outperforms them in certain difficult cases.

This chapter is an extended version of the literature (Okubo & Haraguchi, 2006). We especially focuses on the algorithmic viewpoint of our method. The remainder of this chapter is organized as follows: In the next section, we introduce a basic terminology used throughout this chapter. Section 3 describes the notion of formal concepts and discusses the correspondence between *FC*s and closed itemsets. Our conceptual document clusters are introduced in Section 4. Section 5 formalizes our problem for finding Top-N δ-Valid *FC*s. Our algorithm for the problem is discussed in Section 6. Some pruning rules are presented in details and a pseudo-code of the algorithm is also given. In Section 7, we conduct our experimentation with a real dataset of web pages. Computational performance of our algorithm is compared with several efficient closed itemset miners. In the final section, we conclude this chapter with a summary and important future directions.

2. Preliminaries

In this chapter, we are concerned with a *simple weighted undirected graph*. A graph is denoted by $G = (V, E, w)$, where V is a set of *vertices*, $E \subseteq V \times V$ a set of *undirected edges* [1] and $w : V \rightarrow \mathbb{R}^+$ a (positive real-valued) *weight function* for vertices.
For any vertices $v, v' \in V$, if $(v, v') \in E$, v is said to be *adjacent* to v' and vice versa. For a vertex $v \in V$, the set of vertices adjacent to v is denoted by $N_G(v)$, where $|N_G(v)|$ is called the *degree* of v. If it is clear from the context, it is simply denoted by $N(v)$.

[1] That is, any edge $(v, v') \in E$ is identified with (v', v).

Object ID	Features
1	a b c d e f
2	b c e
3	b e
4	a b d e f
5	b d
6	a d f
7	c d f

Fig. 1. Formal Context

For any pair of vertices v and v' in V $(v \neq v')$, if $(v, v') \in E$, then G is said to be *complete*.
For a subset V' of V, a graph $G(V')$ defined by $G(V') = (V', E \cap V' \times V', w)$ is called a *subgraph* of G and is said to be *induced by* V'. If the subgraph is complete, then it is called a *clique* in G. A clique is simply referred to as the set of vertices by which it is induced. Note here that any subset of a clique is also a clique.
For a clique Q, its *size* is defined by $|Q|$. Since each vertex in G is assigned a weight, it would be reasonable to evaluate cliques by providing an adequate evaluation function based on vertex weights.
For cliques Q and Q', if $Q \subset Q'$, then Q' is called an *expansion* of Q. Moreover, if there exists no clique Q'' such that $Q \subset Q'' \subset Q'$, Q' is called an *immediate expansion* of Q. If a clique Q has no immediate expansion, that is, any proper superset of Q is not a clique, then Q is said to be *maximal*. A maximal clique whose size is largest among all maximal ones is especially called a *maximum clique*. In general, a maximum clique is not uniquely found in G.

3. Formal concept analysis

Formal Concept Analysis (*FCA*) (Ganter & Wille, 1999) is a theory of data analysis which identifies *conceptual structures among objects* (*individuals*). We first introduce some terminologies for *FCA*.

3.1 Formal concepts

Let $\mathcal{O}$ be a set of *objects* (*individuals*) and $\mathcal{F}$ a set of *features* (*attributes*). Assume we have a binary relation $R \subseteq \mathcal{O} \times \mathcal{F}$, where a tuple $(x, y) \in R$ means that the object x is associated with the feature y (that is, x has y). A triple of $\mathcal{O}$, $\mathcal{F}$ and R, $< \mathcal{O}, \mathcal{F}, R >$, is called a *formal context*.
A formal context is often represented as a table. Figure 1 shows an example of a formal context in a table format. For example, the object 2 is associated with the features b, c and e.
Under a formal context $< \mathcal{O}, \mathcal{F}, R >$, for each object $x \in \mathcal{O}$, the set of features with which x is associated is denoted by $\mathcal{F}(x)$, that is, $\mathcal{F}(x) = \{y \mid (x, y) \in R\}$.
Given a formal context $< \mathcal{O}, \mathcal{F}, R >$, for a set of objects $X \subseteq \mathcal{O}$ and a set of features $Y \subseteq \mathcal{F}$, we define two mappings $\varphi : 2^{\mathcal{O}} \to 2^{\mathcal{F}}$ and $\psi : 2^{\mathcal{F}} \to 2^{\mathcal{O}}$, respectively, as follows.

$$\varphi(X) = \{y \in \mathcal{F} \mid \forall x \in X, (x, y) \in R\} = \bigcap_{x \in X} \mathcal{F}(x) \quad \text{and}$$

$$\psi(Y) = \{x \in \mathcal{O} \mid Y \subseteq \mathcal{F}(x)\}.$$

The former computes the set of features shared by every object in X. The latter, on the other hand, returns the set of objects each of which is associated with all of the features in Y.

Based on the mappings, a *formal concept* (FC in short) under the formal context is defined as a pair of an object set $X \subseteq \mathcal{O}$ and a feature set $Y \subseteq \mathcal{F}$, (X, Y), such that $\varphi(X) = Y$ and $\psi(Y) = X$. Especially, X and Y are called the *extent* and *intent* of the concept, respectively. From the definition, it is obvious that $\psi(\varphi(X)) = X$ and $\varphi(\psi(Y)) = Y$. That is, a formal concept is defined as a pair of *closed* sets of objects and features under the composite mappings. We often denote the composite mappings $\psi \circ \varphi$ and $\varphi \circ \psi$ by E and I, respectively.

For a set of objects $X \subseteq \mathcal{O}$, $\varphi(\psi(\varphi(X))) = I(\varphi(X)) = \varphi(X)$ holds. In other words, $\varphi(X)$ is always closed under I. Therefore, $\varphi(X)$ can be the intent of an FC. More precisely speaking, for any set of objects X, we can uniquely obtain an FC, $(\psi(\varphi(X)), \varphi(X)) = (E(X), \varphi(X))$. Similarly, for a set of features $Y \subseteq \mathcal{F}$, we can always consider its corresponding FC, $(\psi(Y), \varphi(\psi(Y))) = (\psi(Y), I(Y))$.

From the definition of the mappings, we can observe the following theoretical properties.

Observation 1.
Let X and X' be subsets of $\mathcal{O}$ such that $X \subseteq X'$. Then $\varphi(X) \supseteq \varphi(X')$ and $E(X) \subseteq E(X')$. Dually, for subsets of $\mathcal{F}$, Y and Y', such that $Y \subseteq Y'$, $\psi(Y) \supseteq \psi(Y')$ and $I(Y) \subseteq I(Y')$ hold. ■

3.2 Formal concept lattice

Given a formal context $< \mathcal{O}, \mathcal{F}, R >$, let $\mathcal{FC}$ be the set of FCs under the context. We introduce here an ordering on $\mathcal{FC}$.

Definition 1. (Partial Ordering on $\mathcal{FC}$)
Let FC_i and FC_j be a pair of formal concepts in $\mathcal{FC}$ such that $FC_i = (X_i, Y_i)$ and $FC_j = (X_j, Y_j)$. Then FC_i *precedes* FC_j, denoted by $FC_i \prec_{fc} FC_j$, iff $X_i \subset X_j$ and $Y_i \supset Y_j$. ■

For a pair of formal concepts FC_i and FC_j such that $FC_i \prec_{fc} FC_j$, we often say that FC_i is more *specific* than FC_j and FC_j is more *general* than FC_i.

The partially ordered set $(\mathcal{FC}, \prec_{fc})$ forms a *lattice*, called a *formal concept lattice*. For the formal context in Figure 1, we have the formal concept lattice shown in Figure 2. In the figure, xyz is an abbreviation of a set $\{x, y, z\}$. The most general concept is put at the top and the most specific one at the bottom. For any pair of FC_i and FC_j, if FC_i immediately precedes FC_j, they are connected by an edge.

3.3 Exact correspondence between formal concepts and closed itemsets

In the field of *Data Mining* (Han & Kamber, 2006), many researchers have investigated *Frequent Itemset Mining* (Agrawal & Srikant, 1994; Han et al., 2007; Pasquier et al., 1999). Particularly, the notion of *closed itemsets* is well-known as a useful lossless condensed representation of itemsets (Pasquier et al., 1999).

Let $\mathcal{I}$ be a set of *items*. A *transaction* T is a subset of $\mathcal{I}$ and is assigned a unique identifier, denoted by $id(T)$. A *transaction database* $\mathcal{TD}$ is given as a (multiple) set of transactions. Let $\mathcal{ID}$ be the set of identifiers of transactions in $\mathcal{TD}$, that is, $\mathcal{ID} = \{id(T) \mid T \in \mathcal{TD}\}$. We can obtain a binary relation $R \subseteq \mathcal{ID} \times \mathcal{I}$ which is defined as $R = \{(id(T), x) \mid T \in \mathcal{TD} \land x \in T\}$. Regarding each transaction in $\mathcal{TD}$ as an object and each item in $\mathcal{I}$ as a feature, we can represent the transaction database as a formal context $< \mathcal{ID}, \mathcal{I}, R >$.

A set of items in $\mathcal{I}$, I, is called an itemset. For a transaction database $\mathcal{TD}$, the *support* (or *frequency*) of I, denoted by $sup(I)$, is defined as $sup(I) = |\{T \in \mathcal{TD} \mid I \subseteq T\}|$. An itemset I is said to be *closed* if there exists no itemset I' such that $I \subset I'$ and $sup(I) = sup(I')$. Since the support of an itemset is defined as the number of transactions containing the itemset, a closed itemset I exactly corresponds to the intent of a formal concept. For the closed itemset I,

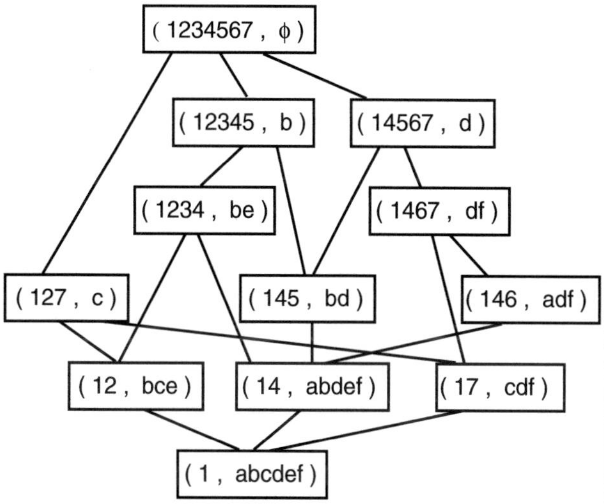

Object ID	Features
1	a b c d e f
2	b c e
3	b e
4	a b d e f
5	b d
6	a d f
7	c d f

Fig. 2. Formal Concept Lattice

furthermore, the set of identifiers of the transactions containing I, denoted by ID_I, is uniquely identified. Particularly, ID_I is closed in the sense that any other transaction never contains I, that is, ID_I also corresponds to the extent of an FC. Therefore, we can always observe the exact correspondence between a closed itemset I and the formal concept (ID_I, I).
From the correspondence, any efficient closed itemset miner would be helpful for finding FCs. For example, `AFOPT` (Liu et al., 2003), `DCI-Closed` (Lucchese et al., 2004) and `LCM` (Uno et al., 2004) are well-known as such efficient systems (algorithms).

4. Conceptual document clusters based on formal concepts

Let $\mathcal{D}$ be a set of *documents* and $\mathcal{T}$ a set of *feature terms*. We assume that each *document* in $\mathcal{D}$ is represented as a set of feature terms in $\mathcal{T}$ appearing in the document. Then, we have a binary relation $R \subseteq \mathcal{D} \times \mathcal{T}$, where a tuple $(d,t) \in R$ means that the term t appears in the document d. Under the assumption, the triple $\mathcal{C} =< \mathcal{D}, \mathcal{T}, R >$ is regarded as a formal context, where for each formal concept (D, T) under $\mathcal{C}$, D is considered as a *document cluster*. It should be emphasized here that we can clearly explain why the documents in D are grouped together. Each document in D shares the set of feature terms T and any other document never contains T. In this sense, D can be viewed as a conceptual document cluster which is definable by the feature terms shared with the documents. Thus, by restricting our document clusters to extents of formal concepts under $\mathcal{C}$, we can explicitly provide conceptual meanings based on their intents.

5. Top-N δ-valid formal concept problem

For a given formal context $\mathcal{C} =< \mathcal{O}, \mathcal{F}, R >$, the number of FCs under $\mathcal{C}$ often becomes large. It is actually impossible for users to check and analyze all of them. Therefore, selectively extracting FCs with a certain degree of quality would be a practical and reasonable approach. Needless to say, quality of an FC is affected by both its extent and intent. For example, a concept with a larger intent might have convincing evidence (similarity) for the grouping of objects (extent). Its extent, however, tends to be smaller. We often consider that concepts with too small extents would not be so meaningful because they might be too specific or exceptional. Conversely, although a concept with a smaller intent will have a larger extent, evidence for the grouping seems to be weak. In other words, the extent would consist of less similar objects. Thus, in order to obtain meaningful *FC*s, it is required to control their quality from the viewpoint of extents and intents. For such a requirement, we formalize our *FC*s to be found as follows:

Constraint on Intents: In order for *FC*s to retain a certain degree of similarity, a constraint on intents is imposed. Concretely speaking, a threshold for evaluation value of intents, δ, is provided. For an *FC*, if its intent value is greater than or equal to δ, then the *FC* is considered to have sufficient quality of intent. Such an *FC* is said to be *δ-valid*.

Preference in Extents: *FC*s with higher evaluation values of extents are preferred among the δ-valid *FC*s. Particularly, given an integer N, the *FC*s with Top-N extent values are extracted.

In order to evaluate extents and intents of *FC*s, we assume that each object $x \in \mathcal{O}$ and feature $y \in \mathcal{F}$ are assigned their positive real-valued weights, referred to as $w_{\mathcal{O}}(x)$ and $w_{\mathcal{F}}(y)$. Then, evaluation functions for extents and intents, $eval_E$ and $eval_I$, are defined with $w_{\mathcal{O}}$ and $w_{\mathcal{F}}$, respectively.
Although we can define various evaluation functions, *increasing monotone* functions are strongly preferred from the computational point of view, where a function f is said to be increasing monotone (under set-inclusion) iff $S \subseteq S'$ implies $f(S) \leq f(S')$ for any pair of sets, S and S'. In what follows, we assume our evaluation functions to be increasing monotone. The reason why such a function is preferable will become clear in the next section.
We can now formalize our problem of finding *Top-N δ-valid formal concepts* as follows:

Definition 2. (Top-N δ-Valid Formal Concept Problem)
Let $\mathcal{C} = < \mathcal{O}, \mathcal{F}, R >$ be a formal context, δ a threshold for admissible evaluation value of intent and N an integer for Top-N. The problem of finding *Top-N δ-valid formal concepts for* $\mathcal{C}$ is to extract the set of formal concepts $\{(X, Y)\}$ such that $eval_I(Y) \geq \delta$ (as constraint) and $eval_E(X)$ is in the top N among such ones (as preference). ■

From the viewpoint of problem specification, our Top-N δ-valid *FC* problem is closely related to *Top-N Frequent Closed Itemset Mining* (Wang et al., 2005) and *Constraint-Based Concept Mining* (Besson et al., 2005).
Given a pair of parameters, N and $minlen$, Top-N Frequent Closed Itemset Mining (Wang et al., 2005) is to find closed itemsets of length at least $minlen$ whose frequencies (supports) are in the top N. Since length (size) of itemsets is a measure which evaluates itemsets, the parameter $minlen$ controls the quality of closed itemsets (that is, intents) to be extracted, as is similar to our problem. Furthermore, frequencies of closed itemsets are equivalent to sizes of their corresponding extents. In case we simply evaluate each intent and extent by their sizes, therefore, our Top-N *FC* problem is identical with the Top-N frequent closed itemset mining. In the framework, however, length and frequency are only measures by which we can evaluate itemsets. On the other hand, in our framework, we can consider various evaluation measures as well as length and frequency. In this sense, our problem can be regarded as a generalization of Top-N closed itemset mining.
Given a pair of parameters, $minsup$ and $minlen$, Constraint-Based Concept Mining (Besson et al., 2005) is a task of finding all closed itemsets I such that $sup(I) \geq minsup$ and $|I| \geq minlen$. That is, this mining task is to compute all frequent closed itemsets with enough length.

Since the frequency of closed itemsets is equivalent to the size of extents, *minsup implicitly* gives some integer N such that the N-th frequency of closed itemsets with enough length is equal to *minsup*. Therefore, if extents are evaluated by their sizes, providing *minsup* in essence corresponds to providing some N for Top-N in our problem. However, the authors consider that providing N is more simple and intuitive than providing *minsup*.

6. Finding top-N δ-valid formal concepts with clique search

In this section, we precisely discuss our algorithm for finding Top-N δ-valid FCs.
Top-N δ-valid FCs can be extracted by finding certain *cliques* in an weighted undirected graph. Before going into details, we present a basic strategy of our search algorithm.

6.1 Basic search strategy

Let $\mathcal{C} =< \mathcal{O}, \mathcal{F}, R >$ be a formal context. For each FC under $\mathcal{C}$, there always exists a set of objects $X \subseteq \mathcal{O}$ such that $E(X) = \psi(\varphi(X))$ and $\varphi(X)$ correspond to the extent and the intent of the FC, respectively. Therefore, by applying the mappings φ and ψ to each set of objects $X \subseteq \mathcal{O}$, we can obtain all of the FCs under $\mathcal{C}$.
Let us consider a *total ordering* on $\mathcal{O} = \{x_1, \ldots, x_{|\mathcal{O}|}\}$, $\prec$, simply defined as $x_i \prec x_j$ iff $i < j$. It is assumed that for each subset $X \subseteq \mathcal{O}$, the elements in X is ordered based on $\prec$.
For a subset of $\mathcal{O}$, $X_i = \{x_{i_1}, \ldots, x_{i_n}\}$, the first element x_{i_1} is denoted by $head(X_i)$ and the last one, x_{i_n}, by $tail(X_i)$. Furthermore, the set of first k elements, $\{x_{i_1}, \ldots, x_{i_k}\}$, is called the *k-prefix* of X_i and is referred to as $prefix(X_i, k)$, where $0 \leq k \leq n$ and $prefix(X_i, 0)$ is defined as ϕ.
We introduce here a *partial ordering* on $2^{\mathcal{O}}$, $\prec_s$, as follows.

Definition 3. (Partial Ordering on $2^{\mathcal{O}}$)
Let X_i and X_j be subsets of $\mathcal{O}$ such that $X_i \neq X_j$. Then X_i *precedes* X_j or X_j *succeeds* X_i, denoted by $X_i \prec_s X_j$, iff X_i is a prefix of X_j, that is, $X_i = prefix(X_j, |X_i|)$. If X_j is a successor of X_i, then X_j is called a *descendant* of X_i. Particularly, X_j is called a *child* of X_i if X_j is an immediate successor of X_i. ■

It can be easily observed that the partially ordered set $(2^{\mathcal{O}}, \prec_s)$ forms a *tree* with the root node ϕ which is well-known as a *set enumeration tree* (Rymon, 1992). Figure 3 shows an example of a set enumeration tree for $\mathcal{O} = \{\mathtt{a}, \mathtt{b}, \mathtt{c}, \mathtt{d}, \mathtt{e}\}$.
For each (non-leaf) subset $X \subseteq \mathcal{O}$ in the tree, its child is simply obtained as $X \cup \{x\}$, where $tail(X) \prec x$. Based on the fact, therefore, any subset of $\mathcal{O}$ can be generated systematically *without any duplications*, starting with the empty set.
In the tree, a simple theoretical property can be observed.

Observation 2.
Let X_i and X_j be subsets of $\mathcal{O}$ such that $X_i \prec_s X_j$. Then, $eval_I(\varphi(X_i)) \geq eval_I(\varphi(X_j))$.

Proof:
It is immediately proved from Observation 1. From $X_i \subseteq X_j$, $\varphi(X_i) \supseteq \varphi(X_j)$ holds. Since $eval_I$ is assumed to be increasing monotone, we have $eval_I(\varphi(X_i)) \geq eval_I(\varphi(X_j))$. ■

As a direct consequence, a simple pruning rule will be available in our search.

Pruning 1.
For a set of objects $X \subseteq \mathcal{O}$, if $eval_I(\varphi(X)) < \delta$ holds, then there is no need to examine any descendant of X. ■

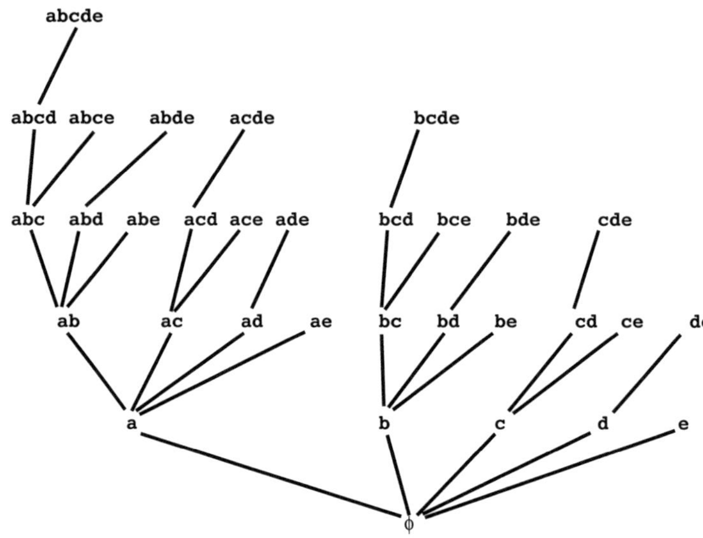

Fig. 3. Set Enumeration Tree

Proof:
It can be easily verified. Let X' be a descendant of X. Since $X \subset X'$, $eval_I(\varphi(X)) \geq eval_I(\varphi(X'))$ holds. From the assumption in the rule, we have $eval_I(\varphi(X')) \leq eval_I(\varphi(X)) < \delta$. This means that no δ-valid FC can be obtained from X'. Thus, we can safely prune any descendant of X. ■

From the above discussion, our search for finding Top-N δ-valid FCs can be performed in *depth-first manner* with the simple pruning. During our search, we maintain a list which stores Top-N δ-valid FCs already found. That is, the list keeps *tentative* Top-N FCs. For a set of objects $X \subseteq \mathcal{O}$, we check whether $eval_I(\varphi(X)) \geq \delta$ holds or not. If it holds, then $(E(X), \varphi(X))$ is a δ-valid FC and the tentative Top-N list is adequately updated for the FC. Then a child of X is generated and the same procedure is recursively performed for the child. If $eval_I(\varphi(X)) < \delta$, we can immediately backtrack without examining any descendant of X. Starting with the initial X of the empty set, the procedure is iterated in depth-first manner until no X remains to be examined. A pseudo-code of our basic algorithm is presented in Figure 4.

6.2 Finding formal concepts by clique search

Although a pruning rule is available, the simple basic algorithm just discussed above is required further improvement for efficient computation. In order to improve it, we try to find our Top-N FCs by *clique search* with *depth-first branch-and-bound* strategy (Balas & Yu, 1986).

6.2.1 Graph construction

Given a formal context $\mathcal{C} =< \mathcal{O}, \mathcal{F}, R >$ and a threshold δ, an weighted undirected graph $G = (\mathcal{O}, E, w_{\mathcal{O}})$, is first constructed, where the set of edges, E, is defined as

$$E = \{(x_i, x_j) \mid x_i, x_j \in \mathcal{O}(i \neq j) \wedge eval_I(\mathcal{F}(x_i) \cap \mathcal{F}(x_j)) \geq \delta\}.$$

That is, if a pair of objects share a set of features whose evaluation value is greater than or equal to δ, then they are connected by an edge.

Input :
$< \mathcal{O}, \mathcal{F}, R >$: a formal context where
$\mathcal{O}$: a set of objtects, $\mathcal{F}$: a set of features and R : a binary relation on $\mathcal{O}$ and $\mathcal{F}$
δ : a threshold for intent value
N : an integer for Top-N
$eval_E$: an evaluation function for extents defined with an weight function $w_{\mathcal{O}}$ for $\mathcal{O}$
$eval_I$: an evaluation function for intents defined with an weight function $w_{\mathcal{F}}$ for $\mathcal{F}$
Output :
$\mathcal{FC}$: the set of δ-valid formal concepts whose extent values are in the top N

```
procedure main() :
    FC ← φ ;  /* Grobal variable */
    min = 0.0 ;  /* Grobal variable */
    for each x ∈ O in predefined order do
        begin
            if eval_I(F(x)) ≥ δ then   /* Pruning 1 */
                TopNFCFindBasic({x}, F(x)) ;
            endif
        end
    return FC ;
```

```
procedure TopNFCFindBasic(X, I) :
    TopNListUpdata((E(X),I)) ;
    for each x ∈ O such that tail(X) ≺ x in predefined order do
        begin
            NewX ← X ∪ {x} ;
            NewI ← I ∩ F(x) ;
                if eval_I(NewI) ≥ δ then /* Pruning 1 */
                    TopNFCFindBasic(NewX, NewI) ;
                endif
        end
```

```
procedure TopNListUpdate(FC) :
    FC ← FC ∪ {FC} ;
    if FC tentatively contains N-th ones then
        min ← N-th extent value ;
        Remove M-th ones from FC such that N < M ;
    endif
```

Fig. 4. Basic Algorithm for Finding Top-N δ-Valid Formal Concepts

6.2.2 Clique enumeration tree

Since each clique Q in G is a subset of $\mathcal{O}$, $(E(Q), \varphi(Q))$ always becomes a formal concept. It should be noted here that from the definition of G, for each δ-valid FC, there always exists a clique Q in G such that $E(Q)$ and $\varphi(Q)$ are the extent and intent of the FC, respectively. Therefore, subsets to be examined in our basic algorithm can be restricted to only cliques in G. Based on δ, thus, we can *statically* excludes many useless subsets from which we can never obtain δ-valid FCs.

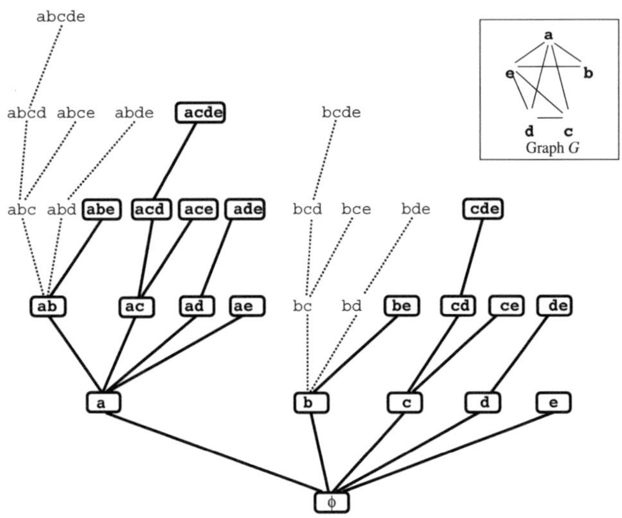

Fig. 5. Clique Enumeration Tree for Graph G

Since any subset of a clique is also a clique, the ordering $\prec_s$ is still valid for cliques and the cliques in G also form a tree, called a *clique enumeration tree*. An example of a clique enumeration tree for a graph G is shown in Figure 5, where any clique in G is boxed.

Needless to say, Pruning 1 is still available in the clique enumeration tree. That is, the constraint based on δ can work not only statically in the graph construction, but also *dynamically* in the search process.

A child of a clique Q is generated by adding a certain vertex (object) to Q. Such an object to be added is precisely defined with a notion of *extensible candidates*

Definition 4. (Extensible Candidates for Clique)
Let $G = (V, E, w)$ be a graph and Q a clique in G. A vertex $v \in V$ adjacent to any vertex in Q is called an *extensible candidate* for Q. The set of extensible candidates is denoted by $cand(Q)$, that is,

$$cand(Q) = \{v \in V \mid \forall u \in Q \ \ (v, u) \in E\} = \bigcap_{v \in Q} N_G(v).$$ ■

Since it is obvious from the definition that for any extensible candidate $v \in cand(Q)$, $Q \cup \{v\}$ always becomes a clique, we can easily generate a child of Q by adding $v \in cand(Q)$ such that $tail(Q) \prec v$. Thus, we can explore a clique enumeration tree in depth-first manner.

6.3 Pruning redundant cliques

As has just been discussed, Pruning 1 excludes useless cliques from which no δ-valid FCs can be obtained. In addition to such useless ones, our clique enumeration tree in general contains redundant cliques whose corresponding FCs are identical. Therefore, it would be desirable for efficient computation to prune such redundant cliques as well. We can observe the following three simple properties of FCs which will be useful for realizing it.

Observation 3.
Let (X, Y) be a formal concept. Then, there always exists a clique Q in G such that $E(Q) = X$ and $head(Q) = head(X)$. ■

Proof:
It is trivial. Since X is a clique in G, X itself can be such a clique Q. Then, it is obvious that $E(Q) = E(X) = X$ and $head(Q) = head(X)$. ■

Observation 4.
Let Q be a clique in G. For any element $\alpha \in E(Q)\backslash Q$, $E(Q \cup \{\alpha\}) = E(Q)$ holds. That is, their corresponding FCs are identical. ■

Proof:
It can be easily proved from Observation 1. Let α be an element such that $\alpha \in E(Q)\backslash Q$. From a property of the mapping φ, $\varphi(Q \cup \{\alpha\}) = \varphi(Q) \cap \varphi(\{\alpha\})$. Moreover, since $\alpha \in E(Q)$, $\varphi(Q) \subseteq \varphi(\{\alpha\})$. Therefore, we have $\varphi(Q \cup \{\alpha\}) = \varphi(Q)$ and $\psi(\varphi(Q \cup \{\alpha\})) = \psi(\varphi(Q))$. ■

Observation 5.
Let Q be a clique in G and $Q \cup \{\alpha\}$ a child of Q. For any element $\beta \in E(Q \cup \{\alpha\})\backslash E(Q)$ such that $\beta \prec \alpha$, there exists Q' such that $E(Q') = E(Q \cup \{\alpha\})$ and Q' is examined prior to $Q \cup \{\alpha\}$ in our depth-first search. ■

Proof:
Let β be an element such that $\beta \in E(Q \cup \{\alpha\})\backslash E(Q)$ and $\beta \prec \alpha$. Since $\beta \notin E(Q)$ and $Q \subseteq E(Q)$, we have $\beta \notin Q$ and then $\beta \notin Q \cup \{\alpha\}$. Therefore, $\beta \in E(Q \cup \{\alpha\})\backslash Q \cup \{\alpha\}$ holds. From Observation 4, $E(Q \cup \{\alpha\} \cup \{\beta\}) = E(Q \cup \{\alpha\})$ holds. It should be noted here that since $\beta \prec \alpha$, $Q \cup \{\alpha\} \cup \{\beta\}$ is processed prior to $Q \cup \{\alpha\}$ in our depth-first search. Thus, the observation can be verified. ■

Each of the above observations provides us a pruning rule to exclude redundant cliques.

Pruning 2.
Let Q be a clique in G. If $head(Q) \neq head(E(Q))$ holds, then Q and its descendants do not have to be examined. ■

Pruning 3.
Let Q be a clique in G. For any element $\alpha \in E(Q)\backslash Q$ such that $tail(Q) \prec \alpha$, $Q \cup \{\alpha\}$ and its descendants do not have to be examined. ■

Pruning 4.
Let Q be a clique in G and $Q \cup \{\alpha\}$ a child of Q. If there exists an element $\beta \in E(Q \cup \{\alpha\})\backslash E(Q)$ such that $\beta \prec \alpha$, then $Q \cup \{\alpha\}$ and its descendants do not have to be examined. ■

A remarkable point we should emphasize is that the pruning rules are safe. In other words, for each formal concept (X, Y), there always exists a clique Q such that $E(Q) = X$ and Q is never pruned with the pruning rules.

Theorem 1.
Pruning 2, 3 and 4 are safe. ■

Proof:
For a formal concept $FC = (X, Y)$, let α_0 be the head element of X, that is, $\alpha_0 = head(X)$. Moreover, assume $P = X \backslash E(\{\alpha_0\}) = \{\alpha_1, \ldots, \alpha_k\}$.

Since $X = E(\{\alpha_0\}) \cup P$,

$$\begin{aligned}\varphi(X) &= \varphi(E(\{\alpha_0\}) \cup P)\\ &= \varphi(E(\{\alpha_0\})) \cap \varphi(P)\\ &= \varphi(\{\alpha_0\}) \cap \varphi(P)\\ &= \varphi(\{\alpha_0\} \cup P).\end{aligned}$$

Therefore, we immediately have

$$X = E(X) = \psi(\varphi(X)) = \psi(\varphi(\{\alpha_0\} \cup P)) = E(\{\alpha_0\} \cup P).$$

For each i $(1 \le i \le k)$, we consider

$$\begin{aligned}D_i &= E(\{\alpha_0\} \cup \{\alpha_1\} \cup \cdots \cup \{\alpha_i\}) \setminus \{\alpha_0\} \cup \{\alpha_1\} \cup \cdots \cup \{\alpha_i\}\\ &= E(\{\alpha_0\} \cup prefix(P,i)) \setminus \{\alpha_0\} \cup prefix(P,i).\end{aligned}$$

In case of $i = 0$, D_0 is defined as $D_0 = E(\{\alpha_0\}) \setminus \{\alpha_0\}$. Observation 4 implies that, for each i $(1 \le i \le k)$, if $\alpha_i \in D_{i-1}$, then

$$E(\{\alpha_0\} \cup prefix(P,i)) = E(\{\alpha_0\} \cup prefix(P,i-1)).$$

On the other hand, if $\alpha_i \notin D_{i-1}$,

$$E(\{\alpha_0\} \cup prefix(P,i)) \supset E(\{\alpha_0\} \cup prefix(P,i-1)).$$

Here, let us consider a subset of P, R, defined as

$$R = \{\alpha_i \in P \mid \alpha_i \notin D_{i-1}\}.$$

Assuming $R = \{\alpha'_1, \ldots, \alpha'_\ell\}$ and $\alpha'_0 = \alpha_0$, P can be represented as a union of $\ell + 1$ (ordered) subsets, $P = P_0 \cup \cdots \cup P_\ell$, where P_i is defined as

$$P_i = \begin{cases} \{\alpha \in P \mid \alpha'_i \preceq \alpha \prec \alpha'_{i+1}\} & \text{if } 0 \le i < \ell,\\ \{\alpha \in P \mid \alpha'_i \preceq \alpha\} & \text{if } i = \ell.\end{cases}$$

That is, each $\alpha \in P$ belongs to a certain P_i. If $\alpha \in P$ is contained in P_i, then the index i is referred to as $f(\alpha)$.

We first verify that for each $\alpha_i \in P$ $(1 \le i \le k)$,

$$E(\{\alpha_0\} \cup prefix(P,i)) = E(\{\alpha'_0\} \cup prefix(R, f(\alpha_i))). \tag{1}$$

The statement can be proved with mathematical induction on the index i of α_i.

In case of $i = 1$, α_1 belongs to P_0 or P_1, that is, $f(\alpha_1)$ is 0 or 1, respectively. For the former, α_1 is in $D_0 = E(\{\alpha_0\}) \setminus \{\alpha_0\}$. Hence, $E(\{\alpha_0\} \cup \{\alpha_1\}) = E(\{\alpha_0\} \cup prefix(P,1)) = E(\{\alpha_0\}) = E(\{\alpha_0\} \cup prefix(R,0))$ holds. For the latter, since $prefix(P,1) = prefix(R,1) = \{\alpha_1\}$, the statement is obviously true.

For the induction step, let us assume that for some i, $E(\{\alpha_0\} \cup prefix(P,i)) = E(\{\alpha'_0\} \cup prefix(R, f(\alpha_i)))$ holds. In case of $\alpha_{i+1} \in D_i$, α_{i+1} belongs to $P_{f(\alpha_i)}$, that is, $f(\alpha_{i+1}) =$

$f(\alpha_i)$. In addition, $E(\{\alpha_0\} \cup prefix(P,i) \cup \{\alpha_{i+1}\}) = E(\{\alpha_0\} \cup prefix(P,i))$ holds. From the assumption, therefore, we have

$$\begin{aligned} E(\{\alpha_0\} \cup prefix(P,i) \cup \{\alpha_{i+1}\}) &= E(\{\alpha_0\} \cup prefix(P,i+1)) \\ &= E(\{\alpha'_0\} \cup prefix(R, f(\alpha_i))) \\ &= E(\{\alpha'_0\} \cup prefix(R, f(\alpha_{i+1}))), \end{aligned}$$

showing the statement is true.

On the other hand, in case of $\alpha_{i+1} \notin D_i$, α_{i+1} belongs to $P_{f(\alpha_i)+1}$ and is particularly identical with $\alpha'_{f(\alpha_i)+1}$. Since $f(\alpha_{i+1}) = f(\alpha_i) + 1$, we also have $\alpha_{i+1} = \alpha'_{f(\alpha_{i+1})}$. From the assumption, therefore, it can be verified that the statement is true as follows.

$$\begin{aligned} E(\{\alpha_0\} \cup prefix(P,i) \cup \{\alpha_{i+1}\}) &= E(\{\alpha_0\} \cup prefix(P,i+1)) \\ &= E(\{\alpha'_0\} \cup prefix(R, f(\alpha_i)) \cup \{\alpha_{i+1}\}) \\ &= E(\{\alpha'_0\} \cup prefix(R, f(\alpha_i)) \cup \{\alpha'_{f(\alpha_i)+1}\}) \\ &= E(\{\alpha'_0\} \cup prefix(R, f(\alpha_i)+1)) \\ &= E(\{\alpha'_0\} \cup prefix(R, f(\alpha_{i+1}))). \end{aligned}$$

As the result, we can conclude the statement is true for any $\alpha_i \in P$ $(1 \leq i \leq k)$.

We can now obtain

$$E(\{\alpha_0\} \cup prefix(P,k)) = E(\{\alpha'_0\} \cup prefix(R, f(\alpha_k))).$$

It is noted here that since $prefix(P,k) = P$ and $prefix(R, f(\alpha_k)) = prefix(R,\ell) = R$, $E(\{\alpha_0\} \cup P) = X = E(\{\alpha'_0\} \cup R)$ holds. This implies that examining $\{\alpha'_0\} \cup R$ is sufficient to obtain the extent X. In order to visit $\{\alpha'_0\} \cup R$ in our depth-first search, we have to take into account the ordered sequence of cliques,

$$\{\alpha'_0\} \cup prefix(R,0) \prec_s \{\alpha'_0\} \cup prefix(R,1) \prec_s \cdots \prec_s \{\alpha'_0\} \cup prefix(R,\ell).$$

Therefore, it should be verified that our pruning rules never exclude any $\{\alpha'_0\} \cup prefix(R,i)$ in the sequence.

For any i $(0 \leq i \leq \ell)$, since $\{\alpha'_0\} \cup prefix(R,i) \subseteq E(\{\alpha'_0\} \cup prefix(R,i)) \subseteq X$ and $\alpha'_0 = \alpha_0 = head(X)$, $head(\{\alpha'_0\} \cup prefix(R,i)) = head(E(\{\alpha'_0\} \cup prefix(R,i)))$ always holds. Hence, Pruning 2 can never prevent us from examining $\{\alpha'_0\} \cup prefix(R,i)$.

In order to show Pruning 3 is safe, we have to verify that for any $\alpha'_i \in R$,

$$\alpha'_i \notin E(\{\alpha'_0\} \cup prefix(R,i-1)) \backslash \{\alpha'_0\} \cup prefix(R,i-1).$$

Let r be the original index of α'_i in P, that is, $\alpha'_i = \alpha_r$ $(\in P)$. Since $\alpha'_i \in R$, $\alpha_r \notin D_{r-1} = E(\{\alpha_0\} \cup prefix(P,r-1)) \backslash \{\alpha_0\} \cup prefix(P,r-1)$. It is, particularly, clear that $\alpha_r \notin E(\{\alpha_0\} \cup prefix(P,r-1))$ because $\alpha_r \notin \{\alpha_0\} \cup prefix(P,r-1)$. From the statement (1), it is noted here that $E(\{\alpha_0\} \cup prefix(P,r-1)) = E(\{\alpha'_0\} \cup prefix(R, f(\alpha_{r-1})))$. Moreover, since $\alpha'_i = \alpha_r$, $f(\alpha_{r-1})$ should be $i-1$. Therefore, $E(\{\alpha_0\} \cup prefix(P,r-1)) = E(\{\alpha'_0\} \cup prefix(R,i-1))$ holds. Since $\alpha'_i \notin E(\{\alpha'_0\} \cup prefix(R,i-1))$, it is clear that $\alpha'_i \notin E(\{\alpha'_0\} \cup prefix(R,i-1)) \backslash \{\alpha'_0\} \cup prefix(R,i-1)$. This means that for each i $(1 \leq i \leq \ell)$, $\{\alpha'_0\} \cup prefix(R,i)$ can never be a target of Pruning 3.

Safeness of Pruning 4 can be confirmed by showing the following statement is true for any i $(1 \leq i \leq \ell)$:

$$\forall \beta \in E(\{\alpha'_0\} \cup prefix(R,i)) \backslash E(\{\alpha'_0\} \cup prefix(R,i-1)), \ \ \alpha'_i \preceq \beta.$$

From Observation 1, for any $X' \subseteq X$, $E(X') \subseteq E(X)$ holds. Moreover, since X is the extent of FC, $E(X) = X$. It implies that for any $X' \subseteq X$, $E(X') \subseteq X$. From $E(\{\alpha_0\}) \cup P = X$ and for any i $(0 \leq i < k)$, $P = prefix(P,i) \cup \{\alpha_{i+1}\} \cup \cdots \cup \{\alpha_k\}$, therefore, we have

$$\begin{aligned} D_i &= E(\{\alpha_0\} \cup prefix(P,i)) \setminus \{\alpha_0\} \cup prefix(P,i) \\ &\subseteq E(\{\alpha_0\}) \cup \{\alpha_{i+1}\} \cup \cdots \cup \{\alpha_k\}. \end{aligned}$$

In other words, for any $\beta \in D_i$, $\beta \in E(\{\alpha_0\})$ or $\alpha_i \prec \beta$. It is, therefore, easy to see that for any $\beta \in E(\{\alpha_0\} \cup prefix(P,i)) \setminus \{\alpha_0\} \cup prefix(P,i-1)$, $\beta \in E(\{\alpha_0\})$ or $\alpha_i \preceq \beta$. From $\{\alpha_0\} \cup prefix(P,i-1) \subseteq E(\{\alpha_0\} \cup prefix(P,i-1))$ and $E(\{\alpha_0\}) \subseteq E(\{\alpha_0\} \cup prefix(P,i-1))$, it is immediately derived that for each $\beta \in E(\{\alpha_0\} \cup prefix(P,i)) \setminus E(\{\alpha_0\} \cup prefix(P,i-1))$, $\alpha_i \preceq \beta$ holds.

Following the argument just before, we assume here that for $\alpha'_i \in R$, its original index in P is r. From the statement (1),

$$\begin{aligned} E(\{\alpha_0\} \cup prefix(P,r)) &= E(\{\alpha'_0\} \cup prefix(R, f(\alpha_r))) \\ &= E(\{\alpha'_0\} \cup prefix(R,i)). \end{aligned}$$

Moreover,

$$\begin{aligned} E(\{\alpha_0\} \cup prefix(P,r-1)) &= E(\{\alpha'_0\} \cup prefix(R, f(\alpha_{r-1}))) \\ &= E(\{\alpha'_0\} \cup prefix(R,i-1)) \end{aligned}$$

because $f(\alpha_{r-1}) = i - 1$. That is,

$$\begin{aligned} & E(\{\alpha_0\} \cup prefix(P,r)) \setminus E(\{\alpha_0\} \cup prefix(P,r-1)) \\ & \quad = E(\{\alpha'_0\} \cup prefix(R,i)) \setminus E(\{\alpha'_0\} \cup prefix(R,i-1)). \end{aligned}$$

Therefore, we can see that for any $\beta \in E(\{\alpha'_0\} \cup prefix(R,i)) \setminus E(\{\alpha'_0\} \cup prefix(R,i-1))$, $\alpha'_i \preceq \beta$ holds.

As the result, in our depth-first search with Pruning 2, 3 and 4, we can surely visit the clique $\{\alpha'_0\} \cup R$ from which the extent X can be obtained. Thus, our prunings are safe. ■

With the help of the prunings, thus, we can safely exclude only cliques from which we certainly obtain duplicate FCs. One might be interested here in whether our removal of duplications is complete or not. We can affirmatively answer to the question. That is, the prunings can *completely* eliminate all of the duplicate FCs.

Theorem 2.
Let $\mathcal{Q}$ be the set of cliques examined in our search with Pruning 2, 3 and 4. Then, for any pair of (different) cliques in $\mathcal{Q}$, their corresponding FCs are not identical. ■

Proof:
We prove the theorem by showing their extents are not identical.
Let Q_i and Q_j be a pair of cliques in $\mathcal{Q}$, where $i \neq j$. There are two cases to be considered.

Case 1 : Q_i and Q_j are comparable under the ordering $\prec_s$.

Case 2 : Q_i and Q_j are not comparable under $\prec_s$.

In each case, we try to verify that $E(Q_i) \neq E(Q_j)$ holds.

Case 1 : Without loss of generality, we assume $Q_i \prec_s Q_j$. There exists a child of Q_i, $Q_i \cup \{\alpha\}$, such that $Q_i \prec_s Q_i \cup \{\alpha\} \preceq_s Q_j$. Since Pruning 3 could not exclude $Q_i \cup \{\alpha\}$, $tail(Q_i) \prec \alpha$ and $\alpha \notin E(Q_i)\backslash Q_i$ hold. Then, we have $\alpha \notin E(Q_i)$.
On the other hand, since $Q_i \cup \{\alpha\} \preceq_s Q_j$, $Q_i \cup \{\alpha\} \subseteq E(Q_i \cup \{\alpha\}) \subseteq E(Q_j)$ holds. This means $\alpha \in E(Q_j)$. Therefore, we obtain $E(Q_i) \neq E(Q_j)$.

Case 2 : Since Q_i and Q_j are not comparable under $\prec_s$, they have common ancestors. Let Q be the maximum (youngest) ancestor among them. That is, Q is equivalent to the maximum common prefix of Q_i and Q_j.
In case of $Q = \phi$, from the definition of the ordering $\prec_s$, $head(Q_i)$ is not equivalent to $head(Q_j)$. Moreover, according to Pruning 2, $head(E(Q_i))$ and $head(E(Q_j))$ should be $head(Q_i)$ and $head(Q_j)$, respectively. Hence, $E(Q_i) \neq E(Q_j)$ holds.
In order to prove $E(Q_i) \neq E(Q_j)$ in case of $Q \neq \phi$, we assume without loss of generality that in our depth-first search, Q_i is examined prior to Q_j. Since $Q \prec_s Q_i$, there exists a child of Q, $Q \cup \{\alpha_i\}$, such that $Q \prec_s Q \cup \{\alpha_i\} \preceq_s Q_i$ Similarly, we can consider another child, $Q \cup \{\alpha_j\}$, such that $Q \prec_s Q \cup \{\alpha_j\} \preceq_s Q_j$. Note here that from the assumption, $tail(Q) \prec \alpha_i \prec \alpha_j$. Since Pruning 4 could not exclude $Q \cup \{\alpha_i\}$, for each $\beta \in E(Q \cup \{\alpha_i\})\backslash E(Q)$, $\alpha_i \preceq \beta$ holds. Similarly, for each $\beta \in E(Q \cup \{\alpha_j\})\backslash E(Q)$, $\alpha_j \preceq \beta$ holds. Furthermore, α_i and α_j are not contained in $E(Q)$ according to Pruning 3. Hence, we have $\alpha_i \in E(Q \cup \{\alpha_i\})$ and $\alpha_i \notin E(Q \cup \{\alpha_j\})$. It should be noted here that by Pruning 4, for any clique Q' such that $Q \cup \{\alpha_j\} \preceq_s Q'$, $E(Q')$ can never contain α_i. That is, $\alpha_i \notin E(Q_j)$. On the other hand, since $Q \cup \{\alpha_i\} \preceq_s Q_i$, it is obvious that $\alpha_i \in E(Q_i)$. Therefore, we can conclude $E(Q_i) \neq E(Q_j)$. ∎

The above prunings are basically based on theoretical properties of *FC*s. In addition to them, we can also enjoy a simple branch-and-bound pruning based on a theoretical property of cliques. It is adopted as a basic pruning mechanism in several efficient algorithms for finding the maximum clique in a given graph (Balas & Yu, 1986; Fahle, 2002; Tomita & Kameda, 2007). This kind of pruning is based on the following simple property.

Observation 6.
For cliques Q and Q' in G such that $Q \subseteq Q'$, $Q \cup cand(Q) \supseteq Q' \cup cand(Q')$. ∎

Proof:
It can be easily proved. Since $Q \subseteq Q'$ and each $v \in cand(Q')$ is adjacent to all vertices in Q', v is adjacent to any vertex in Q, that is, $v \in cand(Q)$. For each vertex $v \in Q'\backslash Q$, $Q \subseteq Q'\backslash\{v\}$. Since such a vertex v is adjacent to all vertices in $Q'\backslash\{v\}$, v is always adjacent to any vertex in Q, that is, $v \in cand(Q)$. Thus, we have $Q \cup cand(Q) \supseteq Q' \cup cand(Q')$. ∎

Let us assume that we have a list of tentative Top-N δ-valid *FC*s already found in our search. Based on the above property, we can obtain a simple but quite effective pruning rule.

Pruning 5.
Let min be the minimum extent value in the tentative list. For a clique Q in G, if $eval_E(Q \cup cand(Q)) < min$, then no descendant of Q has to be examined.

Proof:
For a clique Q, let Q' be a descendant of Q, that is, $Q \subset Q'$. Since $E(Q')$ is also a clique containing Q', $Q \subset Q' \subseteq E(Q')$. There always exists a maximal clique in G, Q_{max}, such that $Q \subset Q' \subseteq E(Q') \subseteq Q_{max}$. Note here that the extensible candidates of Q_{max} becomes ϕ because Q_{max} is maximal. From Observation 6, therefore, $Q_{max} \subseteq Q \cup cand(Q)$ holds. Then, we also have $E(Q') \subseteq Q \cup cand(Q)$. It gives an inequality $eval_E(E(Q')) \leq eval_E(Q \cup cand(Q))$. From the assumption in the pruning rule, we know $eval_E(E(Q')) < min$. This means that the FC obtained from Q', $(E(Q'), \varphi(Q'))$, can never be in Top-N because its extent value is less than the tentative N-th value of extents. Therefore, we can safely prune any descendant of Q as useless ones. ■

In the pruning rule, thus, $eval_E(Q \cup cand(Q))$ can work as an *upper bound* of evaluation values we can observe by expanding Q.

Remark: If our evaluation function $eval_E$ is simply defined as size, the upper bound can be represented as

$$eval_E(Q \cup cand(Q)) = |Q \cup cand(Q)| = |Q| + |cand(Q)|.$$

In this case, the upper bound can be further improved.

Let Q_{max} be a maximum clique which is an expansion of Q. From the definition of $cand(Q)$, $Q_{max} \subseteq Q \cup cand(Q)$ holds. Since $cand(Q)$ is in general not a clique, we can consider a maximum clique Q'_{max} in $G(cand(Q))$, the subgraph of G induced by $cand(Q)$, such that $Q_{max} = Q \cup Q'_{max}$. Therefore, if we can compute any upper bound K for the size of a maximum clique in $G(cand(Q))$, we have

$$|Q_{max}| = |Q \cup Q'_{max}| = |Q| + |Q'_{max}| \leq |Q| + K \leq |Q| + |cand(Q)|.$$

That is, $|Q| + K$ can work as a better (tighter) upper bound of evaluation values we can obtain by expanding Q.

Upper bounds for the size of a maximum clique have been widely utilized in efficient branch-and-bound algorithms for finding a maximum clique (Fahle, 2002; Tomita & Kameda, 2007). The literature (Fahle, 2002) has summarized several classes of upper bounds. According to the argument in (Fahle, 2002), the (*vertex*) *chromatic number* χ can be tightest among well-known upper bounds. However, identifying χ is an NP-complete problem. Therefore, *approximations* of χ are computed in algorithms previously proposed. For more detailed discussion, see the literature (Fahle, 2002; Tomita & Kameda, 2007).

6.4 Algorithm for finding top-N δ-valid formal concepts

With the help of the pruning rules, we can design a depth-first branch-and-bound algorithm for finding Top-N δ-valid FCs. The pruning rules are adequately incorporated into the basic algorithm previously presented. A pseudo-code of our algorithm is shown in Figure 6.

7. Experimental results

We present in this section our experimental results. An example of document cluster actually extracted is presented. Since this chapter mainly focuses on the algorithmic viewpoint, we also discuss the empirical computational performance of our algorithm.

Input :
$< \mathcal{O}, \mathcal{F}, R >$: a formal context where
$\mathcal{O}$: a set of objects, $\mathcal{F}$: a set of features, and R : a binary relation on $\mathcal{O}$ and $\mathcal{F}$
δ : a threshold for intent value
N : an integer for Top-N
$eval_E$: an evaluation function for extents defined with an weight function $w_{\mathcal{O}}$ for $\mathcal{O}$
$eval_I$: an evaluation function for intents defined with an weight function $w_{\mathcal{F}}$ for $\mathcal{F}$
Output :
$\mathcal{FC}$: the set of δ-valid formal concepts whose extent values are in the top N

```
procedure main() :
    FC ← φ ;  /* Global variable */
    min = 0.0 ;  /* Global variable */
    G ← (O, E, w_O) where
          E = {(x_i, x_j) | x_i, x_j ∈ O(i ≠ j) ∧ eval_I(F(x_i) ∩ F(x_j)) ≥ δ} ;  /* Global variable */
    for each x ∈ O in predefined order do
        begin
            if eval_I(F(x)) ≥ δ then   /* Pruning 1 */
                TopNFCFind({x}, F(x), φ, N_G(x)) ;
        end
    return FC ;
```

```
procedure TopNFCFind(X, I, Prev, Cand) :
    if head(X) ≠ head(E(X)) or   /* Pruning 2 */
          ∃x ∈ E(X)\Prev such that x ≺ tail(X) then   /* Pruning 4 */
        return ;
    else
        TopNListUpdata((E(X), I)) ;
    endif
    for each x ∈ Cand\E(X) such that tail(X) ≺ x in predefined order do   /* Based on Pruning 3 */
        begin
            NewX ← X ∪ {x} ;
            NewI ← I ∩ F(x) ;
            NewCand ← Cand ∩ N_G(x) ;
            if eval_I(NewI) < δ then /* Pruning 1 */
                continue ;
            endif
            if FC tentatively contains N-th ones and
                    eval_E(NewX ∪ NewCand) < min then   /* Pruning 5 */
                continue ;
            else
                TopNFCFind(NewX, NewI, E(X), NewCand) ;
            endif
        end
```

```
procedure TopNListUpdate(FC) :
    FC ← FC ∪ {FC} ;
    if FC tentatively contains N-th ones then
        min ← N-th extent value ;
        Remove M-th ones from FC such that N < M ;
    endif
```

Fig. 6. Algorithm for Finding Top-N δ-Valid Formal Concepts

Extent :

`http : //news.bbc.co.uk/sport3/worldcup2002/hi/`
`matches_wallchart/south_korea_v_poland/default.stm` [10]
`http : //news.bbc.co.uk/sport3/worldcup2002/hi/`
`matches_wallchart/tunisia_v_japan/default.stm` [265]

⋮

`http : //news.bbc.co.uk/sport3/worldcup2002/hi/`
`team_pages/france/newsid_2097000/2097020.stm` [328]
`http : //news.bbc.co.uk/sport3/worldcup2002/hi/`
`matches_wallchart/england_v_brazil/`
`newsid_2049000/2049924.stm` [562]

Intent:

`Russia`, `Belgium`, `go`, `bbc`, ... etc.

Fig. 7. Example of 500.0-Valid *FC* for *WorldCup*

Our algorithm has been implemented in language *C* and compiled by *gcc* with the optimization of *O3* on *FreeBSD*. For comparison in the viewpoint of computational efficiency, two closed itemset miners, `AFOPT` (Liu et al., 2003) and `LCM` (Uno et al., 2004), have been also compiled. All of the systems have been run on a PC with Xeon 2.4 GHz CPU and 1GB main memory.

7.1 Dataset

For the experimentation, we have prepared a dataset, *WorldCup*, which is a collection of web pages. They have been retrieved with Google SOAP Search API [2] under the key words, "World Cup" and { "Germany", "France", "Brazil", "Korea", "Japan", "ticket" }. The number of documents (pages) is 5,971. Each document corresponds to a snippet retrieved by Google API. After *Stemming Process* with *Porter Stemmer* (Porter, 1980), we have discarded any words whose document frequencies are out of the range of $[50, 700]$. The remaining words are regarded as feature terms and the number of them is 2,824.

Each document has been *linearly* assigned a weight according to its rank. Moreover, each feature term has been given the *IDF* value as its weight. Each extent and intent have been evaluated by the sum of individual weights.

7.2 Extracted document clusters

Figure 7 shows an example cluster extracted from *WorldCup*, under $N = 50$ and $\delta = 500.0$. It is 33-th one. In the figure, each URL is accompanied with its rank on the right. A point worthy to remark is that the cluster consists of web pages with their ranks within a wide range. Since we usually browse web pages only with relatively higher ranks, lower-ranked pages are almost discarded in many cases, regardless of their contents. However, if such a lowly ranked page is concerned with some feature terms shared with several higher-ranked ones, we can expect that it is probably valuable. Thus, our cluster can make such hidden useful pages visible. A similar effect has been also observed in (Haraguchi & Okubo, 2010; 2006b; Okubo et al., 2005).

[2] It is no longer available.

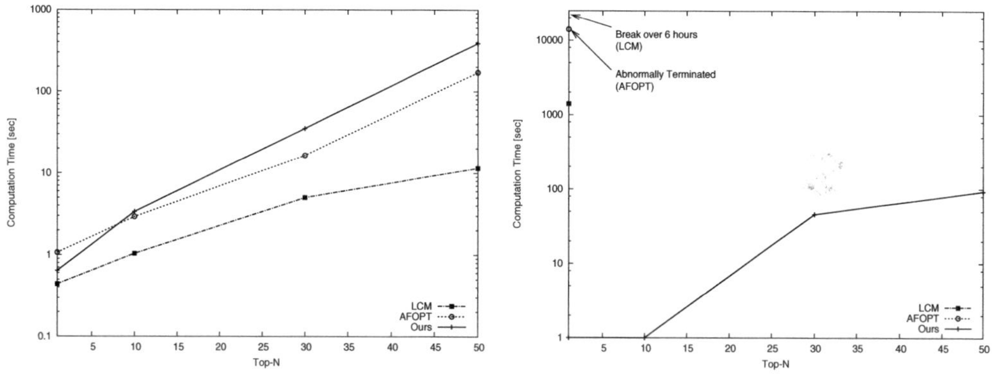

(a) $\delta = 80$ (b) $\delta = 120$

Fig. 8. Computation Time under Various Top-N for *WorldCup*

7.3 Computational performance

As has been discussed, any closed itemset miner would be helpful for finding Top-N δ-valid FCs. We compare computational performance of our algorithm with some of efficient closed itemset miners. Such a system usually enumerates all frequent closed itemsets under a given minimum support threshold ($minsup$). Therefore, we can naively obtain Top-N FCs by first enumerating frequent closed itemsets including Top-N FCs and then choosing the targets from them. Since the former task is the dominant part of the whole process, we particularly report on computation times for the task.

It is noted here that weights of objects (transactions) and features (items) are out of considerations in these miners. Therefore, each object and feature are assigned uniform weights, 1.0. Then each extent and intent are evaluated by the weight sum, that is, by their sizes.

For the comparison, `LCM` (Uno et al., 2004) and `AFOPT` (Liu et al., 2003) have been selected as very fast frequent closed itemset miners. Their implementations are available at *Frequent Itemset Mining Implementations Repository* [3]. In order to find Top-N δ-valid FCs by the systems, we have to provide some $minsup$ under which all of the Top-N FCs can be enumerated as frequent ones. However, we have no idea about an adequate $minsup$ in advance. If a given $minsup$ is too high, some δ-valid FCs will be lost because a higher $minsup$ forces us to extract only smaller closed itemsets equivalent to intents with lower evaluation values. Conversely, if a $minsup$ is too low, we will obtain a large number of closed itemsets, even though we can find all of the targets from them. The most adequate value of $minsup$ is given as the extent size of the N-th δ-valid FCs. Under the optimal $minsup$, the number of closed itemsets to be enumerated can be minimized. In our experimentations, the closed itemset miners are executed under the optimal $minsup$ in each problem setting. It should be emphasized here that it is certainly advantageous to the miners.

For the dataset *WorldCup*, we try to find Top-N δ-valid FCs under $\delta = 80$ and $\delta = 120$. For each δ setting, we observe computation times changing the parameter N. After the execution of our system for each problem setting, `LCM` and `AFOPT` have been given the N-th extent size as the optimal $minsup$. The results are shown in Figure 8.

From the figure, we guess that in case of lower δ, the closed itemset miners can quickly enumerate candidates including the targets. `LCM` is especially a system worthy to remark.

[3] `http://fimi.cs.helsinki.fi/`

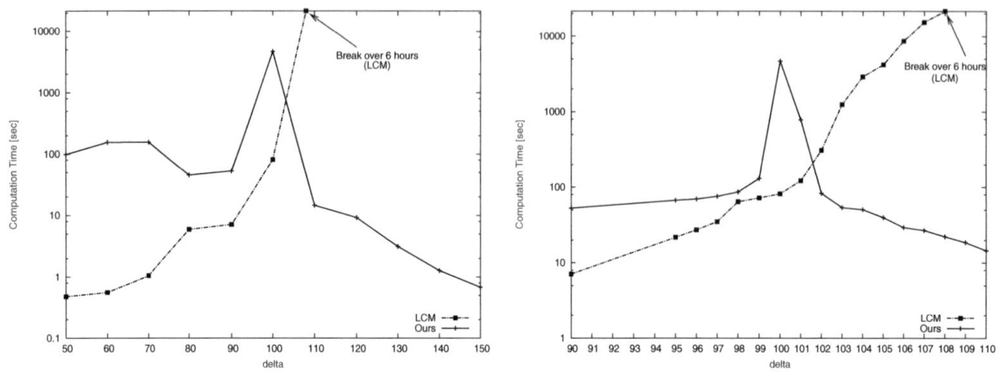

(a) (b) Around $\delta = 100$

Fig. 9. Computation Time under Various δ for *WorldCup* ($N = 30$)

As the result, they will find final targets faster than our system does. However, the authors emphasize here that although they have been ideally given the best *minsup* for each problem, we never know such best values of *minsup* in actual situations.

On the other hand, in case of higher δ, our system outperforms the other systems. These miners have failed to enumerate the closed itemsets within 6 hours. As δ becomes higher, the miners are given a lower *minsup*. It is well known that in such a *minsup*-based system, a lower *minsup* brings just a small reduction of the search space. In other words, under such a lower *minsup*, the number of frequent (closed) itemsets becomes quite huge. The figure seems to reflect this fact.

In order to analyze such a performance behavior more precisely, we observe computation times by `LCM` and our system changing the parameter δ under $N = 30$. The results are shown in Figure 9 (a). From the figure, as we have guessed just above, in lower range of δ, `LCM` can enumerate the closed itemsets including Top-N FCs much faster than our system. On the other hand, in higher range of δ, our system outperforms `LCM`. In particular, since the performance curves cross in a range around $\delta = 100$, detailed curves around the range are shown in Figure 9 (b).

As is shown in Figure 9 (b), the performance curves cross between $\delta = 101$ and $\delta = 102$. Roughly speaking, the computational performance of `LCM` is primary affected the number of frequent closed itemsets, and that of our system the number of FCs we examined in our search. Therefore, we also observe these numbers in order to precisely compare the performance in more detail.

The results are presented in Figure 10 (a) and the detailed curves around $\delta = 100$ are also shown in Figure 10 (b). The curves cross between $\delta = 100$ and $\delta = 101$. In a strict sense, this observation is slightly different from the case of computation time. This observation stems from the difference between the processing cost for each closed itemset and that for each FC. The latter cost (that is, ours) is slightly higher than the former. Since `LCM` can enumerate a more number of frequent closed itemsets, we have had such slight different observations. Therefore, the authors consider that they are consistent.

We observe an exponential growth in the number of closed itemsets `LCM` has actually enumerated, as is shown in Figure 10. The fact can be clearly explained as follows. The parameter δ corresponds to some threshold for the minimum size of itemsets we can accept. Furthermore, frequencies (supports) of itemsets are monotonically decreasing, as itemsets

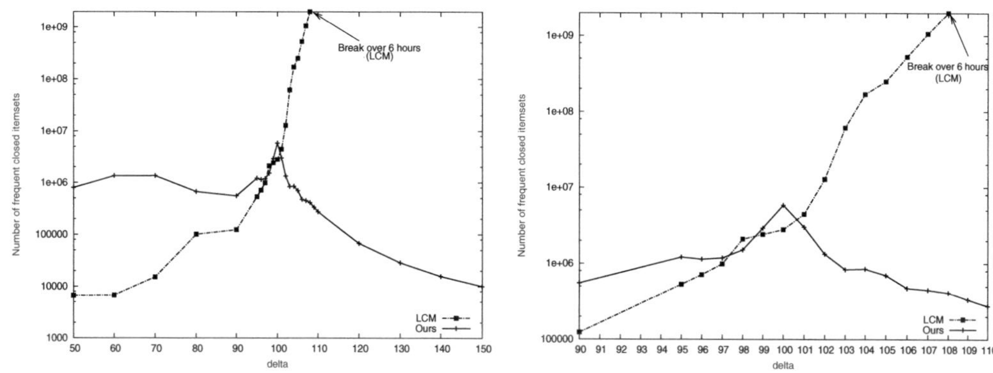

(a) (b) Around $\delta = 100$

Fig. 10. Number of frequent closed itemsets and examined *FC*s for *WorldCup* ($N = 30$)

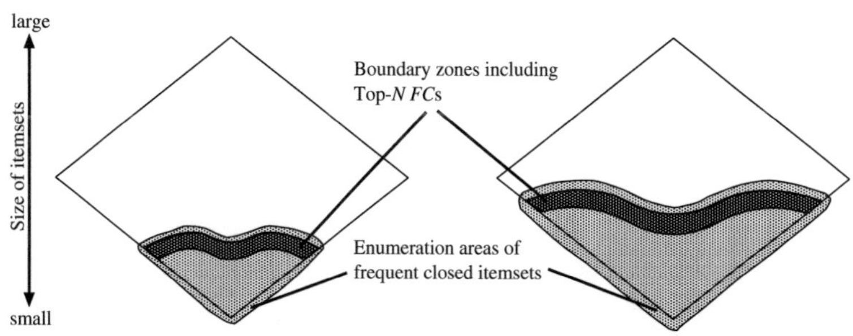

(a) lower δ (b) higher δ

Fig. 11. Boundary Zones including Top-N δ-valid *FC*s and enumeration areas of frequent closed itemsets in itemset-lattices

become larger. Our task of finding Top-N *FC*s is equivalent to extract closed itemsets with enough sizes and Top-N frequencies. Intuitively speaking, therefore, our targets of Top-N δ-valid *FC*s can be found in some boundary zone determined by δ, as is illustrated in Figure 11. If frequent closed itemset miners like `LCM` is used for finding Top-N *FC*s, they have to enumerate the closed itemsets in the lower part of the itemset lattice including the boundary zone. In case of lower δ, since such a boundary zone lies lower in the lattice, the number of closed itemsets will not be so large (Figure 11 (a)). Therefore, they can enumerate all of them very quickly as we have observed above. On the other hand, as δ gets higher, a boundary zone in the lattice rises and the number of closed itemsets to be enumerated will drastically increase (Figure 11 (b)).

From these figures, in higher range of δ, any algorithms for finding frequent closed itemsets are no longer practical for our Top-N δ-valid *FC* problem, even though they are quite helpful in lower range of δ. The authors, however, expectantly assert that in order to find *FC*s which are actually interesting for us, we need to provide a relatively higher value for δ. Under a lower δ, we will obtain *FC*s with larger extents (clusters). Such large clusters seem to be ordinary and not so interesting for us. The authors expect that clusters which are not too large would provide us valuable information in practical sense. In order to find such interesting clusters, we are required to give a relatively higher value of δ. We can, therefore, consider our algorithm to be suitable and effective for this purpose.

8. Concluding remarks

In this chapter, we discussed a method for conceptual clustering of documents. Since our document clusters are extracted as extents of formal concepts, each document cluster can be provided a clear conceptual meaning in terms of feature terms. Our task was formalized as the Top-N δ-valid FC problem. We designed an efficient depth-first branch-and-bound algorithm which is an improved version of our previous algorithm with some new pruning rules. The safeness and completeness of the prunings were verified with theoretical proofs. Our experimental results showed that our document clusters can be extracted with reasonable computation time. Furthermore, we verified that our algorithm outperforms several efficient closed itemset miners in certain problem settings.

Document clusters we can actually extract are much affected by terms we provide as features. In case of web pages, it might depend on the result of converting HTML sources into texts. We need to adequately remove useless terms such as advertisements. Those points should be further investigated as important future work.

Quality of our clusters will be also related to how we assign a weight to each feature term and document. We need to analyze relationship between weight assignment and quality of clusters in more details.

It is important to investigate the scalability of our algorithm. By conducting further experimentations, we need to observe its computational performance for datasets with the order of hundreds thousands.

Needless to say, our method is not only for datasets of documents (web pages). We can apply the method to any dataset in which each object to be clustered can be represented as a set of features, like *relational data*. Applying the method to other practical domain will be interesting work.

9. References

Agrawal, R. & Srikant, R. (1994). Fast Algorithms for Mining Association Rules, *Proceedings of the 20th International Conference on Very Large Databases - VLDB'94*, pp.487 – 499, ISBN 1-55860-153-8, Santiago de Chile, September 1994, Morgan Kaufmann Publishers, CA.

Balas, E. & Yu, C. S. (1986). Finding a Maximum Clique in an Arbitrary Graph, *SIAM Journal on Computing*, Vol. 15, No. 4, pp. 1054 – 1068, ISSN 0097-5397.

Besson, J.; Robardet, C. & Boulicaut, J. (2005). Constraint-Based Concept Mining and Its Application to Microarray Data Analysis, *Intelligent Data Analysis*, Vol. 9, No. 1, pp. 59 – 82, ISSN 1088-467X.

Fahle, T. (2002). Simple and Fast: Improving a Branch and Bound Algorithm for Maximum Clique, *Proceedings of the 10th European Symposium on Algorithms - ESA'02*, LNCS 2461, pp. 485 – 498, ISBN 3-540-44180-8, Rome, September 2002, Springer, Berlin.

Ganter, B & Wille, R. (1999). *Formal Concept Analysis: Mathematical Foundations*, Springer, ISBN 978-3540627715, Berlin.

Han, J.; Cheng, H.; Xin, D. & Yan, X. (2007). Frequent Pattern Mining - Current Status and Future Directions, *Data Mining and Knowledge Discovery*, Vol. 15, No. 1, pp. 55 – 86, ISSN 1384-5810.

Han, J. & Kamber, M. (2006). *Data Mining - Concepts and Techniques (Second Edition)*, Morgan Kaufmann Publishers, ISBN 1-55860-901-6, CA.

Haraguchi, M. & Okubo, Y. (2010). Pinpoint Clustering of Web Pages and Mining Implicit Crossover Concepts, In: *Web Intelligence and Intelligent Agents*, Usmani, Z. (Ed.), pp. 391 – 410, INTECH, ISBN 978-953-7619-85-5, Rijeka.
(Online version : http://sciyo.com/articles/show/title/pinpoint-clustering-of-web-pages-and-mining-implicit-crossover-concepts)

Haraguchi, M. & Okubo, Y. (2007). An Extended Branch-and-Bound Search Algorithm for Finding Top-*N* Formal Concepts of Documents, In: *New Frontiers in Artificial Intelligence, JSAI 2006 Conference and Workshops, Tokyo, Japan, June 5-9, 2006, Revised Selected Papers* , Washio, T., Satoh, K., Takeda, H. and Inokuchi, A. (Eds.), LNCS 4384, pp. 276 – 288, Springer, ISBN 3-540-69901-5, Berlin.

Haraguchi, M. & Okubo, Y. (2006a). An Extended Branch-and-Bound Search Algorithm for Finding Top-*N* Formal Concepts of Documents, *Proceedings of the 4th Workshop on Learning with Logics and Logics for Learning - LLLL'06*, pp. 41 – 47, Tokyo, June 2006, JSAI, Tokyo.

Haraguchi, M. & Okubo, Y. (2006b). A Method for Pinpoint Clustering of Web Pages with Pseudo-Clique Search, In: *Federation over the Web, International Workshop, Dagstuhl Castle, Germany, May 1 - 6, 2005, Revised Selected Papers*, Jantke, K. P., Lunzer, A., Spyratos, N. and Tanaka, Y. (Eds.), LNAI 3847, pp. 59 – 78, Springer, ISBN 3-540-31018-5, Berlin.

Hotho, A.; Staab, S. & Stumme, G. (2003). Explaining Text Clustering Results Using Semantic Structures, *Proceedings of the 7th European Conference on Principles of Data Mining and Knowledge Discovery - PKDD'03*, LNCS 2838, pp. 217 – 228, ISBN 3-540-20085-1, Cavtat-Dubrovnik, September 2003, Springer, Berlin.

Liu, G.; Lu, H.; Yu, J. X.; Wei, W. & Xiao, X. (2003). AFOPT: An Efficient Implementation of Pattern Growth Approach, *Proceedings of the IEEE ICDM Workshop on Frequent Itemset Mining Implementations - FIMI'03*, http://ftp.informatik.rwth-aachen.de/Publications/CEUR-WS/Vol-90/, ISSN 1613-0073.

Lucchese, C.; Orlando, S. & Perego, R. (2004). DCI-Closed: A Fast and Memory Efficient Algorithm to Mine Frequent Closed Itemsets, *Proceedings of the IEEE ICDM Workshop on Frequent Itemset Mining Implementations - FIMI'04*, http://ftp.informatik.rwth-aachen.de/Publications/CEUR-WS/Vol-126/, ISSN 1613-0073.

Okubo, Y. & Haraguchi, M. (2006). Finding Conceptual Document Clusters with Improved Top-N Formal Concept Search, *Proceedings of the 2006 IEEE/WIC/ACM International Conference on Web Intelligence - WI'06*, pp. 347 – 351, ISBN 0-7695-2747-7, Hong Kong, December 2006, IEEE Computer Society, CA.

Okubo, Y.; Haraguchi, M. & Shi, B. (2005). Finding Significant Web Pages with Lower Ranks by Pseudo-Clique Search, *Proceedings of the 8th International Conference on Discovery Science - DS'05*, LNAI 3735, pp. 346 – 353, ISBN 3-540-29230-6, Singapore, October 2005, Springer, Berlin.

Okubo, Y. & Haraguchi, M. (2003). Creating Abstract Concepts for Classification by Finding Top-*N* Maximal Weighted Cliques, *Proceedings of the 6th International Conference on Discovery Science - DS'03*, LNAI 2843, pp. 418 – 425, ISBN 3-540-20293-5, Sapporo, October 2003, Springer, Berlin.

Pasquier, N.; Bastide, Y.; Taouil, R. & Lakhal, L. (1999). Efficient Mining of Association Rules Using Closed Itemset Lattices, *Information Systems*, Vol. 24, No. 1, pp. 25 – 46, ISSN 0306-4379.

Porter, M. F. (1980). An Algorithm for Suffix Stripping, *Program: Electronic Library and Information Systems*, Vol. 14, No. 3, pp. 130 – 137, ISSN 0033-0337.

Rymon, R. (1992). Search through Systematic Set Enumeration, *Proceedings of International Conference on Principles of Knowledge Representation Reasoning - KR'92*, pp. 539 – 550, ISBN 1-55860-262-3, Cambridge, October 1992, Morgan Kaufmann Publishers, CA.

Tomita, E. & Kameda, T. (2007). An Efficient Branch-and-Bound Algorithm for Finding a Maximum Clique with Computational Experiments, *Journal of Global Optimization*, Vol. 37, No. 1, pp. 95 – 111, ISSN 0925-5001.

Uno, T.; Kiyomi, M. & Arimura, H. (2004). LCM ver. 2: Efficient Mining Algorithm for Frequent/Closed/Maximal Itemsets, *Proceedings of the IEEE ICDM Workshop on Frequent Itemset Mining Implementations - FIMI'04*, `http://ftp.informatik.rwth-aachen.de/Publications/CEUR-WS/Vol-126/`, ISSN 1613-0073.

Vakali, A.; Pokorný, J. & Dalamagas, T. (2004). An Overview of Web Data Clustering Practices, *Current Trends in Database Technology - EDBT 2004 Workshops, EDBT 2004 Workshops PhD, DataX, PIM, P2P&DB, and ClustWeb, Heraklion, Crete, Greece, March 14-18, 2004, Revised Selected Papers*, Lindner, W., Mesiti, M., Türker, C., Tzitzikas, Y. and Vakali, A. (Eds.), LNCS 3268, pp. 597 – 606, Springer, ISBN 3-540-23305-9, Berlin.

Wang, J.; Han, J.; Lu, Y. & Tzvetkov, P. (2005). TFP: An Efficient Algorithm for Mining Top-K Frequent Closed Itemsets, *IEEE Transactions on Knowledge and Data Engineering*, Vol. 17, No. 5, pp. 652 – 664, ISSN 1041-4347.

20

Dissimilar Alternative Path Search Algorithm Using a Candidate Path Set[1]

Yeonjeong Jeong and Dong-Kyu Kim
Expressway & Transportation Research Institute, Seoul National University
South Korea

1. Introduction

There is a growing need for navigation services providing multiple dissimilar alternative paths that reflect a variety of user preferences and a dynamic/stochastic variety of travel time and cost. Providing multiple dissimilar paths, in addition to the shortest path based on a certain attribute (travel cost, time or length), may contribute to extending the market of navigation services and attract new customers since navigation users may prefer other attributes, such as driving convenience and fewer right/left turns, to just saving some minutes of driving time.

The traditional method for searching multiple paths is the K-shortest path search method, which provides paths in the order of cost (Yen, 1971; Shier, 1976; 1979; Martins, 1984; Azevedo et al., 1993). However, the multiple paths found by this method tend to be very similar to each other and cannot truly be called alternative paths. A reasonable alternative path should not only have acceptable attribute value(s) but should also be dissimilar to previously identified paths in terms of the links used (Park et al., 2002).

To avoid unreasonable searches for the multiple paths, some methods were suggested in the previous literature. Barra et al. (1993) suggested a link penalty method. In this method, links of a path which was searched in the previous step have a penalty and the next path is searched using a shortest path search algorithm with consideration of the penalties of links. The link penalty method has no way of evaluating the quality of the set of the paths it generates in terms of the spatial differences and the costs of the paths while it can be easily used due to its simplicity (Akgün et al., 2000). Furthermore, this method cannot consider the cost constraint of the alternative paths while generalized cost is one of the most important to select alternative paths in navigation services. The link penalty method is, therefore, not suitable for the path search algorithm for navigation services.

Meng et al. (2005) and Martí et al. (2009) formulated the multiple dissimilar path problems as a multi-objective problem and suggested several solution algorithms. These problems have multiple objectives varying with the purpose of researches such as minimizing average or total costs of the paths, minimizing total population exposed and maximizing the average of the dissimilarity between the paths. However, it takes significant time to solve the multi-objective problem while these problems can produce the paths that meet the given

---

[1] A preliminary version of this paper has appeared in Jeong (2010) writen in Korean.

conditions. The multi-objective problem is not suitable for the application of navigation services since search time also is important as much as dissimilarity in navigation services.
On the other hand, Park et al. (2002) and Jeong et al. (2010) formulated the multiple dissimilar path problems as using cost (time) and dissimilarity constraints. Each of methods has one objective function, such as minimizing the cost of alternative path (Park et al., 2002) or minimizing the shared length ratio between an alternative path and the previous searched path (Jeong et al., 2010). The method suggested in Park et al. (2002) is based on the efficient vector labeling approach (EVL) wherein a cost constraint is used for pruning a transportation network and an overlap constraint is applied to maintain the dissimilarity of alternative paths. The method developed by Jeong et al. (2010) provides dissimilar alternative paths satisfying both user-specified allowable shared length ratio with already searched paths and travel cost ratio against the shortest path. These methods can find alternative dissimilar paths in rational time but they cannot sometimes provide the number of alternative paths required due to their strict constraints.
The candidate path set (CPS) method is another one to use the candidate path set to provide the number of paths required considering dissimilarity. The method suggested in Jeong et al. (2007) establishes a candidate path set based on path deviation by executing the shortest-path algorithm only once. The CPS method provides candidate paths based on the previously searched paths, and thus can provide more various paths than the classical k-shortest path search algorithm. The merit of the CPS is that dissimilarity is not used as a strict constraint but a criterion for selecting alternative paths. In the next section, we will explain the CPS algorithm based on Jeong et al. (2007) with a travel cost constraint and a dissimilarity selecting criterion.

2. Proposed algorithm

2.1 Algorithm

Step 1 Find shortest paths from each node to a destination

Find all-to-one shortest paths from each node to a destination node s.

Denote the shortest path from some node h to a destination node s by P_1^{hs}.

For our interesting origin node r and destination node s,

$$A^{rs} = A^{rs} \cup \{P_1^{rs}\}$$

$$UB = \alpha \times C[P_1^{rs}]$$

Step 2 Update candidate path set

When $P_k^{rs} = \{r, 1, 2, \ldots, (j-1), j, s\}$

step 2-1

$$R_k^{rj} = P_k^{rs} - \{s\},\ C[R_k^{rj}] = C\left[P_k^{rs}\right] - c^{js},\ L[R_k^{rj}] = L\left[P_k^{rs}\right] - \ell^{js}$$

If $R_k^{rj} \in C^{rj}$

then go to step 3

otherwise

$$P_c^{rs} = R_k^{rj} + P_1^{hs}$$

$$C[P_c^{rs}] = C[R_k^{rj}] + c^{jh} + C[P_1^{hs}]$$

$$L[P_c^{rs}] = L[R_k^{rj}] + \ell^{jh} + L[P_1^{hs}]$$

$$(\text{where, } h \in O^j,\ h \neq r, 1, 2, \ldots, (j-1), j, s)$$

$$C^{rj} = C^{rj} \cup \{R_k^{rj}\}$$

If $C[P_c^{rs}] \leq UB$

then $B^{rs} = B^{rs} \cup \{P_c^{rs}\}$

step 2-2

$j = j - 1$

$R_k^{rj} = R_k^{r(j+1)} - \{j+1\}$, $C[R_k^{rj}] = C[R_k^{r(j+1)}] - c^{j(j+1)}$, $L[R_k^{rj}] = L[P_k^{r(j+1)}] - \ell^{j(j+1)}$

If $R_k^{rj} \in C^{rj}$

then go to step 3

otherwise

$$P_c^{rs} = R_k^{rj} + P_1^{hs}$$

$$C[P_c^{rs}] = C[R_k^{rj}] + c^{jh} + C[P_1^{hs}]$$

$$L[P_c^{rs}] = L[R_k^{rj}] + \ell^{jh} + L[P_1^{hs}]$$

$$(\text{where, } h \in O^j,\ h \neq r, 1, 2, \ldots, j, (j+1))$$

$$C^{rj} = C^{rj} \cup \{R_k^{rj}\}$$

If $C[P_c^{rs}] \leq UB$

then $B^{rs} = B^{rs} \cup \{P_c^{rs}\}$

If $j = r$

then go to step 3

otherwise go to step 2-2

Step 3 select $k+1^{th}$ alternative path

$$P_{k+1}^{rs} = \underset{P_C^{rs} \in B^{rs}}{\operatorname{argmin}} \frac{1}{K} \sum_{k=1}^{K} \frac{L\left[P_k^{rs} \cap P_c^{rs}\right]}{L\left[P_k^{rs}\right]} \quad \left(P_k^{rs} \in A^{rs}\right)$$

If user accepts that path

then the algorithm ends

otherwise go to step 2

where,

k	: Number of alternative paths
h, i, j	: Node Index (node r is an origin and node s is a destination)
α	: User-specified allowable travel cost ratio
UB	: Travel cost constraint (upper bound of alternative path cost)
O^j	: Set of nodes linked from node j
$<i,j>$	: Link between node i and node j

c^{ij} : Cost of link between node i and node j

ℓ^{ij} : Length of link between node i and node j

A^{rs} : Set of alternative paths from node r to node s

B^{rs} : Set of candidate paths from node r to node s

C^{rj} : Set of subpaths for avoiding of making same candidate paths

P_k^{rs} : k^{th} Alternative path from node r to node s $(P_k^{rs} \in A^{rs})$, which is a set of continuous nodes $P_k^{rs} = \{r,1,2,\ldots,(j-1),j,s\}$

P_c^{rs} : Candidate path from node r to node s $(P_c^{rs} \in B^{rs})$, which is a set of continuous nodes $P_c^{rs} = \{r,1,2,\ldots,(j-1),j,s\}$

R_k^{rj} : Subpath of P_{k-1}^{rs} from node r to node j, which is a set of continuous nodes $R_k^{rj} = \{r,1,2,\ldots,(j-1),j\}$

$R_k^{rj} + P_1^{hs}$: Path adding R_k^{rj} and P_1^{hs} with link $<j,h>$

$R_k^{rj} - \{j\}$: Path excluding node j from R_k^{rj}

$C[P_k^{rs}]$: Cost of path P_k^{rs}

$L[P_k^{rs}]$: Length of path P_k^{rs}

$L[P_k^{rs} \cap P_c^{rs}]$: Length of overlapped link between P_k^{rs} and P_c^{rs}

2.2 Illustrative example

In this subsection, we explain how the CPS algorithm works using an example network of Fig. 1, which consists of 9 nodes and 12 undirected links. In Fig. 1, the alphabetical characters within each circle mean node indices; the numbers in front of the parentheses denote link indices; two numbers in the parentheses are cost and length of each link, respectively. In this example, the user-specified allowable travel cost ratio, α, is set to 1.3, which means that we include paths with the travel cost not higher than UB by 30% into the candidate path set .

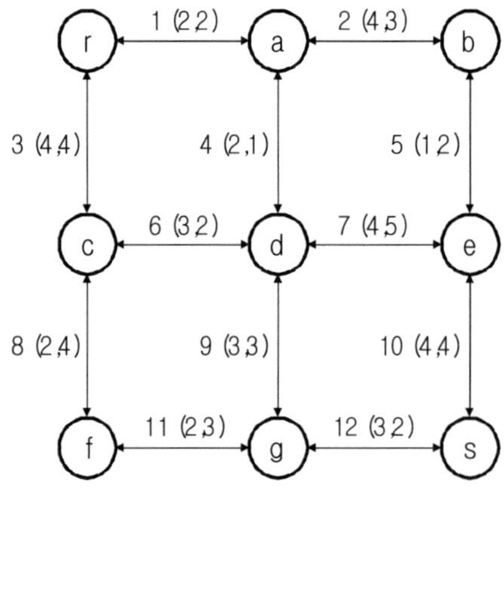

Fig. 1. Example network

2.2.1 Finding the 1st alternative path (the shortest path)

First of all, we found P_1^{hs} from all nodes to a destination node s using a reverse shortest path search algorithm as shown in Fig. 2. Table 1 shows the cost and length of all P_1^{hs}. After then, the shortest path, $P_1^{rs} = \{r,a,d,g,s\}$, is found as shown in Fig. 3. At this time, the minimum travel cost becomes '10', and travel cost constraint, UB is set to '13' as shown in Table 2.

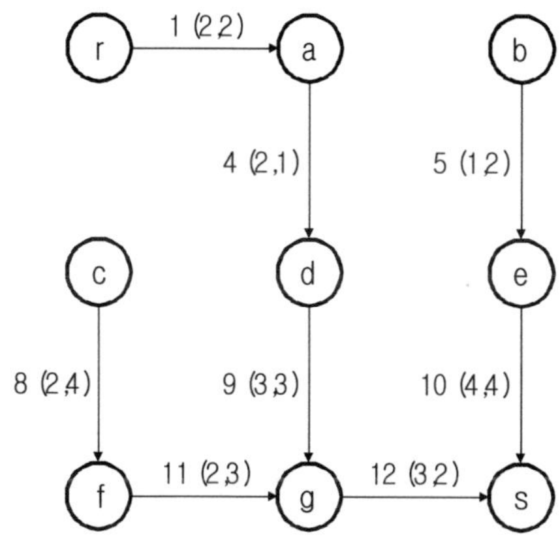

Fig. 2. Shortest paths to node s

h	r	a	b	c	d	e	f	g
$C[P_1^{hs}]$	10	8	5	7	6	4	5	3
$L[P_1^{hs}]$	8	6	6	9	5	4	5	2

Table 1. Path costs and lengths of shortest paths

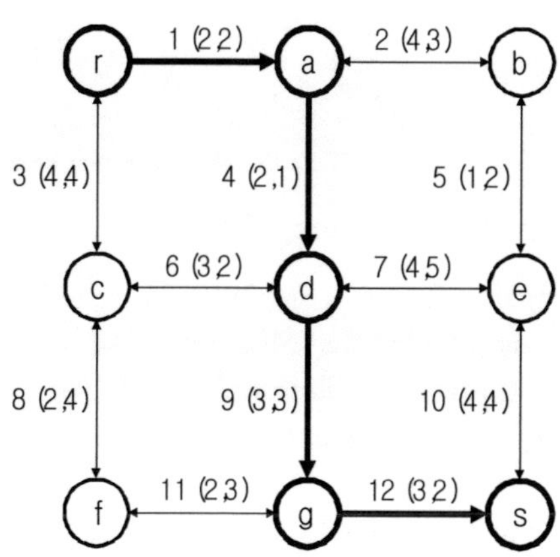

Fig. 3. The 1st shortest path

k	R_k^{rj}	$C[R_k^{rj}]$	h	P_c^{rs}	$C[P_c^{rs}]$	O.R.	P_k^{rs}	$C[P_k^{rs}]$
1							r,a,d,g,s	10

Table 2. Result of the 1st shortest path

2.2.2 Finding the 2nd alternative path

First, we make a subpath, $R_2^{rg} = \{r,a,d,g\}$, by deleting link 12 between node g and node s. The cost of this subpath is calculated as '7' subtracting the cost '3' of deleted link 12 from the cost '10' of $C[P_1^{rs}]$. Then, this subpath is stored in C^{rg}. Node f linked from node g by link 11 is considered as a candidate node for the next path search.

The candidate path set is made as follows: The shortest path from node f to a destination node s has been already determined as P_1^{fs} in the step 1. Therefore, the path adding R_2^{rg} and P_1^{fs}, $R_2^{rg} + P_1^{fs} = \{r,a,d,g,f,g,s\}$, may be the candidate path for the next alternative path. The cost of this path is calculated as '14' by adding the cost '2' of c^{gf} and the cost '5' of $C[P_1^{fs}]$ to the cost '7' of $C[R_2^{rg}]$. This path cost '14' is higher than the user-specified allowable cost ($\alpha \times UB = 13$), and thus the path, $R_2^{rg} + P_1^{fs}$, cannot be included into the candidate path set.

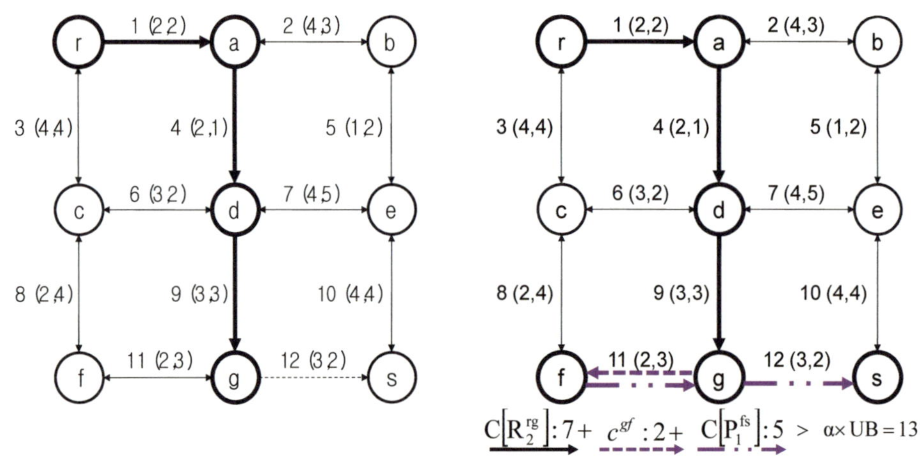

Fig. 4. Updating candidate path set by using subpath R_2^{rg}

Next, a subpath, $R_2^{rd} = \{r,a,d\}$ is investigated by deleting link 9 between node d and node g. The cost of this subpath is calculated as '4' subtracting the cost '3' of deleted link 9 from the cost '7' of $C[R_2^{rg}]$. Then, this subpath is stored in C^{rd}. Node c linked by link 6 and node e linked by link 7 from node d are considered as the next candidate nodes for the next path search.

In the same way mentioned above, two candidate paths, $R_2^{rd} + P_1^{cs} = \{r,a,d,c,f,g,s\}$ and $R_2^{rd} + P_1^{es} = \{r,a,d,e,s\}$, are made for the next alternative path since the shortest paths from node c and node e to a destination node s , as P_1^{cs} and P_1^{es} have been already determined in the step 1. The cost of the path, $R_2^{rd}+P_1^{cs}$, is calculated as '14' adding the cost '3' of c^{dc} and the cost '7' of $C[P_1^{cs}]$ to the cost '4' of $C[R_2^{rd}]$ and this path cannot be also included into the candidate path set since its cost is higher than the user-specified allowable cost. On the other hand, the cost of the path, $R_2^{rd}+P_1^{es}$ is calculated as '12' adding the cost '4' of c^{de} and the cost '4' of $C[P_1^{es}]$ to the cost '4' of $C[R_2^{rd}]$. We can include this path, $R_2^{rd}+P_1^{es}$, into the candidate path set since its cost is not higher than the user-specified allowable cost.

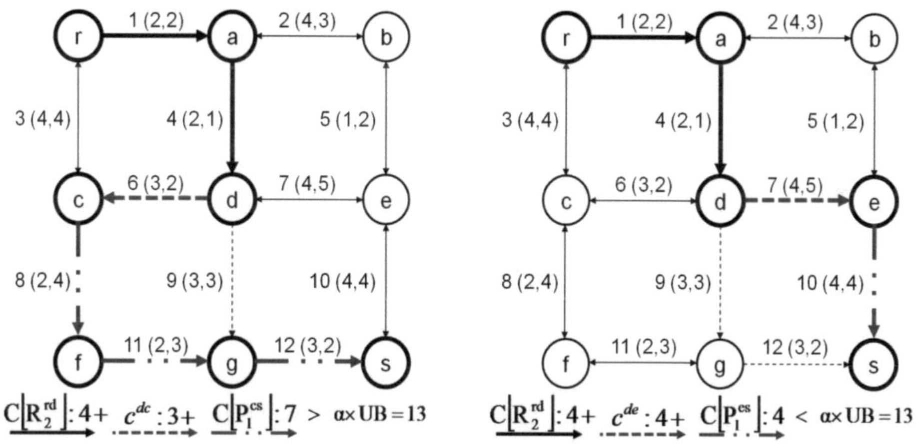

Fig. 5. Updating candidate path set by using subpath R_2^{rd}

Next, a subpath, $R_2^{ra}=\{r,a\}$, is made by deleting link 4 between node a and node d . After calculating the cost of this subpath as '2', this subpath is stored in C^{ra} and node b linked from node a by link 2 is considered as the next candidate. The cost of the path, $R_2^{ra}+P_1^{bs}=\{r,a,b,e,s\}$, can be calculated as '11' adding the cost '4' of c^{ab} and the cost '5' of $C[P_1^{bs}]$ to the cost '2' of $C[R_2^{ra}]$. This path, $R_2^{ra}+P_1^{bs}$, can be also included into the candidate path set since its cost is not higher than the user-specified allowable cost.

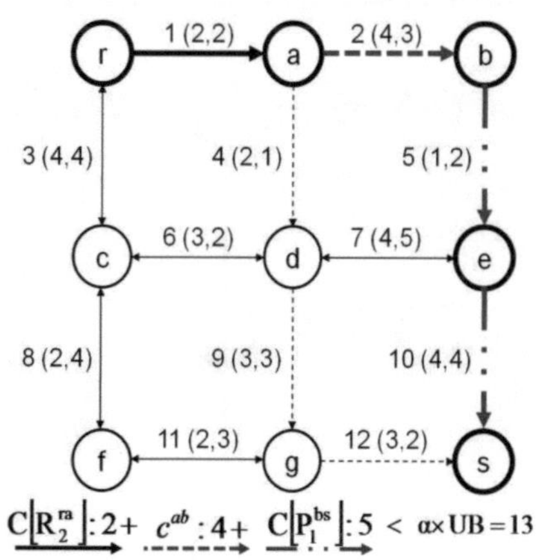

Fig. 6. Updating candidate path set by using subpath R_2^{ra}

Finally, we make a subpath, $R_2^{rr} = \{r\}$, by deleting link 1 between node r and node a. The cost of this subpath is calculated as '0'. This subpath is stored in C^{rr} and node c linked from node r by link 3 will be the next candidate node for the next path search. The path $R_2^{rr} + P_1^{cs} = \{r,c,f,g,s\}$ may be the candidate path for the next alternative path since the shortest path from node c to a destination node s has been already determined as P_1^{cs} in the step 1. The cost of this candidate path is calculated as '11' adding the cost '4' of linked c^{rc} and the cost '7' of $C[P_1^{cs}]$ to the cost '0' of $C[R_2^{rr}]$. And we can also include this path, $R_2^{rr} + P_1^{cs}$, into the candidate path set since its cost is not higher than the user-specified allowable cost.

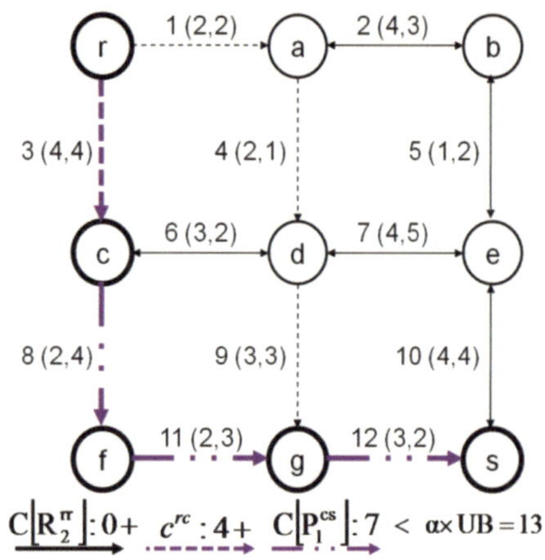

Fig. 7. Updating candidate path set by using subpath R_2^{rr}

Because we have made all subpaths to an origin node r using the shortest path P_1^{rs}, we can select the second alternative path, P_2^{rs} in the step 3. First, we calculate the overlap length ratios of all the paths in the candidate path set by dividing overlapped length of candidate path and the shortest path by the length '8' of the shortest path. The overlapped length ratio of the path, $\{r,a,b,e,s\}$, is the smallest one among the candidate paths, so this path becomes the second alternative path and is deleted in the candidate path set.

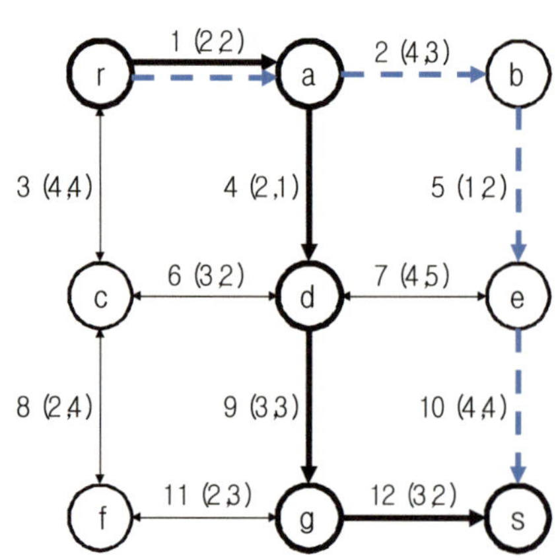

Fig. 8. 1st path and 2nd path

k	R_k^{rj}	$C[R_k^{rj}]$	h	P_c^{rs}	$C[P_c^{rs}]$	O.R.[2]	P_k^{rs}	$C[P_k^{rs}]$
1							r,a,d,g,s	10
2	r,a,d,g	10-3	f	r,a,d,g,f,g,s	7+2+5=14[3]		r,a,b,e,s	11
	r,a,d	7-3	c	r,a,d,c,f,g,s	4+3+7=14			
			e	r,a,d,e,s	4+4+4=12	3/8		
	r,a	4-2	b	r,a,b,e,s	2+4+5=11	2/8		
	r	2-2	c	r,c,f,g,s	0+4+7=11	2/8		

Table 3. Result of finding the 2nd alternative path

2.2.3 Finding the 3rd alternative path

Next, we will find the third alternative path P_3^{rs} from an origin node r to a destination node s using the second alternative path P_2^{rs}.

First, in the same way mentioned above, we make a subpath, $R_3^{re} = \{r,a,b,e\}$, by deleting link 10 between node e and node s. The cost of this subpath is calculated as '7' subtracting the cost '4' of deleted link 10 from the cost '11' of $C[P_2^{rs}]$. Then, this subpath is stored in C^{re}. Node d linked from node e by link 7 is considered as the first candidate node for the third shortest path search. The cost of the path, $R_3^{re} + P_1^{ds} = \{r,a,b,e,d,g,s\}$, is calculated as '17' adding the cost '4' of c^{ed}, the cost '6' of $C[P_1^{ds}]$ and the cost '7' of $C[R_3^{re}]$. This path cost '17' is higher than the user-specified allowable cost ($\alpha \times UB = 13$), and thus the path, $R_3^{re} + P_1^{ds}$, cannot be included into the candidate path set.

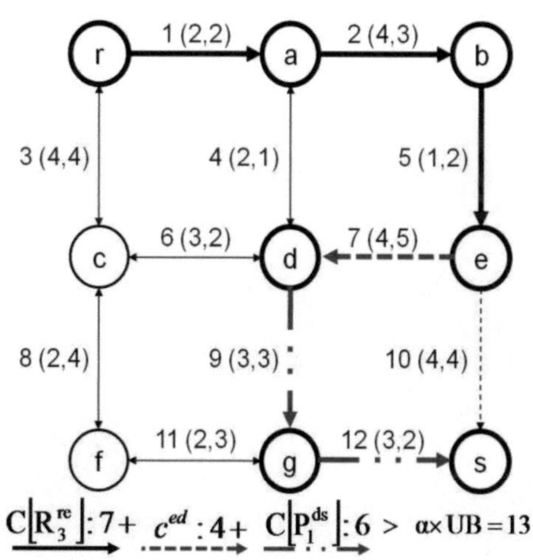

Fig. 9. Updating candidate path set by using subpath R_3^{re}

[2] The overlapped length ratio

[3] The search stops because the path cost is higher than the user-specified allowable cost.

Next, a subpath, $R_3^{rb} = \{r,a,b\}$, is made by deleting link 5 between node b and node e. The cost of this subpath is calculated as '6' subtracting the cost '1' of deleted link 5 from the cost '7' of $C[R_3^{re}]$. Then, this subpath is stored in C^{rb}. Because there is no node linked from node b, the search stops.

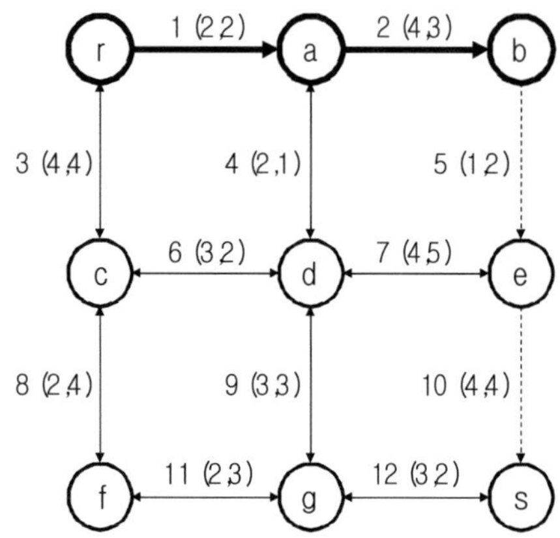

Fig. 10. Updating candidate path set by using subpath R_3^{rb}

Next, we make and investigate a subpath, $R_3^{ra} = \{r,a\}$, by deleting link 2 between node a and node b. The cost of this subpath is calculated as '2' subtracting the cost '4' of deleted link 2 from the cost '6' of $C[R_3^{rb}]$. This subpath, however, has been already included in C^{ra} during the second alternative path search process. Therefore, the search stops and we can select the third alternative path, P_3^{rs} in the step 3.

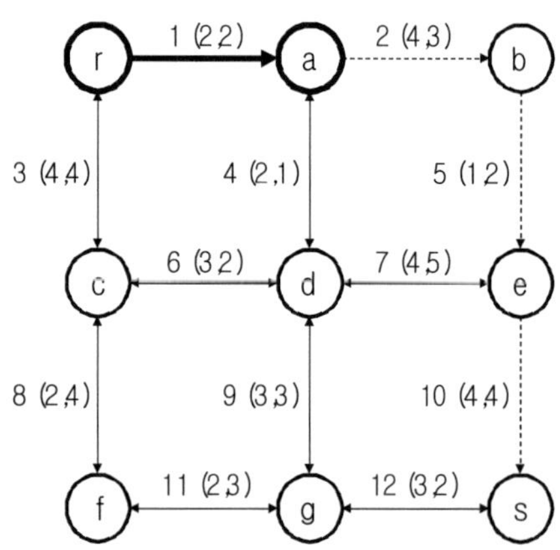

Fig. 11. Updating candidate path set by using subpath R_3^{ra}

First, we calculate the average overlapped length ratios between each path in the candidate path set and the alternative paths. The average overlapped length ratio of the path, $\{r,c,f,g,s\}$ is the smallest one among the candidate paths, so this path becomes the third alternative path and is deleted in the candidate path set.

k	R_k^{rj}	$C[R_k^{rj}]$	h	P_c^{rs}	$C[P_c^{rs}]$	O.R.	P_k^{rs}	$C[P_k^{rs}]$
1							r,a,d,g,s	10
2	r,a,d,g	10-3	f	r,a,d,g,f,g,s	7+2+5=14		r,a,b,e,s	11
	r,a,d	7-3	c	r,a,d,c,f,g,s	4+3+7=14			
			e	r,a,d,e,s	4+4+4=12	$\frac{1}{2}\times(\frac{3}{8}+\frac{6}{12})$		
	r,a	~~4-2~~	~~b~~	~~r, a, b, e, s~~	~~2+4+5=11~~	~~2/8~~		
	r	2-2	c	r,c,f,g,s	0+4+7=11	$\frac{1}{2}\times(\frac{2}{8}+0)$		
3	r,a,b,e	11-4	d	r,a,b,e,d,g,s	7+4+6=17		r,c,f,g,s	11
	r,a,b [4]	7-1						
	r,a [5]	6-4						

Table 4. Result of finding the 3rd alternative path

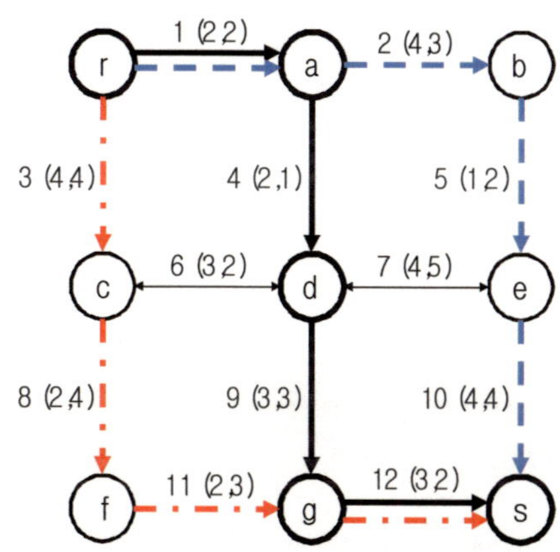

Fig. 12. 1st path, 2nd path and 3rd path

3. Computational results

To check the performance, all methods were applied to a real Chicago and Philadelphia networks[6]. The Chicago network consists of 12,982 nodes and 39,018 links. And the

---

[4] This search stops since there is no node linked from node b.

[5] This search stops for avoiding of making same candidate paths since this subpath has been already included in the set of subpaths

[6] We used 'chicago_network.txt' and 'philadelphia_network.txt' from http://www.bgu.ac.il/~bargera/tntp/.

Philadelphia network consists of 13,389 nodes and 40,003 links. We used 'cost' columns of both network data as link costs but substituted the 'ftime' value '0.01' for '0'. We used C++ for programming and implemented the solution algorithm using a computer with Pentium Core2 Quad 2.66 GHz processor, a Windows XP operating system, and 2 GB DDR RAM.
First of all, we tested 100 iterations of the algorithm to make candidate path sets from node 25 to node 10348 based on the Philadelphia network. Table 5 shows the number of candidate path and CPU time to the iteration. This test shows the method can provide candidate paths quickly.

iteration	# of Candidate Paths	CPU time	iteration	# of Candidate Paths	CPU time
0	1	0.141	10	274	0.234
1	48	0.141	20	450	0.359
2	91	0.156	30	629	0.547
3	91	0.156	40	847	0.812
4	137	0.172	50	971	1.016
5	137	0.172	60	1,136	1.312
6	175	0.187	70	1,278	1.609
7	218	0.203	80	1,463	2.031
8	256	0.219	90	1,544	2.297
9	274	0.234	100	1,669	2.703

Table 5. Test result of making candidate path sets

We compared the results of the EVL method and the CPS method to evaluate the suitability of these methods for navigation services that finds multiple alternative paths. We selected randomly 1,000 O-D (origin-destination) pairs on the Chicago network and 100 O-D pairs on the Philadelphia network for searching for the shortest path and 9 alternative dissimilar paths. This test determines whether the method can provide as many alternative paths as users want; the larger the number of the paths, the better the method.
In Tables 6 and 7, the figures in parentheses refer to the specified values of constraints. For example, 1.1 and 2.0 of the 'user allowable travel cost ratio' mean that the paths having travel cost higher than the shortest path by 10% and 100%, respectively, should not be selected for the next alternative path. In the same manner, 0.5 and 0.8 of the 'user allowable overlapped length ratio' mean that the paths having 50% and 80% or more overlapped length ratios with already searched paths, respectively, should not be selected. The value of

the overlapped length ratio constraint of the CPS method is 1.0 since it does not employ the constraint.

Table 6 shows the average numbers of paths searched by each method. The results show that the stronger the cost and overlap constraints, the fewer paths were searched. The CPS method, which uses only the cost constraint, searched alternative paths close to the number of paths to be required (K=9). Because CPS does not consider the overlap constraint, it can provide almost as many alternative paths as users may want.

		User allowable travel cost ratio							
		Chicago network				Philadelphia network			
		Strong (1.1)		Weak (2.0)		Strong (1.1)		Weak (2.0)	
User allowable overlapped length ratio	Strong (0.5)	EVL	2.56	EVL	7.75	EVL	1.74	EVL	7.49
	Weak (0.8)	EVL	4.47	EVL	7.68	EVL	3.61	EVL	7.41
	None (1.0)	CPS	8.80	CPS	8.97	CPS	8.83	CPS	8.91

Table 6. Average numbers of paths searched (K=9)

Table 7 shows the average CPU computation time required for each method. This test determines which method can provide alternative paths more quickly, so the smaller the value, the better the method. The EVL method prunes the network using the cost constraint. Therefore, the average CPU computation time of the EVL method increases rapidly as the cost constraint weakens while its computation time was not significantly influenced by the overlap constraint. The CPS method searched the number of paths required more quickly because it did not consider the overlap constraint.

		User allowable travel cost ratio							
		Chicago network				Philadelphia network			
		Strong (1.1)		Weak (2.0)		Strong (1.1)		Weak (2.0)	
User allowable overlapped length ratio	Strong (0.5)	EVL	0.86	EVL	4.22	EVL	1.31	EVL	6.05
	Weak (0.8)	EVL	0.95	EVL	4.12	EVL	1.55	EVL	6.08
	None (1.0)	CPS	0.50	CPS	0.56	CPS	0.51	CPS	0.62

Table 7. Average CPU computation times (sec)

Tables 8 and 9 show the average overlap ratios for the case when one or more alternative paths are searched and for the overall sample data (1,000 and 100 O-D pairs), respectively. As shown in Table 8, when one or more alternative paths were searched, CPS's average overlapped length ratio is higher than that of EVL which has the overlap constraint.
However, it is too early to conclude that EVL has better performances than CPS since the result of Table 8 did not reflect the cases when no alternative path was searched. When there is no alternative path, a driver is provided only one path. Therefore, in the result of Table 8, the overlapped length ratio was set to 1.0 when there was no alternative path.
As shown in Table 9, the result of CPS is similar to that of EVL if the result of no alternative path is included. In other words, considering only the case when one or more alternative paths were searched, the EVL with the overlapped length ratio constraint searched more dissimilar paths than CPS; however, in general conditions including the case when no alternative path was searched, whether a method considered the overlap constraint or not does not influence the results. Summarizing all the results, then, the CPS method finds more number of dissimilar alternative paths with similar overlap ratios to the EVL more quickly.

		User allowable travel cost ratio							
		Chicago network				Philadelphia network			
		Strong (1.1)		Weak (2.0)		Strong (1.1)		Weak (2.0)	
User allowable overlapped length ratio	Strong (0.5)	EVL	0.30	EVL	0.27	EVL	0.33	EVL	0.27
	Weak (0.8)	EVL	0.57	EVL	0.52	EVL	0.58	EVL	0.52
	None (1.0)	CPS	0.60	CPS	0.56	CPS	0.58	CPS	0.50

Table 8. Average overlap ratios for the cases when one or more alternative paths were searched

		User allowable travel cost ratio							
		Chicago network				Philadelphia network			
		Strong (1.1)		Weak (2.0)		Strong (1.1)		Weak (2.0)	
User allowable overlapped length ratio	Strong (0.5)	EVL	0.49	EVL	0.28	EVL	0.49	EVL	0.31
	Weak (0.8)	EVL	0.62	EVL	0.53	EVL	0.63	EVL	0.55
	None (1.0)	CPS	0.60	CPS	0.56	CPS	0.59	CPS	0.51

Table 9. Average overlap ratios for the overall sample data

4. Conclusions

In this chapter, we explained that the candidate path set is made by executing a shortest path search algorithm only once and compared the efficient vector labeling method (EVL) and the candidate path set method (CPS) to investigate the conditions for dissimilar paths-search algorithms by which drivers can select their own best path.

Navigation services should provide dissimilar alternative paths until their users are satisfied with a path based on their own criteria. This study suggests the method of selecting the path having the minimum average overlapped length ratio with a previously searched path as the alternative path from among paths that satisfy only the cost constraint. A test based on a real Chicago and Philadelphia networks showed that the proposed method can provide the number of alternative dissimilar paths required more rapidly. The generalized cost constraints are applied to all conditions at the same ratio since the travel cost stems from the entire path. On the other hand, the overlap constraints can vary among the alternative paths. For example, a driver may search for alternative paths until a path is provided that does not include the section he or she does not want. Therefore, navigation services must provide alternative paths to satisfy the various needs of users.

Drivers can select their own best paths from the alternative paths provided by using the information on several alternative paths and can see to what degree the alternative path provided by the service or that they select on their own is better than other paths. Drivers can also become familiar with unfamiliar regions by using different paths.

5. References

Akgün, V., Erkut, E., and Batta, R. (2000). On Finding Dissimilar Paths, *European Journal of Operational Research*, Vol. 121, pp. 232-246, 0377-2217

Azevedo, J. A., Costa, M. E. O. S., Madeira, J. J. E. R. S., and Martins, E. Q. V. (1993). An Algorithm from the Ranking of Shortest Paths, *European Journal of Operational Research*, Vol. 69, pp. 97-106, 0377-2217

Barra, T., Perez, B. and Anez, J. (1993). Multidimensional Path Search and Assignment, *Proceedings of 21st PTRC Summer Annual Conference*, pp. 307-319, Manchester, England, PTRC

Jeong, Y. J., Hong, Y., and Kim, T. J. (2007). Flexible Multipath Search Algorithm for Multipurpose Location-based Activities, *Transportation Research Record: Journal of the Transportation Research Board*, No. 2039, pp. 50-57, 0361-1981

Jeong, Y. J., Kim, T. J., Park, C. H., and Kim, D. -K. (2010). A Dissimilar Alternative Paths-Search Algorithm for Navigation Services: A Heuristic Approach, *KSCE: Journal of Civil Engineering*, Vol. 14, No. 1, pp.41-49, 1226-7988

Jeong, Y. J. (2010). A Dissimilar Paths Search Algorithm for a Multi-purpose Trip, Ph.D. Dissertation, Seoul National University.

Martí, R., Luis González Velarde, J., and Duarte, A. (2009). Heuristics for the Bi-Objective Path Dissimilarity Problem. *Computers and Operations Research*, Vol. 36, No. 11, pp. 2905-2912, 0305-0548

Martins, E. Q. V. (1984). An Algorithm for Ranking Paths that May Contain Cycles. *European Journal of Operational Research*, Vol. 18, pp. 123-130, 0377-2217

Meng, Q., Lee, D. -H., Cheu, R. L. (2005). Multiobjective Vehicle Routing and Scheduling Problem with Time Window Constraints in Hazardous Material Transportation. *ASCE: Journal of Transportation Engineering*, Vol. 131, No. 9, pp. 699-707, 0733-947X

Park, D., Sharma, S. L., Rilett, L. R., and Chang, M. (2002). Identifying Multiple Reasonable Alternative Routes: Efficient Vector Labeling Approach. *Transportation Research Record: Journal of the Transportation Research Board*, No. 1783, pp. 111-118, 0361-1981

Shier, R. D. (1976). Iterative Methods for Determining the K Shortest Paths in a Network. *Networks*, Vol. 6, pp. 205-229, 0028-3045

Shier, R. D. (1979). On Algorithms from Finding the K Shortest Paths in a Network. *Networks*, Vol. 9, pp. 195-214, 0028-3045

Yen, J. Y. (1971). Finding the K shortest Loopless Paths in a Network. *Management Science*, Vol. 17, pp. 712-716, 0025-1909

21

Pattern Search Algorithms for Surface Wave Analysis

Xianhai Song
Changjiang River Scientific Research Institute, Wuhan, Hubei 430010
China

1. Introduction

In recent years Rayleigh waves have been used increasingly as a nondestructive tool to obtain near-surface S-wave velocity, one of the key parameters in environmental and engineering applications (Miller et al., 1999a, 1999b; Park et al., 1998, 1999; Xia et al., 1999, 2003; Foti et al., 2002; Beaty and Schmitt, 2003; Tian et al., 2003; Zhang and Chan, 2003; Lin and Chang, 2004; O'Neill et al., 2003; Ryden et al., 2004; and Song et al., 2006). Utilization of surface wave dispersive properties may be roughly divided into three steps: field data acquisition, dispersion-curve picking, and inversion of phase velocities (Xia et al., 2004). Inversion of Rayleigh wave dispersion curves is one of the key steps in surface wave analysis to obtain a shallow subsurface S-wave velocity profile (Rix, 1988; Lai et al., 2002).
However, inversion of high-frequency Rayleigh wave dispersion curves, as with most other geophysical optimization problems, is typically a nonlinear, multiparameter inversion problem. Dal Moro et al. (2007) have demonstrated the high nonlinearity and multimodality by a synthetic model. Consequently, local optimization methods, e.g. matrix inversion, steepest descent, conjugate gradients, are prone to being trapped by local minima, and their success depends heavily on the choice of a good starting model (Boschetti et al., 1996) and the accuracy of the partial derivatives. Thus, global optimization methods that can overcome this limitation are particularly attractive for surface wave analysis (e.g., Meier and Rix, 1993; Yamanaka and Ishida, 1996; and Beaty et al., 2002).
Pattern search algorithms are a direct search method well suitable for the global optimization of highly nonlinear, multimodal objective functions (Lewis and Torczon, 1999). Pattern search algorithms have recently been used and tested to optimize complex mathematical problems characterized by the large numbers of local minima and/or maxima (Lewis and Torczon, 2000). However, few attempts have been made to address real-world geophysical problems, especially for the inversion of surface wave data. In this chapter, In this chapter, I first implemented and tested a Rayleigh wave dispersion curve inversion scheme based on GPS Positive Basis 2N, a commonly used pattern search algorithm. Incorporating complete poll and complete search strategies based on GPS Positive Basis 2N into the inverse procedure greatly enhances the performance of pattern search algorithms because the two steps can effectively locate the promising areas in the solution space containing the global minima and significantly reduce the computation cost, respectively. The calculation efficiency and stability of the inversion scheme are tested on three synthetic models. Secondly, effects of the number of data points, the reduction of the frequency range

of the considered dispersion curve, errors in P-wave velocities and density, the initial S-wave velocity profile as well as the number of layers and their thicknesses on inversion results are investigated to further evaluate the performance of the proposed approach. Thirdly, I implemented an investigation to fully exploit and utilize the potentiality of pattern search algorithms and to further enhance their performance for surface wave analysis. I investigate effects of different inversion strategies, initial mesh size and final mesh size, expansion factor and contraction factor, as well as inclusion of noise in surface wave data on the performance of the approaches, by three synthetic earth models. Fourthly, a comparative analysis with genetic algorithms is made to further highlight the advantages of the proposed inverse procedure. Finally, the performance of pattern search algorithms is verified by a real-world example from Henan, China.

2. Fundamentals on pattern search algorithms

As described above, pattern search algorithms are a direct search method well capable of solving global optimization problems of irregular, multimodal objective functions, without the need of calculating any gradient or curvature information, especially for addressing problems for which the objective functions are not differentiable, stochastic, or even discontinuous (Torczon, 1997). As opposed to more traditional local optimization methods that use information about the gradient or partial derivatives to search for an optimal solution, pattern search algorithms compute a sequence of points that get closer and closer to the globally optimal point. At each iteration, the algorithms poll a set of points, called a **mesh**, around the current point – the point computed at the previous iteration of the algorithms, looking for a point whose objective function value is lower than the value at the current point. If this occurs, the poll is called **successful** and the point they find becomes the current point at the next iteration. If the algorithms fail to find a point that improves the objective function, the poll is called **unsuccessful** and the current point stays the same at the next iteration. The mesh is formed by adding the current point to a scalar multiple (called **mesh size**) of a set of vectors (called a **pattern**). In addition to polling the mesh points, pattern search algorithms can perform an optional step at every iteration, called **search**. At each iteration, the search step applies another optimization method to the current point. If this search does not improve the current point, the poll step is performed (Lewis and Torczon, 2002).

Pattern search algorithms use the Augmented Lagragian Pattern Search (ALPS) to solve nonlinearly constrained problems (Conn et al., 1991). The ALPS attempts to solve a nonlinear optimization problem with nonlinear constraints, linear constraints, and bounds using Lagrange multiplier estimates and penalty parameters (Lewis and Torczon, 2002). ALPS begins by using an initial penalty parameter and a starting point X0 for starting the optimization process. Pattern search algorithms minimize a sequence of subproblems, which are approximations of the original problem. When the subproblems are minimized to a required accuracy and satisfy feasibility conditions, the Lagrangian estimates are updated. Otherwise, the penalty parameter is increased by a penalty factor. This results in a new subproblem formulation and a minimization problem. These steps are repeated until the stopping criteria are met. For a more detailed description of the algorithms, the interested reader can refer to several excellent publications that extensively cover the subject (e.g., Conn et al., 1991; Torczon, 1997; Lewis and Torczon, 1999, 2000, 2002; Audet and Dennis, Jr., 2003; and Kolda et al., 2003).

3. Pattern search algorithms for surface wave analysis

We implemented a series of MATLAB tools based on the GADS (Genetic Algorithms and Direct Search) Optimization Toolbox of MATLAB 7.1 for surface wave analysis. We have worked on SWIPSA, a software package for Surface Wave Inversion via Pattern Search Algorithms. The codes being developed aim at performing nonlinear inversion of the fundamental and/or higher mode Rayleigh waves using pattern search algorithms.

In the current study, we implemented and tested a Rayleigh wave dispersion curve inversion scheme based on GPS Positive basis 2N, a commonly used pattern search algorithm. GPS Positive basis 2N is the Generalized Pattern Search (GPS) algorithm with the maximal positive basis set 2N vectors, where N is the number of independent variables (which in our case involve S-wave velocities) in the optimization problem. The algorithm uses fixed direction vectors to compute the set of points forming the mesh.

Complete poll method based on GPS Positive basis 2N is incorporated into the inversion procedure to discover the most promising domain in the solution space for a good valley. In general, if a pattern search algorithm finds a point in the mesh that improves the objective function at the current point, it stops the poll and sets that point as the current point for the next iteration. When this occurs, some mesh points might not get polled. Some of these unpolled points might have an objective function value that is even lower than the first one the pattern search finds. Especially for problems in which there are the large numbers of local minima and/or maxima of the object functions, it is sometimes preferable to make the pattern search poll all the mesh points at each iteration and choose the one with the best objective function value (Lewis and Torczon, 1999). Although a complete poll can make the pattern search run significantly longer, this enables the algorithm to explore more points at each iteration and thereby potentially avoid a local minimum that is not the global minimum.

Complete search method based on GPS Positive basis 2N is also adopted to reduce the total function evaluations (the number of times the objective function was evaluated) and the number of iterations (Lewis and Torczon, 1999). This choice is justified by the fact that computation time and efficiency are improved in our latter tests.

The expansion factor and contraction factor control how much the mesh size is expanded or contracted at each iteration. During the inversion procedure, we adopt the values suggested by the GADS Toolbox. We set the initial mesh size at 1, expansion factor at 2, contraction factor at 0.5, initial penalty at 10, and penalty factor at 100, which means the GPS algorithm multiplies the mesh size by 2 after each successful poll and multiplies the mesh size by 0.5 after each unsuccessful poll.

In this chapter, we focus our attention on inversion results of fundamental-mode Rayleigh wave dispersion curves for a near-surface S-wave velocity profile by fixing other parameters, namely P-wave velocities (or Poisson's ratio), density, and thickness, to their known values or good estimates. The reduction of the computation time and the fact that the S-wave velocity is the most important parameter affecting the Rayleigh wave propagation (Xia et al., 1999) are the main reasons for these choices.

To simulate more realistic cases where no a priori information is available, an initial S-wave velocity profile (a starting point X0) with a uniform constant-velocity half-space is adopted. This is a simple and efficient scheme obtained by averaging maximum and minimum phase velocities, which is given by Eq. (1):

$$V_{S0} = (V_R^{\max} + V_R^{\min}) / 2 \quad \text{(For all layers)} \tag{1}$$

The pattern search algorithm presented here is designed to treat the explicit lower and upper bound constraints that are present in the least-squares problem. To fully evaluate the capability of the algorithm and further simulate realistic cases where no a priori information is available, we use a wider search scope of the solution space. The lower and upper bounds of the search areas are 100 and 1000 m/s, respectively, for every layer in all of the latter tests. By design, these boundary values are approximately 100-150% off the true values.

The procedure will set out to find the global minimum of rms (root-mean-square) error misfit between the measured and the predicted phase velocities. The objective function is defined as:

$$F = \left\| \mathbf{V}_{\mathbf{R}}^{\text{obs}} - \mathbf{V}_{\mathbf{R}}^{\text{theo}}) \right\| / \sqrt{m} \tag{2}$$

where $\mathbf{V}_{\mathbf{R}}^{\text{obs}}$ is an $m \times 1$ vector of the observed Rayleigh wave phase velocities, $\mathbf{V}_{\mathbf{R}}^{\text{theo}}$ is an $m \times 1$ vector of the theoretical Rayleigh wave phase velocities, m is the number of dispersion points (phase velocities versus frequency), and $\|\cdot\|$ denotes the *Euclidean* norm of a vector. Forward modeling of the dispersion curves is based on Knopoff's method (Schwab and Knopoff, 1972).

The algorithm is terminated at the 300th iteration in our inversion procedure or when the error misfit reaches a certain previously fixed value.

4. Synthetic data inversion

To examine and evaluate the efficiency and stability of the pattern search algorithm, three synthetic earth models are used. These models are designed to simulate situations commonly encountered in shallow engineering site investigations. As shown in Table 1, Model A, which consists of one homogeneous layer lying over a half-space with downwardly increasing S-wave velocities, represents a simple two-layer geologic structure. Model B (Table 2) with three layers over a half-space represents a simple multilayer ground condition. Model C (Table 3), characterized by four layers lying over a half-space with a 2-m-thick low velocity layer between two higher S-wave velocity layers, models a real complex subsurface structure actually analyzed and validated on a roadbed test site in Henan, China (Song et al., 2006).

Layer Number	S-wave velocity (m/s)	P-wave velocity (m/s)	Density (g/cm³)	Thickness (m)
1	200	416	1.8	6
Half-space	500	1041	2.0	Infinite

Table 1. Model A. Earth model parameters of one layer over a half-space.

Layer Number	S-wave velocity (m/s)	P-wave velocity (m/s)	Density (g/cm³)	Thickness (m)
1	200	416	1.8	2
2	250	520	1.8	4
3	300	625	1.8	6
Half-space	400	833	1.8	Infinite

Table 2. Model B. Earth model parameters of three layers over a half-space.

Layer Number	S-wave velocity (m/s)	P-wave velocity (m/s)	Density (g/cm³)	Thickness (m)
1	200	346	1.8	2
2	150	765	1.8	2
3	200	663	1.8	4
4	300	995	1.8	4
Half-space	400	1327	1.8	Infinite

Table 3. Model C. Earth model parameters of four layers over a half-space.

In the current analysis, a commonly used frequency range of 5-100 Hz (30 data points) was employed. Fig. 1 shows modeled fundamental-mode dispersion curves from all these three synthetic models.

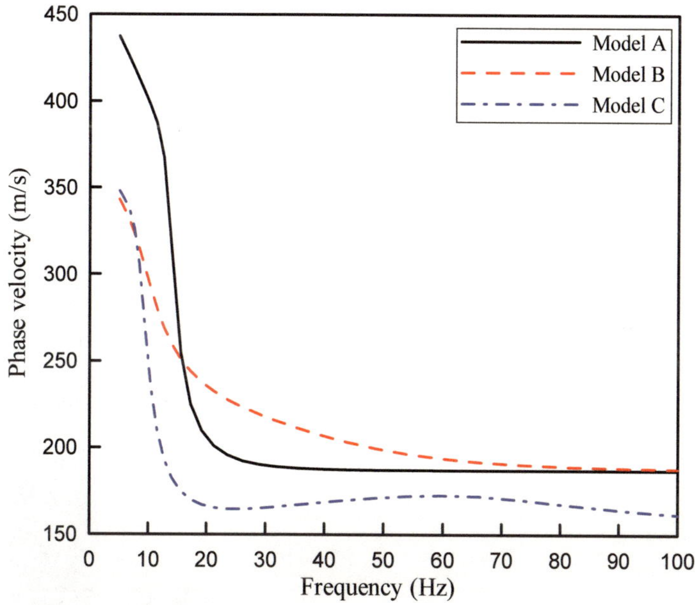

Fig. 1. Modeled fundamental-mode dispersion curves from Model A (solid line), Model B (dashed line), and Model C (dashed-and-dotted line).

4.1 Two-layer model

Fig. 2 demonstrates inversion results of the simple two-layer model (Model A) using the pattern search algorithm, which provide valuable insight into the performance of the proposed inversion scheme. Initial S-wave velocities are all 300 m/s for the layer and half-space, which are estimated by Eq. (1). Other inversion parameters have been mentioned in preceding section.

The convergence curve in Fig. 2a illustrates a typical characteristic of a pattern search algorithm. It shows a very fast initial convergence at the first 10 iterations, followed by progressively slower improvements as it approaches the optimal solution. Fig. 2b shows the mesh size at each iteration. The mesh size increases after each successful iteration and decreases after each unsuccessful one. The best point does not change after an unsuccessful poll. For example, the poll at iteration 1 is unsuccessful. As a result, the algorithm halves the mesh size with contraction factor set to 0.5. We can see that the objective function value computed at iteration 2 is less than the value at iteration 1 (Fig. 2a), which indicates the poll at iteration 2 is successful. Thus, the algorithm doubles the mesh size with expansion factor set to 2 (Fig. 2b). Clearly, the poll at iteration 3 is unsuccessful. As a result, the function value remains unchanged from iteration 2 and the mesh size is halved. The inverse process is terminated after 20 iterations because the error misfit converged to approximately zero. As shown in Fig. 2c, in 20 iterations the pattern search algorithm only performs approximately 58 function evaluations to locate the promising region in the solution space containing the global minima. For this simple model, The S-wave velocities are exactly resolved (Fig. 2d). In practice, the two-layer model may be useful for estimation of static correction (Xia et al., 1999).

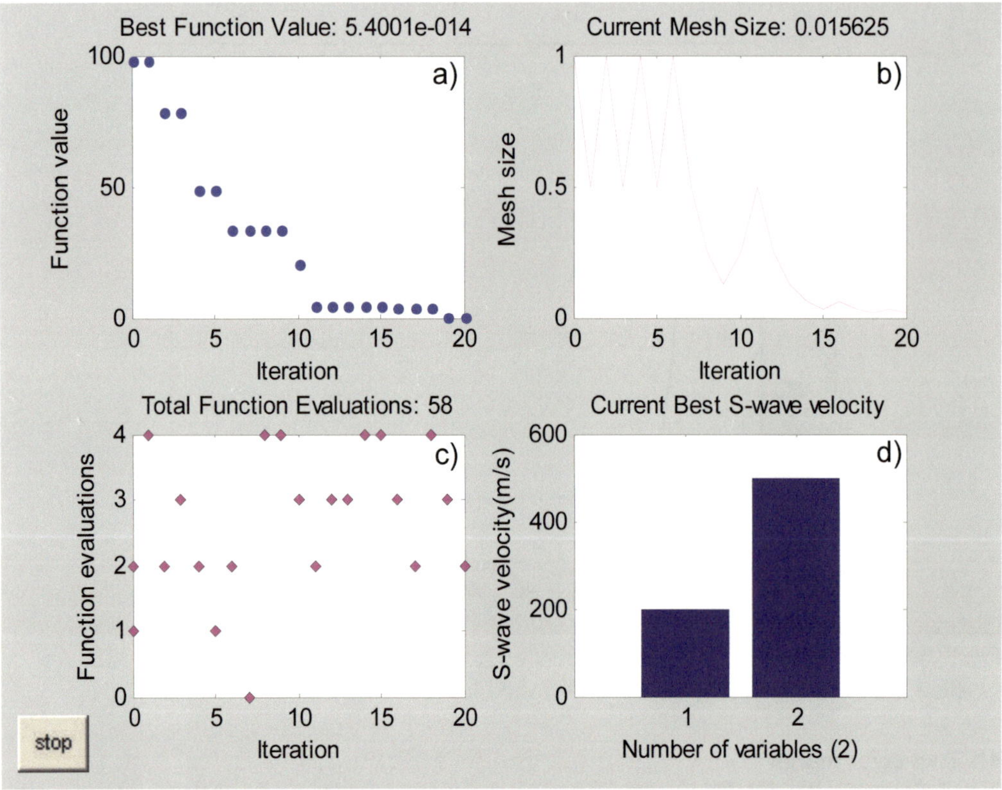

Fig. 2. Inversion results of Model A using pattern search algorithms. (a) The objective function value of the best point obtained at each iteration. (b) Mesh size as a function of iterations. (c) The number of function evaluations performed at each iteration. (d) Inverted S-wave velocities.

4.2 Multilayer models

The multilayer model (Model B) will help us to compare the performance of the algorithm with Model A. Initial S-wave velocities are all 250 m/s for the 4-layer model. Fig.3 illustrates inversion results of Model B using the proposed algorithm. Similar to Fig. 2, the objective function values improve rapidly at the first 20 iterations and then level off at the next 20 iterations (Fig. 3a). The small misfit suggests that the algorithm found the global minimum. However, it should be noted that the algorithm stops after 40 iterations. In 40 iterations the pattern search algorithm implements approximately 269 function evaluations (Fig. 3c) to search for the global optimal solution (Fig. 3d). The implementation gives the evidence that Model B is relatively more complex than Model A, as can be further verified by the fact that the maximum number (8) of function evaluations in each iterative process in Fig. 3c is greater than that (4) in Fig. 2c. Nonetheless, S-wave velocities are still accurately reconstructed (Fig. 3d).

The proposed inversion scheme is further tested on the complex multilayer model (Model C). Initial S-wave velocities are also 250 m/s for each layer of this complex model. Fig. 4 demonstrates inversion results of Model C using the pattern search algorithm. As can be seen in Fig. 4a, the misfit value decreased rapidly in the first 40 iterations and then gradually in the next 40 iterations. As expected, the algorithm stops after a larger number of iterations (80 in this inversion). In 80 iterations the algorithm carried out 677 function evaluations to discover the most promising domains for a good valley. Moreover, we should notice that the maximum number (10) of function evaluations during each implementation in Fig. 4c is greater than the number (8) in Fig. 3c, indicating that Model C is more complex than Model B. It is encouraging that S-wave velocities for all layers of Model C are still unambiguously imaged (Fig. 4d). The low velocity layer is well depicted.

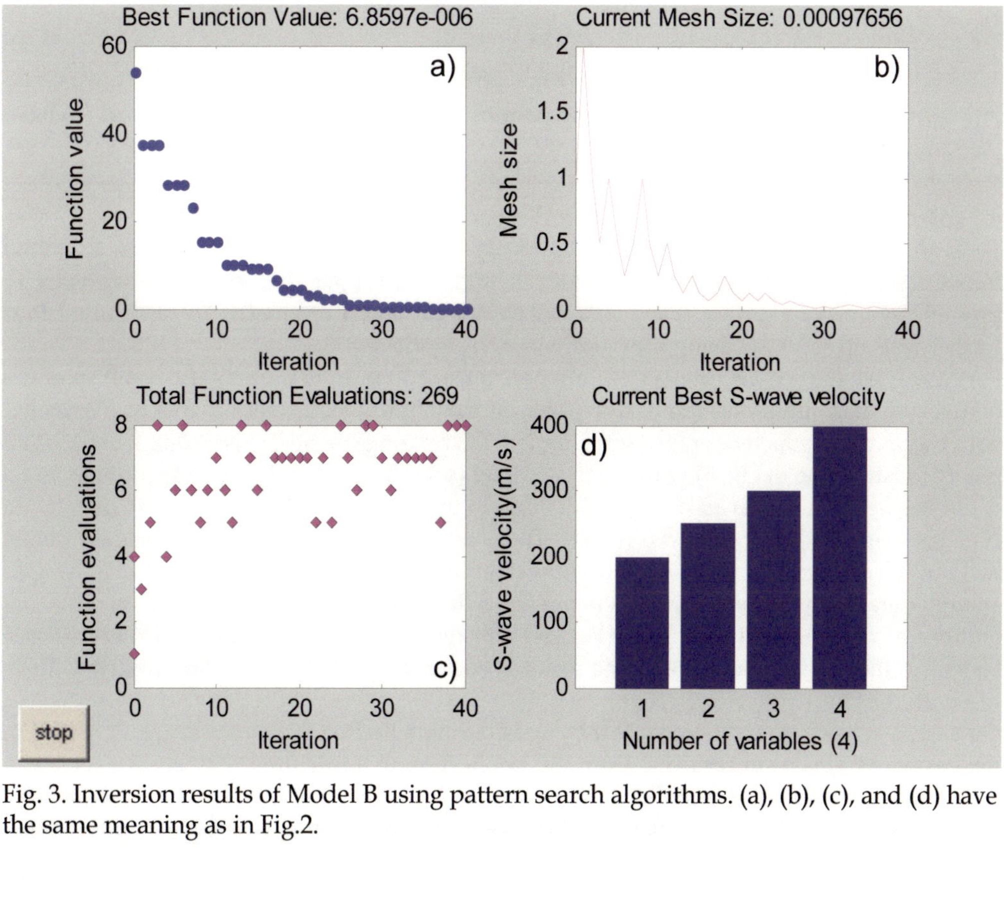

Fig. 3. Inversion results of Model B using pattern search algorithms. (a), (b), (c), and (d) have the same meaning as in Fig.2.

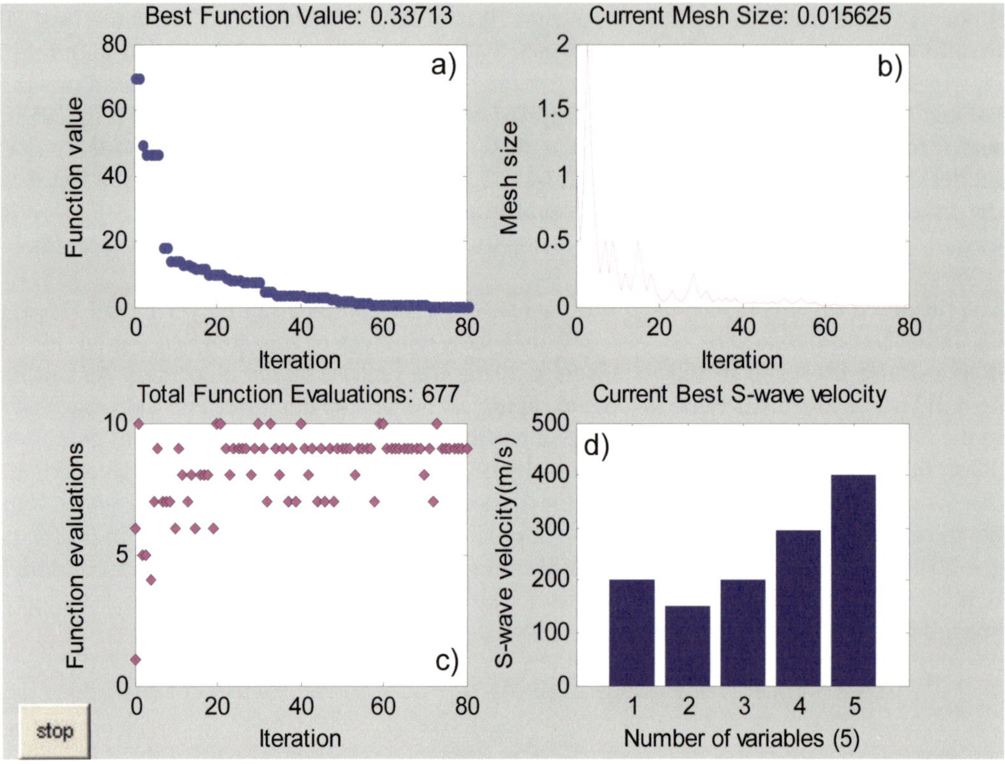

Fig. 4. Inversion results of Model C using pattern search algorithms. (a), (b), (c), and (d) have the same meaning as in Fig. 2.

4.3 Effects of four different aspects on the performance of the algorithm

To evaluate the influences of four different aspects (the number of data points, a limited frequency range, errors in P-wave velocities and density, and the initial S-wave velocity profile) involved in surface wave analysis on the proposed approach, we performed four further tests on Model C using the pattern search algorithm.

For case 1, we reduce the number of data points from 30 to 15 to investigate the effect of the number of data points on the performance of the algorithm. Inversion was implemented with the same parameters previously adopted. Comparing the inversion result from 15 data points (dashed line in Fig. 5) with the true model (solid line in Fig. 5), there appears to be no decreases in accuracy because of the reduction in the number of data points and visually no changes compared with the true model. Thus, we remark that the number of data points will not have a significant influence on implementation of the proposed algorithm as long as enough data points have uniformly encountered the depths of interest. Usually, an excessive number of data points (more than needed) will require more computational time without benefit to the inversion accuracy. The result is consistent with previous findings (Rix, 1988; Xia et al., 1999).

For case 2, we performed another test by considering a limited frequency range. In practice, the frequency spectrum resulting from the application of a low-frequency source such as a sledgehammer over unconsolidated sediments often suffers from lack of high frequencies (Dal Moro et al., 2007). We have experienced this situation a number of times when processing surface wave data. Fig. 5 shows the S-wave velocity profile inverted when only a frequency range of 5-50 Hz is used (dashed-and-dotted line). As can be seen, the solution does not significantly differ from the true model. Values in the shallower portion, however, appear somehow less precise.

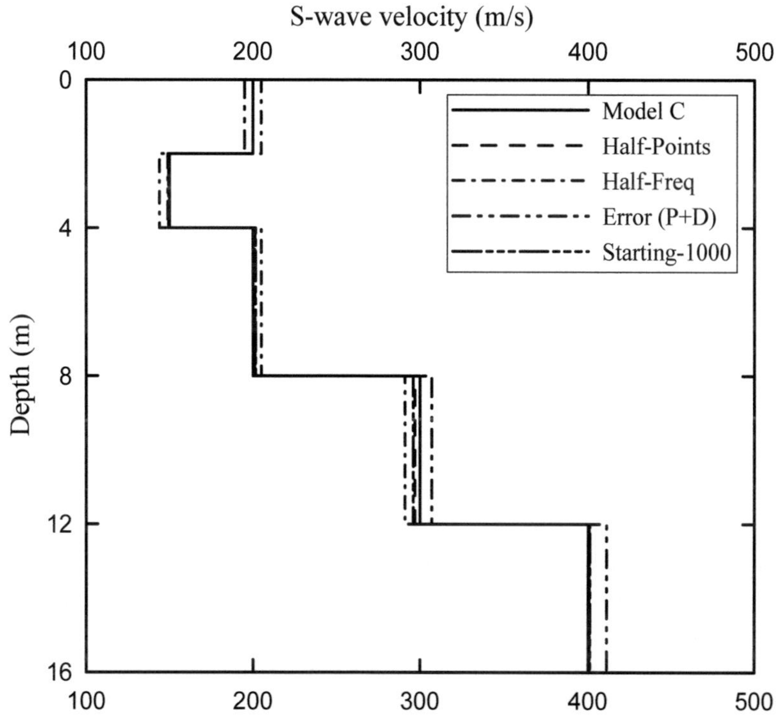

Fig. 5. Effects of the number of data points, limited frequency range, errors in P-wave velocities and density, and the starting point on inversion results of Model C using pattern search algorithms.

For case 3, we introduce a 25% random error generated by a uniform distribution in both P-wave velocities and density to test the performance of the algorithm in more realistic conditions. In the real world, estimation errors in P-wave velocities and density always exist, especially for situations in which no a priori information is available. Fig. 5 illustrates the retrieved S-wave velocity profile for this case (dashed-and-dotted-dotted line). Clearly, S-wave velocities for the first three layers are well delineated. The maximum error occurs at layer 5, which is 3%. This test has also given support to our inversion choice and the suggestion by Xia et al. (1999) that it is impossible to invert Rayleigh wave dispersion curve for P-wave velocities and density.

For case 4, we study the effect of the starting point X0 on the calculation efficiency and stability of the proposed inversion procedure. It is well known that local optimization methods are prone to being trapped at local minima, and their success depends heavily on the choice of a good starting model. Our modeling results demonstrate that pattern search methods have features that make them less likely to be trapped by spurious local minimizers than do methods that use derivatives. For this reason we are using pattern search algorithm as a global optimization technique. How does the choice of a starting point influence the performance of the algorithm? In the following test, let us consider an extreme value 1000 m/s for all layers as an initial point at which the pattern search algorithm starts the optimization, which is approximately 300% off the maximum phase velocity of the true model. It is important to notice that the excessive choice of a starting point does not compromise the accurate reconstruction of the retrieved model and no visual differences can be found (dashed-dotted-dotted-dotted line in Fig. 5). Predictably, a much larger number of iterations (120) and more function evaluations (828) are taken for the algorithm to converge (Fig. 6). However, our testing results show that, for the extreme initial value of 1000 m/s, local optimization techniques such as Levenberg-Marquardt (Xia et al., 1999) and Occam's algorithm (Lai et al., 2002) did not converge.

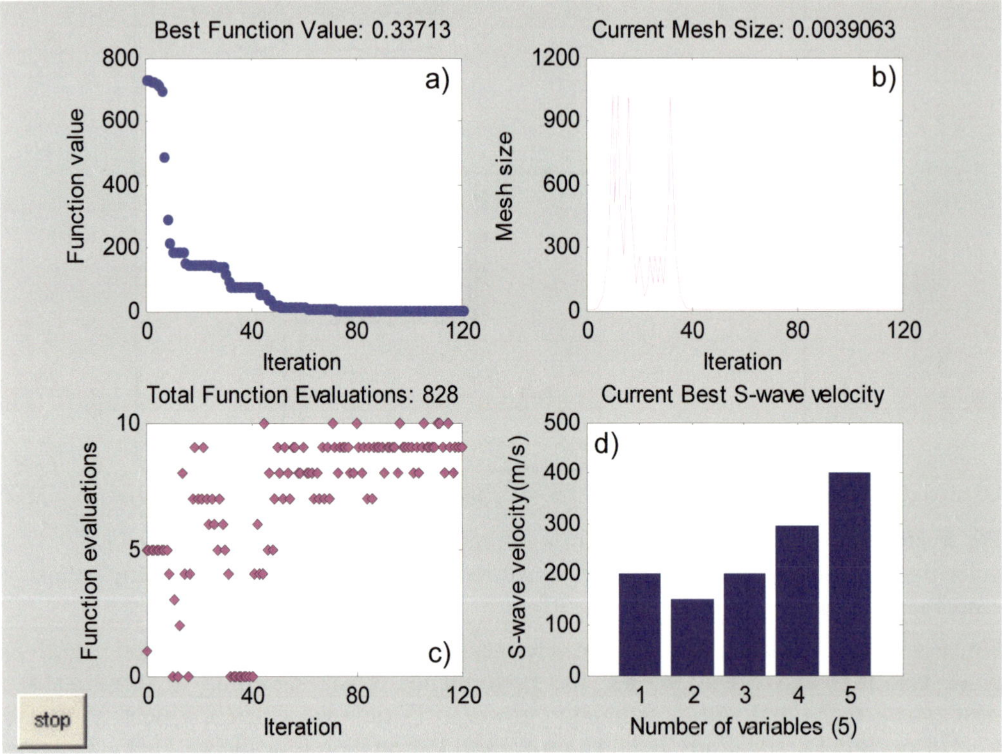

Fig. 6. Inversion results of Model C using pattern search algorithms with extreme initial S-wave velocities of 1000 m/s for all layers. (a), (b), (c), and (d) have the same meaning as in Fig.2.

4.4 Effects of the number of layers and their thicknesses on the algorithm

In practice, the number of layers and their thicknesses may not be always a priori known in subsurface studies. In such situations it may be necessary to overparameterize the vertical profile with a larger number of thin layers. But how would the algorithm behave in this case? To further examine the performance of the algorithm in this realistic condition, we invert Model A again with a 6-layer model, each thin layer being 1.2 m thick. Initial S-wave velocities are all 300 m/s for the new 6-layer model. It is exciting that the two-layer model is still unambiguously resolved although we subdivide the two-layer subsurface into six thin layers

(Fig. 7d). As expected, the algorithm stops after a larger number of iterations (120 in this inversion) (Fig. 7a). In 120 iterations the algorithm performs 1185 function evaluations (Fig. 7c) to discover the most promising domains for a good valley. It should be pointed out that the sampling of the measured phase velocity curve provides the vertical resolution. With a large number of thin layers, a narrow sampling of the dispersion curve is necessary to resolve the S-wave velocity in each layer. We adopt a narrow sampling (120 dispersion points) to resolve the S-wave velocity in each layer in this inversion. However, we should also realize that, for any noisy data, we have to make a trade-off between the resolution and error of an inverted model, to obtain stable results. We can reduce the error in the deduced S-wave velocity model by reducing the resolution of the retrieved model (increasing thicknesses of layers).

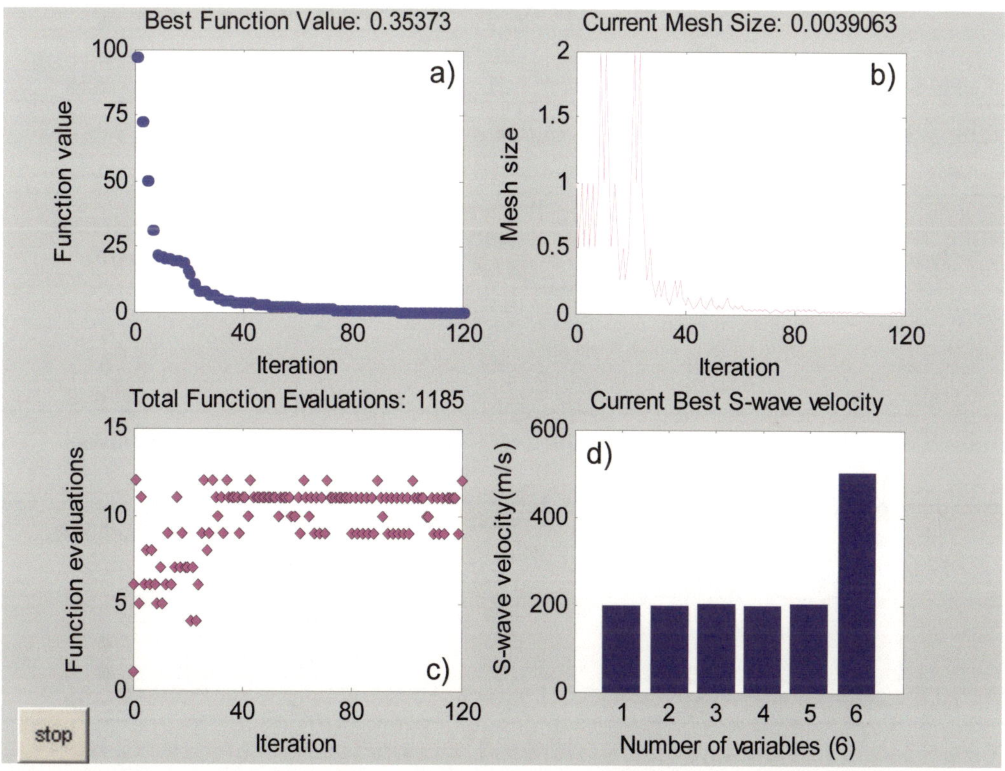

Fig. 7. Inversion results of Model A using a pattern search algorithm with a 6-layer model, each thin layer being 1.2 m thick. (a), (b), (c), and (d) have the same meaning as in Fig. 2.

5. Effects of different inversion strategies on performance of the algorithm

GPS Positive Basis 2N and GPS Positive Basis N+1 are two commonly used inversion strategies in pattern search algorithms. They are the generalized pattern search (GPS) algorithm with the maximal positive basis set 2N vectors and the minimal positive basis set N+1 vectors, respectively, where N is the number of independent variables (which in our case involve S-wave velocities) in the optimization problem. The strategies use fixed direction vectors to define the pattern and compute the set of points forming the mesh.

To investigate and evaluate effects of the above described two inversion strategies on the performance of pattern search algorithms, three synthetic earth models are used. These models are designed to simulate situations commonly encountered in shallow engineering site investigations. As shown in Table 4, Model D represents a multilayer geologic structure with downwardly increasing S-wave velocities. Model E (Table 5) with a soft layer trapped between two stiff layers models a real complex pavement structure containing a low velocity layer. Model F (Table 6), characterized by a stiff layer sandwiched between two soft layers, simulates a multilayer ground condition containing a high velocity layer.

Layer Number	S-wave velocity (m/s)	P-wave velocity (m/s)	Density (g/cm^3)	Thickness (m)
1	200	735	1.9	2
2	250	919	1.9	4
3	300	1102	1.9	6
Half-space	400	1470	1.9	Infinite

Table 4. Model D: A four-layer model with downwardly increasing S-wave velocities

Layer Number	S-wave velocity (m/s)	P-wave velocity (m/s)	Density (g/cm^3)	Thickness (m)
1	200	611	1.9	2
2	160	673	1.9	4
3	260	1093	1.9	6
Half-space	400	1681	1.9	Infinite

Table 5. Model E: A four-layer model with a soft layer trapped between two stiff layers

Layer Number	S-wave velocity (m/s)	P-wave velocity (m/s)	Density (g/cm^3)	Thickness (m)
1	120	441	1.9	2
2	250	919	1.9	4
3	200	1020	1.9	6
Half-space	400	1470	1.9	Infinite

Table 6. Model F: A four-layer model with a stiff layer sandwiched between two soft layers

Fig.8 demonstrates inversion results of Model D using GPS Positive Basis 2N. During the inversion procedure, we set the initial mesh size at 1, expansion factor at 2, and contraction factor at 0.5. The convergence curve in Fig. 8a illustrates a typical characteristic of a pattern search algorithm. It shows a very fast initial convergence at the first 20 iterations, followed by progressively slower improvements as it approaches the optimal solution. Fig. 8b shows the mesh size at each iteration. The mesh size is doubled after each successful iteration and is halved after each unsuccessful one. The best point does not change after an unsuccessful poll. The inverse process is terminated after 36 iterations because the error misfit converged to zero. As shown in Fig. 8c, in 36 iterations the algorithm performs approximately 252 function evaluations to locate the promising region in the solution space containing the global minima. For this four-layer model, the S-wave velocities are exactly resolved (Fig. 8d). The relative errors between the inverted S-wave velocities and the true model (Table 4) are zero.

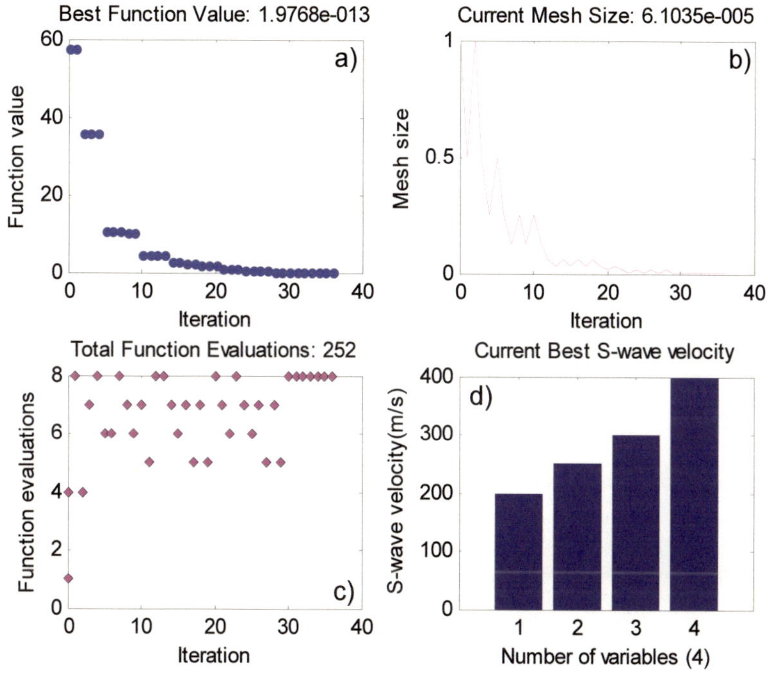

Fig. 8. Inversion results of Model D using GPS Positive Basis 2N. (a), (b), (c), and (d) have the same meaning as in Fig. 2.

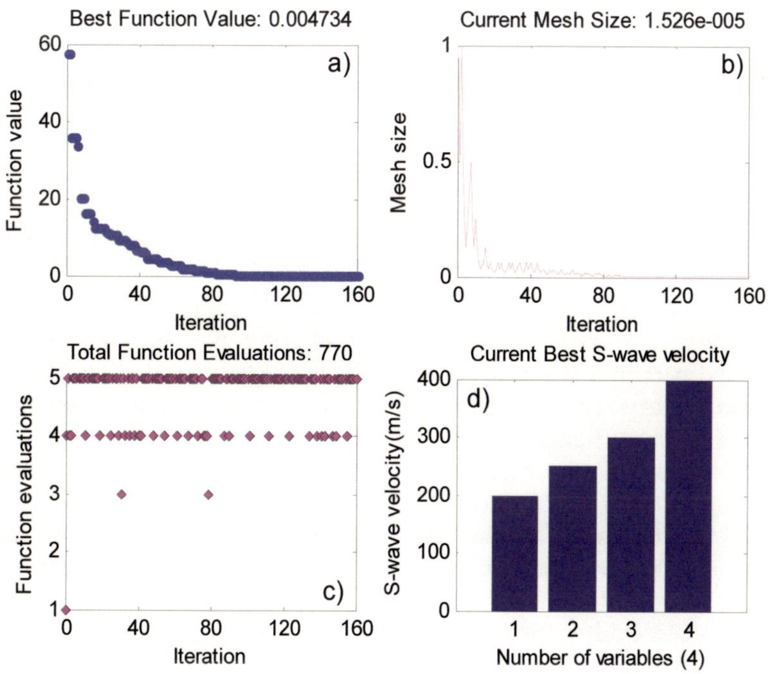

Fig. 9. Inversion results of Model D using GPS Positive Basis N+1. (a), (b), (c), and (d) have the same meaning as in Fig. 2.

Fig.9 illustrates inversion results of Model D using GPS Positive Basis N+1 with the same inversion parameters described above. As shown in Fig. 9a, the misfit value decreased rapidly in the first 80 iterations and then gradually in the next 80 iterations. The algorithm stops after a larger number of iterations (160 in this inversion). In 160 iterations the algorithm carried out 770 function evaluations (Fig. 9c) to discover the most promising domains containing the global minima (Fig. 9d).
Figs.10 and 11 show inversion results of Model E using the above mentioned two inversion strategies with the same inversion parameters described above, respectively. Figs.12 and 13 report inversion results of Model F using the two inversion strategies, respectively. We can draw the same conclusion as Figs. 8 and 9 by analyzing Figs. 10-13.

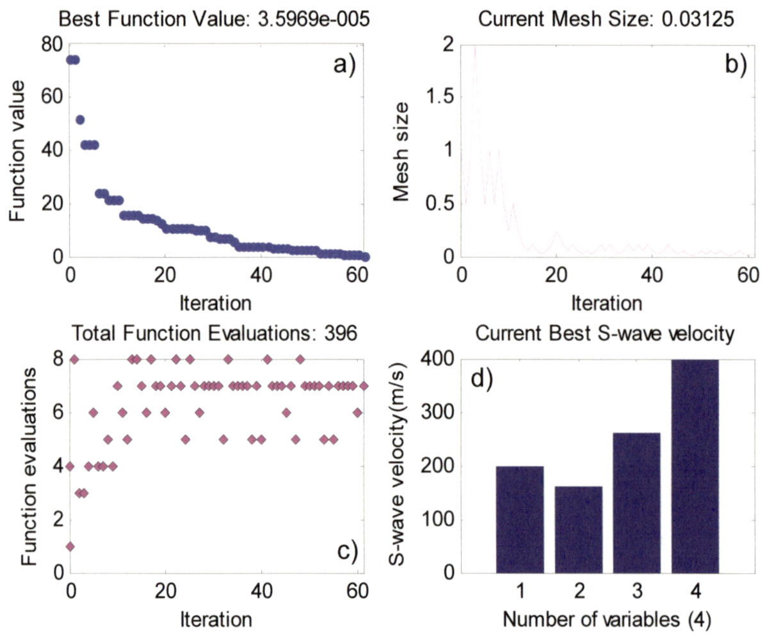

Fig. 10. Inversion results of Model E using GPS Positive Basis 2N. (a), (b), (c), and (d) have the same meaning as in Fig. 2.

Comparing Fig. 8 with Fig. 9, Fig. 10 with Fig. 11, and Fig. 12 with Fig. 13, provides valuable insights into the performance of the above mentioned two inversion strategies. We understand that a pattern search might sometimes run faster using GPS Positive basis N+1 as the inversion strategy because the algorithm searches fewer points at each iteration (the maximum number of function evaluations is 5 in Figs. 9, 11 and 13c). However, as can be seen in Figs. 9, 11 and 13, the strategy, especially when it is applied to complex global optimization problems of highly nonlinear, multiparameter, and multimodal objective functions, might suffer from the high computational cost (770, 1200, and 948 function evaluations in Figs. 9, 11, and 13c, respectively) due to its slow convergence and its wandering near the global minimum in the final stage of search. In contrast, although the strategy based on GPS Positive Basis 2N can make the pattern search run longer because of exploring more points at each iteration (the maximum number of function evaluations is 8 in Figs. 8, 10 and 12c), this enables the algorithm to effectively locate the promising areas in the solution space containing the global minima by looking in more directions at each

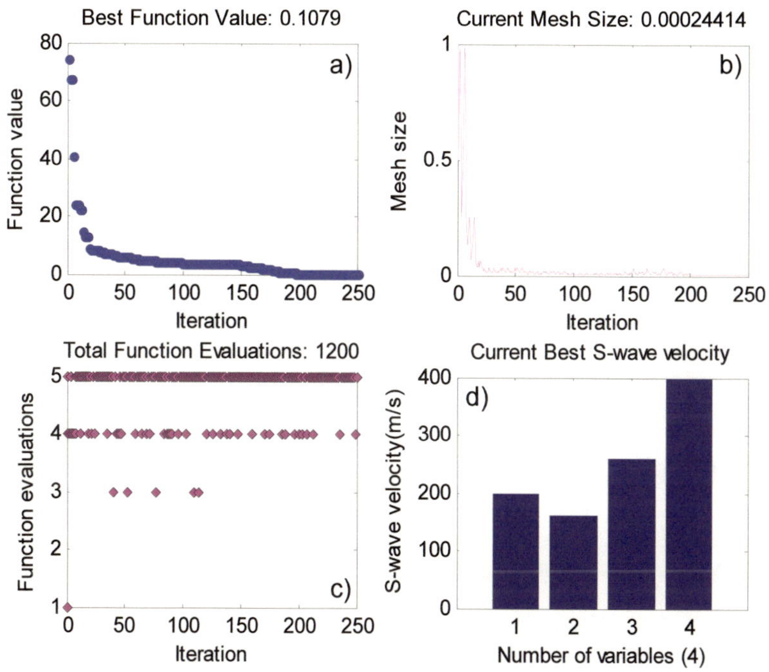

Fig. 11. Inversion results of Model E using GPS Positive Basis N+1. (a), (b), (c), and (d) have the same meaning as in Fig.2.

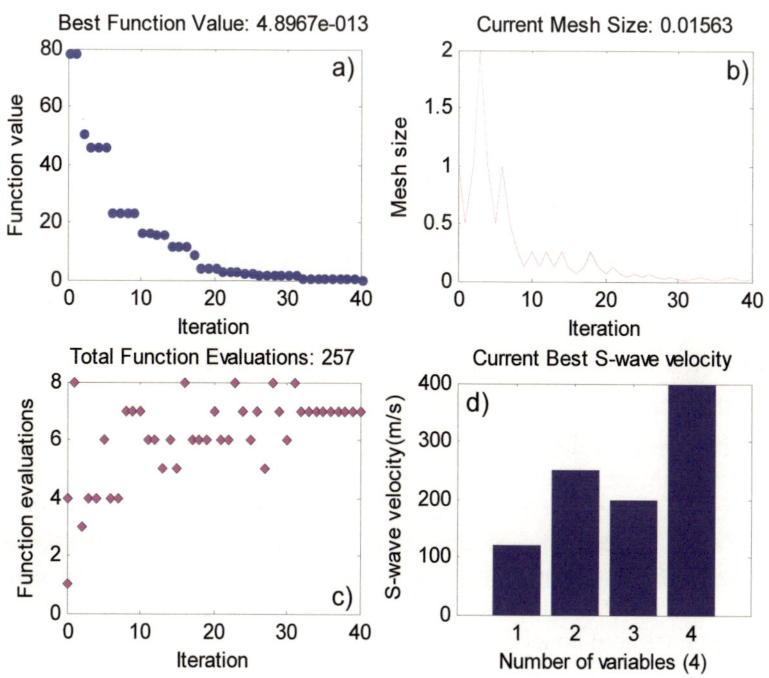

Fig. 12. Inversion results of Model F using GPS Positive Basis 2N. (a), (b), (c), and (d) have the same meaning as in Fig. 2.

iteration and thereby potentially reduces the computational effort (252, 396, and 257 function evaluations in Figs. 8, 10 and 12c, respectively) due to its faster convergence at the neighborhood of the global minimum in the final stage of exploratory moves. For example, using GPS Positive Basis 2N as the inversion strategy reduces the total function count – the number of times the objective function was evaluated – by almost 68 percent.

Therefore, unless otherwise noted, we will use GPS Positive Basis 2N as the inversion strategy in all of the latter tests because the strategy is preferable to that based on GPS Positive Basis N+1 for solving highly nonlinear global optimization problems.

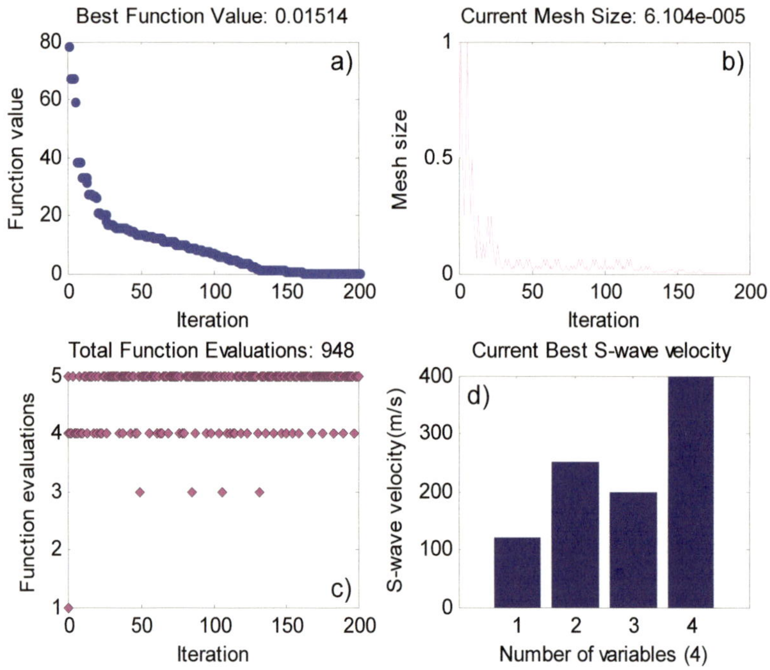

Fig. 13. Inversion results of Model F using GPS Positive Basis N+1. (a), (b), (c), and (d) have the same meaning as in Fig.2.

6. Effects of initial mesh size and final mesh size on performance of the algorithm

The initial mesh size Δ_0 is the length of the shortest vector from the initial point $\mathbf{X}_0$ to a mesh point. Δ_0 should be a positive scalar. To scale the initial mesh size correctly, we take some experimentation using Model D. Table 7 reports effects of five different initial mesh sizes (1, 2, 4, 8, and 16) on the performance of the algorithm. For each experimentation, results from the first 8 iterations are listed. During the trials, we set the expansion factor at 2 and contraction factor at 0.5. As shown in Table 7, an excessive large Δ_0 will require more computational time without benefit to the implementation of the algorithm. Clearly, the first successful poll occurs when the initial mesh size equals to 0.5. Thus, setting the initial mesh size at 0.5 should be considered good in the current study. This choice is also justified by the fact that the computation time and efficiency are improved in our latter tests.

Iter	Δ_0 =1		Δ_0 =2		Δ_0 =4		Δ_0 =8		Δ_0 =16	
. No	f(x)	Δ_k	f(x)	Δ_k	f(x)	Δ_k	f(x)	Δ_k	f(x)	Δ_k
0	57.74	1	57.74	2	57.74	4	57.74	8	57.74	16
1	57.74	0.5	57.74	1	57.74	2	57.74	4	57.74	8
2	36.00	1	57.74	0.5	57.74	1	57.74	2	57.74	4
3	36.00	0.5	36.00	1	57.74	0.5	57.74	1	57.74	2
4	36.00	0.25	36.00	0.5	36.00	1	57.74	0.5	57.74	1
5	10.51	0.5	36.00	0.25	36.00	0.5	36.00	1	57.74	0.5
6	10.51	0.25	10.51	0.5	36.00	0.25	36.00	0.5	36.00	1
7	10.51	0.125	10.51	0.25	10.51	0.5	36.00	0.25	36.00	0.5
8	10.39	0.25	10.51	0.125	10.51	0.25	10.51	0.5	36.00	0.25

Table 7. Effects of different initial mesh sizes on performance of pattern search algorithm.

7. Effects of expansion factor and contraction factor on performance of the algorithm

The expansion factor and contraction factor control how much the mesh size is expanded or contracted at each iteration. The multilayer model (Model D) will help us to investigate the influences of expansion factor and contraction factor on the performance of the proposed inversion procedure.

Fig. 14 demonstrates effects of expansion factor on the performance of the pattern search algorithm. During the inversion procedure, we set the initial mesh size at 0.5, which is suggested in the preceding section, expansion factor at 1, and contraction factor at 0.5, which means the pattern search multiplies the mesh size by 1 after each successful poll (i.e., not allow expansions) and multiplies the mesh size by 0.5 after each unsuccessful poll. Comparing the inversion results from Fig. 14 with the inversion results from Fig. 8, there appears to be no differences in accuracy. However, forcing the steps to be non-increasing (Fig. 14) can make the pattern search converge faster and further avoid its wandering near the global minimum in the final stage of exploratory moves. For example, the procedure with expansion factor set to 1 (not allowing expansions) reduces the total function evaluations from 252 (Fig. 8c) to 125 (Fig. 14c), which is almost 50 percent, and reduces the number of iterations from 36 to 17. Furthermore, note that at the first iteration the pattern search performs a successful poll (Fig. 14a) by scaling the initial mesh size correctly, as can be further verified in our latter tests.

Thus, we remark that the expansion steps are often a waste of computational effort. If an initial mesh size can be scaled correctly (which may take some experimentation), then there is rarely any advantage to aggressively allowing expansions. This is particularly true as the algorithm converges and the final mesh size should go to zero. As this occurs the expansion steps usually yield very little improvement and make the algorithm wander at the neighborhood of the global minimum.

Fig. 15 demonstrates how contraction factor affects the behavior of the pattern search. During the inversion procedure, we set the initial mesh size at 0.5, expansion factor at 1, and contraction factor at 0.25. As can be seen, the mesh size decreases faster with contraction factor set to 0.25 (Fig. 15b), as compared with the above value of 0.5 (Fig. 14b), and the deduced solution (Fig. 15d) does not differ from the true model. The approach, however, takes somewhat longer (157 function evaluations in Fig. 15c) to locate that best solution. Although not being addressed in this analysis, the same is true when the contraction factor is set to 0.75, as compared with the value of 0.5.

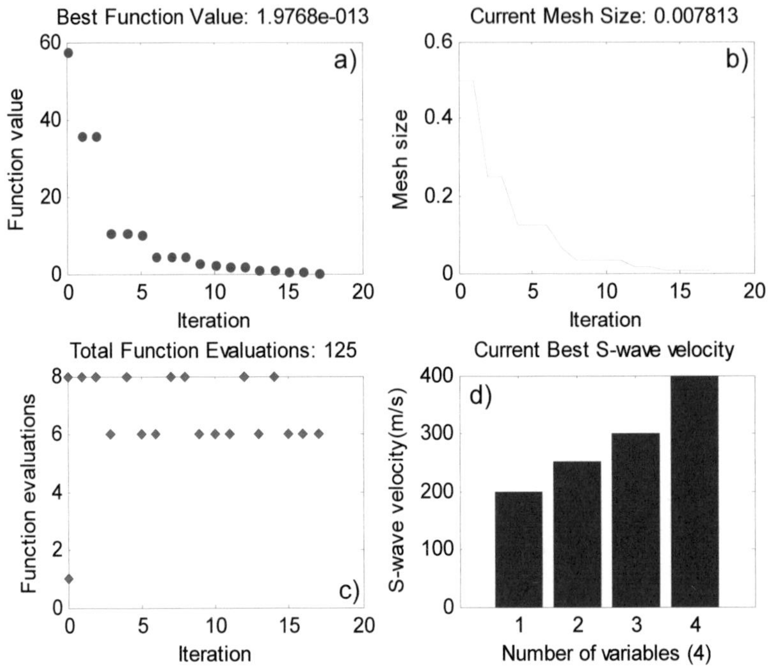

Fig. 14. Effects of expansion factor on performance of pattern search algorithm. (a), (b), (c), and (d) have the same meaning as in Fig. 2.

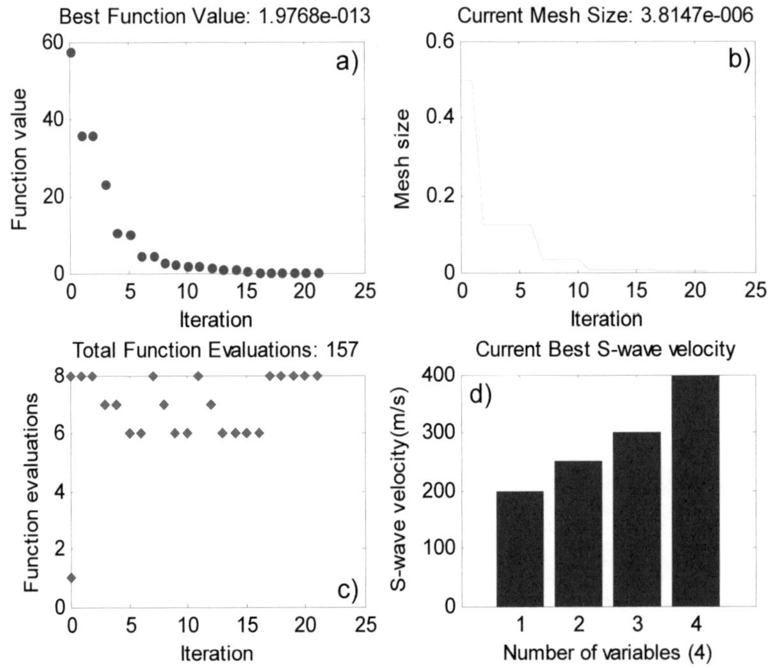

Fig. 15. Effects of contraction factor on performance of pattern search algorithm. (a), (b), (c), and (d) have the same meaning as in Fig. 2.

Therefore, we conclude that it is a wise strategy to continue the implementation of the algorithm with steps of the same magnitude until no further decrease in the objective function is realized, at which point the step size should be halved. This corresponds to setting expansion factor $\Lambda = 1$ and contraction factor $\theta = 1/2$. The insights issued in this section also give support to previous findings (Torczon, 1997; Lewis and Torczon, 1999).

8. Effects of inclusion of noise in surface wave data on performance of the algorithm

In practice, picked surface wave phase velocities are inevitably noisy. To further examine and evaluate effects of inclusion of noise in surface wave data on the performance of the algorithm, we introduced a 10% random error generated by a uniform distribution in surface wave phase velocities of three four-layer models (solid dots in Figs. 16, 18, and 20). Noise that had an amplitude of 10% of the phase velocity were added at each frequency.

The performance of the proposed inversion scheme in this realistic condition is illustrated in Figs. 17, 19, and 21, respectively. During the inversion procedure, we adopt the parameters suggested by the above insights. We set the initial mesh size at 0.5, expansion factor at 1, and contraction factor at 0.5. Dashed lines in Figs. 16, 18, and 20 display initial S-wave velocities used in the inverse process.

As shown in Figs. 17a, 19a, and 21a, the misfit values significantly decrease in the first 10 iterations, and then gradually converge to a similar constant value, which suggests that the algorithm has completed the exploration for the global minimum. As the algorithm converges and approaches the optimal solution, the final mesh size quickly goes to zero (Figs. 17b, 19b, and 21b). The inverse process is terminated after 19, 38, and 30 iterations, respectively, to prevent transferring errors in data into the desired models. Because of a correct choice for the inversion parameters, the algorithm performs only 137, 266, and 204 function evaluations (Figs. 17c, 19c, and 21c), respectively, to search for the global minima. Figs. 17d, 19d, and 21d report the best solutions of the implementation. It can be noted that

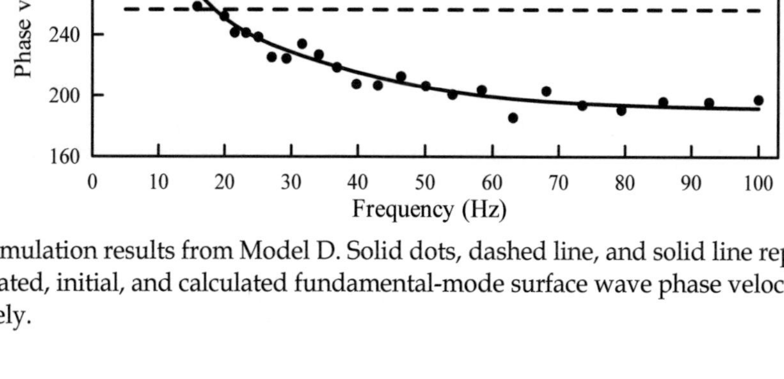

Fig. 16. Simulation results from Model D. Solid dots, dashed line, and solid line represent contaminated, initial, and calculated fundamental-mode surface wave phase velocities, respectively.

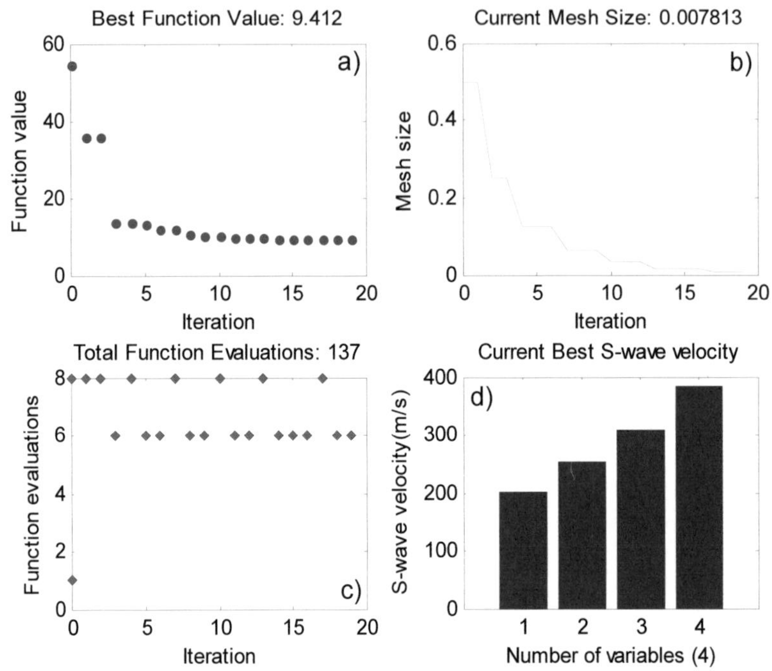

Fig. 17. Effects of inclusion of noise in surface wave data from Model D on performance of pattern search algorithm. (a), (b), (c), and (d) have the same meaning as in Fig. 2.

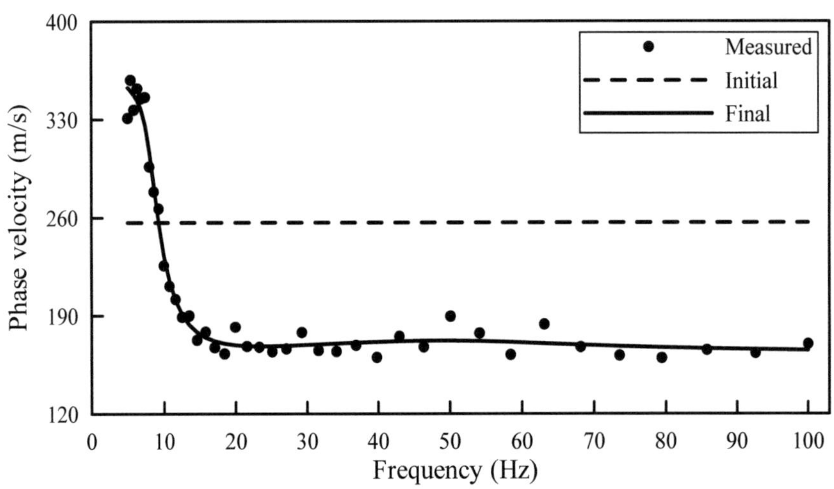

Fig. 18. Simulation results from Model E. Solid dots, dashed line, and solid line represent contaminated, initial, and calculated fundamental-mode surface wave phase velocities, respectively.

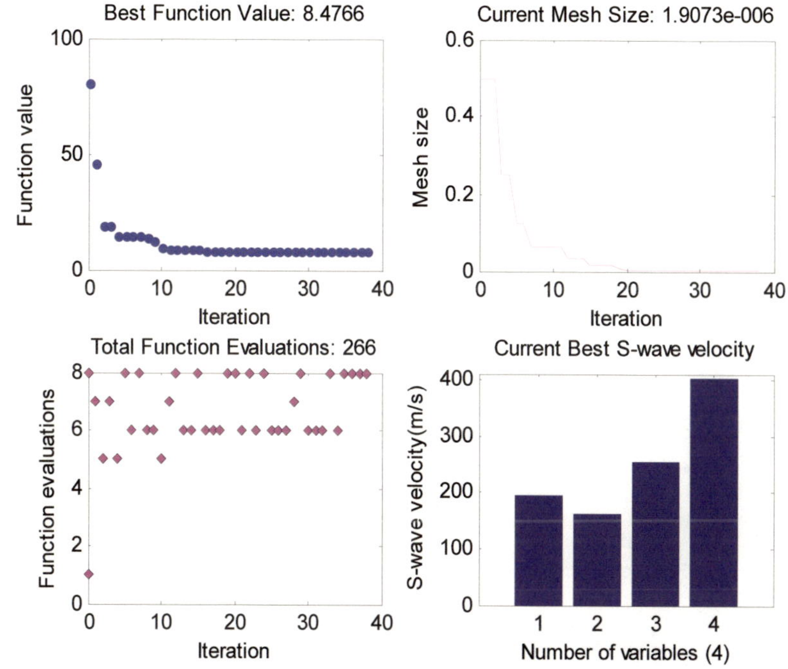

Fig. 19. Effects of inclusion of noise in surface wave data from Model E on performance of pattern search algorithm. (a), (b), (c), and (d) have the same meaning as in Fig. 2.

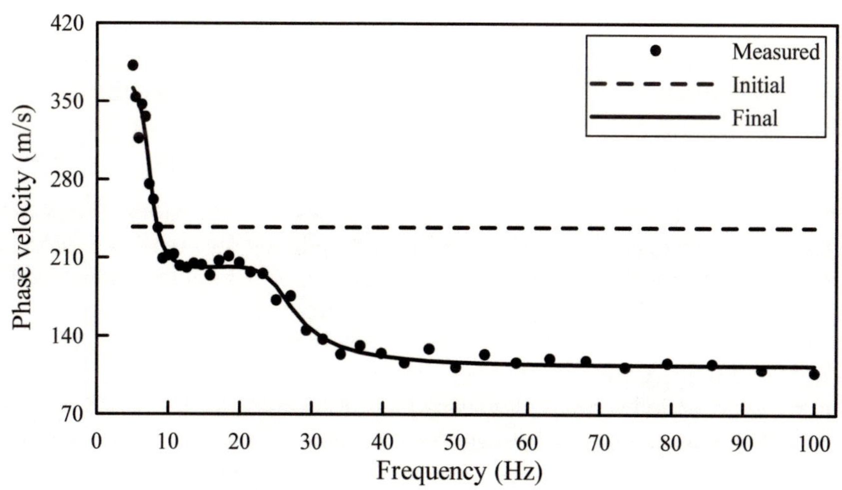

Fig. 20. Simulation results from Model F. Solid dots, dashed line, and solid line represent contaminated, initial, and calculated fundamental-mode surface wave phase velocities, respectively.

S-wave velocities for the first three layers of three four-layer models are well delineated, and the relative errors are all not more than 3%. Maximum errors occur at layer 4, which are approximately 4%. The modeled dispersion curves (solid line in Figs. 16, 18, and 20) from the best solutions (Figs. 17d, 19d, and 21d) also fit the measured phase velocities (solid dots in Figs. 16, 18, and 20) reasonably well.
So, we realize that pattern search algorithms possess stronger immunity with respect to noise and should be considered good not only in terms of accuracy but also in terms of computation effort when they are applied to high-frequency surface wave inversion.

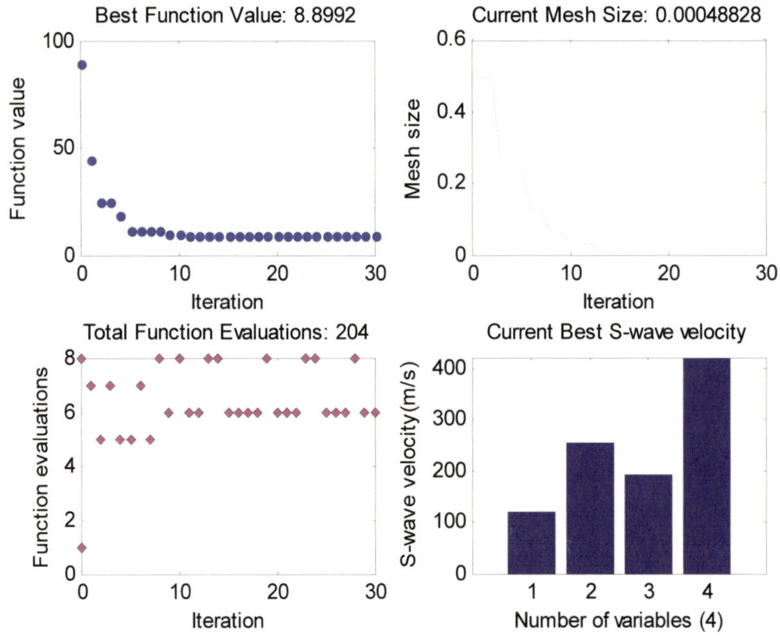

Fig. 21. Effects of inclusion of noise in surface wave data from Model F on performance of pattern search algorithm. (a), (b), (c), and (d) have the same meaning as in Fig. 2.

9. Comparison between pattern search algorithms and genetic algorithms

Pattern search methods proceed by conducting a series of exploratory moves about the current iteration before declaring a new iteration and updating the associated information. It is important to point out that all of the final solutions in our tests are determined by one computation instead of the average model derived from multiple trials because pattern search process is deterministic. This advantage greatly reduces the computation cost. To further highlight this feature, we use Model D again to implement a Rayleigh wave dispersion curve inversion scheme by genetic algorithms (GA) as developed by Yamanaka and Ishida (1996). According to the suggestions of Yamanaka and Ishida (1996), we set the population size at 20, crossover probability at 0.7, and mutation probability at 0.02. The algorithm is terminated at the 150th iteration. A final solution is determined from an average of 20 trials due to random constructions in a GA procedure.
Fig. 22 summarizes genetic algorithm inversion results of Rayleigh wave dispersion curves. As shown in Fig. 22a, the misfit values averaged from 20 inversions rapidly decrease in the

first 70 generations, and then gradually converge to zero in the next 80 generations, indicating that the algorithm has found the global minimum. The final solution from GA (dashed line in Fig. 22b) is identical to the true model while GA performs a total of 60, 000 function evaluations in 20 trials for a final desired model. In contrast, the pattern search algorithm pursues only 252 function evaluations (Fig. 8c) to search the global minimum. Since most of the computational time is spent in the calculation of those forward problems in function evaluations, the proposed scheme applied to nonlinear inversion of surface wave

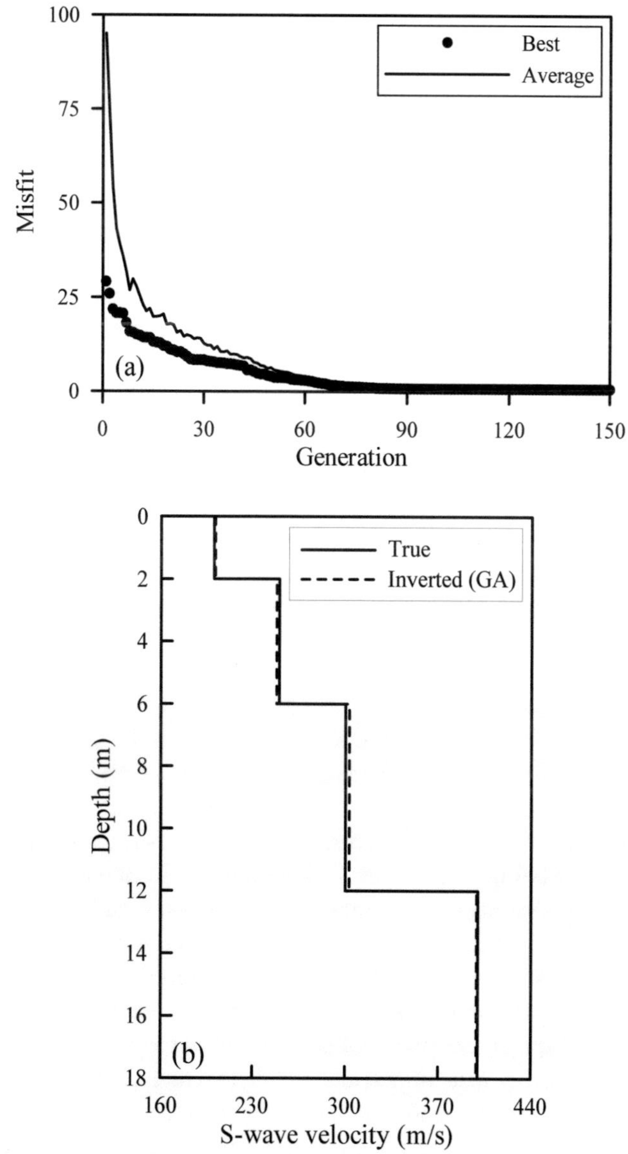

Fig. 22. Inversion results of Model D by a genetic algorithm. (a) Misfit value obtained from an average of 20 trials as a function of generation. (b) True (solid line) and inverted (dashed line) S-wave velocity profiles. The inverted model (b) is an average result from 20 inversions.

data should be considered good not only in terms of accuracy but also in terms of computation effort due to its global and deterministic search process, especially when compared to the application of genetic algorithms to surface wave inversion using the current inversion parameters.

10. Field data inversion

Modeling results presented in the previous section demonstrated the calculation efficiency and reliability of the inverse procedure. To further explore the performance of the algorithm described above, surface wave data acquired from a highway roadbed survey in Henan, China have been reanalyzed in the present study using pattern search algorithm. The surface topography of the tested roadbed is flat, without any obvious relief. The surficial layer of the roadbed has been rolled many times. A number of boreholes were used to obtain priori geologic information, and to evaluate the accuracy and efficiency of the surface wave method. Borehole SK01-06-12 (with a maximum depth of drilling of 14.5 m) reveals a 1.4-m-thick soft clay layer between a stiff surficial layer (compact sand and clay) and a gravel soil layer with mixed alluvial deposit. The soft clay layer usually leads to serious subsidence and deformation of a highway.

Based on our previous modeling result that an excessive number of data points will simply increase the computational cost without benefit to accuracy of the solution, we resample the resulting dispersion curve (Song et al., 2006) using 44 data points with a frequency range of 8-70 Hz (solid dots in Fig. 23) without compromising data accuracy. It is worth noticing that the measured dispersion curve (solid dots in Fig. 23) is characterized by an inversely dispersive trend (an abrupt variation and discontinuity) within the frequency range of 15-30 Hz, which is likely owing to the inclusion of higher modes in the fundamental mode data when a low velocity layer is present.

Similar to the inverse strategy of Model C, a 6-layer subsurface structure was adopted to perform a pattern search algorithm inversion of the observed dispersion curve. Estimated Poisson's ratio and density are 0.4 and 1.8 g/cm^3 for each layer of the 6-layer model, respectively, and are kept constant in the inverse process because the accuracy of the deduced model is insensitive to these parameters. Initial S-wave velocities approximately estimated by Eq. (1) are 250 m/s for all layers (dashed lines in Fig. 23 and Fig. 25).

The performance of the algorithm for the real example is illustrated in Fig. 24. We terminate the inversion process at a 6 m/s error level (80 iterations) to prevent transferring errors in data into the desired model. Because, in most cases, the best match with the measured data does not necessarily obtain the best inversion results (Xia et al., 2003; Song et al., 2007). Similar to Fig. 4a, the misfit values significantly decrease in the first 20 iterations, and then converge to a similar constant value (Fig. 24a), which suggests that the algorithm had completed the exploration of the good valley. In fact such behavior is common to most optimization techniques. Because of complexity of the real example, in 80 iterations the pattern search algorithm performs total 846 function evaluations (Fig. 24c) to discover the most promising areas in the solution space containing the global minima. The maximum number (12) of function evaluations during each inversion gives another evidence of complexity of the real example (Fig. 24c). Fig. 24d reports the best solution of the implementation. Clearly, the low velocity layer (the soft clay layer) has been well imaged.

The characteristic of the calculated dispersion curve from the best model is also similar to that of the modeled dispersion curve from Model C (dashed-and-dotted line in Fig. 1).

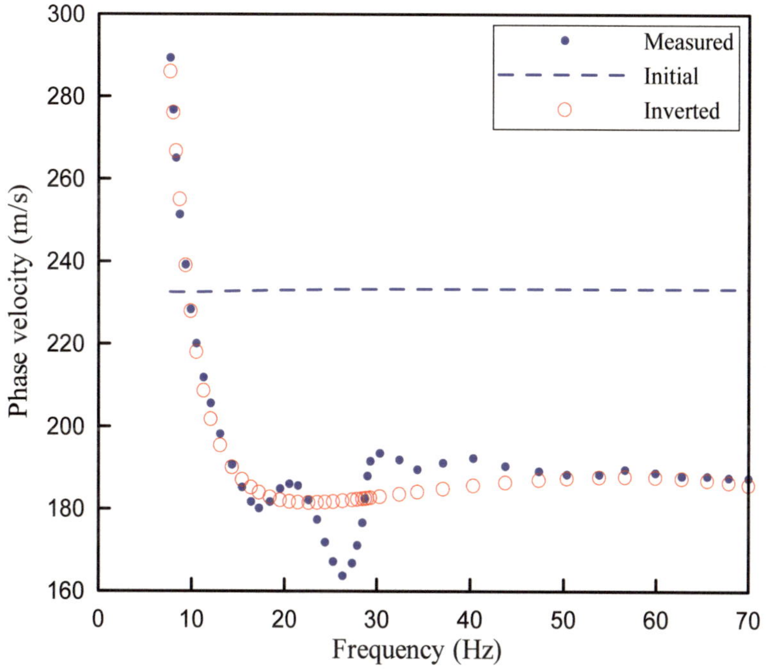

Fig. 23. A real-world example from roadbed survey in Henan, China. Solid dots, dashed line, and open circles represent measured, initial, and forwardly calculated fundamental-mode dispersion curves, respectively.

The inverted model is in acceptable agreement with borehole measurements (diamonds with a solid line in Fig. 25), especially for layer 1, layer 3, and layer 4; misfits are all not more than 4%. However, three greater misfits occur at layer 2, layer 5, and layer 6,which are approximately 8%, 5%, and 13%, respectively, although the modeled dispersion curve (open circles in Fig. 23) from the best solution (Fig. 25d) fits the measured phase velocities (solid dots in Fig. 23) reasonably well. A couple of factors, including a limited frequency spectrum,estimation errors in P-wave velocities and density, higher modes and the inclusion of noise (e.g., body waves) in the data, are likely responsible for these discrepancies. Nonetheless the real example should be considered a successful application to nonlinear inversion of Rayleigh wave dispersion curves using pattern search algorithms. Higher modes are relatively more sensitive to the fine S-wave velocity structure than is the fundamental mode and therefore the accuracy of S-wave velocities can be further improved by incorporating higher-mode data into the inversion process (Beaty and Schmitt, 2003; Xia et al., 2003). Efforts should be made to fully exploit higher-mode Rayleigh waves for imaging and characterizing shallow subsurface more accurately, especially for the inversely dispersive site.

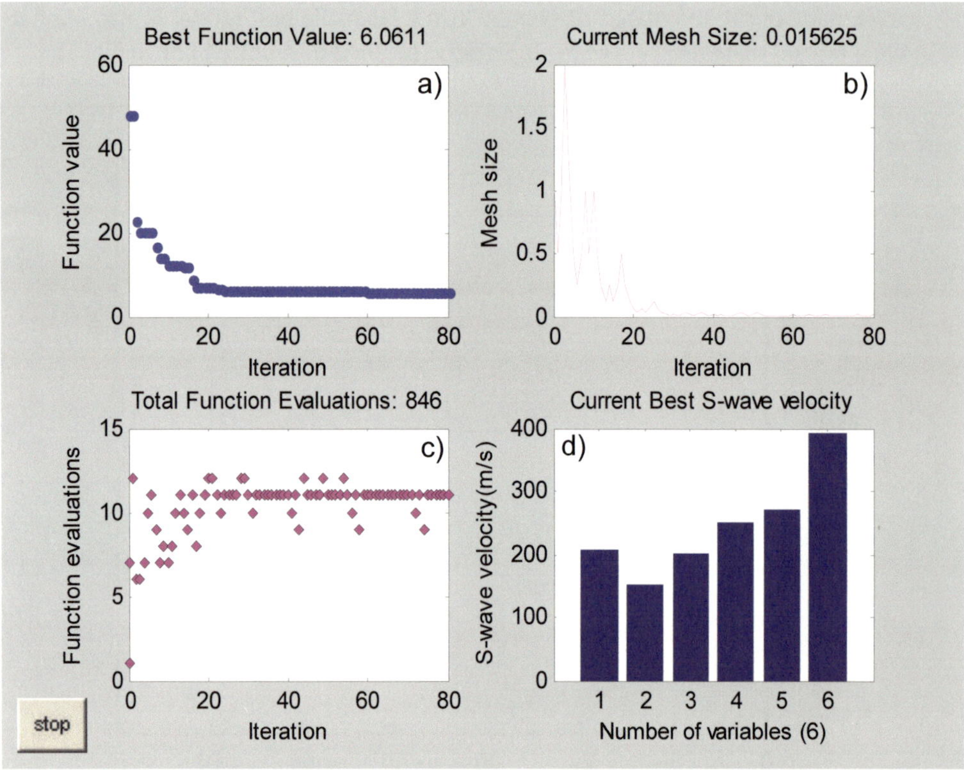

Fig. 24. Inversion results of the real-world example using pattern search algorithms. (a), (b), (c), and (d) have the same meaning as in Fig. 2.

11. Discussion and conclusions

From our successful inversions of synthetic and observed surface wave data, we confidently conclude that pattern search algorithms can be applied to nonlinear inversion of Rayleigh wave dispersion curves. In the current study, we are using pattern search as a global optimization technique. We remark that pattern search algorithms have a number of significant advantages compared with local optimization techniques. Firstly, the algorithms are well suited for solving problems characterized by highly nonlinear, multimodal objective functions, without the need of derivative calculations. This feature can be particularly useful to solve problems for which the objective functions are not differentiable, stochastic, or even discontinuous. However, local optimization methods may not be available in these cases. Secondly, pattern search methods have features that make them less likely to be trapped by spurious local minimizers than do methods that use derivatives. However, local optimization methods are prone to being trapped by local minima, and their success depends heavily on the choice of a good starting model. Thirdly, because pattern search algorithms require only calculating a forward model, they are easily incorporated into inversion of higher-mode Rayleigh waves as well as other geophysical inverse problems. Also, the accuracy of the partial derivatives is key in determining accuracy of the derived model. Because pattern search algorithms are based only on direct solution space

sampling, any kind of linearization of the problem to be solved is avoided, with the consequent elimination of the errors involved in such approximation.
In the present work, we adopted a simple initial S-wave velocity profile and a wider searching scope, performed an extreme initial value (1000 m/s), and subdivided a two-layer subsurface (Model A) into six thin layers, to test the capability of the pattern search algorithm and to simulate more realistic cases where no a priori information is available. The results of numerical tests for both synthetic and actual field data that show that pattern search algorithms possess obvious advantages compared to local-search methods. For example, if the resulting dispersion curve suffers from a serious lack of the frequency spectrum and/or a serious contamination by the inclusion of noises (e.g., body waves) in near-surface applications, in such situations an extreme initial value and a wider searching scope may be necessary for locating a global minimum. When this occurs, local-search methods fail to correctly reconstruct the subsurface model and the initial S-wave velocities determined by Eq. (1) do not work for gradient methods, but Eq. (1) is good enough to start the pattern search algorithm.

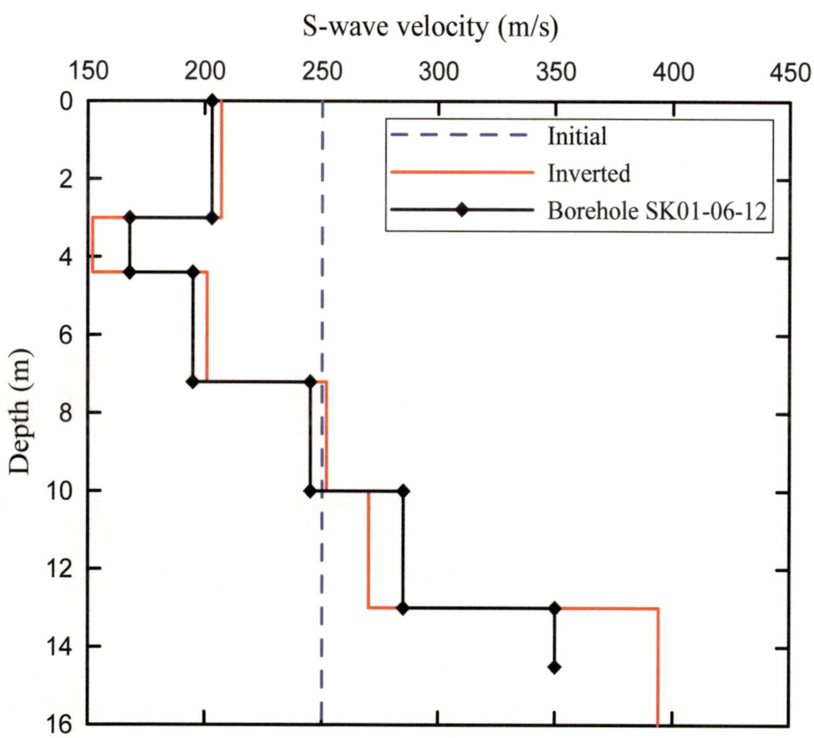

Fig. 25. Initial (dashed line), inverted (solid line), and borehole measurement (solid line with diamonds) S-wave velocity profiles.

12. Acknowledgements

This research is funded by Changjiang River Scientific Research Institute Science Foundation (Nos.YWF0906; CKSF2010009) of China. The authors extend their thanks to Professor Jianghai Xia for his constructive discussion on surface wave technique.

13. References

Audet, C., Dennis, Jr., J.E., 2003. Analysis of Generalized Pattern Searches. SIAM Journal on Optimization 13(3), 889-903.

Boschetti, F., Dentith, M.C., List, R.D., 1996. Inversion of seismic refraction data using genetic algorithms. Geophysics 61(6), 1715-1727.

Beaty, K.S., Schmitt, D.R., Sacchi, M., 2002. Simulated annealing inversion of multimode Rayleigh-wave dispersion curves for geological structure. Geophysical Journal International 151, 622-631.

Beaty, K.S., Schmitt, D.R., 2003. Repeatability of multimode Rayleigh-wave dispersion studies. Geophysics 68, 782-790.

Conn, A. R., Gould, N. I. M., Toint, P. L., 1991. A globally convergent augmented Lagrangian algorithm for optimization with general constraints and simple bounds. SIAM Journal on Numerical Analysis 28(2), 545-572.

Dal Moro, G., Pipan, M., Gabrielli, P., 2007. Rayleigh wave dispersion curve inversion via genetic algorithms and Marginal Posterior Probability Density estimation. Journal of Applied Geophysics 61(1), 39-55..

Foti, S., Sabuelli, L., Socco, L.V., Strobbia, C. 2002. Spatial sampling issues in f-k analysis of surface waves. Proceedings of the Symposium on the Application of Geophysics to Engineering and Environmental Problems (SAGEEP 2002), Las Vegas, Nevada, February 10-14, 2002, 11 pp., available on CD-ROM.

Forbriger, T., 2003. Inversion of shallow-seismic wavefields: I. Wavefield transformation. Geophysical Journal International 153, 719-734.

Kolda, T. G., Lewis, R. M., Torczon, V., 2003. Optimization by direct search: New perspectives on some classical and modern methods, SIAM Review 45, 385–482.

Lewis,R.M.,Torczon,V.,1999. Pattern Search Algorithms for Bound Constrained Minimization. SIAM Journal on Optimization 9(4), 1082-1099.

Lewis,R.M.,Torczon,V.,2000. Pattern Search Methods for Linearly Constrained Minimization. SIAM Journal on Optimization 10(3), 917-941.

Lewis, R. M., Torczon, V., 2002. A globally convergent augmented Lagrangian pattern search algorithm for optimization with general constraints and simple bounds. SIAM Journal on Optimization 12(4), 1075-1089.

Lai, C.G., Rix, G.J., Foti, S., Roma, V., 2002. Simultaneous measurement and inversion of surface wave dispersion and attenuation curves. Soil Dynamics and Earthquake Engineering 22 (9-12), 923-930.

Lin, C.-P., Chang, T.-S. 2004. Multi-station analysis of surface wave dispersion. Soil Dynamics and Earthquake Engineering 24(11), 877-886.

Meier, R.W. Rix, G.J., 1993. An initial study of surface wave inversion using artificial neural networks. Geotechnical Testing Journal 16(4), 425-431.

Miller, R., Xia, J., Park, C., Ivanov, J., Williams, E., 1999a. Using MASW to map bedrock in Olathe, Kansas. in Expanded Abstracts, Society of Exploration and Geophysics, pp. 433-436.

Miller, R.D., Xia, J., Park, C.B., Ivanov, J., 1999b. Multichannel analysis of surface waves to map bedrock. The Leading Edge 18, 1392-1396.

O'Neill, A., Dentith, M., List, R., 2003. Full-waveform P-SV reflectivity inversion of surface waves for shallow engineering applications. Exploration Geophysics 34, 158-173.

Park, C.B., Miller, R.D., Xia, J., 1998. Imaging dispersion curves of surface waves on multi-channel recording. Technical Program with Biographies, SEG, 68th Annual Meeting, New Orleans, Louisiana, pp. 1377-1380.

Park, C.B., Miller, R.D., Xia, J., 1999. Multichannel analysis of surface waves. Geophysics 64(3), 800-808.

Rix, G.J., 1988. Experimental study of factors affecting the spectral analysis of surface waves method. PhD Dissertation, The University of Texas at Austin.

Ryden, N., Park, C.B., Ulriksen, P., Miller, R.D, 2004. Multimodal approach to seismic pavement testing. Journal of Geotechnical and Geoenvironmental Engineering 130(6), 636-645.

Schwab, F.A., Knopoff, L., 1972. Fast surface wave and free mode computations. In: Bolt, B.A. (Ed.), Methods in Computational Physics. Academic Press, New York, pp. 87-180.

Sambridge, M., 1999a. Geophysical inversion with a neighbourhood algorithm—I. Searching a parameter space. Geophysical Journal International 138(2), 479-494.

Sambridge, M.,1999b. Geophysical inversion with a neighbourhood algorithm—II. Appraising the ensemble. Geophysical Journal International 138(3), 727-746.

Song,X.H., Gu, H.M., Liu, J.P., 2006. Occam's inversion of high-frequency Rayleigh wave dispersion curves for shallow engineering applications. Geophysical Solutions for Environment and Engineering: Proceedings of the 2nd International Conference on Environmental and Engineering Geophysics (ICEEG), June 4-9, 2006, Wuhan, China, Science Press USA Inc., Vol 1, p124-130.

Song, X. H., Gu, H. M., 2007. Utilization of multimode surface wave dispersion for characterizing roadbed structure. Journal of Applied Geophysics 63(2), 59-67.

Torczon, V., 1997. On the convergence of Pattern Search Algorithms. SIAM Journal on Optimization 7(1), 1-25.

Tian, G., Steeples, D.W., Xia, J., Miller, R.D., Spikes, K.T., Ralston, M.D. 2003. Multichannel analysis of surface wave method with the autojuggie. Soil Dynamics and Earthquake Engineering 23(3), 243-247.

Xia, J., Miller, R.D., Park, C.B., 1999. Estimation of near-surface shear-wave velocity by inversion of Rayleigh wave. Geophysics 64(3), 691-700.

Xia, J., Miller, R.D., Park, C.B., Tian, G., 2003. Inversion of high frequency surface waves with fundamental and higher modes. Journal of Applied Geophysics 52(1), 45-57.

Xia, J., Miller, R.D., Park, C.B., Ivanov, J., Tian, G., Chen, C., 2004. Utilization of high-frequency Rayleigh waves in near-surface geophysics. The Leading Edge 23(8), 753-759.

Yamanaka H., Ishida H., 1996. Application of genetic algorithm to an inversion of surface wave dispersion data. Bulletin of the Seismological Society of America 86, 436-444.

Zhang, S.X., Chan, L.S., 2003. Possible effects of misidentified mode number on Rayleigh wave inversion. Journal of Applied Geophysics 53, 17-29.

22

Vertex Search Algorithm of Convex Polyhedron Representing Upper Limb Manipulation Ability

Makoto Sasaki[1], Takehiro Iwami[2], Kazuto Miyawaki[3], Ikuro Sato[4], Goro Obinata[5] and Ashish Dutta[6]
[1]*Iwate University,*
[2]*Akita University,*
[3]*Akita National College of Technology*
[4]*Miyagi Cancer Center Research Institute,*
[5]*Nagoya University*
[6]*Indian Institute of Technology Kanpur*
[1-5]*Japan,*
[6]*India*

1. Introduction

In the evaluation of robot manipulator, all possible velocities, accelerations, and forces at the end-effector can be represented as a polyhedra using the concept of manipulability (Yoshikawa, 1990). This evaluation method, which is commonly used in the field of robotics, provides effective knowledge for evaluation of the manipulability of upper and lower limbs considering both the kinematics and dynamics of the system (Sasaki et al., 2008, 2010).
The manipulability of the upper and lower limbs in three-dimensional task space is expressed as an invisible six-dimensional polytope. For such evaluation, a slack variable is generally introduced in order to search for the vertex of the polytope (Shim & Yoon, 1997; Chiacchio et al., 1997; Lee, 2001). However, it is extremely difficult to search for the region of a higher-dimensional polytope accurately using conventional methods because of their huge computational complexity, and it is also difficult to formulate an objective function in the case of linear programming.
In this chapter, we present a manipulating force polytope reflecting an individual's joint torque characteristics as a new evaluation method for assessing the manipulability of an upper limb. We also present a visualization algorithm and a vertex search algorithm for a higher-dimensional polytope based on the geometric characteristic of joint torque space. The effectiveness of the method proposed for quantitative evaluation of the individual's manipulability of the upper limb is confirmed through the presented experimental result.

2. Seven degree of freedom upper-limb model

Figure 1 portrays a seven DOF-rigid-link model of the upper limb. In the model, θ_1, θ_2, and θ_3 represents the shoulder flexion(+)/extension(-), adduction(+)/abduction(-), and external rotation(+)/internal rotation(-) respectively. In addition, θ_4 is elbow flexion(+)/extension(-);

θ_5, θ_6, θ_7 signify wrist supination(+)/pronation(-), palmar flexion(+)/dorsiflexion(-), and radial flexion(+)/ulnar flexion(-) respectively. The physical parameters of each link, e.g., mass, center of gravity, inertia matrix, are calculated using regression equations based on the body weight and link length (Ae et al., 1992). In general, the dynamic equation of motion of the upper limb is given as

$$\boldsymbol{\tau} = \boldsymbol{M}(\boldsymbol{\theta})\ddot{\boldsymbol{\theta}} + \boldsymbol{h}(\boldsymbol{\theta},\dot{\boldsymbol{\theta}}) + \boldsymbol{g}(\boldsymbol{\theta}) + \boldsymbol{J}^T\boldsymbol{F}, \tag{1}$$

where $\boldsymbol{\tau} \in \boldsymbol{R}^l$ is a joint torque vector, $\boldsymbol{\theta} \in \boldsymbol{R}^l$ is a joint angle vector, $\boldsymbol{M}(\boldsymbol{\theta}) \in \boldsymbol{R}^{l \times l}$ is an inertia matrix, $\boldsymbol{h}(\boldsymbol{\theta},\dot{\boldsymbol{\theta}}) \in \boldsymbol{R}^l$ are centrifugal and coriolis terms, $\boldsymbol{g}(\boldsymbol{\theta}) \in \boldsymbol{R}^l$ is a gravity term, $\boldsymbol{J} \in \boldsymbol{R}^{n \times l}$ is a Jacobian matrix, $\boldsymbol{F} \in \boldsymbol{R}^n$ is a hand force vector, $l\,(=7)$ is the number of joints, and $n\,(\leq 6)$ represents the degrees of freedom of the hand force vector. Because the net joint torque for generating the hand force can be written as

$$\tilde{\boldsymbol{\tau}} = \boldsymbol{\tau} - \boldsymbol{M}(\boldsymbol{\theta})\ddot{\boldsymbol{\theta}} - \boldsymbol{h}(\boldsymbol{\theta},\dot{\boldsymbol{\theta}}) - \boldsymbol{g}(\boldsymbol{\theta}), \tag{2}$$

the relation between the joint torque and the hand force is given as

$$\tilde{\boldsymbol{\tau}} = \boldsymbol{J}^T\boldsymbol{F}. \tag{3}$$

This equation means that an individual's hand force characteristic is obtained by substituting measurable joint torque characteristics into $\boldsymbol{\tau}$. Because the joint torque characteristics vary according to the joint angle and direction of rotation, the maximum joint torque that can be generated at an arbitrary condition is given as

$$\tilde{\tau}_{imax} = \tau_{imax}(\theta_i) - M_i(\boldsymbol{\theta})\ddot{\boldsymbol{\theta}} - h_i(\boldsymbol{\theta},\dot{\boldsymbol{\theta}}) - g_i(\boldsymbol{\theta}) \tag{4}$$

$$\tilde{\tau}_{imin} = \tau_{imin}(\theta_i) - M_i(\boldsymbol{\theta})\ddot{\boldsymbol{\theta}} - h_i(\boldsymbol{\theta},\dot{\boldsymbol{\theta}}) - g_i(\boldsymbol{\theta}), \tag{5}$$

where $\tau_{imax}(\theta_i)$ and $\tau_{imin}(\theta_i)$ signify the maximum joint torque that can be generated at joint angle θ_i in a positive direction or a negative direction, and $i\,(=1,2,\cdots,l)$ is the joint number.

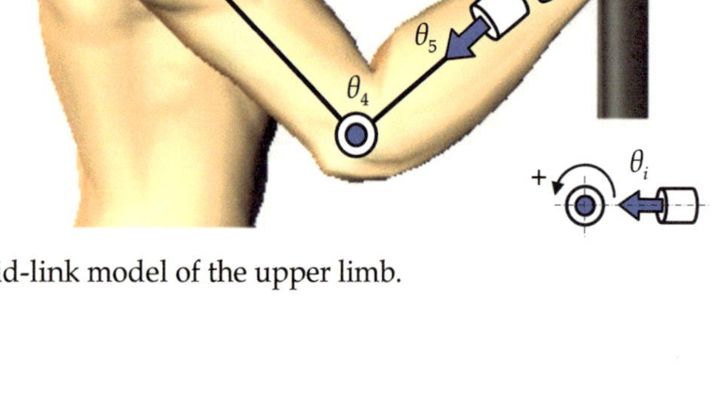

Fig. 1. Seven-rigid-link model of the upper limb.

These joint torques can be quantified using a Cybex (Cybex Inc.) or Biodex machine (Medical Systems Inc.). Therefore, all the possible hand forces encountered during daily life motion is given by the joint torque that satisfies the following conditions.

$$\tilde{\tau}_{imin} \leq \tilde{\tau}_i \leq \tilde{\tau}_{imax} \tag{6}$$

3. Manipulating force polytope considering joint torque characteristics

3.1 Derivation of the polytope

All the hand forces that can be generated during a daily life motion is given by the joint torques satisfying the condition of Eq. (6). The set of all hand forces can be calculated using Eq. (6) and

$$F = (J^T)^{-1}\tilde{\tau} . \tag{7}$$

This set of forces can be expressed as a convex polytope in n-dimensional hand force space. The convex polytope is called the manipulating force polytope. For a redundant manipulator such as the human upper limb $(l > n)$, in general, the set of hand forces cannot be calculated directly because J^T is not a regular matrix. The pseudo-inverse matrix $(J^T)^+$ is a general solution that minimizes the error norm $\left\|\tilde{\tau} - J^T F\right\|$ and it is introduced instead of $(J^T)^{-1}$

$$F = (J^T)^+\tilde{\tau} , \tag{8}$$

(Chiacchio et al., 1997). However, Eq. (3) does not always have a solution for hand force because all joint torque space cannot be covered with the range space $R(J^T)$ of J^T, as shown in Fig. 2 (Asada & Slotine, 1986). In other words, a unique solution is not guaranteed and $\tilde{\tau}$ of both sides of the following equation cannot be equated.

$$\tilde{\tau} = J^T F = J^T (J^T)^+ \tilde{\tau} = \tilde{\tau} \tag{9}$$

Therefore, to obtain the manipulating force polytope for a human upper limb, searching the subspace of the joint torque space given by $R(J^T)$ and projecting it to the hand force space is required.

Here, because the null space $N(J)$ of J is an orthogonal complement of $R(J^T)$, the following relation can be written

$$N(J) = \{R(J^T)\}^{\perp} . \tag{10}$$

In addition, the singular value decomposition of Jacobian matrix J is given as

$$J = U\Sigma V^T = [U_1 \;\; U_2]\begin{bmatrix} S & 0 \\ 0 & 0 \end{bmatrix}\begin{bmatrix} V_1^T \\ V_2^T \end{bmatrix} , \tag{11}$$

where $\Sigma \in R^{n \times l}$ is a diagonal matrix with arranged nonzero singular values of J such as $S = \mathrm{diag}(s_1, s_2, \cdots, s_r)$, $U \in R^{n \times n}$ is an orthogonal matrix, $U_1 \in R^{n \times r}$ and $U_2 \in R^{n \times (n-r)}$ are submatrices of U, $V \in R^{l \times l}$ is an orthogonal matrix, $V_1 \in R^{l \times r}$ and $V_2 \in R^{l \times (l-r)}$ are submatrices of V, and r is the rank of J. Because the column vector v_t $(t=1,2,\cdots,r)$ of V_1 is equal to the base vector of Eq. (10), $R(J^T)$ is represented as the space covered by r base vectors of dimension l. By projecting to the hand force space the joint torque's subspace given by $R(J^T)$, the manipulating force polytope is obtainable.

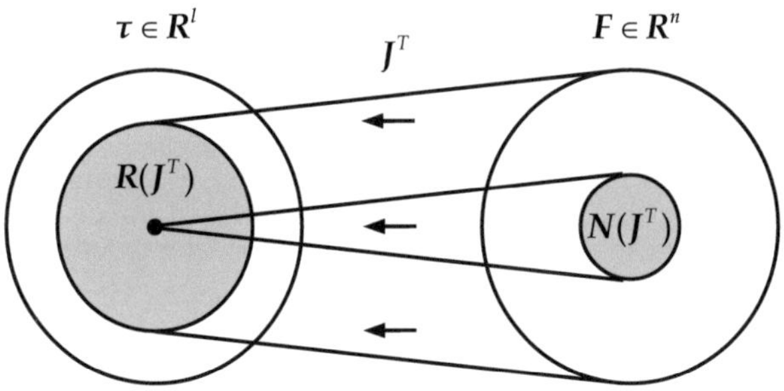

Fig. 2. Null space and range space of J^T.

3.2 Vertex search algorithm for higher dimensional polytope

In order to search for the vertex of the convex polytope, a slack variable is generally introduced. However, the vertex search using a linear programming method such as the simplex method engenders huge computational complexity and a complex definition of the objective function. Especially, it is extremely difficult to search for all vertexes of a high-dimensional polytope. Therefore, we propose a new vertex search algorithm.

The vertex search algorithm is based on the geometric characteristic that the points of intersection between the l-dimensional joint torque space and the space covered by r base vectors of dimension l exist in the $(l-r)$-dimensional face of joint torque space. The algorithm is explained using a three-dimensional rectangle in Fig. 3 for clarification.

For $l=3$ and $r=2$, the two-dimensional plane covered by two base vectors intersects with a side (= one dimension) of a three-dimensional rectangle (see Fig. 3(a)). Because its side is a common set of two planes, the number of joint torque components equal to the maximum joint torque $\tilde{\tau}_{imax}$ or the minimum joint torque $\tilde{\tau}_{imin}$ is equal to two. For $l=3$ and $r=1$, the one-dimensional straight line covered by a base vector intersects with a face (= two dimension) of a three-dimensional rectangle (see Fig. 3(b)). The number of joint torque components equal to $\tilde{\tau}_{imax}$ or $\tilde{\tau}_{imin}$ is then equal to one. Consequently, generalizing the geometric characteristics shows that the space covered by r base vectors of dimension l intersects with the $(l-r)$-dimensional face of the l-dimensional joint torque space. It also reveals that the number of joint torque components equal to $\tilde{\tau}_{imax}$ or $\tilde{\tau}_{imin}$ is equal to r.

By defining the points of intersection between the l-dimensional joint torque space and the range space $R(J^T)$ of J^T is written as

$$K=[k_1,k_2,\cdots,k_r]^T, \tag{12}$$

the subspace of the joint torque space is given as

$$T=k_1v_1+k_2v_2+\cdots+k_rv_r=V_1K. \tag{13}$$

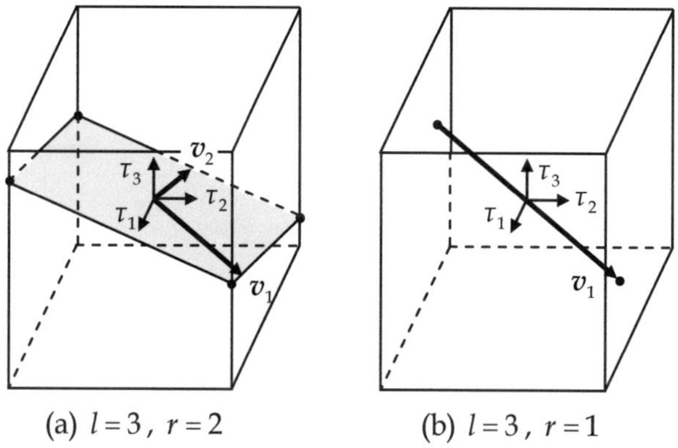

Fig. 3. Vertexes of l-dimensional convex polytopes.

Equation (13) can also be written as

$$\begin{bmatrix} T_1 \\ T_2 \end{bmatrix} = \begin{bmatrix} \tau_1 \\ \vdots \\ \tau_r \\ \hline \tau_{r+1} \\ \vdots \\ \tau_l \end{bmatrix} = \begin{bmatrix} k_1 v_{11} + k_2 v_{21} + \cdots + k_r v_{r,1} \\ \vdots \\ k_1 v_{1,r} + k_2 v_{2,r} + \cdots + k_r v_{r,r} \\ \hline k_1 v_{1,r+1} + k_2 v_{2,r+1} + \cdots + k_r v_{r,r+1} \\ \vdots \\ k_1 v_{1,l} + k_2 v_{2,l} + \cdots + k_r v_{r,l} \end{bmatrix} = \begin{bmatrix} V_{11} \\ V_{12} \end{bmatrix} K, \tag{14}$$

where $T_1 \in R^r$ and $T_2 \in R^{l-r}$ are submatrices of $T \in R^l$, and where $V_{11} \in R^{r\times r}$ and $V_{12} \in R^{(l-r)\times r}$ are the submatrices of the base vector V_1. From this equation, the relation between T_1 and T_2 is obtained as

$$T_2 = V_{12} K = V_{12} V_{11}^{-1} T_1 . \tag{15}$$

Because there are 'r' joint torque components equal to $\tilde{\tau}_{imax}$ or $\tilde{\tau}_{imin}$ in the intersection points, we can define T_1 as shown below:

$$T_{11} = \begin{bmatrix} \tau_1 \\ \vdots \\ \tau_r \end{bmatrix} = \begin{bmatrix} \tilde{\tau}_{1max} \ or \ \tilde{\tau}_{1min} \\ \vdots \\ \tilde{\tau}_{rmax} \ or \ \tilde{\tau}_{rmin} \end{bmatrix} \tag{16}$$

The intersection points K are obtained by judging whether the joint torque component of T_2 calculated from Eqs. (15) and (16) satisfies the condition of the joint torque in Eq. (6). Therefore only when T_2 satisfies this condition, the joint torque T is calculated from K,

$$K = V_{11}^{-1} T_1 = V_{12}^{-1} T_2 , \tag{17}$$

And it becomes the vertex of the l-dimensional convex polytope. Herein, the number of combinations which select the n equations from l equations in Eq. (14) and define V_{11} is ${}_lC_r$, while the number of combinations defining T_1 in Eq. (16) is 2^r. All vertexes of the l dimensional convex polytope can be found by calculating the intersection points in all combinations. The manipulating force polytope based on human joint torque characteristics is finally expressed by calculating the convex hulls of all the vertexes projected using Eq. (8) on the hand force space. This is done because the vertex of the l-dimensional convex polytope defined by the proposed algorithm always guarantees the unique solution shown in Eq. (9).

3.3 Example

As a simple example of numerical analysis, the three DOF model of the upper limb (three DOF planar redundant manipulator) shown in Fig. 4 is examined. The link lengths L_1, L_2, and L_3 are 0.3, 0.2, and 0.1 m, and joint angles θ_1, θ_2, and θ_3 are 10, 30, and 30 deg, respectively. Maximum joint torques $\tilde{\tau}_{1max}$, $\tilde{\tau}_{1min}$, $\tilde{\tau}_{2max}$, $\tilde{\tau}_{2min}$, $\tilde{\tau}_{3max}$, and $\tilde{\tau}_{3min}$ are 3.5, 3, 2.5, 2, 1.5, and 1 Nm, respectively. Jacobian matrix described in Eq. (6) becomes

$$\begin{aligned} J &= \begin{bmatrix} -L_1S_1 - L_2S_{12} - L_3S_{123} & -L_2S_{12} - L_3S_{123} & -L_3S_{123} \\ L_1C_1 + L_2C_{12} + L_3C_{123} & L_2C_{12} + L_3C_{123} & L_3C_{123} \end{bmatrix} \\ &= \begin{bmatrix} -0.275 & -0.223 & -0.094 \\ 0.483 & 0.187 & 0.034 \end{bmatrix} \end{aligned} . \tag{18}$$

By calculating the singular value decomposition of Jacobian matrix, each matrix $\boldsymbol{U}$, $\boldsymbol{\Sigma}$, and $\boldsymbol{V}$ described in Eq. (11) are obtained as

$$\boldsymbol{U} = \begin{bmatrix} -0.567 & 0.824 \\ 0.824 & 0.567 \end{bmatrix}, \tag{19}$$

$$\boldsymbol{\Sigma} = \begin{bmatrix} 0.626 & 0 & 0 \\ 0 & 0.108 & 0 \end{bmatrix}, \tag{20}$$

$$\boldsymbol{V} = \begin{bmatrix} 0.884 & 0.443 & 0.149 \\ 0.448 & -0.716 & -0.535 \\ 0.130 & -0.540 & 0.832 \end{bmatrix}. \tag{21}$$

All vertexes of the three-dimensional convex polyhedron in joint torque space can be founded using the vertex search algorithm proposed in section 3.2,.

$$\tilde{\boldsymbol{\tau}} = \begin{bmatrix} -3.000 \\ -2.000 \\ -0.750 \end{bmatrix}, \begin{bmatrix} 3.500 \\ 2.500 \\ 0.982 \end{bmatrix}, \begin{bmatrix} -3.000 \\ 1.500 \\ 1.500 \end{bmatrix}, \begin{bmatrix} 3.500 \\ -0.583 \\ -1.000 \end{bmatrix}, \begin{bmatrix} -1.598 \\ -2.000 \\ -1.000 \end{bmatrix}, \begin{bmatrix} 0.598 \\ 2.500 \\ 1.500 \end{bmatrix}. \tag{22}$$

The two-dimensional manipulating force polyhedron is finally expressed by calculating the convex hulls of all the vertexes projected using Eq. (8).

$$\boldsymbol{F} = \begin{bmatrix} 7.207 \\ -2.114 \end{bmatrix}, \begin{bmatrix} -9.846 \\ 1.649 \end{bmatrix}, \begin{bmatrix} -22.981 \\ -19.284 \end{bmatrix}, \begin{bmatrix} 16.747 \\ 16.773 \end{bmatrix}, \begin{bmatrix} 11.901 \\ 3.459 \end{bmatrix}, \begin{bmatrix} -19.561 \\ -9.887 \end{bmatrix}. \tag{23}$$

Figure 5 portrays the 2-dimensional manipulating force polyhedron which presents the set of all possible hand forces.

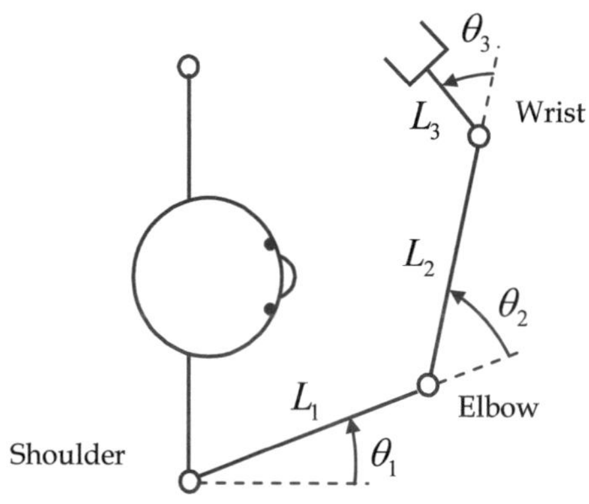

Fig. 4. Three DOF model of the upper limb.

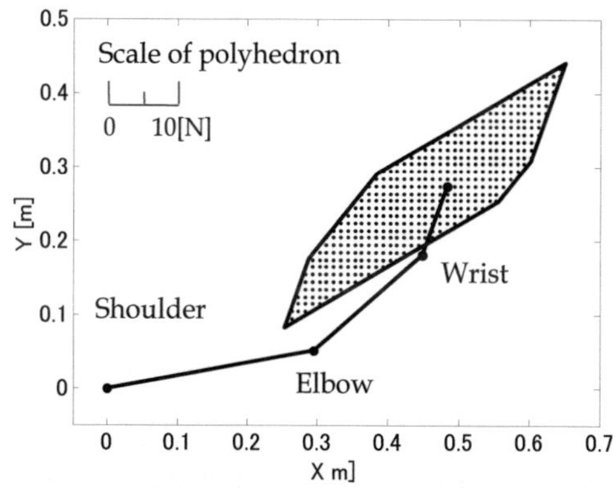

Fig. 5. Two dimensional manipulating force polyhedron.

4. Experimental validation

The proposed evaluation method is verified by comparing the manipulating force polytope based on the maximum joint torque with the measured hand force characteristics

4.1 Measurement of maximum joint torque

In order to calculate the manipulating force polytope reflecting an individual's joint torque characteristics, it is indispensable to measure the maximum joint torque $\tau_{imax}(\theta_i)$ and $\tau_{imin}(\theta_i)$ in advance. For these studies, a Cybex machine (Cybex Inc.) was used for measuring them. The device can measure the maximum joint torque continuously at every joint angle in both the positive and negative directions.

For our experiment, we measured the maximum joint torque produced by the concentric contraction for every pair of movement directions; flexion and extension, adduction and abduction, and external rotation and internal rotation at the shoulder; flexion and extension

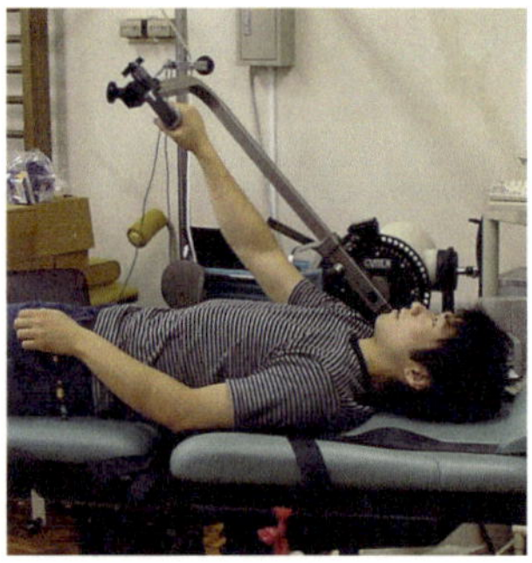

(a) Shoulder flexion/extension

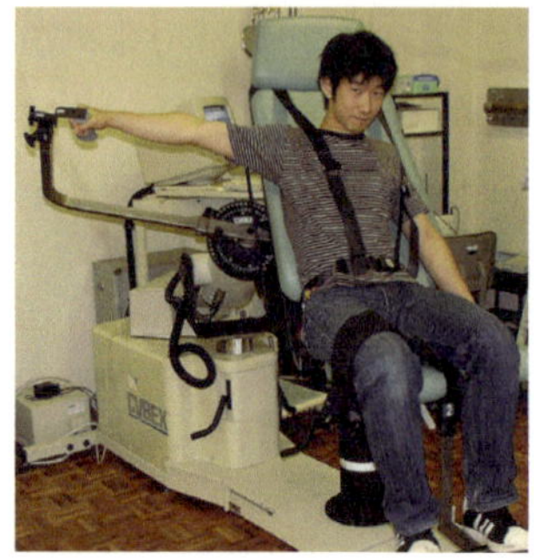

(b) Shoulder adduction/abduction

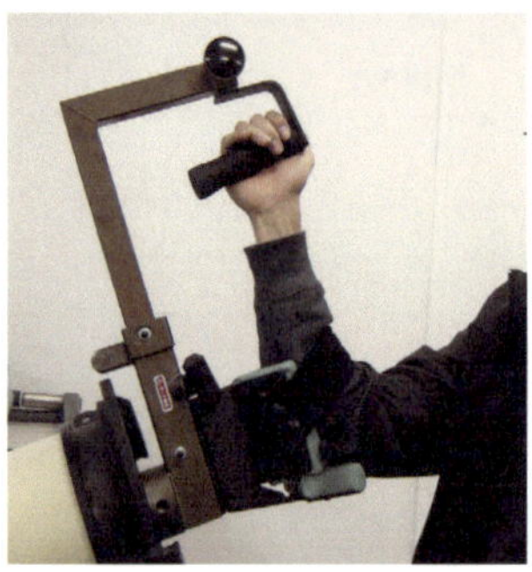

(c) Shoulder external/internal rotation

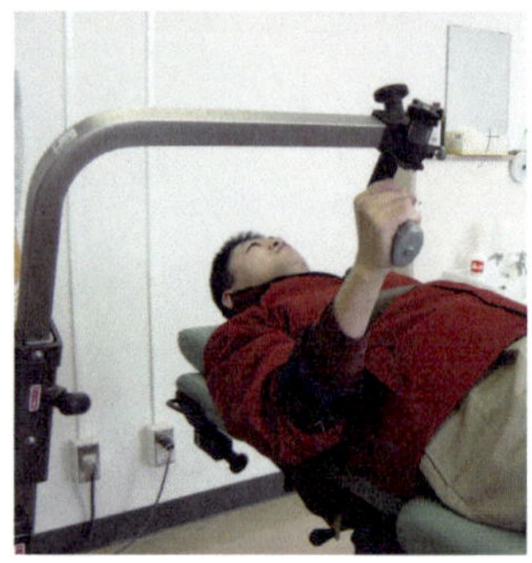

(d) Elbow flexion/extension

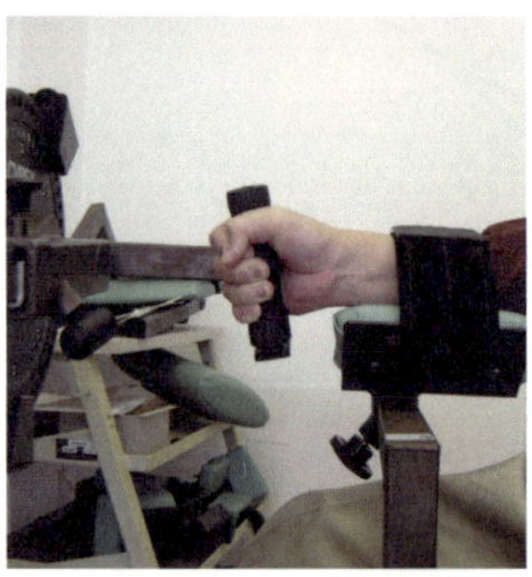

(e) Wrist supination/pronation

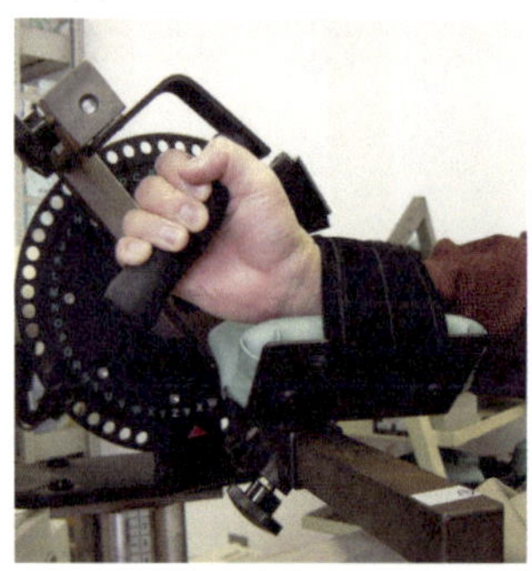

(f) Wrist palmar flexion/dorsiflexion

(g) Wrist radial flexion/ulnar flexion

Fig. 6. Measurement of maximum joint torque.

at the elbow; and supination and pronation, palmar flexion and dorsiflexion, and radial flexion and ulnar flexion at the wrist (see Fig. 6). The participant in the experiment was a person with a spinal cord injury (60 years old, 170 cm, 55 kg, and L2 lumbar injury). The Ethical Committee approved the study protocol, which was fully explained to all subjects in both spoken and written forms, particularly addressing the purpose of the study and the precise procedures to be used and any possible adverse effect.

4.2 Measurement of the hand force and joint angle

Figure 7 shows a measurement system comprising a six-axis force sensor (IFS-105M50A20-I63; Nitta Corp.) and a three-dimensional magnetic position and orientation sensor (Fastrak;Polhemus). The subject added the hand force in eight directions using maximum effort. The hand force applied to the grip was measured using a six-axis force sensor. The receiver to detect the position and posture was put to the hand and the humerus. The joint position and angle of the upper limb, which has 7 degrees of freedom, was calculated using the method developed by Oikawa and Fujita (2000). During this measurement, the subject's upper body was fixed to the back of a chair by belts to eliminate the influence of upper body movements on maximum hand force measurements. The measurements were taken at a sampling frequency of 20 Hz.

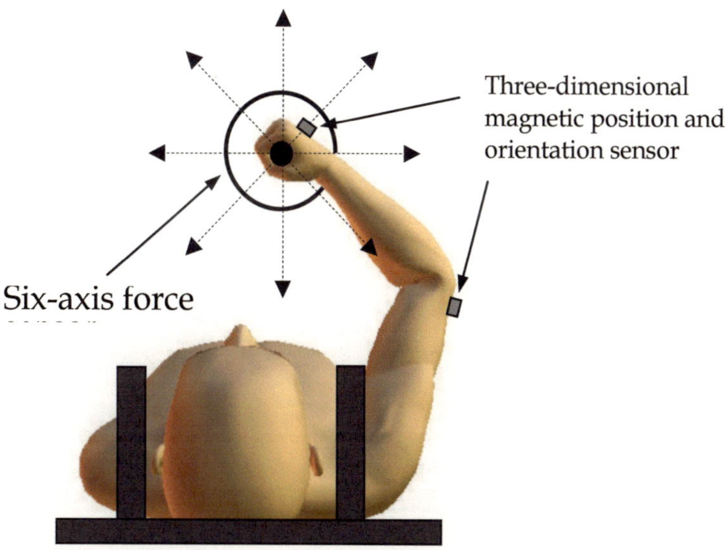

Fig. 7. Measurement system for hand force and upper limb posture.

4.3 Results

Figure 8 depicts a typical example of the maximum joint torque measured using the Cybex device. It is very clear that the ellipsoid described above, which does not consider human joint torque characteristics, is insufficient to evaluate the manipulability of upper limbs because even the joint torque characteristics of healthy person vary greatly according to the joint angle and rotational direction.

Figure 9 portrays the manipulating force polytope, as calculated from the maximum joint torque and posture of the upper limb. The polytope, projected to the two-dimensional plane, represents the set of all the possible hand forces on the horizontal plane, demonstrating a

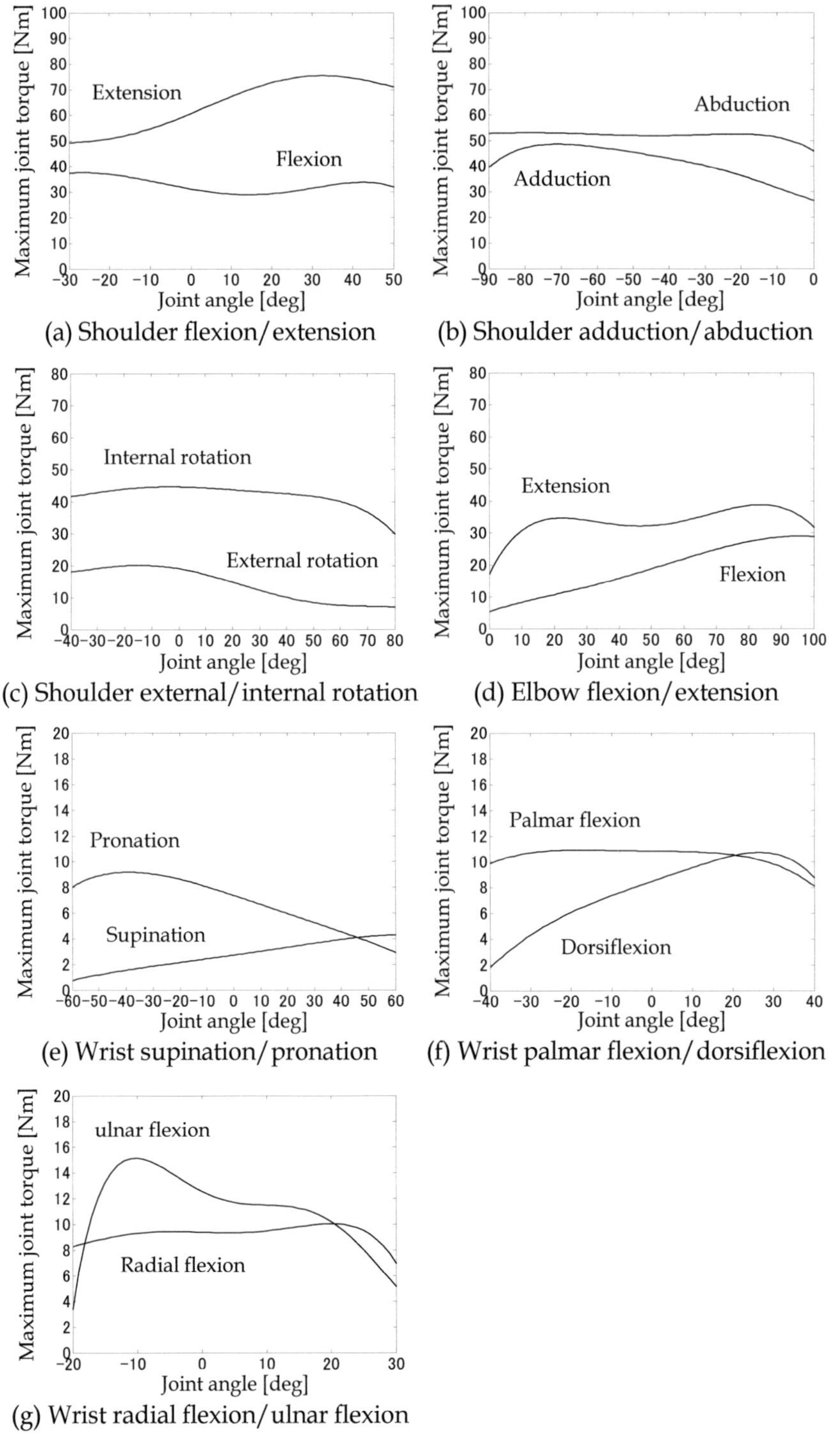

Fig. 8. Measurement results of maximum joint torque.

hexagonal shape. This type of shape of the manipulating force polytope agrees with the findings of Oshima et al. (1999) that the distribution of the hand force vector in a two-dimensional plane is a hexagonal shape. In addition, the hand force vector (gray arrow) presumed from the manipulating force polytope approximately corresponds to the measured hand force (black arrow). The effectiveness of the method proposed for quantitative evaluation of an individual's manipulability of the upper limb can be confirmed through the presented experimental result, but it is necessary to perform further verification to achieve a more accurate evaluation.

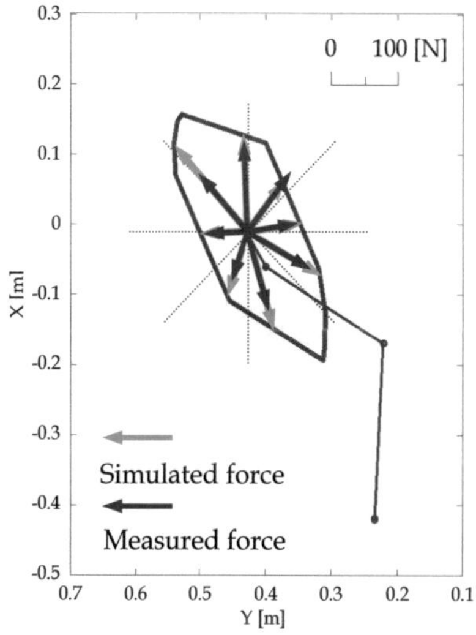

Fig. 9. Manipulating force polytope and hand force.

5. Conclusion

This chapter has presented a manipulating force polytope based on the human joint torque characteristics for evaluation of upper limb manipulability. As described in sections 3, the proposed methods are based on the relation between the joint torque space and the hand force space. Therefore, it is certain that more accurate evaluation can be achieved by expanding these concepts and by considering the relations among muscle space, joint torque space, and hand force space. However, the development of a three-dimensional musculoskeletal model of a human is a respected research area in the field of biomechanics. This is because it is difficult to model an individual's muscle properties strictly, such as the maximum contraction force, the origin, the insertion and the length of each muscle. Also, because of this fact, the proposed evaluation method is a realistic technique by which the influence of the remaining muscle strength or paralysis can be modeled directly and easily as the individual's joint torque characteristics. Nevertheless, further improvements are necessary to achieve a more accurate evaluation because the bi-articular muscle characteristics cannot be accounted sufficiently using the method of separately measuring the maximum joint torque characteristics of each joint.

Through our investigations, we have solved two problems to express the manipulating force polytope based on the measured maximum joint torque. The first is to reflect the human joint torque characteristics depending on the joint angle and the rotational direction into the formulation of the manipulating force polytope. The second is to derive a new vertex search algorithm for higher-dimensional polytopes to search for all vertexes of convex polytopes without oversight by an easy calculating formula with few computational complexities. It is certain that the proposed methods are effective not only for evaluation of the manipulability of human upper limbs but also for the evaluation of a robot manipulator's manipulation capability because no reports, even in the robotics literature, have described solutions to these problems. Therefore, the proposed methods can probably contribute to progress in the field of robotics in a big way, offering useful new findings.

6. Acknowledgements

The authors gratefully acknowledge the support provided for this research by a Japan Society of Promotion of Science (JSPS) Grant-in-Aid for Young Scientists (B) 22700572.

7. References

Ae, M.; Tang, H.P. & Yokoi, T. (1992). Estimation of inertia properties of the body segments in Japanese athletes, In: *Biomechanism*, Vol. 11, pp. 23–32, The Society of Biomechanisms Japan, ISBN 978-4-13-060132-0.

Asada, H. & Slotine, J.-J.E. (1986). *Robot Analysis and Control*, John Wiley and Sons, ISBN 0-471-83029-1.

Chiacchio, P.; Bouffard-Vercelli, Y. & Pierrot, F. (1997). Force polytope and force ellipsoid for redundant manipulators. *Journal of Robotic Systems*, Vol. 14, No. 8, pp. 613–620, ISSN 0741-2223.

Lee, J. (2001). A structured algorithm for minimum $l\infty$-norm solutions and its application to a robot velocity workspace analysis. *Robotica*, Vol. 19, pp. 343–352, ISSN 0263-5747.

Oikawa, K. & Fujita K. (2000). Algorithm for calculating seven joint angles of upper extremity from positions and Euler angles of upper arm and hand. *Journal of the Society of Biomechanisms*, Vol. 24, No. 1, pp. 53–60, ISSN 0285-0885.

Oshima, T.; Fujikawa, T. & Kumamoto, M. (1999). Functional evaluation of effective muscle strength based on a muscle coordinate system consisted of bi-articular and mono-articular muscles: contractile forces and output forces of human limbs. *Journal of the Japan Society for Precision Engineering*, Vol. 65, No. 12, pp. 1772–1777, ISSN 0912-0289.

Sasaki, M.; Kimura, T.; Matsuo, K.; Obinata, G.; Iwami, T.; Miyawaki, K. & Kiguchi, K. (2008). Simulator for optimal wheelchair design. *Journal of Robotics and Mechatronics*, Vol. 20, No. 6, pp. 854–862, ISSN 0915-3942.

Sasaki, M.; Iwami, T.; Miyawaki, K.; Sato, I.; Obinata, G. & Dutta, A. (2010). Higher dimensional spatial expression of upper limb manipulation ability based on human joint torque characteristics. *Robot Manipulators, New Achievements*, INTECH, pp.693-718, ISBN 978-953-307-090-2.

Shim, I.C. & Yoon, Y.S. (1997). Stabilization constraint method for torque optimization of a redundant manipulator, *Proceedings of the 1997 IEEE International Conference on Robotics and Automation*, pp. 2403–2408, ISBN 0-7803-3612-7, Albuquerque, NM, April, 1997.

Yoshikawa, T. (1990). *Foundations of Robotics: Analysis and Control*, MIT Press, ISBN 0-262-24028-9.

23

Modeling with Non-cooperative Agents: Destructive and Non-Destructive Search Algorithms for Randomly Located Objects

Dragos Calitoiu[1] and Dan Milici[2]
[1]Carleton University
[2]Stefan cel Mare University
[1]Canada
[2]Romania

The problem of plastic anti-personal mine detection is well known. These devices are typically 75mm in diameter and between 25mm to 50mm in thickness. Some types contain no metal, but their explosive (RDX, TNT) can be considered as a dielectric material with a dielectric constant between 3.5 and 4.0. This electromagnetic property enables a radar to identify mines. It is true that the radars operating "through the air" provide a high detection rate. However, in the case of operating "into the ground", the problems are significant and inherently reduce performance. Target identification is done in the presence of the air-ground interface, which usually produces a higher amplitude signal than an anti-personal mine Chignell (1998). This context can justify why the difficulties of detecting anti-personal mines are formidable. A family of search mobots controlled by a new algorithm proposed in this research could be a solution[1] for operating on the ground.

In this Chapter we[2] address the general question of what is the best strategy to search efficiently for randomly located objects (target sites). We propose a new agent based algorithm for searching in an unpredictable environment. The originality of our work consists in applying a non-cooperative strategy, namely the distributed Goore Game model, as opposed to applying the classical collaborative and competitive strategies, or individual strategies. This research covers both the destructive search and the non-destructive search. The first occurs when the agent visits the target only one time. The latter can be performed in either of the two cases - if the target becomes temporarily inactive or if it leaves the area.

The proposed algorithm has two versions: one when the agent can move with a step equal to unity and the other when the step of the agent follows a Levy flight distribution. The second version is inspired by the work of A.M. Reynolds *et al.* Reynolds (2006a;b; 2007; 2008a;b; 2009); Reynolds & Rhodes (2009); Rhodes & Reynolds (2007) where he braced the use of Levy processes when resources are sparsely distributed within unpredictable environments.

The Chapter is organized as follows. The Goore Game is presented in the next section. In Section 2 we introduce the terminology of the Learning Automata, methodology used for

---

[1] The main application of our proposed algorithm is anti-personal mine detection. However, this research can be extended to any type of exploration on ground or aerial using uninhabited aerial vehicle (on Earth or for conducting planetary science missions).

[2] The first author is also member of OPTIMOD Research Institute, Ottawa.

implementing the behavior of the players for the Goore Game. The motivation due to Levy flight for selecting the search step is described in Section 3. The proposed search algorithm and the results of the simulations are presented in Section 4 (for destructive search) and Section 5 (for non-destructive search). Finally, Section 6 concludes the Chapter.

1. Goore game

Goore Game is an example of self-organization and self-optimization game studied in the field of artificial intelligence. It was presented by Tsetlin in 1963 Tsetlin (1963) and analyzed in detail in Narendra & Thathachar (1989) and Thathachar & Arvind (1997). The informal formulation follows.

"*Imagine a large room containing N cubicles and a raised platform. One person (voter) sits in each cubicle and a Referee stands on the platform. The Referee conducts a series of voting rounds as follows. On each round the voters vote either "Yes" or "No" (the issue is unimportant) simultaneously and independently (they do not see each other) and the Referee counts the fraction, f, of "Yes" votes. The Referee has a unimodal performance criterion $G(f)$, which is optimized when the fraction of "Yes" votes is exactly f_0. The current voting round ends with the Referee awarding a dollar with probability $G(f)$ and assessing a dollar with probability $1 - G(f)$ to every voter independently. On the basis of their individual gains and losses, the N voters then decide, again independently, how to cast their votes on the next round. No matter how many players there are, after enough trials, the number of "Yes" votes will approximate Nf_0.*"

Each player plays solely in a greedy fashion, voting each time the way that seems to give the player the best payoff. This is somewhat unexpected. Greed affects outcomes in an unpredictable manner: a player does not attempt to predict the behavior of other players. Instead, each player performs by trial and error and simply preferentially repeats those actions that produce the best result for that player.

The essence of the Goore Game is a random walk that is strongly biased toward the global optimum. Some of the game's features Oommen et al. (1999) which render it both non-trivial and intriguing are:

- The game is a non-zero-sum game.
- Unlike the games traditionally studied in the AI literature (Chess, Checkers, etc.) the game is essentially a distributed game.
- The players of the game are ignorant of all of the parameters of the game. All they know is that they have to make a choice, for which they are either rewarded or penalized. They have no clue as to how many other players there are, how they are playing, or even of how/why they are rewarded/penalized.
- The stochastic function used to reward or penalize the players, after measuring their performance as a whole, can be completely arbitrary, as long as it is uni-modal.
- The game can achieve a globally optimal state with N-players without having to explicitly dictate the action to each player. The players self-organize and self-optimize based on the reward function.

The Goore Game can be representative for many real-life scenarios as recruitment of motor units Thathachar & Arvind (1997) (as working muscles) to perform a certain task, such as exerting a force to lift a weight. In this setting, each motor unit contributes either a fixed magnitude of force or none at all. Function of the specificity of the job, it will be mandatory to recruit the correct number of motor units. If there are more motor units than actually needed, this will exert more force than necessary. On contrast, if there are less motor units, they may

not be able to perform the task at all. The problem is one of employing the right number of working units to perform the task.
The game was initially studied in the general learning domain and was considered an interesting pathological game. Recently, it was applied in QoS (Quality of Service) support in wireless sensor networks Iyer & Kleinrock (2003), Chen & Varshney (2004), in controlling wings with integrated check-valve electrostatic actuators Ho et al. (2002), and in cooperative mobile robotics Cao et al. (1997), Tung & Kleinrock (1996).

2. Some fundamentals of learning automata

Due to the solid theoretical basis that has been established within the Learning Automata (LA) field during the last decades, and particularly due to the results concerning games, we decided to implement our searching algorithm using LA.
LA have been used Narendra & Thathachar (1989), Poznyak & Najim (1997), Lakshmivarahan (1981) to model biological learning systems and to find the optimal action that is offered by a Random Environment[3]. Learning is realized by interacting with the Environment and by processing its responses to the actions that are chosen, while gradually converging toward an ultimate goal. The environment evaluates the performance of LA and directs the learning process performed by the LA. Thus, the LA's overall performance is gradually improved. In this respect, the process of learning is based on a learning loop involving two entities: the Random Environment (RE) and the LA.
The RE offers to the automaton a set of possible actions $\{\alpha_1, \alpha_2, \ldots, \alpha_r\}$ to choose from. The automaton chooses one of those actions, say α_i, which serves as an input to the RE. Since the RE is "aware" of the underlying penalty probability distribution of the system, depending on the *penalty probability* c_i corresponding to α_i, it produces a response (β) to the LA that can be a *reward* (typically denoted by the value $\beta = 0$), or a *penalty* (typically denoted by the value $\beta = 1$). The reward/penalty information (corresponding to the action) provided to the LA helps it to choose the subsequent action. By repeating the above process, through a series of Environment-Automaton interactions, the LA finally attempts to learn the *optimal* action from the Environment. The Learning process is presented in Figure 1.

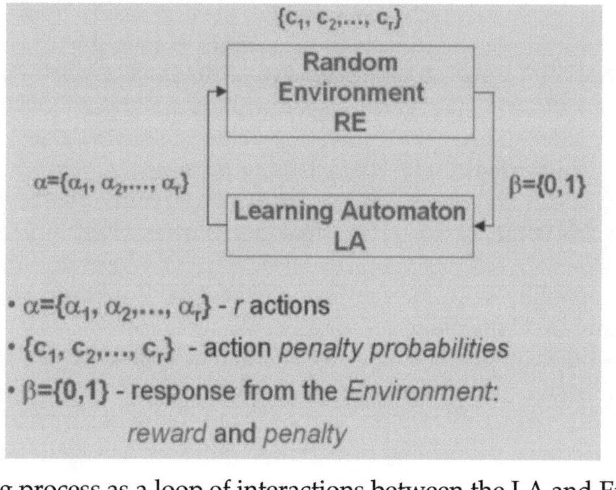

Fig. 1. The Learning process as a loop of interactions between the LA and Environment.

[3] The first author thanks Dr. John B. Oommen for introducing him in the field of Learning Automata.

2.1 The continuous linear reward-inaction scheme

When the Goore Game was first investigated, Tsetlin utilized his so-called Tsetlin automaton to solve it. Later, more research was done in the LA area and many families of LA proved to solve the Goore Game efficiently. In our research, we are using a very fast LA: the continuous Linear Reward-Inaction scheme (L_{RI}) that was introduced by Norman Norman (1968). This scheme is based on the principle that whenever the automaton receives a favorable response (i.e., a reward) from the environment, the action probabilities are updated, whereas if the automaton receives an unfavorable response (i.e., a penalty) from the environment, the action probabilities are unaltered.

The probability updating equations for this scheme are characterized by a parameter θ ($0 < \theta < 1$) and can be simplified to be as below Norman (1968):

$$\begin{array}{l} p_1(t+1) = p_1(t) + (1-\theta) \times (1 - p_1(t)) \\ \text{if } \alpha(t) = \alpha_1, \text{ and } \beta(t) = 0 \\ p_1(t+1) = \theta \times p_1(t) \\ \text{if } \alpha(t) = \alpha_2, \text{ and } \beta(t) = 0 \\ p_1(t+1) = p_1(t) \\ \text{if } \alpha(t) = \alpha_1 \text{ or } \alpha_2, \text{ and } \beta(t) = 1 \end{array} \tag{1}$$

Note that if action α_i is chosen, and a reward is received, the probability $p_i(t)$ is increased, and the other probability $p_j(t)$ (i.e., $j \neq i$) is decreased. If either α_1 or α_2 is chosen, and a penalty is received, $P(t)$ is unaltered.

Equation (1) shows that the L_{RI} scheme has the vectors $[1,0]^T$ and $[0,1]^T$ as two absorbing states - one of which it converges to. Therefore, the convergence of the L_{RI} scheme is dependent on the nature of the initial conditions and probabilities.

3. Levy flight

The solution presented in this research has two components: the first one is motivated by the strategy involving distributed control; the second one is inspired by the moves made by the animal world. In the previous sections, we introduced the Goore Game and its implementation with LA. In this section, we present the inspiration from the animal world.

Animals move for various reasons: to search for sources of food that are not accessible in the immediate vicinity of the animal, to search for a mate, to avoid predators, to visit a watering hole or to search for a site on which to lay eggs Reynolds & Rhodes (2009). The complexity of the searching strategy depends on the knowledge about the environment. If the environment is unchanging or wholly predictable, animals may develop knowledge of where to locate resources and exploit that knowledge. However, where resource availability is unknown or unpredictable (and this is the scenario investigated in our research), animals have to conduct non-oriented searches with little or no prior knowledge of where resources are distributed. Consequently, the capability to locate resources efficiently will minimize the risk of starvation and potentially minimize exposure to competitors and predators.

The first suggestion that movement patterns of some biological organisms may have Levy flight characteristics came from Shlesinger and Klafter Shlesinger & Klafter (1986). These particular movements consist in random sequences of independent flight-segments whose lengths, l, are drawn from a probability distribution function, having a power-law tail

$$p(l) \approx l^{-\mu}, \tag{2}$$

where $1 < \mu < 3$.

Over recent years, theoretical and field studies provided evidence that many organisms adopt Levy flight[4] movement pattern when they are searching for resources. Honeybees (Apis mellifera), Drosophhila, aphid, microzooplankton, wandering albatross (Diomedea exulans) are a few examples Reynolds (2006a)-Reynolds (2008a), Benhamou (2008).
In general, individual random Levy-flight searching strategies are less efficient than an equidistant (Archimedian) spiral search. However, such a spiral search can only work if navigation and target detection are precise enough geometrically to ensure that all areas are explored and the intervening regions are not missed. In the scenario when the objective of the search is missed, there is no second chance of encountering it because the trajectory is an ever-expanding spiral. A.M. Reynolds mentioned in Reynolds (2008b) that adopting a spiral-search pattern would be disastrous if the navigation and detection systems are even slightly erroneous. A systematic spiral-searching strategy can only be used initially, when cumulative navigational errors are relatively small but should be abandoned in favour of a random looping-searching strategy at latter times.
For the completeness of our analysis, we present now the comparison between individual Brownian search and Levy flight search. For many years, the Brownian motion was the most used model for describing non-oriented animal movement Kareiva & Shigesda (1983)-Okubo & Levin (2002). An individual trajectory through space is regarded as being made up of a sequence of distinct, randomly oriented move step-lengths drawn from a Gaussian distribution. The main difference between the Brownian walk and the Levy flight is due to what (or who) decides the length of the movements[5]. In the Brownian walk, it is considered that the scale of the movement is defined by the organism; in contrast, in the Levy flight, the larger scale of the movement is determined by the distribution of the targets (food or prey). This difference explains why Levy flight is more flexible and suitable for the scenario when the animal has to adapt to the environmental changes.
The last conclusion encourages exploring the maximization of search efficiency. All of the above comments on searching strategies are presented in the context of individuals. However, we propose an algorithm that is collective and has a distributed control: it is able to coordinate independent searching agents, in a des-centralized fashion.
Until now, in addition to the individual models of search for food, the collective models used were developed in a collaborative and competitive manner (see Particle Swarm Optimization, where an entire swarm - flock of birds, school of fish, herd of insects - has a collaborative[6] effect of searching for food). To the best of our knowledge, this is the first research to present a search algorithm using non-cooperative players.

4. Destructive search

This section contains details regarding the algorithm and the corresponding results associated to the destructive search.

---

[4] Strictly speaking, the pattern identified should be named Levy walk because it contains continuous movements rather than discrete jumps. However, we are following the literature that uses Levy flight and Levy walk synonymously.

[5] The main consequence of this difference can be evaluated in swarms or flocks Cai et al. (2007); Viswanathan et al. (1996; 1999). In t steps, a Brownian-walker unit visits $t/\ln(t)$ new sites whereas a Levy flight unit visits t. However, in t steps, a swarm of N Brownian-walker units visit $t\ln(N/\ln(t))$ new sites whereas a swarm of N Levy flight units visit Nt.

[6] Examples of wolves making choices in how to search an area for food can be applied to optimize autonomous vehicles in search of data Plice et al. (2003).

4.1 The algorithm for the destructive search

The algorithm contains two types of actions that each LA can select: *Action 1* means "move", whereas *Action 2* means "stay". The "search" process can be added to each of these actions, namely we can have *Action 1* as "move" and "search", and *Action 2* as only "stay" or *Action 1* as only "move", and *Action 2* as "stay" and "search".
The formal procedure is presented below:

Initialization:
Randomly distribute N agents is the area of radius R_1;
Randomly associated to each agent a probability P_{i1};
Set $Flag\_i\_move$=0 for each agent;

FOR $j = 1$ TO *Nr_iter* DO:
Moving the agents:
For each agent i DO:
Generate a random number M_i;
IF $M_i < P_{i1}$ THEN DO:
$Flag\_i\_move$=1;
Randomly rotate the agent;
Compute D_{ij} the distance between the agent and the rest of $N - 1$;
IF (neighborhood is empty) AND ($D_{ij} < R_2$) AND (neighborhood is unvisited)
THEN (MOVE 1 Step);
END IF;
END IF;
END DO;

Feedback from Referee:
Compute $f = \sum(Flag\_i\_move)$ for all N agents;
Compute $G(f)$;

Updating probabilities for agents
FOR each agent DO:
Generate a random number S_i;
IF ($S_i < G(f)$) THEN:
IF ($flag\_i\_move$ = 1) THEN increase P_{i1}
ELSE decrease P_{i1};
END IF;
END IF;
END DO;
Set $Flag\_i\_move$=0 for each agent;

END DO;

Remarks:

- As we mentioned earlier, our proposed algorithm can be applied on two versions, function of how the resources are distributed in the environment.
    1. Version 1: the movement step is equal to unity.

2. Version 2: the movement step follows a Levy flight distribution described by $l \in [1;5]$ and $\mu = 2$).

- A comment can be made regarding the order of actions to be taken. From the decision point of view, if the condition $M_i < P_{i1}$ is satisfied, the agent will select *Action 1* (in our case, the agent is allowed to move). The agent will be rewarded by the Referee (in general, by the Environment) function of the decision taken. The second step after making the decision is to see if he has an empty space unvisited where to move AND if he satisfies the distance condition: his distance to the farthest neighbor agent must be less than R_2. If these conditions are satisfied, the agent can move on the field. We presented these aspects in detail to make it easier for the reader to understand the difference between the decision of selecting *Action 1* (to move) and the real process on the field. The probabilities are updated only function of the decision and not of the real move on the field. It is true that it is possible to test a new version of the algorithm, namely version 3, where the $Flag\_i\_move$ becomes equal to unity only after the movement step is completely done, namely (MOVE 1 STEP) AND ($Flag\_i\_move$). However, the distance condition is very powerful and will affect the convergence provided by the GG algorithm. The version 3 can succeed if the settings θ (the constant involved in updating probabilities), N, R_1 and R_2 are carefully selected.

4.2 Simulation results

In this subsection, we present four families of simulations: one obtained with Version 1 of the algorithm and three obtained with different settings of Version 2 of the algorithm (namely three different values for the length of the movement step). We depict only the graphical results obtained after enough iterations that are not allowed more movements, for each version of the proposed algorithm. However, we present in Table 1 the area covered by N=10 agents (players) in four settings: Version 1 and Version 2 with the same $\mu = 2$ and $l = 2$, $l = 3$ and $l = 4$. Each setting was run 25 simulations. In each of these settings, we used $N = 10$ agents, with $R_1 = 10$ and $R_2 = 40$. All the agents are L_{RI} with $\theta = 0.1$. The performance criterion $G(\cdot)$ used by the Referee is $G(x) = 0.9 \times e^{-\frac{(0.7-x)^2}{0.0625}}$, as presented in Figure 2. The reader can see that the maximum was covered from Version 1; the increase in the length of the movement decreases the total area covered by the agents.
In Figure 3 (left), we present the result corresponding to Version 1 of the algorithm, namely when the movement step is equal to unity. In Figures 3 (right) and 4 we present the results corresponding to Version 2 of the algorithm, namely when the movement step follows a Levy flight with $l = 2$ in the first graph, with $l = 3$ in the second graph, and $l = 4$ in the third graph. The exponent of the distribution is always $\mu = 2$. The reader can observe the size of the steps as being very close to the agents that cannot move. Many of them have a probability P_1 equal to unity. Thus, they can move from the point of view of the decision maker. However, the distance constraint will not allow them to realize the movement on the field.

5. Non-destructive search

This section contains details regarding the algorithm and the corresponding results associated to the non-destructive search.

5.1 The algorithm

As in previous section, the algorithm contains two types of actions that each LA can select: *Action 1* means "move", whereas *Action 2* means "stay". The "search" process can be added

Iteration	Version1	$l=2$	$l=3$	$l=4$
1	218	516	406	381
2	196	337	535	455
3	185	584	370	428
4	147	608	471	526
5	132	490	569	412
6	190	510	366	524
7	134	511	411	368
8	180	703	625	534
9	184	433	452	429
10	197	582	462	331
11	138	443	638	486
12	129	569	556	280
13	332	389	441	510
14	127	450	435	441
15	165	525	502	400
16	168	300	540	538
17	218	302	521	394
18	235	422	364	504
19	217	430	588	385
20	225	372	417	597
21	252	441	474	544
22	247	501	391	346
23	130	432	624	373
24	111	568	405	430
25	113	428	383	360
Mean	182.80	473.84	477.84	439.04
Standard Deviation	52.98	97.71	86.90	79.96

Table 1. Destructive Search: The area covered by N=10 agents in four settings: Version 1 ($l = 1$) and Version 2 (with the same $\mu = 2$ and $l = 2$, $l = 3$ and $l = 4$). Each setting was run 25 simulations. The average and the standard deviation are presented.

to each of these actions, namely we can have *Action 1* as "move" and "search", and *Action 2* as only "stay" or *Action 1* as only "move", and *Action 2* as "stay" and "search".
The formal procedure is presented below:

Initialization:
Randomly distribute N agents is the area of radius R_1;
Randomly associated to each agent a probability P_{i1};
Set $Flag\_i\_move$=0 for each agent;

FOR $j = 1$ TO Nr_iter DO:
Moving the agents:
For each agent i DO:
Generate a random number M_i;
IF $M_i < P_{i1}$ THEN DO:

Iteration	Version1	$l = 2$	$l = 3$	$l = 4$
1	876	822	716	613
2	848	757	766	589
3	1031	1017	745	623
4	1024	906	564	516
5	1021	993	752	796
6	766	834	782	528
7	928	750	572	606
8	1140	897	533	451
9	873	1006	882	374
10	1042	934	860	666
11	903	762	803	476
12	898	921	779	363
13	947	893	654	475
14	855	1086	857	434
15	1261	674	604	553
16	1062	950	643	697
17	1016	680	575	509
18	1112	831	727	610
19	983	955	1096	674
20	1178	499	716	365
21	1029	879	694	649
22	1011	958	740	573
23	908	987	619	594
24	1107	828	791	629
25	852	876	762	402
Mean	986.84	867.8	729.28	550.6
Standard Deviation	118.44	129.75	123.48	113.05

Table 2. Non-Destructive Search: The area covered by N=10 agents in four settings: Version 1 ($l = 1$) and Version 2 (with the same $\mu = 2$ and $l = 2$, $l = 3$ and $l = 4$). Each setting was run 25 simulations. The average and the standard deviation are presented.

Flag_i_move=1;
Randomly rotate the agent;
Compute D_{ij} the distance between the agent and the rest of $N - 1$;
IF (neighborhood is empty) AND ($D_{ij} < R_2$)
THEN (MOVE 1 Step);
END IF;
END IF;
END DO;

Feedback from Referee:
Compute $f = \sum(Flag\_i\_move)$ for all N agents;
Compute $G(f)$;

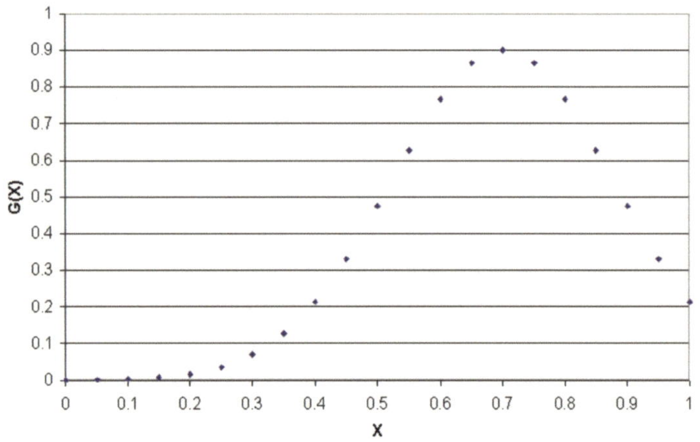

Fig. 2. The function $G(x) = 0.9 \times e^{-\frac{(0.7-x)^2}{0.0625}}$ has its maximum value for x=0.7.

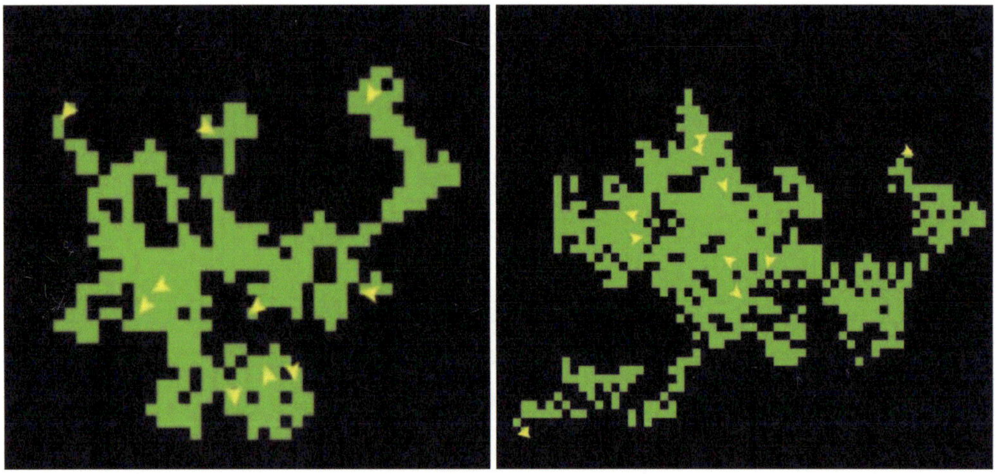

Fig. 3. Destructive Search: (Left)The simulation made with Version 1. (Right) The simulation made with Version 2: Levy flight with $\mu = 2$ and $l = 2$.

Updating probabilities for agents

FOR each agent DO:
Generate a random number S_i;
IF ($S_i < G(f)$) THEN:
IF ($flag\_i\_move$ = 1) THEN increase P_{i1}
ELSE decrease P_{i1};
END IF;
END IF;
END DO;
Set $Flag\_i\_move$=0 for each agent;

Fig. 4. Destructive Search: (Left) The simulation made with Version 2: Levy flight with $\mu = 2$ and $l = 3$. (Right) The simulation made with Version 2: Levy flight with $\mu = 2$ and $l = 4$.

END DO;

Remarks:

- As we mentioned earlier, our proposed algorithm can be applied on two versions, function of how the resources are distributed in the environment.
  1. Version 1: the movement step is equal to unity.
  2. Version 2: the movement step follows a Levy flight distribution described by $l \in [1;5]$ and $\mu = 2$).
- Again, a comment can be made regarding the order of actions to be taken. The steps are the same as in the previous section. However, the difference from the destructive search consist in the freedom to mode into an already visited empty space.

6. Simulation results

In this section, we present four families of simulations: one obtained with Version 1 of the algorithm and three obtained with different settings of Version 2 of the algorithm (namely three different values for the length of the movement step). We depict only the graphical results obtained after enough iterations that are not allowed more movements, for each version of the proposed algorithm. However, we present in Table 2 the area covered by N=10 agents (players) in four settings: Version 1 and Version 2 with the same $\mu = 2$ and $l = 2, l = 3$ and $l = 4$. Each setting was run 25 simulations. In each of these settings, we used $N = 10$ agents, with $R_1 = 10$ and $R_2 = 40$. All the agents are L_{RI} with $\theta = 0.1$. The performance criterion $G(\cdot)$ used by the Referee is $G(x) = 0.9 \times e^{-\frac{(0.7-x)^2}{0.0625}}$, as presented in the previous section. The reader can see that the maximum was covered from Version 1; the increase in the length of the movement decreases the total area covered by the agents.

In Figure 5 (left), we present the result corresponding to Version 1 of the algorithm, namely when the movement step is equal to unity. In Figures 5 (right) and 6 we present the results corresponding to Version 2 of the algorithm, namely when the movement step follows a Levy flight with $l = 2$ in the first graph, with $l = 3$ in the second graph, and $l = 4$ in the third graph. The exponent of the distribution is always $\mu = 2$. The reader can observe the size of the steps as being very close to the agents that cannot move. Many of them have a probability P_1 equal to unity. Thus, they can move from the point of view of the decision maker. However, the distance constraint will not allow them to realize the movement on the field.

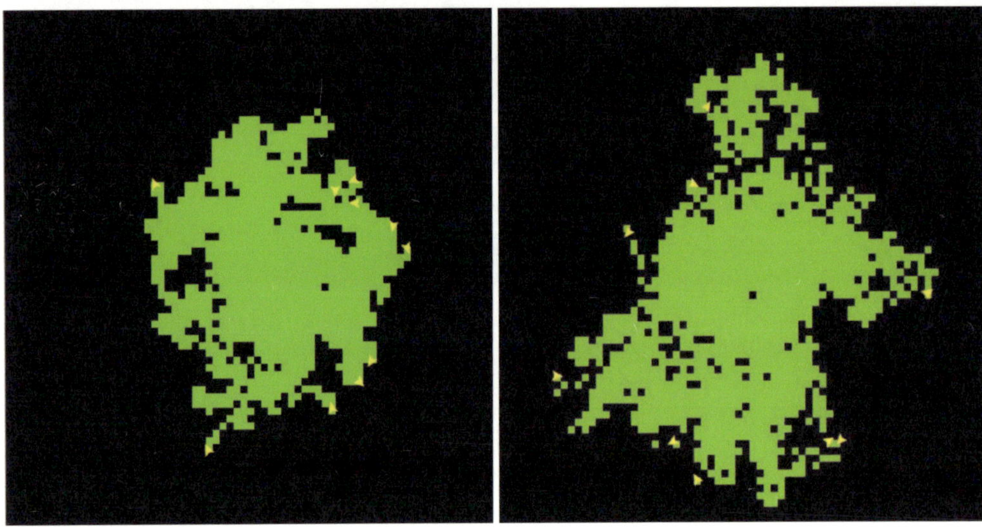

Fig. 5. Non-Destructive Search: (Left) The simulation made with Version 1. (Right) The simulation made with Version 2: Levy flight with $\mu = 2$ and $l = 2$.

7. Conclusions

This paper presents a new agents-based algorithms which can be used for identifying efficient search strategies for locating objects (e.g. mines) distributed over large areas. The originality of our work consists in applying a non-cooperative non-zero sum game, namely the distributed Goore Game model. As opposed to the classical collaborative and competitive strategies, the agents are not aware of the actions of the other agents.

We investigated two methods, namely the destructive search and the non-destructive search. The proposed algorithm has two versions: one when the agent can move with a step equal to unity and the other when the step of the agent follows a Levy flight distribution. The latter version is inspired by the work of Reynolds, motivated by biological examples. We present the area covered in each simulation function of the length of the movement step. The reader can evaluate the benefit of each version.

In the case of the non-destructive search, the reader can observe a trade off between the maximum of area covered and the freedom to search far from the initial center. The Version 1 of the algorithm covers the greatest area. However, the Version 2 of the algorithm is able to search after targets at a greater distance from the initial center.

In the case of the destructive search, the reader can observe that the Version 2 of the algorithm covers the greatest area. Increasing l will stabilize the variation of the searching area (the standard deviation is decreasing).

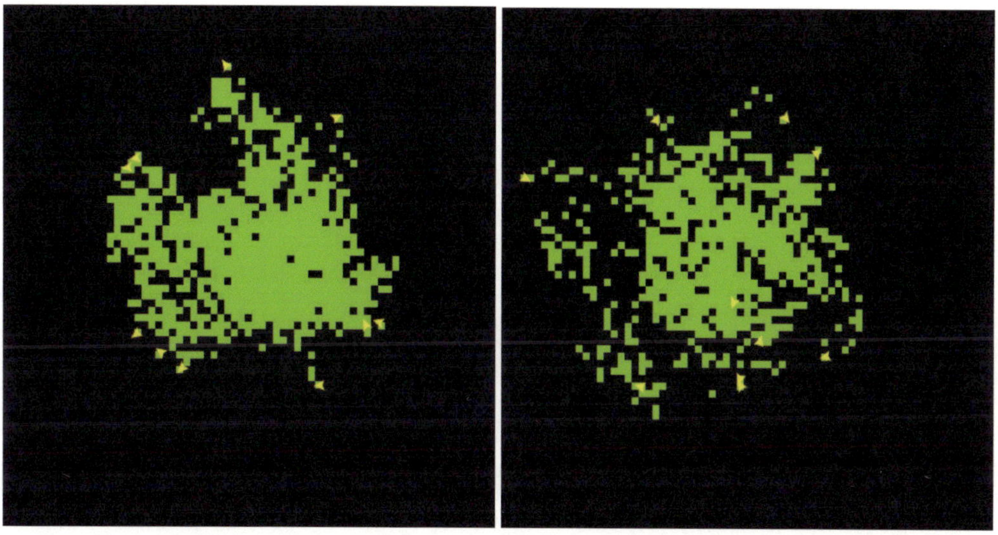

Fig. 6. Non-Destructive Search: (Left)The simulation made with Version 2: Levy flight with $\mu = 2$ and $l = 3$. (Right) The simulation made with Version 2: Levy flight with $\mu = 2$ and $l = 4$.

The future direction of this research are: i) producing a sensitivity analysis of the search problem, namely how the area covered by the agents depends on N, R_1, R_2 and G and ii) comparing the benefits of destructive vs. non-destructive search algorithms.

8. References

Benhamou, S. (2008). How many animals really do the Levy walk? reply, *Ecology* Vol. 89(No. 8): 2351–2352.

Cai, X., Zeng, J., Cui, Z. & Tan, Y. (2007). Particle Swarm Optimization using Levy probability distribution, *L.Kand, Y.Liu and S. Zeng (Eds): ISICA 2007, LNCS 4683* pp. 353–361.

Cao, Y., Fukunaga, A. & Kahng, A. (1997). Cooperative mobile robotics: Antecedents and directions, *Autonomous Robots* Vol. 4(No. 1): 1–23.

Chen, D. & Varshney, P. (2004). QoS support in wireless sensor networks: A survey, *The 2004 International Conference on Wireless Networks (ICWN 2004)* pp. 227–233.

Chignell, R. (1998). MINREC - a development platform for anti-personel mine detection and recognition, *Detection of abandoned land mines, Conference publication no. 458*, IEE, Edinburg, U.K., pp. 64–76.

Ho, S., Nassef, N., Pornsin-Sirirak, N., Tai, Y.-C. & Ho, C.-M. (2002). *Flight dynamics of small vehicles*, ICAS CONGRESS, Toronto, Canada.

Iyer, R. & Kleinrock, L. (2003). Qos control for sensor networks, *IEEE International Conference on Communications* Vol. 1: 517–521.

Kareiva, P. & Shigesda, N. (1983). Analysis insect movement as a correlated random walk, *Oecologia* Vol. 56: 234–238.

Lakshmivarahan, S. (1981). *Learning Algorithms Theory and Applications*, Springer-Verlag, Berlin.

Narendra, K. & Thathachar, M. (1989). *Learning Automata: An Introduction*, Prentice-Hall Inc., Upper Saddle River, NJ.

Norman, M. F. (1968). On linear models with two absorbing barriers, *Journal of Mathematical Psychology* Vol. 5: 225–241.

Okubo, A. & Levin, S. (2002). *Diffusion and ecological problems: modern perspectives*, Springer-Verlag, New-York.

Oommen, B., Granmo, O. & Pederson, A. (1999). Using stochastic AI techniques to achieve unbounded resolution in finite player Goore game and its applications, *Proceedings of IEEE-CIG'07, the 2007 IEEE Symposium on Computational Intelligence and Games*, IEEE, Hawaii, pp. 161–167.

Plice, L., Pisanich, G. & Young, L. (2003). Biologically inspired behavioural strategies for autonomous aerial explorers on Mars, *Proceedings of the 2003 IEEE Aerospace Conference, Big Sky* 1: 1–304.

Poznyak, A. & Najim, K. (1997). *Learning Automata and Stochastic Optimization*, Springer-Verlag, Berlin.

Reynolds, A. (2006a). On the intermittent behavior of foraging animals, *Europhysics Letters* Vol. 75(No. 4): 517–520.

Reynolds, A. (2006b). Optimal scale-free searching strategies for the location of moving targets: New insights on visual cued mate location behaviour in insects, *Physics Letters A* Vol. 360: 224–227.

Reynolds, A. (2007). Avoidance of specific odour trails results in scale-free movement patterns and the execution of an optimal searching strategy, *Europhysics Letters* Vol. 79: 30006–30011.

Reynolds, A. (2008a). How many animals really do the Levy walk? comment, *Ecology* Vol. 89(No. 8): 2347–2351.

Reynolds, A. (2008b). Optimal random Levy-loop searching: new insights into the searching behaviours of central-place foragers, *Europhysics Letters* Vol. 82(No. 2): 20001–20006.

Reynolds, A. (2009). Adaptive Levy walks can outperform composte Brownian walks in non-destrcutive random searching scenarios, *Physica A* Vol. 388: 561–564.

Reynolds, A. & Rhodes, C. (2009). The Levy flight paradigm: random search patterns and mechanisms, *Ecology* Vol. 90: 877–887.

Rhodes, C. & Reynolds, A. (2007). The influence of search strategies and homogeneous isotropic turbulence on planktonic contact rates, *Europhysics Letters* Vol. 80: 60003–60012.

Shlesinger, M. & Klafter, J. (1986). *Growth and Form, H.E.Stanley and N.Ostrowski (Eds)*, Martinus Nijhof Publishers, Amsterdam.

Thathachar, M. & Arvind, M. (1997). Solution of Goore game using models of stochastic learning automata, *Journal of Indian Institute of Science* (No. 76): 47–61.

Tsetlin, M. (1963). Finite automata and the modeling of the simplest forms of behavior, *Uspekhi Matem Nauk* Vol. 8: 1–26.

Tung, B. & Kleinrock, L. (1996). Using finite state automata to produce self-optimization and self-control, *IEEE Transactions on parallel and distributed systems* Vol. 7(No. 4).

Viswanathan, G., Afanasyev, V., Buldyrev, S., Murphy, E., Prince, P. & Stanley, H. E. (1996). Levy flight search patterns of wandering albatrosses, *Nature* Vol. 381: 413–415.

Viswanathan, G., Buldyrev, S., Havlin, S., da Luz, M. G., Raposo, E. P. & Stanley, H. E. (1999). Optimizing the success of random searches, *Nature* Vol. 401: 911–914.

24

Extremal Distribution Sorting Algorithm for a CFD Optimization Problem

K.Yano and Y.Kuriyama
Mie University
Gifu University
Japan

1. Introduction

The numerical simulator for fluid analysis based on computational fluid dynamics (CFD) is focused on analyzing the behavior of a fluid around an object, or its thermal hydraulics. CFD is a technique that considers the Navier-Stokes equation and energy conservation law and uses the mass conservation method. With the development of computing power and the price plummet of personal computers, the CFD simulator has become a useful and realistic tool(Stefano et al., 2005). Furthermore, CFD is now used not only for analyzing of the behavior of a fluid but also for optimization of a fluid's shape or flow for improved quality or performance. That said, the optimization with a CFD simulator for improved quality or performance still has many problems. For example, the solution space formed by the solution of optimization using a CFD simulator has become a multimodal space with a lot of local minimums, as shown in Fig. 1. Furthermore, the optimizations for practical use become more complication because these applications require more variables and constraints.

As a method of searching efficiently for a complex solution space, the meta-heuristic algorithm(Pablo, 2003) is a heuristic technique. As an algorithm with the greatest general

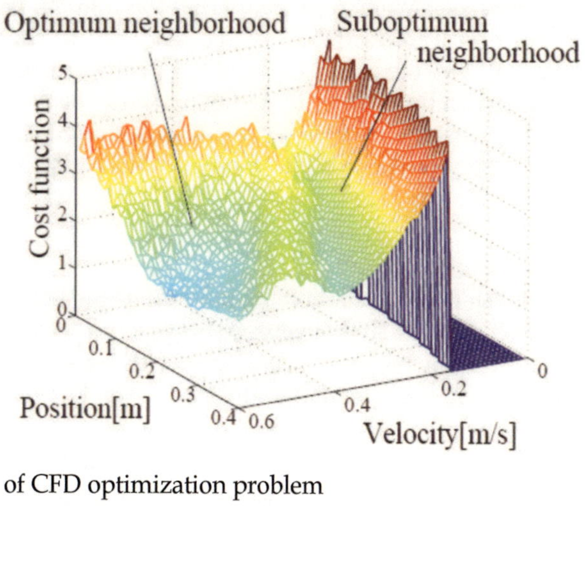

Fig. 1. Solution space of CFD optimization problem

versatility, the genetic algorithm (GA) is generally used (Kokolo et al., 2000). However, in cases such as analyzing a problem that has a lot of local solution, the solution that incorporates the general GA is highly likely to derive local solution, and thus it is difficult to derive the global optimized solution. Of course, this problem can be solved by enlarging the number of population members, the number of generations and the mutation evolution; on the other hand, the computational time for one condition was a few minutes and the optimization requires hundreds of repeated computations. Thus the optimization using the CFD simulator needs a lot of time to finish the task.

The purpose of this study was to design a solution search algorithm using fewer populations and generations to derive the optimized solution more efficiently for an optimization problem by using a CFD simulator. Specifically, focusing on an extremal solution in a multimodal space, we propose the Extremal Distribution Sorting Algorithm (EDSA), which searches intensively at the improving point in the nearly extremal solution. The proposed method makes it possible to derive the global optimized solution quickly with few repeated computation. The effectiveness of the proposed method is shown through experiments in actual die-casting plants for deriving the optimum plunger input.

In this study, the design of the Extremal Distribution Sorting Algorithm (EDSA) is described and applied to actual die-casting plant. In section 2, the algorithm of EDSA is indicated. The EDSA are based on GA, a big feature of EDSA is using the approximate curve to search the extreme value. In section 3, the EDSA is applied the actual optimization problem of die-casting plant, and the GA is also applied to compare the performance. Finally, section 4 concludes with the effectiveness of the proposed algorithm.

2. Extremal distribution sorting algorithm

In this study, to derive the optimum solution in a multimodal space in a CFD optimization problem with low calculation frequency, we propose the Extremal Distribution Sorting Algorithm (EDSA). The EDSA distinguishes an progressive area and analyzes the solution space of a CFD optimization problem and the tendency toward the improvement of the solution by using the approximation curve of the evaluation value and the extreme value. An outline of the EDSA is presented in **Fig.** 2. The possibility of getting into the local minimum is high only when searching for the optimization solution neighbourhood, and all that simply. Therefore, the EDSA searches for the tendency to the improvement of the solution and aims at an efficient optimized calculation by comprehending the distribution of the solution in the entire solution space. In addition, a loop of an optimization group is treated as a generation, the best solution in a generation is treated as an elite, the following optimization group of the present analytical optimization group is treated as a next generation.

3.1 Deriving the extreme value

Though all individuals inside the generation are handled as the next generation candidates in the GA, an excellent individual is analyzed by priority in the EDSA. Thus the n-dimensional CFD optimization problem is replaced with two-dimensional space by the evaluation value and one variable, and the algorithm searches for the tendency to the solution to each variable by repeating the operation n times. First, each extreme value and the neighborhood of the evaluation value and the approximation curve are obtained. When the evaluation value of the CFD simulator is assumed to be $f(x)$, the extreme value cannot

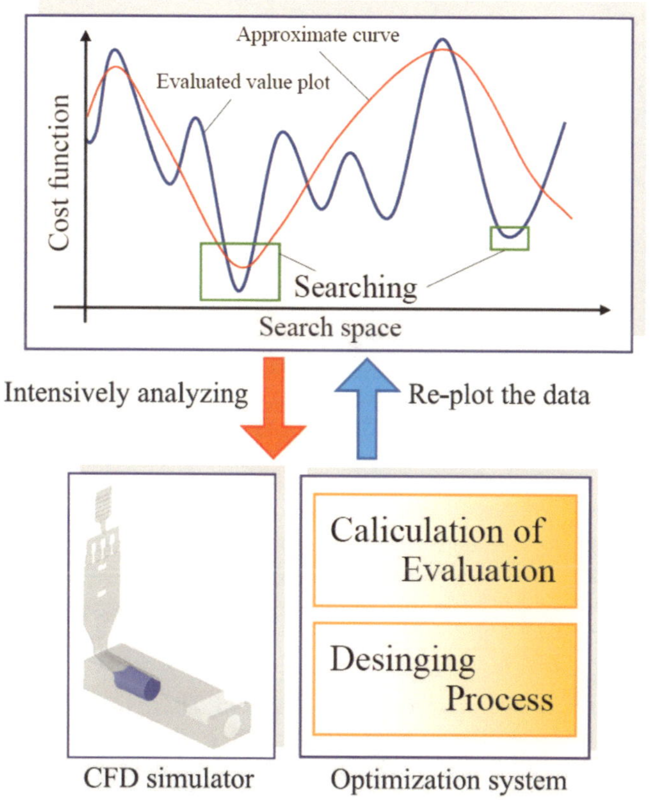

Fig. 2. Extremal distribution sorting algorithm

$$\left(f\left(x_{i+1,k}\right)-f\left(x_{i,k}\right)\right)\times\left(f\left(x_{i,k}\right)-f\left(x_{i-1,k}\right)\right)<0<\left(f\left(x_{i,k}\right)-f\left(x_{i-1,k}\right)\right) \quad (1)$$

$$\left(f\left(x_{i+1,k}\right)-f\left(x_{i,k}\right)\right)\times\left(f\left(x_{i,k}\right)-f\left(x_{i-1,k}\right)\right)<0, \quad \left(f\left(x_{i,k}\right)-f\left(x_{i-1,k}\right)\right)<0 \quad (2)$$

be derived by the differentiation because it is discontinuous. Therefore, whether *k*th variables and the *i*th individual is an extreme value is judged by using the following Equation 1 and Equation 2.

When Equation 1 is filled at the same time, x_i ; k is the maximum value. When Equation 2 is filled at the same time, x_i ; k is the minimum value. When x_i ; k is judged as an extreme value, x_i is preserved as an extreme value. When thinking about the extreme value neighborhood of x_i ; k, the minimum unit e_k of the variable is used. Afterwards, the two points x_i ; k +e_k and xi ; k e_k that adjoin x_i ; k are substituted for the extreme value. The extreme value and the neighborhood are calculated in the same way for the approximation curve, and the individual is preserved.

3.2 Deriving the approximate curve

The approximation curve of the evaluation value to comprehend the tendency to the solution is derived. It depends on a complex solution space by using the approximation curve, and it searches for the area where the improvement of the solution is expected. The approximation curve used to search for the solution is derived by the least-squares method, as follows Equation 3, where N : the number of samples, n:the degree of the CFD optimization problem, m:the degree of the approximation curve, x_i ; k : the k th, i th individual, J_i : the evaluation value of i th individual. The degree of the approximation curve m is changed in proportion to the number of samples N. Condition m is that 5th dimensions are assumed to be the maximum degree in this study.

$$\begin{pmatrix} N & \sum_{i=0}^{N} x_{i,k} & \sum_{i=0}^{N} x_{i,k}^2 & \cdots & \sum_{i=0}^{N} x_{i,k}^m \\ \sum_{i=0}^{N} x_{i,k} & \sum_{i=0}^{N} x_{i,k}^2 & \sum_{i=0}^{N} x_{i,k}^3 & \cdots & \sum_{i=0}^{N} x_{i,k}^{m+1} \\ \vdots & \vdots & \vdots & \ddots & \vdots \\ \sum_{i=0}^{N} x_{i,k}^m & \sum_{i=0}^{N} x_{i,k}^{m+1} & \sum_{i=0}^{N} x_{i,k}^{m+2} & \cdots & \sum_{i=0}^{N} x_{i,k}^{2m} \end{pmatrix} \begin{pmatrix} a_0 \\ a_1 \\ \vdots \\ a_m \end{pmatrix} = \begin{pmatrix} \sum_{i=0}^{N} y_i \\ \sum_{i=0}^{N} x_{i,k} \cdot J_i \\ \vdots \\ \sum_{i=0}^{N} x_{i,k}^m \cdot J_i \end{pmatrix} \tag{3}$$

3.3 Election of the next generation individual

After deriving the extreme value of the CFD simulator from the evaluation value and the approximation curve, the next generation's candidates are elected based on those tendencies. Note that the approximation curve is not a curve that passes the extreme value that actually exists. There is a possibility that the extreme value is not more excellent than an actual evaluated value because the approximation curve is composed of the value of the guess. Naturally, the opposite possibility can exist, too. Then, only the individual to which the improvement of the solution is expected and the individual with a higher evaluation value are left as election candidate. And, the parents of the next generation are elected from among these candidates. The parents are elected based on the extreme value of the evaluation value. First, a set of the individual with a bad extreme value and its neighborhood is assumed to be X_b. A set of the penalty X_p is also listed it based on X_b to exclude the next generation's candidates. Moreover, an individual that doesn't fill the restriction is added to X_p. Next, a set of the individual with a good extreme value and its neighborhood is assumed to be X_g. Note that if the extreme value whose evaluation value is larger than the mean value of the maximum value $\overline{f}(x_g)$,

$$f(x_g) > \overline{f}(x_g) \tag{4}$$

only the extreme value that fills Equation 4 is preserved as a set of candidate X_c, which makes an inquiry into X_p. If there is a corresponding individual to X_p in X_c, it is excluded from X_c. The conceptual diagram of the above operation is shown in Fig.3.

In addition, the candidate's exclusion is done based on the following conditions. When you compare the extreme value of the approximation curve with that of the evaluation value, the latter is preserved by priority because it is dependable. A good extreme value of the evaluation value is assumed to be x_g. In addition, only the individual that fills Equation 4 is made a candidate x_c from among x_g. A bad extreme value of the evaluation value is assumed to be x_b, and its neighborhood is assumed to be x_{g+e}, x_{b+e}. A good extreme value of the approximation curve is assumed to be x_{Ag}, and a bad extreme value of the approximation curve is assumed to be x_{Ab}, and the neighborhood is assumed to be x_{Ag+e}, x_{Ab+e}. Candidates are chosen based on the following condition:

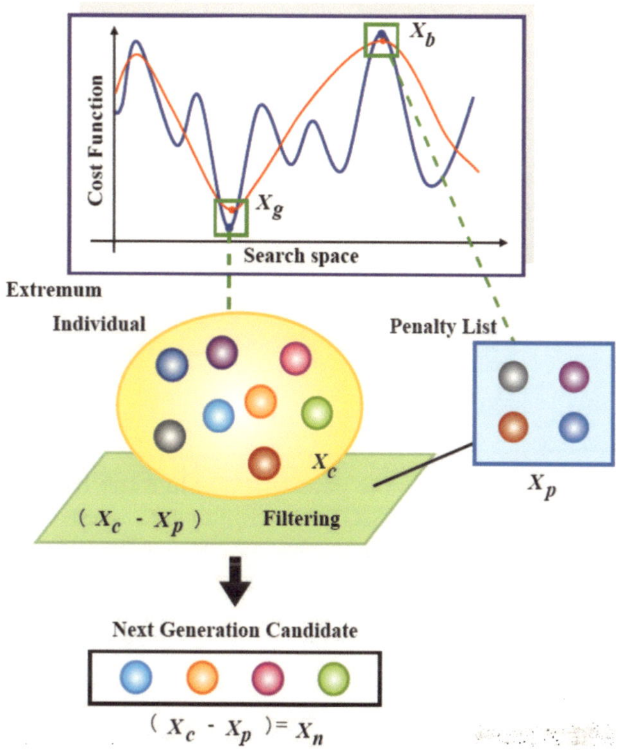

Fig. 3. The individual selection

$$x_c > x_b > x_{g+e} > x_{Ag} > x_{b+e} > x_{Ab} > x_{Ag+e} > x_{Ab+e} \tag{5}$$

Candidates are preserved as x_n based on Equation 5. The best solution in a generation is added to the candidate as the elite to continue the improvement of the solution. Finally, these candidates are preserved as the parents of the next generation individual x_n.

3.4 Simplex crossover

The parents individual that generates the next generation individual is elected from X_n. The roulette selection is applied to the election method. The roulette selection is the method of selecting the individual according to the selection rate corresponding to the evaluation value. The probability P_i that a certain individual is selected is expressed in Equation 6.

$$P_i = \frac{f(x_i)}{\sum_{j=1}^{N_g} f(x_j)} \tag{6}$$

In the use of Equation 6 and simplex crossover (SPX), next generation individuals are generated. The conceptual diagram of SPX is shown in Fig.4.
SPX is a crossover method for a real-coded genetic algorithm (RCGA)(Shigeyoshi et al. 1999). The RCGA uses the crossover method for treating not the variable as bit strings but the real vectors. Especially, it is an effective crossover method for solving a continuous optimization problem, and it is an effective way to consider the dependence among

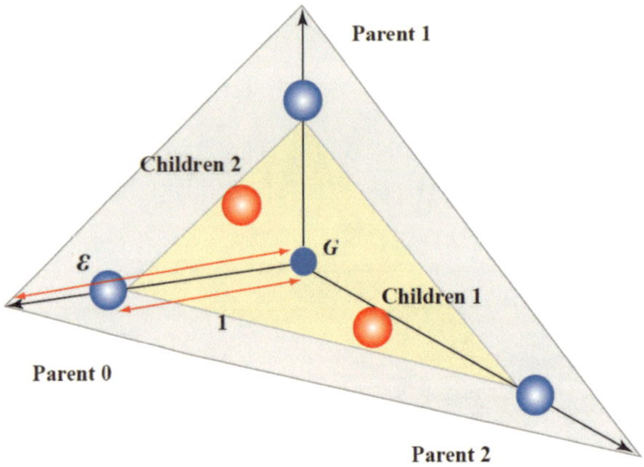

Fig. 4. Simplex crossover

variables. Moreover, information on the parents individual can be easily passed on to the child individual(Isao et al. 1997). The RCGA has several kinds of crossover methods.

In the proposal algorithm, in spite of the dependence among variables or the scale problem, SPX is employed to deal with any optimization problems. Moreover, the n dimensional CFD optimization problem is replaced with two-dimension space by the evaluation value and one variable. The individual with the extreme value of each variable is distinguished. Therefore, other values of the variables can be operated as crossover while maintaining the value of a variable that became an extreme value.

The procedure of SPX is as fellows. When the intended CFD optimization problem is R_n, n+1 th parents $P\vec{x}_0,...,P\vec{x}_n$ are elected from Xn according to Equation 6. Next, the barycentric position G is derived based on the parents.

$$\vec{G} = \frac{1}{n+1}\sum_{i=1}^{k}\overrightarrow{Px_i} \tag{7}$$

The range of formation of the next generation is decided based on G, and the next generation individual is generated by using the uniform random number.

$$\overrightarrow{p_0} = \vec{G} + \varepsilon(\overrightarrow{Px_0} - \vec{G}) \tag{8}$$

$$\vec{c}_0 = \vec{0} \tag{9}$$

$$\overrightarrow{p_j} = \vec{G} + \varepsilon(\overrightarrow{Px_j} - \vec{G}) \tag{10}$$

$$\overrightarrow{c_j} = r_{j-1}\left(\overrightarrow{P_{j-1}} - \overrightarrow{P_j} + \overrightarrow{c_{j-1}}\right),\ (j = 1,\cdots,n) \tag{11}$$

Note that r_{j-1} is calculated from the uniform random number $u(0,1)$ in section [0,1].

$$r_{j-1} = \left(u(0,1)\right)^{\frac{1}{j+1}} \tag{12}$$

And, the next generation C_x is the following equation.

$$\vec{c_0} = \overrightarrow{x_n} + \overrightarrow{C_n} \tag{13}$$

When the relation between the number of individuals in generation N and the degree of the CFD optimization problem k is $N > k$, the selection of the parents and the generation of the next generation individuals are repeated until the number of individuals reaches N. And, if the restriction is not filled or does not conform to penalty lists Xp, the next generation individual is not preserved.

3. Application to Die-casting

3.1 Evaluation of air entrapment

Our fluid analysis software was a 3D fluid calculation program using calculus of finite differences for treating a wide range of flows from an incompressible flow to a flow accompanied by an adjustable surface, flow accounting for compaction, and flow accompanied by solidification. The free surface is calculated by the Volume Of Fluid(VOF). The geometric for a complex obstacle is recognized by Fractional Area Volume Obstacle Representation(FAVOR). Fig.5 shows an overview of the mesh setting, and Table 1 shows the parameters of the mesh setting which was used by past study(Ken'ichi et al. 2008).

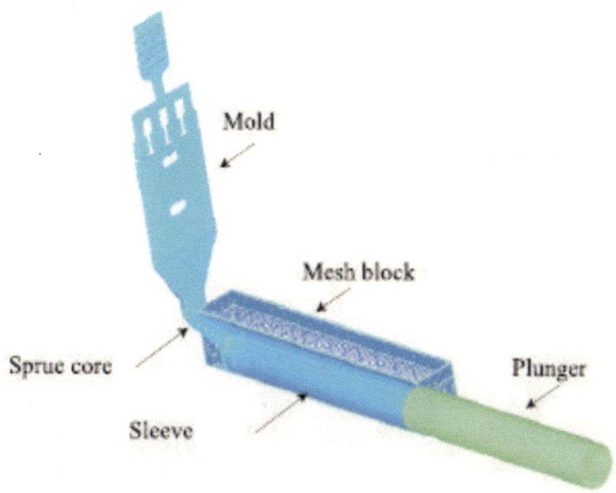

Fig. 5. Mesh setting for CFD simulation

	Cell size	Number of cell
X-direction	0.004	20
Y-direction	0.002~0.006	132
Z-direction	0.0022~0.0035	29
Total number of cell		76,560

Table 1. Mesh parameter

As seen in Fig.5, the sleeve is symmetrical to the X axis. Thus, the analyzing area is set as only a one-sided model to reduce the analyzing time to, only about ten minutes. Table 1 shows the minimum settings to do calculations quickly and accurately, and the mesh parameter is set so that the rough mesh is used around the start point of the sleeve because the velocity is low and the fluid is stable in the section. On the other hand, the fine mesh is

used around the end point of the sleeve because the breaks of the wave at an early stage of filling cause dispersion by collision with the sprue core in the section.
In this study, the plunger tip was flat, and we used hot working die steels (SKD61) for the die, sleeve, and plunger. Aluminum alloy of ADC12 is assumed as the molten metal. Table 2 shows the fluid properties of ADC12. We set the die temperature during pouring to 110 to 150°C (steady state) and the molten metal temperature in the melting furnace to 660 to 680°C. We used Yushiro AZ7150W as a parting agent.

Density of fluid	2700 kg/m³
Viscosity of fluid	0.0030 Pa•s
Specific heat	1100J/(kg•K)
Thermal conductivity	100.5 W(m•K)
Initial temperature	653.15 K

Table 2 . Fluid properties of ADC12

Using the fluid analysis software to determine the air entrapment amount in molten metal caused by plunger movement in the sleeve, we calculated the air entrapment amount on the liquid surface assuming that a turbulent eddy surface, i.e., turbulent strength exceeds gravity and we analyzed stabilization of surface tension and the range of liquid elements lifted on the free surface. V_a : air entrapment column fraction, F_f :fluid volume fraction, and V_f :cell volume fraction (ratio of an obstacle area to a fluid area) calculated by fluid analysis software in each mesh cell are multiplied by the column of each mesh cell and summed. Equation 14 calculates air entrapment amount $a(t)$.

$$a(t) = \sum_{k=1}^{n} V_{ak} F_{fk} V_{fk} V_{ck} \tag{14}$$

where V_c is the volume of a mesh cell and n the total of mesh cells. In experiments, we could not strictly measure the air entrapment amount caused by actual plunger movement, and it is difficult to evaluate $a(t)$, so we used air entrapment amount $a(t_{fill})$ at the completion of filling the sleeve ($t=t_{fill}$)resulting from analysis with index A representing the ease of air entrapment. We fixed acceleration at 0.05 m and changed low velocity v_l from 0.20 to 0.60 m every 0.01 m/s to analyze air entrapment until sleeve filling. Simulation confirmed the break of an initial wave and scattering due to collision the break of an initial wave and

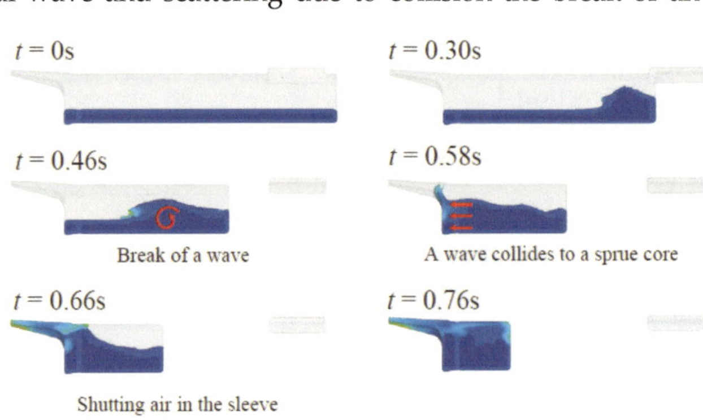

Fig. 6. Simulation result of $v_l = 0.50$ m/s

scattering due to collision with the sprue core at 0.37 m/s or more (Fig.5). Air surrounded by the sleeve wall, plunger, and molten metal was also confirmed at t = 0.66 s. These phenomena are expressed as "air shutting".
Even if velocity is decelerated to less than or equal to 0.23 m/s, however, a big wave is generated by reclusion between the return wave and plunger (Fig.6 (vl=0.21 m/s)) and air shutting is also generated by molten metal. This implies that low-velocity projection alone cannot prevent air entrapment and suppress product defects.

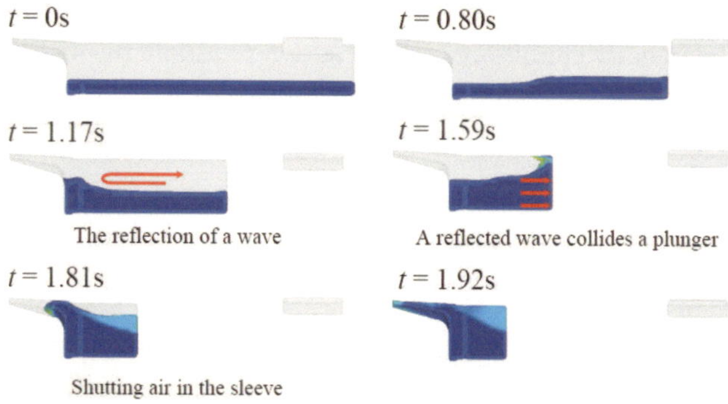

Fig. 7. Simulation result of v_l=0.21 m/s

3.2 Setting the cost function

The actual casting plants can be control the multistep velocity, and the velocity pattern, which has five phases, is derived from past studies. Thus, in this study the velocity is set by v_1,v_2,v_3, and the acceleration distance is set by x_1, x_2. The plunger velocity is expressed as shown in Fig.8, where x_{fill} is filling position which is a constant value.
The optimization problem was defined with a cost function equivalent to the sum of the weighted quantity of air entrainment and the weighted filling time, as shown in Equation 15,

$$\text{minimize} \quad : \quad J = w_a A(v_i(t), x) + w_t t_f(v_i(t), x) + K_p + A_{\text{shut}} \tag{15}$$

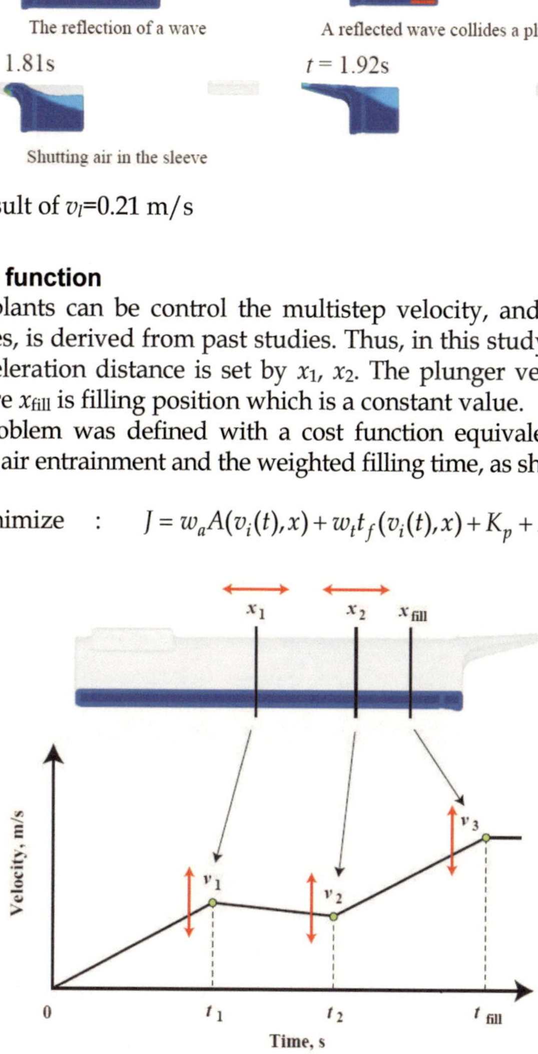

Fig. 8. Die-casting simulation model

$$\text{subject to} \quad : \quad \begin{array}{ll} 0.02 \le v_i \le 0.60 & (i = 1 \sim 3) \\ 0.02 \le x_i \le 0.35 & (i = 1 \sim 2) \\ 0 \le t_{\text{fill}} \le 0.35 & \\ A_{\text{shut}} \le 2.0 & \end{array} \qquad (16)$$

where A is the quantity of air entrainment, t_{fill} is the filling time, x is the acceleration distance, and $w_a = 1.0$ and $w_t = 0.1$ are the weighting factors, where K_p is the penalty. Each time the penalty conditions shown in Equation 16 hold, the penalty $K_p = 108$, which is big enough to avoid the penalty conditions, will be added to satisfy the specifications. And A_{shut} is the volume of trapped air to avoid air surrounded by the sleeve wall, plunger, and molten metal when the plunger injection is switched from low speed to high speed. A_{shut} is defined as shown in Fig.9.

Three parameters are introduced to calculate the quantity of air shutting.

- D_1: Volume/opening column of fluid in the Y cross section.
- D_2: Threshold of air entrapment amount.
- D_3: Calculation time step.

We used fluid analysis of t were each time interval specified by D_3 to output the cell column fraction and the fraction of fluid for calculating the filling per sleeve cross section.

We calculated the space volume at the back where the fraction of fluid is behind $D_1 \times 100\%$ for the cross section and defined the maximum space volume as the amount of air shutting A_{shut} m^3. If plunger velocity input is designed to enable the air entrapment amount to be decreased using this simulator, good results will be obtained in actual projection experiments.

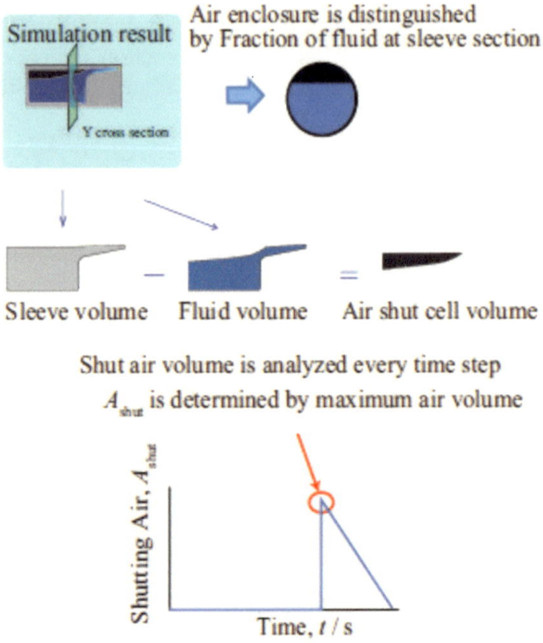

Fig. 9. The relationship of the air entrapment to velocity and switching position by using the CFD simulator

3.3 Optimum result of die-casting

The parameters for the EDSA are shown in Table 3, and the parameters for the GA to be compared with the EDSA are shown in Table 4, where the initial population is the same for each algorithm, allowing us to calculate under the same conditions.

Parameter	Numerics
Number of generation	60
Number of population	30
Number of elite preservation	2
Order of fitting curve	5

Table 3. Parameters for EDSA

Parameter	Numerics
Number of generation	60
Number of population	30
Number of elite preservation	1
Crossover fraction	0.80
Mutation fraction	0.01

Table 4. Parameter for GA

The results of calculating using the EDSA and the GA are shown in Fig.10. Fig.11 shows the process of calculating. The result of the optimization shown in Table 5, the GA has good convergence at the early stage. However, the GA is stopped at the early stage, and finally the solution converges by the 31st generation. The reason is that the solution fell into the spot of a local solution. The results show that the GA can't be used to derive the optimum solution without an enormous amount of calculation.

On the other hand, the EDSA took a long time until convergence, but it is continued to calculate at the maximum generation, and compared with the GA, the solution derived by using the EDSA is better than the solution derived by using the GA. Based on these results, we conclude that the proposed method can derive the optimized solution with few repeated computations.

3.4 Verification by experiment

Experiments for an actual die-casting plant were performed with the obtained optimum velocity input derived using the EDSA and the GA. The plunger velocity used in the experiment is shown in Table 6. The result of the blister examination is shown in Fig.12. Fig.12 is the total area of the air bubble that appeared on the test piece surface after the blister examination is shown.

Parameter	EDSA	GA
Cost function	0.3441	0.4622
Air entrainment	0.1682	0.2737
Filling time	1.76 s	1.89 s
Optimum termination	41	19

Table 5. Performance comparison sample

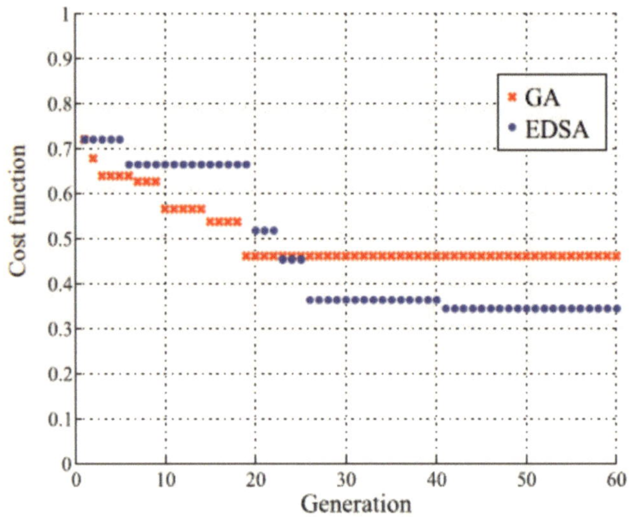

Fig. 10. Optimization result of EDSA and GA

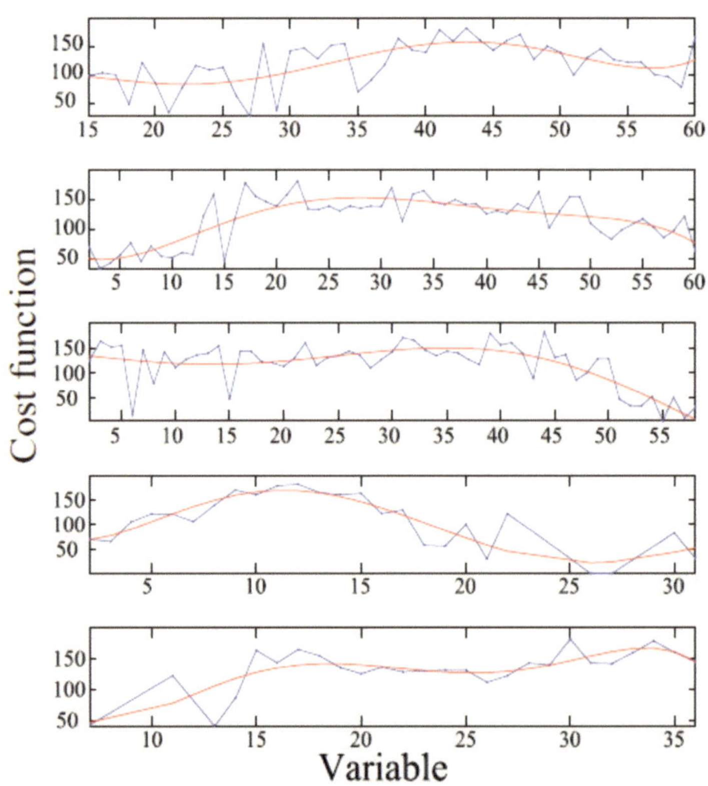

Fig. 11. Optimization process of EDSA

The amount of air entrainment by the CFD simulator is also indicated in Fig.12 for comparison. As seen in the Fig.12, there is a significant difference in the amount of air entrainment between the experimental result and the simulation result. However, seen from the relative scale, the amount of air entrainment using the EDSA is better than that resulting from using the GA. From the results of the amount of air entrainment by the CFD simulator and experimental result, the amount of air entrainment using the EDSA is better than that resulting from using the GA.

EDSA	Time s	Velocity m/s	Position m
1	1.23	0.26	0.160
2	1.34	0.50	0.200
3	1.76	0.29	0.367

GA	Time s	Velocity m/s	Position m
1	1.32	0.22	0.145
2	1.62	0.44	0.245
3	1.87	0.56	0.367

Table 6. Calculated optimum plunger velocity by using EDSA and GA

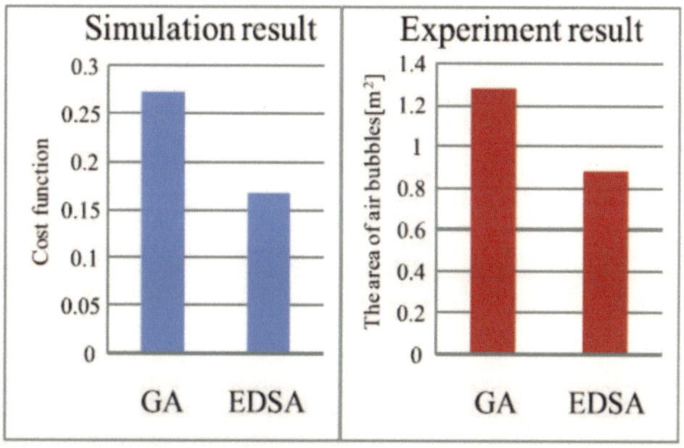

Fig. 14. Experimantal results and simulation results.

4. Conclusion

The purpose of this study was to design a search algorithm that used smaller number of populations and a generation that can derive the optimized solution more efficiently for an optimization problem using a CFD simulator. Specifically, focusing on the extremal solution in the multimodal space, we proposed the Extremal Distribution Sorting Algorithm (EDSA), which searches intensively for the improvement point in the nearly extremal solution. The proposed method makes it possible to derive the global optimized solution quickly with few repeated computations. The effectiveness of the proposed method is shown through experiments in actual die-casting plants for deriving the optimum plunger input. The proposed method can derive the optimized solution with few repeated computation. Finally, the effectiveness of the proposed method was clarified by experimental results, which showed that the amount of air entrainment by using the EDSA was better than that resulting from using the GA.

5. Reference

Stefano P., Carlo P. & Martin M., (2005). "Integrating Multibody Simulation and CFD : toward Complex Multidisciplinary Design Optimization," *JSME international journal. Ser. B, Fluids and thermal engineering*, Vol.48, No.2, pp. 224-228

Pablo M., (2003)."gentle introduction to memetic algorithm," *Handbookof Metaheuristics*, pp. 105-144

Kokolo I.& Shigenobu K., (2000). "GA based on the UV-structure Hypothesis and Its Application to JSP," 6th Parallel Problem Solving from Nature, pp. 273-282

Ken'ichi. Y., Koutarou H., Yoshifumi K.& Seishi N., (2008) . "Optimum Velocity Control of Die Casting Plunger Accounting for Air Entrapment and Shutting, (2008)" *International Journal of Automation Technology*, Vol.2, No.4, pp. 259-265

Shigeyoshi T.& Masayuki Y., (1999). "Simplex Crossover in Real Coded Genetic Algorithms," *Proceedings of the Annual Conference of JSAI*, Vol.13, pp. 452-454

Isao O., Hiroshi S. and Shigenobu. K., (1997). "A Real-coded Genetic Algorithm for Function Optimization Using Unimodal Normal Distribution Crossover," *Proc. 7th Int'l Conf. on Genetic Algorithms*, pp.246-253